★

AMERICAN FOOD WRITING
An Anthology with Classic Recipes

★

A Special Publication of
THE LIBRARY OF AMERICA

American ★ ★ ★ ★ ★
Food Writing

AN ANTHOLOGY WITH CLASSIC RECIPES

★ ★ ★ ★ ★   Edited by Molly O'Neill

Some of the material in this volume is reprinted
with the permission of holders of copyright and publication rights.
Acknowledgments are on page 729.

Distributed to the trade by Penguin Putnam Inc.
and in Canada by Penguin Books Canada Ltd.

Designed by Mark Melnick
Composed in Wessex with Coquette headings

Library of Congress Control Number: 2007920143

ISBN: 978-1-59853-005-6

10 9 8 7 6 5 4 3 2 1

Printed in the United States of America

American Food Writing: An Anthology
is published with a gift in honor of
SARAH PORTER BOEHMLER,
Chef and Hostess extraordinaire

Contents

Introduction

by Molly O'Neill

I spent the food revolution in restaurant kitchens, newsrooms, and the editorial offices of magazines. The battle lines had been drawn, and I was for fresh herbs, not dried ones; for flaky, kosher salt and against grainy, iodized salt; for sweet butter, not the salted variety. I was pro fresh whole chickens and opposed to frozen and deconstructed birds. You would have recognized me instantly: I wore a heavy-gauge, all-cotton chef's apron, used only Henckels knives, and cooked primarily in the copper pans and enamelware that I had hauled home from E. Dehillerin, *le spécialiste du matériel de cuisine*, in Paris. You would not, however, have seen the blinders that permitted me and my co-generationists to believe that we were the first Americans to recognize food as something more than fuel and to dedicate ourselves to improving the nation's table.

We were not, of course, the first. Culinary reform of one sort or another has a long and continuous history in America, and from early on, American writers have seen food as a window into the wider culture—a sign of our values and our ideals, a measure of our civilization. What is distinctive about American food writing is how constant and close to the surface is its sense of moral struggle. The tussle changes form. If the Puritans of the Massachusetts Bay Colony, for instance, reviled the sin of gluttony (even while managing to eat very well), today's green gourmets denounce eating chemically induced, industrially processed food. But the essential tension in the American appetite has remained constant. Different impulses gain ascendancy in different eras—one generation venerates abstemious control and another champions whole-hog indulgence—and this, in turn, mirrors a central conflict in American culture.

In the nineteenth century, for instance, cookbooks and books of household management assumed a close connection between a well-run kitchen and a sound personal morality; and as this view was popularized, the kitchen became, increasingly, a zone of female autonomy. But the Victorian ideal of domestic efficiency was not universally embraced. At the beginning of *Huckleberry Finn* (1884), for instance, Mark Twain uses food to express the pull between the sedate gentility associated with Huck's would-be reformer the Widow Douglas and the anarchic free-for-all of life beyond her civilizing ways. Allowing that there was nothing really the matter with the widow's victuals, Huck adds: "… that is, nothing only everything was cooked by itself. In a barrel of odds and ends it is different; things get mixed up, and the juice kind of swaps around, and the things go better."

Although food has always been used to assert (and acquire) status in the United States, there is, as well, always a powerful undercurrent of Huck—a populist counter-pull, championing simple, rustic eating against the more formalized, pulled-up manners of upward climbers. This has often been a way of pitting honest poverty against decadent wealth, with the implication that those without duplicity have no need to hide behind artifice and confection. To sing the praises of naïve cooking is to return to Eden, to begin the civilizing process again, to have another crack at getting it right.

From Joel Barlow's sophisticated mock-heroic celebration of the rough-hewn simplicity of American hasty pudding in 1796 to Gary Nabhan's contemporary search for the primal tortilla, the urge to resist civilization—whether conceived as foreign sophistication, plutocratic excess, or technologized mass-production—has coursed through American food writing. Sometimes the resistance is overt, as with Huck Finn; sometimes it is tacit. In Joseph Mitchell's "Mr. Barbee's Terrapin," for instance, the reader is led delicately but surely to suppose that the diamond-back turtle prized by privileged northerners and fussed over by their chefs is actually far more succulent when prepared simply by the family that raises it on a muddy island off the coast of Georgia.

Whether implicit or explicit, the tension between the civilized and the wild is a constant in American food writing. It expresses itself in various binary oppositions: between refined and rough, elite and democratic, professional and amateur, expensive and affordable, foreign and home-grown. From time to time, this tension also comes to the fore as it did in 1975, when Craig Claiborne, the *New York Times* food critic, published an account of a $4,000 dinner that he shared in Paris with his frequent collaborator, the chef and cookbook writer, Pierre Franey. The meal was composed of 31 dishes and nine wines and it did not matter that Mr. Claiborne had actually won the dining experience in a charity auction; the public outrage was, he told me once, "reminiscent of the lynch mobs in Mississippi." Russell Baker quickly responded with a satire called "Francs and Beans," which appeared on the op-ed page of *The New York Times*: "The meal opened with a 1975 Diet Pepsi served in a disposable bottle. Although its bouquet was negligible, its distinct metallic aftertaste evoked memories of tin cans one had licked experimentally in the first flush of childhood's curiosity."

Mark Twain could not have crafted a more American hoopla. This confrontation had a dramatic effect on my generation. Along with the rest of the country, we'd fallen in love with fine food when we were children, at least since 1963 when Julia Child's French Chef series premiered on TV. Most of the other food writers we read and cooked from—Craig and Mary Francis and Michael Field and A. J. Liebling and Waverley Root—were also devout Francophiles. But we were embarrassed by the $4,000 meal and troubled by the elitism of French cuisine. Seeing ourselves as more populist, more natural, less fuddy-duddy than our predecessors, we set about inventing something more inclusive, more individual, less effete: the New American Cuisine. Before you could say "Blackened Redfish" we had, like Huck, "lit out for the territories," and there was the New Cajun Cuisine, the New New England Cuisine, the New Tex Mex, the New California Cuisine ...

But we were merely living another episode of an old drama. While serving as ambassador to France, Thomas Jefferson developed a taste for French cuisine; his journals note his attempts to bring the fruits and vegetables and grapevines home to Monticello, and ever since, Euro-envy has continued to alternate with native chauvinism in American food writing. Charles Ranhofer detailed the French-inspired meals that *le tout* New York favored during the latter half of the 1800s, while in the same era Henry Ward Beecher waxed nostalgic on the day-long labor of making an old-fashioned apple pie.

With the Woodstock generation, food became a cultural tender, a means of establishing a generational identity distinct from that of our parents. Again, it turns out that this is an old story: every generation declares its tastes—and its identity—by rejecting something that the previous generation holds dear. If one takes the long view, this ritual is not without its ironies.

To food revolutionists, for instance, iceberg lettuce was the embodiment of everything wrong with food—big, mass-produced, and bred not for flavor but for its ease of shipping and handling and its all-but-eternal shelf life. We crusaded for tiny, varied garden greens with texture and taste. But even as we built a culture that the writer David Kamp would eventually christen "The United States of Arugula," we were embracing the very thing that a previous generation had scorned.

A glimpse of that earlier era occurs in an episode of Mary McCarthy's *The Group*, as one college friend and her beau, a gourmet cook, share their excitement for modern ingredients with another, less up-to-the-minute college friend: "'Have you tasted the new Corn Niblets?' asked Kay. Dottie shook her head. 'You ought to tell your mother about them. It's the whole-kernel corn. Delicious. Almost like corn on the cob. Harold discovered them.' She considered. 'Does your mother know about iceberg lettuce? It's a new variety, very crisp, with wonderful keeping powers. After you've tried it, you'll never want to see the old Boston lettuce again ...'"

"Food writing" as such is a relatively recent—almost a contemporary—invention. The selections in this anthology tilt to the current era because food writing since, say, World War II has been richer, more varied, more lyrical than much of what came before. (We do, however, find foreshadowings of the more specialized food writing of our day in a variety of sources and in every phase of American history: journals, letters, novels, poems, travel accounts, autobiographies, histories, ethnographic studies, all represented in this volume.) When addressing the subject of food, women were consigned to the role of advice-giver in the Victorian household manual tradition and, until recently, did not express the full range of their experience. The appetite for food writing that evoked food's sensual pleasures was limited to a small, relatively privileged world. And then, beginning in the mid-twentieth century, all that changed, and there was an explosion of lively, diverse, mouth-watering food prose.

The admission of women to the bon vivant club of gourmets was key to this shift. M.F.K. Fisher was the crucial figure here, and her ability to describe the world and herself in visceral and affecting terms demonstrated the poetic possibilities of the subject. Fisher took the memoirist's approach, and her intimate accounts of daily life gave food writing an emotional weight it had never carried before. In *The Gastronomical Me* (1943), she wrote: "People ask me: Why do you write about food, and eating and drinking? Why don't you write about the struggle for power and security, and about love, the way others do? They ask it accusingly, as if I were somehow gross, unfaithful to the honor of my craft. The easiest answer is to say that, like most other humans, I am hungry. But there is more than that. It seems to me that our three basic needs, for food and security and love, are so mixed and mingled and entwined that we cannot straightly think of one with the others. So it happens that when I write of hunger, I am really writing about love and the hunger for it, and warmth and the love of it and the hunger for it ... and then the warmth and richness and fine reality of hunger satisfied ... and it is all one."

Many of her successors see food as an end in itself–and end up producing something like food porn–but the most successful memoirists write about food and the self in order to write about the human condition, human appetite, human yearnings. Gael Greene's celebration of her own insatiable hungers as she analyzed the food in New York restaurants becomes a portrait of female destiny in a modern and liberated world; Laurie Colwin's tales of daily life cast domesticity as both the added burden and the potential bonus of the modern working wife and mother.

The contemporary food writer uses taste and sensation to discover and explain what makes her human. If I were to name this genre it would be: "My Awakening and What I Ate," and it is the modern coming-of-age story. Some instances of it, like Anthony Bourdain's *Kitchen Confidential*, are set in the kiln and clatter of restaurant kitchens and are, sometimes literally, trials by fire. Others, like Ruth Reichl's *Garlic and Sapphires*, take place on the other side of the kitchen door, and chronicle the emergence of self-awareness, taste by savored (or rejected) taste. Still others, like Sara Suleri's *Meatless Days*, use taste to measure the distance between cultures.

Food keeps one in the present. The physical sensation of a flavor in the mouth is an antidote to the flavorlessness of our increasingly abstract and virtual world. A good piece of apple pie is not just about the apples or about the crust, it is, instead, about the collision of tensions––soft and firm, sweet and sour, salty and buttery. Likewise, a good piece of food writing is never just about the food; it is, among other things, about place and time, desire and satiety, the longing for home and the lure of the wider world. In a good piece of food writing, dozens of other tensions skittle just beneath the surface of these basic conflicts: the civilized competes with the wild, the idiosyncratic tugs at convention, self-control campaigns to squelch self-indulgence. A meal, like the written account of it, is a declaration of self.

Writers tend to be more direct, less circumspect when writing about food. They can be off-hand and intimate, passionate, opinionated—and visceral. To consider dinner in all its aspects—the hollow anticipation of it, the imagining and the crafting of it, the look and the smell of it, the feeling of it in the mouth, the millions of flavor notes that the tongue sounds (remember this! and that!)—is a rare opportunity for a writer. One can look outside the self, describing the outer world as a journalist does; one can also use the poet's discipline and write from the inside, listening to the chords of memory and response summoned by taste, fearlessly following each backward in time.

The range of voices and disparate approaches gathered here tell the tale of a culture in search of itself and, eternally, in search of a cuisine to call its own, from the first days of optimism and wide-eyed wonder at New World plenty through all the stages of a developing nation. The rapid growth of industrial food processing in the nineteenth and early twentieth centuries triggered in some a yearning for the reassurances of older, home-centered ways; and a similar response was evoked in the 1960s, when even wider and more inexorable industrial developments resulted in a taut stretch of plastic wrap between food and the people shopping for it. At such times Americans long to scurry back to Eden, to a time when an individual was in sole charge if not of his fate then at least of his dinner.

Food also opens other worlds. As the American appetite has become over the past half century more adventuresome, the enthusiasm for reading about the food of disparate cultures has grown—and so has the body of literature that opens doors to the tastes and habits of far-flung worlds. Cooking has always been a necessity; today it is also a pastime, an obsession, an entertainment, a spectator sport. Food is what we think about when we worry the future. What will we eat? asks Eric Schlosser in *Fast Food Nation*. What indeed? asks Michael Pollan in *The Omnivore's Dilemma*. The subject is infinitely elastic and so, it seems, is appetite for reading about food in America today.

Why? Perhaps because reading about food reminds us that we are human and alive and a tangle of contradictions, some of which can be eased by a meal and some of which can be resolved by remembering and imagining what it feels like to bite off a piece of the world, to pull it across the tongue, to swallow it. Perhaps we read about food to recall the meals we've already eaten and to picture the ones we'd like to tuck into at some later date. Or maybe we read about food to avoid eating, a nation of armchair gourmets protecting our waistlines and arteries, eating nothing but words.

But at the deepest level I think we Americans read about food to remember how it feels to be hungry and to deserve a meal, to imagine being windswept and exhausted, shivering and lonely; to feel, as the early explorers did, wracked by the appetite born of long odds and great hope. We read about food to feel the things that thoughts of food can fix. Which is just about everything. Every meal, after all, is a new beginning.

Molly O'Neill

Pehr Kalm

from Travels into North America

From the beginning, bounty was part of the covenant. New World explorers wrote—sometimes, admittedly, with promotional ends in view—of waters so thick with fish that simply by walking across the backs of them one could cross a bay; fresh cod, wrote Plymouth colonist Edward Winslow in 1621, was so plentiful that it was "but coarse meate with us." Pehr Kalm (1716–1779), a Finnish botanist and agricultural economist, was one of the most assiduous of those who set about cataloging these riches. Dispatched by the Royal Swedish Academy of Sciences to search for seeds and plants that could have a commercial value in the Old World, Kalm arrived in 1748, established a home base in the Scandinavian expatriate communities in southern New Jersey, and over the next four years traveled widely and wrote extensively about natural phenomena such as Niagara Falls, as well as New World food products and foodways.

In awe of the natural larder, he writes with wide-eyed wonder and a sense of abundant possibility, as intrigued by the diversity of the cooks he encountered as he is by the ingredients at their disposal. His descriptions here—of preparing pumpkins and apple dumplings and a hot cabbage dish that sounds like an ur–cole slaw—show the interplay of Native American, British, and Dutch culinary habits in the colonial kitchen. Supersizing may have been the manifest destiny of a nation settled for its bounty; and as Kalm's observations on oysters here suggest, the urge to industrialize that bounty is as old as the nation itself.

■ ■ ■

Oysters. About New York they find they find innumerable quantities of excellent oysters, and there are few places which have oysters of such an exquisite taste and of so great a size. They are pickled and sent to the West Indies and other places, which is done in the following manner. As soon as the oysters are caught, their shells are opened, and the fish washed clean; some water is then poured into a pot, the oysters are put into it, and they are boiled for a while; the pot is then taken off the fire again and the oysters taken out and put upon a dish till they are almost dry. Then some nutmeg, allspice and black pepper are added, and as much vinegar as is thought sufficient to give a sourish taste. All this is mixed with half the liquor in which the oysters are boiled, and put over the fire again. While boiling great care should be taken to skim off the thick scum. At last the whole pickling liquid is poured into a glass or earthen vessel, the oysters are put into it, and the vessel is well stopped to keep out the air. In this manner, oysters will keep for years, and may be sent to the most distant parts of the world.

The merchants here buy up great quantities of oysters about this time, pickle them in the above-mentioned manner, and send them to the West Indies, by which they frequently make a considerable profit; for the oysters, which cost them five shillings of their currency, they commonly sell for a pistole, or about six times as much as they give for them, and sometimes they get even more. The oysters which are thus pickled have a very fine flavor, but cannot be fried. The following is another way of preserving oysters: they are taken out of the shells, fried in butter, put into a glass or earthen vessel with the melted butter over them, so that they are fully covered with it and no air can get to them. Oysters prepared in this manner have likewise an agreeable taste, and are exported to the West Indies and other parts.

Oysters are here reckoned very wholesome, and some people assured us that they had not felt the least inconvenience after eating a considerable quantity of them. It is also a common rule here that oysters are best in those months which have an "r" in their names such as September, October, etc. but that they are not so good in other months. However, there are poor people who live all year long upon nothing but oysters and a little bread.

—

Apple-dumplings. One apple dish which the English prepare is as follows: take an apple and pare it, make a dough of water, flour and butter. Roll it thin and enclose apple in it. This is then bound in a clean linen cloth, put in a pot and boiled. When done it is taken out, placed on table and served. While it is warm, the crust is cut on one side. Thereupon they mix butter and sugar, which is added to the apples; then the dish is ready. They call this apple dumpling, sometimes apple pudding. It tastes quite good. You get as many dumplings as you have apples.

—

Pumpkins. A certain kind of oblong and large gourds were called "pumpkins" in Dutch. They were much used by the Dutch, the English, the Swedes and others here in America. The French in Canada had also some use for them, but not as much as those mentioned before. They ripen in the middle of September here in Albany and are able to stand a fair amount of cold. The natives both in Canada and in the English provinces plant a considerable amount of them, yet I think that they came here first from Europe. They were delicious eating and they were prepared in various ways. Sometimes they were cut in two or more parts, placed before the fire and roasted. Frequently they were boiled in water and then eaten. It was customary to eat them this way with meat. Here at Albany the Dutch made a kind of porridge out of them, prepared in the following way. They boiled them first in water, next mashed them in about the same way as we do turnips, then boiled them in a little of the water they had first been boiled in, with fresh milk added, and stirred them while they were boiling. What a delicious dish it became! Another way of preparing these which I observed, was to make a thick pancake of them. It was made by taking the mashed pumpkin and mixing it with corn-meal after which it was either boiled or fried. Both the gruel and the pancake were pleasing to my taste, yet I preferred the former. The Indians do not raise as many pumpkins as they do squashes. Some mix flour with the pumpkins when making the porridge mentioned above, others add nothing. They often make pudding and even pie or a kind of tart out of them. Pumpkins can be preserved throughout the winter until spring, when kept in a cellar where the cold cannot reach them. They are also cut into halves, the seeds removed, the two halves replaced and the whole put into an oven to roast. When they are roasted, butter is spread over the inside while it is still hot so that the butter is drawn into the pumpkins after which they are especially good eating.

—

Cabbage Salad. My landlady, Mrs. Visher, prepared to-day an unusual salad which I never remember having seen or eaten. She took the inner leaves of a head of cabbage, namely, the leaves which usually remain when the outermost leaves have been removed, and cut them in long, thin strips, about $1/12$ to $1/6$ of an inch wide, seldom more. When she had cut up as much as she thought necessary, she put them upon a platter, poured oil and vinegar upon them, added salt and some pepper while mixing the shredded cabbage, so that the oil etc. might be evenly distributed, as is the custom when making salads. Then it was ready. In place of oil, melted butter is frequently used. This is kept in a warm pot or crock and poured over the salad after it has been served. This dish has a very pleasing flavor and tastes better than one can imagine. She told me that many strangers who had eaten at her house had liked this so much that they not only had informed themselves of how to prepare it, but said that they were going to have it prepared for them when they reached their homes.

Travels into North America (1770; first published 1753–61)

Ice Cream

* 2 bottles of good cream * 6. yolks of eggs. * 1/2 lb sugar. *

mix the yolks & sugar.

put the cream on a fire in a casserole, first putting in a ſtick of Vanilla.

when near boiling take it off & pour it gently into the mixture of eggs & sugar.

stir it well.

put it on the fire again stirring it thoroughly with a spoon to prevent it's ſticking to the casserole.

when near boiling take it off and ſtrain it thro a towel.

put it in the Sabottiere.

then set it in ice an hour before it is to be served. put into the ice a handful of salt.

put salt on the coverlid of the Sabotiere & cover the whole with ice.

leave it ſtill half a quarter of an hour.

then turn the Sabottiere in the ice 10 minutes.

open it to loosen with a spatula the ice from the inner sides of the Sabotiere.

shut it & replace it in the ice.

open it from time to time to detach the ice from the sides.

when well taken (prise) ſtir it well with the Spatula.

put it in moulds, juſtling it well down on the knee.

then put the mould into the same bucket of ice.

leave it there to the moment of serving it.

to withdraw it, immerse the mould in warm water, turning it well

till it will come out & turn it into a plate.

*

Thomas Jefferson, holograph manuscript (1780s)

Jefferson was the first American to write a recipe for ice cream.

Joel Barlow

from The Hasty-Pudding

It is a perennial American dilemma: to venerate the simple and natural, or to strive toward the cultivated and complex? Where would dinner be without this push-pull between wholesomeness and debauchery? In his mock-heroic poem *The Hasty-Pudding* (1793), Joel Barlow (1754–1812) resolves the dilemma by praising the purity and goodness of aboriginal America—as symbolized by cornmeal porridge eaten with milk—in a sophisticated satire. Barlow was the kind of early American renaissance man who managed in the course of his life to combine the functions of poet, chaplain, entrepreneur, realtor, diplomat, and sometimes radical public intellectual. He weathered the upheavals of the French Revolution, negotiated the release of Americans held by the Dey of Algiers, and died in Poland when caught up in Napoleon's retreat from Russia. As a culinary historian, it should be noted, he avails himself of some poetic license: the legendary pudding was not, as he suggests, originally the handiwork of a "lovely squaw," but rather a local adaptation of a British dish, a wheat gruel that could be made on the run.

■ ■ ■

A POEM, IN THREE CANTOS.

WRITTEN AT CHAMBERY, IN SAVOY, JANUARY, 1793.

Omne tulit punctum qui miscuit utile dulci.
He makes a good breakfast who mixes pudding with molasses.

CANTO I.

Ye Alps audacious, thro' the heav'ns that rise,
To cramp the day and hide me from the skies;
Ye Gallic flags, that o'er their heights unfurl'd,
Bear death to kings, and freedom to the world,
I sing not you. A softer theme I chuse,
A virgin theme, unconscious of the Muse,
But fruitful, rich, well suited to inspire

The purest frenzy of poetic fire.

    Despise it not, ye Bards to terror steel'd,
Who hurl your thunders round the epic field;
Nor ye who strain your midnight throats to sing
Joys that the vineyard and the still-house bring;
Or on some distant fair your notes employ,
And speak of raptures that you ne'er enjoy.
I sing the sweets I know, the charms I feel,
My morning incense, and my evening meal,
The sweets of Hasty-Pudding. Come, dear bowl,
Glide o'er my palate, and inspire my soul.
The milk beside thee, smoking from the kine,
Its substance mingled, married in with thine,
Shall cool and temper thy superior heat,
And save the pains of blowing while I eat.

    Oh! could the smooth, the emblematic song
Flow like thy genial juices o'er my tongue,
Could those mild morsels in my numbers chime,
And, as they roll in substance, roll in rhyme,
No more thy awkward unpoetic name
Should shun the Muse, or prejudice thy fame;
But rising grateful to th' accustom'd ear,
All Bards should catch it, and all realms revere!

    Assist me first with pious toil to trace
Thro' wrecks of time thy lineage and thy race;
Declare what lovely squaw, in days of yore,
(Ere great Columbus sought thy native shore)
First gave thee to the world; her works of fame
Have liv'd indeed, but liv'd without a name.
Some tawny Ceres, goddess of her days,
First learn'd with stones to crack the well-dry'd maize,
Thro' the rough seive to shake the golden show'r,
In boiling water stir the yellow flour:
The yellow flour, bestrew'd and stir'd with haste,
Swells in the flood and thickens to a paste,

Then puffs and wallops, rises to the brim,
Drinks the dry knobs that on the surface swim;
The knobs at last the busy ladle breaks,
And the whole mass its true consistence takes.

    Could but her sacred name, unknown so long,
Rise, like her labors, to the son of song,
To her, to them, I'd consecrate my lays,
And blow her pudding with the breath of praise.
If 'twas Oella, whom I sang before,
I here ascribe her one great virtue more.
Not thro' the rich Peruvian realms alone
The fame of Sol's sweet daughter should be known,
But o'er the world's wide climes should live secure,
Far as his rays extend, as long as they endure.

    Dear Hasty-Pudding, what unpromis'd joy
Expands my heart, to meet thee in Savoy!
Doom'd o'er the world thro' devious paths to roam,
Each clime my country, and each house my home,
My soul is sooth'd, my cares have found an end,
I greet my long-lost, unforgotten friend.

    For thee thro' Paris, that corrupted town,
How long in vain I wandered up and down,
Where shameless Bacchus, with his drenching hoard,
Cold from his cave usurps the morning board.
London is lost in smoke and steep'd in tea;
No Yankey there can lisp the name of thee;
The uncouth word, a libel on the town,
Would call a proclamation from the crown.*
For climes oblique, that fear the sun's full rays,
Chill'd in their fogs, exclude the generous maize;
A grain whose rich luxuriant growth requires
Short gentle showers, and bright etherial fires.

    But here, tho' distant from our native shore,

*A certain king, at the time when this was written, was publishing proclamations to prevent American principles from being propagated in his country.

With mutual glee we meet and laugh once more.
The same! I know thee by that yellow face,
That strong complexion of true Indian race,
Which time can never change, nor soil impair,
Nor Alpine snows, nor Turkey's morbid air;
For endless years, thro' every mild domain,
Where grows the maize, there thou art sure to reign.
    But man, more fickle, the bold licence claims,
In different realms to give thee different names.
Thee the soft nations round the warm Levant
Polanta call, the French of course *Polante*;
Ev'n in thy native regions, how I blush
To hear the Pennsylvanians call thee *Mush!*
On Hudson's banks, while men of Belgic spawn
Insult and eat thee by the name *Suppawn.*
All spurious appellations, void of truth;
I've better known thee from my earliest youth,
Thy name is *Hasty-Pudding!* thus our sires
Were wont to greet thee fuming from their fires;
And while they argu'd in thy just defence
With logic clear, they thus explain'd the sense:—
"In *haste* the boiling cauldron, o'er the blaze,
Receives and cooks the ready-powder'd maize:
In *haste* 'tis serv'd, and then in equal *haste*,
With cooling milk, we make the sweet repast.
No carving to be done, no knife to grate
The tender ear, and wound the stony plate;
But the smooth spoon, just fitted to the lip,
And taught with art the yielding mass to dip,
By frequent journeys to the bowl well stor'd,
Performs the hasty honors of the board."
Such is thy name, significant and clear,
A name, a sound to every Yankey dear,
But most to me, whose heart and palate chaste
Preserve my pure hereditary taste.

There are who strive to stamp with disrepute
The lucious food, because it feeds the brute;
In tropes of high-strain'd wit, while gaudy prigs
Compare thy nursling man to pamper'd pigs;
With sovereign scorn I treat the vulgar jest,
Nor fear to share thy bounties with the beast.
What though the generous cow gives me to quaff
The milk nutritious; am I then a calf?
Or can the genius of the noisy swine,
Tho' nurs'd on pudding, thence lay claim to mine?
Sure the sweet song, I fashion to thy praise,
Runs more melodious than the notes they raise.

My song resounding in its grateful glee,
No merit claims; I praise myself in thee.
My father lov'd thee thro' his length of days;
For thee his fields were shaded o'er with maize;
From thee what health, what vigor he possest,
Ten sturdy freemen from his loins attest;
Thy constellation rul'd my natal morn,
And all my bones were made of Indian corn.
Delicious grain! whatever form it take,
To roast or boil, to smother or to bake,
In every dish 'tis welcome still to me,
But most, my Hasty-Pudding, most in thee.

Let the green Succatash with thee contend,
Let beans and corn their sweetest juices blend,
Let butter drench them in its yellow tide,
And a long slice of bacon grace their side;
Not all the plate, how fam'd soe'er it be,
Can please my palate like a bowl of thee.

Some talk of Hoe-cake, fair Virginia's pride,
Rich Johnny-cake this mouth has often tri'd;
Both please me well, their virtues much the same;
Alike their fabric, as allied their fame,
Except in dear New-England, where the last

Receives a dash of pumpkin in the paste,
To give it sweetness and improve the taste.
But place them all before me, smoaking hot,
The big round dumplin rolling from the pot;
The pudding of the bag, whose quivering breast,
With suet lin'd, leads on the Yankey feast;
The Charlotte brown, within whose crusty sides
A belly soft the pulpy apple hides;
The yellow bread, whose face like amber glows,
And all of Indian that the bake-pan knows—
You tempt me not—my fav'rite greets my eyes,
To that lov'd bowl my spoon by instinct flies.

The New-York Magazine, January 1796

Johny Cake, or Hoe Cake.

Scald 1 pint of milk and put to 3 pints of indian meal, and half pint of flower—bake before the fire. Or scald with milk two thirds of the indian meal, or wet two thirds with boiling water, add salt, molasses and shortening, work up with cold water pretty stiff and bake as above. ¶

Amelia Simmons, *American Cookery* (1796)

The earliest known American cookbook, *American Cookery* (published in four editions between 1796 and 1808), is notable for considering American ingredients such as watermelon, Jerusalem artichokes, pumpkins, molasses, or, in this recipe, the almighty corn meal.

Meriwether Lewis

from The Journals of Lewis & Clark

It seems likely that Meriwether Lewis (1774–1809), who served as Thomas Jefferson's private secretary before joining William Clark on the expedition through the territories newly acquired in the Louisiana Purchase, shared Jefferson's appreciation for the finer things. Jefferson's overseer, Edmund Bacon, noted that "Meriwether Lewis' mother made very nice hams. And every year I used to get a few from her for [the President's] use." As this excerpt from the expedition journal shows, Lewis placed great importance on turning the raw into the cooked. His account of the process of making *boudin blanc* from buffalo and beef and frying it in bear fat—the cook, by the way, was Toussaint Charbonneau, French-Canadian husband of the celebrated Sacagawea—makes it clear that, like wilderness exploration, sausage-making is heavy, dirty work: work that creates, in Lewis's words, "pangs of keen appetite."

■ ■ ■

Thursday May 9th 1805. Capt C. killed 2 bucks and 2 buffaloe, I also killed one buffaloe which proved to be the best meat, it was in tolerable order; we saved the best of the meat, and from the cow I killed we saved the necessary materials for making what our wrighthand cook Charbono calls the *boudin blanc,* [NB: *poudingue*] and immediately set him about preparing them for supper; this white pudding we all esteem one of the greatest delacies of the forrest, it may not be amiss therefore to give it a place. About 6 feet of the lower extremity of the large gut of the Buffaloe is the first mosel that the cook makes love to, this he holds fast at one end with the right hand, while with the forefinger and thumb of the left he gently compresses it, and discharges what he says *is not good to eat,* but of which in the squel we get a moderate portion; the mustle lying underneath the shoulder blade next to the back, and fillets are next saught, these are needed up very fine with a good portion of kidney suit [suet]; to this composition is then added a just proportion of pepper and salt and a small quantity of flour; thus far advanced, our skilfull opporater C–o seizes his receptacle, which has never once touched the water, for that would intirely distroy the regular order of the whole procedure; you will not forget that the side you now see is that covered with a good coat of fat provided the animal be in good order; the operator sceizes the recepticle I say, and tying it fast at one end turns it inwards and begins now with repeated evolutions of the hand and arm, and a brisk motion of the finger and thumb to put in what he says is *bon pour manger*; thus by stuffing and compressing he soon distends the recepticle to the utmost limmits of it's power of expansion, and in the course of it's longtudinal progress it drives from the other end of the recepticle a much larger portion of the [*blank*] than was previously discharged by the finger and thumb of the left hand in a former part of the operation; thus when the sides of the recepticle are skilfully exchanged the outer for the iner, and all is compleatly filled with something good to eat, it is tyed at the other end, but not any cut off, for that would make the pattern too scant; it is then baptised in the missouri with two dips and a flirt, and bobbed into the kettle; from whence after it be well boiled it is taken and fryed with bears oil untill it becomes brown, when it is ready to esswage the pangs of a keen appetite or such as travelers in the wilderness are seldom at a loss for.—

The Journals of the Lewis & Clark Expedition (1987; written 1805)

John Pintard

Letters to His Daughter, 1819–32

Like many men of means in his era, John Pintard (1759–1844) devoted considerable energy to stocking the family larder. A successful merchant who was deeply involved in New York City's emerging municipal culture (he was, among other things, founder of the New-York Historical Society), Pintard loved good produce and went to great lengths to lay aside food in its season, to keep an eye on market prices and quality, and to exchange the specialties of his region with those of far-flung places. His daughter, Eliza Davidson, to whom the letters excerpted here were addressed, lived in New Orleans, and Pintard regularly shipped her butter and eagerly awaited her return gifts of oranges and pecans. Difficulty in shipping could mean waiting another year to refine the procedure and try again, but try they did, driven by equal measures of familial affection, regional pride, and an appetite for the hard-to-get.

■ ■ ■

December 6, 1819. Your sister is a dear good girl, possessed of intrinsic merit as a housekeeper. This summer she made her first essay & has been peculiarly successful in preparing her confectionary. Thro' fear of failure, as she was determined to do all herself, her experiment was on a small scale. She will however send you a trifling sample of each kind by Mr. Townsend, and another year I hope to be able, if you find them passable, prepare as much as you may wish of our northern fruits, to give a little variety to your more abundant kinds. She likewise has made, agreeably to our family receipts, Cherry & Raspberry Brandy Noyau & Persico, all to my taste exquisitely fine & superior to any imported, and this entirely herself, as she insisted on preparing compounding & infusing all the ingredients with her own hands. Last evening Gov. Clinton, Drs. Hosack & Francis took coffee & passed the evening & extolled their flavour. She is equally successful with her pastry & is very fond of the kitchen department, & enjoys the peculiar felicity of not only seeing to a good dish but relishing it when dressed. Mama however objects, and properly to her exposing herself to the consequences of super-intending the kitchin. She carves a Turky, Goose, or duck with the dexterity

of a Surgeon and with her needle she is very dexterous in millinery, man-
tuamaking, Tayloring & fancy work.

—

August 28, 1820. You speak of the abundance but dearness of your Market, in consequence of forestalling, which altho we have laws & penalties to
restrain are the practice here to a gross extent. But such has been the uncommon productiveness of the season, that Fruits & vegetables, Peaches
excepted, have been very cheap. For instance, on Saturday I bought 24 large
ears of Indian Corn, for one shilling, a peck of Sky beans, small Lima beans,
for *ninepence.* Eight musk melons for one shilling! each as large as I have
paid eighteen pence a piece three years ago. A powerful watermelon at least
10 pounds for eighteen pence, which would have been cheap formerly for
half a dollar. But Butchers meat is high, 10d. for the prime pieces. Poultry is
excessively dear. Aunt Helen dined with us yesterday & your Sister wished
to make a chicken pye. I paid five shillings for a very handsome pair which
is exorbitant. Our Bread is very large. Butter however is $^1/_9$ per lb. I mean the
choicest, for breakfast & tea, by the piggen $^1/_3$. Fall butter I expect will be at
one shilling the best down to ninepence. So that the substantial comforts of
life are very reasonable. A Dollar goes as far as two formerly.

—

October 24, 1820. This day Master Samuel sails for Savanna to pass the
winter with his uncle Mr. Nicholas Bayard. His health is extremely delicate,
tho to us small eaters his appetite appears to be voracious. He does not eat
but devours butter, certainly uses more than all of us together. Indeed this
is a family accomplishment, for it would be uncivil to call it failing, owing
entirely to his Father, who, to the great annoyance of my dear good Uncle,
used to gorge his children. I have more than once I think reprobated this
practice, the consequences of exciting appetite instead of restraining it tends
to gluttony. Simplicity in food is easier preached than practiced, & I confess
I like mine a little piquant, without which my appetite would fail me, but I
never eat to satiety, and seldom have to complain of dispepsy a fashionable
malady especially among high luxurious livers, who riot all winter and go
to the Springs in Summer to disgorge and prepare for another campaign.
In your Southern climate especially heavy rich sauces, must engender bile
& create a feverish excitement, and predisposition to typhus at least. Some

think moderation consists in sobriety, but abstinence in diet is also requisite to health. More, says the old proverb, dig their graves with their Teeth than their Tankard. Probably in the olden time, the Lenten fast was instituted to work off the ill effects of the Festive season of Xmas and New Year, and did we pursue the weekly abstinence on Fridays, enjoined by Holy Church, I am persuaded there would be less of the modern acute diseases.

—

November 4, 1820. By the Ship Pacific you will receive I hope as advised in my letter by Capt. Smith 2 Firkins choice butter packed in Salt, 1 Barrel buckwheat, 2 Firkins Newtown pippins, 1 Box Sweetmeats & 1 bundle Brooms. I attended bright & early to put these articles on board which will probably arrive as soon as this letter. It gratifies me to find that the experiment of the butter succeeded last winter, & will again. By leaving the 2nd Firkin unopened I mean the barrel, until the 1st is used you will have the luxury of good sweet butter throughout the winter, & if the Buckwheat meal, should not get heated on the passage, I shall have afforded a delicious regale to your darlings. Do you mix it with Indian Meal? Which Mama considers a great addition to the excellence of the cakes, half of each, I think, but this to your palate. I suppose your hominy husband does not relish this northern luxury. The apples, should they arrive sound, will be a fine treat for the children, a reward for good lessons. The pippins are not the largest, but being hand picked, promise to keep better than those that are shaken. Cheap as they are, I gave the best price to ensure the best fruit. At all events enough may arrive sound to gratify the bairns. If apples have been as redundant on the Ohio as in this quarter, you will have them in any quantity & very reasonable. Indeed great quantities are shipped I see on board of every vessel destined for N.O. so that you can afford to treat your little ones with apple dumplings & molasses, a wholesome diet, every week. In old times in my good uncles family, and I suppose every other, there were stated days for every dish, salt fish on Saturday, roast Turkey Sunday, the remainder of Saturdays salt, or dumb fish, hashed up with vegetables & warmed in the Frying pan for Monday, Roast beef Wednesday, pease porridge & sausages on Thursday, Apple dumplings Friday, Pancakes Tuesday. This was pretty much the winter course, and always Alamode on Saturday in summer, which was served up cold on Sunday to prevent cooking, or else veal forced meat ball pie. Hasty pudding all winter long for supper, & buckwheat cakes, which came into vogue just before the revolutionary war, for breakfast. In Philadelphia this article is or used to be considered such a treat, as to be served up at tea in large domestic parties, where they are always prepared the size of the gridle, and cut into quarters. Thus you have the courses of old fashion good feeding when abundance of the best was afforded at a very cheap rate. I have heard my good old uncle repeatedly say that an excellent dinner of the best of the market could be provided within the compass of a single dollar, and that there were not many persons who could afford to give so extravagant a dinner!

—

March 17, 1821. St. Patricks a winters day with a sprinkle of snow last night, after two unusual warm days. Yesterday the splendid procession of Butchers paraded our principal streets, with the carcases of the 52 Fat Oxen exhibited at the Cattle Show on Monday. The train was composed of as many Butchers Carts besides horsemen & bands of musick, colours flying, tag rag & bobtail accompanying and reached from Mechanic Hall to Wall Street. At night the markets were illuminated, & this morning the exhibition of Fat Beef exceeded anything ever displayed in this city, which has never been as distinguished for fine beef as Philadelphia but will, if encouraged, soon be on a par, both as to meats and butter, in which our sister city has so long excelled.

—

May 30, 1821. This morning I saw green peas in market from Virginia the first at ²⁄₆ half peck. Cheap enough but they could have no flavour. The difference of a single day is perceptible. Vegetables can only be tasted in perfection, gathered the same day. I can get asparagus, occasionally, cut the same morning by paying extra, 3d to 6d a bunch. Some very fine at one shilling I purchased this morning. When cleaning, Mama makes it a rule to give the good women she employs good dinners, it makes them grateful & always willing to come in preference whenever wanted.

—

January 23, 1822. Yesterday 22nd our new market (Fulton) was opened. It is an elegant quadrangular structure, superior in accommodation perhaps to any thing of the kind, probably even in Europe. The abundant display of every variety of Meats, Fish & Game, exceeded any thing that I have witnessed in this city.   —

September 21, 1826. An elegant day. We shall see hereafter whether this day be an emblem of January. I have just seen your tub of butter nicely packed in a half barrel of salt. It will be sent aboard the Lavinia this morning, I hope in time to go in the run. Stickler says that it comes from one of the best dairies in Orange County & equal in quality to what he sent us this morning which was a nosegay. We have 2 small covered tubs holding 6 lbs each, one of which is received every Thursday morning & the empty one returned. The butter comes from Mr. Ellison's dairy near Newburgh & is superior in quality. Thus the trouble of tasting & rejecting in the market is saved & it comes cheaper by 3d. a lb. It astonishes one to see the immense quantity of butter that comes weekly to this city from Orange, Dutchess & Westchester Counties, besides all Long island. Butter is the great staple article for breakfast & tea among all classes. The idea of restraining children from a liberal use of good fresh butter is exploded, & they almost live upon bread & butter in this city.   —

December 28, 1830. I recollect well, in my youth, or rather childhood to have always heard my good Uncle say when there was any thing delicate on the table, that it was a pity to eat it alone. Tho' far from profuse he kept a good table & always well cooked. This was inherited from our ancestors who not gross were always delicate feeders. I partake of it myself as does our darling when she remarked that the very idea of dinner nauseated her, when abroad—always the same roasted meat, without variety or shadow of change. She was not used to this at Mothers table. Some would call this epicurism & a vitiated appetite. It is not so. Ploughmen & labourers may by hard work, relish & gorge solid junks of boiled pork & raw beef, but surely in the preparation of viands, taste may be consulted, & instead of chicken stewed to rags, a nice fricasee, or your voluptuous gumbo may be prepared without the aid of witchcraft, that will give a relish to the most fastidious appetite. I know nothing more disgusting or provoking than to see a good dish spoiled, always an evidence of a negligent housekeeper.   —

January 24, 1832. Your sister purchased last week, a Dutch oven on an improved plan. It is very accommodating, as placed before the fire it bakes Johnny Cakes, pies &c. as well as roast small joints & cooks a beef stake on the gridiron. I thought it such a convenience that I have ordered one for my dear daughter.   —

January 26, 1832. On my way down I called to see whether the "Boston roasting & baking oven" was completed & had it covered with paper as well as I could to preserve it from scratching. William took it down & put it in the care of the steward with your brothers directions to put it in the baggage room which he saw done, so that I got these jobs off my hands in good season. I have added 2 oval tin pudding dishes & 3 smaller pans, obtained at another shop, so that you can forthwith make an experiment whether the oven will bake a chicken pie & pudding, as quickly as your sisters, whose cook in one hour, day before yesterday prepared the above dishes, for dinner, one after the other. It bakes cakes admirably, & serves to roast coffee to perfection, in short it is adapted for almost every culinary, except stews & fricasees, which are better prepared in casseroles.   —

February 17, 1832. I wish to mention before it escapes me that our Cook gave us yesterday a fine steak prepared for the first time in the Boston Oven. It was admirably cooked, & more juicy than when broiled on the gridiron where much of the gravy runs to waste. This experiment will answer for you likewise. Our Cook considers the oven the best kitchen article she ever used.

Letters from John Pintard to His Daughter (1940; written 1819–32)

John M. Duncan

A Virginia Barbecue

Barbecue is an Anglo adaptation of *barbacoa,* a word the Spanish borrowed from the Arawak to describe the outdoor cooking they encountered among Native Americans in the New World. Smoky pit cooking had become ritualized—although by no means standardized—by the time the publisher and bookseller John M. Duncan (1795?–1825) traveled from his native Glasgow to America in 1818. Invited to join Bushrod Washington (a favorite nephew of George, and owner of Mount Vernon) for an afternoon barbecue, Duncan discovered a cotillion-like "rural fête." What Duncan assumed was a local practice that was in fact spreading all over the new nation. By the middle of the 19th century, no settled portion of the United States would lack for its own characteristic paean to the carnivorous appetite *en plein air*. Debates about the best meat (pork for the South, beef for Texans), the proper smoke (cool or hot), the best sauce (thick and tomatoey in the Mexican manner or vinegar-steeped with hot peppers in the manner of the Atlantic seaboard), and the appropriate accompaniments were already beginning to rage. And they continue, mostly among men. Barbecue is a guy thing, a throwback to the spit-roasted woolly mammoth perhaps. It tends to be written about today (and debated in endless detail) like a sporting event, which in fact it has become: thousands of tiny local competitions are rapidly giving way to several major barbecue leagues, with their own playoffs, world series—and six-figure purses.

■ ■ ■

After having spent an hour or two at Mount Vernon, Judge Washington politely invited us to accompany him to a Barbecue, which was to take place in the afternoon close by the road to Alexandria. The very term was new to me; but when explained to mean a kind of rural fête which is common in Virginia it was not difficult to persuade us to accept the invitation.

The spot selected for this rural festivity was a very suitable one. In a fine wood of oaks by the road side we found a whole colony of black servants, who had made a lodgement since we passed it in the morning, and the blue smoke which was issuing here and there from among the branches, readily suggested that there was cooking going forward.

Alighting from my horse and tying it under the shadow of a branching tree I proceeded to explore the recesses of the wood. At the bottom of a pretty steep slope a copious spring of pure water bubbled up through the ground, and in the little glen through which it was stealing, black men, women and children, were busied with various processes of sylvan cookery. One was preparing a fowl for the spit, another feeding a crackling fire which curled up round a large pot, others were broiling pigs, lamb, and venison, over little square pits filled with the red embers of hickory wood. From this last process the entertainment takes its name. The meat to be *barbecued* is split open and pierced with two long slender rods, upon which it is suspended across the mouth of the pits, and turned from side to side till it is thoroughly broiled. The hickory tree gives, it is said, a much stronger heat than coals, and when completely kindled is almost without smoke.

Leaving the busy negroes at their tasks—a scene by the way which suggested a tolerable idea of an encampment of Indians preparing for a feast after the toils of the chase—I made my way to the outskirts of the wood, where I found a rural banqueting-hall and ball room. This was an extensive platform raised a few feet above the ground, and shaded by a closely interwoven canopy of branches. At one side was a rude table and benches of most hospitable dimensions, at the other a spacious dancing floor; flanking the long dining table, a smaller one groaned under numerous earthen vessels filled with various kinds of liquors, to be speedily converted, by a reasonable addition of the limpid current from the glen judiciously qualified by other ingredients, into tubfulls of generous toddy.

A few of the party had reached the barbecue ground before us, and it was not long ere we mustered altogether about thirty ladies and somewhere about an hundred gentlemen. A preliminary cotillon or two occupied the young and amused the older, while the smoking viands were placed upon the board, and presently Washington's March was the animating signal for conducting the ladies to the table. Seating their fair charge at one side, their partners lost no time in occupying the other, and as there was still some vacant space, those who happened to be nearest were pressed in to occupy it. Among others the invitation was extended to me, and though I observed that several declined it, I was too little acquainted with the tactics of a barbecue, and somewhat too well inclined to eat, to be very unrelenting in my refusal. I soon however discovered my false move. Few except those who wish to dance choose the first course; watchfulness to anticipate the wants of the ladies, prevent those who sit down with them from accomplishing much themselves, the dance is speedily resumed, and even those who like myself do not intend to mingle in it regard the rising of the ladies as a signal to vacate their seats. A new levy succeeds, of those who see more charms in a dinner than a quadrille, and many who excused themselves from the first requisition needed no particular solicitation to obey the second. The signal for rising did not seem on this occasion to excite much notice; and some prolonged their sitting till they had an opportunity of bestowing on the third levy, the pleasure of their company. Some experiments began now to be made upon the virtues of the toddy, and it was not long ere the capacious lakes began to be effectually drained off. Let me not be misunderstood however; I saw not the slightest approach to intemperance. Jollity and good humour were not wanting, but there was nothing which trenched upon sobriety either in speech or behaviour. There might be others present besides Judge Washington who had seats on the bench, but the judicial dignity was no way compromised by any part of the proceedings.

While local politics and other matters engrossed the conversation at table, others less inclined to the sedentary position stationed themselves round the dancers. The cotillon was the favourite figure, and the platform was just large enough to admit of two at a time. There "music rose with its voluptuous swell," and exercise flushed the cheek, and enjoyment brightened the eye of the fair Virginians.

But the sun drove on in its diurnal career; and as my poor steed had fasted since early in the morning, I thought it time to take leave of the entertainment and make the best of my way to Alexandria. I left them about five o'clock, and learned that very shortly after, the assembly broke up.

Travels through Part of the United States and Canada in 1818 and 1819 (1823)

Jean Anthelme Brillat-Savarin

Exploit of the Professor

Jean Anthelme Brillat-Savarin (1755–1826), a lawyer like his forebears, was mayor of his birthplace, Belley in east-central France, when he was forced to flee in the wake of the French Revolution in 1793. A period of exile in the United States provided the occasion for this account of hunting wild turkey in Hartford, Connecticut, from his masterpiece *The Physiology of Taste* (1825). Few books on food have had a wider influence. "Tell me what you eat, and I shall tell you what you are," Brillat-Savarin wrote in the book's introductory aphorisms, and this dictum—along with Proust and his madeleine—remains perhaps food writing's most abused cliché. Gourmands defending their priorities also like this quote from Brillat-Savarin: "The discovery of a new dish confers more happiness on humanity than the discovery of a new star." When the book's translator M.F.K. Fisher was asked why she wrote about food rather than "serious" topics, she quoted Brillat-Savarin. Julia Child did the same when questioned first by feminists and later by animal-rights activists. There is no doubt that for Brillat-Savarin, food came first. After bagging his wild turkey, he doesn't really listen to his host's heartfelt account of a populist Utopia, having more important questions to consider: "I was considering how best I might cook my turkey," he writes, "and I was not without some worries, for I feared that in Hartford I might not find all the ingredients I would need."

■ ■ ■

While I was in Hartford, in Connecticut, I had the good luck to kill a wild turkey. This deed deserves to go down in history, and I shall recount it all the more eagerly since I myself am its hero.

A worthy old landowner (AMERICAN FARMER) had invited me to come hunt on his property; he lived in the backwoods of the State (BACK GROUNDS), promised me partridges, grey squirrels, and wild turkeys (WILD COCKS), and gave me the privilege of bringing with me one or two of my chosen friends.

As a result, one fine day of October 1794 we set out, Monsieur King and I, mounted on two hired nags, with the hope of arriving by nightfall at Monsieur Bulow's farm, situated five whole ungodly leagues from Hartford.

M. King was a hunter of an extraordinary kind: he loved the sport passionately, but when he had killed any game he looked on himself as a murderer, and delivered himself of sensitive moral speculations and elegies on the final passing of his victims, which of course did not in the least keep him from starting the hunt all over again.

Although our road was hardly more than a track, we arrived without accident, and were received with that kind of cordial and wordless hospitality which expresses itself by its actions, which is to say that in a very few minutes all of us had been looked after, refreshed, and lodged—men, horses, and dogs according to their particular needs.

We spent some two hours in looking over the farm and its dependencies. I could describe all of that if I wished to, but I much prefer picturing to the reader M. Bulow's four fine daughters (BUXUM LASSES), for whom our visit was a great event.

Their ages ranged from sixteen to twenty; they were radiant with freshness and good health, and there was about all of them such simplicity, such graceful naturalness, that their most ordinary actions endowed them with a thousand charms.

Shortly after we returned from our walk we sat down around a plentifully laden table: a handsome piece of CORN'D BEEF, a STEW'D goose, and a magnificent leg of mutton, then root-vegetables of all kinds (PLENTY), and at the two ends of the table two enormous jugs of an excellent cider, of which I could not drink enough.

When we had proved to our host that we were genuine hunters, at least in our appetite, he began to talk of the real purpose of our visit: he described to the best of his ability the places where we would find our game, the landmarks which we must watch for to guide us safely back again, and above all the farms where we could find refreshment.

During this conversation the ladies had prepared some excellent tea, of which we drank several cups; then they showed us to a room with two beds in it, where the day's exercise and the good food soon sent us off into a delicious sleep.

The next morning we set out for the hunt a little late, and soon coming to the edge of the clearings made by M. Bulow's workmen, I found myself for the first time in my life in virgin forest, where the sound of the axe had never been heard.

I wandered through it with delight, observing the benefits and the ravages of time, which both creates and destroys, and I amused myself by following every period in the life of an oak tree, from the moment it emerges two-leaved from the earth until that one when nothing is left of it but a long black smudge which is its heart's dust.

M. King chided me for my wandering attention, and we took up the hunt more seriously. First of all we killed some of those pretty little grey partridges which are so plump and so tender. Then we knocked down six or seven grey squirrels, highly thought of in that country; and finally our lucky start led us into the midst of a flock of wild turkeys.

They arose, one after another, in quick noisy flight, screaming loudly. M. King fired first, and ran ahead: the others were by now out of range; then the laziest of them rose from the earth not ten paces from me; I fired at it through a break in the woods, and it fell, stone dead.

Only a hunter will understand the bliss such a lucky shot gave me. I picked up the superb winged creature, and stood admiring it from every angle for a good quarter-hour, when I heard M. King cry out for help; I ran to him, and found that he was only calling me to aid him in the search for a turkey which he declared he had killed, but which had nonetheless completely disappeared.

I put my dog on the scent, but he led us into thickets so dense and thorny that a serpent could not have gone through them, and we were forced to give up, which threw my companion into a temper which lasted until we returned to the farm.

The rest of our hunt is hardly worth describing. On the way back, we lost ourselves in the boundless woods, and were in great danger of having to spend the night in them, had it not been for the silvery voices of the young Bulows and the deep bass of their father, who had been kind enough to come in search of us, and who helped lead us out of the forest.

The four sisters had put on their full battle dress; freshly laundered frocks, new sashes, pretty hats and neatly shining shoes told that they had gone to some expense for our benefits; and as for me, I was willing enough to be my most agreeable to the one of these young ladies who took my arm with as much a proprietary air as any wife.

When we got back to the farm we found supper ready for us; but, before starting to eat, we sat down for a few minutes before a lively blazing fire which had been lighted, even though the weather would not have seemed to call for it. We found it very comforting indeed, and were refreshed by it almost magically.

This custom doubtless came from the Indians, who always have a fire burning in their wigwams. Perhaps it is also a custom given to us by Saint Francis of Sales, who once said that a fire is good twelve months of the year. (*Non liquet.*)

We ate as if we were starved; a generous bowl of punch helped us to finish off the evening, and a discussion in which our host talked much more freely than the day before held us late into the night.

We talked of the War of Independence, in which M. Bulow had served as a ranking officer; of M. de La Fayette, steadily greater in the minds of the Americans, who always spoke of him familiarly by his title (THE MARQUIS); of agriculture, which during that period was enriching the United States, and finally of my own dear France, which I loved much more since I had been forced to leave it.

From time to time, as an interlude in our conversation, M. Bulow would say to his oldest daughter: "Mariah! Give us a song." And she sang to us without more urging, and with a charming shyness, the national air YANKEE DUDDE, and the lament of Queen Mary and the one of Major Andrew, both of them very popular in this country. Mariah had taken a few lessons, and there in the backwoods was thought to be something of an artist; but her singing was praiseworthy mainly because of the quality of her voice, which was at once sweet, fresh, and unaffected.

The next day we left, in spite of the friendliest protests, for even in America I had certain duties to perform. While the horses were being saddled, M. Bulow, having drawn me to one side, spoke in the following profoundly interesting way:

"You see in me, my dear sir, a happy man, if such there be on earth: everything around you and all that you have so far observed is a product of what I own. These stockings I wear were knitted by my daughters; my shoes and my clothes come from my own sheep; they help also, with my gardens and barnyards, to furnish me with simple nourishing food; and what makes our government so admirable is that here in Connecticut there are thousands of farmers just as happy as I am, and whose doors, like mine, are never bolted.

"Taxes here are almost nothing; and as long as they are paid we can sleep in peace. Congress does everything in its power to help our newborn industry; agents come from every direction to buy up whatever we have to sell; and I have cash on hand for a long time, for I have just sold for twenty-four dollars a barrel the wheat I usually get eight for.

"All this is the result of the liberty which we have fought for and founded on good laws. I am master in my own house, and you will not be astonished to know that we never hear the sound of the drum here, nor, except for the fourth of July, the glorious anniversary of our independence, do we ever see soldiers, or uniforms, or bayonets."

During the whole of our trip homeward I was plunged in profound thought. It may be believed that I was pondering the parting speech of M. Bulow, but I had something quite different on my mind: I was considering how best I should cook my turkey, and I was not without some worries, for I feared that in Hartford I might not find all the ingredients I would need— and I was determined to raise a worthy monument to the spoils of my skill.

I inflict on myself a painful sacrifice in leaving out the details of the elaborate preparations I made for the fitting and distinguished way I planned to entertain my American dinner guests. It is enough to say that the partridge wings were served *en papillote*, and the grey squirrels simmered in Madeira.

As for the turkey, which was our only roast, it was charming to look at, flattering to the sense of smell, and delicious to the taste. And as the last morsel of it disappeared, there arose from the whole table the words: "VERY GOOD! EXCEEDINGLY GOOD! OH! DEAR SIR, WHAT A GLORIOUS BIT!"*

---

*The flesh of the wild turkey is darker and with a stronger flavor than that of the domestic bird.

I have learned with pleasure that my estimable colleague, M. Bosc, has shot them in Carolina, and that he found them delicious and much better than the ones we raise in Europe. He advises anyone who plans to grow them to give them the greatest possible liberty, and to take them out into the fields and even the woods, there to add to their flavor and bring them as nearly as possible to the state of the truly wild species. (ANNALES D'AGRICULTURE, pamphlet issued February 28, 1821.)

The Physiology of Taste, (1825; translated by M.F.K. Fisher, 1949)

To Make a Chowder

Four pounds of fish are enough to make a chowder, for four or five people,—half dozen slices of salt pork in the bottom of the pot,—hang it high, so that the pork may not burn,—take it out when done very brown,—put in a layer of fish, cut in lengthwise slices,—then a layer formed of crackers, small or sliced onions, and potatoes sliced as thin as a four-pence, mixed with pieces of pork you have fried; then a layer of fish again, and so on. Six crackers are enough. Strew a little salt and pepper over each layer; over the whole pour a bowl full of flour and water, enough to come up even with the surface of what you have in the pot. A sliced lemon adds to the flavor. A cup of Tomato catsup is very excellent. Some people put in a cup of beer. A few clams are a pleasant addition. It should be covered so as not to let a particle of steam escape, if possible. Do not open it, except when nearly done, to taste if it be well seasoned.

Lydia Maria Child, *The Frugal Housewife* (1830)

A great illustration of the whole chowder technique–the word used to imply layering of ingredients.

Frederick Marryat

from A Diary in America

When the popular British novelist Frederick Marryat (1792–1848) visited America in the late 1830s, he made himself quite unpopular with some of his public criticism of the new nation. By the time he left, he had been threatened by mobs and burned in effigy. In this passage from his 1839 *Diary in America*, however, he takes it upon himself to defend American cooking against the complaints of a native son (novelist James Fenimore Cooper, whose 1825 political treatise *The American Democrat* attempts, like other works of its time, to diagnose a national tendency to dyspepsia). Marryat's argument—that fine cooking exists in direct proportion to "the refinement of the population"—plays out as a contrast between the cooking he enjoyed in New York City at Delmonico's (then the country's premier restaurant) and the dishes such as "cornbread and common doings" (cornbread and fat pork) that appear as "you advance into the country and the population recedes."

■ ■ ■

I must now enter into a very important question, which is that of eating and drinking. Mr. Cooper, in his remarks upon his own countrymen, says, very ill-naturedly—"The Americans are the grossest feeders of any civilized nation known. As a nation, their food is heavy, coarse, and indigestible, while it is taken in the least artificial forms that cookery will allow. The predominance of grease in the American kitchen, coupled with the habits of hearty eating, and of constant expectoration, are the causes of the diseases of the stomach which are so common in America."

This is not correct. The cookery in the United States is exactly what it is and must be everywhere else—in a ratio with the degree of refinement of the population. In the principal cities, you will meet with as good cookery in private houses as you will in London, or even Paris; indeed, considering the great difficulty which the Americans have to contend with, from the almost impossibility of obtaining good servants, I have often been surprised that it is so good as it is. At Delmonico's, and the Globe Hotel at New York, where you dine from the Carte, you have excellent French cookery; so you have at Astor House, particularly at private parties; and, generally speaking, the cooking at all the large hotels may be said to be good; indeed, when it is considered that the American table-d'hôte has to provide for so many people, it is quite surprising how well it is done. The daily dinner, at these large hotels, is infinitely superior to any I have ever sat down to at the *public* entertainments given at the Free-Masons' Tavern, and others in London, and the company is usually more numerous. The bill of fare of the table-d'hôte of the Astor House is *printed every day*. I have one with me which I shall here insert, to prove that the eating is not so bad in America as described by Mr. Cooper.

Astor House, *Wednesday, March 21, 1838.*
Table-d' Hôte.

Vermicelli Soup
Boiled Cod Fish and Oysters
    Do.   Corn'd Beef
    Do.   Ham
    Do.   Tongue
    Do.   Turkey and Oysters
    Do.   Chickens and Pork
    Do.   Leg of Mutton
Oyster Pie
Cuisse de Poulet Sauce Tomate
Poitrine de Veau au Blanc
Salade de Volaille
Ballon de Mouton au Tomate
Tête de Veau en Marinade
Roast Goose
    Do.   Turkey
    Do.   Chickens
    Do.   Wild Ducks
    Do.   Wild Goose
    Do.   Guinea Fowl

Casserolle de Pomme de Terre
    garnie
Compote de Pigeon
Rolleau de Veau à la Jardiniére
Côtellettes de Veau Sauté
Filet de Mouton Piqué aux
    Ognons
Ronde de Bœuf
Fricandeau de Veau aux Epinards
Côtelettes de Mouton Panée
Macaroni au Parmesan
Roast Beef
    Do.   Pig
    Do.   Veal
    Do.   Leg of Mutton
Roast Brandt
Queen Pudding
Mince Pie
Cream Puffs
Dessert.

There are some trifling points relative to eating which I shall not remark upon until I speak of society, as they will there be better placed. Of
course, as you advance into the country, and population recedes, you run
through all the scale of cookery until you come to the "*corn bread, and common doings,*" (i.e. bread made of Indian meal, and fat pork,) in the far West.
In a new country, pork is more easily raised than any other meat, and the
Americans eat a great deal of pork, which renders the cooking in the small
taverns very greasy; with the exception of the Virginian farm taverns,
where they fry chickens without grease in a way which would be admired
by Ude himself; but this is a State receipt, handed down from generation to
generation, and called *chicken fixings.* The meat in America is equal to the
best in England; Miss Martineau does indeed say that she never ate good
beef during the whole time she was in the country; but she also says that an
American stage-coach is the most delightful of all conveyances, and a great
many other things, which I may hereafter quote, to prove the idiosyncracy
of the lady's disposition; so we will let that pass, with the observation that
there is no accounting for taste. The American markets in the cities are well
supplied. I have been in the game market, at New York, and seen at one time
nearly three hundred head of deer, with quantities of bear, racoons, wild
turkies, geese, ducks, and every variety of bird in countless profusion. Bear I
abominate; racoon is pretty good. The wild turkey is excellent; but the great
delicacies in America are the terrapin, and the canvas-back ducks. To like
the first I consider as rather an acquired taste. I decidedly prefer the turtle,
which are to be had in plenty, all the year round; but the canvas-back duck is
certainly well worthy of its reputation. Fish is well supplied. They have the
sheep's head, shad, and one or two others, which we have not. Their salmon
is not equal to ours, and they have no turbot. Pine-apples, and almost all the
tropical fruits, are hawked about in carts in the Eastern cities; but I consider
the fruit of the temperate zone, such as grapes, peaches, &c., inferior to the
English. Oysters are very plentiful, very large, and, to an English palate,
rather insipid. As the Americans assert that the English and French oysters
taste of copper, and that therefore they cannot eat them, I presume they do;
and that's the reason why we do not like the American oysters, copper being
better than no flavour at all.

I think, after this statement, that the English will agree with me that there are plenty of good things for the table in America; but the old proverb says, "God sends meat, and the devil sends cooks;" and such is, and unfortunately must be the case for a long while, in most of the houses in America, owing to the difficulty of obtaining, or keeping servants.

A Diary in America (1839)

POTTED LOBSTER.

¶ Parboil the lobster in boiling water well salted. Then pick out all the meat from the body and claws, and beat it in a mortar with nutmeg, mace, cayenne, and salt, to your taste. Beat the coral separately. Then put the pounded meat into a large potting can of block tin with a cover. Press it down hard, having arranged it in alternate layers of white meat and coral to give it a marbled or variegated appearance. Cover it with fresh butter, and put it into a slow oven for half an hour. When cold, take off the butter and clarify it, by putting it into a jar, which must be set in a pan of boiling water. Watch it well, and when it melts, carefully skim off the buttermilk which will rise to the top. When no more scum rises, take it off and let it stand for a few minutes to settle, and then strain it through a sieve.

¶ Put the lobster into small potting-cans, pressing it down very hard. Pour the clarified butter over it, and secure the covers tightly.

¶ Potted lobster is used to lay between thin slices of bread as sandwiches. The clarified butter that accompanies it is excellent for fish sauce.

¶ Prawns and crabs may be potted in a similar manner.

Eliza Leslie, *Directions for Cookery* (1837)

Leslie was perhaps the most famous culinary writer of the 19th century. The practice of butter-sealing delicate and perishable ingredients was much used in the United States at the time she wrote.

Nathaniel Hawthorne

This Day's Food

The lingering gloom of Puritanism that pervades Hawthorne's novels and stories is notable by its absence in this passage from his journals, a sketch of the idyllic early days of his married life. Hawthorne (1804–1864) had married Sophia Peabody about seven weeks before this entry was written, and the two were living in the Old Manse in Concord. The novelist had not long before spent eight months as a member of the Utopian community Brook Farm, but here he depicts himself as the self-sufficient Adam of his own personal paradise. An early American dream is perfectly realized as he and Sophia enjoy a meal that "comes directly and entirely from beneficent Nature, without the intervention of any third person between her and us."

■ ■ ■

Wednesday, August 24th, 1842.

I left my Sophie's arms at five o'clock this morning, to catch some fish for dinner. On my way through the orchard, I shook our summer apple-tree, and ate the golden apple which fell from it. Methinks these early apples, which come as a golden promise before the treasures of autumnal fruit, are almost more delicious than anything that comes afterwards. We have but one such tree in our orchard; but it supplies us with a daily abundance, and promises to do so for at least a week to come. Meantime, other trees begin to cast their ripening windfalls upon the grass; and when I taste them, and perceive their mellowed flavor and blackening seeds, I feel somewhat overwhelmed with the impending bounties of Providence. I suppose Adam, in Paradise, did not like to see his fruits decaying on the ground, after he had watched them through the sunny days of the world's first summer. However, insects, at the worst, will hold a festival upon them; so that they will not be thrown away, in the great scheme of nature. Moreover, I have one advantage over the primeval Adam, inasmuch as there is a chance of disposing of my superfluous fruits among people who inhabit no Paradise of their own.

Passing a little way down along the river-side, I threw in my line, and soon drew out one of the smallest possible fish. It seemed to be a pretty good morning for the angler—an autumnal coolness in the air; a clear sky, but with a fog along the lowlands and on the surface of the river, which a gentle breeze sometimes condensed into wreaths. At first, I could barely discern the opposite shore of the river; but as the sun arose, the vapors gradually dispersed, till only a warm smoky tint was left along the water's surface. The farm-houses, across the river, made their appearance out of the dusky cloud;—the voices of boys were heard, shouting to the cattle as they drove them to pasture;—a mower whet his scythe, and set to work in a neighboring meadow. Meantime, I continued to stand on the oozy margin of the stream, beguiling the little fish; and though the scaly inhabitants of our river partake somewhat of the character of their native element, and are but sluggish biters, still I contrived to pull out not far from two dozen. They were all bream—a broad, flat, almost circular fish, shaped a good deal like a flounder, but swimming on their edges, instead of their flat sides. As far as mere pleasure is concerned, it is hardly worth while to fish in our river, it is so much like angling in a mud-puddle; and one does not attach the idea of freshness and purity to the fish, as we do to those which inhabit swift, transparent streams, or haunt the shores of the great briny deep. Standing on the weedy margin, and throwing the line over the elder-bushes that dip into the water, it seems as if we could catch nothing but frogs and mud-turtles, or reptiles akin to them; and even when a fish of reputable aspect is drawn out, you feel a shyness about touching him. As to our river, my little wife expressed its character admirably, last night; she said "it was too lazy to keep itself clean." I might write pages and pages, and only obscure the impression which this brief sentence conveys. Nevertheless, we made bold to eat some of my fish for breakfast, and found them very savory; and the rest shall meet with due entertainment at dinner, together with some shell-beans, green corn, and cucumbers from our garden; so that this day's food comes directly and entirely from beneficent Nature, without the intervention of any third person between her and us.

The American Notebooks (1972; written 1842)

James M. Sanderson

Above All Other Birds

James M. Sanderson (1815?–1871) brings an unabashed patriotism to his praises here for the canvas-back duck–the succulent native bird that fed on wild celery and was the darling of East Coast tables from the colonial era until the early 20th century, by which time the species had almost been eaten into extinction. A hotel manager by profession, Sanderson was clearly a gourmet at heart: he sought out recipes for local favorites like terrapin and pumpkin pie, wrote learned articles on champagne and cookery, presided over elaborate banquets (including one in New York featuring dishes from Shakespeare), and urged his compatriots to imagine a day when the culinary arts in America might begin to rival their European counterparts. With the outbreak of the Civil War, he volunteered his services as a "missionary cook," and published *Camp Fires and Camp Cooking; or, Culinary Hints for the Soldier* (1862), in an effort to aid the Union cause: "Beans, badly boiled, kill more than bullets, and fat is more fatal than powder." Sadly, love of good eating also seems to have led Sanderson into some scandalous behavior: while a prisoner of war in Richmond, his fellow inmates accused him, in his role as commissary, of keeping the best food for himself and his circle while others starved. Though exonerated of official charges, he exiled himself to London soon after the war and never returned to the land of the canvas-back.

■ ■ ■

Only look, through your mind's eye, at the catalogue, and from the extended list select the numerous luxuries that each season presents. The winter, the spring, the summer, and the autumn, spread out before us their extensive stock, and seem to invite an unlimited enjoyment. But of all the luxuries bestowed upon man, the *canvass-back duck* stands out in bold relief from the rest of the feathered tribe. Seatsfield says, "had Lucullus known of it, he would have deprived Columbus of the honor of the discovery of our part of the world. No European imperial table can boast a dish so tender, so aromatic and so juicy; the meat really melts on your tongue, and the fat runs over your lips do what you will; it is a genuine gastronomic feast." Featherstonhaugh, with all his excessive loyalty and affection for the land that gave

him birth, says, "it is an exemplary bird, which seems to take–*sua sponte*–
the most indefatigable pains to qualify himself for a favorable reception in
the best society; for in the first instance he makes himself exceedingly fat
by resorting to the low marshy lands of the Susquehanna, to feed upon the
ripe seed of the *zizania aquatica*, a sort of wild rice which abounds there; and
then, at a proper season, betakes himself to an esculent root growing in the
sedgy bands of the river, to give the last finish to the tenderness, the juiciness, and the delicate flavor which distinguishes him *above all other birds*
when brought to table. But justice must be done to him by an abler artist,
or great as his intrinsic qualities are, he may be reduced to a condition that
entitles him even to be pitied by the humble scavenger duck.

"I had heard a great deal of this inestimable bird, before it was presented to me under the auspices of Barnum, and was somewhat surprised
and disappointed, at seeing him place on the table, with great solemnity, a
couple of birds on a dish without a single drop of gravy in it. Now every one
knows that a quantum suff. of good gravy is to English rôtis what fine sunny
weather is to the incidents of life, enabling them to pass along smoothly
and pleasantly; and, therefore, as soon as I had a little recovered from my
alarm, I could not help telling Barnum, that I was afraid I should not like
his canvass-back. Upon which, asking our permission, he took up the carving
knife, and making two incisions in the fat breast of the birds, the dish instantly became *filled* with the desired fluid. Had I not seen this, I could not
have believed it! Then came the action of the *réchauffoirs*, the dismember-
ment of the birds, scarcely warmed through at the fire, the transference of
their delicate flesh to our hot plates, and its reconcoction in their own gravy,
with currant jelly, a soupcon of château margeau, and a small quantity of
fine loaf sugar. We were three of us to these two birds, and the great Barnum
had the satisfaction of hearing us declare, that the only defect they had, consisted in their not being of the size of turkeys."

William Penn, also, in one of his letters says, "There are plenty of ducks
in the Delaware; some very delicious when cooked with a little berry called
cranberry."

But the high admiration of these gentlemen is not equal to the classic,
the Lamb-like description of Buckstone. His eulogium of the canvass-back

duck, in his journey to the South, is certainly equal to the roast-pig of
Elia, and we regret we cannot give it from memory. Wilson, however,
in his Ornithology, says, "the canvass-back, in the rich, juicy, tenderness
of its flesh, and its delicacy of flavor, stands unrivalled by the whole of
its tribe, in this, or perhaps any other part of the world. At our public
dinners, hotels, and particular entertainments, the canvass-backs are
universal favorites." We have also the permission of one of our most celebrated novelists, to say that he always pays them (the canvass-backs) the
greatest respect, by eating all he can get. But it is not to the Tourist, to
the Ornithologist, or to the Novelist, that this delicious bird is indebted
for its fame, nor is it through this channel alone, that its name is to reach
posterity. Joel Barlow has sung its praises in his Columbiad, and many of
the more recent if not more meritorious Poets have carried it upon the
wings of their imaginations to the highest pinnacle of fame, and, if not
cut short by Father Miller, many ages will pass before they are forgotten.
The plan of catching them, is also given in numbers, by the author of
the Foresters, and we want only the delicate pen of Willis, to make the
canvass-back one of the choicest of our national dishes. Indeed, it is the
belief that this bird was especially intended by Providence as the proper
food for the Presidents of this Republic. The place where they abound
in the greatest perfection, being in close contiguity with the Capital, is
strong evidence of the fact, and if we look at the age of the several venerated patriots that have filled the office—at the Republican simplicity
with which the sceptre has been wielded—at the clear sight, and prudent
forethought with which they have been enabled to view and resist the
encroachments of our aristocratic neighbors, it must have been owing to
the influence of the canvass-back duck upon the system. The fact, also,
that our much respected and venerated incumbent has been rejuvenized,
and taken to himself a young and beautiful wife, is an illustration of our
position, and establishes, beyond a doubt, the efficacy of canvass-backs,
and towards this Republic the peculiar intentions of Heaven. The governments of Europe, we all know, are obliged to protect the persons of
their sovereigns, with a retinue, and an expense almost equal to the dis-
bursements of our government. A cook to his august Majesty receives

a salary nearly equal to our President; and yet, with all his skill, is unable to produce a single dish that will afford the nutriment of a canvass-back duck. A physician is alike compensated, and when we compare the ages of the parties, the Republican, without these appendages, outlives the most robust sovereign of the world. Then why is it so? Because, with a chafing-dish, a spoonful of claret, and a little currant jelly, he prepares the dinner that Providence has already cooked upon the wing.

Mirror for Dyspeptics (1844)

TO DRESS MACARONI A LA SAUCE BLANCHE.

Take a quarter of a pound of macaroni, boil it in water, in which there must be a little salt. When the macaroni is done, the water must be drained from it, and the saucepan kept covered; roll two table-spoonfuls of butter in a little flour; take a pint of milk, and half a pint of cream; add the butter and flour to the milk, and set it on the fire, until it becomes thick. This sauce ought to be stirred the whole time it is boiling, and always in the same direction. Grate a quarter of a pound of parmesan cheese; butter the pan in which the macaroni is to be baked, and put in first, a layer of macaroni, then one of grated cheese, then some sauce, and so on until the dish is filled; the last layer must be of cheese, and sauce with which the macaroni is to be well covered. Ten minutes will bake it in a quick oven.   —*Italian Receipt.*

Sarah Rutledge, *The Carolina Housewife* (1847)

An early version of macaroni and cheese, presented by the daughter of a signer of the Declaration of Independence.

George G. Foster

The Eating-Houses

George G. Foster (1814?–1856) had spent years traveling around the country working on small newspapers before he began to publish his series *New York in Slices* in the *New York Tribune* in 1848. The runaway success of these lively snapshots of city life led promptly to a sequel, *New York by Gas-Light* (1850). "The Eating-Houses" offers a lively picture of the hurly-burly of urban dining in an era when appetites were large, the beef was butchered on Washington Street, and the public eating houses were mostly a man's domain. Foster fell on hard times later in his career—he served nine months in prison for forgery—and his *New York Times* obituary described him as "a remarkable example of the worthlessness of a brilliant talent unguided by a moral purpose, or a decent regard for the proprieties of civilized society."

■ ■ ■

"Beefsteakandtatersvegetábesnumbertwenty—Injinhardandsparrowgrass-numbérsixteen!" "Waiter! Waiter! WA-Y-TER!" "Comingsir"—while the rascal's *going* as fast as he can! "*Is* that beef killed for my porterhouse steak I ordered last week?" "Readynminitsir, comingsir, dreklysir—twonsixpence, biledamand cabbage shillin, ricepudn sixpnce, eithteenpence—at the barf you please—lobstaucensammingnumberfour—yes sir!" Imagine a continuous stream of such sounds as these, about the size of the Croton river, flowing through the banks of clattering plates and clashing knives and forks, perfumed with the steam from a mammoth kitchen, roasting, boiling, baking, frying, beneath the floor—crowds of animals with a pair of jaws apiece, wagging in emulation of the one wielded with such terrific effect by SAMSON—and the thermometer which has become ashamed of itself and hides away behind a mountain of hats in the corner, melting up *by degrees* to boiling heat—and you will have some notion of a New York eating-house. We once undertook to count these establishments in the lower part of the City, but got surfeited on the smell of fried grease before we got half through the first street, and were obliged to go home in a cab. We believe, however, that there can't be less than a hundred of them within half a mile of the Exchange.

They are too important a "slice" of New York to be overlooked, and strangers who stop curiosity-hunting after they have climbed the big clock-case at the head of Wall-street, haven't seen half the sights.

A New York eating-house at high tide is a scene which would well repay the labors of an antiquarian or a panoramist, if its spirit and details could be but half preserved. Every thing is done differently in New York from anywhere else—but in eating the difference is more striking than in any other branch of human economy. A thorough-bred diner-down-town will look at a bill of fare, order his dinner, bolt it and himself, and be engaged in putting off a lot of goods upon a greenhorn, while you are getting your napkin fixed over your nankeens (we think the cotton article preferable) and deciding whether you will take ox-tail or mock-turtle. A regular down-towner surveys the kitchen with his nose as he comes up-stairs—selects his dish by intuition, and swallows it by steam and the electro-galvanic battery. As to digesting it, that is none of his business. He has paid all liabilities to his stomach, and that is all he knows or cares about the matter. The stomach must manage its own affairs—he is not in that "line."

Not less than thirty thousand persons engaged in mercantile or financial affairs, dine at eating-houses every day. The work commences punctually at twelve; and from that hour until three or four the havoc is immense and incessant. Taylor at Buena Vista was nothing to it. They sweep every thing—not a fragment is left. The fare is generally bad enough—not nearly equal to that which the cook at the Home above Bleecker saves for the beggars, (generally her own thirteen cousins, "just come over.") It is really wonderful how men of refined tastes and pampered habits, who at home are as fastidious as luxury and a delicate appetite can make them, find it in their hearts—or stomachs either—to gorge such disgusting masses of stringy meat and tepid vegetables, and to go about their business again under the fond delusion that they have dined. But "custom," they say, does wonders; and it seems that the fear of losing it makes our merchant-princes willing to put up with and put down warm swill in lieu of soup, perspiring joints for delicate *entrées*, and corn meal and molasses instead of *meringues à la crême à la rose*.

There are three distinct classes of eating-houses, and each has its model or type. Linnæus would probably classify them as Sweenyorum, Browniverous, and Delmonican. The Sweenyorum is but an extension downward of the Browniverous, which we have already described. The chief difference to be noted between the two is, that while at Brown's the waiters *actually do* pass by you within hail now and then, at Sweeney's no such phenomenon ever by any possibility occurs. The room is laid out like the floor of a church, with tables and benches for four, in place of pews. Along the aisles (of Greece, if you judge by the smell) are ranged at "stated" intervals, the attentive wait- ers, who receive the dishes, small plate sixpnce, large plate shillin, as they are cut off by the man at the helm, and distribute them on either side, with surprising dexterity and precision. Sometimes a nice bit of rosegoose, ten- der, may be seen flying down the aisle, without its original wings, followed closely in playful sport by a small plate bilebeef, vegetables, until both ar- rive at their destination; when goose leaps lightly in front of a poet of the Sunday press, who ordered it probably through a commendable preference for a brother of the quill; while the fat and lazy beef dumps itself down with perfect resignation before the "monstrous jaws" of one of the b'hoys, who has just come from a fire in 49th-street, and is hungry, *some!*

At Brown's we get a bill of fare, with the "extras" all honestly marked off and priced at the margin. But at Sweeney's we save our sixpence and dis- pense with superfluities. The bill of fare is delivered by a man at the door, regularly engaged for that purpose, and is as follows:

> Biledlamancapersors.
> Rosebeefrosegoorosemuttonantaters—
> Biledamancabbage, vegetables—
> Walkinsirtakaseatsir.

This is certainly clear and distinct as General Taylor's political opinions, and does away with a great deal of lying in print, to which bills of fare as well as newspapers are too much addicted. The Sweeney, or sixpenny cut, is frequented by a more diversified set of customers than either of the others. It is not impossible to see, here, Professor Bush dining cheek-by-jowl with a hod-man off duty, nor to find a blackleg from Park-row seated opposite the police-officer whose manifest destiny it will be one of these days to take him to quod—unless he should happen to have money enough about him to pay for being let go. The editor, the author, the young lawyer, the publisher,

the ice-cream man round the corner, the poor physician on his way to patients who don't pay, the young student of divinity learning humility at six
shillings a week; the journeyman printer on a batter, and afraid to go home
to his wife before he gets sober; in short, all classes who go to make up the
great middle stripe of population, concentrate and commingle at Sweeney's.
Yet all these varied elements never effervesce into any thing in the slightest
degree resembling a disturbance; for eating is a serious business—especially
when you have but sixpence and no idea whether the next one has been
coined.

It is true that Sweeney's "is emphatically a sixpenny eating-house"—
but you must take care what you are about, or you may as well have dined
at the Astor.—Unless you know how it is done, you will be nicely done
yourself. If you indulge in a second piece of bread, a pickle, a bit of cheese,
&c., &c., your bill will be summed up to you something after this fashion:—
"Clamsoup sixpnce, rosebeef large, shilln, roastchikn eighteen, extra bread
three, butter sixpnce, pickle sixpnce, pudn sixpnce, cheese three, claret
(logwood and water alumized) two shilln—seven shilln." If you wish to dine
cheaply, be contented with a cheap dinner. Call simply for a small plate of
roast beef mixed, (this means mashed turnips and potatoes in equal quantities.) After you have eaten this frugal dish,—and it is as much as any one
really *needs* for dinner,—you may send for "bread, hard," drink a tumbler of
cool Croton, pay one shilling for the whole, and go about your business like
a refreshed and sensible man.

There is still another class of eating-houses, which deserve honorable
mention—the cake and coffee shops, of which "Butter-cake Dick's" is a favorable sample.—The chief merit of these establishments is that they are kept
open all night, and that hungry Editors or belated idlers can get a plate of
biscuits with a lump of butter in the belly for three cents, and a cup of coffee
for as much more—or he can regale himself on pumpkin pie at four cents
the quarter-section, with a cup of Croton, fresh from the hydrant, gratis. The
principal supporters of these luxurious establishments, however, are the
firemen and the upper circles of the newsboys, who have made a good business during the day, or have succeeded in pummeling some smaller boy and
taking his pennies from him. Here, ranged on wooden benches, the butter-
cakes and coffee spread ostentatiously before them, and their intelligent faces

supported in the crotch of their joined hands, these autocrats of the press, and the b'hoys, discuss the grave questions as to whether Fourteen was at the fire in Front-street first, or whether it is all gas. Here also are decided in advance the relative merits and speed of the boats entered for the next regatta, and points of great pith and moment in the science of the Ring are definitively settled. As midnight comes and passes, the firemen, those children of the dark, gather from unimaginable places, and soon a panorama of red shirts and brown faces lines the walls and fills the whole area of the little cellar. They are generally far more moderate than politicians and less noisy than gentlemen. At the first tingle of the fire-bell they leap like crouching greyhounds, and are in an instant darting through the street towards their respective engine-houses—whence they emerge dragging their ponderous machines behind them, ready to work like Titans all night and all day, exposing themselves to every peril of life and limb, and performing incredible feats of daring strength, to save the property of people who know nothing about them, care nothing for them, and perhaps will scarcely take the trouble to thank them.

But of all this by itself. The type of eating-house of which we have not spoken is the expensive and aristocratic *restaurant* of which Delmonico's is the only complete specimen in the United States—and this, we have it on the authority of travelled epicures, is equal in every respect, in its appointments and attendance as well as the quality and execution of its dishes, to any similar establishment in Paris itself. We have not left ourselves room in this number to speak in detail of this famous *restaurant*, nor of its *habitués*. It well deserves, however, a separate notice; and a look through its well-filled yet not crowded saloons, and into its admirable *cuisine* will enable us to pass an hour very profitably—besides obtaining a dinner which , as a work of art, ranks with a picture by Huntingdon, a poem by Willis, or a statue by Powers—a dinner which is not merely a quantity of food deposited in the stomach, but is in every sense and to all the senses a great work of art.

New York in Slices (1849)

TO MAKE CORN BREAD. FOUR EGGS TO A QUART OF MILK, A POUND OF BUTTER TO SIX POUNDS OF MEAL. STIR WELL UNTIL IT IS ABOUT THE THICKNESS OF GOOD MOLASSES. A TEA-CUPFUL OF MOLASSES TO SIX POUNDS OF MEAL TO WHICH ADD A TEA-SPOONFUL OF SALÆRATUS. GREASE YOUR PANS WELL WITH BUTTER. PUT IT IN A GOOD HOT OVEN; BAKE THREE QUARTERS OF AN HOUR.

Tunis G. Campbell, *Hotel Keepers, Head Waiters, and Housekeepers' Guide* (1848)

Campbell preached abolition while working as a baker and a hotel steward.

Herman Melville

Chowder

In one of the most buoyant chapters in *Moby-Dick* (1851), Melville's whalers Ishmael and Queequeg, after a suite of omens (coffin and tombstones and gallows) seeming to portend no good for their approaching voyage on the *Pequod*, are granted momentary respite in a paradise of chowder: "Chowder for breakfast, and chowder for dinner, and chowder for supper." Such is Melville's power of evocation that few American literary passages stir such deep and immediate craving. If they could just stay on land in the quintessentially fishy precincts of the Try Pots, all might turn out quite differently: but even here Melville (1819–1891) cannot resist ending the brief chapter with the image of a young seaman impaled on his own harpoon.

■ ■ ■

It was quite late in the evening when the little Moss came snugly to anchor, and Queequeg and I went ashore; so we could attend to no business that day, at least none but a supper and a bed. The landlord of the Spouter-Inn had recommended us to his cousin Hosea Hussey of the Try Pots, whom he asserted to be the proprietor of one of the best kept hotels in all Nantucket, and moreover he had assured us that cousin Hosea, as he called him, was famous for his chowders. In short, he plainly hinted that we could not possibly do better than try pot-luck at the Try Pots. But the directions he had given us about keeping a yellow warehouse on our starboard hand till we opened a white church to the larboard, and then keeping that on the larboard hand till we made a corner three points to the starboard, and that done, then ask the first man we met where the place was: these crooked directions of his very much puzzled us at first, especially as, at the outset, Queequeg insisted that the yellow warehouse—our first point of departure—must be left on the larboard hand, whereas I had understood Peter Coffin to say it was on the starboard. However, by dint of beating about a little in the dark, and now and then knocking up a peaceable inhabitant to inquire the way, we at last came to something which there was no mistaking.

Two enormous wooden pots painted black, and suspended by asses' ears, swung from the cross-trees of an old top-mast, planted in front of an old doorway. The horns of the cross-trees were sawed off on the other side, so that this old top-mast looked not a little like a gallows. Perhaps I was over sensitive to such impressions at the time, but I could not help staring at this gallows with a vague misgiving. A sort of crick was in my neck as I gazed up to the two remaining horns; yes, *two* of them, one for Queequeg, and one for me. It's ominous, thinks I. A Coffin my Innkeeper upon landing in my first whaling port; tombstones staring at me in the whalemen's chapel; and here a gallows! and a pair of prodigious black pots too! Are these last throwing out oblique hints touching Tophet?

I was called from these reflections by the sight of a freckled woman with yellow hair and a yellow gown, standing in the porch of the inn, under a dull red lamp swinging there, that looked much like an injured eye, and carrying on a brisk scolding with a man in a purple woollen shirt.

"Get along with ye," said she to the man, "or I'll be combing ye!"

"Come on, Queequeg," said I, "all right. There's Mrs. Hussey."

And so it turned out; Mr. Hosea Hussey being from home, but leaving Mrs. Hussey entirely competent to attend to all his affairs. Upon making known our desires for a supper and a bed, Mrs. Hussey, postponing further scolding for the present, ushered us into a little room, and seating us at a table spread with the relics of a recently concluded repast, turned round to us and said–"Clam or Cod?"

"What's that about Cods, ma'am?" said I, with much politeness.

"Clam or Cod?" she repeated.

"A clam for supper? a cold clam; is *that* what you mean, Mrs. Hussey?" says I; "but that's a rather cold and clammy reception in the winter time, ain't it, Mrs. Hussey?"

But being in a great hurry to resume scolding the man in the purple shirt, who was waiting for it in the entry, and seeming to hear nothing but the word "clam," Mrs. Hussey hurried towards an open door leading to the kitchen, and bawling out "clam for two," disappeared.

"Queequeg," said I, "do you think that we can make out a supper for us both on one clam?"

However, a warm savory steam from the kitchen served to belie the apparently cheerless prospect before us. But when that smoking chowder came in, the mystery was delightfully explained. Oh, sweet friends! hearken to me. It was made of small juicy clams, scarcely bigger than hazel nuts, mixed with pounded ship biscuit, and salted pork cut up into little flakes; the whole enriched with butter, and plentifully seasoned with pepper and salt. Our appetites being sharpened by the frosty voyage, and in particular, Queequeg seeing his favorite fishy food before him, and the chowder being surpassingly excellent, we dispatched it with great expedition: when leaning back a moment and bethinking me of Mrs. Hussey's clam and cod announcement, I thought I would try a little experiment. Stepping to the kitchen door, I uttered the word "cod" with great emphasis, and resumed my seat. In a few moments the savory steam came forth again, but with a different flavor, and in good time a fine cod-chowder was placed before us.

We resumed business; and while plying our spoons in the bowl, thinks I to myself, I wonder now if this here has any effect on the head? What's that stultifying saying about chowder-headed people? "But look, Queequeg, ain't that a live eel in your bowl? Where's your harpoon?"

Fishiest of all fishy places was the Try Pots, which well deserved its name; for the pots there were always boiling chowders. Chowder for breakfast, and chowder for dinner, and chowder for supper, till you began to look for fish-bones coming through your clothes. The area before the house was paved with clam-shells. Mrs. Hussey wore a polished necklace of codfish vertebra; and Hosea Hussey had his account books bound in superior old shark-skin. There was a fishy flavor to the milk, too, which I could not at all account for, till one morning happening to take a stroll along the beach among some fishermen's boats, I saw Hosea's brindled cow feeding on fish remnants, and marching along the sand with each foot in a cod's decapitated head, looking very slip-shod, I assure ye.

Supper concluded, we received a lamp, and directions from Mrs. Hussey concerning the nearest way to bed; but, as Queequeg was about to precede me up the stairs, the lady reached forth her arm, and demanded his harpoon; she allowed no harpoon in her chambers. "Why not?" said I; "every true whaleman sleeps with his harpoon—but why not?" "Because it's dangerous," says she. "Every since young Stiggs coming from that unfort'nt v'y'ge of his, when he was gone four years and a half, with ony three barrels of *ile*, was found dead in my first floor back, with his harpoon in his side; ever since then I allow no boarders to take such dangerous weepons in their rooms a-night. So, Mr. Queequeg" (for she had learned his name), "I will just take this here iron, and keep it for you till morning. But the chowder; clam or cod to-morrow for breakfast, men?"

"Both," says I; "and let's have a couple of smoked herring by way of variety."

Moby-Dick (1851)

PEACH LEATHER.

Peel very ripe, soft peaches; mash them fine, and strain through a colander. If the peaches are not very sweet, add a little sugar. Butter well panes of glass, and spread the paste smoothly upon them. Put in the sun to dry; when dry on one side, turn it, and when perfectly dry, roll and keep in boxes. When not convenient to use the glass, butter strips of cloth, and spread upon well-seasoned boards.

Annabella P. Hill, *Mrs. Hill's New Cook Book* (1867)

Mrs. Hill's was the major Southern cookbook published in the aftermath of the Civil War. Pickled shrimp and peach leather are among the quintessential Southern dishes of their time.

Henry David Thoreau

In his classic *Walden* (1854), Henry David Thoreau (1817–1862) investigates the possibilities of a self-sufficient mode of life—a life in harmony with nature, free from the system of entanglements, compromises, and sacrifices commonly known as civilization. Having first obtained for himself a rudimentary shelter near Walden Pond, he turned of course to the question of what to eat. And here, as in most things in *Walden*, he found ample satisfaction in bare essentials: purslane, a weed he gathered in the local cornfields, made a good dinner simply "boiled and salted." Even bread—one of the most basic and elemental parts of an everyday diet, as the proverb would have it—he realized he could simplify. A well-puffed loaf, it was conventionally believed, was the only healthy and wholesome kind. But Thoreau challenges his readers to see such claims for what they may be—propaganda for costly yeast and wheat flour—and to consider the moral superiority of an unleavened bread made of rough-ground, native corn. His notes on watermelon, taken from his late manuscript writings, likewise affirm his underlying credo: "Our diet . . . must answer to the season." A major spiritual ancestor of many today who look for locally grown, organic foods, Thoreau seems not, however, to have been especially motivated by a concern for flavor—for the better *taste* of natural fare. To critics who questioned his austerities, he had a simple answer: "I can live on board nails."

■ ■ ■

Bread

I learned from my two years' experience that it would cost incredibly little trouble to obtain one's necessary food, even in this latitude; that a man may use as simple a diet as the animals, and yet retain health and strength. I have made a satisfactory dinner, satisfactory on several accounts, simply off a dish of purslane (*Portulaca oleracea*) which I gathered in my cornfield, boiled and salted. I give the Latin on account of the savoriness of the trivial name. And pray what more can a reasonable man desire, in peaceful times, in ordinary noons, than a sufficient number of ears of green sweet-corn boiled, with the addition of salt? Even the little variety which I used was a yielding to the demands of appetite, and not of health. Yet men have come to such a pass that they frequently starve, not for want of necessaries, but for want of luxuries; and I know a good woman who thinks that her son lost his life because he took to drinking water only.

The reader will perceive that I am treating the subject rather from an economic than a dietetic point of view, and he will not venture to put my abstemiousness to the test unless he has a well-stocked larder.

Bread I at first made of pure Indian meal and salt, genuine hoe-cakes, which I baked before my fire out of doors on a shingle or the end of a stick of timber sawed off in building my house; but it was wont to get smoked and to have a piny flavor. I tried flour also; but have at last found a mixture of rye and Indian meal most convenient and agreeable. In cold weather it was no little amusement to bake several small loaves of this in succession, tending and turning them as carefully as an Egyptian his hatching eggs. They were a real cereal fruit which I ripened, and they had to my senses a fragrance like that of other noble fruits, which I kept in as long as possible by wrapping them in cloths. I made a study of the ancient and indispensable art of bread-making, consulting such authorities as offered, going back to the primitive days and first invention of the unleavened kind, when from the wildness of nuts and meats men first reached the mildness and refinement of this diet, and travelling gradually down in my studies through that accidental souring of the dough which, it is supposed, taught the leavening process, and through the various fermentations thereafter, till I came to "good, sweet, wholesome bread," the staff of life. Leaven, which some deem the soul of bread, the *spiritus* which fills its cellular tissue, which is religiously preserved like the vestal fire,—some precious bottle-full, I suppose, first brought over in the Mayflower, did the business for America, and its influence is still rising, swelling, spreading, in cerealian billows over the land,—this seed I regularly and faithfully procured from the village, till at length one morning I forgot the rules, and scalded my yeast; by which accident I discovered that even this was not indispensable,—for my discoveries were not by the synthetic but analytic process,—and I have gladly omitted it since, though most housewives earnestly assured me that safe and wholesome bread without yeast might not be, and elderly people prophesied a speedy decay of the vital forces. Yet I find it not to be an essential ingredient, and after going without it for a year am still in the land of the living; and

I am glad to escape the trivialness of carrying a bottle-full in my pocket, which would sometimes pop and discharge its contents to my discomfiture. It is simpler and more respectable to omit it. Man is an animal who more than any other can adapt himself to all climates and circumstances. Neither did I put any sal soda, or other acid or alkali, into my bread. It would seem that I made it according to the recipe which Marcus Porcius Cato gave about two centuries before Christ. "Panem depsticium sic facito. Manus mortariumque bene lavato. Farinam in mortarium indito, aquæ paulatim addito, subigitoque pulchre. Ubi bene subegeris, defingito, coquitoque sub testu." Which I take to mean—"Make kneaded bread thus. Wash your hands and trough well. Put the meal into the trough, add water gradually, and knead it thoroughly. When you have kneaded it well, mould it, and bake it under a cover," that is, in a baking-kettle. Not a word about leaven. But I did not always use this staff of life. At one time, owing to the emptiness of my purse, I saw none of it for more than a month.

Every New Englander might easily raise all his own breadstuffs in this land of rye and Indian corn, and not depend on distant and fluctuating markets for them. Yet so far are we from simplicity and independence that, in Concord, fresh and sweet meal is rarely sold in the shops, and hominy and corn in a still coarser form are hardly used by any. For the most part the farmer gives to his cattle and hogs the grain of his own producing, and buys flour, which is at least no more wholesome, at a greater cost, at the store. I saw that I could easily raise my bushel or two of rye and Indian corn, for the former will grow on the poorest land, and the latter does not require the best, and grind them in a hand-mill, and so do without rice and pork; and if I must have some concentrated sweet, I found by experiment that I could make a very good molasses either of pumpkins or beets, and I knew that I needed only to set out a few maples to obtain it more easily still, and while these were growing I could use various substitutes beside those which I have named, "For," as the Forefathers sang,—

> "we can make liquor to sweeten our lips
> Of pumpkins and parsnips and walnut-tree chips."

Finally, as for salt, that grossest of groceries, to obtain this might be a fit occasion for a visit to the seashore, or, if I did without it altogether, I should probably drink the less water. I do not learn that the Indians ever troubled themselves to go after it.

Thus I could avoid all trade and barter, so far as my food was concerned, and having a shelter already, it would only remain to get clothing and fuel. The pantaloons which I now wear were woven in a farmer's family,—thank Heaven there is so much virtue still in man; for I think the fall from the farmer to the operative as great and memorable as that from the man to the farmer;—and in a new country fuel is an encumbrance. As for a habitat, if I were not permitted still to squat, I might purchase one acre at the same price for which the land I cultivated was sold—namely, eight dollars and eight cents. But as it was, I considered that I enhanced the value of the land by squatting on it.

There is a certain class of unbelievers who sometimes ask me such questions as, if I think that I can live on vegetable food alone; and to strike at the root of the matter at once,—for the root is faith,—I am accustomed to answer such, that I can live on board nails. If they cannot understand that, they cannot understand much that I have to say. For my part, I am glad to hear of experiments of this kind being tried; as that a young man tried for a fortnight to live on hard, raw corn on the ear, using his teeth for all mortar. The squirrel tribe tried the same and succeeded. The human race is interested in these experiments, though a few old women who are incapacitated for them, or who own their thirds in mills, may be alarmed.

Watermelons

Watermelons. The first are ripe from August seventh to twenty-eighth (though the last is late), and they continue to ripen till they freeze; are in their prime in September.

John Josselyn, an old resident in New England, speaks of the watermelon as one of the plants "proper to the country." He says that it is "of a sad grass-green color, or more rightly sap green; with some yellowness admixed when ripe."

September is come with its profusion of large fruits. Melons and apples seem at once to feed my brain.

How differently we fare now from what we did in winter! We give the butcher no encouragement now, but invite him to take a walk in our garden.

I have no respect for those who cannot raise melons or who avoid them as unwholesome. They should be spending their third winter with Parry in the arctic regions. They seem to have taken in their provisions at the commencement of the cruise, I know now how many years ago, and they deserve to have a monument erected to them of the empty cans which held their preserved meats.

Our diet, like that of the birds, must answer to the season. This is the season of west-looking, watery fruits. In the dog-days we come near to sustaining our lives on watermelon juice alone, like those who have fevers. I know of no more agreeable and nutritious food at this season than bread and butter and melons, and you need not be afraid of eating too much of the latter.

When I am going a-berrying in my boat or other carriage, I frequently carry watermelons for drink. It is the most agreeable and refreshing wine in a convenient cask, and most easily kept cool. Carry these green bottles of wine. When you get to the field you put them in the shade or in water till you want them.

When at home, if you would cool a watermelon which has been lying in the sun, do not put it in water, which keeps the heat in, but cut it open and place it on a cellar bottom or in a draught of air in the shade.

There are various ways in which you can tell if a watermelon is ripe. If you have had your eye on the patch much from the first, and so know the history of each one and which was formed first, you may presume that those will ripen soonest. Or else you may incline to those which lie nearest to the center of the hill or root, as the oldest.

Next, the dull, dead color and want of bloom are as good signs as any. Some *look* green and livid, and have a very fog of bloom on them, like a mildew. These are as green as a leek through and through, and you'll find yourself in a pickle if you open one. Others have a dead dark-greenness, the circulations coming less rapid in their cuticles and their blooming period passed, and these you may safely bet on.

If the vine is quite lively, the death of the quirl at the root of the stem is almost a sure sign. Lest we should not discern it before, this is placed for a sign that there is redness and ripeness within. Of two, otherwise similar, take that which yields the lowest tone when struck with your knuckles, that is, which is hollowest. The old or ripe ones ring bass; the young, tenor or falsetto. Some use the violent method of pressing to hear if they crack within, but this is not to be allowed. Above all no tapping on the vine is to be tolerated, suggestive of a greediness which defeats its own purpose. It is very childish.

One man told me that he couldn't raise melons because his children *would cut them all up.* I think that he convicted himself out of his own mouth. It was evident that he could not raise children in the way they should go and was not fit to be the ruler of a country, according to Confucius's standard. I once, looking by a special providence through the blinds, saw one of his boys astride of my earliest watermelon, which grew near a broken paling, and brandishing a case-knife over it, but I instantly blowed him off with my voice before serious damage was done—and I made such an ado about it as convinced him that he was not in his father's dominions, at any rate. This melon, though it lost some of its bloom then, grew to be a remarkably large and sweet one, though it bore, to the last, a triangular scar of the tap which the thief had designed on it.

The farmer is obliged to hide his melon patch far away in the midst of his corn or potatoes. I sometimes stumble on it in my rambles. I see one to-day where the watermelons are intermixed with carrots in a carrot bed and so concealed by the general resemblance of the leaves at a little distance.

It is an old saying that you cannot carry two melons under one arm. Indeed, it is difficult to carry one far, it is so slippery. I remember hearing of a lady who had been to visit her friends in Lincoln, and when she was ready to return on foot, they made her the rather onerous present of a watermelon. With this under her arm she tript it glibly through the Walden Woods, which had a rather bad reputation for goblins and so on in those days. While the wood grew thicker and thicker, and the imaginary dangers greater, the melon did not grow any lighter, though frequently shifted from arm to arm; and at length, it may have been through the agency of one of those mischievous goblins, it slipt from under her arm, and in a moment lay in a dozen pieces in the middle of the Walden road. Quick as thought the trembling traveller gathered up the most luscious and lightest fragments with her handkerchief, and flew rather than ran with them to the peaceful streets of Concord.

If you have any watermelons left when the frosts come, you may put them into your cellar and keep them till Thanksgiving time. I have seen a large patch in the woods frozen quite hard, and when cracked open they had a very handsome crystalline look.

Watermelons, said to be unknown to the Greeks and Romans. It is said to be one of those fruits of Egypt which the Jewish people regretted in the desert under the name of *abbattichim.*

The English botanists may be said to know nothing about watermelons. The nearest that Gerarde gets to our watermelon is in his chapter on "Citrull Cucumbers," where he says, "The meat or pulp of Cucumer Citrill which is next unto the bark is eaten."

In Spence's *Anecdotes* it is said that Galileo used to compare Ariosto's *Orlando* to a melon field. "You may meet with a very good thing here and there in it, but the whole is of very little value." Montaigne says, quoting Aurelius Victor, "The emperor Dioclesian, having resigned his crown and retired to 'private life,' was some time after solicited to resume his charge, but he announced, 'You would not offer to persuade me to this, had you seen the fine condition of the trees I have planted in my orchard, and the fair melons I have sowed in my garden.'" Gosse, in his *Letters from Alabama,* says of the watermelon, "I am not aware that it is known in England; I have never seen it exposed in the London markets," but it is abundant all over the United States; and in the South:

> The very negroes have their own melon "patches," as well as their peach orchards, and it is no small object of their ambition to raise earlier or finer specimens than their masters. . . . [It] may be considered as the best realization of the French princess's idea of "ice with the chill taken off." . . . A cart-load is brought home from the field nearly every evening, to supply the demand of the family for the next day; for during this torrid weather, very little business but the eating of watermelons is transacted. If a guest call, the first offering of friendship is a glass of cold water as soon as seated; then there is an immediate shout for watermelons, and each taking his own, several are destroyed before the knife is laid down. The ladies cut the hard part, near the rind, into stars, and other pretty shapes, which they candy as a conserve for winter.

"Bread": *Walden* (1854); "Watermelons": *Wild Fruits* (2000; written 1859–62)

Irish Potato Pudding.

(One that will do for Passover.)—Boil six large potatoes in their skins; let them remain till next day, then peel them and grate on a horseradish-grater very light; then beat up six eggs, separately, the whites to a snow; add six ounces of sifted sugar, a pinch of salt, two ounces of ground almonds, and the grated rind of a lemon; beat all lightly together, and bake or steam in a mould with four ounces of melted fat.

Esther Levy, *Jewish Cookery Book* (1871)

In this recipe from the first known Jewish-American cookbook, the Irish potato pudding is billed as "One that will do for Passover" and resembles a potato kugel.

Frederick Douglass

from My Bondage and My Freedom

In these passages from *My Bondage and My Freedom* (1855), the second of his three auto-biographies, Frederick Douglass (1818–1895) offers a study in unsustainable contrasts: the slaves on the Maryland plantation where he spent his early youth subsist, barely, on a diet of "ash cake," while guests in the big house are treated to an almost unbelievably luxurious spread, the likes of which are easier to find in the annals of ancient Rome than in American food literature. It may have been the memory of want that made Douglass as attentive as he was to these contrasts. ("I have often been so pinched with hunger," he later recalled, "as to dispute with 'Nep,' the dog, for the crumbs which fell from the kitchen table. Many times have I followed, with eager step, the waiting-girl, when she shook the table-cloth, to get the crumbs and small bones flung out for the dogs and cats.") Yet if there is a distinctly bitter schadenfreude in his sense that his master's groaning table will yield nothing but gout, dypepsia, and other complaints, there may also be a redemptive lesson. After reading this passage, the sight of a lavish table begs certain questions: Who isn't here? What are the hidden costs?

■ ■ ■

As a general rule, slaves do not come to the quarters for either breakfast or dinner, but take their "ash cake" with them, and eat it in the field. This was so on the home plantation; probably, because the distance from the quarter to the field, was sometimes two, and even three miles.

The dinner of the slaves consisted of a huge piece of ash cake, and a small piece of pork, or two salt herrings. Not having ovens, nor any suitable cooking utensils, the slaves mixed their meal with a little water, to such thickness that a spoon would stand erect in it; and, after the wood had burned away to coals and ashes, they would place the dough between oak leaves and lay it carefully in the ashes, completely covering it; hence, the bread is called ash cake. The surface of this peculiar bread is covered with ashes, to the depth of a sixteenth part of an inch, and the ashes, certainly, do not make it very grateful to the teeth, nor render it very palatable. The bran, or coarse part of the meal, is baked with the fine, and bright scales run through the bread.

This bread, with its ashes and bran, would disgust and choke a northern man, but it is quite liked by the slaves. They eat it with avidity, and are more concerned about the quantity than about the quality. They are far too scantily provided for, and are worked too steadily, to be much concerned for the quality of their food. The few minutes allowed them at dinner time, after partaking of their coarse repast, are variously spent. Some lie down on the "turning row," and go to sleep; others draw together, and talk; and others are at work with needle and thread, mending their tattered garments. Sometimes you may hear a wild, hoarse laugh arise from a circle, and often a song. Soon, however, the overseer comes dashing through the field. "*Tumble up! Tumble up*, and to w*ork*, w*ork*," is the cry; and, now, from twelve o'clock (midday) till dark, the human cattle are in motion, wielding their clumsy hoes; hurried on by no hope of reward, no sense of gratitude, no love of children, no prospect of bettering their condition; nothing, save the dread and terror of the slave-driver's lash. So goes one day, and so comes and goes another.

—

The close-fisted stinginess that fed the poor slave on coarse corn-meal and tainted meat; that clothed him in crashy tow-linen, and hurried him on to toil through the field, in all weathers, with wind and rain beating through his tattered garments; that scarcely gave even the young slave-mother time to nurse her hungry infant in the fence corner; wholly vanishes on approaching the sacred precincts of the great house, the home of the Lloyds. There the scriptural phrase finds an exact illustration; the highly favored inmates of this mansion are literally arrayed "in purple and fine linen," and fare sumptuously every day! The table groans under the heavy and blood-bought luxuries gathered with pains-taking care, at home and abroad. Fields, forests, rivers and seas, are made tributary here. Immense wealth, and its lavish expenditure, fill the great house with all that can please the eye, or tempt the taste. Here, appetite, not food, is the great *desideratum*. Fish, flesh and fowl, are here in profusion. Chickens, of all breeds; ducks, of all kinds, wild and tame, the common, and the huge Muscovite; Guinea fowls, turkeys, geese, and pea fowls, are in their several pens, fat and fatting for the destined vortex. The graceful swan, the mongrels, the black-necked wild goose; partridges, quails, pheasants and pigeons; choice water fowl, with all their strange varieties, are caught in this huge family net.

Beef, veal, mutton and venison, of the most select kinds and quality, roll bounteously to this grand consumer. The teeming riches of the Chesapeake bay, its rock, perch, drums, crocus, trout, oysters, crabs, and terrapin, are drawn hither to adorn the glittering table of the great house. The dairy, too, probably the finest on the Eastern Shore of Maryland—supplied by cattle of the best English stock, imported for the purpose, pours its rich donations of fragrant cheese, golden butter, and delicious cream, to heighten the attraction of the gorgeous, unending round of feasting. Nor are the fruits of the earth forgotten or neglected. The fertile garden, many acres in size, constituting a separate establishment, distinct from the common farm—with its scientific gardener, imported from Scotland, (a Mr. McDermott,) with four men under his direction, was not behind, either in the abundance or in the delicacy of its contributions to the same full board. The tender asparagus, the succulent celery, and the delicate cauliflower; egg plants, beets, lettuce, parsnips, peas, and French beans, early and late; radishes, cantelopes, melons of all kinds; the fruits and flowers of all climes and of all descriptions, from the hardy apple of the north, to the lemon and orange of the south, culminated at this point. Baltimore gathered figs, raisins, almonds and juicy grapes from Spain. Wines and brandies from France; teas of various flavor, from China; and rich, aromatic coffee from Java, all conspired to swell the tide of high life, where pride and indolence rolled and lounged in magnificence and satiety.

Behind the tall-backed and elaborately wrought chairs, stand the servants, men and maidens—fifteen in number—discriminately selected, not only with a view to their industry and faithfulness, but with special regard to their personal appearance, their graceful agility and captivating address. Some of these are armed with fans, and are fanning reviving breezes toward the over-heated brows of the alabaster ladies; others watch with eager eye, and with fawn-like step anticipate and supply, wants before they are sufficiently formed to be announced by word or sign.

These servants constituted a sort of black aristocracy on Col. Lloyd's plantation. They resembled the field hands in nothing, except in color, and in this they held the advantage of a velvet-like glossiness, rich and beautiful. The hair, too, showed the same advantage. The delicate colored maid rustled in the scarcely worn silk of her young mistress, while the servant men were equally well attired from the overflowing wardrobe of their young masters; so that, in dress, as well as in form and feature, in manner and speech, in tastes and habits, the distance between these favored few, and the sorrow and hunger-smitten multitudes of the quarter in the field, was immense; and this is seldom passed over.

Let us now glance at the stables and carriage house, and we shall find the same evidences of pride and luxurious extravagance. Here are three splendid coaches, soft within and lustrous without. Here, too, are gigs, phætons, barouches, sulkeys and sleighs. Here are saddles and harnesses—beautifully wrought and silver mounted—kept with every care. In the stable you will find, kept only for pleasure, full thirty-five horses, or the most approved blood for speed and beauty. There are two men here constantly employed in taking care of these horses. One of these men must be always in the stable, to answer every call from the great house. Over the way from the stable, is a house built expressly for the hounds—a pack of twenty-five or thirty—whose fare would have made glad the heart of a dozen slaves. Horses and hounds are not the only consumers of the slave's toil. There was practiced, at the Lloyd's, a hospitality which would have astonished and charmed any health-seeking northern divine or merchant, who might have chanced to share it. Viewed from his own table, and *not* from the field, the colonel was a model of generous hospitality. His house was, literally, a hotel, for weeks during the summer months. At these times, especially, the air was freighted with the rich fumes of baking, boiling, roasting and broiling. The odors I shared with the winds; but the meats were under a more stringent monopoly—except that, occasionally, I got a cake from Mas' Daniel. In Mas' Daniel I had a friend at court, from whom I learned many things which my eager curiosity was excited to know. I always knew when company was expected, and who they were, although I was an outsider, being the property, not of Col. Lloyd, but of a servant of the wealthy colonel. On these occasions, all that pride, taste and money could do, to dazzle and charm, was done.

Who could say that the servants of Col. Lloyd were not well clad and cared for, after witnessing one of his magnificent entertainments? Who could say that they did not seem to glory in being the slaves of such a master? Who, but a fanatic, could get up any sympathy for persons whose every movement was agile, easy and graceful, and who evinced a consciousness of high superiority? And who would ever venture to suspect that Col. Lloyd was subject to the troubles of ordinary mortals? Master and slave seem alike in their glory here? Can it all be seeming? Alas! it may only be a sham at last! This immense wealth; this gilded splendor; this profusion of luxury; this exemption from toil; this life of ease; this sea of plenty; aye, what of it all? Are the pearly gates of happiness and sweet content flung open to such suitors? *far from it!* The poor slave, on his hard, pine plank, but scantily covered with his thin blanket, sleeps more soundly than the feverish voluptuary who reclines upon his feather bed and downy pillow. Food, to the indolent lounger, is poison, not sustenance. Lurking beneath all their dishes, are invisible spirits of evil, ready to feed the self-deluded gormandizers with aches, pains, fierce temper, uncontrolled passions, dyspepsia, rheumatism, lumbago and gout; and of these the Lloyds got their full share.

My Bondage and My Freedom (1855)

George Martin Lane

The Lay of the One Fish-Ball

George Martin Lane (1823–1897) was a professor at Harvard College and the author of learned works on Latin grammar and pronunciation. But the professor also wrote humorous light verse, like this lament of a budget-strapped student in search of a good meal. The song had staying power—as "One Meat Ball" it was a hit for Josh White in the 1940s.

■ ■ ■

The boys of Harvard University set the following pathetic ballad a-going, and it is now a popular song. It records the melancholy experience of one of the students:

1. There was a man went up and down,
   To seek a dinner through the town.
2. What wretch is he who wife forsakes,
   Who best of jam and waffles makes?
3. He feels his cash to know his pence,
   And finds he has but just six cents.
4. He finds at last a right cheap place,
   And enters in with modest face.
5. The bill of fare he searches through,
   To see what his six cents will do.
6. The cheapest viand of them all,
   "Twelve-and-a-half cents for two Fish-ball."
7. The waiter he to him doth call,
   And gently whispers—"*one* Fish-ball."
8. The waiter roars it through the hall,
   The guests they start at "*one* Fish-ball."
9. The guest then says, quite ill at ease,
   "A piece of bread, Sir, if you please."
10. The waiter roars it through the hall,
    "We don't give bread with *one* Fish-ball."

MORAL

11. Who would have bread with his Fish-ball,
    Must get it *first*, or not at all.
12. Who would Fish-balls with fixins eat,
    Must get some friend to stand a treat.

Tomato Catsup.

1 peck ripe tomatoes.

1 ounce salt.

1 ounce mace.

1 tablespoonful black pepper.

1 teaspoonful cayenne.

1 tablespoonful cloves (powdered).

7 tablespoonfuls ground mustard.

1 tablespoonful celery seed (tied in a thin muslin bag).

Cut a slit in the tomatoes, put into a bell-metal or porcelain kettle, and boil until the juice is all extracted and the pulp dissolved. Strain and press through a cullender, then through a hair sieve. Return to the fire, add the seasoning, and boil *at least* five hours, stirring constantly for the last hour, and frequently throughout the time it is on the fire. Let it stand twelve hours in a stone jar on the cellar floor. When cold, add a pint of strong vinegar. Take out the bag of celery seed, and bottle, sealing the corks. Keep in a dark, cool place.

Tomato and walnut are the most useful catsups we have for general purposes, and either is in itself a fine sauce for roast meat, cold fowl, game, etc.

Marion Harland, *Common Sense in the Household* (1871)

An early recipe for the classic American condiment. Marion Harland was a best-selling novelist.

Henry Ward Beecher

Apple-Pie

"I don't have time to cook" is a common enough complaint among busy people; we would like to have more time for food, but life's other demands interfere. And yet for the Beechers—that astonishingly overachieving Yankee family—accomplishment in the ministry, in politics, in education, and in the arts seems to have gone hand-in-hand with an abiding interest in eating well and everything that entails. Sister Catharine, founder of colleges and advocate of reform in the education of women, also wrote one of her century's leading home-ec manuals, *A Treatise on Domestic Economy* (1841). Sister Harriet, the famous novelist, published extensively on cookery as well (see pages 76-82 in this volume). And here, brother Henry (1813-1887), the most celebrated preacher of *his* day, turns his formidable attention to one of the humbler icons of the American kitchen, apple pie.

■ ■ ■

How often people use language without the slightest sense of its deep, interior meaning! Thus, no phrase is more carelessly or frequently used than the saying, *"Apple-pie order."* How few who say so reflect at the time upon either apple-pie or the true order of apple-pie! Perhaps they have been reared without instruction. They may have been born in families that were ignorant of apple-pie; or who were left to the guilt of calling two tough pieces of half-cooked dough, with a thin streak of macerated dried apple between them, of leather color, and of taste and texture not unbecoming the same,—an apple-pie! But from such profound degradation of ideas we turn away with gratitude and humility, that one so unworthy as we should have been reared to better things.

We are also affected with a sense of regret for duty unperformed; for great as have been the benefits received, we have never yet celebrated as we ought the merits of apple-pie. That reflection shall no longer cast its shadow upon us.

"Henry, go down cellar, and bring me up some Spitzenbergs." The cellar was as large as the whole house, and the house was broad as a small pyramid.

The north side was windowless, and banked up outside with frost-defying tan-bark. The south side had windows, festooned and frescoed with the webs of spiders, that wove their tapestries over every corner in the neighborhood, and, when no flies were to be had, ate up each other, as if they were nothing but politicians, instead of being lawful and honorable *arachnidœ*. On the east side stood a row of cider-barrels; for twelve or twenty barrels of cider were a fit provision for the year,—and what was not consumed for drink was expected duly to turn into vinegar, and was then exalted to certain hogsheads kept for the purpose. But along the middle of the cellar were the apple-bins; and when the season had been propitious, there were stores and heaps of Russets, Greenings, Seeknofurthers, Pearmains, Gilliflowers, Spitzenbergs, and many besides, nameless, but not virtueless. Thence selecting, we duly brought up the apples. Some people think anything will do for pies. But the best for eating are the best for cooking. Who would make jelly of any other apple, that had the *Porter*? who would bake or roast any other sweet apple, that had the *Ladies' Sweeting*,—unless, perhaps, the *Talman Sweet*? and who would put into a pie any apple but *Spitzenberg*, that had *that*? Off with their jackets! Fill the great wooden bowl with the sound rogues! And now, O cook! which shall it be? For at this point the roads diverge, and though they all come back at length to apple-pie, it is not a matter of indifference which you choose. There is, for example, one made without under-crust, in a deep plate, and the apples laid in, in full quarters; or the apples being stewed are beaten to a mush, and seasoned, and put between the double paste; or they are sliced thin and cooked entirely within the covers; or they are put without seasoning into their bed, and when baked, the upper lid is raised, and the butter, nutmeg, cinnamon, and sugar are added; the whole well mixed, and the crust returned as if nothing had happened.

But O be careful of the paste! Let it not be like putty, nor rush to the other extreme, and make it so flaky that one holds his breath while eating for fear of blowing it all away. Let it not be plain as bread, nor yet rich like cake. Aim at that glorious medium, in which it is tender, without being fugaciously flaky; short, without being too short; a mild, sapid, brittle thing, that lies upon the tongue, so as to let the apple strike through and touch the *papillœ* with a mere effluent flavor. But this, like all high art, must be a thing of inspiration or instinct. A true cook will understand us, and we care not if others do not!

Do not suppose that we limit the apple-pie to the kinds and methods enumerated. Its capacity in variation is endless, and every diversity discovers some new charm or flavor. It will accept almost every flavor of every spice. And yet nothing is so fatal to the rare and higher graces of apple-pie as inconsiderate, vulgar spicing. It is not meant to be a mere vehicle for the exhibition of these spices, in their own natures. It is a glorious unity in which sugar gives up its nature as sugar, and butter ceases to be butter, and each flavorsome spice gladly evanishes from its own full nature, that all of them, by a common death, may rise into the new life of apple-pie! Not that apple is longer apple! *It*, too, is transformed. And the final pie, though born of apple, sugar, butter, nutmeg, cinnamon, lemon, is like none of these, but the compound ideal of them all, refined, purified, and by fire fixed in blissful perfection.

But all exquisite creations are short-lived. The natural term of an apple-pie is but twelve hours. It reaches its highest state about one hour after it comes from the oven, and just before its natural heat has quite departed. But every hour afterward is a declension. And after it is one day old, it is thenceforward but the ghastly corpse of apple-pie.

But while it is yet florescent, white or creamy yellow, with the merest drip of candied juice along the edges, (as if the flavor were so good to itself that its own lips watered!) of a mild and modest warmth, the sugar suggesting jelly, yet not jellied, the morsels of apple neither dissolved nor yet in original substance, but hanging as it were in a trance between the spirit and the flesh of applehood, then, when dinner is to be served at five o'clock, and you are pivotted on the hour of one with a ravening appetite, let the good dame bring forth for luncheon an apple-pie, with cheese a year old, crumbling and yet moist, but not with base fluid, but oily rather; then, O blessed man, favored by all the divinities! eat, give thanks, and go forth, "*in apple-pie order!*"

Eyes and Ears (1862)

MAKING SHORTCAKE IN CAMP

★ ★ ★

Take the top of your provision box, or one of the boards from the bottom of your boat (camp supposed to be on the shores of Lake Superior). As it will probably be rough, cover it with a napkin, then you have a good pasteboard. Get your Indian guide to find a smooth sapling, peel off the bark, scrape it smooth, and then you have your rolling-pin. Mix half a pound of butter in half a pound of flour; but as you have probably left your scales at home, measure three or four tablespoonfuls of butter and one quart of flour; add a small spoonful of salt. Wet it with the coldest water you can get, roll it out about one-third of an inch thick, and of a shape suitable to your cooking utensil. If you are so luxurious as to have a camp-stove or baker, you can cut the paste into cakes and bake them as you would in civilized life; but if you take things after the manner of the aborigines, you will pour the grease from the frying-pan in which the salt pork has been cooked, and put the sheet of paste into it, cooking it over some coals drawn from the fire. There is still another way. If you can find a smooth, flat stone, heat it thoroughly in the fire; then withdraw it, and having dusted it with flour, bake your cake upon it. Eaten with a good mug of tea, a thin slice of pork, brown and crisp, and a broiled trout, all seasoned with good appetite, nothing can be more delicious.

National Cookery Book (1876)

This cookbook, published in conjunction with Philadelphia's celebration of the bicentennial in 1876, is a portrait of the national table.

Walt Whitman

A Great Treat of Ice Cream

The years that Walt Whitman (1819–1892) spent tending to the wounded in Washington, D.C., military hospitals during the Civil War found expression both in great poems like "The Wound-Dresser" and in letters home. Here, writing to his mother, he offers a moving account of his attempt to comfort his patients with a rare treat: ten gallons of ice cream, a solitary sweet note in a ward of sadness, a little bit of deliverance to dying men. Ice cream was enough of a novelty that some of the soldiers had never encountered it before.

■ ■ ■

Washington, June 3, 1864.

Mother, if this campaign was not in progress I should not stop here, as it is now beginning to tell a little upon me, so many bad wounds, many putrefied, and all kinds of dreadful ones, I have been rather too much with—but as it is, I certainly remain here while the thing remains undecided. It is impossible for me to abstain from going to see and minister to certain cases, and that draws me into others, and so on. I have just left Oscar Cunningham, the Ohio boy—he is in a dying condition—there is no hope for him—it would draw tears from the hardest heart to look at him—he is all wasted away to a skeleton, and looks like some one fifty years old. You remember I told you a year ago, when he was first brought in, I thought him the noblest specimen of a young Western man I had seen, a real giant in size, and always with a smile on his face. O what a change. He has long been very irritable to every one but me, and his frame is all wasted away. The young Massachusetts 1st artillery boy, Cutter, I wrote about is dead. He is the one that was brought in a week ago last Sunday badly wounded in breast. The deaths in the principal hospital I visit, Armory-square, average one an hour.

I saw Capt. Baldwin of the 14th this morning; he has lost his left arm—is going home soon. Mr. Kalbfleisch and Anson Herrick, (M. C. from New York) came in one of the wards where I was sitting writing a letter this morning, in the midst of the wounded. Kalbfleisch was so much affected by the sight that he burst into tears. O, I must tell you, I gave in Carver hospital a great treat of ice cream, a couple of days ago—went round myself through about 15 large wards–(I bought some ten gallons, very nice). You would have cried and been amused too. Many of the men had to be fed; several of them I saw cannot probably live, yet they quite enjoyed it. I gave everybody some–quite a number of Western country boys had never tasted ice cream before. They relish such things as oranges, lemons, etc. Mother, I feel a little blue this morning, as two young men I knew very well have just died. One died last night, and the other about half an hour before I went to the hospital. I did not anticipate the death of either of them. Each was a very, very sad case, so young. Well mother, I see I have written you another gloomy sort of letter. I do not feel as first rate as usual.

WALT.

The Wound Dresser: A Series of Letters Written from the Hospitals in Washington during the War of
   Rebellion (1898; written 1864)

HAYES' CAKE ⚘ TILDEN CAKE

HAYES' CAKE.

One cup sugar, half cup butter, three eggs beaten well together, level tea-spoon soda stirred in half cup sour milk, two small cups flour; flavor with lemon, pour in small dripping-pan, bake half an hour, and cut in squares. —*Miss Flora Ziegler, Columbus*

TILDEN CAKE.

One cup butter, two of pulverized sugar, one of sweet milk, three of flour, half cup corn starch, four eggs, two tea-spoons baking-powder, two of lemon extract. —*Mrs. T. B., Chicago, Ill.*

Estelle Woods Wilcox, ed., *Buckeye Cookery and Practical Housekeeping* (1877)

A touch of political symbolism: the cakes are named for the Republican and Democratic candidates in the contested election of 1876.

Harriet Beecher Stowe

from Cookery

Between writing *Uncle Tom's Cabin* (1852) and a multitude of other works of fiction, Harriet Beecher Stowe (1811–1896) found time to venture into the field of the domestic arts. With her sister Catharine she co-wrote *The American Woman's Home; or Principles of Domestic Science* (1869), and under the pseudonym Christopher Crowfield she published *House and Home Papers* (1865), from which this spirited discussion of the proper way to prepare meat is taken. Like other culinary reformers of her day, Stowe embraced the methods of the Gallic kitchen, comparing them favorably with British and American ways. But she's careful to avoid the appearance of elitism or epicurean indulgence in making her case for the French, fearing her readers will accuse her of promoting "niceties" and "whim-whams." Instead, she praises French cuisine for its Yankee practicality and "utilitarian good sense."

■ ■ ■

The third head of my discourse is that of *Meat*, of which America furnishes, in the gross material, enough to spread our tables royally, were it well cared for and served.

The faults in the meat generally furnished to us are, first, that it is too new. A beefsteak, which three or four days of keeping might render practicable, is served up to us palpitating with freshness, with all the toughness of animal muscle yet warm. In the Western country, the traveller, on approaching an hotel, is often saluted by the last shrieks of the chickens which half an hour afterward are presented to him *à la* spread-eagle for his dinner. The example of the Father of the Faithful, most wholesome to be followed in so many respects, is imitated only in the celerity with which the young calf, tender and good, was transformed into an edible dish for hospitable purposes. But what might be good housekeeping in a nomadic Emir, in days when refrigerators were yet in the future, ought not to be so closely imitated as it often is in our own land.

In the next place, there is a woful lack of nicety in the butcher's work of cutting and preparing meat. Who that remembers the neatly trimmed mutton-chop of an English inn, or the artistic little circle of lamb-chop fried in bread-crumbs coiled around a tempting centre of spinach which can always be found in France, can recognize any family-resemblance to these dapper civilized preparations in those coarse, roughly hacked strips of bone, gristle, and meat which are commonly called mutton-chop in America? There seems to be a large dish of something resembling meat, in which each fragment has about two or three edible morsels, the rest being composed of dry and burnt skin, fat, and ragged bone.

Is it not time that civilization should learn to demand somewhat more care and nicety in the modes of preparing what is to be cooked and eaten? Might not some of the refinement and trimness which characterize the preparations of the European market be with advantage introduced into our own? The housekeeper who wishes to garnish her table with some of those nice things is stopped in the outset by the butcher. Except in our large cities, where some foreign travel may have created the demand, it seems impossible to get much in this line that is properly prepared.

I am aware, that, if this is urged on the score of æsthetics, the ready reply will be, "O, we can't give time here in America to go into niceties and French whim-whams!" But the French mode of doing almost all practical things is based on that true philosophy and utilitarian good sense which character-ize that seemingly thoughtless people. Nowhere is economy a more careful study, and their market is artistically arranged to this end. The rule is so to cut their meats that no portion designed to be cooked in a certain manner shall have wasteful appendages which that mode of cooking will spoil. The French soup-kettle stands ever ready to receive the bones, the thin fibrous flaps, the sinewy and gristly portions, which are so often included in our roasts or broilings, which fill our plates with unsightly *débris*, and finally make an amount of blank waste for which we pay our butcher the same price that we pay for what we have eaten.

The dead waste of our clumsy, coarse way of cutting meats is immense. For example, at the beginning of the present season, the part of a lamb de-nominated leg and loin, or hind-quarter, sold for thirty cents a pound. Now this includes, besides the thick, fleshy portions, a quantity of bone, sinew, and thin fibrous substance, constituting full one third of the whole weight. If we put it into the oven entire, in the usual manner, we have the thin parts overdone, and the skinny and fibrous parts utterly dried up, by the application of the amount of heat necessary to cook the thick portion. Supposing the joint to weigh six pounds, at thirty cents, and that one third of the weight is so treated as to become perfectly useless, we throw away sixty cents. Of a piece of beef at twenty-five cents a pound, fifty cents' worth is often lost in bone, fat, and burnt skin.

The fact is, this way of selling and cooking meat in large, gross portions is of English origin, and belongs to a country where all the customs of society spring from a class who have no particular occasion for economy. The practice of minute and delicate division comes from a nation which acknowledges the need of economy, and has made it a study. A quarter of lamb in this mode of division would be sold in three nicely prepared portions. The thick part would be sold by itself, for a neat, compact little roast; the rib-bones would be artistically separated, and all the edible matters scraped away would form those delicate dishes of lamb-chop, which, fried in bread-crumbs to a golden brown, are so ornamental and so palatable a side-dish; the trimmings which remain after this division would be destined to the soup-kettle or stew-pan. In a French market is a little portion for every purse, and the far-famed and delicately flavored soups and stews which have arisen out of the French economy are a study worth a housekeeper's attention. Not one atom of food is wasted in the French modes of preparation; even tough animal cartilages and sinews, instead of appearing burned and blackened in company with the roast meat to which they happen to be related, are treated according to their own laws, and come out either in savory soups, or those fine, clear meat-jellies which form a garnish no less agreeable to the eye than palatable to the taste.

Whether this careful, economical, practical style of meat-cooking can ever to any great extent be introduced into our kitchens now is a question. Our butchers are against it; our servants are wedded to the old wholesale wasteful ways, which seem to them easier because they are accustomed to them. A cook who will keep and properly tend a soup-kettle which shall receive and utilize all that the coarse preparations of the butcher would require her to trim away, who understands the art of making the most of all these remains, is a treasure scarcely to be hoped for. If such things are to be done, it must be primarily through the educated brain of cultivated women who do not scorn to turn their culture and refinement upon domestic problems.

When meats have been properly divided, so that each portion can receive its own appropriate style of treatment, next comes the consideration of the modes of cooking. These may be divided into two great general classes: those where it is desired to keep the juices within the meat, as in baking, broiling, and frying,—and those whose object is to extract the juice and dissolve the fibre, as in the making of soups and stews. In the first class of operations, the process must be as rapid as may consist with the thorough cooking of all the particles. In this branch of cookery, doing quickly is doing well. The fire must be brisk, the attention alert. The introduction of cooking-stoves offers to careless domestics facilities for gradually drying-up meats, and despoiling them of all flavor and nutriment,—facilities which appear to be very generally laid hold of. They have almost banished the genuine, old-fashioned roast-meat from our tables, and left in its stead dried meats with their most precious and nutritive juices evaporated. How few cooks, unassisted, are competent to the simple process of broiling a beefsteak or mutton-chop! how very generally one has to choose between these meats gradually dried away, or burned on the outside and raw within! Yet in England these articles *never* come on table done amiss; their perfect cooking is as absolute a certainty as the rising of the sun.

No one of these rapid processes of cooking, however, is so generally abused as frying. The frying-pan has awful sins to answer for. What untold horrors of dyspepsia have arisen from its smoky depths, like the ghosts from witches' caldrons! The fizzle of frying meat is as a warning knell on many an ear, saying, "Touch not, taste not, if you would not burn and writhe!"

Yet those who have travelled abroad remember that some of the lightest, most palatable, and most digestible preparations of meat have come from this dangerous source. But we fancy quite other rites and ceremonies inaugurated the process, and quite other hands performed its offices, than those known to our kitchens. Probably the delicate *côtelettes* of France are not flopped down into half-melted grease, there gradually to warm and soak and fizzle, while Biddy goes in and out on her other ministrations, till finally, when thoroughly saturated, the dinner-hour impends, she bethinks herself, and crowds the fire below to a roaring heat, and finishes the process by a smart burn, involving the kitchen and surrounding precincts in volumes of Stygian gloom.

From such preparations has arisen the very current medical opinion that fried meats are indigestible. They are indigestible, if they are greasy; but French cooks have taught us that a thing has no more need to be greasy because emerging from grease than Venus had to be salt because she rose from the sea.

There are two ways of frying employed by the French cook. One is, to immerse the article to be cooked in *boiling* fat, with an emphasis on the present participle,—and the philosophical principle is, so immediately to crisp every pore, at the first moment or two of immersion, as effectually to seal the interior against the intrusion of greasy particles; it can then remain as long as may be necessary thoroughly to cook it, without imbibing any more of the boiling fluid than if it were inclosed in an egg-shell. The other method is to rub a perfectly smooth iron surface with just enough of some oily substance to prevent the meat from adhering, and cook it with a quick heat, as cakes are baked on a griddle. In both these cases there must be the most rapid application of heat that can be made without burning, and by the adroitness shown in working out this problem the skill of the cook is tested. Any one whose cook attains this important secret will find fried things quite as digestible and often more palatable than any other.

In the second department of meat-cookery, to wit, the slow and gradual application of heat for the softening and dissolution of its fibre and the extraction of its juices, common cooks are equally untrained. Where is the so-called cook who understands how to prepare soups and stews? These are precisely the articles in which a French kitchen excels. The soup-kettle, made with a double bottom, to prevent burning, is a permanent, ever-present institution, and the coarsest and most impracticable meats distilled through the alembic come out again in soups, jellies, or savory stews. The toughest cartilage, even the bones, being first cracked, are here made to give forth their hidden virtues, and to rise in delicate and appetizing forms. One great law governs all these preparations: the application of heat must be gradual, steady, long protracted, never reaching the point of active boiling. Hours of quiet simmering dissolve all dissoluble parts, soften the sternest fibre, and unlock every minute cell in which Nature has stored away her treasures of nourishment. This careful and protracted application of heat and the skilful use of flavors constitute the two main points in all those nice preparations of meat for which the French have so many names,—processes by which a delicacy can be imparted to the coarsest and cheapest food superior to that of the finest articles under less philosophic treatment.

French soups and stews are a study,—and they would not be an unprofitable one to any person who wishes to live with comfort and even elegance on small means.

John Bull looks down from the sublime of ten thousand a year on French kickshaws, as he calls them:—"Give me my meat cooked so I may know what it is!" An ox roasted whole is dear to John's soul, and his kitchen-arrangements are Titanic. What magnificent rounds and sirloins of beef, revolving on self-regulating spits, with a rich click of satisfaction, before grates piled with roaring fires! Let us do justice to the royal cheer. Nowhere are the charms of pure, unadulterated animal food set forth in more imposing style. For John is rich, and what does he care for odds and ends and parings? Has he not all the beasts of the forest, and the cattle on a thousand hills? What does he want of economy? But his brother Jean has not ten thousand pounds a year,—nothing like it; but he makes up for the slenderness of his purse by boundless fertility of invention and delicacy of practice. John began sneering at Jean's soups and ragouts, but all John's modern sons and daughters send to Jean for their cooks, and the sirloins of England rise up and do obeisance to this Joseph with a white apron who comes to rule in the kitchens.

There is no animal fibre that will not yield itself up to long-continued, steady heat. But the difficulty with almost any of the common servants who call themselves cooks is, that they have not the smallest notion of the philosophy of the application of heat. Such a one will complacently tell you concerning certain meats, that the harder you boil them the harder they grow,—an obvious fact, which, under her mode of treatment, by an indiscriminate galloping boil, has frequently come under her personal observation. If you tell her that such meat must stand for six hours in a heat just below the boiling-point, she will probably answer, "Yes, Ma'am," and go on her own way. Or she will let it stand till it burns to the bottom of the kettle,—a most common termination of the experiment. The only way to make sure of the matter is either to import a French kettle, or to fit into an ordinary kettle a false bottom, such as any tinman may make, that shall leave a space of an inch or two between the meat and the fire. This kettle may be maintained as a constant *habitué* of the range, and into it the cook may be instructed to throw all the fibrous trimmings of meat, all the gristle, tendons, and bones, having previously broken up these last with a mallet.

Such a kettle will furnish the basis for clear, rich soups or other palatable dishes. Clear soup consists of the dissolved juices of the meat and gelatine of the bones, cleared from the fat and fibrous portions by straining when cold. The grease, which rises to the top of the fluid, may thus be easily removed. In a stew, on the contrary, you boil down this soup till it permeates the fibre which long exposure to heat has softened. All that remains, after the proper preparation of the fibre and juices, is the flavoring, and it is in this, particularly, that French soups excel those of America and England and all the world.

English and American soups are often heavy and hot with spices. There are appreciable tastes in them. They burn your mouth with cayenne or clove or allspice. You can tell at once what is in them, oftentimes to your sorrow. But a French soup has a flavor which one recognizes at once as delicious, yet not to be characterized as due to any single condiment; it is the just blending of many things. The same remark applies to all their stews, ragouts, and other delicate preparations. No cook will ever study these flavors; but perhaps many cooks' mistresses may, and thus be able to impart delicacy and comfort to economy.

As to those things called hashes, commonly manufactured by unwatched, untaught cooks, out of the remains of yesterday's repast, let us not dwell too closely on their memory,—compounds of meat, gristle, skin, fat, and burnt fibre, with a handful of pepper and salt flung at them, dredged with lumpy flour, watered from the spout of the tea-kettle, and left to simmer at the cook's convenience while she is otherwise occupied. Such are the best performances a housekeeper can hope for from an untrained cook.

But the cunningly devised minces, the artful preparations choicely flavored, which may be made of yesterday's repast,—by these is the true domestic artist known. No cook untaught by an educated brain ever makes these, and yet economy is a great gainer by them.

House and Home Papers (1865)

Mother's RICE PUDDING

One cup rice, ten cups milk; bake five hours.

"Why, Aunt Jane, that is the shortest receipt I ever saw," said Mabel.

"That's all there is of it," answered her aunt, "except that of course any cook would know that there should be a little salt added—perhaps a teaspoonful. You must wash the rice carefully to get out any specks of dirt in it, put it into a buttered baking-dish with the milk and salt, shut the oven door and forget all about it, if your fire is steady and slow. If the fire is a quick one, the damper has to be turned so as to shut off the heat. In this long, slow process of heating, the watery part of the milk evaporates, and the rich, creamy remainder becomes so incorporated with the rice, that there is no need of butter or eggs. If you want to make it still better, throw in a cupful of raisins, not stoned, but just carefully picked over, after the pudding has been in about half an hour. You may just stir them up in it; it will do no harm."

"Any sauce with it, Aunt Jane?"

"I don't care for sauce with it myself, but you may make some hard sauce, in case the others should wish for it. It may be made as soon as you have set in the pudding, and then left in the ice-box until dinner-time."

"Won't you let me write down some more receipts, aunty?"

"Oh yes, a dozen of them if you want them, and the other girls can copy them into their books afterwards. I'll give you some that you can use next winter."

Elizabeth Stansbury Kirkland, *Six Little Cooks* (1877)

Randolph Harrison

from The Philosophy of Frying

North of the Mason-Dixon line, deep-fat frying has occasionally been suspect: "The frying-pan," writes Harriet Beecher Stowe, "has awful sins to answer for." But in the South, fried foods are more typically approached with a kind of reverence. In the following piece, taken from an essay in the *Southern Planter and Farmer*, Randolph Harrison (1830–1900)—a retired Confederate colonel who lived at Ampthill Plantation in Virginia's Cumberland County—tries to examine his subject scientifically. His cool prose gives way, however, to gushes about "the very poetry of fried chicken." (His plantation, by the way, is now a bed and breakfast.)

■ ■ ■

"The philosophy of frying!" An important, if *homely* branch of domestic economy; let it not be despised as a subject too trivial to be noticed. In the hey-day of phlebotomy it was said that "the lancet killed more than the sword." The frying-pan, in unskilled hands, is a more deadly implement than the lancet—and the millions that use it, from Maine to California, are almost all unskilful.

"Frying," as commonly practised, is in this wise: The food, to be cooked, is put with a modicum of lard, or fat meat, in a pan barely warmed, or at most slightly heated, then placed on the fire and held there while the viands are turned about until "done," when they are served up, reeking with grease; and might safely be warranted to give dyspepsia to any but the genuine corn-field negroes of blue blood.

The true theory of frying depends upon this principle: that while, as is well known, water cannot be heated above 212°F., oil or animal fat can easily be carried to about 800°, and, in fact, should be for the purpose indicated. The frying should really be a boiling in oil or fat, which should be deep enough to cover the articles; having first raised it to the proper temperature, which may be tested by immersing a crumb of bread, (if the bread is almost instantly turned to a rich, brown hue, the heat is sufficient) then the pieces are plunged into the bath of boiling fat, and removed as soon as done, which will be in a time incredibly short to those who have not tested this method of cookery, and the effect is magical, nothing can be more delicate than meat cooked in this way.

If everything shall have been artistically done, not a drop of grease will be found adhering to the beautifully browned surface of fish, flesh or fowl. The effect of the intense heat is instantly to shrivel, and as it were hermetically seal the integument, keeping in all the juices and preserving all the flavor and delicacy in a way that, perhaps, no other process can equal.

Those who have travelled Westward (by the White Sulphur Springs) in the good old days when railroads, those vile centralizers, had not broken up all the good inns of the country, will remember that celebrated hostelry, "Callaghan's;" everything there was good, but it had a specialty for fried chicken, a celebrity almost as extensive as that of the "London Tavern" for turtle soup, or, the "Rocher de Cancale" for oysters; it was the very poetry of fried chicken—to have eaten it was something to be remembered as an era in one's life. It was said that a distinguished lady of Baltimore, Madame B., once stopped there a day or two for the purpose of finding out the secret process by which such superb results were achieved. Whether the artist (cooks are notoriously jealous!) was cajoled into allowing her thunder to be stolen, I cannot say, but it was afterwards told to me, and was actually as I have described.

There was another tavern in Lower Virginia, more humble, because in a less frequented route, where the fried chicken was, as at Callaghan's, all that it ought to be. The landlady disclosed the secret to a gentleman who told the writer—she too had been led by genius to artistic excellence.

Science and high art must corroborate each other—frequently art, guided by intuition, arrives at its ends long before scientific research has made plain the way—so in the instances I have mentioned. But, now, he who runs may read, and there is no more excuse for bad frying, except the overweening love of darkey cooks for "fat." It is so hard for the most honest of them to resist its seductive influences that they will be apt to appropriate so much as not to leave enough for the "hot bath" I have described. The mistress will have to superintend the operation.

Southern Planter and Farmer, April 1876

⁙ MEAT-FLAVORING ⁙

As the housekeeper is sometimes hurried in preparing a dish, it will save time and trouble for her to keep on hand a bottle of meat-flavoring compounded of the following ingredients.

2 chopped onions.

3 pods of red pepper (chopped).

2 tablespoonfuls brown sugar.

1 tablespoonful celery seed.

1 tablespoonful ground mustard.

1 teaspoonful turmeric.

1 teaspoonful black pepper.

1 teaspoonful salt.

Put all in a quart bottle and fill it up with cider vinegar. A tablespoonful of this mixed in a stew, steak, or gravy, will impart not only a fine flavor, but a rich color. Keeping this mixture on hand will obviate the necessity of the housekeeper looking through various spice boxes and packages to get together the requisite ingredients for flavoring, and will thus save her time and trouble.

Marion Cabell Tyree, *Housekeeping in Old Virginia* (1878)

The "meat flavoring" is a powerfully seasoned (hot peppers, mustard, onion, brown sugar, inter alia) vinegar that shows how off the mark it is to call pre-modern American food bland.

George Augustus Sala

The Tyranny of Pie

Pie—the national scourge and the national glory, the quintessentially American obsession that has worked its way into countless song titles and proverbial expressions—finds an appropriate chronicler in George Augustus Sala (1828–1895), a prolific British journalist who brought a colorful and bombastic style to his coverage of the American scene.

■ ■ ■

Almost everything that I behold in this wonderful country bears traces of improvement and reform—everything except Pie. The national manners have become softened—the men folk chew less, expectorate less, curse less; *the newspapers are not half so scurrilous as our own**; the Art idea is becoming rapidly developed; culture is made more and more manifest; even "intensity" in æsthetics is beginning to be heard of and Agnosticism and other "isms" too numerous to mention find exponents in "Society," and the one absorbing and sickening topic of conversation is no longer the Almighty Dollar—but to the tyranny of Pie there is no surcease. It is a Fetish. It is Bohwani. It is the Mexican carnage god Huitchlipotchli, continually demanding fresh victims. It is Moloch. Men may come and men may go; the Grant "Boom" may be succeeded by the Garfield "Boom;" but Pie goes on for ever. The tramp and the scallawag, in pants of looped and windowed raggedness, hunger for Pie, and impetuously demand nickel cents wherewith to purchase it; and the President of the United States, amid the chastened splendour of the White House, can enjoy no more festive fare. The day before we left New York one of the ripest scholars, the most influential journalists (on

---

*The modern American press seems to me to offend only against good taste in their omnivorous appetite of interviewing celebrated or notorious individuals (and the interviewing nuisance has become common enough in England), and in their fondness for filling their columns with brief personalities sometimes very quaint, but usually almost childishly frivolous and quite harmless.

the Democratic side) the brightest wits and most genial companions in the States lunched with us. He would drink naught but Château Yquem; but he partook twice, and in amazing profusion of Pumpkin Pie. They gave me Pie at the Brevoort, and I am now fresh from the consumption of Pie at the Mount Vernon, Baltimore. Two more aristocratic hotels are not to be found on this continent. I battled strongly against this dyspepsia-dealing pastry at first; but a mulatto waiter held me with his glittering eye, and I yielded as though I had been a two-years child. The worst of this dreadful pie—be it of apple, of pumpkin, of mulberry, or of cranberry—is that it is so very nice. It is made delusively flat and thin, so that you can cut it into conveniently-sized triangular wedges, which slip down easily. Pardon this digression; but Pie really forms as important a factor in American civilisation as the *pot-au-feu* does in France. There is no dish at home by which we nationally stand or fall. The "roast beef of Old England" sounds very well to the strains of Mr. Dan Godfrey's band at a dinner at the Freemason's Tavern; but sirloin of beef is fourteen pence a pound, and there are hundreds of thousands of labouring English people who never taste roast beef from year's end to year's end—save when they happen to get into gaol or into the workhouse at Christmastide.

America Revisited (1882)

Emily Dickinson

Black Cake

Raised in a household where Lydia Maria Child's *The Frugal Housewife* (1829) was a family favorite, Emily Dickinson (1830–1886) grew up learning cookery among other chores, eventually concentrating on breads and desserts. Her niece Martha Dickinson Bianchi later evoked an aunt with a flair for the forbidden and the indulgent: "I was usually left with her while both families went to church on Sabbath mornings and well remember being escorted by her down to the cool hoarding cellar, past the wine closet to a mysterious cupboard of her own, where she dealt me such lawless cake and other goodies, that even a child of four knew it for excess, sure to be followed by disaster later in the day. There was an unreal abandon about it all such as thrills the prodigality of dreaming." Here is a recipe for one such "lawless cake," enclosed in a letter of 1883 to her friend Mrs. J. Howard Sweetser.

■ ■ ■

Dear Nellie

Your sweet beneficence of Bulbs I return as Flowers, with a bit of the swarthy Cake baked only in Domingo.

Lovingly,
Emily

Black Cake–

2 pounds Flour–
2 Sugar–
2 Butter–
19 Eggs–
5 pounds Raisins–
1 ½ Currants–
1 ½ Citron–
½ pint Brandy–
½–Molasses–
2 Nutmegs–

> 5 teaspoons
>   Cloves–Mace–Cinnamon–
> 2 teaspoons Soda–

Beat Butter and Sugar together–
Add Eggs without beating–and beat the mixture again–
Bake 2 $\frac{1}{2}$ or three hours, in Cake pans, or 5 to 6 hours in Milk pan,
    if full–

The Letters of Emily Dickinson (1986; written 1883)

Frank Hamilton Cushing

from Zuñi Breadstuff

In the years that Frank Hamilton Cushing (1857–1900) spent with the Zuñi of New Mexico, he pioneered the anthropological approach of observing by participating; he was inducted into the tribe's Bow Priesthood and was given the name Tenatsali, or "medicine flower." Edmund Wilson wrote of Cushing that he "was an admirable writer—almost as much as a literary man as he was a technical expert," and went on to note that "though he praises the Zuñi cuisine . . . he shudders at the memory of his first attempts to emulate their eating habits." If he never quite acquired a taste for the strange dishes typically served up at a Zuñi feast, Cushing nonetheless describes them with the kind of heightened attention, intelligence, and curiosity that great food writing demands.

■ ■ ■

The menu of a Zuñi feast, what though made up from a single course, is as extensive and varied a one, sometimes, as that of the most luxurious of civilized dinners. To be sure, no fish graces or leads on in such a meal to the more substantial meats, and the soups, though copious in kind as in abundance, are hopelessly mixed up with even the desserts, in the serving of it. But an examination of the illustrations contemplated in and brought over from our last chapter, will not fail to speedily display anew the amplitude of resource in Zuñi cookery.

Piled high on more than one flat basket-tray (*a, d*) are the sheets and rolls of paper-bread or *he'-we*—the sheets dully symbolizing the green earth and blue sky in their colors; the rolls, not less, the six chief hues of the rainbow. On special occasions these bulky wafers are reinforced by one or two deep basket-bowls of puffy, double-lobed wheaten loaves like overgrown bakers' rolls (fig. *a*), but browner and thicker-skinned outside, light-buff and porous, coarse-grained, yet quite as spongy, within. Then there are the *tchu'-tsi-kwah-na-mu-we*, or "skinned-corn-paste-loaves," neatly done up, like druggists' packets, in wrappers of corn-husk (fig. *i*); and if not further like drugs, medicinal, still, like them again in that they are certainly

VARIETIES OF COOKED FOODS

good medicine for the disease of hunger; best, however, when that disease is acutest. Partaking somewhat of the nature of these latter (for they are well done up and cooked by boiling) are the crescent-shaped, soft, sweet, and sticky *â'-te-a-mu-we* (fig. *b*), bright in their twisted envelopes of green corn-leaves, yet as yellow inside of this exterior as the squash-blossoms with which they have been seasoned. Neither less yellow, less sticky, nor less a delicacy, although decidedly less sweet and more saline, like over-done "Indian pudding" in which salt has gained mastery over the molasses, is the *k̓os'-he-pa-lo-k̓ia* in its sooty, unsteady, little cooking-pot with its rim of upturned, rather singed corn-shucks (fig. *h*). Capping this feast in their resistless, yea relentless, attractiveness to the Zuñi palate, are the husk-beswathed slabs of red *he'-pa-lo-k̓ia* (fig. *c*). Nor is there lack of more solid foods; for, could such a stuff as green syrup with gigantic pills of "blue-mass" floating about in it, be readily imagined, I would ask my readers to kindly draw such a pleasing picture, the more vividly to realize the appearance of the big bowl of *mu'-k̓iä-li-we*, or dumpling soup, than he will by merely examining fig. *f.* This bowl of slimy breadstuff swelters, but does not out-steam; the equally generous trencher of stewed meat-joints and toasted hominy (fig. *e*) which stands beside it in the middle of this oval array. Of all dishes most indispensable to Zuñi dinners, this over-seethed, vastly rich and greasy, vermilion-colored, pepper-scummed, diabolical *olla podrida*, ranks next to the universal *he'-we*. No wonder that within convenient reach of it, tilted up over a primitive plate of sandstone, is a skewer of broiled meat-shreds; or, more often, a spindle of suet and tidbit-stuffed sheep-intestines (fig. *j*), browned to brittleness at the periphery but somewhat underdone toward the center. This dietic bobbin, however hot and reeking, must be, if one would have it relish at its best, returned to the coals repeatedly, during its unwinding course at a long dinner. On another sandstone plate lies the blood-pudding, composed of chopped liver, lights, suet, salt, pepper, coarse browned meal, brains, and clotted blood, rammed into a large intestine and baked or boiled until, what with swelling and congealing when allowed to grow cold, it looks like a hugely distended Bologna sausage, and tastes like unspiced head-cheese. Less digestible, moreover, it certainly is not. In the nature of *entrées* are other preparations precisely like this last in outward appearance (fig. *k*). A typical one of these is the same kind of large intestines stuffed with its own half-digested contents, thoroughly enhanced by the liberal addition of salt, red pepper, and parched meal, then roasted for three hours or more to solidity and shining brownness in front of a raging fire of embers. Most unprepossessing in its semblance is this unassimilated meal of some sheep or roebuck; but to the vegetable-famished Zuñi (no less than it proved to my own taste after a preliminary training of some months in the native dietary) it is a most grateful change, a promoter of appetite, and an excellent digester of some of the poisons above catalogued. A really superior sauce or condiment—never absent from luncheons and rarely so from other meals—at least in the height of the chile season, is the pepper, onion, salt, coriander-leaf, and water paste, served in the lava-stone trough in which it has been freshly macerated and crushed (fig. *g*). Save that it completes the list of our illustrations (fig. *l*) there would be no need to mention the ever-present jar or earthen box of salt and chile-colorado or red-pepper meal—which (having been toasted) looks and smells like snuff; but tastes like the wrong end of a lighted cigarette (until you get used to it)!

The dishes already described are but the repastorial bulwarks of Zuñi; for in addition to them one may frequently see corn, sweet or common, cooked on the cob in the various ways long ago mentioned; either stewed beans, or beans in large bunches (pods and all) boiled until soft, and eaten as asparagus is eaten; fried, roasted, or baked squash; boiled pumpkin; snaky coils of desiccated melon strips—simmered with or without dried peaches, or the peaches stewed without the melon strips, both sweet without sugaring; greens made from water-cress or young milkweed pods; small game, served with a rich gravy of squash-seed meal, and often the grinning, pop-eyed heads of larger game or domesticated animals, buried over night in a fire-surmounted cist of stone, and black as the sable of a dead coal from the singeing they have thereby been subjected to. The ears, hoofs, and tails of deer, antelope, and cattle, first scorched in blazing fire, then boiled a day or two, also show up at the larger Zuñi dinners in the shape of thick gelatinous soups. Finally, most curious of all the eatables of these motly meals, are parched locust-chrysalides, or *chum'-al-li.* These incipient, though active insects are industriously dug in great numbers from the sandy soil of the cañon woodlands, by the women, who go forth to their lowly chase, like berry-pickers, in merry shoals. They are then confined in little lobe-shaped cages of wicker, brought home toward evening, and at once both cleaned and "fattened," by immersion over night in warmish water, of which, if they be a lively lot, they absorb so much as to increase in individual bulk before morning to more than twice their natural size. Then they are taken out and treated to a hot bath in melted tallow, which causes them to roll up and die, after which they are salted and parched as corn is, in an earthen toasting-pot, over a hot—very hot—fire.

Such a meal as this, eaten as promiscuously as it has been described, is not to be seen every day; but if one eliminate from it the locusts and other fancy dishes, retaining the meat and bean-stews, *he'-we,* and some other varieties of breadstuff, he will have the representative dinner, or evening meal, of every well-to-do Zuñi household almost every day (except during melon and green-corn time) throughout the year.

Zuñi Breadstuff (1920; first published 1884–85)

CHICKEN CROQUETTES

Boil chicken very tender, pick to pieces, take all gristle out, then chop fine. Beat two eggs for one chicken and mix into meat; season with pepper and salt; make into cakes oblong shaped; powder crackers and roll them into the powder, after dipping them into two eggs beaten moderately well. Then have your lard very hot, and fry just before sending them to the table.

Abby Fisher, *What Mrs. Fisher Knows About Old Southern Cooking* (1881)

Born a slave, Mrs. Fisher moved to San Francisco after the Civil War and with her husband created a business that manufactured pickles and preserves, among other items. Like this classic chicken croquette, all her recipes are Southern.

John Burroughs

My Sugar-Making Days

John Burroughs (1837–1921) grew up on a farm in the Catskills and became famous for his eloquent nature essays, a form he did much to popularize. Here, in a nostalgic evocation of country ways from his collection *Signs and Seasons* (1886), maple-syrup making becomes a ritual that distills a place and time into a single indelible taste.

■ ■ ■

One of the features of farm life peculiar to this country, and one of the most picturesque of them all, is sugar-making in the maple woods in spring. This is the first work of the season, and to the boys is more play than work. In the Old World, and in more simple and imaginative times, how such an occupation as this would have got into literature, and how many legends and associations would have clustered around it! It is woodsy, and savors of the trees; it is an encampment among the maples. Before the bud swells, before the grass springs, before the plow is started, comes the sugar harvest. It is the sequel of the bitter frost; a sap-run is the sweet good-by of winter. It denotes a certain equipoise of the season; the heat of the day fully balances the frost of the night. In New York and New England, the time of the sap hovers about the vernal equinox, beginning a week or ten days before, and continuing a week or ten days after. As the days and nights get equal, the heat and cold get equal, and the sap mounts. A day that brings the bees out of the hive will bring the sap out of the maple-tree. It is the fruit of the equal marriage of the sun and the frost. When the frost is all out of the ground, and all the snow gone from its surface, the flow stops. The thermometer must not rise above 38° or 40° by day, or sink below 24° or 25° at night, with wind in the northwest; a relaxing south wind, and the run is over for the present. Sugar weather is crisp weather. How the tin buckets glisten in the gray woods; how the robins laugh; how the nuthatches call; how lightly the thin blue smoke rises among the trees! The squirrels are out of their dens; the migrating water-fowls are streaming northward; the sheep and cattle look wistfully toward the bare fields; the tide of the season, in fact, in just beginning to rise.

Sap-letting does not seem to be an exhaustive process to the trees, as the trees of a sugar-bush appear to be as thrifty and as long-lived as other trees. They come to have a maternal, large-waisted look, from the wounds of the axe or the auger, and that is about all.

In my sugar-making days, the sap was carried to the boiling-place in pails by the aid of a neck-yoke and stored in hogsheads, and boiled or evaporated in immense kettles or caldrons set in huge stone arches; now, the hogshead goes to the trees hauled upon a sled by a team, and the sap is evaporated in broad, shallow, sheet-iron pans,—a great saving of fuel and of labor.

Many a farmer sits up all night boiling his sap, when the run has been an extra good one, and a lonely vigil he has of it amid the silent trees and beside his wild hearth. If he has a sap-house, as is now so common, he may make himself fairly comfortable; and if a companion, he may have a good time or a glorious wake.

Maple sugar in its perfection is rarely seen, perhaps never seen, in the market. When made in large quantities and indifferently, it is dark and coarse; but when made in small quantities—that is, quickly from the first run of sap and properly treated—it has a wild delicacy of flavor that no other sweet can match. What you smell in freshly cut maple-wood, or taste in the blossom of the tree, is in it. It is then, indeed, the distilled essence of the tree. Made into syrup, it is white and clear as clover-honey; and crystallized into sugar, it is as pure as wax. The way to attain this result is to evaporate the sap under cover in an enameled kettle; when reduced about twelve times, allow it to settle half a day or more; then clarify with milk or the white of an egg. The product is virgin syrup, or sugar worthy the table of the gods.

Signs and Seasons (1886)

CHICKEN CHARTREUSE

Chop very fine *nine ounces*, or *a heaping cup*, of *cold cooked chicken*; add the inside of *two sausages*, or *two ounces* of *lean, cooked ham*, chopped fine, *three tablespoonfuls* of *powdered bread crumbs*, *one tablespoonful* of *capers*, or *one tablespoonful* of *chopped parsley*, *two tablespoonfuls* of *lemon juice* or *vinegar*, a *speck* of *cayenne*, *two eggs*, well beaten, and enough *hot soup stock* to make it quite moist. Add *salt* and *pepper* to taste, the amount depending upon the seasoning in the sausages. The sausages may be omitted, and a larger amount of chicken used. Butter a small mould, and pack the meat in closely to within an inch of the top to allow for swelling. Put it on a trivet in a kettle, and steam three hours. If no uncooked meat be used, one hour will be sufficient. Cool it in the mould; when ready to serve, dip the mould quickly into warm water and loosen the meat around the edges with a thin knife and remove the mould. It may be served plain or moulded in jelly.

Mary Lincoln, *Mrs. Lincoln's Boston Cookbook* (1884)

A major American cookbook, as important as Fannie Farmer. "Chartreuses" were elegant dishes of assorted finely chopped ingredients steamed in a mold.

Ward McAllister

Success in Entertaining

Samuel Ward McAllister (1827–1895) was the self-appointed arbiter of New York society from the 1860s to the 1890s. Born into a socially prominent judicial family in Savannah, he was a lawyer in California during the Gold Rush before returning East, where he married an heiress and set about fashioning himself into a tastemaster for New York's old-money circles. His celebrated coinage "The Four Hundred" supposedly derived from the number of people who could fit into Mrs. Astor's ballroom. McAllister overstepped the line with the publication of his memoir *Society As I Have Found It* (1890), from which this wonderful description of planning a dinner party for the Gilded Age is taken; the Four Hundred felt their privacy had been violated and shunned the author thereafter.

■ ■ ■

"We may live without love,—what is passion but pining?
But where is the man who can live without dining?"—

Owen Meredith.

The first object to be aimed at is to make your dinners so charming and agreeable that invitations to them are eagerly sought for, and to let all feel that it is a great privilege to dine at your house, where they are sure they will meet only those whom they wish to meet. You cannot instruct people by a book how to entertain, though Aristotle is said to have applied *his* talents to a compilation of a code of laws for the table. Success in entertaining is accomplished by magnetism and tact, which combined constitute social genius. It is the ladder to social success. If successfully done, it naturally creates jealousy. I have known a family who for years outdid every one in giving exquisite dinners–(this was when this city was a small community)–driven to Europe and passing the rest of their days there on finding a neighbor outdoing them. I myself once lost a charming friend by giving a better soup than he did. His wife rushed home from my house, and in despair, throwing up her hands to her husband, exclaimed, "Oh! what a soup!" I related this to my cousin, the distinguished *gourmet*, who laughingly said: "Why did you not at once invite them to pork and beans?"

The highest cultivation of social manners enables a person to conceal from the world his real feelings. He can go through any annoyance as if it were a pleasure; go to a rival's house as if to a dear friend's; "Smile and smile, yet murder while he smiles." A great compliment once paid me in Newport was the speech of an old public waiter, who had grown gray in the service, when to a *confrère* he exclaimed: "In this house, my friend, you meet none but quality."

In planning a dinner the question is not to whom you owe dinners, but who is most desirable. The success of the dinner depends as much upon the company as the cook. Discordant elements—people invited alphabetically, or to pay off debts—are fatal. Of course, I speak of ladies' dinners. And here, great tact must be used in bringing together young womanhood and the dowagers. A dinner wholly made up of young people is generally stupid. You require the experienced woman of the world, who has at her fingers' ends the history of past, present, and future. Critical, scandalous, with keen and ready wit, appreciating the dinner and wine at their worth. Ladies in beautiful toilets are necessary to the elegance of a dinner, as a most exquisitely arranged table is only a solemn affair surrounded by black coats. I make it a rule never to attend such dismal feasts, listening to prepared witticisms and "twice-told tales." So much for your guests.

The next step is an interview with your *chef*, if you have one, or *cordon bleu*, whom you must arouse to fever heat by working on his ambition and vanity. You must impress upon him that this particular dinner will give him fame and lead to fortune. My distinguished cousin, who enjoyed the reputation of being one of the most finished *gourmets* in this country, when he reached this point, would bury his head in his hands and (seemingly to the *chef*) rack his brain seeking inspiration, fearing lest the fatal mistake should occur of letting two white or brown sauces follow each other in succession; or truffles appear twice in that dinner. The distress that his countenance wore as he repeatedly looked up at the *chef*, as if for advice and assistance, would have its intended effect on the culinary artist, and *his* brain would at once act in sympathy.

The first battle is over the soup, and here there is a vast difference of opinion. In this country, where our servants are oftentimes unskilled, and have a charming habit of occasionally giving ladies a soup shower bath, I invariably discard two soups, and insist to the protesting *chef* that there shall be but one. Of course, if there are two, the one is light, the other heavy. Fortunately for the period in which we live, our great French artists have invented the *Tortue claire*, which takes the place of our forefathers' Mock Turtle soup, with forcemeat balls, well spiced, requiring an ostrich's digestion to survive it. We have this, then, as our soup. The *chef* here exclaims, "Monsieur must know that all *petites bouchées* must, of necessity, be made of chicken." We ask for a novelty, and his great genius suggests, under pressure, *mousse aux jambon*, which is attractive to the eye, and, if well made, at once establishes the reputation of the artist, satisfies the guests that they are in able hands, and allays their fears for their dinner.

There is but one season of the year when salmon should be served hot at a choice repast; that is in the spring and early summer, and even then it is too satisfying, not sufficiently delicate. The man who gives salmon during the winter, I care not what sauce he serves with it, does an injury to himself and his guests. Terrapin is with us as national a dish as canvasback, and at the choicest dinners is often a substitute for fish. It is a shellfish, and an admirable change from the oft repeated *filet de sole* or *filet de bass*. At the South, terrapin soup, with plenty of eggs in it, was a dish for the gods, and a standard dinner party dish in days when a Charleston and Savannah dinner was an event to live for. But no Frenchman ever made this soup. It requires the native born culinary genius of the African.

Now when we mention the word terrapin, we approach a very delicate subject, involving a rivalry between two great cities; a subject that has been agitated for thirty years or more, and is still agitated, i.e. the proper way of cooking terrapin. The Baltimoreans contending that the black stew, the chafing dish system, simply adding to the terrapin salt, pepper, and Madeira, produce the best dish; while the Philadelphians contend that by fresh butter and cream they secure greater results. The one is known as the Baltimore black stew; the other, as the Trenton stew, this manner of cooking terrapin originating in an old eating club in Trenton, N.J. I must say I agree with the Philadelphians.

And now, leaving the fish, we come to the *pièce de resistance* of the dinner, called the *relévé*. No Frenchman will ever willingly cook a ladies' dinner and give anything coarser or heavier than a *filet de bœuf*. He will do it, if he has to, of course, but he will think you a barbarian if you order him to do it. I eschew the mushroom and confine myself to the truffle in the treatment of the *filet*. I oftentimes have a *filet à la mœlle de bœuf*, or *à la jardinière*. In the fall of the year, turkey *poults à la Bordelaise*, or *à la Toulouse*, or a saddle of Southdown mutton or lamb, are a good substitute. Let me here say that the American turkey, as found on Newport Island, all its feathers being jet black and its diet grasshoppers, is exceptionally fine.

Now for the *entrées*. In a dinner of twelve or fourteen, one or two hot *entrées* and one cold is sufficient. If you use the truffle with the *filet*, making a black sauce, you must follow it with a white sauce, as a *riz de veau à la Toulouse*, or a *suprême de volaille*; then a *chaud-froid*, say of *pâté de foie gras en Bellevue*, which simply means *pâté de foie gras* incased in jelly. Then a hot vegetable, as artichokes, sauce *Barigoule*, or *Italienne*, or asparagus, sauce *Hollandaise*. Then your *sorbet*, known in France as *la surprise*, as it is an ice, and produces on the mind the effect that the dinner is finished, when the grandest dish of the dinner makes its appearance in the shape of the roast canvasbacks, woodcock, snipe, or truffled capons, with salad.

I must be permitted a few words of and about this *sorbet*. It should never be flavored with rum. A true Parisian *sorbet* is simply "*punch à la Toscane*," flavored with *Maraschino* or bitter almonds; in other words, a homœopathic dose of prussic acid. Then the *sorbet* is a digestive, and is intended as such. *Granit*, or water ice, flavored with rum, is universally given here. Instead of aiding digestion, it impedes it, and may be dangerous.

A Russian salad is a pleasing novelty at times, and is more attractive if it comes in the shape of a *Macedoine de legumes*, Camembert cheese, with a biscuit, with which you serve your Burgundy, your old Port, or your Johannisberg, the only place in the dinner where you can introduce this latter wine. A genuine Johannisberg, I may say here, by way of parenthesis, is rare in this country, for if obtained at the Chateau, it is comparatively a dry wine; if it is, as I have often seen it, still lusciously sweet after having been here twenty years or more, you may be sure it is not a genuine Chateau wine.

The French always give a hot pudding, as pudding *suedoise*, or a *croute au Madère*, or *ananas*, but I always omit this dish to shorten the dinner. Then come your ices. The fashion now is to make them very ornamental, a *cornucopia* for instance, but I prefer a *pouding Nesselrode*, the best of all the ices if good cream is used.

Society As I Have Found It (1890)

ROMAN·PVNCH

ROMAN PUNCH. N°. 1.

Grate the yellow rind of four lemons and two oranges upon two pounds of loaf sugar. Squeeze the juice of the lemons and oranges; cover the juice and let it stand until the next day. Strain it through a sieve, mix with the sugar; add a bottle of champagne and the whites of eight eggs beaten to a stiff froth. It may be frozen or not, as desired. For winter use snow instead of ice.

ROMAN PUNCH. N°. 2.

Make two quarts of lemonade, rich with pure juice lemon fruit; add one tablespoonful of extract of lemon. Work well, and freeze; just before serving, add for each quart of ice half a pint of brandy and half a pint of Jamaica rum. Mix well and serve in high glasses, as this makes what is called a semi or half-ice. It is usually served at dinners as a *coup de milieu*.

Mrs. F. L. Gillette & Hugo Ziemann, *The White House Cook Book* (1887)

Mixed drinks—shrubs, syllabubs, punches, and toddies—were the rage after dinner in the late 19th century. Roman Punch was the most popular of them all.

Henry Adams

from History of the United States

In his recent *Henry Adams and the Making of America* (2005), Garry Wills has argued that *History of the United States during the Administrations of Jefferson and Madison* is the neglected masterpiece of American historiography. The work's first six chapters, a rapid, trenchant portrait of America in all its aspects in 1800, constitute a classic in their own right. This survey of the emerging nation's eating habits–described with a serious attention that foreshadows more modern approaches to history-writing–forms part of this prelude.

■ ■ ■

The standard of comfort had much to do with the standard of character; and in the United States, except among the slaves, the laboring class enjoyed an ample supply of the necessaries of life. In this respect, as in some others, they claimed superiority over the laboring class in Europe, and the claim would have been still stronger had they shown more skill in using the abundance that surrounded them. The Duc de Liancourt, among foreigners the best and kindest observer, made this remark on the mode of life he saw in Pennsylvania:–

> "There is a contrast of cleanliness with its opposite which to a stranger is very remarkable. The people of the country are as astonished that one should object to sleeping two or three in the same bed and in dirty sheets, or to drink from the same dirty glass after half a score of others, as to see one neglect to wash one's hands and face of a morning. Whiskey diluted with water is the ordinary country drink. There is no settler, however poor, whose family does not take coffee or chocolate for breakfast, and always a little salt meat; at dinner, salt meat, or salt fish, and eggs; at supper again salt meat and coffee. This is also the common regime of the taverns."

An amusing, though quite untrustworthy Englishman named Ashe, who invented an American journey in 1806, described the fare of a Kentucky cabin:–

"The dinner consisted of a large piece of salt bacon, a dish of hominy, and a tureen of squirrel broth. I dined entirely on the last dish, which I found incomparably good, and the meat equal to the most delicate chicken. The Kentuckian eat nothing but bacon, which indeed is the favorite diet of all the inhabitants of the State, and drank nothing but whiskey, which soon made him more than two-thirds drunk. In this last practice he is also supported by the public habit. In a country, then, where bacon and spirits form the favorite summer repast, it cannot be just to attribute entirely the causes of infirmity to the climate. No people on earth live with less regard to regimen. They eat salt meat three times a day, seldom or never have any vegetables, and drink ardent spirits from morning till night. They have not only an aversion to fresh meat, but a vulgar prejudice that it is unwholesome. The truth is, their stomachs are depraved by burning liquors, and they have no appetite for anything but what is high-flavored and strongly impregnated by salt."

Salt pork three times a day was regarded as an essential part of American diet. In the "Chainbearer," Cooper described what he called American poverty as it existed in 1784. "As for bread," said the mother, "I count that for nothing. We always have bread and potatoes enough; but I hold a family to be in a desperate way when the mother can see the bottom of the pork-barrel. Give me the children that's raised on good sound pork afore all the game in the country. Game's good as a relish, and so's bread; but pork is the staff of life . . . My children I calkerlate to bring up on pork."

Many years before the time to which Coopper referred, Poor Richard asked: "Maids of America, who gave you bad teeth?" and supplied the answer: "Hot soupings and frozen apples." Franklin's question and answer were repeated in a wider sense by many writers, but none was so emphatic as Volney:—

"I will venture to say," declared Volney, "that if a prize were proposed for the scheme of a regimen most calculated to injure the stomach, the teeth, and the health in general, no better could be invented than that of the Americans. In the morning at breakfast they deluge their stomach with a quart of hot water, impregnated with tea, or so slightly with coffee that it is mere colored water; and they swallow, almost without chewing, hot bread, half baked, toast soaked in butter, cheese of the fattest kind, slices of salt or hung beef, ham, etc., all which are nearly insoluble. At dinner they have boiled pastes under the name of puddings, and the fattest are esteemed the most delicious; all their sauces, even for roast beef, are melted butter; their turnips and potatoes swim in hog's lard, butter, or fat; under the name of pie or pumpkin, their pastry is nothing but a greasy paste, never sufficiently baked. To digest these viscous substances they take tea almost instantly after dinner, making it so strong that it is absolutely bitter to the taste, in which state it affects the nerves so powerfully that even the English find it brings on a more obstinate restlessness than coffee. Supper again introduces salt meats or oysters. As Chastellux says, the whole day passes in heaping indigestions on one another; and to give tone to the poor, relaxed, and wearied stomach, they drink Madeira, rum, French brandy, gin, or malt spirits, which complete the ruin of the nervous system."

An American breakfast never failed to interest foreigners, on account of the variety and abundance of its dishes. On the main lines of travel, fresh meat and vegetable were invariably served at all meals; but Indian corn was the national crop, and Indian corn was eaten three times a day in another form as salt pork. The rich alone could afford fresh meat. Ice-chests were hardly known. In the country fresh meat could not regularly be got, except in the shape of poultry or game; but the hog cost nothing to keep, and very little to kill and preserve. Thus the ordinary rural American was brought up on salt pork and Indian corn, or rye; and the effect of this diet showed itself in dyspepsia.

History of the United States during the Administrations of Thomas Jefferson (1884)

Bran Jelly

Select some clean wheat bran, sprinkle it slowly into boiling water as for Graham mush, stirring briskly meanwhile with a wooden spoon, until the whole is about the consistency of thick gruel. Cook slowly in a double boiler for two hours. Strain through a fine wire sieve placed over the top of a basin. When strained, reheat to boiling. Then stir into it a spoonful or so of sifted Graham flour, rubbed smooth in a little cold water. Boil up once; turn into molds previously wet in cold water, and when cool, serve with cream or fruit juice.

Mrs. E. E. Kellogg, *Science in the Kitchen* (1893)

John Harvey Kellogg's sanitarium at Battle Creek, Michigan, offered salvation to victims of the Gay Nineties table; his wife, Mrs. E. E. Kellogg, supervised the sanitarium's School of Cookery. The role of grains and the regulation of bowels were of great concern to the Kelloggs, but his cornflake solution found a more sustained audience than her recipe for bran jelly.

Charles Ranhofer

from The Epicurean

Charles Ranhofer (1836–1899), born in France, was for over 30 years the chef at Delmonico's in New York City. Regarded in its day as the best in the country, the restaurant served an extensive menu that combined French and American specialties, and was famous for original dishes: Ranhofer claimed fame for Lobster Newberg and, after the Alaskan territory was purchased, helped popularize Baked Alaska. He also introduced new edibles such as avocadoes, which the menu called "alligator pears." Ranhofer's encyclopedic cookbook *The Epicurean* (1894), with a scope comparable to Escoffier's *Le Guide Culinaire* (1903), set a gold standard of dining for homes presumed to be equipped with a sizeable staff of servants.

■ ■ ■

TABLE SERVICE
The service must be performed silently, a look alone from the steward sufficing for each man to do his duty. Every article handed round must be on a silver salver.

THE SERVICE

Oysters.—Little Neck clams are passed around, beginning on one side by the lady on the right and the other side by the gentleman on the right, these being the most distinguished guests; change this method at each course, those being served last before, being the first now.

The butler will pour out the Chablis, stating the name of each wine he serves.

Soup.—There are usually two soups to select from. While serving green turtle offer at the same time lemon cut in quarters.

Sherry should be served with this course.

Side Dishes.—Pass hot hors-d'œuvre; these are served on warm plates. Serve the cold hors d'œuvre at the same time, and should the guest prefer the latter, remove the hot plate at once and substitute a cold one for it.

Sherry or Xeres should accompany this course.

Fish.—If there be two kinds of fish, offer the selection, and pass around the one preferred; should it be boiled or braized fish, have potatoes served at the same time; if broiled or sautéd thinly sliced seasoned fresh cucumbers must accompany it, and if fried fish such as whitebait, serve with thin slices of buttered brown bread and quarters of lemon.

Serve Rhine wine or white Bordeaux.

Removes or Solid Joints.—The removes may be placed on the table before being taken off for carving; if it be a saddle of venison, it should be cooked rare, passing currant jelly at the same time. A saddle of mutton must also be rare and very hot; it can be cut lengthwise at an angle in thin slices or across, although the first way is preferable; serve both these on very hot plates, and have one or two vegetables accompanying them.

Serve champagne.

Entrées.—The entrées must be served one after the other without placing them on the table beforehand; they must be served on hot plates with one vegetable for each entrée, to be either passed round separately or else carefully laid on the same plate, unless it is desired that they be dressed; in this case dress and present to each guest. Serve Bordeaux at the first entrée, and an extra quality of wine at the last; continue serving champagne to those who prefer to drink it until the roast.

INTERVAL—SECOND SERVICE

Iced Punch or Sherbet.—Should there be no ladies present, cigarettes can be handed round at the same time. Remove the two white wine and sherry glasses, and replace them by those used for Burgundy, also remove the cold side dishes. Ten to fifteen minutes must now be allowed between the courses.

Roasts.—The roast may be displayed on the table before carving, this being frequently requested by epicures; should there be several roasts, carve them all at the same time and pass them round according to desire, adding a little watercress for poultry, and should there be canvas-back duck, let currant jelly and fried hominy be served with also a mayonnaise of celery.

Serve the Burgundy from bottles laid flat in baskets holding the basket in the right hand and a white napkin in the left.

Cold.—Serve the cold dishes after the roast, these to be either goose livers (foies-gras) with truffles or boned turkey. The foies-gras must have a spoon to remove it with, and the boned turkey be cut into thin slices, and offer both to the guest at the same time, accompanied by green salads.

Serve Johannisberg or Vin de Paille.

Now remove everything from the table with the exception of the dessert, and to avoid using a brush lift up the extra napkins in front of each person, folding them in two so that the table is neat and clean without being obliged to use a brush or scraper. Lay the dessert plates on the table, and continue the service for the hot dessert.

Hot Sweet Entremets.—Make a distinct service for the hot entremets, then serve the cheese.

Serve a fine Laffitte Bordeaux.

Cold Sweet Entremets.—Make another service for the cold entremets and ices.

Dessert.—Instead of serving the cheese after the hot entremets it may be done now, which is in fact its proper place; pass around the fresh fruits, stewed, candied and dried fruits, bonbon cases, bonbons, mottoes, ices, strawberries and raspberries with cream when in season, passing cakes around at the same time.

Serve Madeira wine, Muscatel and Frontignan, also plates of salted almonds.

THE CONCLUSION OF THE DINNER

It is now time for the hostess to bow, push back her chair and prepare to rise, this being a signal for the ladies to retire; after they have returned to the drawing-room, coffee is passed round on a salver containing spoons, hot water, sugar and cream. A few moments later another waiter comes forward with an empty tray to remove the cups the ladies hand him.

The gentlemen partake of their coffee in the dining-room; at the same time serve them Kirsch, brandy, chartreuse, cigars and cigarettes. The doors are closed and the ladies and waiters have retired so as to allow the gentlemen more freedom to talk among themselves, still it will be necessary to enter the drawing-room and dining-room occasionally in order to see whether anything be needed so as to avoid being called as much as possible.

After half an hour or so, the gentlemen will rejoin the ladies in the drawing-room and then tea is served. The tea service is accomplished by passing around on trays, tea, sugar, hot water, cream, cups, spoons and slices of lemon. A few moments later another waiter removes the empty cups on a tray.

After the tea the service is considered to be ended.

The Epicurean (1894)

Lobster à la Newberg or Delmonico

- - -

(HOMARD À LA NEWBERG OU
À LA DELMONICO)

- - -

Cook six lobsters each weighing about two pounds in boiling salted water for twenty-five minutes. Twelve pounds of live lobster when cooked yields from two to two and a half pounds of meat and three or four ounces of lobster coral. When cold detach the bodies from the tails and cut the latter into slices, put them into a sautoir, each piece lying flat and add hot clarified butter; season with salt and fry lightly on both sides without coloring; moisten to their height with good raw cream; reduce quickly to half and then add two or three spoonfuls of Madeira wine; boil the liquid once more only, then remove and thicken with a thickening of egg-yolks and raw cream. Cook without boiling, incorporating a little cayenne and butter; warm it up again without boiling, tossing the lobster lightly, then arrange the pieces in a vegetable dish and pour the sauce over.

Charles Ranhofer, *The Epicurean* (1894)

Elizabeth Robins Pennell

Spring Chicken

Elizabeth Robins Pennell (1855–1936), little remembered now, could reasonably be called the M.F.K. Fisher of her day, and she surely remains one of the most cosmopolitan and sophisticated of American food writers. Born in Philadelphia, she moved to London in 1884; with her husband, the illustrator Joseph Pennell, her circle over the next three decades came to include artists and writers such as George Bernard Shaw, Henry James, and James Whistler. Asked to contribute a culinary column to the fashionable *Pall Mall Gazette*, she initially doubted her abilities (her only qualifications, she later wrote, "were the healthy appetite and the honest love of a good dinner usually considered unbecoming to the sex"). But she rose to the occasion, assembling a legendary collection of cookbooks for consultation (they're now in the Library of Congress), and crossing the Channel regularly in search of epicurean experience. Collected in *The Feasts of Autolycus: The Diary of a Greedy Woman* (1896; later retitled *The Delights of Delicate Eating*), her columns address topics like "The Virtue of Gluttony," "The Triumphant Tomato," and "Indispensable Cheese." Whatever the subject, she is a master at encouraging a refined enthusiasm for good food, and found "no less art in eating well than in painting well or writing well."

■ ■ ■

Gluttony, it has been written—and with wisdom—deserves nothing but praise and encouragement. For two reasons. "Physically, it is the result and proof of the digestive organs being perfect. Morally, it shows implicit resignation to the commands of nature, who, in ordering man to eat that he may live, gives him appetite to invite, flavour to encourage, and pleasure to reward." But there is a third reason, too often overlooked even by the professional glutton: love of good eating is an incentive to thought, a stimulus to the imagination. The man of the most active mind and liveliest fancy is he who eats well and conscientiously considers each dish as it is set before him.

The test seldom fails. Run through the list of poets and painters of your acquaintance; do not they who eat best write the finest verse and paint the strongest pictures? Those who pretend indifference and live on unspeakable messes are betrayed in the foolish affectation and tedious eccentricity of their work; those who feel indifference are already beyond hope and had better far be selling tape across counters or adding up figures in loathsome ledgers. Memory, borrowing from her store-house of treasures, lingers with tender appreciation and regret upon one unrivalled breakfast, exquisitely cooked, exquisitely served, and exquisitely eaten, when lilacs were sweet and horse-chestnuts blossoming in the boulevards and avenues of Paris. And he upon whose table the banquet was spread is an artist who towers head and shoulders above the pigmies of his generation. It were rash, indeed, to maintain that because he eats daintily therefore he paints like the master he is; but who, on the other hand, would dare aver that because he paints supremely well therefore is he the prince of *gourmets*? Here cause and effect are not to be defined by cold logic, not to be labelled by barren philosophy. One thing alone is certain; if love of good eating will not create genius it can but develop it.

Consequently, it would be impossible to think too much of what you are eating to-day and purpose to eat to-morrow. It is your duty above all things to see that your food is in harmony with place and season. The question now is, what beast or bird is fitting holocaust for the first warm months of spring? Beef is too heating, too substantial; mutton too monotonous, veal too prosaic. Lamb hath charm, but a charm that by constant usage may be speedily exhausted. Does not mint sauce pall at times? Place, then, your trust in the poultry-yard that your pleasure may be long in the spring.

To begin with, poultry pleases because of its idyllic and pastoral associations. The plucked birds, from shop windows, flaunting their nakedness in the face of the world, recall the old red-roofed farmhouse among the elms, and the pretty farmer's daughter in neat, fresh gingham, scattering grain in the midst of her feathered favourites; they suggest the first cool light of dawn and the irrepressible cock crowing the glad approach of day; in a word, they are reminders of the country's simple joys—unendurable at the time, dear and sacred when remembered in town.

The gentle little spring chicken is sweet and adorable above all its kindred poultry. It is innocent and guileless as Bellini's angels, dream-like and strange as Botticelli's. It is the very concentration of spring; as your teeth meet in its tender, yielding flesh, you think, whether you will or no, of violets and primroses, and hedgerows white with may; you feel the balmy breath of the south wind; the world is scented for you with lilac and narcissus; and, for the time being, life is a perfect poem. But—why is there always a but?—your cook has it in her power to ruin the rhythm, to make of melodious lyric the most discordant prose. No less depends upon the being who cooks the chicken than upon the hen who laid the egg. If hitherto you have offended through heedlessness, see now that you approach the subject with a determination to profit.

Of all ways of cooking a spring chicken, frying is first to be commended; and of all ways of frying the American is most sympathetic. Fried chicken! To write the word is to be carried back to the sunny South; to see, in the mind's eye, the old, black, fat, smiling *mammie*, in gorgeous bandana turban, and the little black piccaninnies bringing in relays of hot muffins. Oh, the happy days of the long ago! It is easy to give the *recipe*, but what can it avail unless the *mammie* goes with it? Another admirable device is in broiling. One fashion is to divide your chicken down the back and flatten it, seeing, as you have a heart within you, that no bones be broken. Set it lovingly on a trivet placed for the purpose in a baking-tin into which water, to the depth of an inch, has been poured. Cover your tin; bake the sweet offering for ten minutes or so; take it from the oven; touch it delicately with the purest of pure olive oil, and for another ten minutes broil it over a good brisk fire. And if in the result you do not taste heaven, hasten to the hermit's cell in the desert, and, for the remainder of your days, grow thin on lentils and dates.

Or, if you would broil your chicken after the fashion of infallible Mrs. Glasse, slit it as before, season it with pepper and salt, lay it on a clear fire at a great distance, broil first the inside, then the out, cover it with delicate bread-crumbs, and let it be of a fine brown, but not burnt. And keep this note carefully in your mind: "You may make just what sauce you fancy."

To roast a spring chicken will do no harm, but let it not be overdone. Twenty minutes suffice for the ceremony. Bacon, in thinnest of thin slices, gracefully rolled, is not unworthy to be served with it. In boiling, something of its virginal flavour may be sacrificed, but still there is compensating gain; it may be eaten with white mushroom sauce, made of mushrooms and cream, and seasoned with nutmeg and mace. Here is a poem, sweeter far than all songs of immortal choirs or the weak pipings of our minor singers.

As the chicken outgrows the childish state, you may go to Monte Carlo in search of one hint at least, for its disposal. There you will learn to cut it into quarters, to stew it in wine and shallots, to add, at the psychological moment, tomatoes in slices, and to serve a dish that baffles description. Or you may journey to Spain, and find that country's kitchen slandered when you eat *poulet au ris à l' Espagnole*, chicken cooked in a *marmite* with rice, artichokes, green and red chillies, and salad oil, and served, where the artist dwells, in the blessed *marmite* itself–in unimaginative London, even, you may buy one, green or brown, whichever you will, at a delightful shop in Shaftsbury-avenue. Again, you may wander to Holland–it is a short journey, and not disagreeable by way of Harwich–and be ready to swear that no fashion can surpass the Dutch of boiling chickens with rice or vermicelli, spicing them with pepper and cloves, and, at table, substituting for sauce sugar and cinnamon. But to omit these last two garnishments will not mean a mortal sin upon your conscience. In more festive mood hasten at once to France, and there you will be no less certain that the way of ways is to begin to broil your chicken, already quartered, but, when half done, to put it in a stew-pan with gravy, and white wine, salt and pepper, fried veal balls, onions, and shallots, and, according to season, gooseberries or grapes. Do you not grow hungry as you read? But wait: this is not all. As the beautiful mixture is stewing–on a charcoal fire if possible–thicken the liquor with yolks of eggs and the juice of lemon, and for ever after bless Mrs. Glasse for having initiated you into these noble and ennobling mysteries.

Braise your chicken, fricassee it, make it into mince, croquettes, krameskies; eat it cold; convert it into galantine; bury it in aspic; do what you will with it, so long as you do it well, it can bring you but happiness and peace.

The Feasts of Autolycus (1896)

Eggs à la Goldenrod

3 hard boiled eggs.	1/2 teaspoon salt.
1 tablespoon butter.	1/3 teaspoon pepper.
1 tablespoon flour.	5 slices toast.
1 cup milk.	Parsley.

Make a thin white sauce with butter, flour, milk, and seasonings. Separate yolks from whites of eggs. Chop whites finely, and add them to the sauce. Cut four slices of toast in halves lengthwise. Arrange on platter, and pour over the sauce. Force the yolks through a potato ricer or strainer, sprinkling over the top. Garnish with parsley and remaining toast, cut in points.

Fannie Merritt Farmer, *The Boston Cooking-School Cook Book* (1896)

Laura Shapiro has written: "Eggs à la Goldenrod was the very essence of what Fannie Farmer wanted to teach the ambitious homemakers who flocked to her classes: how to make plain, wholesome breakfast ingredients look so decorative and non-nutritive you could even serve them to ladies."

Annie D. Tallent

Bill of Fare on the Plains

At the other end of the spectrum from the Gilded Age trappings of Delmonico's was the hard life of the trail during the country's westward expansion. Annie D. Tallent (1827–1901), born in York, New York, traveled with the Gordon Expedition from Sioux City, Iowa, into the Black Hills of Dakota Territory after gold was discovered in 1874. After her days panning for gold, she became superintendent of schools in Pennington County, South Dakota.

■ ■ ■

Perhaps some of my readers may like to know how we fared during our long journey over the plains. Well, until the settlements were left behind, we lived on the fat of the land through which we passed, being able to procure from the settlers along the route many articles which we were after compelled to do entirely without.

From that time to the end of our journey, or rather until we returned to civilization, the luxuries of milk, eggs, vegetables, etc., could not, of course, be had for love or money.

Our daily "bill of fare," which, in the absence of menu cards, was stereotyped on memory's tablets, consisted of the following articles, to wit: For breakfast, hot biscuit, fried bacon, and black coffee; for dinner, cold biscuit, cold baked beans, and black coffee; for supper, black coffee, hot biscuit, and baked beans warmed over. Occasionally, in lieu of hot biscuits, and for the sake of variety, we would have what is termed in camp parlance, flapjacks. The men did the cooking for the most part, I, the while, seated on a log or an inverted water bucket, watching the process through the smoke of the camp fire, which, for some unexplainable reason, never ceased for a moment to blow directly in my face, shift as I might from point to point of the compass. I now recall how greatly I was impressed with the dexterity and skill with which they flopped over the flapjacks in the frying-pan. By some trick of legerdemain, they would toss up the cake in the air, a short distance, where it would turn a partial somersault, then unfailingly return to the pan the other side up. After studying the modus operandi, for some time one day, I asked permission to try my skill, which was readily granted by the cook, who doubtless anticipated a failure. I tossed up the cake as I had seen them do, but much to my chagrin, the downcoming was wide of the mark. The cake started from the pan all right, but instead of keeping the perpendicular, as by the laws of gravitation it should have done, it flew off, at a tangent, in a most tantalizing manner, and fell to the ground several feet away from the pan, much to the amusement of the boys. I came to the conclusion that tossing pancakes was not my forte.

To relieve the monotony of our daily fare, our tables (?) were quite frequently provided with game of various kinds, such as elk, deer, antelope, grouse, etc., large bands of antelope being seen almost daily along the route over the plains. Each outfit had their own hunters, who supplied, for the most part, their respective messes, with game, but Capt. Tom Russell, who was the real "Nimrod" of the party, and a crack shot, bagged much more game than he needed, which surplus was distributed among the camps. Besides being a good hunter and skillful marksman, Capt. Tom Russell ever proved himself a brave and chivalrous gentleman, during the long, trying journey, and somehow I always felt safer when he was near.

There were several others in the party, too, who won the reputation of being skilled hunters, and judging by the marvelous stories told of the great number of deer, elk, and other animals killed, which could not be brought into camp, they deserved to stand at the head of the profession. If there is anything in the wide world, more than another, of which the average man feels proud, it is of the quantity of game he captures.

Speaking of game brings to mind an experience, the very remembrance of which always causes an uprising and revolution in the region of the principal organ of digestion. Some of the boys, in their very commendable desire to provide the camp with game, one day captured an immense elk, bringing in the choicest parts for distribution among the different messes, and judging from the flavor and texture of the flesh of the animal it must have been a denizen of the Hills since the time of the great upheaval, and to make a bad matter worse, our chef for the day conceived the very reprehensible idea of cooking the meat by a process called "smothering."

Having a deep-seated, dyed-in-the-wool antipathy to smothered meats of all kinds, I employed all the force of my native eloquence in trying to persuade him to adopt some more civilized method of cooking, but no, he was determined to smother it or not cook it at all, as by that process, he said, all the flavor of the meat would be retained, and he continued: "If my way doesn't suit you, cook it yourself." Accordingly it was cooked his way and brought to the table—the word table is here used figuratively—and truth compels me to admit that it looked very tempting, so, as I was abnormally hungry that night, I conveyed to my mouth, with a zeal and alacrity worthy of a batter cause, an exceedingly generous morsel of the meat; but, oh, ye shades of my ancestors! it was speedily ejected and then and there I pronounced it the most villainous morsel I had ever tasted in all my checkered career, and the cook was compelled to concur in that opinion. "Ugh!" although more than two decades have passed since then, I can taste it yet. The trouble, however, was more in the elk than in the cooking.

All formality was thrown to the winds at meal time, each one helping himself or herself with a liberality and abandon, that was truly astonishing and, I might add, alarming, in view of the fact that our larders were becoming rapidly depleted, and that we were completely cut off from our base of supplies. Our coffee was drank from tin cups and our bacon and beans eaten from tin plates. Yes, we had knives and forks—not silver, nor even silver-plated, yet we enjoyed our meals, for with appetites whetted with much exercise and fresh air we were always ravenously hungry, and could eat bacon and beans with the keenest relish.

Strange as it now seems, while journeying over the plains I was for the most time blessed, or cursed, with a voracious, almost insatiable appetite—in fact, was always hungry during my waking hours, and what is most remarkable, none of the others were afflicted with the malady.

At the outset of the journey I had protested strongly against the kind of food on which we were being regaled, declaring that I never could be tempted to each such abominable stuff, and prophesying my own demise from starvation within a month. Later, however, as I trudged along on foot in the rear of the wagon, I would often, between meals, stealthily approach the wagon, surreptitiously raise the lid of the "grub" box and abstract therefrom a great slice of cold bacon and a huge flapjack as large around as the periphery of a man's hat—and a sombrero hat, at that—and devour them without ever flinching or exhibiting the slightest disgust.

The Black Hills; or Last Hunting Ground of the Dakotas (1899)

Henrietta Sowle

from I Go A-Marketing

Apparently less concerned about woman suffrage than about ensuring an adequate supply of lobsters, Henrietta Sowle (1865–?) embodies her era's often unconflicted appreciation of the pleasures of the table. Sowle was a columnist at the Boston *Transcript*, where the items in *I Go A-Marketing* (1900) originally appeared under the by-line "Henriette."

■ ■ ■

About the only time when I am really anxious to have the right to vote is when some legislation tending toward the preservation of the lobster is on the docket. Then, if I had the opportunity, I should not only vote with both hands for a "close season" on that delectable shellfish, but I should lecture as long as I could get any one to listen to me, either on Boston Common or in Faneuil Hall, in an endeavor to induce others, men and women, to vote with me. I believe I should even resort to bribery where I thought it would do—and I am a fair judge of individuals who don't require their "inducements" to be too heavily coated with sugar—in order to put it through.

As matters are now there are almost as many ways for preparing lobster as there are lobsters in the sea, and in order to try them all you would better be about it before the supply is utterly exhausted, or some one in authority calls "time."

For devilling lobsters I have a budget of recipes, but this seems to be about the best one in the lot: Split the lobster, after it is boiled, in two lengthwise, and put it into a baking-pan; season with salt and cayenne, and pour over it plenty of melted butter, and bake in a hot oven for five minutes. Just before serving spread over it a sauce of melted butter thickened with flour and seasoned with a few drops of lemon juice, a sprinkling of mustard, and a little Madeira or sherry wine.

Lest you should get so attached to this devilled lobster of mine, I hasten to put here an alluring sounding recipe, hoping you may be induced to try it before forming the devilled lobster habit. First fry a sliced onion in enough butter so that there will be no browning of it. Take out the onion in two or three minutes, as it is only intended to flavor the butter, and then fry in this butter the diced meat of two boiled lobsters for two or three minutes. Sprinkle in some chopped parsley and salt and pepper as you like it. Pour over the lobster a pint of white wine, and as soon as this gets to the boiling point take out the lobster and put it on slices of toast. Into the boiling wine put all the butter from the lobsters, just a few chopped mushrooms, if they are at hand, and pour over the slices of lobster toast. Have this just as hot as possible when sending to table, and you will find the alluringness of this dish is not in the telling of it only.

A lobster tartlet is a gastronomical dream, let me tell you, while we are on the subject, and after you try it you will be telling the same story. You should have tartlet moulds made of the very best puff paste, which you fill with diced cold boiled lobster, chopped cooked mushrooms, a caper or two, and a bit of mayonnaise.

Lobster *à la* Newberg is such a staple dish that it seems almost like plagiarizing something or somebody to put it on record here. However, as no list of lobster dishes is correct without it, here it shall go. Cut the boiled lobster into two-inch pieces and fry over a tremendously hot fire, either in a chafing dish or on a range, for just two or three seconds; lessen the heat then, or pull the frying-pan into cooler quarters, while you cover the lobster with thick, rich cream. Let this come to a threat to boil, then stir in say three egg yolks to a pint of cream, the yolks stirred in a little cream, till it thickens a bit. Just a dash of sherry, say two tablespoonfuls, and there you are.

For stuffing lobster tails cut the meat of the lobsters up rather finely, and add to it half its quantity of mushrooms. Fry in butter a bit, dilute with a little cream, season highly with cayenne and salt and fill the half tails with the mixture. Coat with bread crumbs that have been stirred about in melted butter, and brown in a hot oven.

The making of lobster croquettes is a pleasant sort of business, for there is so much anticipation of good to come stirred in with it. Cut the meat—don't chop it—rather finely: moisten with a bit of cream and the butter from the lobster. Mould and roll in crumbs and fry a golden brown.

Don't go to seasoning these croquettes very highly or the delicacy will depart from them. But you know that. And do you know that you may add to almost any sauce used for boiled or baked fish some diced cooked lobster to the benefit of everything and everybody concerned? Well, you may—my word for it.

I Go A-Marketing (1900)

HAMBURG STEAK

2 pounds of lean beef

1 rounding teaspoonful of salt

1 tablespoonful of grated onion

1 saltspoonful of pepper

Purchase the upper portion of the round or the rump steak; trim off the fat and skin and put the meat twice through a meat chopper; add the pepper and onion, and form at once into small steaks, being careful to have them of even thickness. Place these on the broiler, broil over a slow fire for ten minutes. It takes longer to broil a Hamburg steak one inch thick than it does an ordinary steak of the same thickness. Dish on a heated plate, dust with salt, put a little butter on top of each and send at once to the table; or, they may have poured over them tomato sauce, or you may serve them with brown or sweet pepper sauce. Where broiling is out of the question, these may be pan broiled.

Sarah Tyson Rorer, *Mrs. Rorer's New Cook Book* (1902)

The Picayune's Creole Cook Book

Calas

When the editors of the New Orleans *Picayune* assembled this classic compilation of Creole recipes at the beginning of the 20th century, they did so out of a fear that traditional ways—along with the "olden negro cooks of ante-bellum days"—were beginning to disappear. And yet today, even as New Orleans struggles to recover from disaster, Creole cooking—that unique, cosmopolitan blend of French, African, English, Native American, and Spanish influences—is still a vital part of the daily life of the city. The Cala women are long gone, but the not dissimilar beignet and the "morning cup of Café au Lait" are still to be had for breakfast in the Vieux Carré, unaffected by the force of Katrina or social change.

■ ■ ■

"Belle Cala! Tout Chaud!"

Under this cry was sold by the ancient Creole negro women in the French quarter of New Orleans a delicious rice cake, which was eaten with the morning cup of Café au Lait. The Cala woman was a daily figure on the streets till within the last two or three years. She went her rounds in quaint bandana tignon, guinea blue dress, and white apron, and carried on her head a covered bowl, in which were the dainty and hot Calas. Her cry, "Belle Cala! Tout Chaud!" would penetrate the morning air, and the olden Creole cooks would rush to the doors to get the first fresh, hot Calas to carry to their masters and mistresses with the early morning cup of coffee. The Cala women have almost all passed away, for, as remarked at the beginning of this book, there is a "new colored woman" in New Orleans, as elsewhere in the south, and she disdains all the pretty olden industries and occupations which were a constant and genteel source of revenue to the old negro mothers and grandmothers. Only two or three of the ancient Cala women remain. The cries of "Belle Cala Toute Chaud!" are now few and far between. Once in a while, like some ghostly voice of the past, one starts up in bed of an early morning as the weak old voice faintly penetrates your chamber. In a second more it is lost in the distance, and you turn over with a sigh for the good old times and the quaint customs of old Creole days, which gave such a beautiful and unique tinge to the life of the ancient quarter.

But the custom of making Calas still remains. In many an ancient home the good housewife tells her daughters just how "Tante Zizi" made the Calas in her day, and so are preserved these ancient traditional recipes.

From one of the last of the olden Cala women, one who has walked the streets of the French Quarter for fifty years and more, the Picayune has gotten the following established Creole recipe:

$\frac{1}{2}$ Cup of Rice.   3 Cups Water (boiling).
3 Eggs. $\frac{1}{2}$ Cup of Sugar.
$\frac{1}{2}$ Cup of Compressed Yeast.
$\frac{1}{2}$ Teaspoonful of Grated Nutmeg.
Powdered White Sugar.   Boiling Lard.

Put three cups of water in a saucepan, and let it boil hard. Wash half a cup of rice thoroughly, and drain and put into the boiling water. Let it boil till very soft and mushy. Take it out and set it to cool. When cold, mash well and mix with the yeast, which you will have dissolved in a half cup of hot water. Set the rice to rise over night. In the morning beat three eggs thoroughly , and add to the rice, mixing and beating well. Add a half cup of sugar and three tablespoonfuls of flour, to make the rice adhere. Mix well and beat thoroughly, bringing it to a thick batter. Set to rise for fifteen minutes longer. Then add about a half teaspoonful of grated nutmeg, and mix well. Have ready a frying pan, in which there is sufficient quantity of lard boiling for the rice cakes to swim in it. Test by dropping in a small piece of bread. If it becomes a golden brown, the lard is ready, but if it burns or browns instantly it is too hot. The golden brown color is the true test. Take a large, deep spoon, and drop a spoonful at a time of the preparation into the boiling lard, remembering always that the cake must not touch the bottom of the pan. Let it fry to a nice brown. The old Cala women used to take the Calas piping hot, wrap them in a clean towel, basket or bowl, and rush through the streets with the welcome cry "Belle Cala! Tout Chaud!" ringing on the morning air. But in families the cook simply takes the Calas out of the frying pan and drains off the lard by laying in a colander or on heated pieces of brown paper. They are then placed in a hot dish, and sprinkled over with powdered white sugar, and eaten hot with Café au Lait.

The above quantity will make six cakes. Increase in proportion.

Calas may also be made of rice flour. In olden days the Cala women used to pound the rice themselves in a mortar till they reduced it to a fine powder or flour. Then it was mixed and set to rise overnight. If the rice flour is used, one tablespoonful of wheat flour is sufficient to bind.

Often in large Creole families, where rice is left over from the day before, the quantity is increased by adding a cup of well-sifted self-raising flour. But these cakes, though very nice and palatable, are not the true "Calas," which are made entirely of rice, with only a little flour to bind, as directed above.

The Picayune's Creole Cook Book (2nd edition, 1901)

Cranberry Sauce
Sauce aux Airelles

Wash the cranberries in cold water, and pick well, rejecting all those that float on top or are in any manner overripe and spoiled. Put them in a porcelain-lined saucepan, with one pint of water, and let them boil over a moderate fire, stirring occasionally with a wooden spoon, and mashing the fruit as much as possible. When the berries have cooked about twenty minutes, remove the saucepan from the fire, and add the sugar, stirring in sufficient to sweeten nicely. Let them cook at least ten or fifteen minutes longer, after adding the sugar, and put into an earthen bowl, and let the sauce cool. Never strain the sauce. Many do, but the Creoles have found out that cranberry jelly is a very poor and insipid sauce, compared with that of the whole fruit, when formed into a sauce in an earthen mold. Liquid cranberry is a very poor apology for the dainty crimson mold of the native fruit. The following directions for cooking this fruit are given in detail, because so few know how to purchase and prepare it properly:

Never, when buying cranberries, select the pale, whitish fruit. They are unripe and unfit for use. Select fine, large, crimson-colored fruit.

Never cook cranberries in a metal saucepan; nor even in one of agate or the brightest tin. The berries absorb the taste, as they are an acid fruit, and your best efforts will fail in making a fine sauce. Use always a porcelain-lined saucepan.

Do not put much water in the cranberries. The proportion of a half a pint cupful to every quart should be rigidly observed.

Never add the sugar to the cranberries until they have first boiled steadily at least twenty minutes, or else the cranberries are liable to burn. After twenty minutes, add sugar to taste. Do not be sparing of the sugar. Be careful to measure out a good, full pint for every quart of berries you are cooking. Take the cranberries off the stove, and stir in the sugar thoroughly, and let them boil again at least ten or fifteen minutes after you have added the sugar. Stir them often to keep from burning.

Never put the cooked cranberries into tin or metal molds. Use always an earthenware bowl or mold.

Never dip the molds into water before putting in the cranberries. Let them be well washed and dried some time, as dipping them into water renders the cranberries bitter. When you wish to remove the cranberries from the bowl or mold, press them on the top, and gently loosen them at the bottom by setting the mold into hot water long enough to warm it through, and thus loosen the cranberries, without warming them.

And, finally, remember never to strain the cranberries, and not to use them on the same day on which they were cooked. Let them stand at least over night, or twenty-four hours, in a cool place, before serving. Serve Cranberry Sauce with Roast Turkey.

Paul Laurence Dunbar

Possum

Born in Dayton, Ohio, to parents who were former slaves, Paul Laurence Dunbar (1872–1906) achieved national and international fame as a poet with such collections as *Majors and Minors* (1895) and *Lyrics of Lowly Life* (1896). Introducing the latter, William Dean Howells called him "the first instance of an American negro who had evinced innate distinction in literature." Dunbar wrote both in "dialect" and in more conventionally literary idioms, but it was the dialect poetry that achieved the widest popularity in his day. Even his casually humorous poems, like "Possum," have an underlying gravity, however; behind the happy-go-lucky mask of dialect Dunbar's sense of irony is always keen.

■ ■ ■

Ef dey 's anyt'ing dat riles me
    An' jes' gits me out o' hitch,
Twell I want to tek my coat off,
    So's to r'ar an' t'ar an' pitch,
Hit's to see some ign'ant white man
    'Mittin' dat owdacious sin—
W'en he want to cook a possum
    Tekin' off de possum's skin.

W'y dey ain't no use in talkin',
    Hit jes' hu'ts me to de hea't
Fu' to see dem foolish people
    Th'owin' 'way de fines' pa't.
W'y, dat skin is jes' ez tendah
An' ez juicy ez kin be;
I knows all erbout de critter—
    Hide an' haih—don't talk to me!

Possum skin is jes lak shoat skin;
    Jes' you swinge an' scrope it down,
Tek a good sha'p knife an' sco' it,
    Den you bake it good an' brown.
Huh-uh! honey, you 's so happy
Dat yo' thoughts is 'mos' a sin
When you 's settin' dah a-chawin'
    On dat possum's cracklin' skin.

White folks t'ink dey know 'bout eatin',
    An' I reckon dat dey do
Sometimes git a little idee
    Of a middlin' dish er two;

But dey ain't a t'ing dey knows of
    Dat I reckon cain't be beat
W'en we set down at de table
    To a unskun possum's meat!

Howdy, Honey, Howdy (1905)

Matzos Pudding

3 matzos (soaked, pressed
and stirred until
smooth),
10 eggs beaten separately,
2 large apples (peeled and
grated),

1 cup goose fat,
1/2 cup white wine,
Grated rind of a lemon,
Sugar to sweeten,
1/2 teaspoon salt.

Stir one-half hour, and lastly fold in the beaten whites. Grease form well, bake in a moderate oven one-half hour and serve with wine sauce, six eggs, one cup weak wine, sugar to taste. Stir constantly until it thickens as it is apt to curdle.

Mrs. Simon Kander, comp., *The "Settlement" Cook Book* (1903)

As a founder of Milwaukee's Settlement (charitable work among immigrants was known as "settlement work") Lizzie Kander established night classes, clubs, a library, a savings bank, and a gymnasium. Her cooking classes were most popular of all. Her compilation of 174 recipes has gone through dozens of editions and was the model for the thousands of community cookbooks that would follow. (The book's official title, *The Way to a Man's Heart*, was quite in earnest, since poor cooking was often a source of marital strife.)

Owen Johnson

from The Great Pancake Record

From traditional small-town pie-eating contests to the annual U.S. Open of Competitive Eating in Las Vegas, sponsored appropriately enough by Alka-Seltzer, Americans have always relished the chance to try to out-eat one another. "The Great Pancake Record" provides a vintage evocation of such contests from the creator of Dink Stover, Owen Johnson (1878–1952).

■ ■ ■

Conover's was not in the catalogue that anxious parents study, but then catalogues are like epitaphs in a cemetery. Next to the Jigger Shop, Conover's was quite the most important institution in the school. In a little white Colonial cottage, Conover, veteran of the late war, and Mrs. Conover, still in active service, supplied pancakes and maple syrup on a cash basis, two dollars credit to second-year boys in good repute. Conover's, too, had its traditions. Twenty-six pancakes, large and thick, in one continuous sitting, was the record, five years old, standing to the credit of Guzzler Wilkins, which succeeding classes had attacked in vain. Wily Conover, to stimulate such profitable tests, had solemnly pledged himself to the delivery of free pancakes to all comers during that day on which any boy, at one continuous sitting, unaided, should succeed in swallowing the awful number of thirty-two. Conover was not considered a prodigal.

This deed of heroic accomplishment and public benefaction was the true goal of Hickey's planning. The test of the Jigger Shop was but a preliminary trying out. With medical caution, Doc Macnooder refused to permit Smeed to go beyond the ten doubles, holding very wisely that the jigger record could wait for a further day. The amazed Al was sworn to secrecy.

It was Wednesday, and the following Saturday was decided upon for the supreme test at Conover's. Smeed at once was subjected to a graduated system of starvation. Thursday he was hungry, but Friday he was so ravenous that a watch was instituted on all his movements.

The next morning the Dickinson House, let into the secret, accompanied Smeed to Conover's. If there was even a possibility of free pancakes, the House intended to be satisfied before the deluge broke.

Great was the astonishment at Conover's at the arrival of the procession.

"Mr. Conover," said Hickey, in the quality of manager, "we're going after that pancake record."

"Mr. Wilkins' record?" said Conover, seeking vainly the champion in the crowd.

"No—after that record of *yours*," answered Hickey. "Thirty-two pancakes— we're here to get free pancakes today—that's what we're here for."

"So, boys, so," said Conover, smiling pleasantly; "and you want to begin now?"

"Right off the bat."

"Well, where is he?"

Little Smeed, famished to the point of tears, was thrust forward. Conover, who was expecting something on the lines of a buffalo, smiled confidently.

"So, boys, so," he said, leading the way with alacrity. "I guess we're ready, too."

"Thirty-two pancakes, Conover—and we get 'em free!"

"That's right," answered Conover, secure in his knowledge of boyish capacity. "If that boy there can eat thirty-two, I'll make them all day free to the school. That's what I said, and what I say goes—and that's what I say now."

Hickey and Doc Macnooder whispered the last instructions in Smeed's ear.

"Cut out the syrup."

"Loosen your belt."

"Eat slowly."

In a low room, with the white rafters impending over his head, beside a basement window flanked with geraniums, little Smeed sat down to battle for the honor of the Dickinson and the record of the school. Directly under his eyes, carved on the wooden table, a name challenged him, standing out of the numerous initials—Guzzler Wilkins.

"I'll keep count," said Hickey. "Macnooder and Turkey, watch the pancakes."

"Regulation size, Conover," cried that cautious Red Dog, "no doubling now. All fair and aboveboard."

"All right, Hickey, all right," said Conover, leering wickedly from the door. "If that grasshopper can do it, you get the cakes."

"Now, Hungry," said Turkey, clapping Smeed on the shoulder. "Here is where you get your chance. Remember, kid, old sport, it's for the Dickinson."

Smeed heard in ecstasy; it was just the way Turkey talked to the eleven on the eve of a match. He nodded his head with a grim little shake and smiled nervously at the thirty-odd Dickinsonians who formed around him a pit of expectant and hungry boyhood from the floor to the ceiling.

"All ready!" sang out Turkey, from the doorway.

"Six pancakes!"

"Six it is," replied Hickey, chalking up a monster 6 on the slate that swung from the rafters. The pancakes placed before the ravenous Smeed vanished like snowflakes on a July lawn.

A cheer went up, mingled with cries of caution.

"Not so fast."

"Take your time."

"Don't let them be too hot."

"Not too hot, Hickey!"

Macnooder was instructed to watch carefully over the temperature as well as the dimensions.

"Ready again," came the cry.

"Ready—how many?"

"Six more."

"Six it is," said Hickey, adding a second figure to the score. "Six and six are twelve."

The second batch went the way of the first.

"Why, that boy is starving," said Conover, opening his eyes.

"Sure he is, " said Hickey. "He's eating 'way back in last week—he hasn't had a thing for ten days."

"Six more," cried Macnooder.

"Six it is," answered Hickey. "Six and twelve is eighteen."

"Eat them one at a time, Hungry."

"No, let him alone."

"He knows best."

"Not too fast, Hungry, not too fast."

"Eighteen for Hungry, eighteen. Hurrah!"

"Thirty-two is a long ways to go," said Conover, gazing apprehensively at the little David who had come so impudently into his domain. "Fourteen pancakes is an awful lot."

"Shut up, Conover."

"No trying to influence him there."

"Don't listen to him, Hungry."

"He's only trying to get you nervous."

"Fourteen more, Hungry—fourteen more."

"Ready again," sang out Macnooder.

"Ready here."

"Three pancakes."

"Three it is," responded Hickey. "Eighteen and three is twenty-one."

But a storm of protest arose.

"Here, that's not fair!"

"I say, Hickey, don't let them do that."

"I say, Hickey, it's twice as hard that way."

"Oh, go on."

"Sure it is."

"Of course it is."

"Don't you know that you can't drink a glass of beer if you take it with a teaspoon?"

"That's right, Red Dog's right! Six at a time."

"Six at a time!"

A hurried consultation was now held and the reasoning approved. Macnooder was charged with the responsibility of seeing to the number as well as the temperature and dimensions.

Meanwhile Smeed had eaten the pancakes.

"Coming again!"

"All ready here."

"Six pancakes!"

"Six," said Hickey. "Twenty-one and six is twenty-seven."

"That'll beat Guzzler Wilkins."

"So it will."

"Five more makes thirty-two."

"Easy, Hungry, easy."

"Hungry's done it; he's done it."

"Twenty-seven and the record!"

"Hurrah!"

At this point Smeed looked about anxiously.

"It's pretty dry," he said, speaking for the first time.

Instantly there was a panic. Smeed was reaching his limit—a groan went up.

"Oh, Hungry."

"Only five more."

"Give him some water."

"Water, you loon; do you want to end him?"

"Why?"

"Water'll swell up the pancakes, crazy."

"No water, no water."

Hickey approached his man with anxiety.

"What is it, Hungry? Anything wrong?" he said tenderly.

"No, only it's a little dry," said Smeed, unmoved. "I'm all right, but I'd like a drop of syrup now."

The syrup was discussed, approved and voted.

"You're sure you're all right?" said Hickey.

"Oh, yes."

Conover, in the last ditch, said carefully, "I don't want no fits around here."

A cry of protest greeted him.

"Well, son, the boy can't stand much more. That's just like the Guzzler. He was taken short and we had to work over him for an hour."

"Conover, shut up!"

"Conover, you're beaten."

"Conover, that's an old game."

"Get out."

"Shut up."

"Fair play."

"Fair play! Fair play!"

A new interruption came from the kitchen. Macnooder claimed that Mrs. Conover was doubling the size of the cakes. The dish was brought. There was no doubt about it. The cakes were swollen. Pandemonium broke loose. Conover capitulated, the cakes were rejected.

"Don't be fazed by that," said Hickey, warningly to Smeed.

"I'm not," said Smeed.

"All ready," came Macnooder's cry.

"Ready here."

"Six pancakes!"

"Regulation size?"

"Regulation."

"Six it is," said Hickey, at the slate. "Six and twenty-seven is thirty-three."

"Wait a moment," sang out the Butcher. "He has only to eat thirty-two."

"That's so—take one off."

"Give him five, Hickey—five only."

"If Hungry says he can eat six," said Hickey, firmly, glancing at his protégé, "he can. We're out for big things. Can you do it, Hungry?"

And Smeed, fired with the heroism of the moment, answered in disdainful simplicity, "Sure!"

A cheer that brought two Davis House boys running in greeted the disappearance of the thirty-third. Then everything was forgotten in the amazement of the deed.

"Please, I'd like to go on," said Smeed.

"Oh, Hungry, can you do it?"

"Really?"

"You're goin' on?"

"Holy cats!"

"How'll you take them?" said Hickey, anxiously.

"I'll try another six," said Smeed, thoughtfully, "and then we'll see."

Conover, vanquished and convinced, no longer sought to intimidate him with horrid suggestions.

"Mr. Smeed," he said, giving him his hand in admiration, "you go ahead; you make a great record."

"Six more," cried Macnooder.

"Six it is," said Hickey, in an awed voice; "six and thirty-three makes thirty-nine!"

Mrs. Conover and Macnooder, no longer antagonists, came in from the kitchen to watch the great spectacle. Little Smeed alone, calm and unconscious, with the light of a great ambition on his forehead, ate steadily, without vacillation.

"Gee, what a stride!"

"By Jiminy, where does he put it?" said Conover, staring helplessly.

"Holy cats!"

"Thirty-nine–thirty-nine pancakes–gee!!!"

"Hungry," said Hickey, entreatingly, "do you think you could eat another–make it an even forty?"

"Three more," said Smeed, pounding the table with a new authority. This time no voice rose in remonstrance. The clouds had rolled away. They were in the presence of a master.

"Pancakes coming."

"Bring them in!"

"Three more."

"Three it is," said Hickey, faintly. "Thirty-nine and three makes forty-two–forty-two. Gee!"

In profound silence the three pancakes passed regularly from the plate down the throat of little Smeed. Forty-two pancakes!

"Three more," said Smeed.

Doc Macnooder rushed in hysterically.

"Hungry, go the limit–the limit! If anything happens I'll bleed you."

"Shut up, Doc!"

"Get out, you wild man."

Macnooder was sent ignominiously back into the kitchen, with the curses of the Dickinson, and Smeed assured of their unfaltering protection.

"Three more," came the cry from the chastened Macnooder.

"Three it is," said Hickey. "Forty-two and three makes–forty-five."

"Holy cats!"

Still little Smeed, without appreciable abatement of hunger, continued to eat. A sense of impending calamity and alarm began to spread. Forty-five pancakes, and still eating! It might turn into tragedy.

"Say, bub—say, now," said Hickey, gazing anxiously down into the pointed face, "you've done enough—don't get rash."

"I'll stop when it's time," said Smeed. "Bring 'em on now, one at a time."

"Forty-six, forty-seven, forty-eight, forty-nine!"

Suddenly, at the moment when they expected him to go on forever, little Smeed stopped, gazed at his plate, then at the fiftieth pancake, and said:

"That's all."

Forty-nine pancakes! Then, and only then, did they return to a realization of what had happened. They cheered Smeed, they sang his praises, they cheered again, and then, pounding the table, they cried in a mighty chorus, "We want pancakes!"

"Bring us pancakes!"

"Pancakes, pancakes, we want pancakes!"

Twenty minutes later, Red Dog and the Egghead, fed to bursting, rolled out of Conover's, spreading the uproarious news.

"Free pancakes! Free pancakes!"

The nearest houses, the Davis and the Rouse, heard and came with a rush.

Red Dog and the Egghead staggered down into the village and over to the circle of houses, throwing out their arms like returning bacchanalians.

"Free pancakes!"

"Hungry Smeed's broken the record!"

"Pancakes at Conover's—free pancakes!"

The word jumped from house to house, the campus was emptied in a trice. The road became choked with the hungry stream that struggled, fought, laughed and shouted as it stormed to Conover's.

"Free pancakes! Free pancakes!"

"Hurrah for Smeed!"

"Hurrah for Hungry Smeed!!"

The Prodigious Hickey (1908)

OLD-FASHIONED
Hickory Nut Cake

Of all the nut cakes there is none better than this old-fashioned one. Cream together one and one-half cups of fine granulated or pulverized sugar and one-half cup of butter. Add three-fourths of a cup of sweet milk, two and one-half cups of flour sifted with two teaspoons of baking powder and one cup of hickory nut meats dredged lightly with flour. Lastly add one-half teaspoon of vanilla and fold in the whites of four eggs beaten to a stiff froth.

Hester Price, in *The Good Housekeeping Hostess* (1904)

This nut cake recipe is one of the foolproof bits of Americana, reinterpreted generation after generation.

Edna Ferber

from Maymeys from Cuba

This excerpt from a story in the collection *Buttered Side Down* (1912), with its description of hungry eyes staring at a display of out-of-season fruits and vegetables, is an intimate, quietly powerful statement of the theme of want in the midst of plenty. Edna Ferber (1885–1968) had a long, successful career as a novelist—her best sellers included *So Big* (1924), *Show Boat* (1926), *Cimarron* (1930), and *Giant* (1950)—and she also achieved celebrity as a playwright and a member of New York's Algonquin Round Table.

■ ■ ■

Just off State Street there is a fruiterer and importer who ought to be arrested for cruelty. His window is the most fascinating and the most heartless in Chicago. A line of open-mouthed, wide-eyed gazers is always to be found before it. Despair, wonder, envy, and rebellion smolder in the eyes of those gazers. No shop window show should be so diabolically set forth as to arouse such sensations in the breast of the beholder. It is a work of art, that window; a breeder of anarchism, a destroyer of contentment, a second feast of Tantalus. It boasts peaches, dewy and golden, when peaches have no right to be; plethoric, purple bunches of English hothouse grapes are there to taunt the ten-dollar-a-week clerk whose sick wife should be in the hospital; strawberries glow therein when shortcake is a last summer's memory, and forced cucumbers remind us that we are taking ours in the form of dill pickles. There is, perhaps, a choice head of cauliflower, so exquisite in its ivory and green perfection as to be fit for a bride's bouquet; there are apples so flawless that if the garden of Eden grew any as perfect it is small wonder that Eve fell for them. There are fresh mushrooms, and jumbo cocoanuts, and green almonds; costly things in beds of cotton nestle next to strange and marvelous things in tissue wrappings. Oh, that window is no place for the hungry, the dissatisfied, or the man out of a job. When the air is filled with snow there is that in the sight of muskmelons which incites crime.

Queerly enough, the gazers before that window foot up the same, year in, and year out, something after this fashion:

Item: One anemic little milliner's apprentice in coat and shoes that even her hat can't redeem.

Item: One sandy-haired, gritty-complexioned man, with a drooping ragged mustache, a tin dinner bucket, and lime on his boots.

Item: One thin mail carrier with an empty mail sack, gaunt cheeks, and an habitual droop to his left shoulder.

Item: One errand boy troubled with a chronic sniffle, a shrill and piping whistle, and a great deal of shuffling foot-work.

Item: One negro wearing a spotted tan top coat, frayed trousers and no collar. His eyes seem all whites as he gazes.

Enough of the window. But bear it in mind while we turn to Jennie. Jennie's real name was Janet, and she was Scotch. Canny? Not necessarily, or why should she have been hungry and out of a job in January?

Jennie stood in the row before the window, and stared. The longer she stared the sharper grew the lines that fright and under-feeding had chiseled about her nose, and mouth, and eyes. When your last meal is an eighteen-hour-old memory, and when that memory has only near-coffee and a roll to dwell on, there is something in the sight of January peaches and great strawberries carelessly spilling out of a tipped box, just like they do in the fruit picture on the dining-room wall, that is apt to carve sharp lines in the corner of the face.

The tragic line dwindled, going about its business. The man with the dinner pail and the lime on his boots spat, drew the back of his hand across his mouth, and turned away with an ugly look. (Pork was up to $14.25, dressed.)

The errand boy's blithe whistle died down to a mournful dirge. He was window-wishing. His choice wavered between the juicy pears, and the foreign-looking red things that looked like oranges, and weren't. One hand went into his coat pocket, extracting an apple that was to have formed the *pièce de resistance* of his noonday lunch. Now he regarded it with a sort of pitying disgust, and bit into it with the middle-of-the-morning contempt that it deserved.

The mail carrier pushed back his cap and reflectively scratched his head. How much over his month's wage would that green basket piled high with exotic fruit come to?

Jennie stood and stared after they had left, and another line had formed. If you could have followed her gaze with dotted lines, as they do in the cartoons, you would have seen that it was not the peaches, or the prickly pears, or the strawberries, or the muskmelon or even the grapes, that held her eyes. In the center of that wonderful window was an oddly woven basket. In the basket were brown things that looked like sweet potatoes. One knew that they were not. A sign over the basket informed the puzzled gazer that these were maymeys from Cuba.

Maymeys from Cuba. The humor of it might have struck Jennie if she had not been so Scotch, and so hungry. As it was, a slow, sullen, heavy Scotch wrath rose in her breast. Maymeys from Cuba. The wantonness of it! Peaches? Yes. Grapes, even, and pears and cherries in snow time. But maymeys from Cuba—why, one did not even know if they were to be eaten with butter, or with vinegar, or in the hand, like an apple. Who wanted maymeys from Cuba? They had gone all those hundreds of miles to get a fruit or vegetable thing—a thing so luxurious, so out of all reason that one did not know whether it was to be baked, or eaten raw. There they lay, in their foreign-looking basket, taunting Jennie who needed a quarter.

Have I told you how Jennie happened to be hungry and jobless? Well, then I sha'n't. It doesn't really matter, anyway. The fact is enough. If you really demand to know you might inquire of Mr. Felix Klein. You will find him in a mahogany office on the sixth floor. The door is marked manager. It was his idea to import Scotch lassies from Dunfermline for his Scotch linen department. The idea was more fetching than feasible.

There are people who will tell you that no girl possessing a grain of common sense and a little nerve need go hungry, no matter how great the city. Don't you believe them. The city has heard the cry of wolf so often that its refuses to listen when he is snarling at the door, particularly when the door is next door.

Where did we leave Jennie? Still standing on the sidewalk before the fruit and fancy goods shop, gazing at the maymeys from Cuba. Finally her Scotch bump of curiosity could stand it no longer. She dug her elbow into the arm of the person standing next in line.

"What are those?" she asked.

The next in line happened to be a man. He was a man without an over-coat, and with his chin sunk deep into his collar, and his hands thrust deep into his pockets. It looked as though he were trying to crawl inside himself for warmth.

"Those? That sign says they're maymeys from Cuba."

"I know," persisted Jennie, "but what are they?"

"Search me. Say, I ain't bothering about maymeys from Cuba. A couple of hot murphies from Ireland, served with a lump of butter, would look good enough to me."

"Do you suppose any one buys them?" marveled Jennie.

"Surest thing you know. Some rich dame coming by here, wondering what she can have for dinner to tempt the jaded palates of her dear ones, see? She sees them Cuban maymeys. 'The very thing!' she says. 'I'll have 'em served just before the salad.' And she sails in and buys a pound or two. I wonder, now, do you eat 'em with a fruit knife, or with a spoon?"

Jennie took one last look at the woven basket with its foreign contents. Then she moved on, slowly. She had been moving on for hours—weeks.

Most people have acquired the habit of eating three meals a day. In a city of some few millions the habit has made necessary the establishing of many thousands of eating places. Jennie would have told you that there were billions of these. To her the world seemed composed of one huge, glittering restaurant, with myriads of windows through which one caught maddening glimpses of ketchup bottles, and nickel coffee heaters, and piles of doughnuts, and scurrying waiters in white, and people critically studying menu cards. She walked in a maze of restaurants, cafés, eating-houses. Tables and diners loomed up at every turn, on every street, from Michigan Avenue's rose-shaded Louis the Somethingth palaces, where every waiter owns his man, to the white tile mausoleums where every man is his own waiter. Everywhere there were windows full of lemon cream pies, and pans of baked apples swimming in lakes of golden syrup, and pots of baked beans with the pink and crispy slices of pork just breaking through the crust. Every dairy lunch mocked one with the sign of "wheat cakes with maple syrup and country sausage, 20 cents."

There are those who will say that for cases like Jennie's there are soup kitchens, Y.W.C.A.'s, relief associations, policemen, and things like that. And so there are. Unfortunately, the people who need them aren't up on them.

Try it. Plant yourself, penniless, in the middle of State Street on a busy day, dive into the howling, scrambling, pushing maelstrom that hurls itself against the mountainous and impregnable form of the crossing policeman, and see what you'll get out of it, provided you have the courage.

Desperation gave Jennie a false courage. On the strength of it she made two false starts. The third time she reached the arm of the crossing police-man, and clutched it. That imposing giant removed the whistle from his mouth, and majestically inclined his head without turning his gaze upon Jennie, one eye being fixed on a red automobile that was showing signs of sulking at its enforced pause, the other being busy with a cursing drayman who was having an argument with his off horse.

Jennie mumbled her question.

Said the crossing policeman:

"Getcher car on Wabash, ride to 'umpty-second, transfer, get off at Blank Street, and walk three blocks south."

Then he put the whistle back in his mouth, blew two shrill blasts, and the horde of men, women, motors, drays, trucks, cars, and horses swept over him, through him, past him, leaving him miraculously untouched.

Jennie landed on the opposite curbing, breathing hard. What was that street? Umpty-what? Well, it didn't matter, anyway. She hadn't the nickel for car fare.

What did you do next? You begged from people on the street. Jennie selected a middle-aged, prosperous, motherly looking woman. She framed her plea with stiff lips. Before she had finished her sentence she found her-self addressing empty air. The middle-aged, prosperous, motherly looking woman had hurried on.

Well, then you tried a man. You had to be careful there. He mustn't be the wrong kind. There were so many wrong kinds. Just an ordinary looking family man would be best. Ordinary looking family men are strangely in the minority. There are so many more bull-necked, tan-shoed ones. Finally Jennie's eye, grown sharp with want, saw one. Not too well dressed, kind-faced, middle-aged. She feel into step beside him.

"Please, can you help me out with a shilling?"

Jennie's nose was red, and her eyes watery. Said the middle-aged family man with the kindly face:

"Beat it. You've had about enough I guess."

Jennie walked into a department store, picked out the oldest and most stationary looking floorwalker, and put it to him. The floorwalker bent his head, caught the word "food," swung about, and pointed over Jennie's head.

"Grocery department on the seventh floor. Take one of those elevators up."

Any one but a floorwalker could have seen the misery in Jennie's face. But to floorwalkers all women's faces are horrible.

Jennie turned and walked blindly toward the elevators. There was no fight left in her. If the floorwalker had said, "Silk negligées on the fourth floor. Take one of those elevators up," Jennie would have ridden up to the fourth floor, and stupidly gazed at pink silk and val lace negligées in glass cases.

Tell me, have you ever visited the grocery department of a great store on the wrong side of State Street? It's a mouth-watering experience. A department store grocery is a glorified mixture of delicatessen shop, meat market, and vaudeville. Starting with the live lobsters and crabs you work your hungry way right around past the cheeses, and the sausages, and the hams, and tongues, and head-cheese, past the blonde person in white who makes marvelous and uneatable things out of gelatine, through a thousand smells and scents—smells of things smoked, and pickled, and spiced, and baked and preserved, and roasted.

Jennie stepped out of the elevator, licking her lips. She sniffed the air, eagerly, as a hound sniffs the scent. She shut her eyes when she passed the sugar-cured hams. A woman was buying a slice from one, and the butcher was extolling its merits. Jennie caught the words "juicy" and "corn-fed."

That particular store prides itself on its cheese department. It boasts that there one can get anything in cheese from the simple cottage variety to imposing mottled Stilton. There are cheeses from France, cheeses from Switzerland, cheeses from Holland. Brick and parmesan, Edam and limburger perfumed the atmosphere.

Behind the counters were big, full-fed men in white aprons, and coats. They flourished keen bright knives. As Jennie gazed, one of them, in a moment of idleness, cut a tiny wedge from a rich yellow Swiss cheese and stood nibbling it absently, his eyes wandering toward the blonde gelatine demonstrator. Jennie swayed, and caught the counter. She felt horribly faint and queer. She shut her eyes for a moment. When she opened them a woman—

a fat, housewifely, comfortable looking woman—was standing before the cheese counter. She spoke to the cheese man. Once more his sharp knife descended and he was offering the possible customer a sample. She picked it off the knife's sharp tip, nibbled thoughtfully, shook her head, and passed on. A great, glorious world of hope opened out before Jennie.

Her cheeks grew hot, and her eyes felt dry and bright as she approached the cheese counter.

"A bit of that," she said, pointing. "It doesn't look just as I like it."

"Very fine, madam," the man assured her, and turned the knife point toward her, with the infinitesimal wedge of cheese reposing on its blade. Jennie tried to keep her hand steady as she delicately picked it off, nibbled as she had seen that other woman do it, her head on one side, before it shook a slow negative. The effort necessary to keep from cramming the entire piece into her mouth at once left her weak and trembling. She passed on as the other woman had done, around the corner, and into a world of sausages. Great rosy mounds of them filled counters and cases. Sausage! Sneer, you *pâté de foies grasers!* But may you know the day when hunger will have you. And on that day may you run into linked temptation in the form Braunschweiger Metwurst. May you know the longing that causes the eyes to glaze at the sight of Thuringer sausage, and the mouth to water at the scent of Cervelat wurst, and the fingers to tremble at the nearness of smoked liver.

Jennie stumbled on, through the smells and the sights. That nibble of cheese had been like a drop of human blood to a man-eating tiger. It made her bold, cunning, even while it maddened. She stopped at this counter and demanded a slice of summer sausage. It was paper-thin, but delicious beyond belief. At the next counter there was corned beef, streaked fat and lean. Jennie longed to bury her teeth in the succulent meat and get one great, soul-satisfying mouthful. She had to be content with her judicious nibbling. To pass the golden-brown, breaded pig's feet was torture. To look at the codfish balls was agony. And so Jennie went on, sampling, tasting, the scraps of food acting only as an aggravation. Up one aisle, and down the next she went. And then, just around the corner, she brought up before the grocery department's pride and boast, the Scotch bakery. It is the store's star vaudeville feature. All day long the gaping crowd stands before it, watching David the Scone Man, as with sleeves rolled high above his big arms, he kneads, and slaps, and molds, and thumps and shapes the dough into toothsome Scotch confections. There was a crowd around the white counters now, and the flat baking surface of the gas stove was just hot enough, and David the Scone Man (he called them Scuns) was whipping about here and there, turning the baking oat cakes, filling the shelf above the stove when they were done to a turn, rolling out fresh ones, waiting on customers. His nut-cracker face almost allowed itself a pleased expression—but not quite. David, the Scone Man, was Scotch (I was going to add, d'ye ken, but I will not).

Jennie wondered if she really saw those things. Mutton pies! Scones! Scotch short bread! Oat cakes! She edged closer, wriggling her way through the little crowd until she stood at the counter's edge. David, the Scone Man, his back to the crowd, was turning the last batch of oat cakes. Jennie felt strangely light-headed, and unsteady, and airy. She stared straight ahead, a half-smile on her lips, while a hand that she knew was her own, and that yet seemed no part of her, stole out, very, very slowly, and cunningly, and extracted a hot scone from the pile that lay in the tray on the counter.

That hand began to steal back, more quickly now. But not quickly enough. Another hand grasped her wrist. A woman's high, shrill voice (why will women do these things to each other?) said, excitedly:

"Say, Scone Man! Scone Man! This girl is stealing something!"

A buzz of exclamations from the crowd—a closing in upon her—a whirl of faces, and counter, and trays, and gas stoves. Jennie dropped with a crash, the warm scone still grasped in her fingers.

Just before the ambulance came it was the blonde lady of the impossible gelatines who caught the murmur that came from Jennie's white lips. The blonde lady bent her head closer. Closer still. When she raised her face to those other faces crowded near, her eyes were round with surprise.

"'S far's I can make out, she says her name's Mamie, and she's from Cuba. Well, wouldn't that eat you! I always thought they were dark complected."

Buttered Side Down (1912)

PERFECTION SALAD

(The author of this recipe won a $100 prize in one of our recipe contests.)

1 envelope Knox Sparkling Gelatine.

1/2 cup cold water.

1/2 cup mild vinegar.

1 pint boiling water

1 teaspoonful salt.

1 cup finely shredded cabbage.

Juice of one lemon.

1/2 cup sugar.

2 cups celery cut in small pieces.

1/4 can sweet red peppers, finely cut.

Soak the gelatine in cold water five minutes; add vinegar, lemon juice, boiling water, sugar and salt. Strain, and when beginning to set add remaining ingredients. Turn into a mold and chill. Serve on lettuce or endive leaves with mayonnaise dressing, or cut in dice and serve in cases made of red or green peppers, or the mixture may be shaped in molds lined with pimentos. A delicious accompaniment to cold sliced chicken or veal.

Mrs. John E. Cooke, in Janet McKenzie Hill, comp., *Dainty Deserts for Dainty People* (1905)

In her book *Perfection Salad: Women and Cooking at the Turn of the Century*, Laura Shapiro uses this salad—perfectly cut vegetables in a pretty gelatin bondage—as a metaphor for the shift from the rural kitchen, where much was grown and prepared by hand, to the urban and industrial one.

Mary Antin

from The Promised Land

The immigrant caught between culinary cultures has become a central theme in American food writing, often serving as a vehicle for deeper questions of loss and assimilation. Mary Antin (1891–1949), in this passage from her autobiography *The Promised Land* (1912), meditates on the remembered flavors of her Polish childhood, before her family immigrated to Boston in the 1890s. In distilling the relation between hunger and memory, she makes a further leap by preferring the imagined dish to any possible reconstruction of it. As she was to say later about the whole process of writing her book: "If you enjoy remembering things, don't put your memories on paper. . . . Chasing elusive memories is like chasing butterflies. The captured butterfly, however delicately mounted, is no longer a butterfly; it is a beautiful carcass."

■ ■ ■

Among the liveliest of my memories are those of eating and drinking; and I would sooner give up some of my delightful remembered walks, green trees, cool skies, and all, than to lose my images of suppers eaten on Sabbath evenings at the end of those walks. I make no apology to the spiritually minded, to whom this statement must be a revelation of grossness. I am content to tell the truth as well as I am able. I do not even need to console myself with the reflection that what is dross to the dreamy ascetic may be gold to the psychologist. The fact is that I ate, even as a delicate child, with considerable relish; and I remember eating with a relish still keener. Why, I can dream away a half-hour on the immortal flavor of those thick cheese cakes we used to have on Saturday night. I am no cook, so I cannot tell you how to make such cake. I might borrow the recipe from my mother, but I would rather you should take my word for the excellence of Polotzk cheese cakes. If you should attempt that pastry, I am certain, be you ever so clever a cook, you would be disappointed by the result; and hence you might be led to mistrust my reflections and conclusions. You have nothing in your kitchen cupboard to give the pastry its notable flavor. It takes history to make such a cake. First, you must eat it as a ravenous child, in memorable twilights, before the lighting of the week-day lamp. Then you must have yourself removed from the house of your simple feast, across the oceans, to a land where your cherished pastry is unknown even by name; and where daylight and twilight, work day and fête day, for years rush by you in the unbroken tide of a strange, new, overfull life. You must abstain from the inimitable morsel for a period of years,—I think fifteen is the magic number,—and then suddenly, one day, rub the Aladdin's lamp of memory, and have the renowned tidbit whisked upon your platter, garnished with a hundred sweet herbs of past association.

Do you think all your imported spices, all your scientific blending and manipulating, could produce so fragrant a morsel as that which I have on my tongue as I write? Glad am I that my mother, in her assiduous imitation of everything American, has forgotten the secrets of Polotzk cookery. At any rate, she does not practise it, and I am the richer in memories for her omissions. Polotzk cheese cake, as I now know it, has in it the flavor of daisies and clover picked on the Vall; the sweetness of Dvina water; the richness of newly turned earth which I moulded with bare feet and hands; the ripeness of red cherries bought by the dipperful in the market place; the fragrance of all my childhood's summers.

Abstinence, as I have mentioned, is one of the essential ingredients in the phantom dish. I discovered this through a recent experience. It was cherry time in the country, and the sight of the scarlet fruit suddenly reminded me of a cherry season in Polotzk, I could not say how many years ago. On that earlier occasion my Cousin Shimke, who, like everyone else, was a storekeeper, had set a boy to watch her store, and me to watch the boy, while she went home to make cherry preserves. She gave us a basket of cherries for our trouble, and the boy offered to eat them with the stones if I would give him my share. But I was equal to that feat myself, so we sat down in a cherry-stone contest. Who ate the most stones I could not remember as I stood under the laden trees not long ago, but the transcendent flavor of the historical cherries came back to me, and I needs must enjoy it once more.

I climbed into the lowest boughs and hung there, eating cherries with the stones, my whole mind concentrated on the sense of taste. Alas! the fruit had no such flavor to yield as I sought. Excellent American cherries were these, but not so fragrantly sweet as my cousin's cherries. And if I should return to Polotzk, and buy me a measure of cherries at a market stall, and pay for it with a Russian groschen, would the market woman be generous enough to throw in that haunting flavor? I fear I should find that the old species of cherry is extinct in Polotzk.

Sometimes, when I am not trying to remember at all, I am more fortunate in extracting the flavors of past feasts from my plain American viands. I was eating strawberries the other day, ripe, red American strawberries. Suddenly I experienced the very flavor and aroma of some strawberries I ate perhaps twenty years ago. I started as from a shock, and then sat still for I do not know how long, breathless with amazement. In the brief interval of a gustatory perception I became a child again, and I positively ached with the pain of being so suddenly compressed to that small being. I wandered about Polotzk once more, with large, questioning eyes; I rode the Atlantic in an emigrant ship; I took possession of the New World, my ears growing accustomed to a new language; I sat at the feet of renowned professors, till my eyes contracted in dreaming over what they taught; and there I was again, an American among Americans, suddenly made aware of all that I had been, all that I had become—suddenly illuminated, inspired by a complete vision of myself, a daughter of Israel and a child of the universe, that taught me more of the history of my race than ever my learned teachers could understand.

All this came to me in that instant of tasting, all from the flavor of ripe strawberries on my tongue. Why, then, should I not treasure my memories of childhood feasts? This experience gives me a great respect for my bread and meat. I want to taste of as many viands as possible; for when I sit down to a dish of porridge I am certain of rising again a better animal, and I may rise a wiser man. I want to eat and drink and be instructed. Some day I expect to extract from my pudding the flavor of manna which I ate in the desert, and then I shall write you a contemporaneous commentary on the Exodus. Nor do I despair of remembering yet, over a dish of corn, the time when I fed on worms; and then I may be able to recall how it felt to be made at last into a man. Give me to eat and drink, for I crave wisdom.

The Promised Land (1912)

BAKED BANANAS

PORTO RICAN FASHION

Select rather green bananas, put them, without removing
the skins, into hot ashes or a very hot oven and bake
until the skins burst open. Send to the table in
a folded napkin. The skins help hold in the
heat and are not to be removed until
the moment of eating. Serve
plenty of butter
with them.

❧

Rufus Estes, *Good Things To Eat* (1911)

Born a slave in Tennessee, Estes worked on Pullman cars and ultimately became a professional chef, working for a subsidiary of U.S. Steel.

Clarence E. Edwords

Around Little Italy

San Francisco acquired early on a reputation for seriousness about the pleasures of food. Clarence E. Edwords (1856–1941), at one time editor of the *San Francisco Chronicle*, offers an atmospheric tour in his 1914 guidebook *Bohemian San Francisco*. The exoticism of the ethnic plays a large role in his sense of the city's culinary distinction, with the shock of unfamiliar aromas and flavors flooding in on the senses of provincial Americans.

■ ■ ■

San Francisco holds no more interesting district than that lying around the base of Telegraph Hill, and extending over toward North Beach, even as far as Fisherman's Wharf. Here is the part of San Francisco that first felt the restoration impulse, and this was the first part of San Francisco rebuilt after the great fire, and in its rebuilding it recovered all of its former characteristics, which is more than can be said of any other part of the rebuilt city.

Here, extending north from Jackson street to the Bay, are congregated Italians, French, Portuguese and Mexicans, each in a distinct colony, and each maintaining the life, manners and customs, and in some instances the costumes, of the parent countries, as fully as if they were in their native lands. Here are stores, markets, fish and vegetable stalls, bakeries, paste factories, sausage factories, cheese factories, wine presses, tortilla bakeries, hotels, pensions, and restaurants; each distinctive and full of foreign life and animation, and each breathing an atmosphere characteristic of the country from which the parent stock came.

Walk along the streets on the side of Telegraph Hill and one can well imagine himself transported to a sunny hillside in Italy, for here he hears no other language than that which came from the shores of the Mediterranean. Here are Italians of all ages, sexes and conditions of servitude, from the padrone to the bootblack who works for a pittance until he obtains enough to start himself in business. If one investigate closely it will be found that many of the people of this part of San Francisco have been here for years and still understand no other language than that of their native home. Why should they learn anything else, they say. Everybody around them, and with whom they come in contact speaks Italian. Here are the Corsicans, with their peculiar ideas of the vendetta and the cheapness of life in general, and the Sicilians and Genoese and Milanese. Here are some from the slopes of Vesuvius or Aetna, with inborn knowledge of the grape and of wine making. All have brought with them recipes and traditions, some dating back for hundreds of years, or even thousands, to the days before the Christian Era was born. It is just the same to them as it was across the ocean, for they hear the same dialect and have the same customs. Do they desire any special delicacy from their home district, they need but go to the nearest Italian grocery store and get it, for these stores are supplied direct from Genoa or Naples. This is the reason that many of the older men and women still speak the soft dialect of their native communities, and if you are so unfortunate as not to be able to understand them, then it is you who are the loser.

Do you wish to know something about conditions in Mexico? Would you like to learn what the Mexicans themselves really think about affairs down in that disturbed republic? Go along Broadway west of Grant avenue, and then around the corner on Stockton, and you will see strange signs, and perhaps you will not know that "Fonda" means restaurant, or that "Tienda," means a store. But these are the signs you will see, and when you go inside you will hear nothing but the gentle Spanish of the Mexican, so toned down and so changed that some of the Castilians profess to be unable to understand it.

Here you will find all the articles of household use that are to be found in the heart of Mexico, and that have been used for hundreds of years despite the progress of civilization in other countries. You will find all the strange foods and all the inconsequentials that go to make the sum of Mexican happiness, and if you can get sufficiently close in acquaintance you will find that not only will they talk freely to you, but they will tell you things about Mexico that not even the heads of the departments in Washington are aware of.

Perhaps you would like to know something about the bourgeoise French, those who have come from the peasant district of the mother country. Go a little further up Broadway and you will begin to see the signs changing from Spanish to French, and if you can understand them you will know that here you will be given a dinner for twenty-five cents on week days and for thirty-five cents on Sundays. The difference is brought about by the difference between the price of cheap beef or mutton and the dearer chicken.

Up in the second story on a large building you may see a sign that tells you meals will be served and rooms provided. One of these is the rendezvous of Anarchists, who gather each evening and discuss the affairs of the world, and how to regulate them. But they are harmless Anarchists in San Francisco, for here they have no wrongs to redress, so they sit and drink their forbidden absinthe, and dream their dreams of fire and sword, while they talk in whispers of what they are going to do to the crowned heads of Europe. It is their dream and we have no quarrel with it or them.

But for real interest one must get back to the slope of Telegraph Hill; to the streets running up from Columbus avenue, until they are so steep that only goats and babies can play on them with safety. At least we suppose the babies are as active as the goats for the sides of the hill are alive with them.

Let us walk first along Grant avenue and do a little window shopping. Just before you turn off Broadway into Grant avenue, after passing the Fior d'Italia, the Buon Gusto, the Dante and Il Trovatore restaurants, we come to a most interesting window where is displayed such a variety of sausages as to make one wonder at the inventive genius who thought of them all. As you wonder you peep timidly in the door and then walk in from sheer amazement. You now find yourself surrounded with sausages, from floor to ceiling, and from side wall to side wall on both ceiling and floor, and such sausage it is !

From strings so thin as to appear about the size of a lady's little finger, to individual sausages as large as the thigh of a giant, they hang in festoons, crawl over beams, lie along shelves, decorate counters, peep from boxes on the floor, and invite you to taste them in the slices that lay on the butcher's block. One can well imagine being in a cave of flesh, yet if you look closely you will discover that sausage is but a part of the strange edible things to be had here.

Here are cheeses in wonderful variety. Cheeses from Italy that are made from goats' milk, asses' milk, cows' milk and mares' milk, and also cheeses from Spain, Mexico, Germany, Switzerland, and all the other countries where they make cheese, even including the United States. These cheeses are of all sizes and all shapes, from the great, round, flat cheese that we are accustomed to see in country grocery stores, to the queer-shaped cacioca-vallo, which looks like an Indian club and is eaten with fruit.

There are dried vegetables and dried fruits such as were never dreamed of in your limited experience, and even the grocer himself, the smiling and cosmopolitan Verga, confesses that he does not know the names of all of them.

As you go out into the street you blink at the transformation, for you have been thousands of miles away. You think that surely there can be nothing more. Wait a bit. Turn the corner and walk along Grant avenue toward the Hill. See, here is a window full of bread. Look closely at it and you will notice that it is not like the bread you are accustomed to. Count the different kinds. Fourteen of them in all, from the long sticks of grissini to the great solid loaves weighing many pounds. Light bread, heavy bread, good bread, soft bread, hard bread, delicate bread, each having its especial use, and all satisfying to different appetites.

Now go a little further to the corner, cross the street and enter the store of the Costa Brothers. It is a big grocery store and while you will not find the sausage and mystifying mass of food products in such lavish display and profuseness, as in the previous place, if you look around you will find this even more interesting, for it is on a different plane. Here you find the delicacies and the niceties of Italian living. At first glance it looks as if you were in any one of the American grocery stores of down-town, but a closer examination reveals the fact that these canned goods and these boxes and jars hold peculiar foods that you are unaccustomed to. Perhaps you will find a clerk who can speak good English, but if you cannot either of the Costa brothers will be glad to show you the courtesy of answering your questions.

Turn around and look at the shelves filled with bottles of wine. Now you feel that you are on safe ground, for you know about wines and can talk about Cresta Blanca, and Mont Rouge, and Asti Colony Tipo Chianti. But wait a minute. Here are labels that you do not understand and wines that you never even heard of. Here are wines whose taste is so delicious that you wonder why it is the whole world is not talking about it and drinking it.

Here are wines from the slopes of Aetna, sparkling and sweet. Here are wines from grapes grown on the warm slopes of Vesuvius, and brought to early perfection by the underground fires. Here are wines from the colder slopes of mountains; wines from Parma and from Sicily and Palermo where the warm Italian sunshine has been the arch-chemist to bring perfection to the fruit of the vine. Here are still wines and those that sparkle. Here the famed Lacrima Christi, both spumanti and fresco, said to be the finest wine made in all Italy, and the spumanti have the unusual quality for an Italian wine of being dry. But to tell you of all the interesting articles to be found in these Italian, and French and Mexican stores, would be impossible, for some of them have not been translated into English, and even the storekeepers would be at a loss for words to explain them.

This is all a part of the Bohemianism of San Francisco, and that is why we are telling you about it in a book that is supposed to be devoted to the Bohemian restaurants. The fact is that San Francisco's Bohemian restaurants would be far less interesting were it not for the fact that they can secure the delicacies imported by these foreign storekeepers to supply the wants of their people.

But do not think you have exhausted the wonders of Little Italy when you have left the stores, for there is still more to see. If you were ever in Palermo and went into the little side streets, you saw the strings of macaroni, spaghetti and other pastes drying in the sun while children and dogs played through and around it, giving you such a distaste for it that you have not eaten any Italian paste since.

But in San Francisco they do things differently. There are a number of paste factories, all good and all clean. Take that of P. Fiorini, for instance, at a point a short distance above Costa Brothers. You cannot miss it for it has a picture of Fiorini himself as a sign, and on it he tells you that if you eat his paste you will get to be as fat as he is. Go inside and you will find that Fiorini can talk just enough English to make himself understood, while his good wife, his sole assistant, can neither speak nor understand any but her native Italian. But that does not bother her in the least, for she can make signs, and you can understand them even better than you understand the English of her husband.

Here you will see the making of raviolis by the hundred at a time. Tagliarini, tortilini, macaroni, spaghetti, capellini, percatelli, tagliatelli, and all the seventy and two other varieties. The number of kinds of paste is most astonishing, and one wonders why there are so many kinds and what is done with them. Fiorini will tell you that each kind has its distinctive use. Some are for soups, some for sauces, and all for special edibility. There are hundreds of recipes for cooking the various pastes and each one is said to be a little better than the others, if you can imagine such a thing.

Turn another corner after leaving Fiorini's and look down into a basement. You do not have to go to the country to see wine making. Here is one of the primitive wine presses of Italy, and if you want to know why some irreverent people call the red wine of the Italians "Chateau la Feet," you have but to watch the process of its making in these Telegraph Hill wine houses. The grapes are poured into a big tub and a burly man takes off his shoes and socks and emulates the oxen of Biblical times when it treaded out the grain. Of course he washes his feet before he gets into the wine tub. But, at that, it is not a pleasant thing to contemplate. Now you look around with wider and more comprehensive eyes, and now you begin to understand something about these strange foreign quarters in San Francisco. As you look around you note another thing. Italian fecundity is apparent everywhere, and the farther up the steep slope of the Hill you go the more children you see. They are everywhere, and of all sizes and ages, in such reckless profusion that you no longer wonder if the world is to be depopulated through the coming of the fad of Eugenics. The Italian mother has but two thoughts—her God and her children, and it is to care for her children that she has brought from her native land the knowledge of cookery, and of those things that help to put life and strength in their bodies.

An Italian girl said to us one day:

"Mama knows nothing but cooking and going to church. She cooks from daylight until dark, and stops cooking only when she is at church."

It was evident that her domestic and religious duties dominated her life, and she knew but two things—to please her God and to care for her family, and without question if occasion demanded the pleasure of her family took precedence.

San Francisco's Latin quarter is appealing, enticing and hypnotizing. Go there and you will learn why San Francisco is a Bohemian city. You will find out that so many things you have thought important are really not at all worth while. Go there and you will find the root of Bohemian restaurants. These people have studied gastronomy as a science, and they have imparted their knowledge to San Francisco, with the result that the Bohemian spirit enters into our very lives, and our minds are broadened, and our views of life and our ideas have a wider scope. It is because of this condition, born on the slopes of Telegraph Hill, that we are drawn out of depressing influences, out of the spirit of self-consciousness, and find a world of pleasure, innocent and educational, the inspiration for which has been handed down through generations of Latins since the days of early Roman empire, which inspiration is still a power for good because it takes people out of themselves and places them where they can look with understanding and speak the language of perception. Little Italy's charm has long been recognized by artists and writers, and many of them began their careers which led to fame and fortune in little cheap rooms on Telegraph Hill. Here have lived many whose names are now known to fame, and to name them would be almost like a directory of world renowned artists and writers. Here is still the memory of Bret Harte and Mark Twain. Here is where Keith had his early studio. Cadenasso, Martinez, and many others know these slopes and love them.

To all these and many more the Latin Quarter of San Francisco possessed a charm they could find nowhere else, and if one desire to bring a saddened look to the faces of many now living elsewhere it is but necessary to talk of the good old days when Bohemia was on Telegraph Hill in San Francisco. Here they had their domicile, and here they foregathered in the little restaurants, whose claims to merit lay chiefly in the fact that they were rarely visited by other than the Italians of the quarter and these Bohemians who lived there.

Here was the inspiration of many a good book and many a famous picture whose inception came from thoughts that crystallized amid these surroundings, and here many a needy Bohemian struggled through the lean days with the help of these kind-hearted Latins. Here they, even as we, were taught something of the art of cooking.

Of course, if one desire to learn various methods of preparing food, it is necessary to keep both eyes open and to ask many questions, seeking the information that sometimes comes from unlooked for sources. Even at that it is not always a good idea to take everything for granted or to accept every suggestion, for you may meet with the Italian vegetable dealer who is so eager to please his customers that he pretends a knowledge he does not possess. We discovered him one day when he had on display a vegetable that was strange to us.

"How do you cook it?" was our question.

"Fry it."

Then his partner shouted his laughter and derision.

"Oh, he's one fine cook. All the time he say 'fry it.' One day a lady she come into da store an' she see da big bucket of ripe olives. Da lady she from the East and she never see olives like dat before. 'How you cook it?' say da lady. 'Fry it,' say my partner. Everything he say fry it."

In another vegetable stand we found an Italian girl, whose soft lisping accent pronounced her a Genoese, and she diffidently suggested "a fine Italian dessert."

> "You take macaroons and strawberries. Put a layer of maca-
> roons in a dish and then a layer of strawberries, cover these with
> sugar, and then another layer of macaroons and strawberries and
> sugar until you have all you want. Over these pour some rum and
> set fire to it. After it is burned out you have a fine dessert."

We bought the macaroons and strawberries on the way home and did not even wait for dinner time to try it. We pronounce it good.

It was made the right way and we advise you to try it, for it is simple and leaves a most delicious memory.

Bohemian San Francisco (1914)

Willa Cather

from My Ántonia

In this delicate depiction of cultural misunderstanding from the novel *My Ántonia* (1918), some midwestern Americans pay a visit to help out a family of recent Bohemian immigrants who are starving in the New World. What they receive in exchange—a little bag of dried wild mushrooms with a "penetrating, earthy odor"—is so little valued by them that it goes uneaten. Only years later will the nature of the gift be appreciated by the youngest of the Americans. Born in Virginia, Willa Cather (1873-1947) moved with her family to Nebraska when she was ten, experiencing firsthand the country's harshness and privation as well as the sort of "otherliness" that she finds in immigrants such as the Shimerdas from Bohemia.

■ ■ ■

Jake helped grandmother to the ground, saying he would bring the provisions after he had blanketed his horses. We went slowly up the icy path toward the door sunk in the drawside. Blue puffs of smoke came from the stovepipe that stuck out through the grass and snow, but the wind whisked them roughly away.

Mrs. Shimerda opened the door before we knocked and seized grandmother's hand. She did not say "How do!" as usual, but at once began to cry, talking very fast in her own language, pointing to her feet which were tied up in rags, and looking about accusingly at every one.

The old man was sitting on a stump behind the stove, crouching over as if he were trying to hide from us. Yulka was on the floor at his feet, her kitten in her lap. She peeped out at me and smiled, but, glancing up at her mother, hid again. Ántonia was washing pans and dishes in a dark corner. The crazy boy lay under the only window, stretched on a gunnysack stuffed with straw. As soon as we entered he threw a grainsack over the crack at the bottom of the door. The air in the cave was stifling, and it was very dark, too. A lighted lantern, hung over the stove, threw out a feeble yellow glimmer.

Mrs. Shimerda snatched off the covers of two barrels behind the door, and made us look into them. In one there were some potatoes that had been frozen and were rotting, in the other was a little pile of flour. Grandmother murmured something in embarrassment, but the Bohemian woman laughed scornfully, a kind of whinny-laugh, and catching up an empty coffee-pot from the shelf, shook it at us with a look positively vindictive.

Grandmother went on talking in her polite Virginia way, not admitting their stark need or her own remissness, until Jake arrived with the hamper, as if in direct answer to Mrs. Shimerda's reproaches. Then the poor woman broke down. She dropped on the floor beside her crazy son, hid her face on her knees, and sat crying bitterly. Grandmother paid no heed to her, but called Ántonia to come and help empty the basket. Tony left her corner reluctantly. I had never seen her crushed like this before.

"You not mind my poor *mamenka*, Mrs. Burden. She is so sad," she whispered, as she wiped her wet hands on her skirt and took the things grandmother handed her.

The crazy boy, seeing the food, began to make soft, gurgling noises and stroked his stomach. Jake came in again, this time with a sack of potatoes. Grandmother looked about in perplexity.

"Haven't you got any sort of cave or cellar outside, Ántonia? This is no place to keep vegetables. How did your potatoes get frozen?"

"We get from Mr. Bushy, at the post-office,—what he throw out. We got no potatoes, Mrs. Burden," Tony admitted mournfully.

When Jake went out, Marek crawled along the floor and stuffed up the door-crack again. Then, quietly as a shadow, Mr. Shimerda came out from behind the stove. He stood brushing his hand over his smooth gray hair, as if he were trying to clear away a fog about his head. He was clean and neat as usual, with his green neckcloth and his coral pin. He took grandmother's arm and led her behind the stove, to the back of the room. In the rear wall was another little cave; a round hole, not much bigger than an oil barrel, scooped out in the black earth. When I got up on one of the stools and peered into it, I saw some quilts and a pile of straw. The old man held the lantern. "Yulka," he said in a low, despairing voice, "Yulka; my Ántonia!"

Grandmother drew back. "You mean they sleep in there,—your girls?" He bowed his head.

Tony slipped under his arm. "It is very cold on the floor, and this is warm like the badger hole. I like for sleep there," she insisted eagerly. "My *mamenka* have nice bed, with pillows from our own geese in Bohemie. See, Jim?" She pointed to the narrow bunk which Krajiek had built against the wall for himself before the Shimerdas came.

Grandmother sighed. "Sure enough, where *would* you sleep, dear! I don't doubt you're warm there. You'll have a better house after while, Ántonia, and then you'll forget these hard times."

Mr. Shimerda made grandmother sit down on the only chair and pointed his wife to a stool beside her. Standing before them with his hand on Ántonia's shoulder, he talked in a low tone, and his daughter translated. He wanted us to know that they were not beggars in the old country; he made good wages, and his family were respected there. He left Bohemia with more than a thousand dollars in savings, after their passage money was paid. He had in some way lost on exchange in New York, and the railway fare to Nebraska was more than they had expected. By the time they paid Krajiek for the land, and bought his horses and oxen and some old farm machinery, they had very little money left. He wished grandmother to know, however, that he still had some money. If they could get through until spring came, they would buy a cow and chickens and plant a garden, and would then do very well. Ambrosch and Ántonia were both old enough to work in the fields, and they were willing to work. But the snow and the bitter weather had disheartened them all.

Ántonia explained that her father meant to build a new house for them in the spring; he and Ambrosch had already split the logs for it, but the logs were all buried in the snow, along the creek where they had been felled.

While grandmother encouraged and gave them advice, I sat down on the floor with Yulka and let her show me her kitten. Marek slid cautiously toward us and began to exhibit his webbed fingers. I knew he wanted to make his queer noises for me—to bark like a dog or whinny like a horse,—but he did not dare in the presence of his elders. Marek was always trying to be agreeable, poor fellow, as if he had it on his mind that he must make up for his deficiencies.

Mrs. Shimerda grew more clam and reasonable before our visit was over, and, while Ántonia translated, put in a word now and then on her own account. The woman had a quick ear, and caught up phrases whenever she heard English spoken. As we rose to go, she opened her wooden chest and brought out a bad made of bed-ticking, about as long as a flour sack and half as wide, stuffed full of something. At sight of it, the crazy boy began to smack his lips. When Mrs. Shimerda opened the bag and stirred the contents with her hand, it gave out a salty, earthy smell, very pungent, even among the other odors of that cave. She measured a teacup full, tied it up in a bit of sacking, and presented it ceremoniously to grandmother.

"For cook," she announced. "Little now; be very much when cook," spreading out her hands as if to indicate that the pint would swell to a gallon. "Very good. You no have in this country. All things for eat better in my country."

"Maybe so, Mrs. Shimerda," grandmother said drily. "I can't say but I prefer our bread to yours, myself."

Ántonia undertook to explain. "This very good, Mrs. Burden,"—she clasped her hands as if she could not express how good,—"it make very much when you cook, like what my mama say. Cook with rabbit, cook with chicken, in the gravy,—oh, so good!"

All the way home grandmother and Jake talked about how easily good Christian people could forget they were their brothers' keepers.

"I will say, Jake, some of our brothers and sisters are hard to keep. Where's a body to begin, with these people? They're wanting in everything, and most of all in horse-sense. Nobody can give 'em that, I guess. Jimmy, here, is about as able to take over a homestead as they are. Do you reckon that boy Ambrosch has any real push in him?"

"He's a worker, all right, mam, and he's got some ketch-on about him; but he's a mean one. Folks can be mean enough to get on in this world; and then, ag'in, they can be too mean."

That night, while grandmother was getting supper, we opened the package Mrs. Shimerda had given her. It was full of little brown chips that looked like the shavings of some root. They were as light as feathers, and the most noticeable thing about them was their penetrating, earthy odor. We could not determine whether they were animal or vegetable.

"They might be dried meat from some queer beast, Jim. They ain't dried fish, and they never grew on stalk or vine. I'm afraid of 'em. Anyhow, I shouldn't want to eat anything that has been shut up for months with old clothes and goose pillows."

She threw the package into the stove, but I bit off a corner of one of the chips I held in my hand, and chewed it tentatively. I never forgot the strange taste; though it was many years before I knew that those little brown shavings, which the Shimerdas had brought so far and treasured so jealously, were dried mushrooms. They had been gathered, probably, in some deep Bohemian forest . . . .

My Ántonia (1918)

BUCKS COUNTY
Apple Butter

A genuine old-fashioned recipe for apple butter, as "Aunt Sarah" made it at the farm. A large kettle holding about five gallons was filled with sweet cider. This cider was boiled down to half the quantity. The apple butter was cooked over a wood fire, out of doors. The cider was usually boiled down the day before making the apple butter, as the whole process was quite a lengthy one. Fill the kettle holding the cider with apples, which should have been pared and cored the night before at what country folks call an "apple bee," the neighbors assisting to expedite the work. The apples should be put on to cook as early in the morning as possible and cooked slowly over not too hot a fire, being stirred constantly with a long-handled "stirrer" with small perforated piece of wood on one end. There is great danger of the apple butter burning if not carefully watched and constantly stirred. An extra pot of boiling cider was kept near, to add to the apple butter as the cider boiled away. If cooked slowly, a whole day or longer will be consumed in cooking. When the apple butter had almost finished cooking, about the last hour, sweeten to taste with sugar (brown sugar was frequently used). Spices destroy the true apple flavor, although Aunt Sarah used sassafras root, dug from the near-by woods, for flavoring her apple butter, and it was unexcelled. The apple butter, when cooked sufficiently, should be a dark rich color, and thick like marmalade, and the cider should not separate from it when a small quantity is tested on a saucer. An old recipe at the farm called for 32 gallons of cider to 8 buckets of cider apples, and to 40 gallons of apple butter 50 pounds of sugar were used. Pour the apple butter in small crocks used for this purpose. Cover the top of crocks with paper, place in dry, cool storeroom, and the apple butter will keep several years. In olden times sweet apples were used for apple butter, boiled in sweet cider, then no sugar was necessary. Small brown, earthen pots were used to keep this apple butter in, it being only necessary to tie paper over the top. Dozens of these pots, filled with apple butter, might have been seen in Aunt Sarah's store-room at the farm at one time.

Edith M. Thomas, *Mary at the Farm* (1915)

H. L. Mencken

In the pages of the Baltimore *Evening Sun*, *The Smart Set*, and *The American Mercury*, Henry Louis Mencken (1880–1956) became America's foremost pundit, decrying the inadequacies of American culture in slashing style. In both his lament for old Baltimore eating and his prescription for the improvement of hot dogs, Mencken blames railway dining cars for the decline in the quality and regional authenticity of American cooking. The cause changes, but the lament remains, as do shades of Mencken's tone—arrogant, outraged, and hyperbolic—in food writing today.

■ ■ ■

The Home of the Crab

That Baltimore is a center of gastronomical debauchery is a delusion still cherished by thousands of Americans who have never been there. It is remarkable how long such notions last. This one, I daresay, was true at some time in the past, but certainly it has not been true since the great fire of 1904. That catastrophe left indelible scars upon the town. It not only changed it physically, and for the worse; it also dethroned the old ruling caste of easygoing, good-living gentry, and turned loose a mob of go-getters, most of them not natives. Baltimore used to run to shady, red-bricked streets, gorgeous victuals and sound liquors; its white marble front steps were almost as famous as its soft crabs, its oysters, its terrapin and its seven-year-old rye. But now it runs to long rows of hideous homes in all the horrible shades of yellow, with front porches fit for railway terminals—and with them have come boulevards and stadiums, and with the boulevards and stadiums, soda water and hot dogs. I remember myself when there were at least twoscore first-rate eating houses in the city: now there are not half a dozen. Two of the best are run by Italians, or at all events, on the Italian plan. The food they offer is, in many ways, the most appetizing in town, but it is Italian, not Baltimorean. When a visitor of civilized tastes honors the town with his presence he doesn't want to eat Italian dishes; he wants to try the Maryland dishes he has heard of all his life—the chicken *à la Maryland*, the planked shad, the Maryland beaten biscuit, the steamed hard crabs, the jowl and sprouts, the soft crabs and so on. Where is he to get them? Maybe, by accident, in some lunchroom. The rest of the eating-houses of the town, ignoring all such local delicacies, serve only the dull, uninspired victuals that are now the standard everywhere in America, from Boston to Los Angeles. Year by year their cuisine comes closer and closer to that of the Pennsylvania Railroad dining-car.

This decay, of course, is not peculiar to Baltimore. It is to be observed all over the United States, and the local causes, when they are discernible at all, are perhaps less potent than the increasing standardization and devitalization that now mark all American life. The American people have become the dullest and least happy race in Christendom. When they seek amusement it is in huge herds, like wild animals. There was a time when even the poorest man, in such a place as Baltimore, at least ate decent food. It was cheap and his wife knew how to cook it, and took pride in the fact. But now the movie parlor engulfs her every afternoon, and what he eats comes mainly out of cans. His midday lunch was once her handiwork, and he washed it down with honest beer. Now he devours hot dogs.

Hot Dogs

The hot dog, as the phrase runs, seems to have come to stay. Even the gastroenterologists have given up damning it, as they have given up damning synthetic gin. I am informed by reliable spies that at their convention in Atlantic City last May they consumed huge quantities of both, and with no apparent damages to their pylorus. In such matters popular instinct is often ahead of scientific knowledge, as the history of liver eating shows so beautifully. It may be that, on some near tomorrow, the hot dog will turn out to be a prophylactic against some malady that now slays its thousands. That this will be the case with respect to gin I am willing to prophesy formally. Meanwhile, hot dog stands multiply, and millions of young Americans grow up who will cherish the same veneration for them that we, their elders, were taught to give to the saloon.

My own tastes in eating run in another direction, and so it is very rarely that I consume a hot dog. But I believe that I'd fall in line if the artists who confect and vend it only showed a bit more professional daring. What I mean may be best explained by referring to the parallel case of the sandwich. When I was a boy there were only three kinds of sandwiches in common use—the ham, the chicken and the Swiss cheese. Others, to be sure, existed, but it was only as oddities. Even the club sandwich was a rarity, and in most eating-houses it was unobtainable. The great majority of people stuck to the ham and the Swiss cheese, with the chicken for feast days and the anniversaries of historic battles. Then came the invasion of the delicatessen business by Jews, and a complete reform of the sandwich. The Jewish mind was too restless and enterprisng to be content with the old repertoire. It reached out for the novel, the dramatic, the unprecedented, as it does in all the arts. First it combined the ham sandwich and the cheese sandwich—and converted America to the combination instanter. Then it added lettuce, and after that, mayonnaise—both borrowed from the club sandwich. Then it boldly struck out into the highest fields of fancy, and presently the lowly sandwich had been completely transformed and exalted. It became, as the announcements said, "a meal in itself." It took on complicated and astonishing forms. It drew on the whole market for materials. And it leaped in price from a nickel to a dime, to a quarter, to fifty cents, even to a dollar. I have seen sandwiches, indeed, marked as much as a dollar and a half.

The rise in price, far from hurting business, helped it vastly. The delicatessen business, once monopolized by gloomy Germans who barely made livings at it, became, in the hands of the Jewish reformers, one of the great American industries, and began to throw off millionaires. Today it is on a sound and high-toned basis, with a national association, a high-pressure executive secretary, a trade journal, and a staff of lobbyists in Washington. There are sandwich shops in New York which offer the nobility and gentry a choice of no less than 100 different sandwiches, all of them alluring and some of them downright masterpieces. And even on the lowly level of the drug-store sandwich counter the sandwich has taken on a new variety and a new dignity. No one eats plain ham and cole-slaw to set it off. At its best it is hidden between turkey, Camembert and sprigs of endive, with anchovies and Russian dressing to dress it.

What I have to suggest is that the hot dog *entrepreneurs* borrow a leaf from the book of the sandwich men. Let them throw off the chains of the frankfurter, for a generation or more their only stay, and go seeking novelty in the vast and brilliant domain of the German sausage. They will be astonished and enchanted, I believe, by what they find there, and their clients will be astonished and enchanted even more. For there are more different sausages in Germany than there are breakfast foods in America, and if there is a bad one among them then I have never heard of it. They run in size from little fellows so small and pale and fragile that is seems a crime to eat them to vast and formidable pieces that look like shells for heavy artillery. And they run in flavor from the most delicate to the most raucous, and in texture from that of feathers caught in a cobweb to that of linoleum, and in shape from straight cylinders to lovely kinks and curlycues. In place of the single hot dog of today there should be a variety as great as that which has come to prevail among sandwiches. There should be dogs for all appetites, all tastes, all occasions. They should come in rolls of every imaginable kind and accompanied by every sort of relish from Worcestershire sauce to chutney. The common frankfurter, with its tough roll and its smear of mustard, should be abandoned as crude and hopeless, as the old-time ham sandwich has been abandoned. The hot dog should be elevated to the level of an art form.

I call upon the Jews to work this revolution, and promise them confidently even greater success than they have found in the field of the sandwich. It is a safe and glorious business, lying wide open to anyone who chooses to venture into it. It offers immense opportunities to men of genuine imagination—opportunities not only for making money but also for Service in its best Rotarian sense. For he who improves the eating of a great people is quite as worthy of honor as he who improves their roads, their piety, their sex life or their safety. He does something that benefits every one, and the fruits of his benefaction live on long after he has passed from this life.

I believe that a chain of hot dog stands offering the novelties I suggest would pay dividends in Baltimore from the first day, and that it would soon extend from end to end of the United States. The butchers and bakers would quickly arise to the chance it offered, and in six months the American repertoire of sausages would overtake and leap ahead of the German, and more new rolls would be invented than you may now find in France. In such matters American ingenuity may be trusted completely. It is infinitely resourceful, venturesome and audacious. I myself am acquainted with sausage-makers in this town who, if the demand arose, would produce sausage of hexagonal or octagonal section, sausages with springs or music boxes in them, sausages flavored with malt and hops, sausages dyed any color in the spectrum, sausages loaded with insulin, ergosterol, anti-tetanus vaccine or green chartreuse.

Nor is there any reason to believe that the bakers would lag behind. For years their ancient art has been degenerating in America, and today the bread that they ordinarily offer is almost uneatable. But when the reformers of the sandwich went to them for aid they responded instantly with both wheat and rye breads of the highest merit. Such breads, to be sure, are not used in the manufacture of drug-store sandwiches, but they are to be found in every delicatessen store and in all of the more respectable sandwich shops. The same bakeries that produce them could produce an immense variety of first-rate rolls, once a demand for them was heard.

I believe in my scheme so thoroughly that I throw it overboard freely, eager only to make life in the United States more endurable. *Soli Deo gloria!* What we need in this country is a general improvement in eating. We have the best raw materials in the world, both quantitatively and qualitatively, but most of them are ruined in the process of preparing them for the table. I have wandered about for weeks without encountering a single decent meal. With precious few exceptions, the hotels of America all cook alike—and what they offer is hard to distinguish from what is offered on railway dining-cars.

"The Home of the Crab": Baltimore *Evening Sun,* June 13, 1927; "Hot Dogs": Baltimore *Evening Sun,* November 4, 1929

PUREE OF PEANUTS

Take 1 pint of peanuts; roast until the shells rub off easily (do not brown); grind very fine; add a saltspoon of salt, 1 teaspoon of sugar; pour on boiling water, and stir until thick as cream. Set in double boiler and boil from 8 to 10 hours; set away and allow to get thoroughly cold; turn out. Can be eaten hot or cold. When sliced, rolled in bread crumbs or cracker dust and fried a chicken brown, it makes an excellent substitute for meat.

A generous layer between slices of bread makes an excellent sandwich.

George Washington Carver, *How To Grow the Peanut and 105 Ways of Preparing It for Human Consumption* (1916)

Carver, born in slavery, taught at Tuskegee and became famous as a consultant on the uses of agricultural products. This recipe grew out of an effort to suggest new uses for peanuts in order to expand the market for the legume.

Sheila Hibben

Eating American

Born Cecile Craik in Montgomery, Alabama, Sheila Hibben (1888–1964) originated the restaurant column for *The New Yorker*. She was also among the first to seriously catalog and appreciate American regional cooking, in articles such as the one that follows, and in landmark collections like *The National Cookbook* (1932) and *American Regional Cookery* (1946). Eleanor Roosevelt tapped her as a food consultant for White House menus; unofficially, she was also an adviser to mystery novelist Rex Stout, providing menus to satisfy the capacious appetite of his gourmand detective Nero Wolfe, along with recipes (see page 204) for his readers.

■ ■ ■

Regional cooking has struck New York. And with such a bang that soon nobody will be left to say, when the subject is brought up: "You mean regional *planning?*" Not since Messrs. Babbitt and More first handed around the undiluted milk of the Word in re Humanism, have so many of us got all mixed up at the start of what shows every sign of rapidly becoming a movement.

Of course, every traveler knows those delightful little Parisian restaurants where *la cuisine régionale* can be had: *beurre blanc* from Nantes, *bouillabaisse* from Marseilles or *garbure béarnaise*. As we sat at Roziers' on the Place St. Michel, have we not often thought how nice it would be if only we got regional dishes in New York? But only a few of us ever realized that our own *plats régionaux* would turn out to be codfish balls and broiled spareribs!

It is the Waldorf-Astoria which has set its sign and seal on our local cooking. And although the result may be highly satisfactory to amateurs of traditional American food, it is doubtless bound to bewilder those of us who have not heard the news of how smart it is to be regional. Upset indeed the ladies from Urbana, Illinois, or Montgomery, Alabama, are likely to be, when, arriving at the Waldorf, reverently expecting lobster *Thermidor* and baked Alaska, they discover that the resident rich and great of New York are demanding, as the last word in culinary effort, a little potlikker and corn pone!

In some of the Waldorf's luxurious modernistic apartments smells are rising that haven't been smelled for thirty years! The housekeeper from Easton, Pennsylvania, may well be edified to see how steamed up Park Avenue is about meat dumplings and corned beef and cabbage. A fine thing it is to know that even the biggest circles lead back home sooner or later, and that, traveling via *crêpes Suzettes* and Peach Melba, you come to rest at corned-beef hash. There is even "picked-up codfish," just as my Aunt Sally has had it every Sunday morning for the last forty years. And wouldn't it give Aunt Sally a turn to see a young man in evening clothes serving her very own codfish out of a silver dish!

Do *you* know what pan dowdy is? Maybe not if you happen to have been born in New England or Alabama, but certainly you must know if your mother was Pennsylvania Dutch. Wisconsin chicken cake is another one that I never heard of. So lost to a patriotic pride in victuals has America become, that I venture to bet the hotelkeepers of Madison never heard of it either, and when the good news reaches Wisconsin of the national importance of its chicken cake, I can see them all reaching for their hats and dashing out to get the recipe from the nearest farmer's wife. Or maybe they will just wire New York for it.

Smartness aside, this revival of native specialties is altogether good, for if anything is going to save our old-fashioned American cooking from going on the rocks, it has got to be a movement. How people could actually get themselves all worked up about saving the grizzly bear of the Rockies, and sit calmly by while such a magnificent dish as South Carolina Hoppin' John faces extinction, was more than I could ever understand! True, New England mutton dumpling at first thought moves me to action no more than Rocky Mountain grizzlies, but to know something about making it is on a par with discovering how the Declaration of Independence starts off. For this country was largely settled on dumplings—Puritan housewives of New England bringing the dumpling tradition across the Atlantic, and nearly a century later, the pioneers taking it with them in the covered wagons. There is even a legend that once when an extra-big train of wagons was crossing the plains back in the thirties, it was found expedient to separate it into two sections, which, for lack of any better basis of division, was done by counting off those who liked boiled dumplings into one group, and those who preferred a crusty ash cake into the other. That plan not only divided the pioneers themselves satisfactorily, but took care of the equipment, too—the pot going along with the dumpling contingent and the ashcake members getting the skillet.

It may already be too late to stem the rising tide of bunk in radio broadcasting about food these days. After listening in on one "food program" last week, I am inclined to think nothing can be done. Moreover, I resent the phrase "listening in" as applied to the entirely unavoidable accident of having a radio turned on me in the office of an advertising agency. What was going on in this particular food hour was what is technically known as a "skit," and portrayed the very voluble agonies of a young housekeeper whose husband has asked a friend in for a little home cooking. Naturally enough, the young housekeeper is telling the grocer all about it, and confiding in him that she can't make a decent pie and that her mayonnaise always curdles. The grocer is a completely broken reed in such a crisis, as all he can offer is: "Well, of course the gentleman *would* expect a nice pie."

Why he would so confidently expect a nice pie is never explained, for, just at that moment, a male customer in the grocery store, of whose presence we have been made aware by a series of radio coughs, gives one special introductory cough and urges the young housekeeper to let him help her out of her difficulties. And does he beg her to give up the pie and mayonnaise fixation and search her heart for something on God's earth that she *does* know how to make? Maybe a baked apple or a French dressing for her salad? Not he! He suggests a PIE MADE BY MAGIC! For he, too, assumes at once that the gentleman would expect a pie—only by this time there is no more talk on anybody's part of its being a *nice* pie. And then, believe it or not, that dreadful man goes on to tell the young housekeeper how to make a pie that requires no cooking—just stirring together Screech Owl Condensed Milk and lemon juice poured over a pie plate lined with graham crackers! Of course, my first instinct was, just as yours undoubtedly is, to warn the husband's friend. But that turns out all right, too, for (would you believe it?) it is the friend who has been giving all this advice in the grocery store—that's what makes it a skit—and if there ever was anybody whom I would like to see confronted with an uncooked condensed-milk graham-cracker magic pie, it is that same advice-bestower!

With such atrocities going on in the name of prosperity and salesman-
ship, what hope is there for posterity and food in this country unless we
rush to the colors of back-to-the-country cooking? Do you remember those
entrancing little maps that used to be (and probably are still) in all French
geographies? The *Départements* of France with the picture of a cheese in
the Seine et Marne, a neat collection of bottles in the Gironde, a jar labeled
"Confiture" in the Meuse and a calculating-looking sardine taking up nearly
the whole of Finisterre. A wonderfully impressive lesson they were in
gourmandise as well as geography, but no more edifying picture than could
be presented of this country, if an able cartographer and a discriminating
glutton would set to work in intelligent coöperation. Our map could have
stars to the North for baked beans and pie for breakfast, and double stars to
the South for crab gumbo and shrimp jumbalaya. It could be captioned EAT
AMERICA FIRST, and would be worth studying.

CAPE COD TURKEY

(STUFFED CODFISH)

1 medium-sized codfish

4 slices salt pork

3 tablespoons butter

1/3 cup soup stock

1 cup bread crumbs

1 small onion

1/2 coffeespoon thyme

1/4 coffeespoon sage

1 hard-boiled egg

salt and pepper

Prepare a freshly caught codfish; wipe well with a damp cloth, and rub inside and out with melted butter, salt, and pepper. Melt 2 tablespoons of butter in a saucepan, and add to it the finely chopped onion. Before the onion begins to brown, add coarsely rolled bread crumbs and let brown a very little. Moisten with the soup stock, and add thyme, sage, chopped hard-boiled egg, and season highly with salt and pepper. Stuff the fish with this mixture, and sew up the cavity. Lay the slices of salt pork in a baking-pan, and put the fish on top of them; dredge with salt and pepper and bake in moderate oven, basting frequently with the grease from the pork. Allow 15 minutes to each pound of fish, and when done serve on a hot platter with quartered lemon.

Sheila Hibben, *The National Cookbook* (1932)

Thomas Wolfe

from Of Time and the River

In this scene from his second novel, *Of Time and the River* (1935), Thomas Wolfe (1900–1938) shows his hero Eugene Gant undergoing an awestruck initiation into undreamed of realms of culinary luxury and abundance as his friend Joel Pierce gives him a tour of the kitchen of the family's Hudson Valley estate. As deprivation meets the promise of total fulfillment, Eugene is overwhelmed by a kind of delirium of wanting: "One was so torn with desire and greedy gluttony as he looked at the maddening plenty of that feast that his will was rendered almost impotent." Wolfe's love of teeming sensory catalogs serves him well in this tour of a spectacularly well-stocked larder.

■ ■ ■

Joel took him downstairs to the kitchen before telling him good-night. They crossed the hall, and passed through the great dining-room. It was also a noble gleaming room of white, as grand and spacious as a room in a château, but warm, and familiar, comforting as home. Then they passed through a service corridor that connected the kitchen and the pantry with the dining-room, and instantly he found himself in another part of this enchanted world—the part that cooked and served and with viewless grace, and magic stealth and instancy—performed the labors of this enchanted house.

It was such a kitchen as he had never seen before—a kitchen such as he had never dreamed possible. In its space, its order, its astounding cleanliness, it had the beauty of a great machine—a machine of tremendous power, fabulous richness and complexity—which in its ordered magnificence, its vast readiness, had the clear and glittering precision of a geometric pattern. Even the stove—a vast hooded range as large as those in a great restaurant— glittered with the groomed perfection of a racing motor. There was, as well, an enormous electric stove that was polished like a silver ornament, the pots and pans were hung in gleaming rows, in vast but orderly profusion ranging from great copper kettles big enough to roast an ox to little pans and skillets just large enough to poach an egg, but all hung there in regimented order, instant readiness, shining like mirrors, scrubbed and polished into gleaming disks, the battered cleanliness of well-used copper, seasoned iron and heavy steel.

The great cupboards were crowded with huge stacks of gleaming china ware and crockery, enough to serve the needs of a hotel. And the long kitchen table, as well as the chairs and woodwork of the room, was white and shining as a surgeon's table: the sinks and drains were blocks of creamy porcelain, clean scrubbed copper, shining steel.

It would be impossible to describe in detail the lavish variety, the orderly complexity, the gleaming cleanliness of that great room, but the effect it wrought upon his senses was instant and overwhelming. It was one of the most beautiful, spacious, thrilling, and magnificently serviceable rooms that he had ever seen: everything in it was designed for use and edged with instant readiness; there was not a single thing in the room that was not needed, and yet its total effect was to give one a feeling of power, space, comfort, rightness and abundant joy.

The pantry shelves were crowded to the ceiling with the growing treasure of a lavish victualling—an astounding variety and abundance of delicious foods, enough to stock a grocery store, or to supply an Arctic expedition—but the like of which he had never seen, or dreamed of, in a country house before.

Everything was there, from the familiar staples of a cook's necessities to every rare and toothsome dainty that the climates and the markets of the earth produce. There was food in cans, and food in tins, and food in crocks, and food in bottles. There were—in addition to such staple products of the canning art as corn, tomatoes, beans and peas, pears, plums and peaches, such rarer relishes, as herrings, sardines, olives, pickles, mustard, relishes, anchovies. There were boxes of glacéd crystalline fruits from California, and little wickered jars of sharp-spiced ginger fruit from China: there were expensive jellies green as emerald, red as rubies, smoother than whipped cream, there were fine oils and vinegars in bottles, and jars of pungent relishes of every sort, and boxes of assorted spices. There was everything that one could think of, and everywhere there was evident the same scrubbed and gleaming cleanliness with which the kitchen shone, but here there was as well, that pungent, haunting, spicy odor that pervades the atmosphere of pantries—a haunting and nostalgic fusion of delicious smells whose exact quality it is impossible to define, but which has in it the odors of cinnamon, pepper, cheese, smoked ham, and cloves.

When they got into the kitchen they found Rosalind there: she was standing by the long white table drinking a glass of milk. Joel, in the swift and correct manner with which he gave instructions, at once eager, gentle and decisive, began to show his guest around.

"And look," he whispered with his soft, and yet incisive slowness, as he opened the heavy shining doors of the great refrigerator—"here's the icebox: if you find anything there you like, just help yourself—"

Food! Food, indeed! The great icebox was crowded with such an assortment of delicious foods as he had not seen in many years: just to look at it made the mouth begin to water, and aroused the pangs of a hunger so ravenous and insatiate that it was almost more painful than the pangs of bitter want. One was so torn with desire and greedy gluttony as he looked at the maddening plenty of that feast that his will was rendered almost impotent. Even as the eye glistened and the mouth began to water at the sight of a noble roast of beef, all crisp and crackly in its cold brown succulence, the attention was diverted to a plump broiled chicken, whose brown and crackly tenderness fairly seemed to beg for the sweet and savage pillage of the tooth. But now a pungent and exciting fragrance would assail the nostrils: it was the smoked pink slices of an Austrian ham—should it be brawny bully beef, now, or the juicy breast of a white tender pullet, or should it be the smoky pungency, the half-nostalgic savor of the Austrian ham? Or that noble dish of green lima beans, now already beautifully congealed in their pervading film of melted butter; or that dish of tender stewed young cucumbers; or those tomato slices, red and thick and ripe, and heavy as a chop; or that dish of cold asparagus, say; or that dish of corn; or, say, one of those musty fragrant, deep-ribbed cantaloupes, chilled to the heart, now, in all their pink-fleshed taste and ripeness; or a round thick slab cut from the red ripe heart of that great watermelon; or a bowl of those red raspberries, most luscious and most rich with sugar, and a bottle of that thick rich cream which filled one whole compartment of that treasure-chest of gluttony, or—

What shall it be now? What shall it be? A snack! A snack!—Before we prowl the meadows of the moon to-night, and soak our hearts in the moonlight's magic and the visions of our youth—what shall it be before we prowl the meadows of the moon? Oh, it shall be a snack, a snack—hah! hah!—it shall be nothing but a snack because—hah! hah!—you understand, we are not hungry and it is not well to eat too much before retiring—so we'll just investigate the icebox as we have done so oft at midnight in America—and we are the moon's man, boys—and all that it will be, I do assure you, will be something swift and quick and ready, something instant and felicitous, and quite delicate and dainty—just a snack!

I think—now let me see—h'm, now!—well, perhaps I'll have a slice or two of that pink Austrian ham that smells so sweet and pungent and looks so pretty and so delicate there in the crisp garlands of the parsley leaf!—and yes, perhaps, I'll have a slice of this roast beef, as well—h'm, now!—yes, I think that's what I'm going to do—say a slice of red rare meat there at the centre—ah-h! there you are! yes, that's the stuff, that does quite nicely, thank you—with just a trifle of that crisp brown crackling there to oil the lips and make its passage easy, and a little of that cold but brown and oh—most—brawny gravy—and, yes sir! I think I *will*, now that it occurs to me, a slice of that plump chicken—some white meat, thank you, at the breast—ah, there it is!—how sweetly doth the noble fowl submit to the swift and keen persuasion of the knife—and now, perhaps, just for our diet's healthy balance, a spoonful of those lima beans, as gay as April and as sweet as butter, a tomato slice or two, a speared forkful of those thin-sliced cucumbers—ah! what a delicate and toothsome pickle they do make—what sorcerer invented them, a little corn perhaps, a bottle of this milk, a pound of butter and that crusty loaf of bread—and even this moon-haunted wilderness were paradise enow—with just a snack—a snack—a snack—

Of Time and the River (1935)

NUT LOAF

There are many variations of this "meat substitute." Nuts are added to many vegetable combinations, but this name is given generally only when there is a marked nut flavor. Every housekeeper can make many variations. Nut loaf is served hot or cold with a suitable sauce. Slices of cold nut loaf may be panfried or brushed with fat and broiled.

> 1 cup chopped nuts
> 2 cups bread crumbs
> 1 teaspoon mixed herbs
> 1 teaspoon salt
> Dash of Paprika
> 1 egg, beaten
> 2 cups Tomato Sauce

The nuts may be of 1 kind or mixed. The crumbs should be from stale bread, but not dry. Mix well, using only enough of the sauce to moisten (about 3/4 cup). Pack in greased mold, steam 30 min. or bake in moderate oven 30 to 35 min. Unmold. Serve hot or cold with the rest of the Tomato Sauce (hot).

Total time 45 to 50 min. (Prep. 15 min.) Serves 10

There are numberless variations. Made a little stiffer this may be made into a Roll and baked on greased baking pan. The following suggestions will only suggest further variety:

Liquid. Use some other sauce than tomato. Brown Sauce or Cheese Sauce, for example. Or use milk.

Egg. Omit or increase to 2.

Crumbs. Instead of crumbs use Mashed Potato, cooked cereal or one of the small forms of Italian paste. Half rice, half crumbs, makes a good loaf.

Carrot. Add 1/2 to 3/4 cup grated (raw).

Celery. Add 1 cup chopped.

Cheese. Add grated cheese up to 1 1/2 cups. A good proportion is 1 1/4 cups each crumbs, nuts and cheese. Cottage Cheese may be used.

Nuts. Use more nuts—up to 1 1/2 cups. Whole nutmeats may be laid over the top.

Seasonings. Add any of the following: 1 tablespoon lemon juice, 1 tablespoon minced parsley, 1 tablespoon Worcestershire Sauce, 1 pimento, minced, 1 teaspoon onion juice or 1 to 2 tablespoons grated onion (better if cooked 2 or 3 min. in 1 tablespoon fat).

Isabel Ely Lord, *Everybody's Cook Book* (1924)

This recipe comes from an enormous compilation prepared under the auspices of the Pratt Institute, displaying state-of-the-art nutritional and home-ec theory in action.

Gertrude Stein

from American Food and American Houses

Gertrude Stein (1874–1946), who grew up in Oakland, California, had been living in Paris for many years before paying a much-heralded return visit to America in 1935. Stein's published works may have been too arcane for most the public, but she was always quite ready to provide copy for the newspapers, as in "American Food and American Houses," written for the *New York Herald Tribune* and excerpted here. Food was a serious matter for Stein, looming large in such works as *Blood on the Dining Room Floor* (1948) and *Tender Buttons* (1914), which devotes one section to "Studies in Description" of such items as roast beef, mutton, cranberries, rhubarb, and custard. ("Custard is this. It has aches, aches when. Not to be. Not to be narrowly. This makes a whole little hill.")

■ ■ ■

Food always remains the same after all it has to be made of flour and butter and eggs and water and meat and fowls and game and fish and shell fish and vegetables and fruit and you have eat it raw or you have to eat it cooked and that is all there is about it and everybody changes a lot about what they do eat, it gets to be a cause, of course there is also salt and pepper and mustard and herbs, and then there are new kinds of fruit, not new kinds of meat and fowls and eggs and butter that is a more difficult matter but new kinds of vegetables and fruit, and then there are oils and vinegar and lemons and sugar, there are quite a lot of new kinds of sugar and then there is honey and maple sugar and then besides it all being raw or being cooked there is it all being hot or being cold or even perhaps being tepid, and there is milk and cream and coffee and chocolate. Well there are really quite a number of things to make different kinds of things to eat and everybody likes it all very much and then they do not like it at all and then they change their minds about it all and then they begin an entirely different way and still always in spite of all the changes the American way is a different way from the French way it really is and that is what I have to say.

As I say the American way is different from the French way and the French way is different from the Italian or the Spanish or the German or the English way. The United States way I imagine is different from the Canadian way I have never been in Canada the Canadian way of eating, and one state is different from another state's way to a certain degree but in general the American way of eating as to what they eat and the order in which they eat it and what they drink with it is the American way.

Not long ago a reporter asked me what are your French friends going to ask you about America. I said do you really want to know what they are going to ask me and are going to keep on asking me about America well it is about what we ate over there.

It is different very different even from what we expected the food we eat and we have gotten to like it, it is going to be a shock to our French friends to hear that we do like it and that it does agree with us because it is not at all food as they understand it as they always understood food.

Some of our older French friends who had at one time or another been in America when we said but what did you eat over there, they just threw their hands up into the air and got excited.

Then when we got them calmed down all that they could say was that it was frightful but they could remember nothing, they said you could not remember you could remember nothing because nothing came in any kind of an order, and that was the most awful it might all come at once, everything might all come at once on the table and on your plate and there seemed no real distinction between a thing being cooked and raw not in America and any way it was awful and they were all thin when they came home from America and excited and really anybody could know that this was so. They really were.

The country in the French country where we live in the summer is a part of France where they are quite certain that they eat better that the food is better that they know more about food being cooked than in any other part of France and besides it is or was the home of Brillat Savarin who wrote the greatest book about French eating and so certainly it is the place where the food is the best food to be eaten in France. Of this they are all quite certain. Madame Recamier too came from that part of France where we always spend our summers and so did the poet Lamartine and they both liked to eat well so it would seem and so that again makes it mean that you eat better there than anywhere else in France and of course to any Frenchman that does mean that you eat better there than anywhere.

Madame Ramier had no children but she had had a niece and her niece married a man named Monsieur Lenormant and he had a son and that son's grandson is now just eighteen and his father is a well known surgeon. The boy eighteen the son is very observing and a patient of his father asked him to go to America with him for two weeks and Henri was of course delighted and went. When he came back we all asked him everything and he was there for only two weeks but we all asked him what he ate and was it as frightful as the older French people said and what he had to say about it.

Well he said you see why Frenchmen do not like it the food in America is because the food is moist. What do you mean we all said. Well he said it is just that, the food is moist, it is very good material much better material than they use in France, the eggs are better the butter very good and the milk much better than in France, the meat much much better than in France the fowls perhaps not so good as grow in France and it is all well and honestly cooked and all served together of course not separately as in France each kind of thing separately and the fruit is better than in France, the vegetables not so good but when you eat it it is all moist.

You see he said French people did not like food moist, if it is moist then how can they drink wine, if the food is not dry there is no reason for drinking wine. Now he said when anything is roasted in America it is juicy and if it is juicy it is moist and if it is moist you do not want to drink wine with it. Their salads made of fruit are juicy and moist and again you do not want to drink wine with it. Their dessert is mostly ice cream and that too is moist and so nobody wants to drink wine with it and to a Frenchman if you cannot drink wine you cannot dine.

We were much struck by what he said and then we came to America and he was right and there is no doubt about it compared with France the food is moist and as it is moist it is not necessary to drink wine with it indeed wine really does not go with it.

There are two things that are very striking when you come back. In the first place desserts have disappeared out of America and the lots of cakes. Salads fruit salads have immensely taken their place. We used always to tell our French friends how many different kinds of desserts how many different kinds of cakes there were in America and how there was no end to the changes in them well that is not true any more not in the North not in the South not in the East not in the Middle West, no that is not true of American eating now anywhere, all kinds of fruit salads have taken their place the place of cake and pudding which make desserts. Then there used to be so many kinds of pancakes, every kind of pancake, that too has disappeared the pancake has pretty well disappeared and I imagine that there are lots of little Americans who have never even heard of them never even heard of the word pancakes. Then in the old days there were very few soups and not really good ones. Now there are lots of kinds of soups and all very good ones.

Then there were the heavy American breakfasts, they have entirely disappeared, nobody seems to need or eat them just what has taken their place well that seems hard to say but they have disappeared and nobody seems to be offered them or want them. Perhaps in the country they still have them but most likely not but certainly not anywhere in a city.

Nevertheless the young Frenchman was right, whatever the changes are and there are certainly very many of them whatever the changes are the one thing remains characteristic of it that the eating is moist.

I remember in 1920 a Frenchwoman weeping because she could find no lettuce anywhere in the Middle West in America not a single one and now you can go nowhere without their insisting upon you having them.

They always drank a good deal of coffee but they do now drink a perfectly extraordinary quantity of coffee. They used to drink cocoa then but that like desserts and pancakes seems to have been entirely forgotten.

So then that is that for the food and it is very interesting. The order in which it is eaten well that seems to be a matter that is to suit the individual eater and that is a terrifying thing to any Frenchman, the order in France is fixed as fixed as anything is existing.

One finds oneself doing strange things. In the old days a girl might have found herself ordering a succession of sweets, now they might begin with tomato juice and follow by a salad and then a water ice, or a man begins with cranberry juice and ham and eggs and then a fruit salad, the only thing that has really and truly remained is pie. They do have pie, they all do have pie, they do not all eat pie, there are a very great many who never eat pie, but anywhere and everywhere if you want pie you can have pie. That is really the only thing really left over. And there are really no new kinds of pie.

They eat much less solid meat, meat is still what they eat but it is not such solid meat, mutton chops are tender and small pork is good but not always, but beef is very good but as I say on the whole meat is not so heavily eaten as it was.

Now what has all this to do with anything, well anything always has something to do with something and nothing is more interesting than that something that you eat.

New York Herald Tribune, April 13, 1935

CHOP SUEY

An iron pot is used in making this dish, greased with 3 tablespoons peanut oil. One cup of raw lean pork is cut in cubes, put in pot and allowed to cook until brown. After the pork is brown a preparation of vegetables, mixed, is placed in pot and allowed to steam, tight-fitting lid making this possible, first cooking it 10 minutes while stirring.

This mixture consists of 2 1/2 cups water, chestnuts cut in cubes, 2 1/2 cups bamboo shoots, 2 cups Chinese greens, cut in small pieces, 2 cups chopped celery, cut in small pieces, 1 cup onion chopped in small pieces, 3 cups canned mushrooms, chopped in small pieces, 5 cups bean sprouts, 1/2 cup chopped salted almonds.

After steaming for 30 minutes chicken stock is added to moisten. Next 2 tablespoonfuls corn starch mixed with chicken stock is added to thicken it. If this becomes too thick a little more chicken stock is added to thin it.

Next a whole roast chicken, cut in dices, being careful to use no skin or fat part of the chicken is put in the iron pot and cooked slowly for 10 or 15 minutes with a cup of "Soy" sauce added to season it and to give it the proper dark color.

(Most of these ingredients are purchased in Chinatown. This recipe takes care of about 8 people.)

Fashions in Food in Beverly Hills (1930)

Chop suey (from the Mandarin *tsa sui*, meaning "odds and ends") was, according to legend, served to Chinese immigrants working on the transcontinental railroad. Not a traditional dish, it was advertised by all Chinese restaurants catering to Americans. This version was offered by Buster Keaton as "His Favorite Dish."

John Steinbeck

Breakfast

The "curious warm pleasure" of a remembered meal is the essence of this brief but affecting story from Steinbeck's 1938 collection *The Long Valley* (later included in his 1939 novel *The Grapes of Wrath*). Simple food shared among people thrown together in transient fashion—"frying bacon and baking bread, the warmest, pleasantest odors I know"—becomes the occasion for a moment of real communion.

■ ■ ■

This thing fills me with pleasure. I don't know why, I can see it in the smallest detail. I find myself recalling it again and again, each time bringing more detail out of a sunken memory, remembering brings the curious warm pleasure.

It was very early in the morning. The eastern mountains were black-blue, but behind them the light stood up faintly colored at the mountain rims with a washed red, growing colder, greyer and darker as it went up and overhead until, at a place near the west, it merged with pure night.

And it was cold, not painfully so, but cold enough so that I rubbed my hands and shoved them deep into my pockets, and I hunched my shoulders up and scuffled my feet on the ground. Down in the valley where I was, the earth was that lavender grey of dawn. I walked along a country road and ahead of me I saw a tent that was only a little lighter grey than the ground. Beside the tent there was a flash of orange fire seeping out of the cracks of an old rusty iron stove. Grey smoke spurted up out of the stubby stovepipe, spurted up a long way before it spread out and dissipated.

I saw a young woman beside the stove, really a girl. She was dressed in a faded cotton skirt and waist. As I came close I saw that she carried a baby in a crooked arm and the baby was nursing, its head under her waist out of the cold. The mother moved about, poking the fire, shifting the rusty lids of the stove to make a greater draft, opening the oven door; and all the time the baby was nursing, but that didn't interfere with the mother's work, nor with the light quick gracefulness of her movements. There was something very precise and practiced in her movements. The orange fire flicked out of the cracks in the stove and threw dancing reflections on the tent.

I was close now and I could smell frying bacon and baking bread, the warmest, pleasantest odors I know. From the east the light grew swiftly. I came near to the stove and stretched my hands out to it and shivered all over when the warmth struck me. Then the tent flap jerked up and a young man came out and an older man followed him. They were dressed in new blue dungarees and in new dungaree coats with the brass buttons shining. They were sharp-faced men, and they looked much alike.

The younger had a dark stubble beard and the older had a grey stubble beard. Their heads and faces were wet, their hair dripped with water, and water stood out on their stiff beards and their cheeks shone with water. Together they stood looking quietly at the lightening east; they yawned together and looked at the light on the hill rims. They turned and saw me.

"Morning," said the older man. His face was neither friendly nor unfriendly.

"Morning, sir," I said.

"Morning," said the young man.

The water was slowly drying on their faces. They came to the stove and warmed their hands at it.

The girl kept to her work, her face averted and her eyes on what she was doing. Her hair was tied back out of her eyes with a string and it hung down her back and swayed as she worked. She set tin cups on a big packing box, set tin plates and knives and forks out too. Then she scooped fried bacon out of the deep grease and laid it on a big tin platter, and the bacon cricked and rustled as it grew crisp. She opened the rusty oven door and took out a square pan full of high big biscuits.

When the smell of that hot bread came out, both of the men inhaled deeply. The young man said softly, "Keerist!"

The elder man turned to me, "Had your breakfast?"

"No."

"Well, sit down with us, then."

That was the signal. We went to the packing case and squatted on the ground about it. The young man asked, "Picking cotton?"

"No."

"We had twelve days' work so far," the young man said.

The girl spoke from the stove. "They even got new clothes."

The two men looked down at their new dungarees and they both smiled a little.

The girl set out the platter of bacon, the brown high biscuits, a bowl of bacon gravy and a pot of coffee, and then she squatted down by the box too. The baby was still nursing, its head up under her waist out of the cold. I could hear the sucking noises it made.

We filled our plates, poured bacon gravy over our biscuits and sugared our coffee. The older man filled his mouth full and he chewed and chewed and swallowed. Then he said, "God Almighty, it's good," and he filled his mouth again.

The young man said, "We been eating good for twelve days."

We all ate quickly, frantically, and refilled our plates and ate quickly again until we were full and warm. The hot bitter coffee scalded our throats. We threw the last little bit with the grounds in it on the earth and refilled our cups.

There was color in the light now, a reddish gleam that made the air seem colder. The two men faced the east and their faces were lighted by the dawn, and I looked up for a moment and saw the image of the mountain and the light coming over it reflected in the older man's eyes.

Then the two men threw the grounds from their cups on the earth and they stood up together. "Got to get going," the older man said.

The younger turned to me. " 'F you want to pick cotton, we could maybe get you on."

"No. I got to go along. Thanks for breakfast."

The older man waved his hand in a negative. "O.K. Glad to have you." They walked away together. The air was blazing with light at the eastern skyline. And I walked away down the country road.

That's all. I know, of course, some of the reasons why it was pleasant. But there was some element of great beauty there that makes the rush of warmth when I think of it.

The Long Valley (1938)

Kenneth Roberts

from Down-East Ambrosia

Kenneth Roberts (1885–1957) is best remembered for his stirring historical novels, among them *Arundel* (1930), *Rabble in Arms* (1933), and *Northwest Passage* (1937). A native of Maine, he shows his strong local feelings in this nostalgic piece about his grandmother's Down-East cooking. When it comes to her recipe for savory ketchup, he brings to bear the same exactness of detail for which his novels were noted.

■ ■ ■

Thursday nights were big nights for the young fry in grandmother's house, because that was the night for boiled dinner; but the biggest night of all was Saturday night. The rich scent of cooking had percolated through the house all day, and above all the other scents had risen the meaty, fruity, steamy odor of baked beans.

Ah, me! Those Saturday-night dinners of baked beans, brown bread, cottage cheese, grandma's ketchup; and for a grand finale, chocolate custards! I can hear myself, a child again, begging and begging for another plate of beans, just one more plate of beans; hear the inexorable voice of authority say firmly, "You've had three plates already!" And in spite of that, I can hear myself, pestlike, continuing to beg, "Just three beans! Just three more!" I usually got three additional beans, no more, no less; and always they were as delicious, as rich, as tantalizing in their toothsome mellowness as the first spoonful had been.

Others may insist on *soufflés*, ragouts, *entremets*, *vol-au-vents*, but I prefer baked beans cooked the way my grandmother used to cook them. Gourmets may have their crêpes Suzette, their peach Melbas, their *biscuit Tortonis*, their *babas au rhum*, if only I can have my grandmother's chocolate custards, sweet, smooth, cooling, and topped with half an inch of thick yellow cream.

I have heard theorists say that those of us who think back so fondly to the simple dishes we enjoyed as children are bemused by memory; that in those far-off days we had the voracious appetites, the cast-iron digestions, the lack of discrimination common to ostriches and the very young: that beans, hash, finnan haddie and all such coarse and common fare are only delicious in retrospect.

Nothing could be farther from the truth. Hash, badly made, is disgusting; beans, poorly baked, are an offense to the palate; tripe, cooked by a mediocre cook, is revolting. But prepared by a State-of-Mainer who has the requisite touch, they are as ambrosial to me today as ever they were.

I once found myself in Palm Beach, Florida, discussing with the owner of a celebrated restaurant what should be set before a luncheon party of twelve. If, I told him, I could get the sort of hash my grandmother made in Maine, the guests would swoon with delight; but of course, I said, it was impossible.

He resented my skepticism. What, he demanded, was impossible about it? He agreed that well-made hash was indeed a dish for an epicure; and he insisted that his chef was just the one to make it.

"You're sure?" I asked. "You're sure he knows how? Everything finely chopped, moist in the center, brown and crisp on the outside?"

He was all assurance. Certainly the chef knew! I was to have no fear! My guests would talk about that hash for months! I was to leave it all to him!

There was considerable talk about that hash when the guests arrived. The thought of genuine Maine hash inflamed them, but when at last it was brought the potatoes were cut in lumps the size of machine-gun bullets, the meat was in chunks, the whole dreadful mixture had been made dry and crumbly over a hot fire. Beyond a doubt, the guests talked about that hash for the remainder of the year, but not in the way the restaurant owner had anticipated.

Years afterward, in the grill of the Barclay in New York, I was scanning the menu with two friends, preparatory to having lunch. What I'd like more than anything, I said, was the sort of hash my grandmother used to make, but that, of course, was impossible outside of Maine. My bitterness led the headwaiter to join in the conversation. His chef, he thought, could make hash that would please me—provided he knew how I liked it. I said that I had doubts; that I liked it chopped fine—extremely fine—moistened a little, cooked over a slow fire on the back of the stove until the bottom was brown and crisp, then folded over like an omelet.

"Yes," the headwaiter said, "he can do it. That's the way he makes the hash he eats himself."

Eagerly, and yet fearing the worst, I ordered hash.

"I'll have some too," one of my companions said.

"So'll I," said the other.

I advised against it. If not made correctly, I told them, it would be terrible, but they persisted. If there was a chance of getting real hash, they wanted it.

To our profound pleasure, the hash was delicious—as good as my grandmother's—and between the three of us we demolished a platterful. I must admit, however, that there was something lacking, though that something wasn't the fault of the chef. The ketchup that was produced to accompany the hash was a brilliant red, sweetish and without character. The chef had made hash for which no State-of-Mainer would need to apologize, but he had no ketchup comparable to my grandmother's to go with it.

Ketchup is an important adjunct to many Maine dishes, particularly in families whose manner of cooking comes down to them from seafaring ancestors. As far as I know, a sweetened ketchup in those families is regarded as an offense against God and man; against nature and good taste. This antagonism to sweetened ketchup is traceable to the days when dozens of Maine sea captains from every Maine town were constantly sailing to Cuba and the West Indies for cargoes of molasses and rum, and to Spain for salt. Captain Marryat, in the novel, Frank Mildmay, describes a shore excursion of ship's officers in Spain, in 1807, and complains of the lavish use of tomato sauce on all sorts of food. The same thing is true in Spain today, as well as in Italy, where it is customary to serve a bowl of hot tomato sauce with macaroni, spaghetti, fettucini, ravioli and many other dishes, so that the diner may lubricate his viands to suit himself. Under no circumstances is this tomato sauce sweetened. It is made by adding hot water to a paste obtained by boiling down tomato juice to a concentrate.

In most parts of early New England, tomatoes were called love apples and were shunned as being poisonous, but that wasn't true among Maine's seafaring families. Sea captains brought tomato seeds from Spain and from the Spanish cities in the West Indies, their wives planted them, and the good cooks in the families experimented with variants of the ubiquitous and somewhat characterless tomato sauce of Cuban and Spanish cooks. The ketchups they evolved, in spite of the aversion to tomatoes throughout early

America, were considered indispensable with hash, fish cakes and baked beans in Maine, even in the days of love apples.

Such was the passion for my grandmother's ketchup in my own family that we could never get enough of it. We were allowed to have it on beans, fish cakes and hash, since those dishes were acknowledged to be incomplete without them; but when we went so far as to demand it on bread, as we often did, we were peremptorily refused, and had to go down in the cellar and steal it—which we also often did. It had a savory, appetizing tang to it that seemed—and still seems—to me to be inimitable. I became almost a ketchup drunkard; for when I couldn't get it, I yearned for it. Because of that yearning, I begged the recipe from my grandmother when I went away from home, and since that day I have made many and many a batch of her ketchup, with excellent results.

> With a large spoon rub cooked tomatoes through a sieve into a kettle, to remove seeds and heavy pulp, until you have one gallon of liquid. One peck of ripe tomatoes, cooked and strained, makes one gallon. This operation is greatly simplified by using one dozen cans of concentrated tomato juice. Put the kettle on the stove and bring the tomato juice almost to a boil. Into a bowl put a pint of sharp vinegar, and in the vinegar dissolve 6 tablespoons of salt, 4 tablespoons of allspice, 2 tablespoons of mustard, 1 tablespoon of powdered cloves, 1 teaspoon of black pepper, $1/4$ teaspoon of red pepper. Stir the vinegar and spices into the tomato juice, set the kettle over a slow fire and let it simmer until it thickens. The mixture must be constantly stirred, or the spices settle on the bottom and burn. If made from concentrated tomato juice, half an hour's cooking is sufficient; but if made from canned tomatoes, the mixture should be allowed to simmer for at least three hours. When the kettle is removed from the fire, let the mixture stand until cold. Then stir and pour into small-necked bottles. If a half-inch of olive oil is poured into each bottle, and the bottle then corked, the ketchup will keep indefinitely in a cool place. It's better if chilled before serving.

My memories of my grandmother's kitchen are fond ones. The stove was large, strategically situated near windows from which the cook could observe the goings and comings of the neighbors and so divert herself while engaged in her duties. As a result her disposition was almost free of the irritability so frequently found among cooks; and one who stood persistently beside the stove on baking days was usually fortunate enough to be allowed to lick the large iron spoons with which the chocolate, orange and vanilla frostings had been applied to the cakes. There was also an excellent chance that the cook's attention would be so caught by an occurrence in the outer world that a deft bystander could thrust a prehensile forefinger into the frosting pan and extract a delectable morsel without detection.

Opposite the stove was the pantry, with a barrel of flour and a barrel of sugar beneath the bread shelf. An excellent confection could be obtained from the sugar barrel by dropping a spoonful of water into it and carefully removing the resulting blob of moist sugar with a fork.

On the bread shelf was a fascinating hen's wing for brushing flour from the shelf into the barrel after an orgy of bread making; and on the cool shelf near the window, where the pans of milk stood overnight to permit the cream to rise, was a magnificent giant clamshell used to skim the cream. If one rose early in the morning, he could not only watch the delicate operation of cream removal but might be allowed to lick the clamshell.

On the floor under the milk shelf were three gray crocks decorated with blue tracings. In one of the crocks were hermits, in another doughnuts, and in the third sugar cookies. These crocks were dangerous to tamper with when freshly filled or almost empty; for the eagle eye of the kitchen's guardian—a muscular lady who wore a bright brown wig and answered to the name of Katie—was quick to discover the larceny; and her tongue promptly announced it in the most agonizingly penetrating voice I ever remember hearing. As a boy, I considered her totally lacking in reticence at such times. When the hermits or doughnuts were about one third gone, however, a reasonable number could be abstracted with almost no peril to the abstractor.

The door to the woodshed, the barn, the grape arbor and the—well, let's call it the Rest Room—was in a third corner; and in the fourth corner was a box-like contrivance over which, on Sunday mornings, I spent many a long hour, engrossed in polishing my grandfather's shoes. Careful as was John Singleton Copley in putting on canvas the likenesses of his sitters, I'm sure he worked no harder with his brushes than I did with mine, applying equal portions of expectoration and blacking to every crease and contour of that respected footgear; then vigorously wielding the polishing brush until my small arms ached.

Every Sunday I was rewarded for my labors with five cents—a vast sum in days when one penny purchased three licorice sticks, five all-day suckers mounted on toothpicks, or two coconut cakes—a delicacy which could be made to last beyond belief if wrapped in the corner of a handkerchief and chewed in that protective covering.

Only on every other Sunday, however, could I take an artist's delight in admiring my own craftsmanship; for my grandmother was a Congregationalist and my grandfather a Baptist, and they tolerantly divided me, so to speak, between them. On one Sunday I was led by my grandmother to the Congregationalist church, to which I went willingly, knowing that at the halfway mark in the service I would be given a peppermint from the mysteriously hidden pocket of my grandmother's black silk dress; and on the following Sunday I went eagerly with my grandfather to the Baptist church, where I was free to crouch on the floor at my grandfather's feet during the longer reaches of the sermon, and contemplate with profound satisfaction the results of my labors in the kitchen.

Yes, I knew the kitchen well; and from occasionally sleeping above it, I became an expert on its intricate and absorbing sounds—not only the rhythmic thumping of the hash chopper, muffled by the mound of potatoes and corned beef through which it was driven by Katie's tireless arms, and the occasional muted rasp when the scattered mound was reassembled for further chopping. How well I knew the delicate gritting of an iron spoon against a saucepan at the culmination of a successful frosting making; the faint bubbling which accompanied the manufacture of doughnuts; the soft clanking that announced the removal of the lid of the mince-meat jar. Many of these sounds, of course, left me unmoved, but others brought me hurriedly down the winding back stairs—so hurriedly that I usually fell the last half-dozen steps, having learned that the compassion aroused by such a fall would unfailingly earn me a doughnut, a frosting spoon to lick, or at the worst a slice of new bread, well buttered and sprinkled with sugar.

My interest in the kitchen will help to explain why I have saved as many of my grandmother's recipes as I could—particularly the recipes for the simple Maine dishes that seem to me the best in the world.

To bake one's own beans, in these enlightened days of canned foods, is doubtless too much trouble, particularly if the cook wishes to spend her Saturday afternoons motoring, playing bridge or attending football games—though many a Maine housewife still persists in the old-fashioned method.

My grandmother's beans were prepared like this: Four cups of small white beans were picked over to eliminate the worm-holed specimens and the small stones that so mysteriously intrude among all beans; then covered with water and left to soak overnight. Early the next morning—usually around five o'clock—they were put in a saucepan, covered with cold water and heated until a white scum appeared on the water. They were then taken off the stove, the water thrown away, and the bean pot produced. In the bottom of the bean pot was placed a one-pound piece of salt pork, slashed through the rind at half-inch intervals, together with a large peeled onion; then the beans were poured into the pot on top of the pork and onion. On the beans were put a heaping teaspoon of mustard, half a cup of molasses and a teaspoon of pepper; the bean pot was filled with boiling water, and the pot put in a slow oven. At the end of two hours, a tablespoon of salt was dissolved in a cup of boiling water and added to the beans. Every hour or so thereafter the cover was removed, and enough boiling water poured in to replace that which had boiled away. An hour before suppertime the cover was taken off for good, the salt pork pulled to the top, and no more water added. Thus the pork, in the last hour, was crisped and browned, and the top layer of beans crusted and slightly scorched. When the beans were served, the pork was saved and the scorched beans skimmed off and thrown away. The two great tricks of bean making seemed to be the frequent adding of water up to the final hour of baking, so that no part of the beans had an opportunity to become dry, and the removal of the cover during the last hour.

The hash trick was simpler. Into a wooden hash bowl were put three cups of cold boiled potatoes and four cups of cold corned beef from which all gristle and fat had been removed. The hash chopper was used on these until the meat and potatoes were in infinitesimal pieces. A frying pan was placed on the stove and a piece of butter the size of two eggs melted in it.

A cup of boiling water was added to the butter; then the chopped potatoes and corned beef were poured in and stirred until hot.

At this point the frying pan was set back on the stove where there was no danger of burning, and the hash tamped down in the pan. At the end of a quarter hour, when a brown crust had formed on the lower side of the hash, a broad-bladed knife was inserted beneath it, and one half was deftly folded over on the other, as an omelet is folded. It was then ready to serve. The important feature in hash making was to make sure that the person who did the chopping shouldn't be too easily satisfied, but should lovingly labor until each piece of potato and each piece of corned beef was cut as small as possible.

The Saturday Evening Post, March 19, 1938

Procure a porterhouse steak 2 inches thick, of fine-grained texture, bright red in color, and well marbled with fat. Trim off excess fat and wipe with a clean cloth. Heat a wire broiler, grease it with some of the fat, and broil the steak over a hot fire for 3 minutes on each side.

PLANKED PORTERHOUSE STEAK

Take a well-seasoned oak plank which has never been washed, but which has been kept scrupulously clean by being scraped with a dull knife and wiped with good olive oil. Lay the steak on the plank, surround with a border of fluffy mashed potatoes, and put in a hot oven (450 F.) for 14 minutes. Five minutes before the end brush the potatoes over with a little melted butter, and salt and pepper the steak. Take from the oven, paint with soft butter, sprinkle with finely chopped parsley, dot with slices of fresh limes, and serve at once.

Rex Stout, *Too Many Cooks* (1938)

The orchid-tending, 286-pound detective Nero Wolfe appeared in countless novels and stories by Rex Stout, and in 1996 a Nero Wolfe Cookbook was assembled from the recipes found in his fiction.

Joseph Mitchell

Mr. Barbee's Terrapin

Joseph Mitchell (1908–1996), longtime essayist and story writer for *The New Yorker*, is most often remembered for his portraits of characters on the margins of the city: the denizens of dive bars, vagabonds, circus freaks. Among the salt-of-the-earth folk he found in New York's Fulton Fish Market—and describes so wonderfully in *Old Mr. Flood* (1948)—the "goormy" was a species to be ridiculed ("Next they'll be putting a cherry on boiled codfish," one jokes). Mitchell himself, if not a man of fancy tastes, had an evident relish for local eateries, markets, and foodways. (In "All You Can Hold for Five Bucks," for instance, he vividly documents the vanishing New York "beefsteak" tradition.) Here, on a trip through his native South, he stops to investigate the source of a metropolitan delicacy, the now-endangered terrapin.

■ ■ ■

Returning from a late vacation, I stopped off in Savannah, Georgia, and made a pilgrimage to Mr. Will Barbee's diamondback-terrapin farm on the Isle of Hope, a small, lush island nine miles below Savannah. I was there on the first day of autumn, when he starts shipping live terrapin to Northern hotels, clubs, sea-food dealers, and luxury restaurants, and was in time to see his Negro foreman barrel up three dozen nine-year-old cows, or females; this, the first shipment of the season, was dispatched to a dealer in Fulton Fish Market. The diamondback is a handsome reptile, whose meat, when stewed with cream, is tender and gelatinous. Gastronomically, it is by far the finest of the North American turtles, and terrapin stew is our costliest native delicacy. Three styles of stew—Philadelphia, Maryland, and Southern—are made in bulk by a man in Fulton Market and sold to families and clubs; Maryland style, in which dry sherry and thick cream are used, costs $10 a quart. In Manhattan hotels the usual price is $3.50 a plate. A live terrapin in New York City brings from $3.50 to $7 retail, according to the length of its belly shell. For the last decade, under the protection of conservation laws, the diamondback has been slowly increasing in numbers in brackish sloughs all along the Eastern seaboard, but it still is scarce enough to make the fecundity of Mr. Barbee's farm of the utmost importance to chefs in New York, Baltimore, Philadelphia, Washington, and New Orleans, the cities in which the stew is most respected. Mr. Barbee is the country's largest shipper; last year he supplied three hundred dozen live terrapin at an average price of $30 a dozen. He also put up four thousand cans of stew meat. In addition, on the porch of a rustic dance pavilion which he operates as a sideline, he sold terrapin dinners to hundreds of Yankee yachtsmen who stopped at the farm on their way to Florida through the Inland Waterway, which skirts the Isle of Hope. His wife, Rose, who looks after the cooking, is revered by yachtsmen, and her terrapin stew, Southern style, is famous from Cape Cod to Key West.

My train arrived at Union Station in Savannah at 9:30 the morning of the day I visited the farm, and an unselfish cab-driver I consulted advised me to check my bag and take a streetcar to the Isle of Hope. "I could drive you there," he said, "but if you want to see some old-fashioned yellow-fever country, you better take the streetcar." I am thankful I followed his advice. The Isle of Hope line is a single-track, Jim Crow, interurban railroad; in its steam-engine days it bore the stirring title Savannah, Thunderbolt & Isle of Hope Railroad. I recommend a trip on it to lovers of Americana. There were only three passengers on the car I boarded. We rattled through Savannah and its suburbs and plunged into a swampy forest of primeval live oaks whose limbs dripped with gloomy Spanish moss. Occasionally we crossed trestles over marshes in which rice was once grown with slave labor, and we passed through a number of small farms whose door-yard bushes were heavy with ripe, crimson pomegranates, the autumn fruit of the South. About five miles out of Savannah, the streetcar rounded a curve and the motorman suddenly put on his brake. A fat milch cow was on the track, grazing on nut grass that grew between the ties. The motorman pulled his whistle cord, but the cow did not budge. Some Gullah Negroes were digging yams in a patch beside the track; one hurried over and kicked the cow and she ambled off. The motorman, who was laughing, stuck his head out and said, "I give you fair warning. Next time she gets on my right of way I'm going to climb out and milk her." The Negro, also laughing, said, "Help yourself, Captain. She's got enough for the both of us."

A short while later we crossed a bridge spanning one of the rice marshes and reached the Isle of Hope. The streetcar line came to an end directly in front of several weatherbeaten frame buildings, on one of which there was a sign: "Alexander M. Barbee's Son. Dance Pavilion. Operating the Only Diamondback Terrapin Farm in the World. Oysters, Shrimp, Fancy Crabmeat. You Are Welcome." This building extended out over the water on piles, and two battered shrimp sloops were tied to the wharf abutting it; later I learned that this water was the Skidaway, a tidal river. I entered the building and found Mr. Barbee behind a counter, opening bottles of Coca-Cola for some shrimp fishermen. I recognized him from a description given by a Northern yachtsman who told me about the farm just before I went on vacation; he said Mr. Barbee looked "like an easygoing country storekeeper who would rather talk about his merchandise than sell it." I introduced myself and told him I was from New York and wanted to see his terrapin farm.

"Well, sir," he said, "I'm glad to see you. I'll show you the whole works, and I'll see that you get all the terrapin stew you can hold. We're going to barrel up a few terrapin for the New York trade today. The season opens up North around the second week of October, and we commence shipping on the first day of autumn. I've got forty-five hundred in my fattening pen ready to go and I want you to see them, but first we'll go up to the breeding farm. It's up the road a ways." He took off his apron and called to his wife, who was upstairs. "We keep house on the second floor of the pavilion," he told me. His wife came downstairs and he introduced us, saying, "Rose, I've invited this gentleman to have dinner with us. Make sure he gets a bait of terrapin." Mrs. Barbee, a pretty, red-cheeked young woman, smiled and said, "Mighty glad to have you."

I followed Mr. Barbee out on the front porch of the pavilion. "Right off the bat," he said, "I better tell you that the most important thing about terrapin meat is its tonic quality. It fills you full of fight. Why do you think so many rich old men eat terrapin? Well, sir, I'll tell you. A terrapin is full of rich, nourishing jelly, and this jelly makes you feel young and spry. To be frank, it's the same as monkey glands. If you were to take and feed terrapin stew to all the people of this country, the birth rate would jump like a flash of lightning. There was a time when the coastal marshes were so full of terrapin they fed the meat to plantation slaves. It was cheaper than sowbelly. Well, I was up to City Hall in

Savannah one day and a man there showed me some old papers he had dug out that said the plantation owners of Chatham County were forced to quit feeding terrapin to slaves because it made them breed too much. They wanted them to breed, of course, but they didn't want them to breed that much. Why, they spent all their time breeding. After all, there's a limit to everything."

We started up an oyster-shell lane that ran beside the river, and I said, "It must be convenient to have the streetcar line end right in front of your pavilion."

"To tell you the truth," Mr. Barbee said, "that's no accident. In a way, that's how the terrapin farm began. My daddy, Alexander Barbee, was a conductor on that road back in steam-engine days. He was French descent, and he liked to eat. He used to buy terrapin the colored people along the railroad would capture in the marshes. At first he just bought a mess now and then for his own table, but in time he took to trading in them, shipping them up to Maryland by the barrel.

"Well, around 1895, diamondbacks got so scarce the price shot up. They had been fished-out. When an old millionaire up North got ready to throw a banquet, he sometimes had to send men up and down the coast to get a supply. So in 1898 it came to pass that my daddy decided to make a stab at raising terrapin in captivity during his off hours from the railroad. Some Northern scientists he wrote to said it was a tom-fool idea, absolutely impossible, but he went out at night with the colored people and bogged around in the salt marshes and got so he understood terrapin better than any man in history. When he got ready to buy land for his terrapin farm, he naturally thought of the end of the railroad line. The land there had always looked good to him. It was the most beautiful scene in the world; when he reached it he could knock off and have a cigar. So he bought a few swampy acres, built a shed, and stocked it with terrapin. Every time he got to the end of the run he would jump out and tend to them. He got them in a breeding mood, and by 1912 they were breeding to such an extent he quit his job on the railroad. From time to time he bought more land down here. He was a unusual man. He played the cornet in a band up in Savannah and he had a high opinion of fun, so he built a dance pavilion down here. The pavilion isn't any gold mine, but we still keep it going. I sort of like it. People come out from Savannah on hot nights in the summer and you know how it is—you like to see them."

We reached the end of the oyster-shell lane and came upon a long, rather dilapidated shed in an oak grove. Green moss was growing on the shingled roof and the whitewash on the clapboards was peeling. There was a big pad-lock on the door. "This shed is the breeding farm," Mr. Barbee said. "They're born in here, and they stay here until they're around nine summers old. At the beginning of the ninth summer they're put in the fattening pen and allowed to eat their heads off. In the autumn, after they've been fattened for four or five months, they're sent to market. You can eat a terrapin when it's five years old, but I think they taste better around nine. Also, it's waste-ful to eat young terrapin, when you consider it takes two nine-year-olds to produce a good pint of clear meat." He unlocked the door but did not open it. Instead, as if he had suddenly changed his mind, he turned around on the steps of the shed and resumed the story of his father.

"Daddy passed away ten years ago and I took charge," he said. "He was quite a man, if I do say so. That white house we passed up there at the bend in the lane was his home. His room is just the way he left it. It's called the Barbee Musical Room, because everything in it plays a tune. Touch the bed, and a music box in the mattress plays a tune. Hang your hat on the rack, and the same thing happens. Pick up anything on the table from a dice cup to a hairbrush, and you get a tune. Why, there's one hundred and fifty objects in that room that'll play a tune if you just touch them. There's a rubberneck wagon up in Savannah that brings tourists down here to the island just to see it, and we employ a colored girl to stay in the room and answer questions. I bet half the yachtsmen that go to Florida in the winter have visited it.

"Three things Daddy truly admired were diamondbacks, music boxes, and William Jennings Bryan. In 1911, just before he quit the railroad, he put a clutch of terrapin eggs in his grip and went up to Washington and called on Mr. Bryan at his hotel. He had one egg that was just before hatching, and he said to Mr. Bryan, 'Sir, I have long been an admirer of yours and I want to ask a favor. I want you to hold this egg in your hand until it hatches out.' I reckon the great statesman was a bit put out, but Daddy argued him into it, and he held the egg until a little bull terrapin hatched out right on his palm. Daddy thanked him and said he was going to name the little fellow William Jennings Bryan, but Mr. Bryan said he thought Toby would be a better name. Daddy kept that terrapin for many years. He would carry it in his coat pocket everywhere he went. He had it trained so it would wink its right eye whenever he said, 'See here, Toby, ain't it about time for a drink?' "

Mr. Barbee laughed. "Yes, sirree," he said, "Daddy was a sight." He swung the shed door open. A rickety catwalk extended the length of the shed, and on each side of it were nine stalls whose floors swarmed with thousands of terrapin of all ages. Some were the size of a thumbnail and some were as big as a man's hand. There was a musky but not unpleasant smell in the shed. The diamondback is a lovely creature. On both sides of its protruding, distinctly snakelike head are pretty, multicolored lines and splotches. The hard shell in which it is boxed glints like worn leather. On the top shell, or carapace, are thirteen diamond-shaped designs, which may be pale gold, silvery, or almost black. Sometimes a terrapin shows up with fourteen diamonds on its shell; Mr. Barbee said that Negroes save these rare shells for good luck. The belly shell, or plastron, is the color of the keys of an old piano. "We measure them by placing a steel ruler on the belly shell," Mr. Barbee said, bending over and lifting a terrapin out of a stall. The creature opened its sinister little jaws, darted its head from left to right, and fought with its claws. "This cow will measure six and a half inches, which means she's around eight years of age. Next year she'll be ready for the stewpot. The price a terrapin brings at retail is largely based on shell length. In New York you'd pay between three and a half and five dollars for a seven-inch cow. An eight-inch one might bring seven dollars." Mr. Barbee noticed that I was watching the terrapin's jaws. "Oh, they never bite," he said.

"Are bull terrapin used in stews?" I asked.

"A bull's meat is tougher but just as palatable," he said. "A bull doesn't grow as big as a cow. You seldom see one longer than five inches. Also, from eggs hatched in captivity we get eighteen cows to every bull. That's a fact I can't explain. Naturally the bulls are overworked, so we strengthen the herd by putting wild bulls in the pen at breeding time. We employ hunters to capture them in the winter, when terrapin hibernate. They don't eat anything from frost until around March. They burrow in the marsh mud and sleep through the winter. They always leave an air hole in the mud, and that's what hunters look for. Some hunters use dogs called terrapin hounds, which are trained to recognize these holes. When a hound finds a hole he bays, and the hunter digs the terrapin out. We buy wild terrapin and ship them right along with our home-grown stock. My terrapin are raised so naturally they taste exactly like wild ones just pulled out of the mud. The difference is impossible to detect."

Mr. Barbee returned the terrapin he had been holding to its stall, and she crawled off. He said that, just as in the wild state, captive cows begin laying eggs in the late spring, nesting in shallow holes which they dig with their hind claws in sand on the stall floors. A cow may lay twice in a season, depositing a total of twenty eggs. The eggs are about the size of pecans and are elastic; they do not crack under pressure. In the tidal marshes the eggs hatch in from two to three months; on the farm they are stolen from the nests and incubated. Just how this is done, Mr. Barbee flatly declined to tell. "That's the Barbee family secret," he said.

An old Negro came into the shed. "Looky, looky, here comes Cooky," he said. He was carrying a bucket. "Jesse Beach, my foreman," Mr. Barbee said. "His bucket is full of crab legs and chopped-up oysters." The old man went down the catwalk, tossing a handful of food into each stall. I had noticed that the moment he entered the shed, the terrapin commenced crawling toward the front of their stalls. "They know Jesse," Mr. Barbee said. The terrapin converged on the food, shouldering each other out of the way, just as puppies do. They ate greedily. "Diamondbacks make wonderful pets," Mr. Barbee said. "I sell a lot of babies for that purpose. They are much more interesting than the dumb little turtles they sell in pet shops."

We followed the old Negro out of the shed and Mr. Barbee locked the door. "We'll take a look at the fattening pen now," he said. We went to one of the shacks alongside the pavilion. It housed a crabmeat cannery, another of the thrifty Mr. Barbee's enterprises. Between the shack and the riverbank, half in the water and half in the shore mud, was a board corral. The shallow, muddy water in it seethed with forty-five hundred full-grown terrapin. "This is a terrapin heaven," Mr. Barbee said. On one side of the corral was a cement walk, and when we stepped on it our shadows fell athwart the water and the terrapin sunning themselves on the surface promptly dived to the bottom. The tips of their inquisitive heads reappeared immediately and I could see hundreds of pairs of beady eyes staring up. "They're fat and sassy," Mr. Barbee said. "There's a pipe leading from the shucking table in the crab cannery right into the pen, and the legs and discarded flesh from the shucked crabs drop right into the water. The terrapin hang around the spout of the pipe and gobble up everything that comes along. Sooner or later those terrapin down there will appear on the finest tables in the country. God knows they're expensive, but that can't be helped. I feed a terrapin nine years before I sell it, and when you think of all the crabmeat and good Georgia oysters those fellows have put away, you can understand why a little-bitty bowl of terrapin stew costs three dollars and a half." While we stood there gazing down into a muddy pool containing more than $11,000 worth of sleek reptiles, the Negro foreman walked up with an empty barrel and a basket of Spanish moss. He doused the moss in the river and made a bed on the bottom of the barrel. The barrel had air holes cut in it. Then he reached in the pool and grabbed six terrapin. He scrubbed them off with a stiff brush and placed them on the wet moss. Then he covered them with moss and placed six more on this layer, continuing the sandwiching process until the barrel contained three dozen. While he was putting the head on the barrel, Mrs. Barbee came to a window of the pavilion and called, "Come to dinner."

The table was laid on the back porch of the pavilion, overlooking the Skidaway, and there was a bottle of amontillado on it. Mr. Barbee and I had a glass of it, and then Mrs. Barbee brought out three bowls of terrapin stew, Southern style, so hot it was bubbling. The three of us sat down, and while we ate, Mrs. Barbee gave me a list of the things in the stew. She said it contained the meat, hearts, and livers of two diamondbacks killed early that day, eight yolks of hard-boiled eggs that had been pounded up and passed through a sieve, a half pound of yellow country butter, two pints of thick cream, a little flour, a pinch of salt, a dash of nutmeg, and a glass and a half of amontillado. The meat came off the terrapins' tiny bones with a touch of the spoon, and it tasted like delicate baby mushrooms. I had a second and a third helping. The day was clear and cool, and sitting there, drinking dry sherry and eating terrapin, I looked at the scarlet leaves on the sweet gums and swamp maples on the riverbank, and at the sandpipers running stiff-legged on the sand, and at the people sitting in the sun on the decks of the yachts anchored in the Skidaway, and I decided that I was about as happy as a human can be in the autumn of 1939. After the stew we had croquettes made of crabmeat and a salad of little Georgia shrimp. Then we had some Carolina whiting that had been pulled out of the Atlantic at the mouth of the Skidaway early that morning. With the sweet, tender whiting, we had butter beans and ears of late corn that were jerked off the stalk only a few minutes before they were dropped in the pot. We began eating at one o'clock; at four we had coffee.

Three afternoons later, back in Manhattan, I visited the terrapin market of New York, which is located in three ancient buildings near the corner of Beekman and Front Streets, in Fulton Market. The largest of these is occupied by Moore & Co., an old black-bean, turtle-soup, and terrapin-stew firm now owned by a gourmet named Francesco Castelli. Each winter it sells around two thousand quarts of diamondback stew. In Mr. Castelli's establishment I saw the barrel of terrapin I had watched Mr. Barbee's foreman pack on the Isle of Hope. "I order a lot of Barbee's stuff and I ordered it from his father before him," Mr. Castelli said. "I also use terrapin from the Chesapeake Bay area, from the Cape Hatteras area of North Carolina, from New Jersey, and Long Island." Mr. Castelli believes that turtle and terrapin meat is the most healthful in the world and likes to tell about a fox terrier which lived in his factory and ate nothing but turtle meat until he died in 1921, aged twenty-five. He uses all his terrapin in his stewpots and sells no live ones.

Live ones are sold by a rather sharp-spoken old Irishman on Front Street named D. R. Quinn, who has been in the business most of his life and has not developed a taste for the meat, and by Walter T. Smith, Inc., also on Front Street. Smith's is sixty-two years old and is one of the largest turtle firms in the world; its cable address, Turtling, is known to many European chefs. It sells all kinds of edible turtles, including treacherous snappers and great 150-pound green turtles out of the Caribbean, from which most turtle soup is made. Snappers, prized for soup in Philadelphia, are not popular here. They can knock a man off his feet with their alligatorlike tails and have been known to snap off the fingers of fishermen; few New York chefs are hardy enough to handle them. I had a talk with Mr. Kurt W. Freund, manager of the firm, and he took me up the sagging stairs to the room in which his tanks are kept and showed me diamondbacks from every state on the Eastern seaboard except Maine. A few were from sloughs on Long Island. He said that in the local trade all terrapin caught from Maryland north are called Long Islands. He said that in the North, terrapin hunting is a fisherman's sideline and that few hunters north of Maryland catch more than a couple of dozen a year.

"I imagine you're under the impression that millionaires buy most of our terrapin," Mr. Freund said. "If so, you're dead wrong. During prohibition the terrapin business was hard hit, and it's just beginning to come back, and for years the poor Chinese laundryman has been the backbone of our trade. I'd say that seventy per cent of the sixteen thousand live diamondbacks sold on this street last year were bought by old Chinese. Come look out this window and see my sign." Hanging from the second-floor window was a red-and-white wooden signboard smeared with Chinese characters. Mr. Freund said the characters were pronounced "gim ten guoy" and meant "diamondback terrapin." He said that each autumn he hires a Chinese to write form letters quoting terrapin prices, which are distributed by the hundred in Chinatown.

"An old Chinese does not run to the drugstore or the doctor when he gets creaky in the joints," Mr. Freund said. "He saves his pennies and buys himself a terrapin. He cooks it with herbs and rice whiskey. Usually he puts so much whiskey in it he gets a spree as well as a tonic. In the autumn and in the spring the old Chinese come in and bargain. They balance terrapin on their palms and deliberate half an hour before making a selection. The turtle has been worshipped in China for centuries. It's supposed to have tonic and aphrodisiac qualities. The local Chinese certainly believe it has. Most of my steady Chinese customers are old laundrymen, and I know that some of them are practically penniless, but they think terrapin meat will do them more good than the finest doctor."

I told Mr. Freund that Mr. Barbee professed to believe that the consumption of terrapin meat is better than monkey glands for regaining youthfulness.

"Seriously," I said, "do you think there's anything to it?"

"I've been around terrapin a good while, and I've eaten the meat myself for years, and I've discussed the matter with scores of old Chinese," Mr. Freund said, "and I wouldn't be surprised."

The New Yorker, October 28, 1939

Nelson Algren

from America Eats

Food historians have only just begun to tap the resources of the "America Eats" project, one of the many ambitious undertakings of the Depression-era Works Progress Administration. Involving hundreds of loosely coordinated correspondents in many corners of the United States—among them Saul Bellow, Arna Bontemps, Zora Neale Hurston, Stetson Kennedy, Eudora Welty, and Richard Wright—the project set out to document the nation's foodways, past and present. Abandoned at the outbreak of World War II, the project's research efforts ended up scattered in various archives, some of them in all likelihood lost. But some—like this account of Midwestern food festivals attributed to Nelson Algren (1909–1981), who headed the Illinois Writers' Project—have begun to appear in print. More are surely to come: these are irreplaceable revelations of America's culinary heritage.

■ ■ ■

The country around East St. Louis, although traditionally French, is now largely dominated by Americans of German extraction. Their influence can be seen in *Wurst Markt* dinners: literally, sausage market. Such a dinner consists of homemade pork sausage, mashed potatoes, all kinds of vegetables, and bread and fruit pies.

The homesteaders lived lives of isolation, but once or twice a year a box social was held at the local schoolhouse. Each young woman brought a box of food. These were auctioned, the buyer sharing the food and becoming the partner for the evening of the young lady whose box he bought, sharing the same schoolroom desk and seat. The owners of the boxes were supposed to be secret. Somehow, though, it nearly always leaked out, and that of the most popular belle often fetched a substantial price. The food usually was crisp fried chicken, several pieces of pie, some slices of cake and not infrequently included some homemade candy and a few bought red apples. But the food wasn't the thing. It was the social get-together that made the box social important.

In neighborhoods where social contact is still difficult, the box social is awaited from year to year. Various superstitions have grown out of these occasions: "fancy box, homely girl" or "too much time spent on the outside, not enough on the inside."

Cakewalks, while not strictly eating occasions, are a related activity. Here, numbers are marked off on a circle on a floor and competitors pay for the privilege of walking around the circle to music. When the music stops the number on a cake is revealed, and the person standing on the corresponding number on the floor captures the cake.

Sauerkraut Day is the largest single-day celebration in Illinois. The town of Forreston, for example, has entertained no less than 20,000 visitors at one time, with fourteen barrels of kraut, a ton of wienies, 30,000 buns, and gallons of coffee.

In central Illinois as in other sections of the country, the immigration of foreigners has exerted a strong influence on what the people eat. Sauerkraut and sauerbraten are today common American foods. In communities with a predominant Scandinavian population, fish puddings and *bakkels* have gained some popularity. The Italians have given us ravioli and gnocchi, the Hungarians goulash and *galuska*, and the Greeks a variety of tasty combination dishes. Every midwestern city of any size has its restaurant where chop suey is served by Chinese, and in communities where there are large numbers of Russians and Armenians, we find adherents who speak very highly of the borsch and *bitochky smetance* of the former and the kebab of the latter.

Along the Wabash, after Yankee and Cavalier had pressed the French adventurers west, Hoosier homesteaders began developing festal customs after the manner of all rural folk who remain in one country for more than one generation.

An apple peelin', for example, was as good an excuse as any for a party.

Upon arrival, each peeler was given a crock of apples and a paring knife. A ten- to twenty-gallon stone jar was placed in the center of a group of five to eight persons. Here the apples which were peeled, cored, and quartered were deposited.

As each peeler finished his batch, the crock was removed and he was handed another full one. All participated in this except the passers, who were usually the host and hostess. The peeling usually ended about 9:30 in the evening, and by this time jars and buckets stood brimming with apples. Each unmarried man kept strict tab on the number of crocks of apples he had peeled, because the winner could kiss any girl he chose. Which invariably brought forth much giggling and good-humored teasing.

Immediately upon finishing the peelin', the men went into the parlor, moved the furniture into the sitting room, took up the homemade rag rug, sprinkled generous quantities of cornmeal and salt over the wide boards of the floor, grouped chairs in one corner for the fiddle, French harp, and "gittar" players, calling out: "Partners to your places, hook up your back bend and tighten your braces."

The day after the peelin', two or three neighborwomen would come over to cook the apple butter. This was done in the backyard in a big copper kettle sitting on four stones over a log fire and stirred with ladles eighteen feet long.

After cooking the butter all day, as a final touch the exact amount of clove oil was dropped into it, and this gave it an indefinable flavor not to be duplicated by factory butter. Then it was sealed in hot, sterile glass jars, cooled, and finally stored in the underground fruit cellar.

Related to the peelin's were stirrings. The hostess of the stirring prepared great kettles of cider which were kept boiling hot. Guests prepared apples which were put in the boiling cider and stirred until apple butter was achieved.

Pumpkin butter was made by boiling the pumpkin in a big kettle, then squeezing the juice out in a press and straining and boiling it down. Perhaps it would be thickened some with apples. They spread it on a piece of bread and thought it was the only butter in the world.

Grease from bears, deer, and coons was often rendered into candles, but when short of candles there was often nothing better than some grease in a dish with a rag set up in the middle. Coon grease was thought especially good for boots.

Following apple picking, bean threshing (with flails), corn husking, Indian summer, and the fall plowing came butchering time. The rites and ceremonies of hog killing naturally occurred after snappy weather had set in so that the pork could be kept fresh longer, which gave to the heating of huge cauldrons of water a certain element of coziness as well as the eternal thrill of fire building. Then there was the sharpening of the knives and the setting up of heavy planks on wooden horses, upon which the scalded hog was laid for the divestment of his hairy covering.

Housework was hustled out of the way and indoor preparations made beforehand as far as possible, for the housewife's share in the activities was but secondary to the outside drama. Bread, pies, and doughnuts were made and pans of beans baked so the stove would be left free for the chief performance. Once the kill was over, fuel was added to the fire, knives were tested along leathern thumbs, and tubs and pans made ready to receive the entrails.

The huge quivering mass was then carried into the kitchen and placed on a table. Over this the housewife bent, to "strip the innards" or "riddle the guts." The fat from these was "tried out" in one kettle and rendered in another.

The advent of spareribs was one of the anticipated seasonal events, like dandelion greens in spring and sweet corn in summer. They came with the first severe freeze of early winter, when butchering time brought a welcome change to the meat diet, as did a mess of greens after a winter of potatoes and cabbage, and bespoke not only a delectable treat in themselves but a round of family dinners and neighborly exchange. For the farmers of a community usually made of butchering a succession of events in order to help each other with the work and to keep the feast of fresh meat going as long as possible.

The family reunion is another old Indiana custom, dating from the calico and blue jeans era. On a Sunday in July or August, fifteen or twenty will be scheduled in the public parks and churchyards of every county seat in the state.

This show really belongs to the mothers, who do most of the work, from organizing to cooking to riding herd on the children. Their part begins early in the morning—or perhaps even the day before—for it is almost universal for each family to bring along the food it will consume and a little extra besides.

If the reunion is being held in a public park, chances are that somebody has brought along a baseball and bat. The men and older boys troop off to the diamond (or cow pasture) and start a vigorous but necessarily brief game of baseball, during which the elders prove to themselves that they're just as spry as ever and the youngsters play all the key positions. The real veterans find or improvise a horseshoe court and pitch horseshoes.

While the ball game is still in full swing and the horseshoe pitchers are still trying for ringers, a little group of men may drift off to a convenient spot behind a building or in a clump of trees. There they stand solemnly and talk in low tones while Uncle John or Cousin Ned opens a bottle of whiskey. In times past it would have been pure Jasper County corn distilled in Uncle John's back lot, but today the art of moonshining is almost gone from the Hoosier hills. There's a drink around and pipes are lighted. But the drinking is quiet and usually slight, for the family reunion is dominated too thoroughly by the older women. For the most part, the presence of the bottle remains a closely guarded secret, betrayed only by Grandpa's insistence on telling the same story three times.

The younger children, in the meantime, are standing shyly at a respectful distance from the main table, eyeing the food with wistful glances and trying to remember which of their fellows are the first cousins from Elwood.

When the baseball game has died away and the whiskey has been downed, dinner is ready and the entire clan assembles. The meat platters are first to move—chicken rolled in flour and fried in shallow fat to a rich, crisp brown, baked ham, beef roasted thoroughly to a heavy, tender darkness, gravied meat loaf kept hot for serving on a big camp-range. Chicken is the favorite with ham, beef, and meat loaf following in that order, but most plates receive at least two different kinds of meat.

The vegetables which follow include potatoes—creamed, scalloped, mashed, and chopped into salad—baked beans, green beans, lima beans, scalloped corn, sliced tomatoes, and fresh or pickled beets. Flanking them are deviled eggs, coleslaw, cottage cheese, and an endless variety of homemade pickles, sauces, relishes, jellies, jams, preserves, butters, and savories. Served at the same time is coffee, no matter how hot the day, poured in an endless stream from the spouts of great coffeepots wielded by tireless women.

When a slacking off in the first rush of eating is indicated by the gradual resumption of conversation, the servers start a second general attack, urging everyone to have another helping of everything. Then, when only the most hardy are still chewing away on chicken legs or wishbones, the cakes are cut—angel food, devil's food, banana, marble, sponge, coconut, orange, burnt sugar, and lazy daisy. These are followed by pumpkin, cherry, apple, mince, peach, blackberry, and custard pies.

America Eats (1992; written c. 1937–41)

M.F.K. Fisher

Mary Frances Kennedy Fisher (1908–1992), a prolific author and frequent contributor to *The New Yorker*, blended gastronomy and autobiography in her work in ways that expanded the horizons of American food writing. Like few before her, she articulated some of the interconnections between eating and other human appetites—for love, for camaraderie, for security. "There is a communion of more than our bodies when bread is broken and wine drunk," she wrote. Memory and desire entwine in her work with taste and smell, the one enhancing the other. Her style, at once lyrical and coolly modern, was a brilliant achievement, and she has become a kind of patron saint for those who would understand and explore the life of the palate. Born in Albion, Michigan, Fisher grew up in Whittier, California, where her father ran the local newspaper. After a few desultory years as a college student and journalist, she moved to Dijon, where her simmering appetites for food and for life came to a boil. She published a score of books in her lifetime—including such classics as *Serve It Forth* (1937), *Consider the Oyster* (1941), *How to Cook a Wolf* (1942), and *The Gastronomical Me* (1943)—and spent the last several decades of her life in Sonoma County, a hero of the Gourmet Revolution.

■ ■ ■

A Lusty Bit of Nourishment

> *Cook, white, must understand oysters. Apply aft. 1 P.M.*
> *Iliffe, 847 E. Allegheny.*
> —Adv. in *Philadelphia Inquirer*, March 1941

The flavor of an oyster depends upon several things. First, if it is fresh and sweet and healthy it will taste good, quite simply . . . good, that is, if the taster like oyster.

Then, it will taste like a Chincoteague or a blue point or a mild oyster from the Louisiana bayous or perhaps a metallic tiny Olympia from the Western coast. Or it may have a clear harsh flavor, straight from a stall in a wintry French town, a stall piled herring-bone style with Portugaises and Garennes, green as death to the uninitiated and twice as toothsome.

Or it may taste firm and yet fat, like the English oysters from around Plymouth.

Then an oyster will taste like what the taster expects, which of course depends entirely on the taster. Myself, since I was seventeen I have expected all oysters to be delicious, and with few exceptions they have been. In the same way, some people wait, if they manage to swallow these shell-fish at all, to gag more or less violently. And they gag.

Oysters can be eaten for themselves, as on the half shell or even in cooked dishes; they can be eaten primarily for the sauce that coats them, as in Oysters à la Rockefeller and all their offspring; and they can be eaten as a flavoring . . . oyster stuffing, for example.

Oyster stuffing, for turkeys naturally, is as American as corn-on-the-cob or steamed coot, as far as Americans know or care. To many families it is a necessary part of Christmas dinner, so that its omission would at once connotate a sure sign of internal disintegration, as if Ma came to church in her corset-cover or Uncle Jim brought his light-o'-love to the children's picnic.

It would mean financial failure too, to leave out those oysters which not so long ago were brought carefully a thousand miles for the fortunate money-bags in Iowa and Missouri who could boast of them in their holiday stuffings. Not every man could buy them, God knows, even if he wanted to, and a Middle Westerner was even prouder than a man from Down East to have these shell-fish on his feast-day.

Perhaps it is because they were somewhat lacking in their first freshness by the time they reached Peoria; perhaps it was because the people of this land so far from seashores were abashed by shells: whatever the reason, oysters in the Middle West were always cooked . . . and still are, mostly. And in spite of evidence, turkey stuffing seems primarily a part of that cookery. In it, oysters are used for their flavor, quite simply.

There are many recipes, from New England cookbooks as well as those spotted brown pamphlets issued yearly by the Ladies' Aids and Guild Societies of small towns beyond the Mississippi. All of them agree that it is almost impossible to put too many oysters in a turkey dressing if you are going to put in any at all.

The method of using them differs, of course, so that one rule will say, "Mince ½ dozen thoroughly and sprinkle throughout the crumbs," and another will command more generously, "Fill cavity of bird with large plump blue points." A fair medium, however, is the following recipe from Mrs. William Vaughn Moody's *Cook Book:**

Dressing for Turkey or Other Fowl with Oysters

1 ½ qts. of fine counts	1 qt. of oyster juice
1 qt. of lightly fried crumbs	salt, pepper, celery salt, and paprika

Wing the oysters. Add the bread crumbs, oyster juice, and seasoning.

I would add, with the Browns in their *Country Cook Book*, that "Perhaps Oyster stuffing is one of the best, but the crumbs, which are mixed with the oysters and oyster liquor, should be literally soaked in melted butter, as should all crumbs that go into a turkey." For myself, I also like a cup or more of finely chopped celery stirred in with the crumbs, rather than Mrs. Moody's celery salt.

There is a recipe in the book Merle Armitage and his wife cooked up called *Fit for a King* which is less conventional, but very good for those who don't want any nonsense about hiding the oysters. It is called, simply enough,

Oyster Stuffing

Toast some thin slices of bread until brown and butter them. Lay 2 slices flat inside the turkey and over them put a good layer of raw oysters seasoned with salt and pepper, lemon juice, and a few pieces of butter. Over this lay two more slices of toast and then a layer of oysters as before. The resulting flavor is delicious.

Between these two recipes there are ten thousand variations, probably, but the general idea of using oysters as a flavoring is no new one to us, any more than it has been for some several thousand years to the Chinese.

They probably are the longest users of these molluscs in such fashion. It has been going on for centuries, like so many other quaint Oriental customs, so that the oldest cookbooks give practically the same recipes used today in Hongkong and the kitchens of bewildered blonde brides in other outposts-of-Empire.

* Charles Scribner's Sons, New York, 1931.

There are two kinds of oysters used in Chinese cooking for their flavor. There is *ho tsee*, the dried oyster, and then there is *ho yeou*, which is so much like our old-fashioned oyster catsup that I wonder if it was not brought back to us by one of those doughty old sea captains whose spirits still search for the Northwest Passage far past Java Head.

Marion Harland's 1873 edition of *Common Sense in the Household* gives a recipe that is probably as good as any outside a Chinese grocery, although other more modern cookbooks are less bound by tee-totalitarianism than she, and more willing to forego vinegar altogether and put in a full quart of sherry for each quart of shellfish. Here is Mrs. Harland's recipe:

Oyster Catsup

1 quart oysters	1 tablespoon salt
1 teacupful cider vinegar	1 teaspoon cayenne pepper, and same of mace
1 teacupful sherry	

Chop the oysters and boil in their own liquor with a teacupful vinegar, skimming the scum as it rises. (It is here that such devil-may-care moderns as the Browns in their *Country Cook Book* say, "To each pint of oysters add a pint of sherry, let come to a boil . . .") Boil three minutes, strain through a hair-cloth, return the liquor to the fire, add the wine, pepper, salt, and mace. Boil fifteen minutes, and when cold, bottle for use, sealing the corks.

Mr. Henry Low, who is an authority on Chinese food, says of a *ho yeou* which might as well be Mrs. Harland's, for all the difference we could know, "Very delicious to serve with cold boiled chicken." In spite of the somewhat Charlie Chan-ish swing to this sentence, the opinion is a good one.

So is his inclusion, in *Cook at Home in Chinese,*[*] of at least one recipe using dried oysters, which can be bought at almost any Oriental grocery store in this country and are very much like the smoked oysters people give you now at cocktail parties, excellent little shriveled things on toothpicks which make your mouth taste hideous unless you drink a lot, which may also make your mouth taste hideous. Probably our smoked oysters could be used as well as *ho tsee*, but I doubt if they should be soaked. Or perhaps I am mistaken.

[*] The Macmillan Company, New York, 1938.

Anyway, here is Mr. Low's recipe for

Dried Oysters with Vegetables

(Ho Tsee Soong)

$\frac{1}{2}$ lb. dried oysters (*ho tsee*)	2 tablespoons oyster sauce
1 cup chopped bamboo shoots	(*ho yeou*)
(*jook tsun*)	$\frac{1}{2}$ teaspoon sugar
1 cup chopped Chinese cabbage	$\frac{1}{2}$ cup water
(*bok choy*)	a pinch of salt
1 cup peeled chopped water	a dash of pepper
chestnuts (*ma tai*)	$\frac{1}{2}$ head shredded Boston lettuce
$\frac{1}{2}$ cup chopped raw lean pork	1 teaspoon gourmet powder
1 clove crushed garlic	(*mei jing*)
1 piece crushed green ginger	2 teaspoons cornstarch

Soak oysters five hours and cut off hard parts. Chop fine. Mix together all chopped ingredients, add ginger, garlic, gourmet powder, salt, pepper and sugar. Put in a hot, well-greased skillet and cook four minutes. Add oyster sauce and water and cook four minutes more. Add cornstarch, which has been made into a smooth paste. Stir, and cook one minute. Arrange lettuce leaves on platter and pour cooked mixture over them.

It is not such a far cry as it seems from the exotic blendings of this Ho Tsee Soong to the pungency of Oysters à la Rockefeller. Both dishes depend almost more upon the herbs that make up their body than they do upon the oysters that are the *raison d'être*, and whether they are "dry and putrid" in a dark kitchen in Chungking or San Francisco, or fresh in New Orleans, the herbs must be prepared with finicky attention.

There are too many legends, really, about Oysters Rockefeller for any one to dare say what he thinks is the true one. It is equally foolish to say what is the true recipe since every gourmet who has ever dined in that nostalgically agreeable room of Antoine's on St. Louis Street figures, after the third or fourth sampling if not the first, that he has at last discovered the secret.

It is true that Mr. Alciatore, like his father and grandfather, has managed to keep his Rockefellers consistently delicious. That is perhaps the reason they are so justly famous, rather than any special secret formula. Other restaurants serve their own versions, which may be a little cheaper or even a little more expensive, and may look almost like Antoine's. But they are undependable, so that sometimes the rock-salt they rest on is half an inch thick and sometimes an inch; sometimes the covering, that little soft green blanket over each oyster, is dark, and sometimes it is lightly mottled, with logical differences in the flavor of the dish itself.

(This simple, apparently difficult secret for success has also been copied by the bar-men in the Roosevelt Hotel in New Orleans, too: unchanging excellence. According to their publicity, they are the only makers of the Original Ramos Gin Fizz, that subtle smooth-like drink which has nourished reporters and politicians and other humans through many a long food-less summer near the simmering bayous.

(Once, for reasons of research, I drank two Ramos fizzes away from the hallowed Roosevelt. They were truly bad. I went back to the hotel, and watched eagerly while the old bar-man put little dashes of this and that together and then handed it all to the strong young stevedore who was chief shaker. I decided that infinite care, unhurried patience, and a never-varying formula were more the secret than any magic element such as dried nectar-crumbs or drops from a Ramos philter.

(I proved this theory, at least to my pleasure, when with infinite care and a certain amount of unhurried patience I too made a Ramos, after a recipe I found which was printed in 1900 for Solari's Grocery. It was easy to assemble, once I located some orange-flower water . . . and it was, Heaven protect me for this blasphemy!, as good as any ever shook up at the Roosevelt.)

Oysters Rockefeller, then, surrounded as they are by pomp and legend, are not impossible to copy. Their miracle is that *chez* Antoine, where the last two Alciatores have served them ever since 1889, they have always been delicious. Probably it is safe to say that they have not varied one jot or tittle in all these years, so that Mr. Roy could feel quite safe in sitting down to the millionth order, complete with photographers and head-waiter-with-wine-basket, to dip into the first succulent shell with only a faint sign of suspicion on his small intelligent face.

The postcards resulting from this occasion are given to every person who eats Oyster à la Rockefeller at Antoine's, and on each one, like the number of your duck in the old days at the Tour d'Argent in Paris (Where else?), is stamped the number of your plate of these famous morsels. It is an endearing bit of *chi-chi*, which is barely marred by the italics under the picture: *The recipe is a sacred family secret.*

That is rather more than *chi-chi*, although equally endearing in its solemnity. It is what could be called an exaggeration of the truth, since, although the Alciatores may use $^3/_4$ of a teaspoon of this or that rather than $^1/_2$, there are many private cooks who have a recipe which is as good, Louisiana gourmets say, as Antoine's own.

This is it, reprinted from *A Book of Famous Old New Orleans Recipes Used in the South for More Than Two Hundred Years:**

Oysters Rockefeller

Procure oysters on the half shell, wash them and drain them, and put them back on the shells. Place ice cream salt to the thickness of about one half inch on a platter and preheat, placing the oysters that are on the half shells on the hot salt and run them in the broiler for five minutes. Then cover with the following sauce and bread crumbs and bake in the hot oven until brown. Serve hot.

Sauce for Oysters Rockefeller

1 cup oyster water	1 oz. herbsaint
1 cup plain water	1 cup best butter
$^1/_4$ bunch shallots	$^1/_4$ bunch spinach
1 small sprig thyme	1 tablespoon Worcestershire sauce
$^1/_2$ cup ground bread crumbs toasted and sifted	2 small stalks green celery

Grind all the vegetables in the chopper. Put the water and the oyster liquor together, and let boil vigorously for about five minutes then add the ground vegetables and cook about twenty minutes or until it's to the consistency of a thick sauce.

Stir in the butter until melted and remove from fire, add the herbsaint, pour sauce over oysters on the shells, sprinkle with bread crumbs return to

---

* For sale at Solari's and other New Orleans stores.

hot oven for five minutes and serve piping hot on the platter in which you cooked them.

(Herbsaint is a cordial made in the deep South from various herbs but mostly anise, so that it tastes very much like that clear *Anis Mono* that used to be served in Spanish pubs, or even like Pernod. Some people say that Antoine's spurns it in Oysters Rockefeller, but I wouldn't know. Myself, I think not.)

It is more than likely that if Mr. Alciatore, to say nothing of his Head Chef Camille Averna, should see this recipe he would toss his head slightly, or perhaps even sneer. However, sacred family secret or no, I still believe that any good cook with skill and, above all, unfailing patience can make Oysters à la Rockefeller that are as like Antoine's as one angel can be like another.

The question is, Who wants to? Perhaps you are an habitué or perhaps you have been to Antoine's once or twice. The inescapable charm of that simple, almost austere room, with mirrors for walls; with the blue gas lamps flickering through all the evening while the electric lights snap on and off for the blazings of *crêpes Suzette* and *cafés brûlots au diable*; with its high cashier's seat at the back and its deft impersonal waiters who let the pantry doors swing wide open now and then to show the ordered shimmer of the wine-glass cupboard: all that makes a family secret much more precious than any recipe, and one that means untellable pleasure to untold amateur gourmets.

Whether they are men like "The Grand Duke Alexis, brother of the Czar of Russia," or Sinclair Lewis, or "Mr. Nobody from Nowhere," they find at Antoine's something remembered, something perhaps never known but recognized, so that dining there is full of ease and mellowness. *Huitres en Coquilles à la Rockefeller* appear magically, prepared with loving patience for each eager diner as if he were the first and only *gastronome*, and their tedious preparation is something that can best be left to Camille Averna's direction.

It should never matter that other people, armed with determination and an almost perfect copy of the Alciatores' recipe, could probably do just as well. Better go once to the little place on St. Louis Street in New Orleans, and eat them as they should be eaten, than struggle doggedly a thousand times with hot salt-beds and spinach-grindings in Connecticut or California. Oysters à la Rockefeller any place but *chez* Antoine are not quite as delicious, not quite as *kosher* nor as *comme il faut*.

There are, of course, at least ten other precious recipes for every thousand humans who have ever cooked an oyster. There are fairly complicated ones, like the following rule contributed to the first number of the magazine *Gourmet* by the Hotel Pierre of New York and its Head Chef Georges Gonneau:

French Creamed Oysters

Put one cup of butter into the top of a lighted chafing-dish; add one tablespoon English mustard, $\frac{1}{4}$ teaspoon anchovy paste; salt, pepper, and a dash of cayenne pepper to taste; stir until mixture is thoroughly blended. Add three cups finely chopped celery and stir almost constantly until celery is nearly cooked. Pour in 1 quart rich, fresh cream slowly, stirring constantly until mixture comes to a boil. Add four dozen oysters, cleaned and free from beard, and cook two minutes. Finally, add $\frac{1}{4}$ cup good sherry wine. Serve on freshly made toast on hot plates, and garnish with quartered lemon and crisp young watercress. Dust each serving with paprika, mixed with a little nutmeg.

This recipe, an excellent way to exercise man's basic fascination for chafing dishes and vice versa, is naturally much simpler than some, even though sautéed ham and mushrooms be added, or truffles; and on the other hand it is a great deal more elaborate than such a one as Marion Harland gave in 1870 and many years before.

She wrote with a passion which was always ladylike in spite of its perhaps ungenteel *gourmandise*, as her period dictated, but she was never squeamish, and her "receipts" are to a large number of *aficionados* as beautifully rounded as the Songs of Solomon. Witness what she said, so long ago and only yesterday, about

Roast Oysters

There is no pleasanter frolic for an Autumn evening, in the regions where oysters are plentiful, than an impromptu "roast" in the kitchen. There the oysters are hastily thrown into the fire by the peck. You may consider that your fastidious taste is marvelously respected if they are washed first. A bushel basket is set to receive the empty shells, and the click of the oyster-knives forms a constant accompaniment to the music of laughing voices.

Nor are roast oysters amiss upon your own quiet supper-table, when the "good man" comes in on a wet night, tired and hungry, and wants "something heartening." Wash and wipe the shell-oysters, and lay them in the oven, if it is quick; upon the top of the stove, if it is not. When they are open, they are done. Pile in a large dish, and send to table. Remove the upper shells by a dexterous wrench of the knife, season the oyster on the lower, with pepper-sauce and butter, or pepper, salt, and vinegar in lieu of the sauce, and you have the very aroma of this pearl of bivalves, pure and undefiled.

Or (she adds, rather in anti-climax), you may open while raw, leaving the oysters upon the lower shells; lay in a large baking-pan, and roast in their own liquor, adding pepper, salt, and butter before serving.

Probably the "pepper sauce" used by Mrs. Harland's frolicking family was made more or less after this old New England recipe:

Roast Oyster Sauce

2　tablespoons butter	4　drops tabasco sauce
juice of 1 lemon	juice of $\frac{1}{2}$ onion

Melt the butter, stir in the other ingredients and pour over oysters. Serve hot.

The Harland recipe is not much different from one given in *Plats du Jour** by Paul Reboux, but its style is as much like his as his own flippant punning words are like the silence that comes now from his once garrulous land of wit and gaiety:

Grilled Oysters

. . . Surely, this recipe would not have the approval of the S.P.C.A. But it is probable that oysters possess a sensitivity analogous to that of the French tax-payer, so that they are incapable of very characteristic reactions. That, then, is why there is little reason for weeping tenderly at the idea that these molluscs must be placed on the grill.

As they submit to the same end that overtook Saint Lawrence, the oysters open. It is exactly like the purse of the government pensioner as Income

*Flammarion, Paris, 1936.

Tax Day rolls around: one does the only possible thing in the presence of bad luck.

Take advantage of their being open to pop in a little melted butter, some pepper, and some bread crumbs. Then close them up again: at this moment they will be too weak to resist you. Let them cook a little. And serve them very hot.

Some people like this very much.

All oysters cooked in sauce, whether their own or manufactured, are necessarily of a certain complexity. They may be as simple as Marion Harland's or Reboux's; they may be coated with the intricacies of *roux* and white-wine sauces. They may even be surrounded by the strange legends of Antoine's, so that their consumption becomes more a rite than the simple manifestation of a hunger.

According to the little black-and-gold booklet published for Antoine's centennial, Oysters à la Rockefeller contain "such rich ingredients that the name of the Multi-Millionaire was borrowed to indicate their value." Some gourmets say that any oyster worthy of its species should not be toyed with and adulterated by such skullduggeries as this sauce of herbs and strange liqueurs. Others, more lenient, say that Southern oysters like Mr. Alciatore's need some such refinement, being as they are languid and soft-tasting to the tongue.

They are, you might say, more like the Southern ladies than the brisk New Englanders. They are delicate and listless . . . and ice is scarce, or used to be . . . and the weather's no good for saving; best cover the bayou-molluscs with a fine New Orleans sauce, or at least a dash or two of red Evangeline. . . .

But further north, men choose their oysters without sauce. They like them cold, straightforward, simple, capable of spirit but unadorned, like a Low Church service maybe or a Boston romance.

And oysters of the North Atlantic Coast are worthy of this more or less unquestioning trust. They are firm and flavorful, and eaten chilled from their own lower shell with a bit of lemon juice squeezed over them they are among men's true delights.

There are, oddly enough, almost as many ways to eat such a simple dish as there are men to eat it.

First, several millennia ago, men cracked the shells and sucked out the tender gray bodies with their attendant juices and their inevitable sharp splinters. Then, when knives came, they pried open the two shells and cupped the lower one in their hands, careful not to spill its colorless elixir. And always, even from the beginning, there have been variations on these two simple processes; there has been invented a series of behavior-rules as complex as the recipes to prevent sea-sickness or how to arrange three tulips in a low jade-green bowl for the local garden show.

If a man cared, and knew all the rules, he would be really frightened to go into a decent oyster-bar and submit his knowledge to the cold eyes of the counter-man and all the local addicts. He would be so haunted by what was correct in that certain neighborhood and how to hold the shell and whether lemon juice should be used and so on that he would probably go instead to a corner drug store and order a double chocolate banana-split.

Fortunately, though, almost everybody who goes into an oyster-bar or even eats in a restaurant is so pleased with the oysters themselves that he eats them in his own fashion without giving a toot or a tinkle about what other people think.

In America, on the East Coast, oysters are usually served on a plate of shaved ice, with small round white crackers in a bowl or vase. Quite often a commendable battery of bottled sauces such as tabasco and horse-radish accompanies the order, and in many restaurants a little cup of red sauce with a tomato base is put in the middle of the plate of ice-and-oysters. Either this little cup of sauce or one of the bottles contains gastronomic heat in one form or another.

In New Orleans' oyster-bars, and all over the Western World in what used to be called "places of the people . . . common places," the procedure is simpler, almost as simple as the English pub-custom of shoving you your oysters, a toothpick to pluck them with, and a shaker of weak vinegar if you're toff enough to want it. Down South there is a long marble or hard wood counter between the customer and the oyster-man, sloping toward the latter. He stands there, opening the shells with a skill undreamed of by an ordinary man and yet always with a few cuts showing on his fingers, putting the open oysters carefully, automatically, on a slab of ice in front of him, while a cat waits with implacable patience at his ankles for a bit of oyster-beard or a caress. He throws the top shells behind him into a barrel, and probably they go into a road or a wall somewhere, later, with cement to bind them.

A man comes into the bare place, which has hard lights, and sawdust on the floor. He mutters "One" or "Two" to the oyster-man, and pulls a handful of square soda-crackers from the tipped glass jar at the end of the counter. If he wants to, he spoons out a cupful of tomato sauce from a big crock.

By then his one or two dozen oysters wait in a line for him upon the cold counter, their shells tipped carefully so that the liquor will lie still in them and not flow down the sloping marble and into the bins of unopened shells underneath. He picks up an oyster on a pointed thin little fork, and holds the shell under his chin while he guides it toward his mouth, having dunked it or not in the garish sauce, and then he swallows it.

If he likes raw oysters he enjoys this ceremony very much. Many do not, and may they long rest happy, if envious. Now, having wasted too many years in shuddering at oysters, I like them. I *thoroughly* like them, so that I am willing to forego comfort and at times even safety to savor their strange cold succulence.

I was quite willing, once at the Old Port in Marseille before things changed, to risk their brassy greenness at a quay-side stand. Once I knowingly ate a "bad one" in the Pompeiian Room at the Bern-Palace rather than cry them shame. And now, after more than a few years of prejudiced acquaintance, I can still say that oysters please me.

Those years, which have not been quite empty of perception, have made me form a few ideas of my own, since it is impossible to enjoy without thought, in spite of what the sensualists say.

I am still very ignorant, but I know that I used to like *Portugaises vertes* and oysters from Garennes, in the times that seem so far from me now . . . as far as the well-fed French people who once plucked the shells with me from their willow baskets on the Rue de la Gare, when the old man sliced open the rough long shells with his knife there or in front of Crespin's in Dijon in the winter, and the little oyster-stalls stood bravely near the stations in all the province-towns of France. The greenness and the tepid brassiness of those shell-fish were at first a shock, and I also thought I should suspect their unhygienic deaths . . . but none ever hurt me, and my palate always benefited as well as my spirit.

In America I think I like best the oysters from Long Island Sound, although I have eaten Chincoteagues and some others from the Delaware Bay that were very good. Farther south, in spite of my innate enthusiasm, I have had to admit that the oysters grow less interesting served in the shell, and almost cry out for such delicious decadences as horse-radish or even cooking, which would be sacrilege in Boston or Bordeaux.

On the Mexican Gulf they are definitely better cooked, although skilled gourmets have insisted otherwise to me, and one man from Corpus Christi once put his gun on the table while he stated quietly that anybody who said Texas blue points weren't the best anywhere was more than one kind of insulting liar. I still prefer cooked oysters in the South, since for me one of the pleasures of eating a raw oyster is the crispness of its flesh (*crisp* is not quite right, and *flesh* is not right, but in the same way you might say that *oyster* is not right for what I mean) . . . and crispness seems not to exist in the warm waters there.

And on the West Coast, I like the metallic tiny bites of the Olympias, and patriotism or no patriotism, find the Japanese-spawned Willapoints from Oregon tasteless and too bulky to be eaten from the shell. One thing, to my mind, should accompany all such oysters served this way as inevitably as soda-crackers go with soup in a drug store or Gilbert with Sullivan or Happy New Year with Merry Christmas: buttered brown bread and lemon.

In the Good Old Days, those good old days so dull to hear about and so delightful to talk of, thin slices of real pumpernickel-ish brown bread (No machine-sliced beige-colored sponge, for God's sake!) and honest-to-Betsy lumps of juicy lemon used to come automatically with every half-dozen of oysters, whether you sat in the circle at the Café de Paris or stood with one foot in the sawdust down near the third-class restaurant of the Nurnberger-Bahnhof. They picked up the sometimes tired flavor of the oysters, and I soon discovered that a few drops of lemon juice on the buttered bread tasted much better than on the shell-fish themselves.

I have thought seriously about this, while incendiary bombs fell and people I knew were maimed and hungry, and I believe that all American oyster-bars and every self-respecting restaurant in this good land which presumes to serve raw oysters in their shells or even naked in a cup, should at once make it compulsory to serve also a little plate of thin-sliced nicely

buttered good dark bread, preferably the heavy fine-grained kind and buttered with sweet butter I should say, and a few quarters of lemon.

I think the oyster-men and the owners of restaurants would find this little
persnicket a paying one, and that even if they charged a few cents extra for the
lemon or the butter or even the bread, like Lipp's and some of the old places in
Europe, they would sell enough more oysters to repay them many times.

And for the person who likes oysters, such a delicate, charming, nostalgic gesture would seem so delicate, so nostalgically charming, so reminis-
cent of a thousand good mouthfuls here and there in the past . . . in other
words, so *sensible* . . . that it would make even nostalgia less a perversion
than a lusty bit of nourishment.

Define This Word

That early spring I met a young servant in northern Burgundy who was
almost fanatical about food, like a medieval woman possessed by the devil.
Her obsession engulfed even my appreciation of the dishes she served, until
I grew uncomfortable.

It was the off season at the old mill which a Parisian chef had bought and
turned into one of France's most famous restaurants, and my mad waitress
was the only servant. In spite of that she was neatly uniformed, and showed
no surprise at my unannounced arrival and my hot dusty walking clothes.

She smiled discreetly at me, said, "Oh, but certainly!" when I asked
if I could lunch there, and led me without more words to a dark bedroom
bulging with First Empire furniture, and a new white bathroom.

When I went into the dining room it was empty of humans . . . a
cheerful ugly room still showing traces of the *petit-bourgeois* parlor it had
been. There were aspidistras on the mantel; several small white tables were
laid with those imitation "peasant-ware" plates that one sees in Paris china
stores, and very good crystal glasses; a cat folded under some ferns by the
window ledge hardly looked at me; and the air was softly hurried with the
sound of high waters from the stream outside.

I waited for the maid to come back. I knew I should eat well and slowly, and suddenly the idea of dry sherry, unknown in all the village *bistros* of the last few days, stung my throat smoothly. I tried not to think of it; it would be impossible to realize. Dubonnet would do. But not as well. I longed for sherry.

The little maid came into the silent room. I looked at her stocky young body, and her butter-colored hair, and noticed her odd pale voluptuous mouth before I said, "Mademoiselle, I shall drink an *apéritif.* Have you by any chance—"

"Let me suggest," she interrupted firmly, "our special dry sherry. It is chosen in Spain for Monsieur Paul."

And before I could agree she was gone, discreet and smooth.

She's a funny one, I thought, and waited in a pleasant warm tiredness for the wine.

It was good. I smiled approval at her, and she lowered her eyes, and then looked searchingly at me again. I realized suddenly that in this land of trained nonchalant waiters I was to be served by a small waitress who took her duties seriously. I felt much amused, and matched her solemn searching gaze.

"Today, Madame, you may eat shoulder of lamb in the English style, with baked potatoes, green beans, and a sweet."

My heart sank. I felt dismal, and hot and weary, and still grateful for the sherry.

But she was almost grinning at me, her lips curved triumphantly, and her eyes less palely blue.

"Oh, in *that* case a trout, of course—a *truite au bleu* as only Monsieur Paul can prepare it!"

She glanced hurriedly at my face, and hastened on. "With the trout, one or two young potatoes—oh, very delicately boiled," she added before I could protest, "very light."

I felt better. I agreed. "Perhaps a leaf or two of salad after the fish," I suggested. She almost snapped at me. "Of course, of course! And naturally our *hors d'oeuvres* to commence." She started away.

"No!" I called, feeling that I must assert myself now or be forever lost. "No!"

She turned back, and spoke to me very gently. "But Madame has never tasted our *hors d'oeuvres*. I am sure that Madame will be pleased. They are our specialty, made by Monsieur Paul himself. I am sure," and she looked reproachfully at me, her mouth tender and sad, "I am sure that Madame would be very much pleased."

I smiled weakly at her, and she left. A little cloud of hurt gentleness seemed to hang in the air where she had last stood.

I comforted myself with sherry, feeling increasing irritation with my own feeble self. Hell! I loathed *hors d'oeuvres*! I conjured disgusting visions of square glass plates of oily fish, of soggy vegetables glued together with cheap mayonnaise, or rank radishes and tasteless butter. No, Monsieur Paul or not, sad young pale-faced waitress or not, I hated *hors d'oeuvres*.

I glanced victoriously across the room at the cat, whose eyes seemed closed.

II

Several minutes passed. I was really very hungry.

The door banged open, and my girl came in again, less discreet this time. She hurried toward me.

"Madame, the wine! Before Monsieur Paul can go on—" Her eyes watched my face, which I perversely kept rather glum.

"I think," I said ponderously, daring her to interrupt me, "I think that today, since I am in Burgundy and about to eat a trout," and here I hoped she noticed that I did not mention *hors d'oeuvres*, "I think I shall drink a bottle of Chablis 1929—*not* Chablis Village 1929."

For a second her whole face blazed with joy, and then subsided into a trained mask. I knew that I had chosen well, had somehow satisfied her in a secret and incomprehensible way. She nodded politely and scuttled off, only for another second glancing impatiently at me as I called after her, "Well cooled, please, but not iced."

I'm a fool, I thought, to order a whole bottle. I'm a fool, here all alone and with more miles to walk before I reach Avallon and my fresh clothes and a bed. Then I smiled at myself and leaned back in my solid wide-seated chair, looking obliquely at the prints of Gibson girls, English tavern scenes, and hideous countrysides that hung on the papered walls. The room was warm; I could hear my companion cat purring under the ferns.

The girl rushed in, with flat baking dishes piled up her arms on napkins, like the plates of a Japanese juggler. She slid them off neatly in two rows on to the table, where they lay steaming up at me, darkly and infinitely appetizing.

"*Mon Dieu!* All for me?" I peered at her. She nodded, her discretion quite gone now and a look of ecstatic worry on her pale face and eyes and lips.

There were at least eight dishes. I felt almost embarrassed, and sat for a minute looking weakly at the fork and spoon in my hand.

"Perhaps Madame would care to start with the pickled herring? It is not like any other. Monsieur Paul prepares it himself, in his own vinegar and wines. It is very good."

I dug out two or three brown filets from the dish, and tasted. They were truly unlike any others, truly the best I had ever eaten, mild, pungent, meaty as fresh nuts.

I realized the maid had stopped breathing, and looked up at her. She was watching me, or rather a gastronomic X-ray of the herring inside me, with a hypnotized glaze in her eyes.

"Madame is pleased?" she whispered softly.

I said I was. She sighed, and pushed a sizzling plate of broiled endive toward me, and disappeared.

I had put a few dull green lentils on my plate, lentils scattered with minced fresh herbs and probably marinated in tarragon vinegar and walnut oil, when she came into the dining room again with the bottle of Chablis in a wine basket.

"Madame should be eating the little baked onions while they are hot," she remarked over her shoulder as she held the bottle in a napkin and uncorked it. I obeyed meekly, and while I watched her I ate several more than I had meant to. They were delicious, simmered first in strong meat broth, I think, and then drained and broiled with olive oil and new-ground pepper.

I was fascinated by her method of uncorking a vintage wine. Instead of the Burgundian procedure of infinite and often exaggerated precautions against touching or tipping or jarring the bottle, she handled it quite nonchalantly, and seemed to be careful only to keep her hands from the cool bottle itself, holding it sometimes by the basket and sometimes in a napkin. The cork was very tight, and I thought for a minute that she would break it. So did she; her face grew tense, and did not loosen until she had slowly worked out the cork and wiped the lip. Then she poured an inch of wine in a glass, turned her back to me like a priest taking Communion, and drank it down. Finally some was poured for me, and she stood with the bottle in her hand and her full lips drooping until I nodded a satisfied yes. Then she pushed another of the plates toward me, and almost rushed from the room.

I ate slowly, knowing that I should not be as hungry as I ought to be for the trout, but knowing too that I had never tasted such delicate savory morsels. Some were hot, some cold. The wine was light and cool. The room, warm and agreeably empty under the rushing sound of the stream, became smaller as I grew used to it.

My girl hurried in again, with another row of plates up one arm, and a large bucket dragging at the other. She slid the plates deftly on to the table, and drew a deep breath as she let the bucket down against the table leg.

"Your trout, Madame," she said excitedly. I looked down at the gleam of the fish curving through its limited water. "But first a good slice of Monsieur Paul's *pâté*. Oh yes, oh yes, you will be very sorry if you miss this. It is rich, but appetizing, and not at all too heavy. Just this one morsel!"

And willy-nilly I accepted the large gouge she dug from a terrine. I prayed for ten normal appetites and thought with amused nostalgia of my usual lunch of cold milk and fruit as I broke off a crust of bread and patted it smooth with the paste. Then I forgot everything but the exciting faint decadent flavor in my mouth.

I beamed up at the girl. She nodded, but from habit asked if I was satisfied. I beamed again, and asked, simply to please her, "Is there not a faint hint of *marc*, or perhaps cognac?"

"*Marc*, Madame!" And she awarded me the proud look of a teacher whose pupil has showed unexpected intelligence. "Monsieur Paul, after he has taken equal parts of goose breast and the finest pork, and broken a certain number of egg yolks into them, and ground them *very*, very fine, cooks all with seasoning for some three hours. *But*," she pushed her face nearer, and looked with ferocious gloating at the *pâté* inside me, her eyes like X-rays, "he never stops stirring it! Figure to yourself the work of it—stir, stir, never stopping!

"Then he grinds in a suspicion of nutmeg, and then adds, very thoroughly, a glass of *marc* for each hundred grams of *pâté*. And is Madame not pleased?"

Again I agreed, rather timidly, that Madame was much pleased, that Madame had never, indeed, tasted such an unctuous and exciting *pâté*. The girl wet her lips delicately, and then started as if she had been pin-struck.

"But the trout! My God, the trout!" She grabbed the bucket, and her voice grew higher and more rushed.

"Here is the trout, Madame. You are to eat it *au bleu*, and you should never do so if you had not seen it alive. For if the trout were dead when it was plunged into the *court bouillon* it would not turn blue. So, naturally, it must be living."

I knew all this, more or less, but I was fascinated by her absorption in the momentary problem. I felt quite ignorant, and asked her with sincerity, "What about the trout? Do you take out its guts before or after?"

"Oh, the trout!" She sounded scornful. "Any trout is glad, truly glad, to be prepared by Monsieur Paul. His little gills are pinched, with one flash of the knife he is empty, and then he curls in agony in the *bouillon* and all is over. And it is the curl you must judge, Madame. A false *truite au bleu* cannot curl."

She panted triumph at me, and hurried out with the bucket.

III

She *is* a funny one, I thought, and for not more than two or three minutes I drank wine and mused over her. Then she darted in, with the trout correctly blue and agonizingly curled on a platter, and on her crooked arm a plate of tiny boiled potatoes and a bowl.

When I had been served and had cut off her anxious breathings with an assurance that the fish was the best I had ever tasted, she peered again at me and at the sauce in the bowl. I obediently put some of it on the potatoes: no fool I, to ruin *truite au bleu* with a hot concoction! There was more silence.

"Ah!" she sighed at last. "I knew Madame would feel thus! Is it not the most beautiful sauce in the world with the flesh of a trout?"

I nodded incredulous agreement.

"Would you like to know how it is done?"

I remembered all the legends of chefs who guarded favorite recipes with their very lives, and murmured yes.

She wore the exalted look of a believer describing a miracle at Lourdes as she told me, in a rush, how Monsieur Paul threw chopped chives into hot sweet butter and then poured the butter off, how he added another nut of butter and a tablespoonful of thick cream for each person, stirred the mixture for a few minutes over a slow fire, and then rushed it to the table.

"So simple?" I asked softly, watching her lighted eyes and the tender lustful lines of her strange mouth.

"So simple, Madame! But," she shrugged, "you know, with a master—"

I was relieved to see her go; such avid interest in my eating wore on me. I felt released when the door closed behind her, free for a minute or so from her victimization. What would she have done, I wondered, if I had been ignorant or unconscious of any fine flavors?

She was right, though, about Monsieur Paul. Only a master could live in this isolated mill and preserve his gastronomic dignity through loneliness and the sure financial loss of unused butter and addled eggs. Of course, there was the stream for his fish, and I knew his *pâtés* would grow even more edible with age; but how could he manage to have a thing like roasted lamb ready for any chance patron? Was the consuming interest of his one maid enough fuel for his flame?

I tasted the last sweet nugget of trout, the one nearest the blued tail, and poked somnolently at the minute white billiard balls that had been eyes. Fate could not harm me, I remembered winily, for I had indeed dined today, and dined well. Now for a leaf of crisp salad, and I'd be on my way.

The girl slid into the room. She asked me again, in a respectful but gossipy manner, how I had liked this and that and the other things, and then talked on as she mixed dressing for the endive.

"And now," she announced, after I had eaten one green sprig and dutifully pronounced it excellent, "now Madame is going to taste Monsieur Paul's special terrine, one that is not even on the summer menu when a hundred covers are laid here daily and we have a headwaiter and a wine waiter, and cabinet ministers telegraph for tables! Madame will be pleased."

And heedless of my low moans of the walk still before me, of my appreciation and my unhappily human and limited capacity, she cut a thick heady slice from the terrine of meat and stood over me while I ate it, telling me with almost hysterical pleasure of the wild ducks, the spices, the wines that went into it. Even surfeit could not make me deny that it was a rare dish. I ate it all, knowing my luck, and wishing only that I had red wine to drink with it.

I was beginning, though, to feel almost frightened, realizing myself an accidental victim of these stranded gourmets, Monsieur Paul and his handmaiden. I began to feel that they were using me for a safety valve, much as a thwarted woman relieves herself with tantrums or a fit of weeping. I was serving a purpose, and perhaps a noble one, but I resented it in a way approaching panic.

I protested only to myself when one of Monsieur Paul's special cheeses was cut for me, and ate it doggedly, like a slave. When the girl said that Monsieur Paul himself was preparing a special filter of coffee for me, I smiled servile acceptance; wine and the weight of food and my own character could not force me to argue with maniacs. When, before the coffee came, Monsieur Paul presented me, through his idolater, with the most beautiful apple tart I had ever seen, I allowed it to be cut and served to me. Not a wince or a murmur showed the waitress my distressed fearfulness. With a stuffed careful smile on my face, and a clear nightmare in my head of trussed wanderers prepared for his altar by this hermit-priest of gastronomy, I listened to the girl's passionate plea for fresh pastry dough.

"You cannot, you *cannot*, Madame, serve old pastry!" She seemed ready to beat her breast as she leaned across the table. "Look at that delicate crust! You may feel that you have eaten too much." (I nodded idiotic agreement.) "But this pastry is like feathers—it is like snow. It is in fact good for you, a digestive! And why?" She glared sternly at me. "Because Monsieur Paul did not even open the flour bin until he saw you coming! He could not, he *could not* have baked you one of his special apple tarts with old dough!"

She laughed, tossing her head and curling her mouth voluptuously.

IV

Somehow I managed to refuse a second slice, but I trembled under her surmise that I was ready for my special filter.

The wine and the fortitude had fled me, and I drank the hot coffee as a suffering man gulps ether, deeply and gratefully.

I remember, then, chatting with surprising glibness, and sending to Monsieur Paul flowery compliments, all of them sincere and well won, and I remember feeling only amusement when a vast glass of *marc* appeared before me and then gradually disappeared, like the light in the warm room full of water-sounds. I felt surprise to be alive still, and suddenly very grateful to the wild-lipped waitress, as if her presence had sustained me through duress. We discussed food and wine. I wondered bemusedly why I had been frightened.

The *marc* was gone. I went into the crowded bedroom for my jacket. She met me in the darkening hall when I came out, and I paid my bill, a large one. I started to thank her, but she took my hand, drew me into the dining room, and without words poured more spirits into my glass. I drank to Monsieur Paul while she watched me intently, her pale eyes bulging in the dimness and her lips pressed inward as if she too tasted the hot, aged *marc*.

The cat rose from his ferny bed, and walked contemptuously out of the room.

Suddenly the girl began to laugh, in a soft shy breathless way, and came close to me.

"Permit me!" she said, and I thought she was going to kiss me. But instead she pinned a tiny bunch of snowdrops and dark bruised cyclamens against my stiff jacket, very quickly and deftly, and then ran from the room with her head down.

I waited for a minute. No sounds came from anywhere in the old mill, but the endless rushing of the full stream seemed to strengthen, like the timid blare of an orchestra under a falling curtain.

She's a *funny* one, I thought. I touched the cool blossoms on my coat and went out, like a ghost from ruins, across the courtyard toward the dim road to Avallon.

"A Lusty Bit of Nourishment": *Consider the Oyster* (1941); "Define This Word": *The Gastronomical Me* (1943)

Marjorie Kinnan Rawlings

from Cross Creek Cookery

The writings of Marjorie Kinnan Rawlings (1896–1953) are imbued with the textures and flavors of Cross Creek, a partly wild corner of north central Florida where she moved in her early 30s to "deliberately cut her civilized ties." Best known for her novel *The Yearling* (1938) and her memoir *Cross Creek* (1942), Rawlings was an enthusiast for the foodways of her chosen region, and in *Cross Creek Cookery* (1942)–written in response to the unexpectedly wide popularity of *Cross Creek*–she provided a rich blend of recipes and anecdotes.

■ ■ ■

The other day I sat in a hotel with friends, planning a wild Mallard duck dinner menu for their consumption later at Cross Creek. A lieutenant sat nearby. He was introduced, and he confessed that he had overheard our plans.

"I never," he said, "listened to a more *voluptuous* conversation."

My wild duck dinner sounds good, it is good, and I think ruefully that it should be good. It not only costs me as much to feed my flock of wild Mallards as to feed two mules, but it makes me ill to kill them for the table. I should never do it, except that the flock so multiplies each year that I cannot afford to keep them all. Fortunately, there are always far too many drakes, so several times a year, having given away as many as possible to new homes, I serve the excess–reluctantly–to a favored few.

Six years ago I had a gift of a setting of wild Mallard eggs from the Carolina marshes. I hatched them under a hen. The original ten ducklings lived a year in the pen. I could not endure their captivity any longer and turned them loose, expecting them to fly at once to the adjacent marshes of Orange Lake. They refused to leave. They are the lords of my manor, gay, noisy and demanding. The ten grew at one time to seventy, which is a lot of ducks. I try to keep the flock down to twenty-five.

My Mallard dinner is especially good, I think, because of the dishes served with the meat, and because the ducks, from their type of feeding, have a finer flavor than either domestic ducks or truly wild ducks. They have an abundance of skimmed milk and clabber along with their grain and their greens. This tenderizes and lightens the meat. They are fatter than the hunter's wild ducks, but not so fat as market ducks.

I am at violent variance with the school of believers in raw or underdone duck. These insist that well-done duck is bound to be hard and dry. Mine are not. The skin is crisp and crusty, the meat is moist and so tender and yielding that it may be cut with a fork. It melts on the tongue like broiled chicken liver. The ducks must be properly aged—after dressing—from three to five days, without freezing. The flavor needs no embellishment, and I do not even use the conventional onion or celery or apple stuffing. I place them, dressed whole, salted and peppered, breast side up, in a tightly covered roasting pan with an inch of hot water in the pan. The oven is hot, four hundred and fifty degrees, for the first fifteen minutes. The heat is then reduced to three hundred and fifty degrees for the remaining time of cooking. Young ducks will roast in a little over an hour. For old ducks, I allow from two to three hours. They should be basted every fifteen minutes with the liquid in the pan. I allow one-half duck per person. An occasional guest can eat a whole duck, but is not encouraged.

A light, rather acid first course is desirable, such as iced melon with lime juice or baked sherried grapefruit. With the ducks I serve giblet gravy, wild rice, braised whole white onions, tiny cornmeal muffins, carrot soufflé or sweet potato in orange baskets or orange fritters, crisp celery, a tart jelly such as currant, wild grape or wild plum or kumquat, a light green salad, such as endive and water cress, with a trace of minced shallots and a tart French dressing made with Tarragon vinegar, any good dry red wine, preferably Burgundy, and again a light, rather acid dessert, such as tangerine sherbet.

I disremember, as we say at the Creek, just when I began shooting chickens for the table. They were my own chickens. They were, and are, game chickens. The breed suits me to a T, because I like to see them running loose instead of cooped in a pen. They are decorative, they take care of themselves except for scratch feed night and morning, they roost in the orange trees, from which the handsome bronze and red rooster assists the coming of the dawn, and they make frying-size chickens, with large meaty breasts, earlier than any other breed. But they are wild as hawks. When there is a man working on the place, or small pickaninnies visiting, it is rather a lark to run one down for the pot. Spectators cheer.

But a hot summer day found old Martha and me alone, with company coming, and we ran chickens until we dropped from exhaustion, and never touched a feather. I remembered that in Alaska my brother and I shot ruffed grouse with rifles, for the birds would not stir from their perches in distant trees across thick ravines, and, once moved to action, were gone instantly behind impenetrable Alaskan foliage so that a wing shot was out of the question. We needed the meat, and it was entirely sporting and made a difficult long shot to use a rifle and aim for the head or neck. When I got back my breath, I loaded my .22 rifle and potted the necessary broilers through the heads.

Came a day when, from too frequent shooting, I had only to appear in the yard with my .22, to have every chicken on the place scatter for the distant woods. I stalked like a panther. When I came within range, the young rooster I was after moved his head every time I fired. A dignified professor and his haughty wife were coming for dinner. I was desperate. I returned to the house for my shotgun and ignominiously, violating all rules of sportsmanship, brought down my bird. Dinner went off nicely, and the professor's grave face brightened as he bit into the succulent breast of chicken, pan-browned and oven-baked in sherry. There was a grinding noise, the professor blanched, and he removed his mouthful of chicken breast and poked at it with his fork. Two little lead pellets rolled to the plate. If it had been one little lead pellet, I should have insinuated that he had best consult his dentist. There were two. It was one of the cowardly moments in my life. I rang for more wine and asked the professor's opinion on James Joyce. There are, simply, people to whom one can explain that one shoots chickens for the table and people to whom one cannot—

Squab-Size Roast Chicken

I have a favorite way of preparing squab-sized chickens, one to one and one-quarter pounds in weight.

For every small whole chicken, prepare stuffing made of one-third cup of dry bread crumbs, sautéd in one tablespoon of butter, and two tablespoons coarsely broken pecan meats. Stuff chickens (or squabs), roll in salted and peppered flour, brown to a golden color in Dora's butter. Place in a casserole or roaster. Drain off from frying pan all but four to six tablespoons of the cooking butter, according to number of chickens. Add two cups boiling water to remaining fat, stirring well to gather up all the browned particles. Pour over chickens. Add one-quarter cup dry sherry for every chicken. Cover tightly and cook in oven at three hundred and fifty degrees until thoroughly tender, about one to one and one-half hours. It is sometimes necessary to add more hot water, as there should be a thin gravy. Fluffy rice is especially good with this dish.

I prepare quail, doves, rabbit, squirrel and even the coarser cuts of venison in this fashion, especially if the age of the game is uncertain. For doves and quail, one-quarter cup of buttered bread crumbs and one tablespoon of pecan meats for stuffing is sufficient. For rabbit, squirrel and venison I use no stuffing, but increase the quantity of hot water, the resulting gravy to be thickened with a little flour and a little chopped parsley added.

I once even prepared, lacking game, a piece of beef in this manner. The occasion irks me still. My friend Phil May asked to bring his friend, Wallace Stevens, the poet, to dinner at Cross Creek. The great man was on a strict diet, he wrote, and must be served only lean meat, a green salad and fruit. I planned my best baked-in-sherry-ham for the rest of the company, and wracked my brains for a method of making of lean meat a delicacy. I decided to prepare the heart of a Boston pot roast of beef in an individual casserole, with sherry. The poet proved delightful but condescending. He began on his beef, looked over at the clove-stuck ham, and announced that he would partake not only of that, but of all the other rich dishes on the table. His diet, it seemed, was not for purposes of health, but for vanity. He was, simply, reducing. I snatched his sherried beef from him, pulled out the bone and tossed it on the hearth to my pointer dog.

Smother-Fried Quail, Dove, Rabbit, Squirrel

I use this method when the game is of uncertain age. Roll the game in salted and peppered flour. Drop in a Dutch oven or deep iron skillet containing one-quarter inch of butter. Brown on all sides. Almost cover with boiling water. Cover tightly and let simmer over open flame or campfire until meat is meltingly tender. Thicken gravy with flour. More salt will be needed.

Deep-Fried Young Quail or Young Dove

Dip quail or dove in milk. Roll well in salted and peppered flour. Drop in kettle of fat hot enough to brown a cube of bread in sixty seconds. Fry until a chestnut brown. Serve with hot grits and butter.

Pan-Fried Young Quail or Dove

Roll quail or dove in salted and peppered flour. Fry in one-half inch of hot butter until tender, turning once. Make gravy by adding flour to butter, one tablespoon flour to every two tablespoons of butter, and rich milk or thin cream, one cup to every tablespoon of flour. More salt.

My friend Dessie is one of Florida's most expert campers. Given an axe and a gun, she can make a good living in the woods. I once saw her bring down a duck on the wing with a .22 rifle. As a cook, I should be extremely cautious about turning her loose in my kitchen, but on a camp, I should take her say-so as to the cooking of any game dish.

How to Fry Venison
(Dessie)

Cut chops, or backstrap, three-quarters of an inch thick, rub with lemon and sprinkle with flour. In an uncovered Dutch oven or iron skillet melt one tablespoon butter and one tablespoon Crisco. Have pan only medium hot over low coals. Add venison and fry six to ten minutes, turning only once. Salt and pepper when done.

Venison is also delicious broiled like steak. It should be aged.

Dessie also gave me gravely a recipe that she calls "Coot Surprise." My comment was that I should be surprised as all get-out if anybody could eat it. I myself consider coots completely inedible. Even Webster's dictionary backs me up in low-rating coots, and says, "They are stupid, and fly slowly, and can hardly be classed as game birds." I have prepared coots hopefully according to all sorts of varying backwoods advice, and always had to throw them out, with the exception of pilau of rice and coot livers and gizzards.

But there are many, including Dessie, who consider them good. For the curious, experimentally inclined, here is her recipe.

Coot Surprise

Skin coots and rub with salt and lemon juice or vinegar. Let stand overnight. Wash, split in halves, and rub with salt and pepper. Dust with flour. Fry in medium deep hot fat in a covered pan until golden brown. Serve with wild rice and green vegetables or a green salad.

Jugged Rabbit

Cut rabbit in pieces. Place in deep pan and cover with red wine, to which is added one teaspoon whole cloves, one teaspoon all-spice, two bay leaves, one teaspoon whole peppercorns. Let stand in cool place for three days. Drain. Roll in salted and peppered flour. Brown in one-quarter inch butter. Cover with hot water and simmer until tender. More hot water may be necessary. Remove rabbit. Stir in one tablespoon flour dissolved in four tablespoons cold water for every cup of gravy. Add one-half teaspoon salt, dash of pepper. Pour over rabbit. One rabbit serves four to six.

Bear Meat

Bears, once so plentiful in Florida that before 1792 William Bartram wrote, "there are still far too many bears in Florida," are becoming scarce. I see no reason for destroying the remaining ones, since they live so far from any domestic clearing that they are no longer a menace, as formerly, to stock. But I must admit that bear meat at the proper season, and properly cooked, is a delicious meat. A male bear in the mating season, like a boar hog, is not fit to eat. A female nursing bear not only has tough and stringy meat, but for humanitarian reasons should never be destroyed. A young male bear in the off-season provides meat better than the best beef. I should happily settle for a stupid steer, but on the occasions when I have had bear meat in the Big Scrub of Florida, I have enjoyed it thoroughly.

Pot Roast of Bear

Place haunch or chuck of bear meat, salted and peppered, in a covered roasting pan with one inch of hot water and one-quarter cup of melted bear fat. Roast in a hot oven, four hundred to four hundred and fifty degrees, basting every fifteen minutes, until tender, from two to four hours. Remove meat from roaster. Stir in flour and extra salt and pepper to browned fat in pan, and add hot water to make gravy of proper consistency. Serve with hominy grits, boiled onions and swamp cabbage.

Bear Steak

Hang rib steaks of bear as long as possible without spoiling. Brush with salt and pepper and melted bear fat or olive oil. Broil over hot live oak coals about twenty minutes, turning twice. Serve with baked sweet potatoes and cole slaw.

Alligator-Tail Steak

Rattlesnake meat is canned commercially in Florida and served as a delicate hors-d'œuvre. I have never tried it and do not intend to. It is said to taste much like canned tuna. *Chacun à son goût.* Bartram wrote in his famous *Travels* that Governor Grant of Florida had a passion for rattlesnake meat "if the snake had not bit himself," but Bartram, as I should have done, "tasted of the meat but could not swallow it."

Steak from the tail of an alligator is another matter. It is truly delicious. It is like liver or veal (which it resembles in texture and coloring) in that it must be cooked very quickly or a very long time. In between, it toughens. Cut strips lengthwise of the tail, four inches long and two inches wide, or cut cross-sections between the vertebræ. Roll in salted and peppered flour and fry quickly in butter. It may also be browned in the butter, hot water and the juice of a lemon added, and simmered for two to two and one-half hours until tender.

A woman wrote me from Mississippi that she and her twelve-year-old son, a great hunter, had read my chapter on foods in *Cross Creek*. A few days later, the young man came on an eight-foot alligator in a Mississippi swamp, and horrified her by dragging it home for her to cook the tail. She wrote that at the moment she was torn between attempting it, and burying the alligator, to face her young son's wrath.

Cross Creek Cookery (1942)

Samuel Chamberlain

from Clémentine in the Kitchen

Originally serialized in the fledgling *Gourmet* magazine, *Clémentine in the Kitchen* (1943) is a lightly fictionalized account of one American family's love affair with French food. After more than 12 years in France, the artist and printmaker Samuel Chamberlain (1895–1975), his wife, Narcissa, and their two daughters were forced by the outbreak of war to return home. Unwilling to break their ties with French cuisine, they took with them their cook, Gabrielle, who then faced the problem of re-creating her native cooking with the materials available in Marblehead, Massachusetts. *Clémentine in the Kitchen* remains a book of immense charm.

■ ■ ■

Clémentine had a lot of adjusting to do before she became reconciled to the way food is purveyed in a small Yankee seaport. She was endlessly perplexed by the myriad of gaudy packages with peppy names in the grocery store. She was puzzled by Mr. Wilcox, the butcher, who never had any veal and who refused bluntly to cut up his sides of beef the way they do in France. Why did the *pâtisseries* sell pots of baked beans on Saturday night, she wanted to know. The corner drug store, nine-tenths of whose space was given over to a magazine stand, a soda fountain, and cigars, cosmetics and pin ball machines, left her totally bewildered. If you could see the funereal little *pharmacie* back in our French town, with two large snakes pickled in alcohol as the only window decoration, you would understand why Clémentine was dismayed, if dazzled. Once on her Thursday off the exploring Clémentine wandered into Jerry's Diner, which happens to be the headquarters of all the high school hep cats. To the accompaniment of "The Jumpin' Jive" on the juke box and the raucous shouts of the exuberant "alligators," she had her evening meal, and came home a shaken woman. It takes a little time for a full-fledged Burgundian to become adjusted to the tempo of Tommy Dorsey.

But *one* local institution was pitched precisely to Clémentine's old world viewpoint—the fish store of Mr. Job Stacy. Repeated coats of white paint, inside and out, could not disguise the antiquity of Stacy's Fish Shop, installed in a low frame building which resembled a pure Cape Cod cottage. Back in the '70s Job's grandfather had cut a many-paned shop window in the street façade of the house, and established the business. Job and his brothers (who do most of the fishing), inherited it as a matter of course. Job takes charge of the shop and his brothers, who are distinctly less personable and given to Saturday night bacchanals, preside at the picturesque old fishermen's shack at the water's edge, where the nets, lobster pots and Newbury-port rum are stored.

There is no hint of pretension in Stacy's Fish Shop. The window contains the same exhibition of giant sea shells, coral curiosities, mounted lobsters and stuffed fish which has been there for years. Once you are inside you will observe a Spartan exhibit of cod liver oil, flanked by a few wooden boxes of salted cod filets and a lonely squad of catsup bottles. Clean sawdust is on the floor. Before you is a small white marble counter, covered with chopped ice which all but conceals a few freshly-caught haddock and cod. That is all you see as you enter Mr. Stacy's shop, except a blackboard. It isn't impressive. But there is one hint that indisputable treasures are concealed in icy bins in the back room. It is that blackboard upon which Job lavishes a fine Spencerian flourish. When the gastronomically-minded Beck family studied this handsome document for the first time, a ray of pure rapture burst through the clouds. We began to realize our enormous good fortune in choosing this small New England seaport as a home. For Job Stacy lists upon his blackboard an almost Utopian stock of freshly-caught fish. He has haddock, mackerel and young cod at excursion rates. And there are handsome butterfish, rock bass, perch and bluefish. He has filets of cusk, plaice and flounder, besides smoked filets and finnan haddie of unimpeachable integrity. His bins hide an ample supply of halibut, swordfish and salmon. He has clams—soft-shelled ones for steaming, Cherrystones for appetizers and, for your chowder, ponderous Quohaugs. He has oysters—Bluepoints, Cotuits and Narragansetts. His lobsters are so alive they are frisky, but he has lobster meat if you prefer it. In season you can find tender young soft-shelled crabs, or you can have shrimps or crabmeat at any time. He has not only the large sea scallops but those rarities of the American *gourmandise*, small Cape scallops as well.

It was natural that Clémentine should share our enthusiasm, once we introduced her to Mr. Stacy and his well-stocked back room. Here was a shop that reminded her of France, and of the amiable Monsieur Chollet who used to sell us *merlan, turbot* and *sole.* Clémentine began to pay almost daily visits to Mr. Stacy's shop, chattering affably in French, a language which he obviously did not understand, until she finally thawed out his Yankee reserve very perceptibly. Meanwhile the Beck family saw the beginning of a dream come true. Our table became beautified with the freshest of Atlantic fish, cooked as a French *Cordon Bleu* would do it.

Here I would like to share our good fortune with you by tearing a few leaves from Clémentine's well-thumbed notebook. There is nothing brilliantly original about any of these recipes. They merely follow the old French fundamentals. But to judge by the comments of our dinner guests, they have opened up a new vista to at least a few New England hostesses. And since they can be achieved rather easily in an American home, we hope that they merit your sympathetic consideration.

Clémentine's approach to the problem of preparing New England fish was refreshing and direct. It never occurred to her to fry fish in deep fat. Fried scallops, fried oysters, fried clams, fried "filet of sole"—the inevitable vocabulary of the restaurant cook in these parts had not become a part of her culinary jargon—and we were just as glad. Clémentine took the simplest and most obvious French path—which was to bake this clean, salt-water fish in white wine with mushrooms. The unassuming haddock and baby cod take on surprising distinction when prepared in this rudimentary manner:

Haddock au Vin Blanc

Place the cleaned fish in a flat baking dish (porcelain, glass or earthenware) with butter, thinly sliced mushrooms and a few small onions. Add salt, pepper, a bay leaf and a sprig of thyme. Sprinkle with bread crumbs and dot with butter. Pour a generous glass of dry white wine in the baking dish and cook in a medium oven until tender, basting now and then. Serve with steamed potatoes and a trickle of lemon juice.

The French cook dorade, pike, sole, flounder and many another fish in this way. An utterly simple recipe, it lends itself to many of our own fish, from fresh and salt waters, and it has the potential power to improve conjugal harmony in American households by at least 3 per cent, especially if the fish is served with a worthy dry white wine.

Scallops are a favorite stand-by in New England, where I'll wager that not one in fifty escapes being fried in deep fat. A few are doubtless broiled on skewers between squares of bacon and served with a *Maître d'Hôtel* sauce. Those are the 50-to-1 shots. Yet Madame Prunier lists fifteen other ways to cook them. Clémentine was impressed when Mr. Stacy delivered a pound of scallops all cleaned and removed from their shells. But she missed the flat shells, which are essential to her method of cooking them. We rescued a dozen or more shells from the Stacy shack by the sea, and Clémentine proceeded with her old familiar *Coquilles St. Jacques au Gratin*, the classic French way of preparing scallops. A few American cook books cite variations of this dish. André Simon and Jeanne Owen both give fine versions, but most of the other books ignore the basic recipe. So here it is, translated from Edouard de Pomiane's amusing brochure, *Le Carnet d'Anna:*

Coquilles St. Jacques au Gratin

Wash sea scallops in cold water and cut each in four pieces. Place them in a casserole and cover with dry white wine. For four servings, add six shallots finely chopped and a quarter of a pound of thinly sliced mushrooms. Allow to boil for ten minutes. Salt slightly and add pepper. Place the scallops in four scallop shells, powder with fine bread crumbs and grated Swiss cheese. Brown in the oven and serve in the shell, very hot.

The same basic recipe can be applied to any firm white fish, and is excellent for dressing up leftovers. Small individual baking dishes can be substituted for the shells, of course, and small onions can replace the shallots. Clémentine carries the same basic idea a little further in a recipe which she has adapted from an obscure French cook book. So much of her own creative ability is shown in this dish that we have always referred to it as "Clémentine's Flounder." It is something of a show piece, yet its ingredients are so simple that it can be achieved by any good cook near a fish store or a frozen foods counter. It works as handsomely with frozen filets of perch as with Job Stacy's freshly-caught flounder. Here it is, and we feel certain you are going to like it, once you try it:

Clémentine's Flounder

For 6 people, select 6 medium-sized flounders, or 12 corresponding filets. Salt the filets slightly, dip in milk, then in flour, and brown lightly on both sides in butter. Place in a long, shallow baking dish.

Dice 6 large scallops and place in a casserole with: butter the size of an egg, a half pound of minced mushrooms (not peeled), a few pinches of herbs, (parsley, tarragon, chives, chervil), a section of garlic, a shallot and a medium-sized onion (all minced), salt and pepper. Cook on a brisk fire for 5 minutes, then slowly for 10 or 15 minutes, stirring often, by which time the water has evaporated. Cover the filets with this savory mixture.

If you have saved the heads and bones of your fish, boil them, strain the liquid and use it as a base for the fairly thick Béchamel sauce which is next on the program. Mix 1 ounce of grated Swiss cheese, 1 ounce of grated Parmesan cheese and half a pint of thick cream with the sauce. Pour this sauce on top of your dish. Add a few dabs of butter, sprinkle lightly with grated cheese and brown in the oven until the juice has reduced by a third. Serve in the baking dish.

If there were space for only two of Clémentine's master fish recipes, the Beck family would be unanimous in choosing this one and Lobster Delmonico for the honor. The latter dish was Clémentine's triumph for the winter. We had the temerity to serve it to a few native sons and daughters of this old seaport town, where there are only two ways to cook lobster. You either boil 'em or you broil 'em, that's all there is to it. But this seraphic dish won our friends over to *la cuisine française* completely, and we think it will enrapture the readers of this book as well. It is adapted from the recipe of Monsieur Baccou, formerly chef of the Restaurant Marguery in Paris. The counterpoint of its two sauces, one with the rich savor of old Port wine, the other an absolutely delicious cream sauce, is superb with the fragrant lobster meat and dry rice. It's extravagant, and perhaps you had better postpone it for the duration. But *some* day try

Lobster Delmonico

For eight persons: 4 lobsters weighing 1 ½ to 2 pounds each; a pint and a half of thick fresh cream; the yolks of 6 eggs; a half pint of good Port wine.

Cooking of the Lobsters. Prepare a *court-bouillon* consisting of a bottle of dry white wine, the same quantity of water, salt, pepper in crushed grains, minced carrots and onions, parsley, thyme and bay leaf. Allow this to cook for 30 minutes. Plunge the live lobsters in the *court-bouillon*, which should be boiling vigorously, and cook for 20 minutes.

Remove the lobsters, and allow to cool. Detach the tail, remove the shell and cut the meat in thick slices. Also remove the large pieces of meat from the claws. Melt butter the size of an egg in a *plat à sauter*, in which you align the pieces of lobster meat. Salt slightly, heat and add a half pint of good Port wine. Allow to cook down slightly. Light the Port with a match, if it is strong enough in alcohol, and allow it to burn out. Then keep hot until time to serve.

The Sauce. Make a *liaison* with fresh cream, 6 yolks of egg, salt, a spot of Cayenne and cook in a double boiler. Stir in gently, piece by piece, a third of a pound of butter, and add lobster roe, if there is any. Serve very hot in a sauce dish.

With the lobster and its two sauces serve dry white boiled rice and, if you want the occasion to be flawless, a glistening Montrachet.

We have always considered these two dishes to be Clémentine's master-pieces of fish cooking, but her biggest piscatorial (or should I say Crustacean) thrill came entirely by accident. On Sunday afternoons she was in the habit of taking long bicycle rides to satisfy her curiosity about this strange new land. The Sunday motorists often stuck their heads out of their car windows and laughed at her, for reasons which mystified her, but she didn't mind.

She returned from one such expedition livid with excitement, and called elatedly to my wife, "*Madame! J'ai trouvé des moules! Des quantités de moules!*" It wasn't the first time that Clémentine had appeared with such news. We all remembered the snails she had discovered in our French garden—and rushed into the kitchen. Wrapped up in somebody's Sunday newspaper were great clusters of small, purplish-black mussels. Clémentine had pedaled far that day, to a rocky promontory jutting out into the Atlantic. Seated on the rocks and watching the waves break at low tide, she suddenly saw something to thrill her thrifty Burgundian soul—great patches of perfectly good mussels, the very same kind of mussels they serve in Prunier's in Paris. Clémentine could conceive of only one course of conduct—to gather several handfuls of these toothsome mollusks at once, wondering in the meantime why they were ignored by all the other Sunday trippers. When the Beck family sat down to great heaping soup plates full of *Moules à la Marinière* the next day, we wondered too.

And, my good New England neighbors, especially you in the State of Maine, something ought to be *done* about this! Quantities of these delicate and absolutely delicious mussels cling to the rocks on your jagged shore! Some of them are within the range of oil refineries, glue factories, creosote mills and disposal plants, and are entirely inedible. But others cling to the clean rocks in bountiful patches, washed only by pure sea water. Your ancestors realized that mussels, when properly washed and steamed, were a dish which any gourmet would cherish. There is a fine old Yankee recipe for mussels dating back to 1763. Why do you fishermen of Maine scorn them now, or use them for bait, rather than exploit them for the multitude of voluptuaries who would welcome them in the markets? Listen to this simple bourgeois French recipe for mussels, gentlemen, and try it some cold winter evening. Perhaps then you will send more of your long-overlooked treasure to the big city markets.

Moules à la Marinière
(A Peasant Version)

Brush and scrape the mussel shells, and wash in several waters, clipping the "beard" with a knife. (Maybe this laborious procedure is the reason mussels aren't popular.) Place 2 quarts of mussels in a pan, add 4 or 5 sections of garlic chopped fine, a good fistful of minced parsley, a little freshly ground pepper and 2 ounces of butter. Salt is not needed. Cover the pan, place over a brisk fire and cook for 5 or 6 minutes, shaking the pan 2 or 3 times. Remove the lid. The mussels are open, ready to be served with the sauce in soup plates.

We await your reaction, gentlemen, with genuine eagerness.

Clémentine in the Kitchen (1943)

Jerre Mangione

from Mount Allegro

In his memoir *Mount Allegro* (1943), Jerre Mangione (1909–1998) looks back on his early life in Rochester, New York's, "Little Sicily" with great warmth and humor; his fondly detailed recollections of family feasts conjure up a lost world. If his account hints at some of the ways in which authentic Italian cooking was transformed on these shores into an Italian-American hybrid—cottage cheese takes the place of a proper ricotta in his father's much-prized cannoli, and the venison, pheasant, and rabbit that might have been served in the old country yield here to the available beef, lamb, and chicken—his intense nostalgia is also a powerful argument for the preservation of Italian traditions. Any food that sounds *this* good ought to be worth going to some trouble for—and indeed, the otherwise "assimilated" children, grandchildren, and further descendants of Italian immigrants continue to this day to rediscover and celebrate their culinary heritage.

■ ■ ■

Great-Uncle Minicuzzu and my Uncles Luigi and Nino were avid guests at nearly every banquet my father gave. They flanked him on both sides at the table, like the disciples of Christ at the Last Supper, and they partook of his wine and cooking as though each meal were their last one.

There was a banquet for as many occasions as my father could imagine, and his imagination was fertile. He once gave a banquet for some relatives who were moving to California and, when they were suddenly obliged to change their plans, he gave another banquet to celebrate their staying. He no sooner had finished with one banquet than he began to talk about the next one. He had the pride of an artist in his cooking, particularly his pastrymaking, and he never denied the story that when the Baron Michele, the richest man in the province of Girgenti, went on his honeymoon to Palermo, he took my father along to prepare his favorite desserts.

He was especially noted for a Sicilian delicacy called *cannolo*, which was unsurpassed by any of the other pastrycooks in Rochester and seldom equaled even in New York and Palermo. As a boy he had been apprenticed to a famous Sicilian pastrycook and he learned his trade well. He might have become a celebrated pastrymaker had he remained in Sicily, but here in America, the land of ice-cream and pie, there was not enough of a market for his products and he became another factory worker, expressing his real talents on holidays and other occasions when he could give banquets for his friends and relatives.

Although his *cannoli* were masterpieces, his recipe for making them was no secret and he willingly itemized it for anyone who wanted to attempt it. Needless to say, no one ever approached his results, though several of his more determined imitators came to his kitchen to watch every move and measurement he made. The ingredients were simple: cottage cheese refined to a smooth paste; tiny bits of chocolate mixed into the paste, and a few drops of a magical spirit known as *cannela* (a liquid cinnamon), whose sharp odor recurs to me with fully as many memories as a cup of tea ever gave Proust. The trick, my father claimed, was not so much in concocting the cream as in preparing the crisp, cylindrical shells that held it.

Like most good art, the *cannoli* looked simple but entailed much more work than would seem necessary to a layman. So that he would have no distractions, my father often started making his *cannoli* at three in the morning. Until dawn, he hovered over the shells like an anxious mother, nursing them to their proper crispness. After the shells were done, there were almonds to be roasted and crushed into golden crumbs that would be sprinkled over the ends of the *cannoli* once they were filled with cream. And always there had to be perfect timing. Judging from the amount of patience *cannoli* required and the small amount my father usually showed, he must have saved a little patience every day so that he would have enough to make his *cannoli* once or twice a year.

The more enthusiasts his *cannoli* bred, the less inclined he was to make them. His explanation was that since he did not have time to make *cannoli* for all his friends and relatives, he would make them for no one but his immediate family. When occasionally he broke this rule, our house would take on the atmosphere of a secret underground society.

My father would solemnly warn us not to tell anyone he was making *cannoli* and, when they were finished, he would count them out carefully into empty shoe-boxes he hoarded for such occasions and sneak them to favored relatives and friends, the right number for each family, begging them not to say a word about the gift to anyone lest someone take offense at being left out.

He never took money for his *cannoli* and would be hurt if anyone tried to pay him. Once he opened a pastry shop and featured *cannoli* as his specialty. For a few months business seemed good; many Sicilians bought many *cannoli*. Yet my father made no money. It was not until he closed the shop that he realized he had failed to charge enough to cover the cost of the ingredients.

In those few months he was in business scores of new *cannoli* addicts were born and, ever afterward, they telephoned hopefully a week before an important holiday like Christmas or Easter to ask if Don Peppino would make a few dozen *cannoli* for them. He enjoyed answering the telephone at such times, even though his answer was usually No, for like any good artist it heartened him to know that his product was still appreciated and in demand.

As temperamental as he was, my father could be relied on to assume responsibility for cooking all Sunday dinners. This sometimes involved preparing at least a half-dozen courses for as many as twenty persons. To show her gratitude, my mother gladly took charge of such details as serving and dishwashing and, when she was certain there were enough guests listening, she complimented him extravagantly not only on his abilities as a cook but also as a carpenter and a paperhanger.

We were all aware of the strategy behind her flattery, yet we realized that she sincerely believed him to be the best cook on earth. When they teased each other, my mother would declare that it was only because of his cooking skill that she had married him, whereupon my father would retort that she could be sure that was not the reason he had married her.

On Sunday mornings he rose earlier than the rest of us and took complete charge of the kitchen, using my mother and one of the children for the menial jobs of peeling, grating, and slicing. His meals had an extravagance about them that was far out of proportion to his salary. To finance them he often had to borrow money. But for him that was less important than sharing the joy and warmth that good food and gay company created.

Like the rest of my relatives, he believed implicitly in the goodness of food and liked to repeat the motto: "Food is the only thing you can take with you when you die." This was not said in any morbid sense, but as encouragement for more eating. If a guest had the temerity to turn down another helping of food, the motto was sprung on him with great gusto if it was obvious that the guest's eating capacity had not yet reached its limits (the guest, of course, was never permitted to decide for himself what those limits might be), and as a polite rebuke if it was clear to the host that his guest could not eat another morsel of food without bursting. My relatives' passionate faith in food as a soul and body builder was, in the last analysis, an expression of their philosophy. If you ate well, you felt well. And if you felt well, all was well with the world.

For weekday suppers a soup course, some spaghetti and meat, followed by a salad, was an ample meal. But on Sundays and holidays it was assumed that your appetite became gargantuan and, besides soup and salad, you were expected to stow away at least three different courses of meat, four or five vegetables, along with celery and fennel, all topped off with pastry, fruits, and nuts.

One of my father's meat courses was usually *brusciuluna*, a combination of Roman cheese, salami, and moon-shaped slivers of hard-boiled egg encased in rolls of beef that had been pounded into tenderness. All this was held together by an engineering feat involving many strings and toothpicks. The other meats served were chicken (two kinds usually—boiled chicken, from which the soup had been made—and roast chicken), lamb, and veal. I daresay that if deer meat, pheasant, and rabbit had been more easily available, they would have been served too.

The accompaniment to all this eating was bread and wine. They went with every meal, as inevitably as a theme runs through a song. You drank wine with everything except the soup—though there were those like my Great-Uncle Minicuzzu and Rosario Alfano who liked to drink wine even with their soup, and were fond of repeating the ancient Sicilian boast that they could drink wine even while riding in a cart bumping over a country road.

Bread was eaten with every course, except with such other flour products as spaghetti and pastry. It would have been considered redundant eating bread with them. My relatives, like all Sicilians, had a deep-seated reverence for bread, and they transferred it to their children to such an extent that none of us, even to this day, can eat food without bread and not feel guilty. It was considered sinful to waste bread, or to permit a loaf of bread to sit upside down, or to eat meat without eating bread. One of the most hospitable gestures a host could make during his campaign to gorge a guest with food was to give his guest permission to eat his meat without bread. Once that permission was granted, no risk of sinning was incurred.

Aside from its traditional association with the body of Christ, bread to my relatives was a daily reminder of the hardships they and their ancestors had endured to survive, a symbol of man's humbleness. They regarded bread as some God-bequeathed friend who would keep their bodies and souls together when nothing else would. And when times were bad, they said to each other, "As long as God grants us a piece of bread, we shall get along."

Possibly because Sicilians, more than any other group of Italians, have suffered greatly in their struggle for existence, their attachment to bread and what it symbolized was stronger and they put their best efforts into making it. They made it finer and tastier than any other Italian bread. They sprinkled sesame seeds over it and wrought it into a dozen different designs expressing their love of life and fear of the Devil. They made loaves with replicas of flowers on them, loaves formed like a woman's braided tresses, loaves to look like giant amulets, and loaves shaped the way you would shape your hand if you met up with the evil eye. The most common kind was the loaf with three gashes cut into its top—a warning to the Devil of what might happen to him if he tried to interfere with the goodness of God.

The only bread that had a finer texture was the bread that was prepared in honor of Saint Joseph on his birthday. It was firmer and sweeter than everyday bread and as fancy as bread could be without being pastry. My relatives knew of no greater culinary tribute to pay a saint. So closely was this bread associated with Saint Joseph that eating it made me feel a little like a cannibal; as much as I liked its taste, I was always careful not to bite into the bread too hard.

Next to bread and wine, *pasta* was the most cherished of foods. My relatives agreed that no matter how much food a man ate, he could not satisfy his appetite if his main meal did not include some form of *pasta*. This might be in the form of noodles or spaghetti served with sauces of butter, or oil and garlic, or *suco* made from meat and tomatoes. If you got bored with noodles or spaghetti, you had the choice of a score of different shapes of macaroni with as many different names, including butterflies, angels' hair, stars, little worms, sparrows' tongues, and big cannons.

If my father knew in advance that his guests were to include a couple who were expected to announce their engagement, he would advertise the situation by serving a tubular macaroni about three inches long known as *mezzo-zittu*, which means half-engaged. And if the couple were already engaged and about to be married, the macaroni he served was *zittu* (engaged), almost twice the size of *mezzo-zittu*. This was about as far as a Sicilian's sense of delicacy would permit him to go. Once they were married, such suggestive symbols were considered superfluous and any kind of macaroni would do.

Mount Allegro: A Memoir of Italian American Life (1943)

S. J. Perelman

Avocado, or the Future of Eating

Sometimes, when scanning the litanies of geographical derivation, cooking lessons, and animal-husbandry disclaimers that are printed with the names of dishes on a menu, I think of this lampoon of the all-natural claims on the menu of a drugstore lunch counter in Los Angeles, one of the countless small comic masterpieces that S. J. Perelman (1904–1979) created for *The New Yorker* over many decades. Ice cream with no "fillers"? Perelman thinks not. Syrups made from cane sugar and real fruits? "If that's a boast, I must say it's a pretty hollow one. . . ."

■ ■ ■

(Note found in an empty stomach off Santa Barbara)
One day not long ago in Los Angeles I found myself, banderillas in hand, facing the horns of a dilemma. I had gone into a Corn Exchange bank to exchange some corn and had fallen into conversation with the manager. He was very affable and insisted I inspect the assets of the branch, which included, among other things, the teeth Bryant Washburn had used in his film career. Issuing into the hot sunlight of the street, I was dismayed to find that it was time for lunch, and since I had forgotten to bring along a bag of pemmican, I would have to eat in Los Angeles—a fairly exact definition of the term "the kiss of death." I looked around me. On my left I could obtain a duplexburger and a Giant Malted Milk Too Thick For a Straw; on my right the feature was barbecued pork fritters and orangeade. Unnerved, I stopped a passing street Arab and courteously inquired where I might find a cheap but clean eating house. Phil the Fiddler (for it was he) directed my steps to a pharmacy bearing the legend "Best Drug Stores, Inc." Merely for the record, I dined off an avocado sandwich on whole wheat and a lime rickey, and flunked my basal-metabolism test later that afternoon. I don't pretend to blame the management for my physical shortcomings; all I want them to do is laugh off their menu, a copy of which I seem to have before me.

In general, "Soda Fountain Suggestions" (Best Drug Stores, Inc.) is an attractively printed job in two colors (three if you count the gravy), and though it can hardly hope to rival the success of *Gone with the Wind*, I suppose there is an audience which will welcome it. The salads and three-decker sandwiches are treated with a certain gaiety and quaint charm which recall *Alice of Old Vincennes.* The banana splits and hot-and-cold Ovaltines are handled with a glib humor in the text, which is more than I can say for the way they are handled behind the fountain. The day I was there, a simply appalling oath escaped the lips of one of the dispensers when he dropped some fudge on his shoe. The authors have included a very disarming foreword short enough to quote in its entirety: "It is our earnest desire to fulfill the name that we have chosen for our chain, THE BEST. We can only accomplish this by serving you best. Any criticisms or suggestions will be appreciated by the management." Only a churl would decline so graceful a gambit. *Messieurs, en garde!*

Specifically, gentlemen, my criticism concerns that cocky little summary of yours at the bottom of the menu. "BEST Soda Fountains," you proclaim flatly, "are BEST because: the ice creams contain no 'fillers' (starch, albumen, etc.); the syrups are made from cane sugar and real fruits; the coffee is a special blend made the modern Silex way with a specially filtered water," and so forth. Lest some of the younger boys in the troop think the millennium has come to the City of Our Lady, Queen of the Angels, what are the facts?

In the first place, you needn't think you can woo me with any such tinsel as "the ice creams contain no 'fillers' (starch, albumen, etc.)." One thing I'll have in my ice cream or it's no dice—and that's fillers. I don't even insist on ice cream as long as I can stuff myself with fillers. You heap my plate with albumen and starch (any kind, even laundry starch) and stand clear. Call me a piggy if you want to, but I just can't get *enough* of that starch.

Quite honestly, your statement that the syrups "are made from cane sugar and real fruits" surprised me. If that's a boast, I must say it's a pretty hollow one. It might interest you to know that back in 1917 the Allied High Command specified *beet* sugar and *false* fruits in all syrups purchased by its commissary department. Didn't know that, did you? Probably too busy evading the draft at the time. Well, you just ask any biochemist his recommendation on sugars, as I did recently; you'll get the same terse answer:

beet sugar and false fruits. I have this cousin of mine who is a perfect wiz at chemistry—really astonishing marks for a boy of nineteen in high school—and no matter what you ask him, he'll give you the same answer: beet sugar and false fruits. Frankly, the family's getting a little worried about it; they have to keep Benny chained to a ring in the floor most of the time.

Furthermore, it's useless to try to creep into my heart with any blandishments like "the coffee is a special blend made the modern Silex way with a specially filtered water." Filtering Los Angeles water robs it of its many nourishing ingredients, not the least of which is chow mein. It is an interesting fact, known to anybody who has ever been interned in that city or its suburbs, that the water possesses a rich content of subgum almond chow mein, Cantonese style, and one or two cases have even been reported where traces of peanut candy and lichee nuts were found. The assertion of a friend of mine that he once saw an Irish houseboy come out of a water faucet, of course, must be regarded as apocryphal. The Irish are a wiry little people, but they are not as wiry as all that. Nor are they ready as yet for the self-government which my distinguished opponents, the gentlemen of the affirmative, claim they should have. And so, honorable judges and ladies and gentlemen, we of the negative conclude that the Irish should not be given their independence because (1) we need them for a coaling station, (2) there is a high percentage of illiteracy, and (3) if we do, Ireland will soon be snatching up Guam—or "chewing Guam," so to speak. I thank you.

Crazy Like a Fox (1944)

Betty MacDonald

That Infernal Machine, the Pressure Cooker

Betty MacDonald (1907–1958) had little idea what she was in for when she allowed her husband to persuade her to go into the poultry business in the Pacific Northwest. Her difficulties in adjusting to rural life—and to married life—became the basis for her first book, *The Egg and I* (1945), a surprise best seller that spawned not only a movie version but a whole series of movies featuring the incidental characters Ma and Pa Kettle. MacDonald's humor has a sharp edge, evident in this passage where the perils of late-summer canning reveal a deeper vein of marital tension.

■ ■ ■

Toward the end of June when the cougar episode had cooled somewhat, Bob and I made several early morning pilgrimages to the abandoned farm and picked five gallons of wild blackberries—and the canning season was on. How I dreaded it! Jelly, jam, preserves, canned raspberries, blackcaps, peas, spinach, beans, beets, carrots, blackberries, loganberries, wild blackberries, wild raspberries, applesauce, tomatoes, peaches, pears, plums, chickens, venison, beef, clams, salmon, rhubarb, cherries, corn, pickles and prunes. By fall the pantry shelves would groan and creak under nature's bounty and the bitter thing was that we wouldn't be able to eat one tenth of it. Canning is a mental quirk just like any form of hoarding. First you plant too much of everything in the garden; then you waste hours and hours in the boiling sun cultivating; then you buy a pressure cooker and can too much of everything so that it won't be wasted.

Frankly I don't like home-canned anything, and I spent all of my spare time reading up on botulism. Bob, on the other hand, was in the thing heart and soul. He stepped into the pantry, which was larger than most kitchens, and exhibited pure joy at the row on row of shining jars. And I couldn't even crack his complacency when I told him that, although the Hickses were at the time using year before last's canned beef, they were busily preparing to can another one hundred and fifty quarts. Women in that country were judged not by their bulging sweaters, but by their bulging pantries. Husbands unashamedly threw open their pantry doors and dared you to have more of anything.

I reminded Bob, as I began hauling out jars, lids, sugar and the pressure cooker, that the blackberries of the summer before tasted like little nodules of worsted and we still had twenty-five quarts. But he was adamant and so "Heigh-ho and away we go"—the summer canning was on.

I crouched beneath the weight of an insupportable burden every time I went out to the garden. Never have I come face to face with such productivity. Pea vines pregnant with bulging pods; bean poles staggering under big beans, middle-sized beans, little beans and more blossoms; carrots with bare shoulders thrust above the ground to show me they were ready; succulent summer squash and zucchini where it seemed only a matter of an hour ago there were blossoms; and I picked a water bucket full of cherries from *one* lower branch of the old-fashioned late cherry tree that shaded the kitchen.

There was more of everything than we could ever use or preserve and no way to absorb the excess. I tried sending vegetables to our families, but the freight rates and ferry fares and time involved (plus the fact that Seattle has superb waterfront vegetable markets) made this seem rather senseless. I sent great baskets of produce to the Kettles, but with Paw on the road every day imploring the farmers to give him anything they couldn't use, even they had too much. I picked peas and took a shopping bag full to Mrs. Kettle, and was embarrassed and annoyed to find two bushel baskets of them sitting on the back porch, covered with swarms of little flies and obviously rotting. There was no market for this excess since the market gardeners supplied the neighboring towns. I became so conscience stricken by the waste that of my own volition I canned seventy-five quarts of string beans and too late noticed that the new farm journal carried a hair-raising account of the deaths from botulism from eating home-canned string beans.

Birdie Hicks took all the blue ribbons at the county fair for canning. She evidently stayed up all night during the summer and early fall to can, for she would come to call on me at seven-fifteen, crisp and combed and tell me—as her sharp eyes noted that I still had the breakfast dishes and the housework to do, the baby to bathe and feed and my floor to scrub before I could get at my canning—that she had just finished canning thirty-six quarts of corn on the cob, twenty-five quarts of tomatoes, eighty-two quarts of string beans and a five-gallon crock of dill pickles. She canned her peaches in perfect halves, stacked in the jars like the pictures in the canning book. They were perfectly beautiful, but tasted like glue. She canned her tomatoes whole and they came out of the jars firm and pretty, but tasted like nothing. Mother had taught me to put a couple of pits and a little brown sugar with my peaches; plenty of clove, onion and finely chopped celery with tomatoes—and anyway, I like the flavor of open-kettle canned fruit and tomatoes.

By the end of the summer the pullets were laying and Bob was culling the flocks. With no encouragement from me, he decided that, as chicken prices were way down, I should can the culled hens. It appeared to my warped mind that Bob went miles and miles out of his way to figure out things for me to put in jars; that he actively resented a single moment of my time which was not spent eye to pressure gauge, ear to steam cock; that he was forever coming staggering into the kitchen under a bushel basket of something for me to can. My first reaction was homicide, then suicide, and at last tearful resignation.

When he brought in the first three culled hens, I acidly remarked that it wasn't only the cooker which operated under pressure. No answer.

Later, because of my remark, he said that I did it on purpose. I didn't, I swear, but I did feel that God had at last taken pity on me—for the pressure cooker blew up. It was the happiest day of my life, though I might have been killed. A bolt was blown clear through the kitchen door, the walls were dotted with bits of wing and giblet, the floor was swimming in gravy, and the thick cast aluminum lid broke in two and hit the ceiling with such force it left two half moon marks above Stove. I was lyrical with joy. I didn't know how it happened and I cared less. I was free! *Free!* F-R-E-E! After supper as I went humming about the house picking pieces of chicken off the picture frames and from the mirror in the bedroom, Bob eyed me speculatively. Then he picked up the Sears, Roebuck catalogue and began looking for a bigger, quicker and sturdier variety of pressure cooker.

The Egg and I (1945)

4 cups flour
2 cups water
1 bunch scallions, chopped fine

Knead the flour and water into a soft dough and then divide into 6 portions. Roll each portion with a rolling pin into a cake of about 1 foot in diameter. Spread

2 tb-sp. chopped scallion
1 tb-sp. lard or vegetable oil
1/2 t-sp. salt

over each cake. Roll up each cake (as you would roll up a carpet) and then twist into a standing spiral, like a fattened water-heater. With the rolling pin, flatten the spiral from top down into a cake of about 1/2 foot in diameter.

Melt 1 tb-sp. of lard or vegetable oil in a deep frying pan. Put in the cake, apply cover, and fry for 2 min. on each side over a medium fire. Turn to a low fire and fry for 3 more min. on each side (that is, 10 min. altogether for each cake) until the outside of the cake has turned light brown, while the inside is still soft. Cut each into six pieces as you do a pie and serve hot.

Fried scallion cake, when properly made, at once takes away that hungry feeling. Sometimes one cake with soup makes a good hearty meal. Millet congee, if you can get millet, is even better than soup.

Buwei Yang Chao, *How to Cook and Eat in Chinese* (1945)

How to Cook and Eat in Chinese was a pioneering book that brought the term "stir-frying" into common use.

Ogden Nash

The Strange Case of Mr. Palliser's Palate

Ogden Nash (1902–1971) wrote enduringly popular light verse that is striking for its formal inventiveness and rhythmic precision. Here the vocabulary of haute cuisine provides him with an occasion for bravura rhyming, in a little tale whose grisly ending hangs on a devilish bit of punning.

■ ■ ■

Once there was a man named Mr. Palliser and he asked his wife, May I be a
    gourmet?
And she said, You sure may,
But she also said, If my kitchen is going to produce a Cordon Blue,
It won't be me, it will be you,
And he said, You mean *Cordon Bleu?*
And she said to never mind the pronunciation so long as it was him and not
    heu.
But he wasn't discouraged; he bought a white hat and the Cordon Bleu Cook
    Book and said, How about some *Huitres en Robe de Chambre?*
And she sniffed and said, Are you reading a cook book for Forever *Ambre?*
And he said, Well, if you prefer something more Anglo-Saxon,
Why suppose I whip up some tasty *Filets de Sole Jackson,*
And she pretended not to hear, so he raised his voice and said, Could I please
    you with some *Paupiettes de Veau à la Grecque* or *Cornets de Jambon
    Lucullus* or perhaps some nice *Moules à la Bordelaise?*
And she said, Kindly lower your voice or the neighbors will think we are
    drunk and *disordelaise,*
And she said, Furthermore the whole idea of your cooking anything fit to
    eat is a farce. So what did Mr. Palliser do then?
Well, he offered her *Œufs Farcis Maison* and *Homard Farci St. Jacques* and
    Tomate Farcie à la Bayonne and *Aubergines Farcies Provençales,* as well
    as *Aubergines Farcies Italiennes,*

And she said, Edward, kindly accompany me as usual to Hamburger Heaven
and stop playing the fool,

And he looked in the book for one last suggestion and it suggested *Croques
Madame*, so he did, and now he dines every evening on *Crème de
Concombres Glacée, Côtelettes de Volaille Vicomtesse,* and *Artichauds à
la Barigoule.*

The New Yorker, March 13, 1948

Jade Snow Wong

from Fifth Chinese Daughter

In this excerpt from her memoir *Fifth Chinese Daughter* (1950), set in San Francisco's Chinatown during the Depression, Jade Snow Wong (1922–2006) recounts some of the lessons involved in "Learning To Be a Chinese Housewife" (as her chapter title puts it): how to shop on a budget for the best meat and produce, how to prepare rice. Ultimately, Wong chose a different path in life than that which her parents, guided "by the nineteenth-century standards of Imperial China," would have envisioned for her; she wrote books (also including *No Chinese Stranger*, published in 1974), became a noted potter, ran a travel business, and lectured throughout Asia. But when it came to cooking, she clearly cherished the firm foundations of her traditional upbringing. "It has been said that food, family, and endurance (in that order) characterize Chinese consciousness," she later wrote. "Each of my children did homework in the kitchen while I coached and cooked, and each is now able to create delicious innovations at the wok."

■ ■ ■

Almost overnight, the life of Jade Snow, heretofore characterized by gravity keyed to propriety, became weighted with the gravity which only anxiety over money can cause.

Now, every day after school she reported immediately to Mama, who gave her the usual fifty cents to purchase groceries for that evening's dinner and tomorrow's breakfast. Lunch was composed of leftovers. With prudent management, it was possible to get a small chicken for twenty cents, three bunches of Chinese greens for ten cents, three whole Rex soles or sand dabs for ten cents, and about a half pound of pork for the remaining ten cents. The household staples, such as rice, oil, salt, soy sauce, and soap were bought by Daddy.

The small chicken would be cut up, bone and all, into pieces which could be handled by chopsticks, marinated like beef or pork with a standard seasoning of a tablespoon each of flour, soy sauce, sugar, and oil and then placed in a bowl for steaming. This dish would be saved for breakfast. The sole to be served at night would be fried with a little chopped fresh ginger root, which was used more frequently than garlic in the Chinese kitchen. Ginger root in this instance neutralized any fishy odor—no fish was ever cooked without it—but it was also indispensable as an herb for the relief of certain types of colds and stomach or intestinal upsets.

The pork was sliced thin and used to make soup stock in which the greens were cooked. The three bunches of greens made sufficient soup and vegetable for both dinner and breakfast. Together with generous bowls of rice this menu fed three adults and three children.

In shopping for groceries, Jade Snow soon learned which stores carried the best of a particular thing; and after scathing criticism from Mama, she learned how shiny a fresh fish should look and how firm it should feel; how solid a head of cabbage should be before it could be considered solid, how an old turnip looked as distinguished from a young one, how pink good pork was, how crisp a bean sprout should be, and how green a young onion. Jade Snow never tried to bargain, as Mama often did from Chinese habit, or to get more than her money's worth by begging or flattery, as she heard fellow shoppers do, but under Mama's watchful checking at home, she certainly had to get her money's worth.

Most of the Chinese vegetables and condiments were purchased at the small general grocery stores, which were a clutter of canned goods on shelves, huge open baskets of vegetables along the wall, cured sausages, dried sea foods, and pressed ducks hanging overhead, jars of preserves and sauces here and there, sawdust on the floor, and always a fat cat watchful for mice. Mama said that they were much like the grocery stores in China.

The meat market was more American-looking with its long, refrigerated counters and white uniformed butchers. For fish, Jade Snow shopped at the stores which usually sold fish at counters in front and live poultry in the back. At the end of Chinatown, however, was one store which sold poultry without selling fish; it was Uncle Jan's store.

Uncle Jan was called "Uncle" because he was Daddy's good friend; also Mama had gone to school with his wife in China. He was Jade Snow's friend too, and she never had to watch him to be sure she got a good chicken.

Uncle Jan never bothered to make an inviting window display; he had paper sacks piled there. But he had more business than any other poultry store—he supplied restaurants, and many Caucasians came to get their chickens from him. Uncle Jan sometimes sat at his counter taking telephone orders, or making entries in his books, but whenever a customer came in, he jumped to wait on him personally. He was a good salesman without apparent effort, for he loved people. He would ask you how you were cooking your chicken, how many you were feeding, and would give you exactly what you wanted at the most reasonable price in Chinatown. He would put his hand into one of the many cages which filled his store to the ceiling and pull out a loudly protesting chicken. By the feel of its breastbone he could tell you when it had been hatched.

When Jade Snow went to Uncle Jan's, he always smiled happily, showing a flash of gold-crowned teeth. A cigar hung perpetually from a corner of his mouth, a cigar which he chewed but didn't smoke. Here and there on the white tile floor, Jade Snow could see little black wads of chewed tobacco. Uncle Jan inevitably asked, "How is your father? He is always working so hard. But so do we all nowadays, with many mouths to feed. And your mother? I still think of her as 'the little one' from habit, for that is what I used to call her in China." After Jade Snow had murmured replies, he might continue, "Why don't you get some squabs instead of chicken today? They are fat and tender."

Jade Snow would be doubtful, "Mama said chicken."

Uncle Jan would grin and wave his hand, "You tell your mother that I want you to have squabs for dinner."

Jade Snow would ask cautiously, "But the price?"

"Don't even think about the price; I will figure it correctly for you."

While live white squabs were killed and dressed by his wife or employees, Uncle Jan would continue his conversation. He never left Jade Snow waiting alone in his store.

"And what about the oldest sister and your other sisters and brothers? Is the little one growing fast? And what about you? Are you being a good scholar? I always have admired the way your father has taken his stand on educating his daughters. He is a scholar while we are just businessmen."

As she left, Uncle Jan would call out with the usual courtesy, "Tell your mother that she is welcome to visit us at our home any time she is free."

And Jade Snow would reply, "Thank you, and you feel free to visit us too." She always felt a warm glow after talking to Uncle Jan. At American

Thanksgiving, for some years now, they had served turkeys given to them by him, for he had a standing agreement with Daddy that if Daddy would help him sell turkeys on the rush day before Thanksgiving, he would receive as a gift as large a fowl as he desired.

By four in the afternoon Jade Snow had usually completed her shopping and rushed home, where Mama would have started dinner preparations. The rice always received first attention. "Get your rice on the stove first," Mama said, "and if it is cooked well, the other accompaniments are secondary. But if the rice is underdone or improperly cooked, the most delicious meat or vegetables cannot make up for it. The reputation of a good cook begins with good rice."

They had only half an hour to prepare dinner, then only twenty minutes for the meal, before it was time for Jade Snow to grab her Chinese books and be off to the Chinese school with Jade Precious Stone. Returning home at eight o'clock, Jade Snow first washed the dinner dishes and then washed the rice for the next morning's breakfast. To wash rice correctly is the first step in cooking rice correctly, and it is considered one of the principal accomplishments or requirements of any Chinese female. When Jade Snow was six, Daddy had stood her on a stool at the kitchen sink in order to teach her himself this most important step, so that he could be personally satisfied that she had a sure foundation.

First, she dipped out the required amount of raw polished white rice from the rice barrel. In their household, the barrel held a hundred pounds of rice, and an abalone shell was the measure. This shell had been used in the family for years; Mama said it was older than Jade Snow. Its luster was dulled, but infallibly, one-and-one-half measurefuls would insure enough rice for one meal (a little more for dinner; a little less for breakfast; and two measures when there was company). The rice was scooped into a heavy aluminum pot with a tight cover, and was washed in the pot.

It was first dampened with a little water, then rubbed for a while with both hands (if you were a child like Jade Snow) or with one hand (if you were a grownup). White starch would come off the rice and bleed into the water. You rinsed after the thorough first rubbing of about a hundred strokes. Then rub, scrub, and rinse again. Rub, scrub, and rinse again. Then rinse, rinse, rinse. Three scrubbings; six rinsings; these were the minimum treatments. When the water came out clear, the rice had been thoroughly cleaned.

Now it was ready for cooking water. Cold water was added until it reached one of Daddy's first knuckle joints above the level of the rice. Jade Snow usually allowed on her fingers a knuckle and a half. Then she checked the quantity of water by tilting the pot gently so that the rice remained undisturbed on the bottom. In this position, the knuckle-or-so of water, if allowed to flow to the edge of the tilted pot, would reach to the diameter of the rice on the bottom of the pot.

The cooking of rice was not less important than the washing. The pot, with its lid tightly in place, was set over a burner with the flame turned high until the water began to bubble and boil over. Then the burner was turned very low, and the steaming rice water was gradually absorbed. Daddy said that this was a most delicate stage in the cooking and that one should never lift the cover of the pot to peer at its contents. Instead, one should give the rice the full benefit of its steam and only by observation of the escaping steam should one conclude how nearly done the rice was. At the first bubbling stage, the steam rose straight up, strongly. At the completion of cooking, the steam curled ever so gently around the edges of the lid.

If by carelessness one forgot to turn down the flame when the water boiled, the rice would scorch. At times, this could happen in the best of families, but Daddy had a remedy. He would place a little saucer or Chinese teacup full of cold water in the pot on top of the rice to absorb the scorched taste.

Ideally, however, the rice would be cooked just right in about a half hour, into tender, smooth, snowy, fluffy, separate morsels. Under no circumstances did one stir or drain or rinse. Of course, this formula for faultless rice which would be beyond reproach of the most critical future mother-in-law depended entirely on the kind of rice which was chosen. During the prolonged waterfront strike in San Francisco, when it was not possible to obtain imported Chinese rice, Daddy bought the only available substitute—blunt-grained California rice. Despite the most careful efforts of Daddy and Mama by turn to coax, treat, and nurse this rice through washing and cooking, the result was a sticky, yellowish mass. The Wongs ate bread for the period of this strike.

Clearly Jade Snow's shopping list never included a few pounds of rice. Choosing a season's supply (about five hundred pounds) required the combined wits of both Daddy and Mama. Where rice was concerned, Daddy was perhaps more opinionated than many other Chinese, because his father used to own a rice store among his other businesses in China, and he had grown up among rice-husking activities.

When the Wongs were dipping into their last fifty pounds of rice in the rice barrel, it was a signal for Daddy to go to his favorite rice dealer, who imported his merchandise from China.

"Fellow Villager, we wish to choose our new supply of rice. May we have some samples of your current stock?" Daddy would ask.

"Good morning, Mr. Wong," the proprietor would reply. "I know you like the firmer type. I have a shipment of such rice, which is whole and smooth, and absorbs very little water. It is also comparatively free of foreign matter."

"That is very important," Daddy would answer, "for our last supply contained an abnormal amount of husks and gravel particles. It would be best if you would let me take home some samples to discuss them with my woman before I order."

The half dozen or more sample packets which the rice dealer supplied were wrapped in squares of cotton material, blue lined with bright pink. Each was labeled with type and price. Once home, Daddy and Mama sat down at their round dining table and carefully opened the little parcels, spreading them out in orderly rows.

Daddy put on his glasses and pointed out to Mama the sample recommended by the rice dealer. "This new import is supposed to take little water and be quite free from grit and husks."

Mama studied it a minute and then pointed to another sample. "However, the grains of this type are formed more perfectly and have a nice shiny fat look on the surface, which shows it is from fresher stock. Rice cooked from these grains will have the firmer texture which we like."

Then she added, "But it costs fifty cents more for each fifty-pound sack. Perhaps we should get the type the rice dealer recommended."

Daddy, who had previously decided on the kind the rice dealer recommended, was suddenly aroused, "What is more important than the rice which we eat twice a day and which is our main food? It is what we are, or we are what it is. Better to have what we want at whatever price, and economize on something else. It is decided—we shall have this most expensive type."

And so Daddy returned the samples and ordered the kind selected. Soon several hundred pounds of rice in its fifty-pound sacks was delivered and stacked in a corner of the store.

Now to the Wong children, this delivery by no means ended the story of buying rice. For the rice came from China packed in double thickness straw-mat sacks, the open ends hand-sewn with strong hemp twine; as re-inforcement, double strips of flexible cane about three-eighths of an inch wide, were wound around the sacks. From each sack of rice Daddy opened to fill the rice barrel, he, who wasted nothing, carefully untied the cane, straightened it out, and saved it to make switches for whipping disobedient or improper children, because Daddy firmly believed that severe whipping was the most effective means of bringing up creditable daughters and il-lustrious sons.

So it was no wonder that the Wong children always watched a delivery of new rice with sad eyes and heavy hearts. It was also no wonder that Little Brother Forgiveness, who as a son dared to be more articulate than his older sisters, would plead unhappily with Daddy when he saw him come home with new rice samples, "Daddy, please don't buy any more rice!"

Fifth Chinese Daughter (1950)

Alfred Kazin

from A Walker in the City

Food memory as geography: recalling the pushcart market in his old neighborhood in the Brownsville section of Brooklyn, Alfred Kazin (1915–1998), in this passage from his memoir *A Walker in the City* (1951), seems to literally walk through time, moving back along the familiar streets until he finds himself once again in the noisy midst of what is beginning to disappear. (In the years since his book was published, it has disappeared altogether.) Kazin, one of the great chroniclers of American literature in such books as *On Native Grounds* (1942) and *Bright Book of Life* (1973), here brings his descriptive gifts to bear on a street theater crammed almost beyond reckoning with sights, sounds, and flavors.

■ ■ ■

On Belmont Avenue, Brownsville's great open street market, the pushcarts are still lined on each other for blocks, and the din is as deafening, marvelous, and appetizing as ever. They have tried to tone it down; the pushcarts are now confined to one side of the street. When I was a boy, they clogged both sides, reached halfway up the curb to the open stands of the stores; walking down the street was like being whirled around and around in a game of blind man's buff. But Belmont Avenue is still the merriest street in Brownsville. As soon as I walked into it from Rockaway, caught my first whiff of the herrings and pickles in their great black barrels, heard the familiarly harsh, mocking cries and shouts from the market women—"*Oh you darlings! Oh you sweet ones, oh you pretty ones! Storm us! Tear us apart! Devour us!*"—I laughed right out loud, it was so good to be back among *them*. Nowhere but on Belmont Avenue did I ever see in Brownsville such open, hearty people as those market women. Their shrewd open-weather eyes missed nothing. The street was their native element; they seemed to hold it together with their hands, mouths, fists, and knees; they stood up in it behind their stands all day long, and in every weather; they stood up for themselves. In winter they would bundle themselves into five or six sweaters, then putting long white aprons over their overcoats, would warm themselves at fires lit in black oil drums between the pushcarts, their figures bulging as if to meet the rain and cold head-on in defiance.

I could hear them laughing and mock-crying all the way to Stone Avenue, still imploring and pulling at every woman on the street—"*Vayber! Vayber! Sheyne gute vayber! Oh you lovelies! Oh you good ones! Oh you pretty ones! See how cheap and good! Just come over! Just taste! Just a little look! What will it cost you to taste? How can you walk on without looking? How can you resist us? Oh! Oh! Come over! Come over! Devour us! Storm us! Tear us apart! BARGAINS BARGAINS!!*" I especially loved watching them at dusk, an hour before supper, when the women would walk through to get the food at its freshest. Then, in those late winter afternoons, when there was that deep grayness on the streets and that spicy smell from the open stands at dusk I was later to connect with my first great walks inside the New York crowd at the rush hour—then there would arise from behind the great flaming oil drums and the pushcarts loaded with their separate mounds of shoelaces, corsets, pots and pans, stockings, kosher kitchen soap, memorial candles in their wax-filled tumblers and glassware, "chiney" oranges, beet roots and soup greens, that deep and good odor of lox, of salami, of herrings and half-sour pickles, that told me I was truly home.

As I went down Belmont Avenue, the copper-shining herrings in the tall black barrels made me think of the veneration of food in Brownsville families. I can still see the kids pinned down to the tenement stoops, their feet helplessly kicking at the pots and pans lined up before them, their mouths pressed open with a spoon while the great meals are rammed down their throats. "*Eat! Eat! May you be destroyed if you don't eat! What sin have I committed that God should punish me with you! Eat! What will become of you if you don't eat! Imp of darkness, may you sink ten fathoms into the earth if you don't eat! Eat!*"

We never had a chance to know what hunger meant. At home we nibbled all day long as a matter of course. On the block we gorged ourselves continually on "Nessels," Hersheys, gumdrops, polly seeds, nuts, chocolate-covered cherries, charlotte russe, and ice cream. A warm and sticky ooze of chocolate ran through everything we touched; the street always smelled faintly like the candy wholesaler's windows on the way back from school. The hunger for sweets, jellies, and soda water raged in us like a disease;

during the grimmest punchball game, in the middle of a fist fight, we would dash to the candy store to get down two-cent blocks of chocolate and "small"—three-cent—glasses of cherry soda; or calling "upstairs" from the street, would have flung to us, or carefully hoisted down at the end of a clothesline, thick slices of rye bread smeared with chicken fat. No meal at home was complete without cream soda, root beer, ginger ale, "celery tonic." We poured jelly on bread; we poured it into the tea; we often ate chocolate marshmallows before breakfast. At school during the recess hour Syrian vendors who all looked alike in their alpaca jackets and black velours hats came after us with their white enameled trays, from which we took *Halvah*, Turkish Delight, and three different kinds of greasy nut-brown pastry sticks. From the Jewish vendors, who went around the streets in every season wheeling their little tin stoves, we bought roasted potatoes either in the quarter or the half—the skins were hard as bark and still smelled of the smoke pouring out of the stoves; apples you ate off a stick that were encrusted with a thick glaze of baked jelly you never entirely got down your throat or off your fingers, so that you seemed to be with it all day; *knishes*; paper spills of hot yellow chick peas. I still hear those peddlers crying up and down the street—"*Árbes! Árbes! Hayse gute árbes! Kinder! Kinder! Hayse gute árbes!*" From the "big" Italians, whom we saw only in summer, we bought watermelons as they drove their great horse-smelling wagons down the street calling up to every window—"Hey you ladies! *Hey ladies! Freschi* and good!"—and from the "small" ones, who pushed carts through the streets, paper cups of shaved ice sprinkled before our eyes with drops of lemon or orange or raspberry syrup from a narrow water bottle.

But our greatest delight in all seasons was "delicatessen"—hot spiced corned beef, pastrami, rolled beef, hard salami, soft salami, chicken salami, bologna, frankfurter "specials" and the thinner, wrinkled hot dogs always taken with mustard and relish and sauerkraut, and whenever possible, to make the treat fully real, with potato salad, baked beans, and french fries which had been bubbling in the black wire fryer deep in the iron pot. At Saturday twilight, as soon as the delicatessen store reopened after the Sabbath rest, we raced into it panting for the hot dogs sizzling on the gas plate just inside the window. The look of that blackened empty gas plate had driven us wild all through the wearisome Sabbath day. And now, as the electric sign blazed up again, lighting up the words JEWISH NATIONAL DELICATESSEN, it was as if we had entered into our rightful heritage. Yet *Wurst* carried associations with the forbidden, the adulterated, the excessive; with spices that teased and maddened the senses to demand more, still more. This was food that only on Saturday nights could be eaten with a good conscience. Generally, we bought it on the sly; it was supposed to be bad for us; I thought it was made in dark cellars. Still, our parents could not have disapproved of it altogether. Each new mouthful of food we took in was an advantage stolen in the battle. The favorite injunction was to *fix yourself,* by which I understood we needed to do a repair job on ourselves. In the swelling and thickening of a boy's body was the poor family's earliest success. "Fix yourself!" a mother cried indignantly to the child on the stoop. "Fix yourself!" The word for a fat boy was *solid.*

A Walker in the City (1951)

Maria Sermolino

from Papa's Table d'Hôte

Maria Sermolino (1895–1991) gives us a behind-the-scenes look at the workings of an Italian family restaurant in Greenwich Village in the early 20th century, when tenderloin of beef was six and a half cents a pound and veal went for seven cents. For its American customers untutored in Italian ways, a restaurant like Gonfarone's offered a learning experience in everything from the proper use of cutlery to the rituals of wine-drinking, and an education in exotic: "'Antipasto,' 'minestrone,' 'spaghetti'—what manner of food was this?" For the immigrant's child watching the scene, the restaurant provided a satisfying taste of cultural one-upmanship as these customers fumbled hopelessly with their pasta. Sermolino later worked as a foreign correspondent and editor for *Life*.

■ ■ ■

The economics of a family brought up in a restaurant are not like those of any other family. The family's rent and food and laundry and heat and servants and entertainment expenses all come directly out of the business. At Gonfarone's there was no fancy bookkeeping or separation of expenditures. Even doctors' bills, I assume (although I do not know), were probably paid by the simple expedient of taking the money out of the cash box. And when the cash balance in the bank was more than enough to meet outstanding obligations, papa and Madama would each take an equal amount and spend it or save it or, as they did more than once, jointly buy a house in the neighborhood as an investment. If they were not mindful of monetary expenditures, neither were they concerned over the number of hours they toiled. A few hands accomplished a great deal and even small profits, when shared by only two, can seem large.

Although for several decades Gonfarone's was probably the largest and most successful of the Italian table d'hôtes, it was but one of many similar restaurants all of whose owners made more than just a comfortable living. It seems as if, for several decades, the American palate could not be satiated with Italian food. During its heyday, Gonfarone's served four to five thousand dinners a week. I can still see the people standing closely packed together in the narrow hall and overflowing on to the stairs and out on Macdougal Street as they waited for tables. Papa would be in the dining-room from noon until midnight, with a few hours' respite in the afternoon, and Madama would be in the pantry, and mama at her cashier's desk, without taking time out for meals until the rush was over. Since they were young (at least papa and mama were) and working for themselves, the busier they were the better they liked it. On marketing days, Madama and papa would get up at five in the morning and go to Washington market where they bought a week's supply of food at one time. (Sometimes papa would sneak home from the Tiro Club on Macdougal Street just in time to leave with Madama.)

The unloading of the trucks full of foodstuffs was a sight to behold. All the deliveries were made through the bar and even on winter days when the blasts of cold air sweeping through the wide open doors at the foot of the basement steps chilled me to the bone, I could not resist watching the spectacle. Big, muscular men would march by with a side of beef, or a carcass of veal, or a whole lamb on their shoulders. Barrels filled with chickens and dripping water from the cracked ice which kept them fresh came rolling on their sides down the wooden tracks placed over the cellar stairs. Sometimes I would shove and kick them over the barroom floor towards the kitchen. There were crates of celery with their green leaves sticking out at the tops and sides, and crates of lettuce and radishes and tomatoes, and burlap bags with potatoes and onions and leeks, and barrels of apples and grapes and the whole place was fragrant with a mixture of scents from things recently taken from the moist earth.

The customer got a great deal for his fifty or sixty cents at Gonfarone's but even at that price there was a margin of profit, because wholesale prices of foodstuffs were so low. (And, I've been told, papa was a shrewd buyer.) Tenderloin of beef cost six and a half cents a pound; veal, seven cents a pound, chicken, nine cents, lamb, eight cents. A barrel of onions cost one dollar and fifty cents, and a bushel of tomatoes was forty cents. Potatoes were a dollar seventy-five a barrel and eggs, by the crate, cost fifteen cents a dozen.

A typical Gonfarone menu, at any time during the first decade of the twentieth century, might have read as follows:

Assorted Antipasto
Minestrone
Spaghetti with Meat or Tomato Sauce
Boiled Salmon with Caper Sauce
Sweetbread with Mushroom Patty
Broiled Spring Chicken or Roast Prime Ribs of Beef
Brussels Sprouts . . Spinach
Boiled or Mashed Potatoes
Green Salad
Biscuit Tortoni or Spumoni
Fresh Fruit . . . . . . Assorted Cheeses
Demi-tasse

This formidable list represented not a choice of items, but a list of all the food a customer could have on a weekday night for fifty cents, including a pint of California red wine. (Imported wine was ten cents extra.) There were day-to-day variations in the menu, but the quantity was always the same. On Saturdays and Sundays the price was sixty cents, but that included half a boiled lobster with mayonnaise. As the cost of food and labor went up, papa realized that one day he would have to raise his prices. For many months he discussed the problem—with Madama, mama, the help and the customers—and then the day came when he took the momentous step. He raised the price from fifty to fifty-five cents.

Although the length and variety of the menu undoubtedly attracted many people to the early Italian table d'hôtes in general, and Gonfarone's in particular, the manner in which the food was prepared and the novelty of the food itself also were important factors. "Antipasto," "minestrone," "spaghetti"—what manner of food was this? There was nothing in American cookery remotely like it. The antipasto consisted of hearts of celery (the big stalks were used for the minestrone), tasty little black olives, several slices of imported Italian salame, sardines, anchovies, sliced tomatoes sprinkled with basil, imported tuna, and a big juicy pimento. (Papa would be horrified if he could see the mountain of cole slaw topped with a shriveled anchovy and a speck of pimento which passes for antipasto today.) The minestrone was a tasty soup made with beef stock and a variety of fresh vegetables with just enough well-cooked beans to make it smooth and rich. The spaghetti, however, was the most intriguing dish.

By the simple act of ordering spaghetti an American was plunged into a foreign experience. Not only was its taste different than anything he had ever eaten, but so was the manner of eating it. Few could master the technique of spaghetti twirling, but they had fun trying. They tangled with the slippery stuff, tried to be neat and politely American in their handling of it, but most often they went down in defeat and *a)* cut it up into short lengths, or *b)* sucked it up like a peasant. Whenever papa had the time, he would stop at one table after another and demonstrate how to eat spaghetti.

Even a novice can master the trick provided he keeps his head and does not panic. The important thing to remember is to hook *exactly one strand* of spaghetti on a tine of the fork at one time and, with the fork held at a right angle either to a spoon or a *bare spot* on the dish, twirl that one long strand completely around the tines. That makes a good mouthful. An Italian peasant is adept at digging into a mound of spaghetti and coming up with several long strands, which he holds high over his mouth and, with head thrown back, sucking them in, but this is not for restaurant dining, in America or Italy. Only cowards and barbarians cut spaghetti with a knife. Thus mutilated it becomes something else, and the eating experience undergoes a change, just as eating a mashed banana is different from eating a whole one, or eating hamburger is not the same as eating steak.

From the standpoint of the restaurateur spaghetti had many advantages. A portion looked like, and was, a lot of food and yet it cost less than two cents a portion—including enough sauce and grated cheese to gratify a glutton. Furthermore, after gorging himself on a mound of spaghetti, a customer's appetite would have lost its edge and small portions of the remaining courses on the menu would abundantly satisfy him.

The profit on food, however, was a minor item. The bar was the gold mine. A forty-gallon barrel of good bar whiskey from Park & Tilford cost about fifty dollars and, at fifteen cents for a three-ounce drink, straight, returned about two hundred and fifty dollars. Mixed with Italian vermouth, imported by the barrel, it made a superb Manhattan cocktail, which, including the maraschino cherry cost about three cents a drink (more or less, depending on how much melted ice was included), and sold for fifteen cents, or two for a quarter. By the case, French champagne cost about two dollars a quart and was on the wine list at four to five dollars a bottle. Lacrima Christi, Bosca or Asti spumante—white sparkling wines from Italy which looked like champagne and, to most Americans frequenting Italian table d'hôtes, tasted like it—cost about nine dollars a case. No customer in a festive mood could resist ordering it at two dollars a bottle, especially since it was served with a champagne flourish with a white napkin wrapped around its neck, and in a silver-plated wine-cooler filled with cracked ice. Furthermore, the cork popped as loudly as a French champagne cork.

As for the "red ink," usually California claret, a pint of it was served, free, with every dinner—a grandiose gesture which greatly impressed Americans who, if they thought of wine at all, considered it a foreign luxury. The restaurateurs of fifty years ago could afford such generosity since, when bought in forty or fifty barrel lots, the cost of the wine was about ten *cents* a gallon.

Labor costs, which have become a nightmare to operators of large restaurants, were practically nonexistent. Amedeo probably was paid about forty dollars a month, the dishwashers about twenty dollars, and, in the very early days, the waiters worked only for their food and tips or, at most, were paid about ten dollars a month. (In some of the fancy uptown restaurants the waiters paid for the privilege of working, because on tips alone they could make up to two hundred dollars a month.) The minimum tip at Gonfarone's was a dime a head (a "sport" might leave a quarter for two) and, since one waiter could serve about fifty customers a day, counting luncheon and dinner, he could make about five dollars a day. Over a busy weekend he might double his take. Furthermore, since controls were lax, even a waiter who tried to be honest might find his pockets unaccountably bulging with dinner money which, somehow, got confused with his tip money. There was so much of it pouring in, that everybody shared.

Papa had a theory that the more money the help made the better they worked. By working hard they helped fill the till for papa and Madama, and if they appropriated the overflow it mattered not to papa. Even when they left, as most of them did after four or five prosperous years, to open rival places of their own, papa bore them no ill will. In fact he sometimes lent them money with which to get started and took parties of his own customers to their table d'hôtes. (Two of the most successful are still flourishing:

Enrico and Paglieri's on West Eleventh Street, founded by the late Enrico Fasani, and Peter's Back Yard on West Tenth Street, founded by the late Peter Galotti. Both men got their start as waiters at Gonfarone's and became papa's close friends. Few of the old guard are now left but, as recently as a decade ago, there were a score or more of ex-Gonfarone waiters—some now owners, others headwaiters—in Italian restaurants about town who, despite my graying hair and Sally Victor hats, still called me "Il Ninìn," as they did forty-odd years ago when I used to dodge their footsteps in Gonfarone's kitchen.)

As stated previously, on an average weekday Gonfarone's would serve more than five hundred meals. On a good Saturday and Sunday it reached twice that number. Holidays were extra dividends because, without added overhead, they brought in additional revenue. Christmas, Thanksgiving, the Fourth of July, Election Day, Labor Day, Decoration Day, Washington's Birthday were all banner days, but the greatest moneymaker of the year was New Year's Eve.

Although it was the most profitable, all of us dreaded New Year's Eve, and papa considered it downright torture. Beginning at 10 P.M. a special New Year's Eve dinner, costing twice as much as the regular meal, was served. No reservations were taken. The people just flowed in, and when every spare chair and table were occupied papa's troubles began. Among the tardy arrivals demanding room there were always the favorite customers whom one did not wish to offend. With his charm, papa worked miracles. No one seemed to mind when he crowded two parties of four around one small table in order to seat eight more. With the aid of folding circular table tops, he would accommodate a party of six in the space usually taken by two. Sometimes when every inch of space seemed occupied, he would resort to the strategy of splitting a big party and seating a few here and a few there at tables with strangers. Under papa's magic touch the dining-room seemed elastic.

At eleven o'clock the waiters distributed noisy rattles, tin horns, bags of confetti, serpentines of colored paper, rakish paper hats, and a handful of uninflated balloons to every table. On that night the food was of no importance. Everyone came to drink and "make whoopee." Most of them drank too much and papa was miserable. Drunks were a nuisance, especially in a jam-packed room, and even the best of them were unpredictable. At the stroke of midnight, whistles shrieked outside and the crowd inside cheered, shouted, blew horns, burst balloons, stood up on chairs and tables, fell over each other, embracing, kissing, back-slapping, singing in groups, but each intoning a different tune.

At midnight hundreds of friends would shout to papa to "come and clink glasses" with them, but midnight was a signal for papa to slip out of the dining-room and join us for a midnight toast. When we were little, grandma would put us to bed and papa would come to our room. Angela and I would huddle wide-eyed and alert watching papa deftly ease the cork out of the champagne bottle and then, like a shot, he would let it go and the cork would hit the ceiling and bounce right back onto our bed. He would stay only a few minutes but never once did he fail to greet the New Year with us. As we grew older, we were permitted to stay up until midnight, in our parlor, and when we were young ladies we would be in the bar, waiting for midnight and our family ceremony. We kissed each other, and each one of us in turn clinked glasses with the other and wished each other a Happy New Year. Then papa would be off to handle the overexuberant mob in the dining-room above.

Papa's Table d'Hôte (1952)

almond cake • torte

The following recipe is the well-known German Mandeltorte.
In order to have the right result the almonds should be put
through a nut grinder, not a meat grinder. This recipe must
be starred as "the" nut cake my friends so frequently ask for.
It may be baked in a loaf or in layers. This amount serves 6
to 8 people.

Sift:

1 cup sugar

Beat:

6 egg yolks

Add the sugar gradually and beat until these ingredients are
very creamy.

Add:

Grated rind and juice of 1 lemon or 1 small orange

1 teaspoon cinnamon

1 cup ground unblanched almonds

1/2 cup toasted white bread crumbs

(1/2 teaspoon almond extract)

Whip until stiff but not dry:

6 egg whites

1/4 teaspoon salt

... cont'd

Fold them lightly into the batter. This cake is very light and consequently difficult to remove from the pan. Bake it in an 8 inch tube pan in a moderate oven 350° for about 40 minutes. Permit it to cool in the pan. Spread it with:

Chocolate Butter Icing

or bake it in two 8 inch layer pans lined with greased waxed paper. Spread between the layers:

Lemon and Orange Filling

Spread the top with:

Confectioners' sugar

When making a large cake, double or triple this recipe and use pans with a removable rim in order to facilitate handling it. Spread the layers with:

Lemon and Orange Filling

Spread the cake with:

White Icing or Chocolate Butter Icing

Irma Rombauer & Marion Rombauer Becker, *The Joy of Cooking* (1952 edition)

Originally self-published by a widowed St. Louis housewife struggling to support her family, *The Joy of Cooking* has sold an estimated 17 million copies in its many editions. When I am asked what cookbook I would like to have on a desert island, I say *Joy*. If you don't know how to cook, *Joy* can teach you; if you do know how, *Joy* can remind you of cooking times and proportions of ingredients.

Ralph Ellison

from Invisible Man

The power of food to define, to limit, and to free is laid out in bravura fashion by Ralph Ellison (1913–1994) in this passage from his novel *Invisible Man* (1952). For a black intellectual in wintry Harlem, a wagonload of baked yams carries with it a heavier freight of potential humiliation. Ellison's protagonist, however, follows his truest impulse: "To hell with being ashamed of what you liked." Punning on Popeye the Sailor's mantra, he declares: "I yam what I am."

■ ■ ■

The streets were covered with ice and soot-flecked snow and from above a feeble sun filtered through the haze. I walked with my head down, feeling the biting air. And yet I was hot, burning with an inner fever. I barely raised my eyes until a car, passing with a thudding of skid chains whirled completely around on the ice, then turned cautiously and thudded off again.

I walked slowly on, blinking my eyes in the chill air, my mind a blur with the hot inner argument continuing. The whole of Harlem seemed to fall apart in the swirl of snow. I imagined I was lost and for a moment there was an eerie quiet. I imagined I heard the fall of snow upon snow. What did it mean? I walked, my eyes focused into the endless succession of barber shops, beauty parlors, confectioneries, luncheonettes, fish houses, and hog maw joints, walking close to the windows, the snowflakes lacing swift between, simultaneously forming a curtain, a veil, and stripping it aside. A flash of red and gold from a window filled with religious articles caught my eye. And behind the film of frost etching the glass I saw two brashly painted plaster images of Mary and Jesus surrounded by dream books, love powders, God-Is-Love signs, money-drawing oil and plastic dice. A black statue of a nude Nubian slave grinned out at me from beneath a turban of gold. I passed on to a window decorated with switches of wiry false hair, ointments guaranteed to produce the miracle of whitening black skin. "You too can be truly beautiful," a sign proclaimed. "Win greater happiness with whiter complexion. Be outstanding in your social set."

I hurried on, suppressing a savage urge to push my fist through the pane. A wind was rising, the snow thinning. Where would I go? To a movie? Could I sleep there? I ignored the windows now and walked along, becoming aware that I was muttering to myself again. Then far down at the corner I saw an old man warming his hands against the sides of an odd-looking wagon, from which a stove pipe reeled off a thin spiral of smoke that drifted the odor of baking yams slowly to me, bringing a stab of swift nostalgia. I stopped as though struck by a shot, deeply inhaling, remembering, my mind surging back, back. At home we'd bake them in the hot coals of the fireplace, had carried them cold to school for lunch; munched them secretly, squeezing the sweet pulp from the soft peel as we hid from the teacher behind the largest book, the *World's Geography*. Yes, and we'd loved them candied, or baked in a cobbler, deep-fat fried in a pocket of dough, or roasted with pork and glazed with the well-browned fat; had chewed them raw—yams and years ago. More yams than years ago, though the time seemed endlessly expanded, stretched thin as the spiraling smoke beyond all recall.

I moved again. "Get yo' hot, baked Car'lina yam," he called. At the corner the old man, wrapped in an army overcoat, his feet covered with gunny sacks, his head in a knitted cap, was puttering with a stack of paper bags. I saw a crude sign on the side of the wagon proclaiming YAMS, as I walked flush into the warmth thrown by the coals that glowed in a grate underneath.

"How much are your yams?" I said, suddenly hungry.

"They ten cents and they sweet," he said, his voice quavering with age. "These ain't none of them binding ones neither. These here is real, sweet, yaller yams. How many?"

"One," I said. "If they're that good, one should be enough."

He gave me a searching glance. There was a tear in the corner of his eye. He chuckled and opened the door of the improvised oven, reaching gingerly with his gloved hand. The yams, some bubbling with syrup, lay on a wire rack above glowing coals that leaped to low blue flame when struck by the draft of air. The flash of warmth set my face aglow as he removed one of the yams and shut the door.

"Here you are, suh," he said, starting to put the yam into a bag.

"Never mind the bag, I'm going to eat it. Here . . ."

"Thanks." He took the dime. "If that ain't a sweet one, I'll give you another one free of charge."

I knew that it was sweet before I broke it; bubbles of brown syrup had burst the skin.

"Go ahead and break it," the old man said. "Break it and I'll give you some butter since you gon' eat it right here. Lots of folks takes 'em home. They got their own butter at home."

I broke it, seeing the sugary pulp steaming in the cold.

"Hold it over here," he said. He took a crock from a rack on the side of the wagon. "Right here."

I held it, watching him pour a spoonful of melted butter over the yam and the butter seeping in.

"Thanks."

"You welcome. And I'll tell you something."

"What's that?" I said.

"If that ain't the best eating you had in a long time, I give you your money back."

"You don't have to convince me," I said. "I can look at it and see it's good."

"You right, but everything what looks good ain't necessarily good," he said. "But these is."

I took a bite, finding it as sweet and hot as any I'd ever had, and was overcome with such a surge of homesickness that I turned away to keep my control. I walked along, munching the yam, just as suddenly overcome by an intense feeling of freedom—simply because I was eating while walking along the street. It was exhilarating. I no longer had to worry about who saw me or about what was proper. To hell with all that, and as sweet as the yam actually was, it became like nectar with the thought. If only someone who had known me at school or at home would come along and see me now. How shocked they'd be! I'd push them into a side street and smear their faces with the peel. What a group of people we were, I thought. Why, you could cause us the greatest humiliation simply by confronting us with something we liked. Not *all* of us, but so many. Simply by walking up and shaking a set of chitterlings or a well-boiled hog maw at them during the clear light of day! What consternation it would cause! And I saw myself advancing upon Bledsoe, standing bare of his false humility in the crowded lobby of Men's House, and seeing him there and him seeing me and ignoring me and me enraged and suddenly whipping out a foot or two of chitterlings, raw, uncleaned and dripping sticky circles on the floor as I shake them in his face, shouting:

"Bledsoe, you're a shameless chitterling eater! I accuse you of relishing hog bowels! Ha! And not only do you eat them, you sneak and eat them in *private* when you think you're unobserved! You're a sneaking chitterling lover! I accuse you of indulging in a filthy habit, Bledsoe! Lug them out of there, Bledsoe! Lug them out so we can see! I accuse you before the eyes of the world!" And he lugs them out, yards of them, with mustard greens, and racks of pigs' ears, and pork chops and black-eyed peas with dull accusing eyes.

I let out a wild laugh, almost choking over the yam as the scene spun before me. Why, with others present, it would be worse than if I had accused him of raping an old woman of ninety-nine years, weighing ninety pounds . . . blind in one eye and lame in the hip! Bledsoe would disintegrate, disinflate! With a profound sigh he'd drop his head in shame. He'd lose caste. The weekly newspapers would attack him. The captions over his picture: *Prominent Educator Reverts to Field Niggerism!* His rivals would denounce him as a bad example for the youth. Editorials would demand that he either recant or retire from public life. In the South his white folks would desert him; he would be discussed far and wide, and all of the trustees' money couldn't prop up his sagging prestige. He'd end up an exile washing dishes at the Automat. For down South he'd be unable to get a job on the honey wagon.

This is all very wild and childish, I thought, but to hell with being ashamed of what you liked. No more of that for me. I am what I am! I wolfed down the yam and ran back to the old man and handed him twenty cents, "Give me two more," I said.

"Sho, all you want, long as I got 'em. I can see you a serious yam eater, young fellow. You eating them right away?"

"As soon as you give them to me," I said.

"You want 'em buttered?"

"Please."

"Sho, that way you can get the most out of 'em. Yessuh," he said, handing over the yams, "I can see you one of these old-fashioned yam eaters."

"They're my birthmark," I said. "I yam what I am!"

"Then you must be from South Car'lina," he said with a grin.

"South Carolina nothing, where I come from we really go for yams."

"Come back tonight or tomorrow if you can eat some more," he called after me. "My old lady'll be out here with some hot sweet potato fried pies."

Hot fried pies, I thought sadly, moving away. I would probably have indigestion if I ate one—now that I no longer felt ashamed of the things I had always loved, I probably could no longer digest very many of them. What and how much had I lost by trying to do only what was expected of me instead of what I myself had wished to do? What a waste, what a senseless waste! But what of those things which you actually didn't like, not because you were not supposed to like them, not because to dislike them was considered a mark of refinement and education—but because you actually found them distasteful? The very idea annoyed me. How could you know? It involved a problem of choice. I would have to weigh many things carefully before deciding and there would be some things that would cause quite a bit of trouble, simply because I had never formed a personal attitude toward so much. I had accepted the accepted attitudes and it had made life seem simple . . .

But not yams, I had no problem concerning them and I would eat them whenever and wherever I took the notion. Continue on the yam level and life would be sweet—though somewhat yellowish. Yet the freedom to eat yams on the street was far less than I had expected upon coming to the city. An unpleasant taste bloomed in my mouth now as I bit the end of the yam and threw it into the street; it had been frost-bitten.

Invisible Man (1952)

⊚ ⊚

Gazpacho

⊚ ⊚

A favorite summer soup with everyone who tries it, this is a West Coast version of the Spanish and South American variety. Almost a liquid salad, there is no better way to start a meal on a broiling summer day.

Rub a large bowl with a cut clove of garlic. Peel 3 pounds of very ripe tomatoes, remove their cores, and chop them in rather small pieces. Don't lose any of that precious juice—pour it and the tomatoes into the bowl. Peel and chop 2 medium-sized cucumbers and add them, along with 1/2 cup each of minced green pepper and onion, and 2 cups of tomato juice or ice water. Next comes 1/3 cup of olive oil, 3 tablespoons of vinegar, plenty of salt and pepper (taste it!), and either a dash of tabasco or a fresh hot red pepper minced into infinitesimal pieces. Chill this very thoroughly and serve with an ice cube in each dish. The Spanish version has lots of layered bread or toast, but we skip that out here. Serves 10 or 12.

1 clove garlic	2 cups tomato juice or ice water
3 pounds tomatoes	1/3 cup olive oil
2 cucumbers	3 tablespoons vinegar
1/2 cup minced green pepper	Salt and pepper
1/2 cup minced onion	Dash of tabasco or 1 small hot red pepper

Helen Evans Brown, *The West Coast Cook Book* (1952)

Regarded as the culinary authority of the West Coast during the 1950s and 1960s, Helen Evans Brown helped turn California specialties such as this recipe for gazpacho into national favorites.

Alice B. Toklas

Food in the United States in 1934 and 1935

Born in San Francisco, Alice B. Toklas (1877–1967) met Gertrude Stein the first day she arrived in Paris in 1907, and for the next 39 years lived with the writer as confidant, lover, cook, secretary, editor, and host of the couple's rue de Fleurus salon, which was attended by Ernest Hemingway, Thornton Wilder, Sherwood Anderson, Picasso, Matisse, and Braque, among many others. *The Alice B. Toklas Cook Book* (1954), from which this account of Stein and Toklas's culinary experiences on their American tour in the 1930s is taken, is perhaps most notorious for its recipe for hash-laced brownies (a recipe contributed by long-time Morocco resident Brion Gysin). The brownies recipe even inspired a late-60s Peter Sellers comedy, *I Love You, Alice B. Toklas!* Actually one might argue that the contribution of cannabis to the New American cuisine has gone unrecognized. The consumption of Alice B. Toklas brownies created a voracious appetite and a willy-nilly charge to the midnight kitchen. It also reduced inhibition and, sometimes, the ability to comprehend and faithfully execute a recipe from a cookbook. Both the divine and the disastrous flowed from those kitchens; so did a sense of cooking as riotous, fun-filled group effort.

■ ■ ■

When during the summer of 1934 Gertrude Stein could not decide whether she did or did not want to go to the United States, one of the things that troubled her was the question of the food she would be eating there. Would it be to her taste? A young man from the Bugey had lately returned from a brief visit to the United States and had reported that the food was more foreign to him than the people, their homes or the way they lived in them. He said the food was good but very strange indeed—tinned vegetable cocktails and tinned fruit salads, for example. Surely, said I, you weren't required to eat them. You could have substituted other dishes. Not, said he, when you were a guest.

At this time there was staying with us at Bilignin an American friend who said he would send us a menu from the restaurant of the hotel we would be staying at when Gertrude Stein lectured in his home town, which he did promptly on his return there. The variety of dishes was a pleasant surprise even if the tinned vegetable cocktails and fruit salads occupied a preponderant position. Consolingly, there were honey-dew melons, soft-shell crabs and prime roasts of beef. We would undertake the great adventure.

Crossing on the *Champlain* we had the best French food. It made me think of a college song popular in my youth, Home Will Never Be Like This. If the food that awaited us at the Algonquin Hotel did not resemble the food on the French Line it was very good in its way, unrivalled T-steaks and soft-shell crabs and ineffable ice creams.

Mr. Alfred Harcourt, Gertrude Stein's editor, had asked us to spend Thanksgiving weekend with Mrs. Harcourt and himself in their Connecticut home, and there we ate for the first time, with suppressed excitement and curiosity, wild rice. It has never become a commonplace to me. Carl Van Vechten sends it to me. To the delight of my French friends I serve

Wild Rice Salad

Steam ¹/₂ lb. wild rice.

¹/₂ lb. coarsely chopped mushrooms cooked for 10 minutes in 3 tablespoons oil and 2 tablespoons lemon juice, 2 hard-boiled eggs coarsely chopped, 1 green pepper finely chopped, 1 ¹/₂ cups shelled shrimps, all lightly mixed and served with

Aïoli or Aïlloli Sauce

Press into a mortar 4 cloves of garlic, add a pinch of salt, of white pepper and the yolk of an egg. With the pestle reduce these ingredients to an emulsion. Add the yolk of an egg. You may continue to make the sauce with the pestle or discard it for a wooden fork or a wooden spoon or a wire whisk. Real Provençal *Aïoli* makers use the pestle to the end. With whatever instrument you will have chosen you will commence to incorporate drop by drop an excellent olive oil. When the egg has absorbed about 3 tablespoons of the oil, add ¹/₂ tablespoon lemon juice. Continuing to stir, now add oil more briskly. When it soon becomes firm again add 1 dessertspoon tepid water (I repeat, tepid water). Continue to add oil, lemon juice and tepid water. The yolk of 1 egg will absorb 1 cup and 2 tablespoons oil, 1 ¹/₂ tablespoons lemon juice and 2 dessertspoons tepid water.

Aïoli is, of course, nothing more than a garlic mayonnaise, a creamy mayonnaise. Mayonnaise with tepid water is creamier than without it. Mayonnaise should have more salt and pepper added to the yolk of egg than *Aïoli* as well as powdered mustard and paprika.

Gertrude Stein said she was not going to lunch or dine with anyone before lecturing, we would eat simply and alone. Before her first lecture she ordered for dinner oysters and honey-dew melon. She said it would suit her. In travelling to a dozen states she deviated as little as possible from that first menu. Occasionally the oysters had to be replaced by fish or chicken. From the beginning the ubiquitous honey-dew melon bored me. Melons to me are a hot-weather refreshment. Rooms heated to 70° and over do not replace the sun. In any case, I prefer the flavour of Spanish melons to honey-dew and Persian melons. So the most fantastic dishes were experimented with, anything except what sounded like drug-store specialities.

Gertrude Stein continued with her satisfactory *régime* on the days of lectures. On the other days we fared more lavishly with friends in their homes and at restaurants, at first in New York, and then an excellent dinner at the inn at Princeton, at the Signet Club at Harvard with half a dozen of its members and no one else at Gertrude Stein's request, and very well at Smith College. Then we stayed with delightful people in an old historic house amidst rare and beautiful furniture and objects and dined and lunched with exquisite eighteenth-century porcelain, crystal and silver on a precious lace tablecloth, and left, quite starved, to find late in the afternoon fifty miles away an unpretentious but carefully cooked meal in a small town—oysters, roast turkey and its accompaniments and an unusually good rice pudding were not beyond our capacity. We asked to see the cook to thank her, and she gave me the recipe for

Rice Pudding

Thoroughly wash ¼ lb. rice, cook in double boiler in 1 quart milk with a pinch of salt. Stir the yolks of 8 eggs with a wooden spoon gradually adding 1 cup sugar and 5 tablespoons flour. Stir for 10 minutes and slowly add 2 cups scalded milk. Place over very low flame, stirring continuously until the mixture coats the spoon. Remove from heat and strain through a sieve, adding 1 teaspoon vanilla extract. When rice is quite tender, add slowly to egg-sugar-milk mixture. Then gently incorporate the beaten whites of 3 eggs. Pour into buttered mould and cook in 350° oven for 20 minutes. Do not remove from mould until tepid. Serve with

Vanilla Cream Sauce

Stir the yolks of 6 eggs thoroughly with 1 cup sugar. Add 2 ¼ cups scalded milk. Stir over very low flame with wooden spoon until the mixture coats the spoon. Remove from flame and add 1 tablespoon best kirsch. Strain through hair sieve. Stir occasionally until cold enough to put into the refrigerator. Before serving gently add 1 cup whipped cream.

Gertrude Stein's and Virgil Thomson's opera was to be given in Chicago. She had never heard it, so when Bobsie Goodspeed telephoned that we ought to fly out there to hear it—there would not be time between lectures to go there by train—Gertrude Stein said she would but only under the protection of Carl Van Vechten. After a perfect performance of *Four Saints in Three Acts*, Bobsie gave a supper party. She was known to have a perfect *cuisine*. Of the many courses I only remember the first and the last, a clear turtle soup and a fantastic *pièce montée* of nougat and roses, cream and small coloured candles. The dessert reminded me of a postcard Virgil Thomson once sent us from the Côte d'Azur, Delightfully situated within sight of the sea, pine woods, nightingales, all cooked in butter. This is the recipe for

Clear Turtle Soup

Soak ½ lb. sun-dried turtle meat in cold water for four days changing the water each day. On the fourth day prepare 1 stalk celery, 1 leek, 1 carrot, 2 onions and 1 turnip. Put 12 peppercorns, 3 cloves, 8 coriander seeds, a sprig of basil, of rosemary, of marjoram and of thyme in a muslin bag. Put the vegetables, the bag of spices and condiments and the turtle meat in a large stewpan. Cover with 4 quarts stock and bring to the boil uncovered, skim thoroughly, cover and simmer gently for 8 hours at least. It may be necessary to add more stock, in which case add very little at a time and be certain that it is boiling. When the turtle meat is quite tender, remove from pan and put aside. Strain the soup through muslin. When the fat rises to the surface, carefully remove all of it. To clarify the soup add the whites of 3 eggs and the juice of $\frac{1}{2}$ lemon. Put over moderate heat and bring to the boil whisking continuously. When it boils, reduce heat, cover. In 10 minutes, strain through muslin. It will have come beautifully limpid. Cut the turtle meat into 1-inch slices, put into strained soup, add salt and a good pinch of cayenne, $\frac{1}{2}$ cup best dry sherry per quart of soup. Serve hot. A tasty, nourishing but light soup.

We were driven through a winter landscape to a women's college where Gertrude Stein had accepted an invitation to dine with some members of the faculty. The dining-room was really a huge mess hall with acoustics that made a pandemonium of the thousands or was it only hundreds of voices. It was the beautiful young women students who were making this demoniacal noise. No wonder we had always thought of the graduates of the college as sirens, tragic and possibly damned. A restricted dinner was served in a manner appropriate to the surroundings. Gertrude Stein asked if she might have a soft-boiled egg and an orange.

After Gertrude Stein had lectured in New England, we went to Wisconsin, Ohio, Illinois and St. Louis, where the cooking was uniformly good with the exception of a superlative lunch given by a friend of Carl Van Vechten at her vast estate near Minneapolis. The drawing-rooms and dining-room were filled with flowers, largely orchids, the first Tiepolo blue ones we had ever seen. The dining-room table had a bowl of several varieties of hot-house grapes with thin tendrils and tender leaves—and the snow steadily falling outside. Our hostess was in the tradition of a Dumas *fils* heroine, though she was, I believe, the original of Carl Van Vechten's Tattooed Countess. It is unnecessary to say that the menu was entirely a French one, and therefore a recipe of one of its courses has no place here. The temptation however is too great. This is the way to prepare

Lobster Archiduc

Thoroughly wash a live lobster weighing not less than 3 lbs. Plunge into boiling water, allow to cool in liquid. Cut it down the middle and then across, take off the two claws, put aside the coral or eggs. In a deep pan melt over hot flame 4 tablespoons butter and 4 tablespoons oil. When it bubbles, put the six pieces of lobster, in their shell, into the pan. Heat thoroughly, turn with a wooden spoon until each piece is coated with the butter and oil. Then cover the pan and reduce the heat. Cook gently for $\frac{1}{2}$ hour. Drain the lobster. Remove all meat from the shell and replace in the pan with the sauce. Replace over heat. Reheat slowly over low flame. Add the coral or eggs, $\frac{1}{4}$ cup brandy, $\frac{1}{2}$ cup best port wine and 2 tablespoons whisky. Season with salt and cayenne pepper. Cover and allow to boil for 5 minutes. Add 2 cups heavy cream. All to boil. Add the yolks of 2 eggs, heat thoroughly but do not allow to boil. Add the juice of $\frac{1}{4}$ lemon and 5 tablespoons butter in very small pieces, turn gently until melted. Serve. This dish has an illusive flavour.

When we were at St. Paul to our surprise and delight there was a telephone message from Sherwood Anderson. He had heard we were in the neighbourhood. He proposed calling for us and driving us down to meet his wife—they were staying with her sister and their brother-in-law—which he did, through miles of ice and snow-drifts, to sweet people and a festival dinner. It was the happiest of meetings. Of all the delicacies served, it is strange to remark that it was the first time we tasted mint jelly.

In Columbus, Ohio, there was a small restaurant that served meals that would have been my pride if they had come to our table from our kitchen. The cooks were women and the owner was a woman and it was managed by women. The cooking was beyond compare, neither fluffy nor emasculated, as women's cooking can be, but succulent and savoury. Later, at Fort Worth, there was a similar restaurant to which Miss Ela Hockaday introduced us. We were to fly out to California and the restaurant packed us a box of food that was the best picnic lunch ever was. It would be a pleasure to be able to order something approaching it when taking a plane today. Has food on the American planes—not the transatlantic flights but on interior routes—improved? It has not in Europe, it is incredibly bad, even worse than on trains. Do they cook these meals in the locomotive and in the fuselage?

At Detroit there was a strange incident at the hotel which seemed sinister to us. The hardened European visitors became frightened. Gertrude Stein had the habit of an hour's walk after the evening meal, improperly spoken of as dinner. To calm her mind, she went off for a walk, but in a short time she returned quite agitated. Not far from the hotel, from the loudspeaker on a tower with a revolving searchlight, a warning was being repeated that no one was to move until a gunman was caught. A murder had just been committed. Suddenly Joseph Brewer's name flashed into my head. Had we not said we would stay with him if we were in his neighbourhood? He was the president of Olivet College. So we telephoned him and said we would like to be rescued. He said he would come to collect us and our bags, which he did the next morning with a large part of his faculty in several cars. It was an invigorating drive through snow and bitter cold sunshine to Lansing, where we had a carefully prepared lunch. For dessert we had an old-fashioned

Bird's-Nest Pudding

Butter a porcelain pudding dish, slice 8 apples into it, sprinkle with sugar. Pour over them a batter made of 1 cup sour cream, 1 cup flour. Mix well, add the yolks of 3 eggs and 1 cup milk in which has been mixed 1 scant teaspoon baking soda. Beat the whites of 3 eggs, fold into mixture. Bake for $\frac{1}{2}$ hour in medium oven. Brush the top with melted butter and sprinkle with sugar. Brown for 10 minutes. Serve with sweetened heavy cream. This is a pudding we should not neglect.

With a couple of days' rest with Joseph Brewer and the students at Olivet we forgot the horrors of Detroit and started off again. With Gertrude Stein's cousins in their home near Baltimore we enjoyed our first southern hospitality. We went to see Scott Fitzgerald in Baltimore who, with tea, offered us an endless variety of canapés, to remind us, he said, of Paris. In Washington southern hospitality continued. There was no disparity between the inspired negress cook and the enormous kitchen over which she presided. The hospitality was so continuous that there was never time to ask her for a recipe from her vast repertoire. She made the cakes, ices, punches and sandwiches for the parties, and the elaborate lunches and dinners that succeeded each other. No trouble at all, she said, when one has all the best material one needs. A dish, my father once said, can only have the flavour of what has gone into the making of it.

In New York we picked up Carl Van Vechten who was going to Richmond with us to introduce us to some of his friends there. On the way we stopped at Charlottesville where Gertrude Stein was to lecture at the University of Virginia, and where we lunched extremely well with some of the faculty, who pleased us with their divided allegiance to Edgar Allan Poe and Julien Green. At an epicurean dinner at Miss Ellen Glasgow's I was paralysed to find myself placed next to Mr. James Branch Cabell, but his cheery, Tell me, Miss Stein's writing is a joke, isn't it, put me completely at my ease so that we got on very well after that.

At William and Mary we lunched in state with the president at the Governor's house. On the road to Charleston we lunched at an old Planter's Hotel copiously and succulently, for which the French have the nice word *plantureux*. We were asked to lunch at Strawberry. Was the exquisite food more seductive than the incredible water gardens, was the preparation of the menus at the Villa Margharita more exciting than the avenues of camellias? I have never been able to decide. Now they are all one. Changing planes at Atlanta, Gertrude Stein was delighted to see on a huge sign near the airport, Buy Your Meat and Wheat in Georgia.

In New Orleans we found Sherwood Anderson again and he took us to lunch at Antoine's and at a smaller restaurant which we preferred where we ate for the first time

Oysters Rockefeller

Place oysters on the half shell in preheated deep dishes filled with sand (silver sand glistens prettily). Cover the oysters thickly with $^1/_4$ chopped parsley, $^1/_4$ finely chopped raw spinach, $^1/_8$ finely chopped tarragon, $^1/_8$ finely chopped chervil, $^1/_8$ finely chopped basil and $^1/_8$ finely chopped chives. Salt and pepper some fresh breadcrumbs, cover the herbs completely, dot with melted butter and put for 4 or 5 minutes in a preheated 450° oven. Serve piping hot.

This dish is an enormous success with French *gourmets*. It makes more friends for the United States than anything I know.

In New Orleans I walked down to the market every morning realising that I would have to live in the dream of it for the rest of my life. How with such perfection, variety and abundance of material could one not be inspired to creative cooking? We certainly do overdo not only the use of the word but the belief in its widespread existence. Can one be inspired by rows of prepared canned meals? Never. One must get nearer to creation to be able to create, even in the kitchen.

Before leaving Miss Henderson gave us two bottles of orange wine, wine that was still being made in her home. It wasn't until some weeks later that we opened one of the bottles in Chicago and found the wine to be pure ambrosia.

In Chicago we stayed in Thornton Wilder's flat. He had said it would be convenient for Gertrude Stein as it was close to the university where she was to lecture. There was an extensive view from the little flat. It was very exciting, compact and comprehensive. The kitchen, though no larger than a dining-room table, permitted one, with its modern conveniences and marketing by telephone, to cook with the minimum of time and effort quite good meals. Those days are still my ideal of happy house-keeping. Once again we had lovely food with Bobsie Goodspeed, and at old-fashioned restaurants with friends and a delicious dinner with Thornton Wilder at a lakeside restaurant. We even had guests for meals at the flat. The meat or fowl delivered in waxed paper was deposited from the outside hall into the refrigerator, as were also the vegetables, cream, milk, butter and eggs.

On to Dallas where we went to stay with Miss Ela Hockaday at her Junior College. It was a fresh new world. Gertrude Stein became attached to the young students, to Miss Hockaday and the life in Miss Hockaday's home and on the campus. Miss Hockaday explained that all good Texas food was Virginian. Miss Hockaday's kitchen was the most beautiful one I have ever seen, all old coppers on the stove and on the walls, with a huge copper hood over the stove. Everything else was modern white enamel. The only recipe I carried away with me was for cornsticks, not knowing in my ignorance that a special iron was required in which to bake them. But when we sailed to go back to France in my stateroom one was waiting for me, a proof of Miss Hockaday's continuing attentiveness. It was my pride and delight in Paris where it was certainly unique. What did the Germans, when they took it in 1944, expect to do with it? And what are they doing with it now?

At the university at Austin the faculty asked some of the students to meet Gertrude Stein after the lecture. A very stiff punch was served, but when I was about to light a cigarette I was asked not to do so. Only men smoked.

Then we were off to God's own country. It was even more so than I remembered it. If there were more people and more houses, there were com-
pensatingly more fields, more orchards, more vegetables and more gardens.
A great part of the United States that we had seen had been new to me, it
was a revelation of the beauty of our country, but California was unequalled.
Sun and a fertile soil breed generosity and gentleness, amiability and appreciation. It was abundantly satisfying. In Pasadena amongst olive and orange groves we saw our first avocado trees and their fruit offered for sale
stacked in great pyramids, almost as common as tomatoes would be later
in the season. Driving north we heard that the desert wild flowers were in
bloom so we took a day off to see them and the date palms. Through acres
of orchards and artichokes, we made our way north to Monterey where
happy days of my youth had been spent in an adobe house where my friend
Señora B. had been born. The story was that General Sherman had courted
her in the garden of her home, and before leaving Monterey had planted a
rose tree later to be known as the Sherman rose. By the time I stayed with
her she was an exquisite wee old lady with flashing black eyes. She would
throw one of her shawls over my shoulders and say with a devilish glint,
Go out and stand under the rose tree and let the tourists from Del Monte
take your photograph. They will try to give you four bits but you may continue to turn your back on them. Señora B. made a simple Spanish sweet
of which *Panoche* is the coarse Mexican version. She made it like this and
unpretentiously called it

Dulce (1)

In a huge copper pan put quantities of granulated sugar, moisten with
cream, turn constantly with a copper spoon until it is done. Then pour into
glasses.

Señora B. said the longer it cooked the better the flavour would be.
Señora B. would start it early in the morning and would entrust it to me when
she went to mass. It was a compliment I could have dispensed with. As she
was so little she stood on a footstool before her charcoal fire. In her simple but
voluminous dark cashmere clothes she looked like a Zurbaran angel.

Here is my version of the

Dulce (2)

Put 2 cups sugar and 1 cup thin cream in a saucepan and bring to a boil.
Then at once lower the heat and cook very slowly, stirring continuously for
about an hour. It will become heavy and stiff and will have the colour of its
flavour. There are people who like it a lot.

We had stopped at Monterey so that Gertrude Stein could see the house
of Señora B. but it was no longer where it had been. A traffic policeman
came up to us and asked us roughly what we were trying to do. To find
Señora B.'s home, I said. It used to be here. That's right, he said, but years ago
one of those rich easterners came out and bought it and carted it away into
the hills. Carted an adobe house away, I muttered. But he wafted us on.

At Del Monte cooking was still of passionate interest to the management
of the hotel. The same careful attention was given to the kitchen as to the vegetable and flower gardens. Grilled chicken and turkey broilers, spring lamb,
cooked on a spit and basted by brushing it with a bunch of fresh mint, served
with gooseberry jelly and an iced *soufflé*, were still unrivalled experiences.

This is the way to make

Gooseberry Jelly

Take the tips and stalks off 6 lbs. gooseberries, put in a pan over a low flame
with 4 pints water. Simmer until the berries are tender. Turn into a jelly
bag and let the juice run through. Weigh the juice. Place over high flame
and boil briskly for 15 minutes. Add equal weight of sugar. Mix thoroughly
and bring to the boil. Boil for 15 minutes or until it jellies.

Here is the recipe for the ineffable

Iced Soufflé

Put 2 cups sugar in heavy enamelled saucepan with 8 yolks of eggs and 1
whole egg over lowest flame. Beat with a rotary beater until it is quite thick.
This will take some time. When it makes pointed peaks when the egg

beater is removed, take from the stove and flavour with 1 tablespoon kirsch or anisette. Place on ice to cool. Pour into a soufflé dish and sprinkle on top 3 macaroons dried in the oven, rolled and strained. Put in the refrigerator for 3 hours. This is a particular favourite with men.

At Del Monte Lodge we ate for the first time abalone, and thought it a delicious food. It was served in a cream sauce in its shell, lightly browned with breadcrumbs without cheese, we gratefully noticed. Abalone has a delicate flavour of its own and requires no barbecue or barbarous adjuncts.

In San Francisco we indulged in gastronomic orgies—sand dabs *meunière*, rainbow trout in aspic, grilled soft-shell crabs, *paupiettes* of roast fillets of pork, eggs Rossini and *tarte Chambord*. The *tarte Chambord* had been a speciality of one of the three great French bakers before the San Francisco fire. To my surprise in Paris no one had ever heard of it.

At Fisherman's Wharf we waited for two enormous crabs to be cooked in a cauldron on the side-walk, and they were still quite warm when we ate them at lunch in Napa County. Gertrude Atherton took us to lunch at a restaurant where the menu consisted entirely of the most perfectly cooked shell-fish, to her club where the cooking was incredibly good, and to dinner at a club of writers where conversation excelled.

And then the dearest friend sent us a basket of fruit and flowers, fit subject for an Italian painter of the Renaissance, and we tasted for the first time passion fruit. We had known passion-fruit syrup in Paris and thought its flavour exquisite (it made a wonderful ice cream). And now we were told that passion fruit was the fruit of the passion-flower vine. Surely not from the passion-flower vine that has climbed a wall in every garden I ever had.

Then the time had come when we would have to leave California, to leave the United States, to go back to France and cultivate our garden in the Ain. Above everything else I enjoyed working in that garden, but leaving the United States was distressful.

It was not until we were on the *Champlain* again that I realised that the seven months we had spent in the United States had been an experience and adventure which nothing that might follow would ever equal.

The Alice B. Toklas Cook Book (1954)

pineapple pie

1 recipe Plain Pastry

1/3 cup flour

1/2 to 1 cup sugar

1/8 teaspoon salt

2 eggs

1 tablespoon lemon juice

2 cups finely chopped fresh pineapple

2 tablespoons margarine

Prepare pastry. Mix together flour, 1/2 cup sugar, and salt. (The amount of sugar used depends upon tartness of the pineapple.) Beat eggs slightly and combine with the flour and sugar mixture. Stir in lemon juice and pineapple; taste and add more sugar as needed. Pour into 9-inch unbaked shell, dot with margarine, and moisten edge with water. Cover with top crust. Bake 10 minutes at 450° F.; reduce heat to 350° F. and bake 35 minutes longer.

Yield: 9-inch pie ∗ (5 to 6 servings)

Carey D. Miller, Katherine Bazore & Mary Bartow, *Fruits of Hawaii* (1955)

May Sarton

Sukiyaki on the Kona Coast

You consult guides and websites, read restaurant reviews, make reservations months in advance: no amount of advance preparation can guarantee a memorable meal. But on occasion, everything effortlessly falls into place. Here, exploring the big island of Hawaii with a friend, the poet, novelist, and memoirist May Sarton (1912–1995) just happens on a faded roadside sign: "sukiyaki dinners by appointment." What follows—an intimate dinner in a lovely setting, prepared and served with pride and grace, the procession of courses revealing a new cuisine—is an experience worth writing about, still vivid in Sarton's precise and lyrical recollection.

■ ■ ■

The single image that will best bring back for me the peculiar pleasure of that evening on the Kona coast of the island of Hawaii is an incongruous one—my friend and I trying to climb the wall of a room empty except for us and the lizards we were trying to catch. They gathered round the horizontal light fixture over a great window that might have been plate glass but was actually open onto the Pacific Ocean, and thus we could get leverage on the lintel, placing one foot on the sill. Of course we were trying to capture lightning, as elusive as thought itself.

In the end it was we, hanging precariously there, who were caught by our polite Japanese host, who did not betray the slightest surprise to see two middle-aged *haoles*, or mainlanders, in this undignified position. He was bringing us coffee, the final ingredient of a remarkable dinner. We got down rather sheepishly and tried to be properly serious, for we had been in the middle of a conversation with him.

Outside we could hear the incessant lapse and fall of the ocean breaking over the reef. Two dilapidated palms were outlined against a sky that was just turning black after a long cloudless red-gold sunset. Every now and then a bard dove gave its plaintive, flutelike trill. Every now and then the palms clattered like paper in the breeze.

We were on the largest of those extinct volcanoes which sit in the middle of the Pacific, the result of quite recent explosions as geologic time goes, and which still pant now and then like whales troubled in sleep, and tremble; and as late as 1955 saw rivers of burning lava run ravaging down to the sea. We had that day walked in forests of huge tree ferns and we had crossed frozen stretches of lava. This sterile substance was the foundation under all we had seen; no single plant, no tree, no bird but had been brought here from somewhere else, far away, the coconuts floated two thousand miles or more, the seed of a flower carried in a bird's craw.

These islands, as they slowly greened over, had attracted human migrants in waves, first the Polynesians bringing taro, dogs, bananas in their canoes and setting up the primitive principalities and powers of what eventually became Hawaiian royalty; the whalers, the sandalwood merchants, the missionaries, the sugar planters and ranchers, the Chinese and Japanese traders and laborers, and finally the tourists. We were among the last to come, and we would not be staying long. But on this evening we felt the enchantment and the peril of living on the island volcano, born in fire, flowering, and slowly dying in an illimitable relentless blue of sea and sky.

An hour before, we had been sitting in the cocktail bar of one of the big hotels, looking out on a swimming pool and at two soft white American men playing shuffleboard. The hotels might be ocean liners, their verandas decks. The same people—or people who seemed interchangeable—inhabited them season after season, changing as little as the sea urchins, purple, white, and black, we had found that morning in a sea pool, making a sort of hotel out of a piece of hole-indented lava. We looked back across the half mile we had just traveled and it seemed a continent away.

It had happened by the merest chance. Driving along the coast that morning, looking for a place to swim, we had noticed a faded sign announcing sukiyaki dinners by appointment, and pointing down a rough dirt road in the middle of dense kiawe brush. On impulse we turned in, bumping and bumped along till we came to a rough clearing where we saw a new Ford and a couple of sleeping mongrel dogs. The ocean was hidden by a series of one-story wooden buildings, more like shacks, somehow welded together. A few papaya trees, banana plants, and coconut palms stood about casually among piles of rubbish and the creeping lantana that flows out over every waste place unless the morning-glories have already taken over. There was no sign of anything resembling a restaurant, and no human being appeared when we slammed the car door and walked gingerly past one of the dogs who woke up to growl.

We had to shout "is anybody home?" a couple of times before a middle-aged Japanese woman came to the door, but she was evidently at a loss in English. She called back into the recesses of the house and finally a young man with black hair standing straight up on his head came out. Yes, they could serve us a dinner at seven that evening, he said, but with such a dead-pan expression that it was impossible to guess whether ours was an exceptional visitation or the routine thing.

At seven that evening we drove back in the fading light, wondering what we had got ourselves in for. This time we were greeted by an older boy, perhaps twenty, in an immaculate pair of khaki pants and bright-flowered Hawaiian shirt. He led us down a passage and around a corner, up some rickety steps, and finally into a bare room, furnished simply with two straight chairs and a table. One wall was open air, looking out over the ocean, the sunset, and in the immediate foreground a large cement platform smoothed down over piles of lava rubble, standing out to sea like a wharf. The table was set with three bowls at each place, napkins, chopsticks, a bottle of soy sauce. That was all.

In this atmosphere, plain to the point of poverty, restful by its very absence of decoration, we stood in the paneless window feeling the soft evening air on our faces, and talked with our host's son, for so he told us he was, introducing his father proudly as a son should, treating him like a great actor who would not, of course, appear in the first few moments: "My father is the chef." As the boy looked out onto the stark landscape of cement and lava he was obviously visualizing a scene that was vivid in his imagination. The building of the platform, he informed us, represented the first arduous step toward the creation of a real restaurant here. "And when I get out of the Army," he said, "we'll be able to go ahead."

The slim line of his body enhanced by bare feet, his relaxed posture against the lintel, his flowered shirt, and his easy grace in talking to strangers seemed far from the usual image of a G.I., but these islanders are remarkable for their social ease and personal dignity. He told us that he was home on furlough after a "terrible" winter in Maine. "I thought I would die of the cold, forty below once."

He had paid for the flight home rather than hang around bumming free rides, for that would have taken nearly a week. Now the precious month was nearly gone; in a few days he would have to go back to the mainland and ship out to Japan. The Army was making a cosmopolitan of him (how casually he could speak of New York!), but it had given him also, clearly, a renewed sense of loyalty to his family and of love for this island. "I could not live anywhere else." I asked if he had relatives in Japan. "A few cousins perhaps, no one close."

He seemed curiously uneager for this experience ahead, one for which I myself envied him. His mother, he told us, though born in Honolulu like his father, had gone back to the home country as a child and thus, he explained, had learned no English, could neither read nor write. His younger brother wanted to be a teacher and perhaps would go to the mainland to study—but they all wanted to stay here, and were involved in life on the island, each in his own way. "I have a little sister, too, seven years old," he said checking a smile, suddenly shy, as if she were a rather particular joy, one perhaps not to be shared. He was an entrepreneur, a man of big dreams who would see that they were realized. He was, one might say, the motive power of the family, and his father was the artist, the man of skills.

"My father will come soon," he announced, as if he sensed that the moment had arrived for the star's entrance onto the stage. As a matter of fact, the bare room was rather like a stage, and our host now stepped onto it with a distinct flourish. He wore a chef's round white cap, and bore in his hands the small stove and utensils for making sukiyaki; he was followed at a discreet distance by his wife, who carried various bowls of ingredients. He greeted us with a smile of authority and graciousness and bade us take our places.

The G.I. son now made a discreet withdrawal, to reappear with a series of dishes which he placed before us. There was a plate of what looked like rather uninteresting noodles but turned out to be a delicious crab-and-noodle salad; our delight was such that our host asked if he might taste it himself. "For that is my wife's doing," he said, "and I myself do not know what she has made for you."

There was a long boat-shaped dish upon which lay dark pink oval slices of raw fish in a basket of shredded green leaves, a delicacy new to me. There was a plate of cucumber salad, and the inevitable bowl of soy sauce with white radish sliced into it. We sat down to this feast, not concealing our pleasure, while our host stood at the end of the table, smiling upon us like a beneficent god.

He had a lean dried-out brown face, thin iron-strong arms that showed below a short-sleeved cotton shirt, and kind shrewd eyes. Evidently he regarded the serving of a meal as a performance and our appreciation of it as an accolade.

While we ate he talked, introducing the next scene of this meal that was also a play with a deprecatory description of his fishing that morning. "I got only two small Kona crabs," he said, "but if you would like them . . ." Two crabs appeared on the table as if he had clapped his hands. They were pink and white, about five inches across; we picked them up to admire them and he came over to show us just how to cut them open. They tasted fresh and clear as the day itself. Meanwhile his wife had appeared shyly in the doorway and murmured something in Japanese.

"Perhaps you would like to taste some of my wife's abalone soup as well?"

Indeed we would. Two bowls of soup were added to the congregation of dishes already on the table. Every now and then the little girl, with very bright eyes, made a brief appearance in the doorway, but vanished if one of us noticed her there. Every now and then my friend and I exchanged a look of delight, of complicity, in the occasion. Meanwhile the preparations for sukiyaki were going gravely forward at the other end of the table.

"Yes," our host told us proudly, "this is island beef. You will find it very tasty." He lifted the veined red slivers into the sauce, one by one, and added mushrooms and scallions like an alchemist. A delicious fume began to rise from the pan. He looked up with a smile, enjoying our anticipation.

"We usually serve twenty people here in an evening," he said casually. "Clubs make a reservation and often we put the stoves on each table, and let the customers be their own cooks."

"They must be good at it," I ventured.

"They think they are." He smiled the smile of the professional, and moved the various ingredients in the pan deftly around. A big bowl of rice was laid on the table. The great moment, the climax of the play, was drawing near. But we had not as yet mentioned anything to drink. Now that we had established ourselves as connoisseurs (at least my friend could do so, for she has lived in the East and uses chopsticks with agility), we felt we might. Tea, perhaps?

"I thought you might like a little warm sake," he said happily, as if we had picked up the right cue. "I am not supposed to serve liquor, but never mind." And soon the small cups appeared and a pot of the slightly bittersweet drink.

"But you must hold out your cup to me," he told us, realizing that our pouring out for ourselves was a lapse in manners we would not have wished to make had we known better. He filled the cups solemnly, and we drank.

The slight tension of preparing the sukiyaki over, our host visibly relaxed while we ate it. "When my boy comes out of the Army we shall get started here, have a real restaurant. You must come back then, when we have twenty tables outside, and an orchestra."

The sun had gone down while we talked, and we looked out into the darkness where the dream grew big. But we did not say how glad we were to be here before it came true and our private play turned into a public performance.

"May I take a little bowl of sukiyaki to my daughter?" he asked when he saw that there was far more than we could eat. "She is very fond of it before she goes to bed."

He came back and we talked of the big issue in the air—statehood for the Territory—about to come up again before Congress.

"Twenty years ago, it must have been, when Roosevelt was President, we voted on this question, 'Yes' or 'No.' And everyone voted 'Yes.' A long time," he said.

There had been the war, of course, when the Nisei from these islands volunteered by the hundreds for the Army, and proved once and for all where they stood. They were too large a minority, too closely interwoven with the island economy, to be persecuted, as our Nisei on the mainland had been persecuted after Pearl Harbor. Here the war had left no such scars. It had consolidated all the races on the islands as Hawaiians.

And now that the Territory had gone Democratic in the 1954 elections, the Japanese were beginning to come into political power. We thought of these things as we sat talking to this man so fully master of his family and of his fate, so confident of his future, "when my boy comes out of the Army."

The moment of silence had arrived that follows on any really good meal, the silence that is the final applause. We took out cigarettes.

"Tea? Coffee?" he asked.

I longed for a cup of coffee but hesitated; it was hardly in the tradition. But fortunately we did ask for coffee, for our host beamed.

"People like my coffee," he said modestly. It was truly his, for he told us he had grown it himself.

I looked at the thin man standing so proudly before us, smiling, and realized that although he worked in a hotel all day, he also managed to find time to catch the fish and crabs we had just eaten, and to pick, roast, and grind the coffee we were about to taste, as well as to cook meals for twenty of an evening and to rear a loyal family.

Our host went out to brew the coffee, and for the first time we noticed the lizards on the wall. The lights had come on, and the lizards had come to bask in the warmth of their artificial sun, immobile until a shadow came near, then moved lightning swift, impossible to catch.

"Geckos," our host said when he came back and found us spread-eagled on the wall. "But you'll never catch one!"

We felt like children who have been given a party and now are behaving a bit rowdily at the end. We sat down chastened to taste the home-grown coffee, and found it excellent.

"But how do you find time?" we asked.

"My wife helps," he said, "and the children, when there is nothing else to do." He managed to get enough out of his few acres to take care of all his customers and have plenty to spare.

When we returned to our hotel room with its balcony that looked out over the reefs and reverberated each time one of the big combers rolled up and broke in a loud peal of thunder, we felt loath to turn in on the *House Beautiful* studio couches, with a big modern lamp standing between them. We sat on the balcony for a long time, watching the combers, lit up by a spotlight from the hotel garden, rise in a marvelous curve, fall, and break into foam.

The Reporter, June 27, 1957

Clementine Paddleford

from A Flower for My Mother

Few food writers have traveled as widely and enthusiastically in the pursuit of culinary lore as Clementine Paddleford (1898–1967), longtime contributor to *Gourmet*, food editor (1936–1966) of the New York *Herald Tribune*, and author of *How America Eats* (1960). James Beard, who met her as she was about to go "out for a cruise on an atomic submarine to see how they all eat," called her "the getting-aroundest person I have ever known"; she even learned to pilot a plane in order to crisscross the country more efficiently. Here, though, Paddleford sticks close to home, evoking her early years in Stockdale, Kansas, in an affectionate passage from her 1958 memoir, *A Flower for My Mother*.

■ ■ ■

Mother took little stock in the notion that there must be money to buy leisure in which to have a good time. She felt money was a prop on which people were inclined to lean too heavily. Why be a beggar in the midst of plenty? Even a garden event was often made a party occasion. The first strawberries of the season were guests of honor at a strawberry-shortcake supper. This fruit was seasonal then, no eating of berries around the calendar.

When the berries were full and red ripe, drooping to the ground under the leaves, my job was to pick half a milk-pail full for the first shortcake. It was as exciting as a treasure hunt, one's hand searching out the heart-shaped fruit deep under the leaves. A sudden glow of crimson—and into the bucket.

The shortcake was baked in a dripping pan, no mangy single biscuit business of "one for you" and "one for me." A rich biscuit dough was used, baked to flaky perfection, then turned to a turkey platter, split in two, the bottom half lavishly buttered. Over this went the crushed berries. On with the top half. More crushed berries over this; whole berries for decoration. The juice ran in rivulets, making a crimson lake in the plate. Hurry this to the table along with a water pitcher of cream. Little else was needed to make a meal. Enough shortcake was made for second and third helpings. Coffee for the ending, and as Mr. Pepys would write, always with such seeming satisfaction, "And so to bed."

And here is the recipe I remember so well. Shortcake dough: Mix and sift three cups sifted flour, five teaspoons baking powder, one-half cup sugar, one teaspoon salt, and a pinch of nutmeg. Cut in one-half cup shortening with two knives or work with pastry blender. Beat one egg until light; combine with one-half cup milk (about) and add gradually to flour mixture to make a soft dough. Turn on a lightly floured board and knead with a light touch; knead quickly while counting to ten. Divide dough into two parts. Roll each into a round or oval, one-fourth inch in thickness. Place rings together with butter between. Bake in a 450° F. oven for twelve to fifteen minutes. Made in this fashion, the layers separate easily when the shortcake is baked, the outside crisp, the inside well done.

The strawberries: Wash two quarts strawberries or more and remove their Robin Hood caps. Lay the largest berries aside to keep whole. Slightly crush remaining berries with potato masher, add one cup sugar, more or less, as the palate dictates. Let ripen in a warmish place until the biscuit bakes. Split the great biscuit. Butter and center on your largest meat platter. Ladle on half of the crushed sweetened fruit, cap with the top layer, add remaining crushed berries. The big berries, those with plump, perfect figures, still wearing their bloom, are jewels for the crown. Pass with a pitcher of thick cream. Those top berries, cold and sweet like wine, the crushed berries, warm and tasting of sugar and sun, the shortcake crunchy and rich of butter—divine in its goodness.

When sweet corn was ready, the very first pick was made a meal all by itself, nothing but roasted ears and bowls of melted butter. We had no fancy corn holders. We just took the ear in hand. It seems to me we are losing much these days when we no longer make a touch contact with the good things of the earth.

By supper's end we were a well-buttered lot, greased from ear to ear. Sweet-corn kernels on clothes and hair, skin in our teeth. A splendid party.

When the first new potatoes and peas came along these were creamed together and eaten with a platter of fried chicken and a wilted lettuce salad.

Fried-mush breakfasts were an eventful meal, to follow usually a Saturday-night bowl supper of mush and milk. The mush was made with yellow corn meal sifted in fine pinches between thumb and finger into a big kettle of boiling salted water—violently boiling. With the other hand the cook stirred.

The rule was a very little corn meal boiled a very long while (like for Injun porridge) in a vast amount of water. When all the meal was in, not a lump remaining, the kettle was pushed to the back of the stove where the mush slowly cooked with sputters and spurts as the slow rising bubbles broke, cooked and cooked until it was the consistency of thick whipped cream.

Mush left over (we always made plenty) was turned into a greased baking pan and put in a cool place until morning. By then it had set and was ready for slicing. Sometimes if there were left-over bacon, this was crumbled and stirred through the warm porridge.

Fried mush for breakfast was slathered with butter, served with a brown-sugar syrup or with sorghum molasses. And sometimes there was honey when the boys had found a bee tree and dared the taking.

The first big snow meant snowflake ice cream. It was made, if possible, while the snow was falling or very soon after. It must be a big snow, several inches deep, to avoid scraping into dirt. It should be a well-frozen snow and fine, not the soft, wet kind. Snow gatherers would hunt for a drift, scrape off the top surface, then scoop a bucketload of the glistening particles.

In the kitchen all would be ready. A custard had been made using a quart of milk, two eggs, one cup of sugar, a pinch of salt and vanilla flavoring. After cooking this was let come to room temperature. Snow was dipped into a big bowl and the custard poured in slowly, a second helper stirring vigorously. More snow, more stirring. As the mixture thickened it chilled and began freezing. When no more snow could be beaten into the mass, snowflake ice cream was served. One of my happiest memories of snowbound afternoons is "Mother and me" lapping into a bowl with big spoons. This nectar had to be eaten in a hurry. "Tastes good," I'd say. "Of course," she'd answer. "Tastes like mittens and vanilla." But the great ingredient was the stirred-in joy.

Therein lies the secret of my mother's cooking. Every last dish seasoned well with love. She knew that eating was more than just filling hollow legs, just as environment is more than a place. This is one of the things she tried to teach her daughter. Cooking should never be made a chore.

A Flower for My Mother (1958)

Peg Bracken

from Good Cooksmanship, or How to Talk a Good Fight

In 1963, Betty Friedan's *The Feminine Mystique* asked women to question the limits of their traditional roles, bringing feminism to a boil. But the pot had clearly been simmering, as this excerpt from *The I Hate to Cook Book* (1960), by one-time advertising copywriter Peg Bracken (born 1918, now retired in Hawaii), humorously suggests. A surprise best seller, the book offers a broadly satirical look at housewifely rivalries and the increasing pressure not just to cook, but to cook with *cordon bleu* sophistication. "Good Cooksmanship" retains its bite, in this later phase of the gourmet revolution, even if some of the details now seem quaintly dated: are today's higher culinary expectations really about pleasure, or just the latest iteration of a system of social constraint?

■ ■ ■

Now once in a while you'll find yourself in a position where you have to talk about cooking. This is usually a sitting-down position with other ladies hemming you in so you can't get away.

Actually, your cooking is a personal thing, like your sex life, and it shouldn't be the subject of general conversation. But women who love to cook often love to talk about it, too, and if you're going to make any sort of showing at all, there are several points to keep in mind.

For instance, words.

Never say "fry" if you don't mean "deep-fat fry." You can say

> "pan fry"
> "pan broil"
> "sauté"
> "brown in butter"
> "sizzle in butter"

or you may go all the way and say "cook it *à la pôele*," which is a French phrase meaning "stew in butter at such a low temperature that the object is cooked before it starts to brown." But "fry" means the way you would cook doughnuts, if you ever did, which you don't, because you can buy perfectly lovely doughnuts all made.

(The boys behind the counter at Joe's Diner aren't aware of these distinctions, of course, and if you ask them to sauté you an egg, or cook one *à la pôele*, there's no telling what sort of an *oeuf* you'd get. But you are not down at Joe's Diner.)

Similarly, if you can possibly avoid it, don't say "onions." Say "shallots," even though you wouldn't know one if you saw one. This gives standing to a recipe that otherwise wouldn't have much. (The same thing is true of "hamburger" versus "ground round" or "ground sirloin." Never say "hamburger," even if you mean "hamburger.") You're on safe territory if anyone calls you on the shallot business, too, because shallot also means a small green onion, as well as some distant and exotic relative of the onion family, so don't worry a bit.

Another one is "cooking sherry." Just say "sherry." Actually, cooking sherry is quite satisfactory for your modest purposes in most hot cooked entrees. It is cheaper to use, too, because you don't nip as you cook, and, moreover, it saves you on salt. But I'm warning you, the cooking buffs will raise their eyebrows. And while we're at it, you might glance over the following greatly abbreviated list:

Naughty Words	*Good Words*
crisp	crispy
hot	piping hot
cold	chilled
put it in the oven	pop in the oven
it tastes good with . . .	it's a good foil for . . .
light brown	golden
hard-boiled	hard-cooked
filling	rib-sticking
top with bacon	garnish with crispy bacon curls

This brings us to another related department, and it is a good thing it does. You've no idea how hard it is to organize a cookbook, with all the different things in it. Next time, I'm going to write a hair-pants Western with just a horse and a hero.

However, the department we now find ourselves in is FANCY GARNISHES, and those mad gay touches that are yours alone. These are the things you see in cookbooks and magazines that have you thinking, "Now that's a cute idea; I ought to *do* that," but you never remember to.

Well, here they are again. I must emphasize, though, that things that seem mad and gay to us who hate to cook are probably pretty ho-hum to the people who love to. You see, when you hate to cook, you are singularly unobservant where cooking and food are concerned. You're also easily impressed; and if you ever do anything so foreign to your nature as floating a lemon slice on black bean soup, you talk about it for weeks afterward.

Well, a lemon slice isn't the only thing you can float on soup.

There's popcorn. Plain movie popcorn or cheese popcorn. It looks pretty and it's easier than croutons.

Then there are chopped walnuts, pecans, or toasted almonds, any one of which is good on cream of chicken or celery soup.

There's also chopped raw celery or green pepper or green onion tops for any sort of soup that needs some additional crispness.

Then there are fancy garnishes in general.

For instance, with any sort of melon you can serve a bowl of chopped crystallized ginger or powdered ginger.

You can garnish nearly any meat, hot or cold, with chutneyed peach halves. You brush the fresh or canned peach halves with melted butter, put them in a 350° oven for ten minutes, then fill the halves with chutney and heat them *another* five minutes.

And to garnish fish, you can dip small bunches of white seedless grapes first in lemon juice or egg white and then in granulated sugar, dry them on a rack, and scatter them around the platter.

Then, if you've bought some frozen chicken pies, you can stud their tops thickly with almonds (blanched but not toasted, because that'll happen while the pies bake) before you put the pies in the oven.

Should you ever be so foolish as to make cream-cheese balls for a canapé, you may stick thin pretzel sticks into them instead of toothpicks. That way the whole thing gets eaten, and you don't have your ash trays overflowing with toothpicks. (This works just as well, of course, with cubed processed loaf cheese.)

Speaking of canapés, a stack of small Mexican tin plates is a good thing to have around. These aren't for the guests' sake, exactly, but for yours. When someone is juggling a drink and a cigarette and a dip-loaded chip, it can be hard on the sofa. The tin plates won't break, as your bread-and-butter ones will, and they look a little special and festive.

This is as good a place as any to digress briefly into the gay mad aspects of the *container* department, or, what you serve things *in*. For instance, the clever hostess often serves her cookies in a brandy snifter! This would seem to leave her the cooky jar to serve her brandy in, but then a lively party is probably what she's after.

You may use tall beer glasses for your parfaits, too. Or middle-sized brandy snifters. Or ordinary water goblets. The only thing to be careful of here is to make sure you have a fine complete glassware service, containing parfait glasses you *could* have used. Otherwise you just look terribly valiant.

Then there are napkin rings. The ordinary person puts napkins in them, but the clever hostess has bottoms put in hers and uses them for cigarette cups. Or instead of serving a liqueur in her elongated liqueur glasses, she puts one or two little flowers in them, like hyacinths or pansies, and puts them between each pair of place settings, instead of having one floral centerpiece. This, of course, uses up her liqueur glasses, but we can assume that she's serving Irish Coffee.

However, this is far too big a field to cover in the small space available here. To sum up: When you are looking for something to put something in, think of an *unlikely* object to put it in—jam in the eggcups, flowers in the chamberpot, bats in the bird cage—and then *do* it.

And so, back to food, and conversations about it. There are four handy words to remember: OF COURSE I ALWAYS . . . This is your leadin for any of those little touches you want to get across. Never cry, "Girls! I tried the darnedest thing the other day, and it tasted just marvelous! What I did was . . ." No, you understate it, you throw it away, with "Of course, I always mix my dry mustard with white wine" and if you're among people who'll believe anything, you can substitute champagne for white wine, for this is highly regarded in certain circles I don't belong to.

The big thing is to remember those four little words, OF COURSE I ALWAYS

. . . add a quarter of a cup of sesame seeds to my sage-onion chicken dressing

. . . drop a couple of chocolate bits into my demitasse for a good mocha taste

. . . dip fish and chops in biscuit mix or pancake flour before I pan broil them

. . . brush steaks or chops with soy sauce before I broil them

. . . add some tarragon or savory to my scrambled eggs

. . . add a little oregano to the garlic in my garlic bread

. . . add a little chervil to my ordinary biscuit mix

. . . add a little brandy to my pumpkin pie

. . . put a little grated orange peel in my cranberry sauce

. . . blend chopped parsley and a dash of lemon juice with butter and put a dollop of it on broiled steaks

. . . put a little red wine in my onion soup

. . . fatigue my lettuce.

This last, incidentally, is a nice gambit in conversations of this sort, because chances are good that someone will ask you what it means. It means to toss your salad greens with just a drop or two of oil–so that each leaf gets a microscopically thin coating–*before* you add your salad dressing. For some reason, it makes the greenery crisper.

Now, there is one more thing we must consider in this chapter: THE SPECIALTY.

These days it is important to have a specialty, because you never can tell on what bright sunny morning you may wake up and discover that you are a celebrity. Perhaps you were the eleven-billionth person to go through the Holland Tunnel, or maybe you had ten children in two years, all quintuplets.

No matter. The reporters will be around, and the second thing they'll ask you for, after your measurements, is your Kitchen Specialty. You owe it to yourself and to your public to have something on tap besides tuna sandwiches.

The I Hate to Cook Book (1960)

John Berry

Toward Fried Chicken

A dish as central to the American experience as fried chicken is bound to elicit strong feelings. In the following pieces, two writers—John Berry (1915–2000), a California-born poet and novelist with an interest in eastern philosophy, and William Styron (1925–2006), a native Virginian—offer distinct perspectives on this iconic food. For Berry, the cook, like other craftsmen, ought to have "personal knowledge of his materials from beginning to end," so he takes his readers not only through the frying but the butchering and plucking of a humble bird. Styron, on the other hand, is content to begin with frozen chicken parts; what matters most, a consideration Berry never mentions, is that the bird be a tender "broiler," not an overgrown "fryer." Neither writer advocates a thick-crusted, Maryland-style, batter-fried bird—they're united in preferring a light dusting of flour to make a nice crispy skin. And both agree on bacon grease as the only acceptable frying medium. But on the crucial question of just how much bacon grease is required, the two men part company. Berry, for whom the holistic act of preparation seems to matter most, is almost cavalierly optimistic about technique: "I find it difficult to believe that any man or woman of good will can bungle the job of frying," he writes. Styron takes a darker view. Most Southern fried chicken is ruined, he complains, "by inattentiveness, by insouciance, but the idea of—well, it's just a chicken to fry, I'll throw it in the pan." It's just possible that these differences might be arbitrary, but no one really believes this when favorite foods are concerned. No difference in measure or timing or protocol is too tiny to matter big time. Families have fallen apart over lard vs. Crisco pie crusts.

■ ■ ■

It is my firm conviction that every carnivore should kill his own meat at least once in his life—once might be enough for a particularly sensitive and observant person to grasp the full significance of the basic act of taking a living creature in his hands and killing it, preparing it, eating it. My objection to hiring others to do one's killing is not based on the idea that one is evading a moral responsibility through some sort of squeamishness—it is painful for me to interest myself in moral problems of any kind: they invariably remind me that I survive by wronging others and thrive only on their uncertain charity. The objection is based rather on considerations of the Craft and of the Life. The craftsman should have personal knowledge of his materials from beginning to end, or his craft will suffer. I would not care to make such a categorical statement about the human being (as differentiated from the craftsman) in the midst of his shadowy and relativistic Life; under these uncontrolled conditions one could not be sure what would take the place of the old misconceptions. I suggest only that here is an important experience that is filled with aesthetic and metaphysical possibilities which must stem from a concrete action; an area of insight as against an area of inblindness. (I hope it is clear that I wish to *encourage* the eating of meat.)

I shall not attempt to outline the manifold possibilities of killing a chicken, of cutting him up in a sensitive way, exploring the points of juncture, admiring perhaps the parallels to one's own body (including the index finger and the thumb, which exist in a modified form on the wings). Why, indeed should one choose a chicken? For several reasons: he is inexpensive, easily obtained, convenient to handle, fiery but of a fairly remote connection, he has a long, vulnerable neck, and he is so inherently delicious that I find it difficult to believe that any man or woman of good will could bungle the job of frying him.

It seems to me of little importance how you kill the chicken, as long as you get blood on your hands (where it belongs, just as clay belongs on a potter's hands and ink on an etcher's) and take care not to cause him unnecessary suffering, since that would be to introduce extraneous moral issues into a highly formal act. A sharp hatchet and a chopping-block under the open sky can be completely satisfactory. Two nails driven into the block near one edge, close together but bent apart somewhat at the top, will be handy for holding the chicken's head still while you stretch his neck across the block. Feelings of grief, dignity, exhilaration, expiation, rage, compassion, voluptuousness and the like will naturally arise in the killer, but they should not be allowed to spoil his aim. A botched beheading means a deep involvement, with unpredictable results.

A chicken freed of his head will leap and leap. This helps the victim to get the blood out of his system. It does little harm provided that you have plenty of room to dodge and don't mind the spouting. It does tend to bruise the chicken, so that you get a little more dark meat than you would otherwise.

A simple way to avoid this is to hold him in a bag during his final convulsions; however, I think this is rather ignominious. When I don't want a chicken to go looking for his head, I quickly pluck a tuft of feathers from his back and lay him on that tuft, on his back. The tuft must coincide with the place from which it was plucked. After a moment he lies quietly and dies. But he must not be touched for at least ten minutes, or he will resume the struggle.

When he has stiffened a little, seize your bloody chicken by the feet and immerse him completely for about two seconds in a big pot of boiling water. This loosens the feathers. Make sure you have dipped the wings well. Throw him on a drainboard and start to work. (There is a way to make him let go of his feathers without scalding, but it is extremely wicked. Any witch will be glad to show you, for a nominal fee.) After you have plucked out all his feathers, you may find that your chicken has hair. In that case, build a big fire and poke him into it briefly, turning him this way and that. This singes away the hair. You are now ready to cut up a naked chicken. Be sure your butcher knife is sharp. Let me persuade you to cut up that chicken thoughtfully. Don't do violence to the form.

A note on waste and other casual methods: I am peevish at people who are so much at home in the world that they take its processes for granted. He who treats the world as his oyster is destined to shatter his bridgework on a pearl. (In this matter the Deity is in full accord with the Greeks.) Save the head, neck, feet, heart, liver, lungs, gizzard and fat. They're all good food. You can use the fat to fry with—it's expensive if you buy it. The other parts are excellent for soup or gravy, or you can fry them along with the rest. (I have sometimes considered those juicy pin-feathers too. I fear the spleen.)

Salt the pieces, drop them into a paper bag with some flour in it, shake them around, bring them out all powdery. Fry them in deep bacon grease that you have saved up—two or three inches of it. (Butter and olive oil cost too much. They also have a way of changing the subject. Butter makes chicken taste like eggs, olive oil makes it taste like peanuts. Bacon grease is piquant and economical and does not detract from the chickenness of the chicken.) Don't let your fire get too hot or you'll burn the chicken black; but you should have a nifty little blaze—not too low or you'll cook him too thoroughly. Try to get the feel of the process without scorching yourself in excess. The lid on the frying pan protects you; it also keeps you from seeing what is happening to the chicken. Be of good cheer. Butter is for blisters.

After about fifteen minutes the pieces might be nicely brown on the bottom. If so, turn them over. When they have cooked a while on the other side (maybe you should add some more grease?), start testing. Pull out a piece and cut into it next to the bone to see if it has stopped being pink. Smaller, thinner pieces get done more quickly than the others, so be sure to take them out first. Don't cook that chicken one minute too long, or you'll have a dry, mediocre bunch of fowl on your hands.

If you're alone, by all means lay manners aside and eat the whole chicken yourself, having fasted beforehand. It will cheer you enormously. If others are present, you must either curb your instincts or provide more chicken. (In running back and forth between the table and the frying pan, practice Zen. The chicken is in the man and the man is in the chicken. Who got there first?) All you need to go with it is a green salad and a bottle of dry, red wine.

The Artists' and Writers' Cookbook (1961)

William Styron

Southern Fried Chicken (with Giblet Gravy)

Here, then, is another view of the proper approach to fried chicken, as proposed by William Styron (1925–2006), the distinguished author of *Lie Down in Darkness* (1951), *The Confessions of Nat Turner* (1969), *Sophie's Choice* (1979), and other modern classics. For Styron, the familiar food inspires the sort of impassioned opinions usually reserved for politics or religion—and he takes it upon himself to lay down the law.

■ ■ ■

Of all indigenous American culinary triumphs, probably the most put-upon, misunderstood, and generally abused is the Southern fried chicken which in its pure state almost no one ever gets to eat. The abuse is usually justifiable. What does "Southern fried chicken" ordinarily conjure up? To many people it signifies only memories of the great automobile routes wending southward from Washington, D.C., through Virginia and the Carolinas and Georgia, and those squat, slatternly roadside restaurants whose signs bid one to EAT (the noun-variant is EATS, and though our language is incontestably the noblest on earth, there is a raw, anorexia-producing quality in such words that makes one understand why French is the gourmet tongue), and whose personnel and glum interiors bespeak such a basic non-interest in food that the effect—were it not for the pervasive air of commerce—is almost ascetic. In such places Southern fried chicken is invariably the specialty, and similarly a travesty and a blight; there is no wonder that Southern fried chicken has received such a bad name, considering the ignominy it has undergone in these miserable establishments.

A sullen, dark scullion-maid is sent next door (it is considered profitable to run these places in conjunction with a chicken yard), instructed to wring the neck of the largest, most superannuated laying hen she can put her hands on. This she does, and then the enormous fowl is most cursorily plucked, eviscerated, and cut up for frying. Frying of course means something called "deep fry," which is to say that the owner has bought a large stainless steel vat, in which it is possible to allow several gallons of peanut oil to simmer for days on end without undergoing any significant evaporation. (It is the odor of rancid peanut oil, incidentally, that numbs the buds of smell, and gives to these places, all of them, such a gray, mercifully half-perceived, oleaginous aroma.) Needless to say, to "deep fry"–to *immerse* rather than properly to fry–is not to fry at all, it is to pickle. As in the pickling process, deep frying allows for maximum permeation (in this instance, of grease) and is at the same time extremely economical, analogously resembling, let us say, the tasteless compression of frozen orange juice, or, even better, that marvel of American food technocracy which Kafka invented– the packaged breakfast cereal which is called not a breakfast food, not even a cereal, but simply "K." But worst of all is that this Southern fried chicken tastes horrible, it is both unpalatable and indigestible (at least that Kellogg product is not downright harmful); and one of our greatest national shames is that we have no central governing body, as the French have with Cognac and Roquefort, which might make mandatory certain controls over what could be, and should be, one of the greatest glories of our native cuisine. As it is, we have grease-soaked, old, pickled chicken, and I should like to venture my conviction that to rectify this disgrace is at the moment at least as important as, say, the winning of a Davis Cup, or possibly even a Nobel Prize for anything.

Southern fried chicken can be sublime. It is basically simple to produce, but one must be attentive and careful always. Most Southern fried chicken (I am not even thinking now of the unspeakable highway restaurants) is ruined in the home by inattentiveness, by insouciance, by the idea of–well, it's just a chicken to fry, I'll throw it in the pan. No attitude could be more disastrous, and for the production of truly great Southern fried chicken it should be remembered that at least one and a half hours of sober, selfless, undeviating effort must be spent in order to produce a satisfactory result. If this discipline be observed (and pride be taken in the fact, that this discipline must be as exacting, and can be as rewarding, as that which created a *coq au vin*), the result may be a triumph. But without discipline, without attentiveness–nothing. You *cannot* go into the other room and booze it up with your waiting guests.

First, the chicken must be very young and very tender, therefore rather small–"broiler" size. Much as one might dislike the idea of frozen

meat, the fact remains that most packaged frozen chicken parts are usually smaller and more tender than those available at the butcher's counter.
Certainly they are more succulent, in the final outcome, than those mammoth legs and breasts sold by the butcher as "fryers," so I suggest that
unless you can get an authentic spring chicken from your butcher, you
choose the frozen parts put up by Birdseye, Swanson, etc. Secondly, the
covering—the carapace. There is a school, developed mainly in the State
of Maryland, which holds that, before cooking, the chicken parts should
be immersed in some sort of "batter." This is absolute rubbish. Southern
fried chicken should have after cooking a firm, well-developed crust—this
is one of its glories—but the "batter" principle simply won't hold up after
pragmatic examination. The "batter," usually made of corn meal and cream
and all sorts of extraneous substances, causes a tough thick shell to form
over the chicken after cooking, so that there is a genuine discreteness involved: "batter," carapace and chicken interior tend to fall apart one from
the other, whereas an indissolubility of chicken and outer covering is
what is needed. Simple flour, therefore, is the answer—flour liberally laced
beforehand with salt and pepper. I cannot emphasize this "no-batter" or
"no-Chicken a la Maryland" principle enough. Naturally people should
eat fried chicken in their fingers, and if you have ever been to a dinner
where fried chicken Maryland-style was served, and have observed how
the superfluous outer covering of "batter" pulls away from the chicken,
without sense or savor, into people's teeth, you will understand what I
mean. Flour—simple flour—on the other hand, merges and melds with the
chicken in cooking, and therefore should always be used. But remember
again that the flour should be seasoned with salt and pepper before dipping the chicken into it. Now we are almost ready, but here come the most
crucial items of all: what kind of fat? how much fat? how long should the
chicken be cooked?

I'm afraid that only bacon fat will really do. Crisco and its imitators, Wes-
son Oil, peanut oil, and so forth, will suffice, but only pure bacon drippings—
uncontaminated by any other kind of fat, especially the tallowy fat of the
lamb—should be used, short of the craziest emergency. I do not know why
this is so, except that chicken fried in bacon fat simply tastes better—I have
tried them all—and that should do, for the purposes of this essay.

As for the second question, it is extremely important to recognize that we are not deep frying; indeed, we are doing almost the exact opposite: we are *shallow* frying, and the more shallow the fat the better. This point is critical, as I tried to indicate earlier about "deep fry" and its consequences. Let us have no facetiousness when we come to this matter: one half inch, repeat, one half inch, *at the most*, is the optimum depth of fat in the pan, and there should be an effort to maintain this depth (more or less and with considerable give and take, in spite of my strictures) throughout the entire cooking process. The possible permeation of fat is at all costs to be avoided, and one half inch more or less, seems to represent a tolerable limit. (There is also a covered pan vs. open pan controversy which enters here, and is not worth dealing with: people who cook with a covered pan—"all wishfully blind," as Hopkins says—are simply not concerned with immediacy, or with the fact that the entire chicken is getting hopelessly soggy with steam.)

Medium heat throughout is best, though it may be high at the very first. There are schools which hold that the fat should be popping hot before the floured chicken parts are added to the pan, but it makes no difference whatever; I have seen superb Southern fried chicken emerge after the parts have been added to the cold fat. Practicality, however, dictates that, generally speaking, the fat *will* be hot, if only because it almost invariably needs to be melted in order to cover the bottom of the pan. The cooking time itself is the most speculative aspect of the whole process. No attention should be paid to cookbooks which ordain no more than 40, or 45, or 50 minutes. Experience has taught me that a leg or a thigh, being relatively small, will usually consume no more than 30 or 35 minutes of cooking time, while a large breast may well take a full hour. Chicken livers (essential to a good giblet gravy) should take no more than eight or ten minutes. In the last analysis, the color of the chicken and the consistency of the crust should be the only determinants. The color should be a rich golden brown, and it is always better to err in favor of over-doneness, rather than that under-doneness, pale and tan in color, which can only result in a certain sogginess. Likewise, the crust itself should be firm and brittle, "crackly" in texture, and again it is better to favor a small amount of overcooking to achieve this end, if necessary. During the cooking process, it must be remembered that *constant turning of the parts* is essential. I cannot emphasize this too much. Only in this way will uniformity of color, crust and general texture be achieved, and only such steady devotion can enable one to produce true Southern fried chicken which incidentally, is best eaten with rice and giblet gravy and *always*, as I have pointed out, conveyed to the mouth with the fingers.

Giblet Gravy:

Remove the chicken from the pan, making sure that excess fat is absorbed by laying parts on paper towels. Pour off all excess fat from pan, except for 2 tablespoonfuls. Add to pan: 2 tablespoonfuls of flour, well salted and peppered. Stir and cook over low heat, adding slowly: 2 cups of milk. Continue to cook, and now add slowly: 1 or 2 cooked chicken livers, finely chopped. Constantly stirring, let simmer over low heat for 8 or 10 minutes, adding more milk should the consistency become too thick. Color again is the determinant. The color of the gravy should be deep brown, and of a thick consistency, in which the pieces of liver float sumptuously. Keep hot and serve immediately. Parsley may be added, and a dash of paprika.

The Artists' and Writers' Cookbook (1961)

Evan Hunter

Pancakes

Barbecue and grilling—and, in some circles, bread baking—are for some reason things about which many American men harbor strong, often misty-eyed, feelings. Here the novelist Evan Hunter (1926–2005) makes a similarly emotional case for pancakes. The almost mystical center of warm, familial, cozy Sunday mornings, they are his ultimate comfort food: hold the fripperies, just fix them out of the box with a little extra cream and serve with butter and syrup in a short stack. Hunter, the author of *The Blackboard Jungle* (1954) and the screenplay for Alfred Hitchcock's *The Birds* (1963), also created, as Ed McBain, some of the most enduringly popular modern American crime novels.

■ ■ ■

You have to understand pancakes.

If you call them griddle cakes or flapjacks, you don't understand them and you might just as well forget ever trying to make them. Griddle cakes are made in restaurants that have shiny aluminum stoves and fake chefs in big white pastry hats; they have nothing whatever to do with pancakes which are made in people's kitchens. Flapjacks are made by gold prospectors in little wooden shacks in Grade-B movies; they also have nothing at all to do with pancakes. If you don't understand the distinction, then you won't understand pancakes, either. All is lost, and you should buy yourself a waffle iron.

You don't cook pancakes. You make them.

You don't say, "I think I'll cook some pancakes this morning." You always say, "I think I'll *make* some pancakes this morning." In fact, you never say that either because there's only one time to make pancakes and that's on Sunday morning, and you don't have to *think* you'll make them, you *know* you'll make them. That is, if you understand them. If you understand pancakes, you instinctively know they are irrevocably linked to Sunday morning, and sleeping late, and people in robes with sleep around the edges of their eyes and dopey sleep-smiles on their mouths as they suggest, "Why don't you make some pancakes?"

You'd make them anyway. This is Sunday morning.

Here's how you make them:

You buy yourself any one of the commercial mixes. Get yourself a big mixing bowl, a tablespoon, and a cup, and spread these out on the table. Now put the box where you can read the recipe. Sometimes, if you leave the box open after using it, you'll find cereal bugs in it the next time you try making pancakes. It's best to put the prepared mix in a container of some kind, but be sure to cut the recipe off the back of the box, or next time you won't know what you're doing.

The only change I make in the prepared mix recipe is to pour in about half a cup of heavy cream which, I find, gives the pancakes a richer taste and texture. Aside from that, pancakes shouldn't be tampered with. Don't go dropping diced apples into the batter, or blueberries, because then you're not making pancakes anymore. You're baking muffins or cakes.

Don't serve pancakes in any fancy way like putting ice cream on them or fruit, or brandy, or whipped cream. Just put a generous lump of butter on top of each pancake in the stack and then liberally pour either syrup or molasses over them. It isn't advisable to put more than four pancakes in a stack. Excessive depth makes them difficult to cut and difficult to handle on the fork. If you put four in a stack, you can serve two people while your next batch is on the griddle. Pancakes don't encourage simultaneous serving, but there's a lively overlap and, as a result, a built-in anticipation, especially when children are sitting at the table waiting to be served. The cook always gets served last or, when the pancakes are especially successful, not at all. That doesn't matter.

What does matter is that everyone be in the kitchen while the pancakes are being made. It's important to joke a little with the cook and to hear the coffee bubbling on the stove and to smell the good heat-containing aroma of the sizzling round patties as they're taken from the griddle and carried to the table. It's important to watch the butter melting, to see the syrup dripping onto the plate. It's important that there be laughter in that kitchen and warmth.

You have to understand pancakes.

The Artists' and Writers' Cookbook (1961)

A. J. Liebling

from The Modest Threshold

Abbott Joseph Liebling (1904–1963) attributed his discovery of the splendors of French cuisine, during a year in Paris ostensibly spent studying medieval literature, to his having had to make do with a modest allowance—"enough money to pay the check but not enough to produce indifference to the size of the total." Unlimited funds, he felt, deterred rather than encouraged the sense of adventure that he considered indispensable: "A man who is rich in his adolecence is almost doomed to be a dilettante at table. This is not because all millionaires are stupid but because they are not impelled to experiment." Liebling went on to become a staff writer for *The New Yorker* who reported on many subjects—World War II, the state of the press in America, boxing—but he returned inevitably to food, the object of his deepest passion. This passage is from *Between Meals: An Appetite for Paris* (1962), his unsurpassed memoir of his culinary education.

■ ■ ■

When I arrived in Paris, I was excited and apprehensive, and determined, if I got the chance, to sell my life dearly at my French friends' side. I had the scene by heart in fantasy: I would snatch up the rifle dropped by a falling *tirailleur* and die lying on my belly on a ridge, in the manner of Robert Jordan in *For Whom the Bell Tolls*, meanwhile snuffing out Huns like candle flames in a shooting gallery (where I had practiced several times before embarking). It is an image of his own demise that often occurs to the writer militant; Mathieu, in Sartre's long novel *La Mort dans l'Ame*, does it that way, firing from a belfry. But after several months of *attente* in a near-normal Paris, unbombed and unexcited, I began to hope that the whole thing would blow over, leaving me with the glory of having covered a war and none of the inconveniences possibly to be anticipated.

During this doldrum period, I met Root for the first time; it was at a weekly luncheon meeting of the Anglo-American Press Association of Paris, at the Restaurant Drouant, which has good oysters. Soon he became a familiar; we had a passion in common. His face in those days was the precise color of the inside of a *châteaubriant* that is between rare and medium rare.

His firm and broad-based jaw appeared to be an ideal instrument of mastication, but his rounded chin and friendly eyes announced a man readier to crunch a lark's carcass than tear a tiger's throat. A kindly and humorous man of wide and disparate interests, he could talk well of many things, but our conversations, from the day I met him, were preponderantly about what we had eaten, or were about to eat, or wished to eat—a topic varied by discussions of what we had drunk or would like to drink with it.

I could now afford to eat wherever I cared to. During my American interim, my appetite had been sharpened; now, returned to Paris, I was ready to fly with the wings of larks, pheasants, and woodcock. I took up quarters at the Hôtel Louvois, on the little square that faces the Rue de Richelieu, thus abandoning the quarter haunted by Villon in favor of one that is sacred to the memory of Stendhal. Villon, although there are no contemporary portraits of him, is conventionally represented by illustrators as he described himself: "Lean, sunken cheeks, starved belly." His passion for good food was a fixation on the unattainable, like Rudel's for La Princesse Lointaine, or Chartier's for La Belle Dame Sans Merci. Stendhal, however, enjoyed having his picture painted and left many likenesses. They all agree in the convexity of his front elevation—a magnificent background for a watch chain, an advantageous stuffing for a brocaded waistcoat. The difference in the profiles of the resident ghosts symbolized the gastronomic disparity between their respective neighborhoods. The Square Louvois was surrounded by fine restaurants.

In the twenties, the Rue Sainte-Anne, a narrow street running from near the Théâtre Français end of the Avenue de l'Opéra to the Rue Saint-Augustin and skirting the Square Louvois *en passant*, had been rendered illustrious by a man named Maillabuau, a gifted restaurateur but a losing horse-player who had no money to squander on décor. He turned his worn tablecloths into an asset by telling his customers that he wasted none of their contributions on frills—all went into the supreme quality of his materials and wines. A place with doormen in uniforms, he would say—a place with deep carpets and perhaps (here a note of horror would enter his voice) an orchestra—was *ipso facto* and *prima facie* a snare. He would then charge twice as much as any other restaurant in Paris. My memories of visits to Maillabuau's—visits that I had enjoyed only by stratagem—were so pleasant that I had chosen the Hôtel Louvois in order to be near it.

All during my year at the Sorbonne, the *Guide du Gourmand à Paris* had served as the Baedeker for my exploratory splurges when I had money enough to try restaurants off my usual beat. The author addressed his book to the gourmand, rather than to the gourmet, he said, because it was impossible to like food if you did not like a lot of it; "gourmet" was therefore a snob word, and a silly one. This predisposed me in his favor. But it was his subject matter that held me captive. The restaurants were categorized as "of great luxury," "middling-priced," "reasonable," and "simple," but all were warranted "good," and there were about a hundred and twenty-five of them. At the head of the "luxury" group was a "first platoon" of six restaurants (of which today only one survives, and that scarcely worthy of mention). Maillabuau, despite the worn tablecloths, figured among the ten others in the "luxury" group. In my own forays, "reasonable" was my ceiling, but I liked to read about the others—those financially unattainable Princesses Lointaines. I knew the description of Maillabuau's by heart:

> Sombre, almost lugubrious front. If the passerby is not warned, never will he suspect that behind that façade, having crossed that modest threshold, he can know the pure joys of gastronomy! How to know, if one is not a gourmand, that here the sole is divine, that the *entrecôte Bercy* has singular merits, that the pâté of venison is beyond equal, that the burgundies (especially the Chambertin) are of the year that they should be, and that the *marc* resembles embalmed gold? How to know that only here, in all Paris, are made ready the fat squab guinea-hens anointed with all the scents of the Midi? Staggering bill, which one never regrets paying.

I had no thought of crossing that modest threshold myself until one warm morning in the late spring of 1927, when it occurred to me that my father, mother, and sister would be arriving in Paris in a few weeks—they were waiting only for the beginning of the summer holiday at the Connecticut College for Women, where my sister was now a sophomore—and that in the natural course of events they would ask me, the local expert, where to dine. My mother and sister favored the kind of restaurant where they saw pretty dresses and where the *plat du jour* was likely to be called "Le Chicken Pie à l'Américaine," but my father had always been a booster for low overhead and quality merchandise; they were the principles that had guided his career as a furrier. Russian sable and ermine—with baum or stone marten if a woman couldn't afford anything better—had always been his idea of decent wear. His views on fur were a little like J. P. Morgan's on yachts—people who had to worry about the cost shouldn't have them. Foxes began and ended, for him, with natural blacks and natural silvers; the notion of a fox bred to specifications would have filled him with horror. Seal had to be Alaskan seal, not what was called Hudson seal, which meant muskrat. Persian lamb had to be *unborn* Persian lamb, not mutton.

As I had anticipated, when my family arrived in Paris they did indeed consult me about the scene of our first dinner together. So Maillabuau's it was. When we arrived before the somber, almost lugubrious front, my mother wanted to turn back. It looked like a store front, except for a bit of scrim behind the plate glass, through which the light from within filtered without éclat.

"Are you sure this is the right place?" she asked.

"It's one of the best restaurants in the world," I said, as if I ate there every day.

My father was already captivated. "Don't give you a lot of hoopla and ooh-la-la," he said, with approval. "I'll bet there are no Americans here."

We crossed the modest threshold. The interior was only half a jump from sordid, and there were perhaps fifteen tables. Old Maillabuau, rubicund and seedy, approached us, and I could sense that my mother was about to object to any table he proposed; she wanted some place like Fouquet's (not in the *Guide du Gourmand*). But between her and Maillabuau I interposed a barrage of French that neither she nor my sister could possibly penetrate, though each chirped a few tentative notes. "I have brought my family here because I have been informed it is the most illustrious house of Paris," I told him, and, throwing in a colloquialism I had learned in Rennes, a city a hundred years behind the times, I added, "We desire to knock the bell."

On hearing me, old Maillabuau, who may have thought for a moment that we were there by mistake and were about to order waffles, flashed a smile of avaricious relief. Father, meanwhile, regarding the convives of both sexes seated at the tables, was already convinced. The men, for the most part, showed tremendous *devantures*, which they balanced on their knees with difficulty as they ate, their wattles waving bravely with each bite. The women were shaped like demijohns and decanters, and they drank wine from glasses that must have reminded Father happily of beer schooners on the Bowery in 1890. "I don't see a single American," he said. He was a patriotic man at home, but he was convinced that in Paris the presence of Americans was a sign of a bunco joint.

"Monsieur my father is the richest man in Baltimore," I told Maillabuau, by way of encouragement. Father had nothing to do with Baltimore, but I figured that if I said New York, Maillabuau might not believe me. Maillabuau beamed and Father beamed back. His enthusiasms were rare but sudden, and this man—without suavity, without a tuxedo, who spoke no English, and whose customers were so patently overfed—appeared to him an honest merchant. Maillabuau showed us to a table; the cloth was diaphanous from wear except in the spots where it had been darned.

A split-second *refroidissement* occurred when I asked for the *carte du jour*.

"There is none," Maillabuau said. "You will eat what I tell you. Tonight, I propose a soup, trout *grenobloise*, and *poulet* Henri IV—simple but exquisite. The classic *cuisine française*—nothing complicated but all of the best."

When I translated this to Father, he was in complete agreement. "Plain food," he said. "No *schmier*." I think that at bottom he agreed that the customer is sure to be wrong if left to his own devices. How often had the wives of personal friends come to him for a fur coat at the wholesale price, and declined his advice of an Alaskan seal—something that would last them for twenty years—in favor of some faddish fur that would show wear in six!

The simplicity of the menu disappointed me; I asked Maillabuau about the *pintadou*, fat and anointed with fragrance. "Tomorrow," he said, posing it as a condition that we eat his selection first. Mother's upper lip quivered, for she was *très gourmande* of cream sauces, but she had no valid argument against the great man's proposal, since one of the purposes of her annual trips to Europe was to lose weight at a spa. On the subject of wines, M. Maillabuau and I agreed better: the best in the cellar would do—a Montrachet to begin with, a Chambertin with the fowl.

It was indeed the best soup—a simple *garbure* of vegetables—imaginable, the best trout possible, and the best boiled fowl of which one could conceive. The simple line of the meal brought out the glories of the wine, and the wine brought out the grandeur in my father's soul. Presented with one of the most stupendous checks in history, he paid with gratitude, and said that he was going to take at least one meal a day *chez* Maillabuau during the rest of his stay. The dessert, served as a concession to my sister, was an *omelette au kirsch*, and Maillabuau stood us treat to the *marc*, like embalmed gold. Or at least he said he did; since only the total appeared on the check, we had to take his word for it. The *omelette au kirsch* was the sole dessert he ever permitted to be served, he said. He was against sweets on principle, since they were "not French," but the *omelette* was light and healthy. It contained about two dozen eggs.

The next day we had the *pintadou*, the day after that a *pièce de bœuf du Charolais* so remarkable that I never eat a steak without thinking how far short it falls. And never were the checks less than "staggering," and never did my father complain. Those meals constituted a high spot in my gastronomic life, but before long my mother and sister mutinied. They wanted a restaurant where they could see some dresses and eat *meringues glacées* and *homard au porto*.

So in 1939, on my first evening in wartime Paris, I went straight from the Louvois to the Rue Sainte-Anne. The Restaurant Maillabuau had vanished. I did not remember the street number, so I walked the whole length of the Rue Sainte-Anne twice to make sure. But there was no Maillabuau; the horses at Longchamp had eaten him.

Between Meals (1962)

Euell Gibbons

How to Cook a Carp (*Cyprinus carpio*)

Published just a year after Julia Child's *Mastering the Art of French Cooking* (1961), amid a surge in interest in French gourmet traditions, Euell Gibbons' *Stalking the Wild Asparagus* (1962) gave new voice to an alternate strain in American culinary history. Forget the *foie gras*: Gibbons' health-conscious, back-to-the-earth perspective sent readers after edibles that could be gleaned in the wilderness. Raised in rural New Mexico, Gibbons (1911–1975) had earned his knowledge the hard way, foraging for wild foods to avoid starvation; later in life, he supplemented his firsthand experience with extensive reading in ethnobotany. He went on to publish many books, including *Stalking the Blue-Eyed Scallop* (1964), *Stalking the Healthful Herbs* (1966), *Euell Gibbons' Beachcombers Handbook* (1967), *Feast on a Diabetic Diet* (1969, with Joseph Gibbons), and *Stalking the Good Life* (1971), and gained the kind of fame (appearing often with Johnny Carson and in commercials for General Foods) that made him susceptible to parody. But Gibbons cannot be dismissed as a mere "health nut." Julia herself might have admired his delicate handling of the neglected carp, a local trash fish he made "mighty fine eating" with careful preparation.

■ ■ ■

When I was a lad of about eighteen, my brother and I were working on a cattle ranch in New Mexico that bordered on the Rio Grande. Most Americans think of the Rio Grande as a warm southern stream, but it rises among the high mountains of Colorado, and in the spring it is fed by melting snows. At this time of the year, the water that rushed by the ranch was turbulent, icy-cold and so silt-laden as to be semisolid. "A little too thick to drink, and a little too thin to plow" was a common description of the waters of the Rio Grande.

A few species of fish inhabited this muddy water. Unfortunately, the most common was great eight- to ten-pound carp, a fish that is considered very poor eating in this country, although the Germans and Asiatics have domesticated this fish, and have developed some varieties that are highly esteemed for the table.

On the ranch where we worked, there was a drainage ditch that ran through the lower pasture and emptied its clear waters into the muddy Rio Grande. The carp swimming up the river would strike this clear warmer water and decide they preferred it to the cold mud they had been inhabiting. One spring day, a cowhand who had been riding that way reported that Clear Ditch was becoming crowded with huge carp.

On Sunday we decided to go fishing. Four of us armed ourselves with pitchforks, saddled our horses and set out. Near the mouth of the ditch, the water was running about two feet deep and twelve to sixteen feet wide. There is a saying in that part of the country that you can't get a cowboy to do anything unless it can be done from the back of a horse, so we forced our mounts into the ditch and started wading them upstream, four abreast, herding the carp before us.

By the time we had ridden a mile upstream, the water was less than a foot deep and so crystal clear that we could see our herd of several hundred carp still fleeing from the splashing, wading horses. As the water continued to shallow, our fish began to get panicky. A few of the boldest ones attempted to dart back past us and were impaled on pitchforks. We could see that the whole herd was getting restless and was about to stampede back downstream, so we piled off our horses into the shallow water to meet the charge. The water boiled about us as the huge fish swirled past us and we speared madly in every direction with our pitchforks, throwing each fish we managed to hit over the ditch bank. This was real fishing—cowhand style. The last of the fish herd was by us in a few minutes and it was all over, but we had caught a tremendous quantity of fish.

Back at the ranch house, after we had displayed our trophies, we began wondering what we were going to do with so many fish. This started a series of typical cowboy tall tales on "how to cook a carp." The best of these yarns was told by a grizzled old *vaquero*, who claimed he had made his great discovery when he ran out of food while camping on a tributary of the Rio Grande. He said that he had found the finest way to cook a carp was to plaster the whole fish with a thick coating of fresh cow manure and bury it in the hot ashes of a campfire. In an hour or two, he said, the casing of cow manure had become black and very hard. He then related how he had removed the fish from the fire, broken the hard shell with the butt of his Winchester and peeled it off. He said that as the manure came off the scales and skin adhered to it, leaving the baked fish, white and clean. He then ended by saying, "Of course, the carp still wasn't fit to eat, but manure in which it was cooked tasted pretty good."

There were also some serious suggestions and experiments. The chief objection to the carp is that its flesh is full of many forked bones. One man said that he had enjoyed carp sliced very thin and fried so crisp that one could eat it, bones and all. He demonstrated, and you really could eat it without the bones bothering you, but it was still far from being an epicurean dish. One cowboy described the flavor as "a perfect blend of Rio Grande mud and rancid hog lard."

Another man said that he had eaten carp that had been cooked in a pressure cooker until the bones softened and became indistinguishable from the flesh. A pressure cooker is almost a necessity at that altitude, so we had one at the ranch house. We tried this method, and the result was barely edible. It tasted like the poorest possible grade of canned salmon flavored with a bit of mud. It was, however, highly appreciated by the dogs and cats on the ranch, and solved the problem of what to do with the bulk of the fish we had caught.

It was my brother who finally devised a method of cooking carp that not only made it fit for human consumption, but actually delicious. First, instead of merely scaling the fish, he skinned them. Then, taking a large pinch, where the meat was thickest, he worked his fingers and thumb into the flesh until he struck the median bones, then he worked his thumb and fingers together and tore off a handful of meat. Using this tearing method, he could get two or three good-sized chunks of flesh from each side of the fish. He then heated a pot of bland vegetable shortening, rubbed the pieces of fish with salt and dropped them into the hot fat. He used no flour, meal, crumbs or seasoning other than salt. They cooked to a golden brown in a few minutes, and everyone pronounced them "mighty fine eating." The muddy flavor seemed to have been eliminated by removing the skin and the large bones. The forked bones were still there, but they had not been multiplied by cutting across them, and one only had to remove several bones still intact with the fork from each piece of fish.

For the remainder of that spring, every few days one or another of the cowboys would take a pitchfork and ride over to Clear Ditch and spear a mess of carp. On these evenings, my brother replaced the regular *cocinero* and we enjoyed some delicious fried carp.

The flavor of carp varies with the water from which it is caught. Many years after the above incidents I attended a fish fry at my brother's house. The main course was all of his own catching, and consisted of bass, catfish and carp, all from Elephant Butte Lake farther down the Rio Grande. All the fish were prepared exactly alike, except that the carp was pulled apart as described above, while the bass and catfish, being all twelve inches or less in length, were merely cleaned and fried whole. None of his guests knew one fish from another, yet all of them preferred the carp to the other kinds. These experiences have convinced me that the carp is really a fine food fish when properly prepared.

Carp can, of course, be caught in many ways besides spearing them with pitchforks from the back of a horse. In my adopted home state, Pennsylvania, they are classed as "trash fish" and one is allowed to take them almost any way. They will sometimes bite on worms, but they are vegetarians by preference and are more easily taken on dough balls. Some states allow the use of gill nets, and other states, because they would like to reduce the population of this unpopular fish, will issue special permits for the use of nets to catch carp.

A good forager will take advantage of the lax regulations on carp fishing while they last. When all fishermen realize that the carp is really a good food fish when prepared in the right way, maybe this outsized denizen of our rivers and lakes will no longer be considered a pest and will take his rightful place among our valued food and game fishes.

Stalking the Wild Asparagus (1962)

Joseph Wechsberg

Dinner at the Pavillon

After the close of the 1938 World's Fair in New York City, the manager of the French Pavillion, Henri Soulé, a one-man ambassador of French cuisine, remained in the city and opened a restaurant. Thanks to the French chefs and cooks who also remained, as well as to the jet planes that allowed French groceries to be flown overnight into New York, Le Pavillon was a serious piece of Paris on 57th Street, a triumph, writes Joseph Wechsberg, "of evil capitalism and good taste." For many, Le Pavillon was mainly a place to see and be seen. But for true epicures, it was a new temple of gastronomy. Joseph Wechsberg (1907–1983), Austrian-born author of the classic *Blue Trout and Black Truffles* (1953), was well-prepared to appreciate Soulé's talents. He brought a genuinely cosmopolitan sensibility to his food writing, an expansive aficionado's perspective. In his account of Le Pavillon, Wechsberg subtly distinguishes between eating in the pursuit of status and eating to transcend the ordinary. The latter can, indeed, be accomplished with a perfect *sole de la Manche au Vermouth* in a room filled with "the laughter of women, the scent of *beurre noisette* and Miss Dior"—but also on a windswept beach with a good hot dog.

■ ■ ■

I had dinner at the Pavillon a while ago with dear friends. We always go there on my last night in New York before I take the boat or plane for Europe. That happens about twice a year—rarely enough to make our dinner something of an experience. This is as it should be. I've had memorable meals in my life but never too many in succession, and there are often long, lean months between these festive occasions. Perhaps that's why I keep my weight and still remember the greatest meals.

Some of my epicurean friends in France, elderly gentlemen gourmets ("no man under forty can be dignified with the title of gourmet," wrote Brillat-Savarin), have taught me to get into the proper frame of mind before a great dinner. They believe in the joy of anticipation; they admonish you to prepare for the gastronomic delights that await you by eating little and avoiding all worry during the day.

I haven't always been able to follow this sensible advice, particularly with regard to avoiding all worry, but on my last visit to the Pavillon I was lucky: nothing happened all day long to spoil my appetite. When I arrived under the canopy of the Pavillon's Fifty-seventh Street entrance, I had a pleasantly empty feeling in the pit of my stomach. A slight, delicious aroma drifted out, indefinable in its composition but tantalizing in its effect. I was glad I'd had only a very light breakfast and a sandwich for lunch. How often did I experience a similar sensation as I drove up in front of Fernand Point's Pyramide, after a leisurely four-hour ride from Switzerland, just in time for that first glass of champagne! Sitting there and watching the people arrive, I've always felt sorry for those who came bored and blasé, like veteran music critics for their sixty-seventh performance of *La Traviata*.

The Fifty-seventh Street entrance was flanked by two Rolls-Royces, a Cadillac, a Bentley and a Lincoln Continental, all with liveried chauffeurs and low license numbers—the proper automotive cachet for the world's most distinguished restaurant. In the citadels of West Germany's Economic Wonderland, status-hungry new-rich may now hire chauffeured Mercedes 300's which will be parked in front of the customer's house for an hour or longer, conveying the impression of an elegant party going on inside. Soulé has a different problem. Too many of his customers take up precious parking space.

The doorman opened the outside door for me, the revolving door turned, and then there was the swishing sound of the curtain going up. At the end of my short walk through the revolving door I found myself on the Pavillon's brightly illuminated stage. It might have been the champagne party in a lavish production of *La Traviata*. Few set designers would have the means of creating the brilliance of this set with its chandeliers and mirrors, the symphony of colors with its shades of red, green and chartreuse, and the superbly populated stage with many stunning Violettas. A beautiful show, efficiently produced and effectively displayed, a composite impression made of lights and mirrors and flowers, of tinkling glasses and the muted clatter of cocktail shakers, the subdued voices of men and the laughter of women, the scent of *beurre noisette* and Miss Dior. It was the perfect picture of a great, elegant restaurant, a triumph of evil capitalism and good taste.

And there was already the moonlike, smiling face of the proprietor who seemed to come sliding on invisible skates over the thick rug, a benign Buddha from the Basque coast, impeccable in his dinner jacket, an amused twinkle in his eyes.

"Good evening. *Enchanté de vous voir.*" The regal welcome of the ambassador of French cuisine in New York.

My attention was caught by a large, round table near the entrance with a *buffet froid*, a three-dimensional epicurean still life designed to stimulate your tastebuds. Instead of the overwhelming profusion of the many cold dishes so often encountered on an hors d'oeuvres wagon, here were only a few carefully chosen delicacies—salmon from Nova Scotia, *foie gras aux truffés* from France, Mediterranean *loup de mer froid, truites en gelée, terrine de canard, boeuf à la mode, chaud-froid de volaille, côte de veau froid à l'estragon,* American roast beef.

It happened to be Wednesday, and shortly before noon a shipment of three hundred pounds of seafood had arrived at 111 East Fifty-seventh Street that had left Orly Airport in Paris that very morning. The fish had been caught in the waters of France during the preceding night and had reached the kitchen of the Pavillon approximately at the same time as some of the great restaurants in France, owing to the modern wonders of jet travel and the archaic distribution system in France where all foodstuffs are sent from the producing regions first to the Halles in Paris, to be returned sometimes to the very places where they came from, after a few people have earned their commissions.

The Pavillon's shipment that day contained *langouste* (crayfish) from Cap Finisterre which would be kept alive for three days, fifteen turbots from Dieppe, each weighing from eight to ten pounds, several *loups de mer*, a sort of glorified striped bass that is found only in the Mediterranean, fresh soles from the Channel, *crevettes roses* (prawns) with a delicious bouquet of the incoming tide, and the first fresh salmon from the Adour in Soulé's Basque homeland, a rare delicacy.

No other restaurant in America offers such gifts from the French seas. Soulé doesn't mind to pay the outrageous freight bill of a dollar per pound, including many pounds of French ice that surround the perishable shipment. The bill was prominently displayed on the cold buffet—a questionable practice, one might say, but permissible under the circumstances in order to further the customers' gastronomic education.

Soulé preceded me to the table where my friends were already waiting. Martin, his deputy, and a waiter stood there, summoned by the restaurant's mysterious communications system. The waiter turned the table to let me in and thereupon faded noiselessly into the chestnut trees of the Champs Elysées in the mural background. Soulé remained for a while near our table, talking softly, trying to make us feel at home—a condition he considers essential to make dinner at the Pavillon a success—and then he too disappeared. No menu was hastily handed to us. They don't do such things at the Pavillon.

We had been assigned what insiders might consider "an especially desirable table" in the Royale. It was closed off on two sides by mirrored columns, giving us a feeling of semi-privacy. We could see everything but were not on display ourselves. And we wouldn't have to overhear other people's intimate confidences. Unlike my friends who live in Manhattan I have not yet developed protective deafness against noisy neighbors at my elbows.

Leaning back against the soft damask of the red banquette I felt profoundly at ease, securely surrounded by the luxurious props of Pavillon comfort—the soft, thick rug under my soles, the white tablecloth under my arms, the chestnut trees of the Champs Elysées on the wall across the room, the silver and glasses reflecting the lights, the flames of the burners on the service wagon, and the small army of captains and waiters moving around quickly yet unobtrusively. The fresh roses in the vase must have been placed there only a few hours ago.

I became aware, as on my previous visits, of the restaurant's cosmopolitan flavor. The decor and the atmosphere were very French but the clientele was definitely American, with a sprinkle of international and extraterritorial epicures. The happy Franco-American alliance at the Pavillon is a long-established fact. From our table I had a pleasant vista of some attractive female club members—Soulé might have accorded them the supreme encomium of chic—a decorative effect that always seems to stimulate my appetite. Doubtless a thoughtful contribution of Grandmaster Soulé, the uncontested world's champion of the *jeu de dames*. That *ces dames* were club members of long standing was obvious. They all knew each other. At the Royale, familiarity breeds no contempt—on the contrary.

Now Martin handed each of us a small, handwritten menu. The ambassador had been considerate enough not to expose us to the strain of having to choose and had designed our dinner himself. It was what he calls the Pavillon's "gourmet" dinner, the most refined, most delicate evening program in the restaurant's gastronomic repertory:

Consommé Royale

Sole de la Manche au Vermouth

Poularde Demi-Deuil

Coeur de Laitue

Bombe Pavillon

Café

The great dinner began with an exquisite prelude: a strong beef broth that was made with chopped ground lean beef, chopped celery, chopped carrots, chopped onions, chopped leeks. It had simmered for four hours, had been strained through a cheesecloth, and was served with the Royale which in culinary parlance denotes a garnish—a sort of custard made of whole eggs and light cream cooked in a mold that is placed in a pan of water, left in the oven until firm, and cut into small pieces.

After a suitable interval this prelude was followed with the *sole de la Manche au Vermouth*. The sole (that had arrived from France only a few hours ago) had been poached with butter, chopped shallots and sweet Italian vermouth, and the sauce was made of the sole's liquid, with cream, egg yolks and butter. The sauce had been reduced until it seemed to be the very essence of flavor. Superb! A great Montrachet was placed in front of us, the wine of which Dumas once said it should be drunk on one's knees, with the head bared. Martin half filled our glasses and set them down with a flourish.

After the sole there was an intermission. It was almost nine o'clock now and every single table in the Royale was occupied. Between the tables captains and waiters worked quietly and intently, with clockwork precision. Soulé seemed to be everywhere at the same time. It was a flawless performance by the Pavillon's ensemble: it was so perfect that it wasn't noticeable.

A waiter presented the *poularde demi-deuil*, and a moment later the Pavillon's *écuyer tranchant* stood behind the small table, ready to perform the carving ceremony. It was a succulent dish—the chicken baked golden brown, the sauce made with a dry white wine and brown sauce, butter and brandy, and garnished with diced carrots, turnips, mushrooms, truffles and celery. And there was the bottle of our favorite wine, the magnificent Château Cheval-Blanc 1937. We lifted our glasses to the ambassador, who acknowledged our tribute with an imperceptible nod.

"Remember," he said, "that there is no substitute for beauty and no compromise with perfection."

The *bombe Pavillon* is a delicious dessert—an elegant coffee-icecream-inside-vanilla-icecream ornament, topped by a mixture of pineapple, apples, peaches and pears cooked in syrup, sprinkled with chopped nuts and with heated kirsch, and lighted.

I tasted very little of it, just to know how good it was. There comes a moment in every man's life when he has to say no. For a short moment I thought how nice it would be to have the delicate bouquet of the Cheval-Blanc accentuated by the taste of a creamy, pale-yellow Brie, the noble cheese that Charles d'Orléans sent to his friends five hundred years ago as a New Year's present. I quickly dismissed the heretical thought. Perhaps it is just as well that some wish should always remain unfulfilled.

The ambassador seemed to have guessed my thought, for suddenly a bottle of his favorite champagne appeared on the table, Moët & Chandon's Dom Pérignon Cuvée 1952, a delicate liquid lovingly blended to bring *joie de vivre* to every man's heart.

I leaned back. A slight mist of happiness seemed to descend between the chestnut trees of the Champs Elysées. This, I knew, was going to be another long-remembered evening whose very memory would help to sustain life in its grimmer moments.

My friends sat in a contented daze. All around us people seemed cheerful and relaxed and at peace with the world and themselves. Something—I don't know what it was—made me think of another memorable meal, a sumptuous three-hour lunch with Henri Soulé out there in his house in Montauk Point, followed by a visit to the fishing piers and a walk between the sandy dunes and the low underbrush that reminded Soulé of the coast of Bretagne.

It had been a magnificent lunch with a *boeuf à la Bourguignonne*, but the smell of the incoming tide had been strong in the air that afternoon, and two hours later, on our way back, we had been hungry again. Soulé had the driver stop at a roadside stand, saying, "Let's get out and have a couple of hot dogs–they're delicious here."

Dining at the Pavillon (1962)

Eugene Walter

The Gumbo Cult

Eugene Walter (1921–1998) grew up in Mobile, Alabama, but lived much of his adult life as an expatriate Southerner in New York, Paris, Rome, and elsewhere. Wherever he found himself, however, he did his best to live up to the ideals of hospitality he had imbibed in his youth. In Rome, Muriel Spark once recalled, "Walter kept the nearest thing to a salon," and for nearly twenty years, "all roads led to him." Here, in an essay first published in *Gourmet* in 1962, Walter recounts some of his efforts, away from home, to make gumbo. He later went on to write the Time-Life "Foods of the World" volume on Southern cooking, along with *Delectable Dishes from Termite Hall* (1982) and *Hints & Pinches* (1991), further explorations of his culinary heritage.

■ ■ ■

On the subject of appetite in general, Monsieur de Saint-Just had this to say in the *Almanach des Gourmands* of 1807:

> *C'est un plaisir; c'est le dernier qu'on quitte.*
> *Est-il éteint? bientôt il ressuscite.*

(A pleasure 'tis; the last that we surrender/Is it impaired? a little time's its mender.) How precisely this describes my feeling for gumbo—a dish I have always considered special, indeed, ritualistic! It was in my grandmother's kitchen that I first saw gumbo prepared, at her table that I first ate it and joined the gumbo cult for life.

My grandmother was a tiny, plump woman, passionately interested in flowers. I really remember little about her, save that she wore clanking amethyst beads and that she smelled good, rather like lemon verbena. At that time there were still a few Indians living in the woods around Mobile, Alabama, remnants and revenants of the tribes that had been moved west by the government. A few old women among these Indians were "boboshillies," who came to town once or twice a week with their herbs, barks, and remedies. The boboshilly who came to my grandmother was tall and thin, and wore a muslin headcloth almost like a turban. She was completely noiseless as she came and went with a market basket full of this and that: I remember bay leaves, bird's-eye peppers, and the important gumbo filé.

This filé is a preparation of dried ground sassafras leaves that have been pounded in a mortar, sifted through a hair sieve, and bottled. It is a thickening agent and is used in many Southern variants of gumbo and jambalaya. It is always added just before serving and is never cooked. It is the ingredient often missing when these dishes are prepared away from the South. But there's no excuse for lacking gumbo filé if you belong to the cult. The specialty food shops have it or can get it for you.

Okra is often used to impart to gumbos a special smoothness, a kind of figured-bass accompaniment to the piquant spices. Okra is the seedpod of a plant belonging to the mallow or hibiscus family: the rose madder and marshmallow are its cousins. Sassafras is native, but okra was brought from Africa by slaves. Sometimes, to confuse things, okra is called *gumbo* (or *gumbo plant*)—both are African words. *Gumbo* means "everything together"—for example, *gumbo ya-ya* means "everybody talking at once." The most subtle gumbos employ okra and filé.

I remember one occasion when a grand or state gumbo was being prepared in my grandmother's kitchen. The boboshilly had come and gone, and my grandmother and two Negro servants were busy washing and chopping and boiling. One was Rebecca, who had been my father's nurse; the other was Estelle, who was mine. It was a cloudy day, and when thunder suddenly crashed and a downpour began, the yard man, Edward, came inside to sit in the corner by the stove and have a cup of coffee. Edward was very religious and, in imitation of Old Testament prophets, he wore long hair and a curly silken beard. I think his origins were either East African or Coptic. I had been given the task of picking pecans for pie and was sitting under the kitchen table.

Father Seydell of St. Joseph's Church was coming to dinner, and the gumbo was to contain crab, shrimp, and chicken. The crabs were banging about in a box under the sink, the lid held down by a brick. Suddenly there was a huge crash of thunder and a blinding yellow-green light. Then a rose-colored globe of fire rolled through the room. Lightning had struck the pecan tree growing in the yard. Rebecca screamed, Estelle crossed herself, and my grandmother looked under the table and said, "Are you there, Humbug?"

But then everybody began to laugh madly, and since I couldn't see what they were finding so amusing, I crawled out and stood up. The electricity had caused Edward's hair and beard to puff out in the most extraordinary way. His head had become an enormous puffball, like a human dandelion puff. He was confused and sputtering. The funny thing was that he couldn't make his hair and beard go down, and they stayed puffed out for the rest of the day. I had been afraid of Edward before this episode; afterwards, we became friends.

This is my grandmother's state gumbo:

Shrimp and Crab Gumbo

In a large soup kettle combine 1 large bunch of celery, chopped, 12 allspice berries and 3 peppercorns, all cracked, 6 cloves, 2 bay leaves, a few sprigs each of thyme and parsley, 1 blade of mace, the peel from $1/4$ lemon, 1 red pepper pod, free of seeds and chopped, and 1 gallon of water. Salt the water liberally, bring it to a boil, and let it boil for a few minutes. Add 4 dozen whole large shrimp. When the water returns to a boil remove the kettle from the heat and let the shrimp cool in the court bouillon. Remove the shrimp and shell and devein them. Bring the court bouillon to a boil. Plunge 6 or 8 good-sized crabs into cold water and then into the boiling court bouillon and cook them for 10 minutes. Remove the kettle from the heat and cool the crabs in the liquid. When they are cool enough to handle, pick the meat from the shells but leave the claws intact. Strain the bouillon.

In a heavy iron skillet combine 2 tablespoons each of melted bacon fat and flour and cook the *roux*, stirring, until it is a rich dark brown. Stir in gradually 1 cup boiling water and 6 ounces concentrated tomato paste. Add 1 bay leaf, 6 allspice berries and 6 peppercorns, all cracked, 3 cloves, a good pinch of cayenne, and a dash of Tabasco. Turn the mixture into a soup kettle and add 2 quarts of the strained court bouillon. Add 3 green peppers, 3 tomatoes, 2 medium slices cooked ham, and 2 stalks of celery, all chopped. Brown 4 onions, sliced, in 4 tablespoons butter. Add 2 garlic cloves, chopped, and a 3-pound chicken, cut into serving pieces. Brown the chicken on all sides. Add the chicken and onions to the soup pot. Pour 1 cup stock into the pan the chicken was cooked in, stir in all the brown bits, and add this to the gumbo. Cook for 30 minutes. Add ½ pound fresh okra, chopped, and simmer the mixture for 1 hour, or until the chicken is tender. Salt to taste. Reheat to serve. Add the reserved shrimp and crab meat and claws 10 minutes before serving. In 5 minutes, stir 1 tablespoon filé powder into 1 cup of the gumbo stock. Remove the kettle from the heat and add the filé and stock. Serve the gumbo with rice and hot buttered French bread. Serves 12 to 16.

Well, that gives you an idea, doesn't it? People are always asking me what gumbo is. As you see, it's not a soup exactly, it's not a stew, not a ragout, it's uniquely and incomparably gumbo! It is as dark and as thick as river mud, unctuous, spicy, and satisfying.

Thackeray, when he came to New Orleans, decided that he liked gumbo even better than the bouillabaisse he had hymned in Marseille. But it was Lafcadio Hearn who went about sampling and jotting down recipes. This nineteenth-century exotic, born of mixed European parentage on a Greek island, lived long in New Orleans, though he settled at last in Japan. He compiled a book of Creole *recettes* which appeared anonymously under the auspices of the New Orleans *Times-Picayune.* He reported dozens of gumbo variations, among them, simple okra *gombo* and *maigre* oyster *gombo.* Which reminds me that although *gumbo* is now the universal spelling, old family manuscript cookbooks in the South spell it *gombaud, goumbaud, goumbo.* One excellent cook but poor speller living near Vicksburg, with its memories of the Civil War, jotted down for me her formula for shrimp *gunboat.*

Here are Lafcadio Hearn's recipes:

Simple Okra Gombo

Chop a pound of beef and half a pound of veal brisket into squares an inch thick; slice three dozen okra pods, one onion, a pod of red pepper, and fry them all together. When brown pour in half a gallon of water; add more as it boils away. Serve with rice as usual.

Maigre Oyster Gombo

Take 100 oysters with their juice, and one large onion; slice the onion into
hot lard and fry it brown, adding when brown a tablespoon of flour and red
pepper. [Caution with that red pepper! He means a tablespoon of flour to
which has been added a pinch of cayenne.] When thick enough pour in the
oysters. Boil together twenty minutes. Stir in a large spoonful of butter and
one or two tablespoons of filee [filé], then take the soup from the fire and
serve with rice.

The Aleutian Islands, of which the Andreanof Islands are a part, are quite
grand and strange. Nobody knows how many thousands of islands and islets
make up this chain, since this is the part of the globe which is geologically
the youngest, bearing out the contention that the moon was born of the
Pacific ocean. There are earthquakes daily, and some of the islands have the
habit of sinking into the sea for unpredictable periods, then rising again just
as nonchalantly. There are no trees, only the thick wind-flattened tundra
grass which springs up in May and June and dies down in September.

The landscape is without doubt the saddest on earth, shrouded in fogs
and snow. The wind, called williwaw, really does blow horizontally from
the North Pole, and one can lean into it until one is walking almost horizontally. Since I came from Alabama and had never seen snow in my life,
I was bewitched by the Aleutians. But many of the other World War II soldiers found the absence of trees depressing. Some of them made a tree of
wood, chicken wire, and burlap, and put a little fence around it with the
sign: "Aleutian National Forest." When the bulldozers were pushing earth
and rock and ice to make an emergency landing strip on the island of Atka,
the mounds piled up by the bulldozer had grotesque shapes which seemed
to yearn to change into faces and figures. I thought of the rock peak Pavel
Tchelitchew designed for the ballet *Apollon Musagète*: at the end of the ballet, in the calm light, it is seen as the heroic head of a sleeping Apollo. But
there was no calm light here; the sun showed itself only five times, and then
fitfully, in the three years I spent on the islands. The ravens seemed to hover
on the brink of human speech. I used to imagine astonishing exchanges between them. With little effort I had taught them to say "hello" and "hi, doc"

and several satisfying obscenities. As I strolled, furred and booted, along the black Bering sands with a pet caribou and two dogs, listening to the ravens cry greetings and oaths through the thickly swirling snow, it is not surprising that I longed nostalgically for the reassurance of a good spicy gumbo and the conviviality it implies.

So I learned to cook on the islands, since the food in the Air Force mess was usually inedible. By dint of much stealing, bargaining, and scrounging of various sorts, and making use of occasional food packages from the States, I was able to provide, for some of my gourmet buddies, one or two interesting suppers a week. A pilot friend of mine who made a regular run down the Aleutian chain brought us gin and other things we required to exist. I kept begging him to bring a can of okra, but he said it was too hard to find. I was longing to try a gumbo. I remember well the night he finally turned up with the okra. The snow was deep and the williwaw was blowing. The runway had been cleared and I waited by the hangar with dogs and caribou. My friend arrived frozen, but smiling.

"You and your okra," he said. "You know what it's really called? Ladyfingers!"

But he had found a tin of okra at Edmonton, in the Alberta province of Canada. I have never heard it called ladyfingers before or since; ladyfingers in the South are a kind of spongy tea cake in the shape that the French call *langue de chat* (cat's tongue). The next day, caribou and dogs and I went to dig clams on the black shores of the Bering Sea, and I made a gumbo of fresh clams, dried onion flakes, tomato paste, celery salt, lemon peel, and the blessed okra, alias ladyfingers. The gumbo was somewhat ersatz, but we enjoyed it anyway.

One winter day in New York after the War, I felt again a persistent, mystical, and not-to-be-denied hunger for a big bowl of gumbo. It's interesting that in New York one can find authentic food of every country on earth, save of the South. What is advertised as Southern fried chicken is usually an ancient fowl encased in a cement mixture and tormented in hot grease for an eternity. Southern biscuits à la New York are pure cannon wadding. Gumbo they've not even heard of. In the summer I lived on Ninth Street where there was a little garden back of the apartment, but when the steam heat came on in October I moved to an unheated flat on Tenth Street for the winter. I hate steam heat; it makes me think I have a brick on my head. It keeps me awake at night and I hear the spines of old leather books cracking open in the nasty, smothery heat. Crack! There's Ovid. Snap! Oh, poor Beddoes! Creak! Pop! Alas, the little two-volume Herrick.

Later on, the composer Donald Ashwander came from Alabama to live in the same building on Tenth Street, and he made his excellent corn bread—baked in an iron skillet—but at first I was quite alone in my nostalgia for Southern dishes. I went over to the Bleecker Street markets to look for okra, and got nowhere. But while shopping for paprika bacon on Third Avenue, I saw garlands of tiny okra festooning the window of a food shop run by an Armenian.

"I want some okra," I began, but that wasn't the name he knew. When I pointed, he said, "Oh, those are Greek peppers."

"But they're neither Greek nor peppers," I protested, adding to myself, "just as the Harmonious Blacksmith is neither harmonious nor blacksmith; as the City Center is neither city nor center; and red sable brushes are made of squirrels' tails." But I took home a garland of the precious pods, which had been strung on cotton thread and dried in the sun, and made a nice

Chicken Gumbo

Have a tender 3 ½-pound chicken cut into serving pieces and brown them in 2 tablespoons bacon fat. Add 1 chorizo (garlic sausage), cut in pieces, and 2 medium slices ham, diced. Add enough additional fat to cover the bottom of the soup kettle and add 2 bunches of celery, 2 onions, and 1 green pepper, all chopped, and 1 pound fresh okra, sliced. Cook, stirring, until all the ingredients are nicely browned. Add 2 ½ cups cooked tomatoes, 2 bay leaves, and the grated rind of 1 lemon. Cover the kettle and simmer the gumbo slowly for 30 minutes. Do not let it boil. Add ½ cup chopped parsley, several cracked peppercorns, and dashes of Tabasco and cayenne. The gumbo should be very highly seasoned. Add 2 ½ quarts chicken stock, cover the pan, and simmer the gumbo for 1 ½ hours. Correct the seasoning and serve with rice.

When I went to live in Paris, I intended to stay only temporarily at the Hôtel Helvétia in the rue de Tournon. It was run by Monsieur and Madame Jordan. He was from the Jura, she from Provence. The woodwork in the entry hall was painted exactly the same color as their yellow cat Nounouche, who was perfectly camouflaged when he sat on the radiator. Since I never succeeded in finding an apartment in Paris, I remained for five years at the Helvétia, which was not without its charms. It was a remodeled eighteenth-century *hôtel particulier* kept well scrubbed and polished by the Jordans. The problem was that cooking was forbidden in the rooms. There was a marble-topped commode in my room, and in it I hid a two-burner alcohol stove, pots and pans, tableware, and other necessary tools. The iron screen of an unused fireplace concealed my modest cellar. I gave rather elaborate dinner parties in this room not much larger than a refrigerator crate. Each guest had to take away a neatly packaged bit of garbage, to prevent discovery of my culinary activities and to discourage mice. One Italian princess, unused to such procedures, left a trail of coffee grounds and *langoustine* shells from my third-floor room to the street. But usually all went well. What with the Riesling cooling in an ice-filled bidet, and candles burning in ormolu candelabra, I managed to create a small oasis against the dire Paris climate. The most memorable dinners centered around a chicken cooked in *vin jaune de Jura* for Jack and Gurney Campbell; a soup of leeks and *merlan* for the Pakistani actress Roshann Dhunjibhoy and the Dutch photographer Otto van Noppen; and shrimp in a fondue sauce for a Finnish darling named Renata Vitzthum von Eckstädt. I'll tell you about these plates another time. What I'm getting at is the time I planned a particular dinner party at which gumbo was a must, since I had three serious eaters coming to dinner: Sally Higginson, Theodora Keogh, and Celestino Mendès-Sargo—all of whom had heard just about enough on the subject of gumbo and demanded to taste it. As usual, the quest for okra began. I hopped into a bus and rushed to Hédiard's, back of the Madeleine.

"Okra?" demanded the fat pink clerk in white apron. "*Qu'est-ce que vous voulez dire?*" He offered mangoes and *loukoumia*, but the magic pods were unknown to him. My gumbo dinner might never have materialized if, shortly after this initial failure, I had not dined in a Greek restaurant with some African friends. The first plate we attacked was a mound of okra.

"*Comment s'appelle ce plat equis?*" I asked cautiously.

"*Ça? Mais, ce sont les bamias.*"

"*Ah, oui, bamias,*" I observed knowingly. But I sought out the head chef to learn his source of supply. He confided that there was a grocery in the rue Hautefeuille that stocked enormous quantities of tinned okra or *bamias.* Next day, armed with a string bag and hope, I set out for the rue Hautefeuille, a narrow, short street off the Boulevard St. Germain. I entered a low-ceilinged, dark *épicerie.*

"*Bamias,*" I mumbled, receiving an uncomprehending glare in return.

"*Bamias,*" I repeated, but then I saw them, rows of fat tins with baroque lithographs of the okra plant. I pointed an adamant, triumphant forefinger.

"*Ça? Mais, ce sont les cornes grecques.*" (Greek horns.)

"That which we call a rose . . ." I muttered, and gave my order.

Anyway, I had my okra, and made for Sally, Theodora, and Celestino a

Gumbo Improvisé dit de Paris

In a large saucepan, sauté 4 leeks and 1 stalk of celery, all chopped, in 2 tablespoons butter. Stir in 2 tablespoons flour and add $\frac{1}{4}$ cup chopped parsley and a few sprigs of thyme. Continue cooking for 1 minute. Scrub 3 dozen mussels, trim off the beards, and steam them open in a little water. Reserve the mussel meat. Add the mussel liquid to the saucepan with enough water to make 1 quart. Add 6 cracked peppercorns, 2 bay leaves, and a good dash each of cayenne and Tabasco. Cover the pan and simmer the gumbo for $1\frac{1}{2}$ hours. Add 8 *langoustines* (or 4 pounds cut-up lobster), 4 tomatoes, skinned and quartered, and 1 large can okra, drained, and cook for 15 minutes. Add $1\frac{1}{2}$ pounds shrimp and cook for 3 minutes. Add the reserved mussels and cook them for a few minutes until their edges curl and the shrimp turns pink. Correct the seasonings and stir in 1 tablespoon butter. Serve with rice.

When I moved to Rome and lived in a tiny house with a pocket-handkerchief terrace and garden, I immediately had okra seeds sent from America. I lovingly tended the green seedlings in the center of a flower bed until a helpful gardener took them for weeds and snatched them out. I gave seeds to Italian farmers at Latina on the Pontine plain, and the plants flourished, but the farmers refused to pick the pods until they were longer then the regulation inch and a half, with the result that when I cooked them they had the texture and flavor of boiled tree trunks.

But down in Calabria, in the neighborhood of what once was Sybaris, okra is cultivated and used in many a savory country dish. It is called Greek pepper there. The okra is a staple of diet in Greece under its name of *bamia*. It has other names–African, Turkish, and Slavic–which I've not yet learned. But okra or ladyfinger or *bamia* or Greek horn or Greek pepper or gumbo or African mallow or what you will, it's a delightful vegetable and will survive the conspiracy to consign it to oblivion. It just occurs to me that I have mentioned okra only in connection with gumbo; actually, it has a fame and career in its own right. If you have a little water boiling in a pot with a little salt, a pinch of sugar, two or three cracked peppercorns, and a twist of lemon peel, you can toss in a peck of okra pods, cook them until they are succulently just right, then drain, butter, and serve them. One picks up each pod by the stem and eats all save this stem. Fried okra is also fine.

Fried Okra with Green Tomatoes

Slice 1 ½ pounds okra and 2 large green tomatoes. Dredge the vegetables in ½ cup corn meal seasoned with salt and pepper, and brown them in 3 tablespoons bacon fat, stirring from time to time. Drain on absorbent paper and sprinkle with salt. Serve immediately.

Gourmet, April 1962

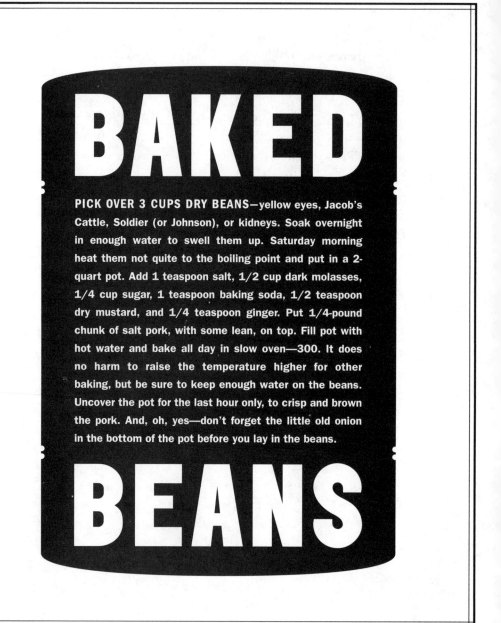

BAKED

PICK OVER 3 CUPS DRY BEANS—yellow eyes, Jacob's Cattle, Soldier (or Johnson), or kidneys. Soak overnight in enough water to swell them up. Saturday morning heat them not quite to the boiling point and put in a 2-quart pot. Add 1 teaspoon salt, 1/2 cup dark molasses, 1/4 cup sugar, 1 teaspoon baking soda, 1/2 teaspoon dry mustard, and 1/4 teaspoon ginger. Put 1/4-pound chunk of salt pork, with some lean, on top. Fill pot with hot water and bake all day in slow oven—300. It does no harm to raise the temperature higher for other baking, but be sure to keep enough water on the beans. Uncover the pot for the last hour only, to crisp and brown the pork. And, oh, yes—don't forget the little old onion in the bottom of the pot before you lay in the beans.

BEANS

John Gould, *Monstrous Depravity* (1963)

For over 60 years, John Gould of Rockland, Maine, chronicled daily life and fading Americana in weekly essays for the *Christian Science Monitor*. His book celebrates the foods of the past, such as these Maine-style baked beans.

James Beard

from Delights and Prejudices

"The secret of good cooking," said James Beard (1903–1985) in an interview shortly before his death, "is, first, having a love of it." For Beard, this love came early, his palate inspired by exposure to fine restaurants in the Pacific Northwest and his mother's hearty boarding house fare. He went on to have one of the more legendary careers in American gastronomy. He preceded Julia Child to the television screen with a program on NBC in 1946, and he published more than a dozen cookbooks, including *Hors d'Oeuvre and Canapés* (1940), *The Fireside Cook Book* (1949), *The Complete Book of Outdoor Cookery* (1955, with Helen Evans Brown), and *Beard on Bread* (1973). Beginning in 1960, he operated the James Beard Cooking School from his home in Greenwich Village, befriending chefs, restaurateurs, food writers, and home cooks. Equally comfortable writing a recipe for *coq au vin* or for a good baking powder biscuit, Beard was a gourmet without snobbery. His memoir *Delights and Prejudices* (1964) is a genuine food lover's picaresque, ranging from stick candy, birthday cakes, and chicken sandwiches to Columbia River salmon, *salad russe*, squab *à la crapaudine*.

■ ■ ■

I always looked forward to Saturday lunches before the theater. They would be quick but exciting, because they were the prelude to a day of gadding about, to the theater (later, to the movies, as they became popular) and to dinner. We often went to the Royal Bakery near the theaters and ate one of their remarkably good clubhouse sandwiches, or chicken sandwiches, salad and tea and some of their extraordinary charlotte russe or marzipan cake. Or we went to Swetlands, where I especially liked the dessert, hot butterscotch on ice cream with toasted almonds. No matter what went before, if I had this dessert I was content with the world. Also, at Swetlands I could stock up on stick candy. And if I was around at the right moment, I would be given a few candied violets. I prized them and picked them out of every box of chocolates that ever came into the house. And I still love their flavor and crystalline texture. I had no taste for chocolate until I grew older.

Two restaurants in Portland, more than any others, advanced my life of good eating. Both had character and offered food which one cannot find any more in cities such as Portland was before the twenties.

One of these restaurants came into my life through a classmate of mine in high school, whose name was Chester Benson. Chester's parents were divorced—his father was tremendously wealthy and a great figure in the development of Oregon—and he lived with his mother and brother not too far from us. Chester and I became good friends—we liked music and theater, and we liked to eat—and our mothers found a common ground of interest as well.

Mrs. Benson was a very good cook, and she made marvelous cakes and pastries for the pleasure of her two sons, and I was often given delicious snacks there and was sometimes invited for lunch. The boys' birthday parties were famous. Mrs. Benson made elaborate preparations for them and would do huge poundcakes, ribboned inside with every imaginable color, heavily iced with royal icing and decorated with silver balls, ornate inscriptions and all sorts of furbelows. They were masterpieces of late Edwardian birthday cake art, and could someone re-create their charm today, he would make a fortune.

At Christmas Mrs. Benson made sugar cookies by the gross. They were crisp, buttery, thoroughly delicious and cut in every imaginable shape with an assortment of cookie cutters I wish I had now. On a certain Saturday before Christmas about twelve or fourteen children and several mothers were invited to the Bensons' for an afternoon of cookie art. Icing of every shade was provided, together with brushes, and the children were given free choice of design. I remember that, between eating and painting, the afternoon was a great success. However, the decorated cookies made a somewhat startling exhibition. Some should have been preserved for the currently popular shows of children's art, although others were better eaten on the spot.

Several years after we became acquainted with the Bensons, Chester's father took over a hotel that had originally been built for someone else. It was named The Benson and was the first great luxury hotel in Portland, more up-to-date than the Edwardian *luxe* of the charming old Portland, with beautifully decorated suites, fine bathrooms and exquisitely appointed dining rooms. And it also provided Portland with its first famous chef, Henri Thiele, a Swiss who had trained in France. This man had a fawning manner and great ambition, but he was a great, creative chef.

Though Mr. and Mrs. Benson were divorced, the boys had charge accounts at their father's hotel, and we were often their guests for dinner or lunch. So it happened that I became a frequent visitor to the hotel, learned to know and admire Thiele and experienced some new and utterly delicious dishes. For example, Thiele did beautiful *paupiettes* of sole, sauced and then garnished with our tiny Olympia oysters, and he did a marvelous crabmeat Newburg, which he served on toasted muffins or toasted brioche, made by him in the hotel bakery. And he did a mutton chop, cut across the saddle in the correct way, served with a stuffed potato, done to order, and an incredible cole slaw shredded into a thin film and flavored with a very tart French dressing containing a little turmeric and hot pepper.

Thiele soon discovered that the Beards loved food, and on occasions when Mother was invited to dine with the Bensons he offered the best of his creative skill. I will never forget the béarnaise sauce he made one evening—as tarragoned as possible and light and fluffy withal—which was served with a roast filet of beef, crusty and rare. The combination was perfection. But Thiele's salmon dishes were his true forte and became the feature of the Columbia Gorge Hotel, which Mr. Benson later built for him. I can remember a whole baked salmon done with cream, and fillets of salmon stuffed with a salmon mousse and then poached in a court bouillon.

And Thiele's Princess Charlotte pudding! I have tried for years and years to duplicate it, from the first days of The Benson, but have never achieved the same quality. It was rather like a fine *bavaroise*, but creamier, with praline in it and a supremely good cassis sauce over it.

I recall visiting Thiele's pastry kitchens, where I saw *petits fours* turned out by a good *pâtissier*, ate some of the creams from the pot and learned a great deal about assembling these little cakes. And I shall never forget a puff paste tart Thiele made with coarsely chopped toasted hazelnuts, a rich pastry cream and a melted sugar and nut topping.

Nor shall I forget his simple dishes, such as grilled liver with a sour cream sauce, very much like the Swiss *suri leberli* but more delicate. And he had a way with the tiny crawfish of the Coast that was sensational, for he combined its meat with avocado and a special sauce of highly seasoned mayonnaise and cream. Then there was the magnificent simplicity of Thiele's steak, done with butter, shallots and pepper and served with his version of roesti.

I shall be forever grateful to the Benson family. Alas, the hotel is no longer owned by the family. It now sports a Trader Vic's, instead of the subtle cookery of Thiele. But Thiele made its name. He reached his high point when he was under the direction of the Bensons. Later, he went into business for himself and became a mass producer without any of the finesse he had brought to his original kitchens. In my files I have a small announcement of the opening of his new business, when he pioneered the practice of sending out lunches to businessmen and office workers. For fifty cents one got three sandwiches, salad, hard-boiled eggs, fruit and pie or cake, and for fifty cents more one could have the addition of two salads, and half a cold chicken. No charge for delivery either. And that was as late as 1924.

The second great Portland restaurant, which still exists in different and more elaborate form, is located in Meier & Frank's department store, run by the two families since the early 1850s. It is a landmark and has a personality unlike that of any other store in America. My father's family traded there in bartering days. Mother had one of the lowest account numbers on the books and felt as much at home there as she did in her own house.

The restaurant began as a novelty and became for a long time the best eating place in all of Portland. It was as hard to get a table there as it is now at "21" in New York. The men's grill has some regulars who have been going there for thirty and forty years or more—every day! This year Meier & Frank opened another fine restaurant in their new shopping-center store, which serves dinner and has a bar, grill and dining room.

One of the best chefs I ever knew was the chef at Meier & Frank's for a number of years, Don Daniels. He was paid extremely well for a chef by those days' standards and was worth it, for he produced food of rare quality—veal birds with a rich, creamy sauce, flavored with dill or tarragon; a beautiful salmi of duckling; and a remarkably good salmon soufflé with a hollandaise sauce. And he did superb clams, shipped from Seaside and Gearhart as fast as possible, which were sautéed *meunière* or with parsley butter and served with an excellent tartar sauce.

Don also served good caviar and wonderful salads, among them one which included chicken, walnuts and his own mayonnaise. His curry of crab was unforgettable, as was his little boned squab with a rice stuffing. Desserts were beyond belief. His Frankco is still one of the greatest frozen desserts ever created. It is made with the heaviest cream possible, whipped and then frozen at a very low temperature. Then it is scooped out in jagged crystalline portions. In my day, this came in maple, cognac, lemon and strawberry, according to the season, and it is still a major attraction at Meier & Frank's. Don also made rich home-style coffeecakes with almond toppings and *streusel*, using butter by the ton. And there was a remarkable black bottom pie. It had a crumb crust and was really two different types of Bavarian cream on a chocolate base. If you cared for that sort of dessert, then it was your dish and a sublime one.

This man was unique, and fortunately the Meiers and Franks understood his genius. He had a true sense of the seasonal aspect of menu building and was one of the first restaurant men to feature seasonal foods when they were at their height. He had an established clientele who wanted the best and paid for it, and he ran the restaurant according to his own gastronomic pleasure. (They are the same ideas, on a smaller scale, which Joseph Baum applied so successfully to the Four Seasons.) I am glad I knew this man and grateful that, for a period of time, I could eat in his restaurant four or five times a week.

San Francisco, during my childhood and early teens, was my dream city. We spent a week or two, sometimes a month, there each year, making the trip usually on the Shasta Limited of the Southern Pacific. This train was my idea of true luxury, and two meals in the diner were heaven (and in those days my family considered Southern Pacific food well below the standards of the great cross-country lines). It was a treat to rise with the Siskiyous and the Coast Ranges rolling by and to breakfast on ham and eggs, sausage and eggs, or occasionally fresh mountain trout which had been taken on during one of the stops—all rather well prepared.

Sometimes we had the thrill of taking a boat trip from Portland aboard *The Beaver, The Bear* or *The Rose City*, which plied their way between Portland, San Francisco and Los Angeles. It was a two-day trip to San Francisco, and the excitement of a short sea voyage made up for the food. At best it was ordinary, but that only gave one greater appetite for the restaurants of San Francisco.

For two wonderful years, during the 1915 fair (the Panama-Pacific International Exposition) and part of the following year, the two great liners *Northern Pacific* and *Great Northern* sailed from Flavel below Astoria to San Francisco and back; and this really was luxury travel. A boat train left from Portland, raced to Flavel at great speed, and soon one was aboard. One of these liners, renamed the *H. F. Alexander*, became one of the fastest ships on the Atlantic during World War I. There wasn't time for much eating aboard either ship—one had dinner and breakfast, and he was ready to dock. But the food was memorable. Dungeness crab and razor clams and Columbia River salmon starred, along with the best of California fruits and vegetables and a great profusion of imported delicacies, such as *foie gras* and occasionally good caviar. I still remember the whole Chinook salmon of enormous proportions in a wine aspic, served with an anchovy mayonnaise remotely related to some of the Provencal sauces. My father loved it, got the recipe, and it became an occasional treat, especially at the beach, where salmon flowed into our house as if it were a tributary of the Columbia.

I can also remember my first *salade russe* aboard one of these ships, and wonderful smallish cantaloupes, somewhat like the Charentais melons, served with delicious ice cream or with fresh raspberries and port.

I cannot describe the excitement of pushing through the Golden Gate in even such a small tub as *The Beaver* or *The Bear*. One had the feeling of having arrived in the Promised Land from afar. (I still succumb to the enchantment of San Francisco each time I go there.) We'd be off to the Palace or the St. Francis, and in later years the Clift. Then without stop there would be theater, music, shopping, visits and eating.

There were great restaurants in those days—Fred Solari's on Maiden Lane, Solari's on Geary Street behind the St. Francis, Marquard's, Tait's at the Beach and Techau Tavern, all of which have disappeared, victims of Prohibition or just tired and gone. But there is still Jack's, a restaurant that has changed comparatively little in all the years I have been going there. It has kept its *fin de siècle* décor and, it would appear, some of its *fin de siècle* personnel. They still serve the same delicious crab, oysters, abalone and fine fish and such specialities as calf's head vinaigrette—and superb sand dabs.

Mother once said, "If I'd been able to get fresh sand dabs every day and the best white asparagus from California throughout the season, I would never have sold the business." This is one of the great fishes of the world and is usually prepared so badly it loses its essential character. This delicate member of the flounder family should be either filleted or cooked whole, and the cooking should be nothing more than the lightest sauté *meunière*. It should be rushed to your table from the pan without further embellishment. This is as tender and as delicious a fish as I have ever eaten anywhere, and if you have never tasted it, make a trip to Jack's one day when you are in San Francisco.

Jack's also produced some excellent squab and chicken, including a wonderful *sauté sec*, which still appears on their menu and is unbelievably simple.

Chicken Sauté Sec

Disjoint a 2- to 2½-pound broiler. Melt 6 tablespoons butter in a skillet, and when it is bubbling, brown the chicken pieces lightly on both sides over a brisk flame. Add salt and pepper to taste. When the chicken is browned to the state you desire, reduce the heat and add ⅓ cup white wine or very dry sherry. Allow the chicken to simmer until it is tender, turning it once or twice during the cooking. Serve it with sautéed potatoes or rice pilaf and a salad.

For some reason San Francisco has always meant squab to me. Once when the family had an apartment there, we used to shop in the markets a great deal and bought squab at two and three for a dollar, and exceedingly good ones at that. Often they were just flattened and broiled *à la crapaudine*, and sometimes they were stuffed with a savory mixture, roasted and basted with white wine and butter—delicious food to be eaten with the fingers, else one would miss some of its goodness. How many times have I watched diners in restaurants too proud to lift bones to mouth. How they massacred the tiny bird! And what miserable return they got. I must say, I have never seen anyone who truly enjoys food who didn't use his fingers when necessary.

Down the alley off Union Square were two famous spots—Fred Solari's and a small French *bistro*, which I found enchanting when I was young. It was of the meal-plus-wine *prix fixe* type of restaurant. The dishes were piled at the table in readiness for customers, and silver, glasses, and linen were also close at hand so that the waiters had a minimum of work before a meal. One was served a huge ironstone tureen of soup, good sourdough bread, an excellent bourgeois dish, a fairly palatable California wine, and cheese and fruit, or sometimes dessert, for about seventy-five cents at lunch and slightly more at dinner. The main dish would be a good *pot-au-feu*, a *boeuf à la mode*, a *daube*, or a *poule-au-pot*. Such hearty, inexpensive dishes would not be ruined if they continued to cook an extra hour while a meal was being served.

We also used to lunch often in the recently demolished Fly Trap. This was as plain as any restaurant could be, but the cooking always remained honest and flavorful. If you wanted good fish or crab, or good chops and steak, you found the Fly Trap had a special quality about it, and this was proven by the loyal patronage of some of the old-timers.

For elegant dining, I think that Marquard's and Tait's at the Beach impressed me more than any other place in San Francisco, with the exception of the Palace Court. Marquard's had a buffet luncheon or hors d'oeuvre luncheon, which used to fascinate me as a child, for I loved the looks of the laden table and the idea of tasting a great many things. And Tait's at the Beach embodied such glamour that I have never forgotten it. But the cuisine at these two places, alas, declined during Prohibition, and I am left only with the recollection of their luxurious air, which, after all, is not the test of a good restaurant.

The Palace Court was another restaurant that prided itself on great food in those days. And with its palms, rich draperies and carpeting and smooth, luxurious service, the hotel was comparable to the best European hostelry. Dishes emanating from its kitchens became classics, for the food, as old San Franciscans know, was impeccable. Game, fine fish and seafood—all the glories of the region—were featured. It was here I learned the joys of the alligator pear, the versatility of the artichoke, the pleasures of ripe citrus fruit. And two famous dishes served there have stayed in my memory.

Crab Legs Palace Court

This dish is still available at the Palace Hotel, though I'm sure not done as well as formerly. Serve as an hors d'oeuvre or as a luncheon dish.

For each serving make a bed of crisp greens. On it place a large slice of tomato. On this place a good-sized artichoke bottom with the inner choke removed and a few leaves left to form a cup. Fill this with *salade russe* (a salad of diced cooked vegetables blended with mayonnaise), top with large Dungeness crab legs, and decorate with thin slices of pimiento. Around the artichoke and the tomato press fine-chopped hard-boiled egg yolk, and serve with a well-flavored Thousand Island dressing. The same dish may be prepared with large lump Atlantic crabmeat or with lobster meat, but the Dungeness crab has a certain delicacy which seems to make the dish more delicious.

The other dish—another Palace original which restaurants elsewhere have copied—is oysters Kirkpatrick. The legend is that they were created for one of the staff at the old Palace. When Helen Brown did her *West Coast Cook Book*, the Palace sent her a recipe which she and I both think is not the original. Nor do she and I agree entirely on the one we first knew. The first one I ever ate, and the one which I had repeatedly, was this:

Oysters Kirkpatrick

For each person arrange 6 oysters in their shells on a bed of coarse salt. Loosen each oyster from its shell, dip it in catchup and return it to shell. Top it with fine-chopped scallions and a strip of partially cooked bacon. Bake at 400° just long enough to heat the oysters and crisp the bacon. Serve at once.

Sometimes a spoonful of grated Parmesan cheese was sprinkled over the bacon before it went to the oven.

Another famous recipe from the Palace, which has been subject to a number of variations since it was first created, was Green Goddess dressing for salads. This was much later than the oysters Kirkpatrick period and it was presumably done for George Arliss when he toured in *The Green Goddess*.

Green Goddess Dressing

Combine 1 quart mayonnaise—and it must be good homemade mayonnaise done with olive oil—with 14 to 16 coarsely chopped anchovies, $\frac{1}{2}$ cup chopped parsley and chives mixed, 3 tablespoons chopped fresh tarragon (or 2 teaspoons dried tarragon, or more to taste), $\frac{1}{3}$ cup tarragon vinegar, and salt and freshly ground black pepper to taste. Beat ingredients together for a few minutes, correct the seasoning and allow the dressing to stand for several hours before serving.

Delights and Prejudices (1964)

BEEF Stroganoff

THERE ARE MANY DIFFERENT VERSIONS OF THIS DISH. Beware of those that specify long cooking. Beef Stroganoff is much better when prepared quickly a few minutes before it is eaten and is one of the specialties that is fun to do at the table if you have an electric skillet or chafing dish.

> 1 1/2 pounds of filet of beef
> 6 tablespoons of butter
> Olive oil
> 2 tablespoons of chopped green onions
> 1/4 cup of white wine or vermouth
> A-1 Sauce or Worcestershire Sauce
> 1 1/2 cups of sour cream
> Salt
> Pepper
> Chopped parsley

Ask the butcher to cut the meat into very thin slices. You can try it yourself, but it is difficult to do a neat job.

Melt 4 tablespoons of the butter in the pan and get it as hot as you can without burning. If you add just a bit of olive oil to the butter it helps prevent it from turning brown. Saute the beef slices in the hot fat very quickly. When they are delicately browned on both sides and done (this takes only a minute or two) remove them to a hot platter. Add remaining butter and the chopped green onions and cook for a minute. Then add white wine or vermouth, a dash or two of A-1 Sauce or Worcestershire Sauce and the sour cream. (Be sure you use the commercial sour cream that you buy at the grocery.) Stir well and heat through, but do not boil or the sour cream will curdle. Salt to taste and pour the sauce over the beef. Top with a sprinkling of freshly ground black pepper and chopped parsley. Serve with rice.

VARIATION: Add 3 tablespoons of chili sauce to the sauce.

James Beard, *The James Beard Cookbook* (1959)

Langston Hughes

from Soul Food

First introduced in the *Chicago Defender* in 1943, Jesse B. Semple, or "Simple," was one of Langston Hughes's most memorable literary creations, a Southern-born Harlem Everyman whose often humorous trials, tribulations, and insights became the subject of a semi-regular column. Collected in *Simple Speaks His Mind* (1950), *Simple Takes a Wife* (1953), *Simple Stakes a Claim* (1957), and other books, Simple and his exploits offered Hughes (1902–1967) a unique foil for commenting on the news of the day and the changing times. Here, in an excerpt from *Simple's Uncle Sam* (1965), he reflects on the pleasures of soul food, the pains of poor restaurant service, and the politics of integration.

■ ■ ■

"You heard, didn't you, about that old colored lady in Washington who went downtown one day to a fine white restaurant to test out integration? Well, this old lady decided to see for herself if what she heard was true about these restaurants, and if white folks were really ready for democracy. So down on Pennsylvania Avenue she went and picked herself out this nice-looking used-to-be-all-white restaurant to go in and order herself a meal."

"Good for her," I said.

"But dig what happened when she set down," said Simple. "No trouble, everybody nice. When the white waiter come up to her table to take her order, the colored old lady says, 'Son, I'll have collard greens and ham hocks, if you please.'

" 'Sorry,' says the waiter. 'We don't have that on the menu.'

" 'Then how about black-eyed peas and pig tails?' says the old lady.

" 'That we don't have on the menu either,' says the white waiter.

" 'Then chitterlings,' says the old lady, 'just plain chitterlings.'

"The waiter said, 'Madam, I never heard of chitterlings.'

" 'Son,' said the old lady, 'ain't you got no kind of soul food at all?'

" 'Soul food? What is that?' asked the puzzled waiter.

"'I knowed you-all wasn't ready for integration,' sighed the old lady sadly as she rose and headed toward the door. 'I just knowed you white folks wasn't ready.'"

"Most ethnic groups have their own special dishes," I said. "If you want French food, you go to a French restaurant. For Hungarian, you go to Hungarian places, and so on."

"But this was an American place," said Simple, "and they did not have soul food."

"The term 'soul food' is still not generally used in the white world," I said, "and the dishes that fall within its category are seldom found yet in any but colored restaurants, you know that. There's a place where jazzmen eat across from the Metropole that has it, and one or two places down in the Village, but those are the only ones I know in Manhattan outside of Harlem."

"It is too bad white folks deny themselves that pleasure," said Simple, "because there is nothing better than good old-fashioned, down-home, Southern Negro cooking. And there is not too many restaurants in Harlem that has it, or if they do, they spoil everything with steam tables, cooking up their whole menu early in the morning, then letting it steam till it gets soggy all day. But when a Negro fries a pork chop *fresh*, or a chicken *fresh*, or a fish *fresh*, I am telling you, it sure is good. There is a fish joint on Lenox Avenue with two women in it that can sure cook fish. But they is so evil about selling it to you. How come some of these Harlem eating places hire such evil-acting people to wait on customers? Them two ladies in this fish place stand behind the counter and look at you like they dare you to 'boo' or ask for anything. They both look mad no sooner than you enter."

"I'll bet they are two sisters who own the place," I said. "Usually by the time Negroes get enough money to own anything, they are so old they are evil. Those women are probably just mad because at their age they have to wait on anybody."

"Then they should not be in business," said Simple.

"I agree," I said. "But on the other hand, suppose they or their husbands have been skimping and saving for years. At last, at the age of forty or fifty they get a little business. What do they want them to do? Give it up just because they have got to the crabby age and should be retiring, before they have anything to retire on?"

"Then please don't take out their age on me when I come in to order a piece of fish," said Simple. "Why them two ladies never ask you what you want politely. They don't, in fact, hardly ask you at all. Them womens looks at customers like they want to say, 'Get out of here!' Then maybe one of them will come up to you and stand and look over the counter.

"You say, 'Have you got any catfish?' She will say, 'No!' And will not say what other kind she has or has not got.

"So you say, 'How about buffalo?' She will say, 'We had that yesterday.'

"Then you will say, 'Well, what have you got today?'

"She will say, 'What do you want?' I have already said twice what I wanted that they did not have. So now I say, 'How about butterfish?'

"She says, 'Sandwich or dinner?'

"I say, 'Dinner.'

"She says, 'We don't sell dinners after ten P.M.'

" 'Then why did you ask me if I wanted a dinner?' says I.

"She says, 'I was paying no attention to the time.'

"I said, 'You was paying no attention to me neither, lady, and I'm a customer. Gimme two sandwiches.'

" 'I am not here to be bawled out by you,' she says. 'If it's sandwiches you want, just say so, and no side remarks.'

" 'Could I please have a cup of coffee?'

" 'We got Pepsis and Cokes.'

" 'A Pepsi.'

"She rummages in the cooler. 'The Pepsis is out.'

" 'A Coke.'

"She comes up with a bottle that is not cold. Meanwhile the fish is frying, and it smells good, but it takes a while to wait, so I say, 'Gimme a quarter to play the juke box.' Three records for a quarter.

"Don't you know that woman tells me, 'We is all out of quarters tonight.'

"So I say, trying to be friendly, 'I'll put in a dime and play just one then. What is your favorite record?'

"Old hussy says, 'There's nothing on there do I like, so just play for yourself.'

" 'Excuse me,' says I, 'I will play "Move to the Outskirts of Town," which is where I think you ought to be.'

"'I wish my husband was here to hear your sass,' she says. 'Is your fish to eat here, or to go?'

"'To go,' I says, 'because I am going before you bite my head off. What do I owe?'

"'How much is two sandwiches to go?' she calls back to the other woman in the kitchen.

"'Prices is gone up,' says the other hussy, 'so charge him eighty cents.'

"'Eighty cents,' she says, 'and fifteen for the Pepsi.'

"'I had a Coke,' I says.

"'The same. You get a nickel change.'

"'From a five-dollar bill?' I says.

"'Oh, I did not notice you give me a five. Claybelle, have you got any change back there?'

"'None.'

"'Neither is I. Mister, you ought to have something smaller.'

"'I do not carry small change around on payday,' says I. 'And what kind of restaurant is this, that can't even bust a five-dollar bill, neither change small change into a quarter for the record player? Don't you-all have nothing in the cash register? If you don't, no wonder, the way you treat a customer! Just gimme my five back and keep your fish.'

"'Lemme look down in my stocking and see what I got there,' she says. And do you know, that woman went down in her stocking and pulled out enough money to buy Harry Belafonte. But she did not have a nickel change.

"So I said, 'Girl, you just keep that nickel for a tip.'

"If that woman owns the place, she ought to sell it. If she just works there, she ought to be fired. If she is the owner's girl friend, was she mine I would beat her behind, else feed her fish until a bone got stuck in her throat. I wonder how come some Harlem places have such evil help, especially in restaurants. Hateful help can spoil even soul food. Dear God, I pray, please change the hearts of hateful help!"

Simple's Uncle Sam (1965)

Vichyssoise

PERHAPS THE MOST POPULAR COLD SOUP in America today is Vichyssoise, to judge by its periodic appearance on almost every restaurant menu in the country during the summer months. Although Vichyssoise, despite its name, originated here and not in France, it remains, nonetheless, another version of the classic *potage Parmentier*, or leek and potato soup, so beloved by the French.

The following recipe is somewhat richer and more sophisticated than its country cousin—which is as it should be; a cold soup tends to be pallid and should be pampered a bit with good stock and thick cream if it is to make any impression on the palate at all.

To serve four or six

4 cups chicken stock, fresh or canned
4 tablespoons butter
2 large leeks, white parts only, finely chopped (about 1 cup)
1 small onion, chopped (about 1/3 cup)
1 small stalk celery, finely chopped (about 1/4 cup)
1 1/2 pints potatoes sliced about 1/4 inch thick
Salt
White pepper
1 cup heavy cream
2 tablespoons finely cut chives

The old adage, "the soup is only as good as the stock," applies particularly to Vichyssoise. Potatoes, apart from their wonderful texture, have little actual flavor when hot, and when cold, even less. If your stock has no character to begin with, your Vichyssoise will be an uninteresting brew indeed. So make your own stock if you can, but if you can't, use canned stock.

Now for the soup:

Melt the 4 tablespoons of butter very slowly in a large, heavy frying pan. As soon as it dissolves, mix into it the chopped onion, celery, and the carefully washed and chopped leeks. Cook slowly for about 20 minutes, stirring every now and then and adjusting the heat so that the vegetables barely color.

When they are soft and translucent, with a rubber spatula transfer them to a 3- or 4-quart saucepan. Pour in the stock, add the sliced potatoes, and bring it all to a boil. Reduce the heat at once, partially cover the pan, and simmer until the potatoes are soft and crumble easily when pierced with a fork.

Now, be firm and avoid the temptation to puree the soup in an electric blender. One of the characteristics of good Vichyssoise is its slightly grainy texture. The blender, no matter how carefully controlled, will reduce the soup to an irretrievable, bland cream. Use a food mill, instead, if you have one; if not, a fairly coarse sieve and the back of a large spoon will do. Whatever implement you use, set it over a large mixing bowl and force the soup through, potatoes, vegetables, and all.

If the puree at this point, seems too coarse in texture, as it may well be if the sieve openings were large ones, force it again through a sieve, this time a finer one. Stir in the seasonings, the white pepper discreetly and the salt liberally; use much more than you would ordinarily, for the cold will dull the soup's flavor later.

Cover the bowl and refrigerate until thoroughly chilled.

Before serving the soup, in chilled cups, stir into it 1 cup of heavy cream, and taste again for salt. If the Vichyssoise seems too thick for your taste, thin it with more cream, heavy or light, and adjust the seasonings accordingly. Garnish each cup with a scant teaspoon of finely cut fresh chives.

AFTERTHOUGHTS:

*Fresh dill, finely cut, makes an interesting departure from the usual chives, or combine equal parts of both. If you can't get either, shred very finely the green stems of scallions, but use them sparingly; the flavor is quite strong.

*A tablespoon or so of good curry powder, mixed into the sauteed vegetables before they are cooked in the stock, will give you a curried Vichyssoise. Try a little apple grated into each cup before garnishing with the chives.

*If, before you add the cupful of cream, the potato puree seems thin, for whatever reason, whip the cream lightly and fold it into the soup just before serving.

Michael Field, *Michael Field's Cooking School* (1965)

Along with Beard, Claiborne, and Julia Child, Michael Field was one of the real movers and shakers in the 1960s gourmet revolution. Eventually he was named editor of the influential Time-Life cookbook series.

LeRoi Jones

Soul Food

The poet Amiri Baraka (b. 1934) was still publishing as LeRoi Jones at the time he wrote this rhapsodic essay, collected in *Home: Social Essays* in 1966. Responding to a claim about African-American culture that he finds outrageous, he answers his own indignant question—"No language? No characteristic food?"—with a catalogue of tastes that is also a linguistic tour de force, practically jumping off the page with the staccato force of its rhythms and assonances.

■ ■ ■

Recently, a young Negro novelist writing in *Esquire* about the beauties of America mentioned that one of the things wrong with Negroes was that, unlike the Chinese, boots have neither a language of their own nor a characteristic cuisine. And this to me is the deepest stroke, the unkindest cut, of oppression, especially as it has distorted Black Americans. America, where the suppliant, far from rebelling or even disagreeing with the forces that have caused him to suffer, readily backs them up and finally tries to become an honorary oppressor himself.

No language? No characteristic food? Oh, man, come on.

Maws are things ofays seldom get to peck, nor are you likely ever to hear about Charlie eating a chitterling. Sweet potato pies, a good friend of mine asked recently, "Do they taste anything like pumpkin?" Negative. They taste more like memory, if you're not uptown.

All those different kinds of greens (now quick frozen for anyone) once were all Sam got to eat. (Plus the potlikker, into which one slipped some throwed away meat.) Collards and turnips and kale and mustards were not fit for anybody but the woogies. So they found a way to make them taste like something somebody would want to freeze and sell to a Negro going to Harvard as exotic European spinach.

The watermelon, friend, was imported from Africa (by whom?) where it had been growing many centuries before it was necessary for some people to deny that they had ever tasted one.

Did you ever hear of a black-eyed pea? (Whitey used it for forage, but some folks couldn't.) And all those weird parts of the hog? (After the pig was stripped of its choicest parts, the feet, snout, tail, intestines, stomach, etc., were all left for the "members," who treated them mercilessly.) Is it mere myth that shades are death on chickens? (Deep fat frying, the Dutch found out in 17th century New Amsterdam was an African speciality: and if you can get hold of a fried chicken leg, or a fried porgie, you can find out what happened to that tradition.)

I had to go to Rutgers before I found people who thought grits were meant to be eaten with milk and sugar, instead of gravy and pork sausage . . . and that's one of the reasons I left.

Away from home, you must make the trip uptown to get really straight as far as a good grease is concerned. People kill chickens all over the world, but chasing them through the dark on somebody else's property would probably insure, once they went in the big bag, that you'd find some really beautiful way to eat them. I mean, after all the risk involved. The fruit of that tradition unfolds everywhere above 100th Street. There are probably more restaurants in Harlem whose staple is fried chicken, or chicken in the basket, than any other place in the world. Ditto, barbecued ribs–also straight out of the South with the West Indians, *i.e.*, Africans from farther south in the West, having developed the best sauce for roasting whole oxen and hogs, spicy and extremely hot.

Hoppin' John (black-eyed peas and rice), hushpuppies (crusty cornmeal bread cooked in fish grease and best with fried fish, especially fried salt fish, which ought to soak overnight unless you're over fifty and can take all that salt), hoecake (pan bread), buttermilk biscuits and pancakes, fatback, *i.e.*, streak'alean-streak'afat, dumplings, neck bones, knuckles (both good for seasoning limas or string beans), okra (another African importation, other name gumbo), pork chops–some more staples of the Harlem cuisine. Most of the food came North when the people did.

There are hundreds of tiny restaurants, food shops, rib joints, shrimp shacks, chicken shacks, "rotisseries" throughout Harlem that serve "soul food"–say, a breakfast of grits, eggs and sausage, pancakes and Alaga syrup– and even tiny booths where it's at least possible to get a good piece of barbe- cue, hot enough to make you whistle, or a chicken wing on a piece of greasy bread. You can *always* find a fish sandwich: a fish sandwich is something you walk with, or "Two of those small sweet potato pies to go." The Muslim temple serves bean pies which are really separate. It is never necessary to go to some big expensive place to get a good filling grease. You *can* go to the Red Rooster, or Wells, or Joch's, and get a good meal, but Jennylin's, a little place on 135th near Lenox, is more filling, or some place like the A&A food shop in a basement up in the 140's, and you can really get away. I guess a square is somebody who's in Harlem and eats at Nedicks.

Home: Social Essays (1966)

Tunnel of Fudge Cake

Ella Rita Helfrich

HOUSTON, TEXAS

Bake-Off® Contest 17, 1966 Prize Winner

THE RECIPE ARGUABLY THE MOST CLOSELY IDENTIFIED with the Bake-Off® Contest, this divine chocolate cake mysteriously develops a "tunnel of fudge" filling as it bakes. Don't scrimp on the nuts, or it won't work!

Cake

1 3/4 cups sugar
1 3/4 cups margarine or butter, softened
6 eggs
2 cups powdered sugar
2 1/4 cups all-purpose flour
3/4 cup unsweetened cocoa
2 cups chopped walnuts*

Glaze

3/4 cup powdered sugar
1/4 cup unsweetened cocoa
4 to 6 teaspoons milk

Heat oven to 350°F. Grease and flour 12-cup Bundt pan or 10-inch tube pan. In large bowl, combine sugar and margarine; beat until light and fluffy. Add eggs 1 at a time, beating well after each addition. Gradually add 2 cups powdered sugar; blend well. By hand, stir in flour and remaining cake ingredients until well blended. Spoon batter into greased and floured pan; spread evenly.

Bake at 350°F. for 58 to 62 minutes.** Cool upright in pan on wire rack 1 hour; invert onto serving plate. Cool completely.

In small bowl, combine all glaze ingredients, adding enough milk for desired drizzling consistency. Spoon over top of cake, allowing some to run down sides. Store tightly covered.

Yield: 16 servings

*Tips: Nuts are essential for the success of this recipe.

**Since this cake has a soft filling, an ordinary
doneness test cannot be used. Accurate oven temperature
and baking times are essential.

High Altitude—Above 3,500 feet: Increase flour to 2 1/4 cups
plus 3 tablespoons. Bake as directed above.

Nutrition Per Serving: Calories 550; Protein 8g;
Carbohydrate 58g; Fat 32g; Sodium 300 mg

Pillsbury: Best of the Bake-Off Cookbook (1996)

Begun in 1949 and as popular as ever, the Pillsbury Bake-Off® is the mother of all cooking contests.

John McPhee

from Oranges

To move from ancient China to contemporary Florida, by way of Renaissance Siena, all in the process of taking a good hard look at oranges, is for John McPhee (b. 1931) pretty much in the ordinary run of things. He is a master of finding the point where tiny details come together to hint at the big picture. McPhee, who won a Pulitzer Prize in 1999, has been honing his unique brand of meditative reporting for *The New Yorker* since 1965, and the results can be savored in such books as *The Pine Barrens* (1968), *The Survival of the Bark Canoe* (1975), *Basin and Range* (1981), and, most recently, *Uncommon Carriers* (2006).

■ ■ ■

The first known reference to oranges occurs in the second book of the *Five Classics*, which appeared in China around 500 B.C. and is generally regarded as having been edited by Confucius. The main course of the migration of the fruit—from its origins near the South China Sea, down into the Malay Archipelago, then on four thousand miles of ocean current to the east coast of Africa, across the desert by caravan and into the Mediterranean basin, then over the Atlantic to the American continents—closely and sometimes exactly kept pace with the major journeys of civilization. There were no oranges in the Western Hemisphere before Columbus himself introduced them. It was Pizarro who took them to Peru. The seeds the Spaniards carried came from trees that had entered Spain as a result of the rise of Islam. The development of orange botany owes something to Vasco da Gama and even more to Alexander the Great; oranges had symbolic importance in the paintings of Renaissance masters; in other times, at least two overwhelming invasions of the Italian peninsula were inspired by the visions of paradise that oranges engendered in northern minds. Oranges were once the fruit of the gods, to whom they were the golden apples of the Hesperides, which were stolen by Hercules. Then, in successive declensions, oranges became the fruit of emperors and kings, of the upper prelacy, of the aristocracy, and, by the eighteenth century, of the rich bourgeoisie. Another hundred years went by before they came within reach of the middle classes, and not until early in this century did they at last become a fruit of the community.

Just after the Second World War, three scientists working in central Florida surprised themselves with a simple idea that resulted in the development of commercial orange-juice concentrate. A couple of dozen enormous factories sprang out of the hammocks, and Florida, which can be counted on in most seasons to produce about a quarter of all the oranges grown in the world, was soon putting most of them through the process that results in small, trim cans, about two inches in diameter and four inches high, containing orange juice that has been boiled to high viscosity in a vacuum, separated into several component parts, reassembled, flavored, and then frozen solid. People in the United States used to consume more fresh oranges than all other fresh fruits combined, but in less than twenty years the per-capita consumption has gone down seventy-five per cent, as appearances of actual oranges in most of the United States have become steadily less frequent. Fresh, whole, round, orange oranges are hardly extinct, of course, but they have seen better days since they left the garden of the Hesperides.

Fresh oranges have become, in a way, old-fashioned. The frozen product made from them is pure and sweet, with a laboratory-controlled balance between its acids and its sugars; its color and its flavor components are as uniform as science can make them, and a consumer opening the six-ounce can is confident that the drink he is about to reconstitute will taste almost exactly like the juice that he took out of the last can he bought. Fresh orange juice, on the other hand, is probably less consistent in flavor than any other natural or fermented drink, with the possible exception of wine.

The taste and aroma of oranges differ by type, season, county, state, and country, and even as a result of the position of the individual orange in the framework of the tree on which it grew. Ground fruit—the orange that one can reach and pick from the ground—is not as sweet as fruit that grows high on the tree. Outside fruit is sweeter than inside fruit. Oranges grown on the south side of a tree are sweeter than oranges grown on the east or west sides, and oranges grown on the north side are the least sweet of the lot. The quantity of juice in an orange, and even the amount of Vitamin C it contains, will follow the same pattern of variation. Beyond this, there are differentiations of quality inside a single orange. Individual segments vary from one another in their content of acid and sugar. But that is cutting it pretty fine. Orange men, the ones who actually work in the groves, don't discriminate to that extent. When they eat an orange, they snap out the long, thin blades of their fruit knives and peel it down, halfway, from the blossom end, which is always sweeter and juicier than the stem end. They eat the blossom half and throw the rest of the orange away.

An orange grown in Florida usually has a thin and tightly fitting skin, and it is also heavy with juice. Californians say that if you want to eat a Florida orange you have to get into a bathtub first. California oranges are light in weight and have thick skins that break easily and come off in hunks. The flesh inside is marvelously sweet, and the segments almost separate themselves. In Florida, it is said that you can run over a California orange with a ten-ton truck and not even wet the pavement. The differences from which these hyperboles arise will prevail in the two states even if the type of orange is the same. In arid climates, like California's, oranges develop a thick albedo, which is the white part of the skin. Florida is one of the two or three most rained-upon states in the United States. California uses the Colorado River and similarly impressive sources to irrigate its oranges, but of course irrigation can only do so much. The annual difference in rainfall between the Florida and California orange-growing areas is one million one hundred and forty thousand gallons per acre. For years, California was the leading orange state, but Florida surpassed California in 1942, and grows three times as many oranges now. California oranges, for their part, can safely be called three times as beautiful.

The color of an orange has no absolute correlation with the maturity of the flesh and juice inside. An orange can be as sweet and ripe as it will ever be and still glisten like an emerald in the tree. Cold—coolness, rather—is what makes an orange orange. In some parts of the world, the weather never gets cold enough to change the color; in Thailand, for example, an orange is a green fruit, and traveling Thais often blink with wonder at the sight of oranges the color of flame. The ideal nighttime temperature in an orange grove is forty degrees. Some of the most beautiful oranges in the world are grown in Bermuda, where the temperature, night after night, falls consistently to that level. Andrew Marvell's poem wherein the "remote Bermudas ride in the ocean's bosom unespied" was written in the sixteen-fifties, and contains a description, from hearsay, of Bermuda's remarkable oranges, set against their dark foliage like "golden lamps in a green night." Cool air comes down every night into the San Joaquin Valley in California, which is formed by the Coast Range to the west and the Sierra Nevadas to the east. The tops of the Sierras are usually covered with snow, and before dawn the temperature in the valley edges down to the frost point. In such cosmetic surroundings, it is no wonder that growers have heavily implanted the San Joaquin Valley with the Washington Navel Orange, which is the most beautiful orange grown in any quantity in the United States, and is certainly as attractive to the eye as any orange grown in the world. Its color will go to a deep, flaring cadmium orange, and its surface has a suggestion of coarseness, which complements its perfect ellipsoid shape.

Among orange groups, the navel orange is an old one. In his *Hesperides, or Four Books on the Culture and Use of the Golden Apples*, Giovanni Battista Ferrari, a Sienese Jesuit priest of the seventeenth century, described it, saying: "This orange imitates to some extent the fertility of the tree which bears it, in that it struggles, though unsuccessfully, to reproduce the fruit upon itself." It is thus a kind of monster. Just beneath the navel-like opening in the blossom end of each navel orange, there is a small and, more or less, fetal orange, usually having five or six pithy segments. The navel strain that we know now originated in Bahia, Brazil, probably as a bud sport, or mutation, of the Brazilian Selecta Orange. In 1870, an American Presbyterian missionary in Bahia was impressed by the seedlessness and rich flavor of this unusual orange with an umbilicus at its blossom end, and sent twelve nursery-size trees to the United States Department of Agriculture in Washington. The department propagated the trees and sent the progeny to anyone who cared to give them a try. In 1873, Mrs. Luther C. Tibbets, of Riverside, California, wrote for a pair of trees, got them, and planted them in her yard. Mrs. Tibbets' trees caught the attention of her neighbors and, eventually, of the world. From them have descended virtually every navel orange grown anywhere on earth today, including the Carter, the Golden Nugget, the Surprise, the Golden Buckeye, the Robertson, and the Thomson. The patriarchal one should by rights be called the Bahia, but merely because of its brief residence in the District of Columbia it has been known for ninety-six years as the Washington Navel Orange.

In the United States, in a typical year, around twenty-five billion oranges are grown. These include, among others, Maltese Ovals, Pope Summers, Nonpareils, Rubys, Sanford Bloods, Early Oblongs, Magnum Bonums, St. Michaels, Mediterranean Sweets, Lamb Summers, Lue Gim Gongs, Drake Stars, Whites, Whittakers, Weldons, Starks, Osceolas, Majorcas, Homosassas, Enterprises, Arcadias, Circassians, Centennials, Fosters, Dillars, Bessies, and Boones, but not—in all of these cases—in any appreciable quantity. Actually, one variety alone constitutes fully half of the total crop. Originally known in California as the Rivers Late Orange and in Florida as the Hart's Tardiff, it was imported into the United States early in the eighteen-seventies in unlabeled packages from the Thomas Rivers Nursery, of Sawbridgeworth, Hertfordshire. The easygoing Mr. Rivers had not only left off the name of the orange trees; he also failed to note where he had found them. They grew to be big, vigorous trees that bore remarkable quantities of almost seedless fruit containing lots of juice, which had a racy tartness in delicious proportion to its ample sugars. As supposedly different varieties, the trees were already beginning to prosper when an orange grower from Spain, traveling in California, felt suddenly at home in a grove of the so-called Rivers Lates. "That," said the Spanish grower, clearing up all mysteries with one unequivocal remark, "is the Late Orange of Valencia."

Out of the bewildering catalogue of orange varieties and strains, the Valencia has emerged in this century as something close to a universal orange. It is more widely and extensively planted than any other. From Florida and California and Central and South America to South Africa and Australia, Valencias grow in abundance in nearly all the orange centers of the world except Valencia. Having given the world the most remunerative orange yet known, Spain now specializes in its celebrated strains of bloods and navels. Only two per cent of the Spanish crop are Valencias, and perhaps only half of that comes from the groves of Valencia itself; much of the remainder grows in old, untended groves near Seville, where cattle wander through and munch oranges on the trees, on either bank of the Guadalquivir.

The Valencia is a spring and summer orange, and the Washington Navel ripens in the fall and winter. The two varieties overlap twice with perfect timing in California—where, together, they are almost all of the total crop— and the orange industry there never stops. In Florida, the Valencia harvest begins in late March and ends in June, and for about four months there is no picking. Florida grows few navel oranges, somewhat to the state's embarrassment. Florida growers tried hard enough, some seventy or eighty years ago, but the Washington Navel, in the language of pomology, proved to be too shy a bearer there. Instead, to meet the fall and winter markets, Florida growers have a number of locally developed early varieties to choose from, and in the main they seem to prefer three: the Pineapple Orange, the Parson Brown, and the Hamlin.

The Pineapple developed in the eighteen-seventies and was so named because its full, heavy aroma gave packinghouse employees the feeling that they were working in Hawaii rather than in Florida. The Pineapple is fairly seedy, usually containing about a dozen seeds, but it is rich in flavor, loaded with juice, and pretty to look at, with its smooth-textured, bright-orange skin and its slightly elongated shape. The skin is weak, though, and highly subject to decay. Most oranges, with appropriate care, will live about a month after they are picked. Pineapple Oranges don't have anything like that kind of stamina. (The Temple Orange and the Murcott Honey Orange, which are not actually oranges, ripen at the same time that Pineapples do. They are natural hybrids, almost certainly tangors—half orange, half tangerine—and they are so sweet that people on diets sometimes eat them before dinner in order to throttle their appetites. Oranges float, but these have so much sugar in them that if you drop one into a bucket of water it will go straight to the bottom. Murcotts were named for Charles Murcott Smith, one of the first men to propagate them. Advertisements have, from time to time, claimed that Temple Oranges were native to the Orient and sacred to a little-known sect of the Buddhist faith, and the seeds from which Florida's trees eventually sprang were stolen from a temple against the resistance of guardian priests. Temple Oranges are in fact named for William Chase Temple, who, long ago, was general manager of the Florida Citrus Exchange.)

Parson Nathan L. Brown was a Florida clergyman who grew oranges to supplement his income; the seedy, pebble-skinned orange that now carries his name was discovered in his grove about a hundred years ago. It tends to have pale-yellow flesh and pale-yellow juice, for, in general, the color of orange juice is light among early-season oranges, deeper in mid-season varieties, and deeper still in late ones.

The seedless, smooth-skinned Hamlin, also named for a Florida grove owner, ripens in October, ordinarily about two weeks ahead of the Parson Brown.

Both Hamlins and Parson Browns, when they are harvested, are usually as green as grass. They have to be ripe, because an orange will not continue to ripen after it has been picked. Many other fruits—apples and pears, for example—go on ripening for weeks after they leave the tree. Their flesh contains a great deal of starch, and as they go on breathing (all fruit breathes until it dies, and should be eaten before it is dead), they gradually convert the starch to sugar. When oranges breathe, there is no starch within them to be converted. Whatever sugars, acids, and flavor essences they have were necessarily acquired on the tree. Hence, an advertisement for "tree-ripened" oranges is essentially a canard. There is no other way to ripen oranges. It is against the law to market oranges that are not tree-ripened—that is to say, oranges that are not ripe. Women see a patch or even a hint of green on an orange in a store and they seem to feel that they are making a knowledgeable decision when they avoid it. Some take home a can of concentrated orange juice instead. A good part, if not all, of the juice inside the can may have come from perfectly ripe, bright-green oranges.

Some oranges that become orange while they are still unripe may turn green again as they ripen. When cool nights finally come to Florida, around the first of the year, the Valencia crop is fully developed in size and shape, but it is still three months away from ripeness. Sliced through the middle at that time, a Valencia looks something like a partitioned cupful of rice, and its taste is overpoweringly acid. But in the winter coolness, the exterior surface turns to bright orange, and the Valencia appears to be perfect for picking. Warm nights return, however, during the time of the Valencia harvest. On the trees in late spring, the Valencias turn green again, growing sweeter each day and greener each night.

Oranges (1967)

Gary Snyder

How to Make Stew in the Pinacate Desert:
Recipe for Locke & Drum

A recipe can sometimes be read as a kind of poem; Gary Snyder (b. 1930) here makes the process literal by making a poem out of a recipe, with little embellishment. Snyder, who was born in San Francisco and grew up near Portland, Oregon, fused his concerns for the environment, Asian and Native American traditions, and modernist poetics into a singular and unmistakable style in such books as *The Back Country* (1968), *Turtle Island* (1974), and *Mountains and Rivers Without End* (1996). Lawrence Ferlinghetti once called Snyder "the Thoreau of the Beat Generation."

■ ■ ■

A. J. Bayless market bent wire roller basket buy up parsnips,
onion, carrot, rutabaga and potato, bell green pepper,
& nine cuts of dark beef shank.
They run there on their legs, that makes meat tasty.

Seven at night in Tucson, get some bisquick for the dumplings.
Have some bacon. Go to Hadley's in the kitchen right beside the
frying steak—Diana on the phone—get a little plastic bag from Drum—
Fill it up with tarragon and chili; four bay leaves; black pepper
corns and basil; powdered oregano, something free, maybe about
two teaspoon worth of salt.

Now down in Sonora, Pinacate country, build a fire of Ocotillo,
broken twigs and bits of ironwood, in an open ring of lava: rake
some coals aside (and if you're smart) to windward,
keep the other half ablaze for heat and light.
Set Drum's fourteen-inch dutch oven with three legs across the embers.

Now put in the strips of bacon.
In another pan have all the vegetables cleaned up and peeled and sliced.
Cut the beef shank meat up small and set the bone aside.
Throw in the beef shank meat,
And stir it while it fries hot,
lots of ash and sizzle—singe your brow—

Like Locke says almost burn it—then add water from the jeep can—
add the little bag of herbs—cook it all five minutes more—and
then throw in the pan of all the rest.
Cover it up with big hot lid all heavy, sit and wait, or drink bud-
weiser beer.

And also mix the dumpling mix aside, some water in some bisquick,
finally drop that off the spoon into the stew.
And let it cook ten minutes more
and lift the black pot off the fire
to set aside another good ten minutes,
Dish it up and eat it with a spoon, sitting on a poncho in the dark.

                                               13.XII.1964

The Back Country (1968)

Julia Child

About the Television Series

A late bloomer by any definition, Julia Child (1912–2004) did not learn about French cooking until 1948, when she was 36. Her subsequent collaboration with Simone Beck and Louisette Bertholle on the now-classic *Mastering the Art of French Cooking* (1961) brought fine cuisine within reach of a great many American home cooks by demystifying it, presenting recipes and techniques in clear, step-by-step instructions. Her nearly accidental introduction to television cooking in 1962, described here, resulted in the public television series "The French Chef." The program enabled home cooks to improve their culinary skills and helped to create an appetite for the proliferation of such programming today. Child made French cooking look appealingly easy. Behind the scenes, however, things did not always go so smoothly.

■ ■ ■

"How in the world did you ever manage to get on television?" is a question frequently asked me. It was purely by accident. My husband, Paul, had resigned from the diplomatic service in 1961, after almost twenty years. We had settled in our great gray pre-Victorian house in Cambridge with its comfortable kitchen, and *Mastering the Art of French Cooking* had just been published. He was planning to write, paint, and photograph; I was to cook, write, and teach. We had even bought ourselves a budget television set, which was so ugly we hid it in an unused fireplace.

One evening a friend we had known in Paris, Beatrice Braude, who was then working at Boston's educational television station, WGBH-TV, suggested it would be a useful push for *Mastering* if I could appear on one of the station's book-review programs. Always happy to do anything for the book, I agreed that it might well be worth thinking about. She persuaded the station and the interview took place with a bit of conversation about food and France, and at one point I beat some egg whites in a large French copper bowl to enliven the talk. The program brought numerous requests for some kind of a cooking program, and WGBH-TV asked me if I would be willing to try three pilots, or experimental half-hour shows, to see whether there might be a real cooking audience out there over the air waves. Paul and I accepted the challenge, although we knew nothing at all about television and had hardly watched a program.

The studio assigned Russell Morash, producer of "Science Reporter," as Producer-Director. Assistant Producer was Ruth Lockwood, who had been working on the Eleanor Roosevelt shows. Because Channel 2's studio had burned almost to the ground a few months before, The Boston Gas Company loaned us its display kitchen. The budget was minute.

Ruth, Paul, and I blocked out a rough sequence of events for three programs: French omelettes, *coq au vin*, and a noncollapsible soufflé, which provided a varied and not-too-complicated sampling of French cooking. After thinking up dozens of titles for the show, we could find nothing better than "The French Chef"; it was short and told a story. Ruth dug around somewhere and came up with the anonymous but spritely musical theme song we are still using. As our own kitchen had enough equipment to furnish a small restaurant, there were no problems in that quarter.

It was out of the question for us to film a live show since we had only two cameras attached by long cables to a mobile bus. Besides, with an absolutely amateur performer, it would have been far too risky. We decided, however, that it would be taped as though it were live. Unless the sky fell in, the cameras failed, or the lights went off, there would be no stops, and no corrections—just a straight thirty minutes from start to finish. This was a good fundamental decision, I think. I hate to stop. I lose that sense of drama and excitement which the uninterrupted thirty-minute limitation imposes. Besides, I would far prefer to have things happen as they naturally do, such as the mousse refusing to leave the mold, the potatoes sticking to the skillet, the apple charlotte slowly collapsing. One of the secrets of cooking is to learn to correct something if you can, and bear with it if you cannot.

The day in June for our first taping, "The French Omelette," Paul and I packed our station wagon with pots, pans, eggs, and trimmings and were off to the Gas Company. Parking was difficult in downtown Boston, so he offloaded inside the main entrance, and I stood over our mound until he returned. How were the two of us to get everything down to the basement of that imposing office building? There was nobody to help, as we were hours ahead of our WGBH camera crew. Office girls and business-suited executives looked disapprovingly at our household pile as they rushed in and out. A uniformed elevator operator said, "Hey, get that stuff out of this lobby!" Eventually Paul located a janitor with a rolling cart and we clanked down to the basement where we unpacked, setting up our wares according to the master plan we had worked out.

Ruth arrived shortly to arrange a dining room setup for the final scene, and to go over our sequence of events. Then came Russ and our camera crew. After a short rehearsal to check lighting and camera angles, Russ said, "Let's shoot it!" And we did. Within the next week, following the same informal system, we taped the other two shows. I still have my notes. There is the map of the free-standing stove and work counter: "Simmering water in large alum. pan, upper R. burner." "Wet sponge left top drawer." "6 eggs in nest of 3 alum. plates w. ramekin." Paul, who was acting as invisible helper, had made himself a sheet of instructions: "When J. starts buttering, remove stack molds." "When soufflé is cheesed, take black saucepan."

On July 26, 1962, after we all had eaten a big steak dinner at our house, we pulled the television set out of hiding and turned it on at 8:30. There was this woman tossing French omelettes, splashing eggs about the place, brandishing big knives, panting heavily as she careened around the stove, and WGBH-TV lurched into educational television's first cooking program. Response to the three shows indicated that there was indeed an audience in New England, Channel 2 suggested we try a series of twenty-six programs, and "The French Chef" was underway. We were to start taping in January, and the first show would be on the air February 11, 1963.

What to pack into each of those thirty minutes? If we showed dishes that were too complicated, we would scare off all but a handful of people. Yet if we remained in the kindergarten, we would soon be a bore. Ruth, Paul, and I decided to start out with a few audience catchers, dishes that were famous, like *boeuf bourguignon*, but easy to make, and then gradually work into the subject. We also wanted to vary the weekly menu and take time to show French techniques, such as how to wield the knife, bone the lamb, clean the leek, whip and fold the egg whites. The idea was to take the bugaboo out of French cooking, to demonstrate that it is not merely good cooking but that it follows definite rules. The simplicity of a *velouté* sauce, for instance, is butter, flour, and seasoned liquid, but the rule is that the flour is cooked in the butter before the liquid is added. Why? (I, myself, will not do anything unless I know why.) "If you don't cook the flour in the butter, your sauce will have the horrid pasty taste of uncooked flour"—I have certainly given tongue to that one a hundred times. Finally we agreed on our program of twenty-six shows, starting with "*Boeuf Bourguignon*" and "French Onion Soup," ending with "Lobster *à l'Américaine*" and "*Crêpes Suzette.*"

In January when we started taping four shows a week, WGBH-TV still had no studio. The shows, like the three pilots, would have to be done where the mobile bus could park and string out cables to its two cameras. Fortunately for us, the Cambridge Electric Company offered their display kitchen located in a large loft room, with ample parking space nearby. We could reach it by a front stairway, by a freight elevator from two floors below, or by an outside iron fire escape that descended into the parking lot. Though our lighting arrangements were makeshift and the sound track was likely to mingle with the roar of the freight elevator, the cooking facilities were fine. The ceiling was high enough for us to hang a mirror over the stove that the camera could peer into when it needed the inside view of a pot. Best of all, we had the whole place to ourselves.

Although we were now an actual and official enterprise, our budget remained small. Paul and I did all the shopping and pre-cooking, and he continued to act as porter and unpacker, as well as chief dishwasher, until we got some volunteer cleaner-uppers for the taping days. Tuesdays and Thursdays were the long cooking rehearsals for the two shows scheduled the following days. Nobody at WGBH had the slightest idea what we were cooking in our loft until the cameras were lugged up the outside fire escape at 10 o'clock on Wednesdays and Fridays, to begin the tapings. We depended on Paul for advice when we were doubtful, and Russ for great openings and closings as well as all the techniques of camera and direction. Otherwise, Ruth Lockwood and I had complete freedom to work up anything we wished and to present it in any manner we chose.

The general pattern of the first three pilot shows seemed to fit my style, so we continued it, perfecting details as we went along. I found I had no sense of timing whatsoever, 1 minute or 5 minutes meant nothing to me as sadly illustrated by our second show and first try at "Onion Soup." I had to show the proper professional way to slice onions fast, the first cooking to soften them, the second cooking to brown them, the several ways to serve the soup; then there was *croûton*-making and gratinéing. I rushed through that program like a madwoman but I got everything in, only to find that when I carried the onion soup to the dining room I had gone so fast we still had 8 minutes left. Agony. I had to sit there and talk for all that time. Russ erased the tape back to about the 15-minute point, but after it happened again, Ruth devised the plan of breaking up the recipe into blocks of time. I could go as fast or slow as I wanted in the allotted time block, but I could not go into the next step until I got the signal.

Signals to the performer are written on placards known as "idiot cards." They are handed to the floor manager, who, by earphones, is plugged into one of the television cameras so he can hear and talk to the director who is shut away in the control room. The floor manager holds the idiot card just under the camera lens, and the performer appears to be gazing right into your eyes but is really reading that message: "Turn on burner number three!" In our case, the floor manager has a big loose-leaf book, and flips the pages according to a time schedule carefully worked out on a stop watch by Ruth. For the onion soup we were very simple: "The Knife & 1st Cook 5 min," "Browning and Simmering 4 min," "Soup in Bowls 2 min," and so forth. Later we became more elaborate, and put key words onto the idiot cards so I would not forget important points. I remember when we did *brioches*, we opened with a shot of three of them: the great big grandfather *brioche*, the middle-sized mother *brioche*, and the little baby *brioche*; we had obviously fallen into the story of Goldilocks and the Three Brioches. The idiot cards read like an Indian massacre—"This Baby; Remove head," "Punch Grandpa," "Slash Mother," "30 sec. Before Wash Hands." Often I am faced with Ruth's helpful reminders: "Stop gasping," "Wipe face," "Don't gallop."

The nonstop taping we have always continued, and in only a few instances, after the disaster of the first onion soup show, have we had to break off, erase, and pick up again. I can remember only half a dozen occasions, some of which were due to electrical failures, others due to me. Once, doing the "Lobster *à l'Américaine*," every time I touched the cooktop I got a short-circuit in the microphone against my chest, and kept clutching my breast in a very odd fashion. It felt like a bee sting. We wiped out back to the worst clutch, and were able to continue in midstream. Another time, "The Flaming

Soufflé" collapsed in its dish on the way to the dining room; I had forgotten to put in the cornstarch. We merely waited for the standby soufflé to come out of the oven and used that. Otherwise we let the gaffes lie where they fell, and on the whole it is just as well.

About halfway through, at the "Beef Gets Stewed Two Ways" show, WGBH-TV moved into its fine new building and we had a beautiful set with the most modern lighting, sound, and equipment. Wonderful as it is, we miss our old loft. It had an intimate atmosphere. We were a happy and independent family of twenty-four, we could eat up all the food ourselves, and even throw a party on occasion. But we could never have done color television there. In the next series, there will be no more gray strawberries, pale and sickly veal, livid lettuce or pallid pickles. Even the tongue will be utterly lifelike as it licks the *mousse au chocolat* off the spoon, and "The French Chef" will have a new dimension.

The French Chef Cookbook (1968)

Coq Au Vin

(CHICKEN IN RED WINE WITH ONIONS, MUSHROOMS, AND BACON)

This popular dish may be called *coq au Chambertin*, *coq au riesling*, or *coq au* whatever wine you use for its cooking. It is made with either white or red wine, but the red is more characteristic. In France it is usually accompanied only by parsley potatoes; buttered green peas could be included if you wish a green vegetable. Serve with it a young, full-bodied red Burgundy, Beaujolais, or Cotes du Rhone.

FOR 4 TO 6 PEOPLE

A 3- to 4-ounce chunk of lean bacon

Remove the rind and cut the bacon into *lardons* (rectangles 1/4 inch across and 1 inch long). Simmer for 10 minutes in 2 quarts of water. Rinse in cold water. Dry.

A heavy, 10-inch, fireproof casserole or an electric skillet
2 Tb butter

Sauté the bacon slowly in hot butter until it is very lightly browned (temperature of 260 degrees for an electric skillet). Remove to a side dish.

2 1/2 to 3 lbs. cut-up frying chicken

Dry the chicken thoroughly. Brown it in the hot fat in the casserole (360 degrees for the electric skillet).

1/2 tsp salt
1/8 tsp pepper

Season the chicken. Return the bacon to the casserole with the chicken. Cover and cook slowly (300 degrees) for 10 minutes, turning the chicken once.

1/4 cup cognac

Uncover, and pour in the cognac. Averting your face, ignite the cognac with a lighted match. Shake the casserole back and forth for several seconds until the flames subside.

3 cups young, full-bodied red wine such as
    Burgundy, Beaujolais, Cotes du Rhone,
    or Chianti
1 to 2 cups brown chicken stock, brown stock, or
    canned beef bouillon
1/2 Tb tomato paste
2 cloves mashed garlic
1/4 tsp thyme
1 bay leaf

Pour the wine into the casserole. Add just enough stock or bouillon to cover the chicken. Stir in the tomato paste, garlic, and herbs. Bring to the simmer. Cover and simmer slowly for 25 to 30 minutes, or until the chicken is tender and its juices run a clear yellow when the meat is pricked with a fork. Remove the chicken to a side dish.

12 to 24 brown-braised onions
1/2 lb. sautéed mushrooms

While the chicken is cooking, prepare the onions and mushrooms.

Salt and pepper

Simmer the chicken cooking liquid in the casserole for a minute or two, skimming off fat. Then raise heat and boil rapidly, reducing the liquid to about 2 1/4 cups. Correct seasoning. Remove from heat, and discard bay leaf.

3 Tb flour
2 Tb softened butter
A saucer
A rubber spatula
A wire whip

Blend the butter and flour together into a smooth paste (*beurre manié*). Beat the paste into the hot liquid with a wire whip. Bring to the simmer, stirring, and simmer for a minute or two. The sauce should be thick enough to coat a spoon lightly.

Arrange the chicken in the casserole, place the mushrooms and onions around it, and baste with the sauce. If the dish is not to be served immediately, film the top of the sauce with stock or dot with small pieces of butter. Set aside uncovered. It can now wait indefinitely.

Shortly before serving, bring to the simmer, basting the chicken with the sauce. Cover and simmer slowly for 4 to 5 minutes, until the chicken is hot through.

Sprigs of fresh parsley

Serve from the casserole, or arrange on a hot platter. Decorate with sprigs of parsley.

Julia Child, Louisette Bertholle, & Simone Beck, *Mastering the Art of French Cooking* (1961)

Nora Ephron

The Food Establishment: Life in the Land of the Rising Soufflé (Or Is It the Rising Meringue?)

As the writer of Hollywood hits including *Silkwood* (1983), *Heartburn* (1986), *When Harry Met Sally* (1989), *Sleepless in Seattle* (1993), and *You've Got Mail* (1998), the more recent of which she also produced and directed, Nora Ephron (b. 1941) has become a celebrity in her own right; if not universally famous, she is at the very least someone who ought to have no trouble getting a good table. Here, though—in a delightful report from her first book, *Wallflower at the Orgy* (1970)—Ephron stands back and watches, bemused, as the outsized egos of "the Food Establishment" vie for preeminence in a field grown increasingly fractious as well as increasingly influential. James Beard, Julia Child, Craig Claiborne, Michael Field, M.F.K. Fisher, Waverley Root: examples of their justly celebrated food writing are included elsewhere in this anthology. Ephron, with her keen sense of the comic, fills in some of the backstory.

■ ■ ■

One day, I awoke having had my first in a long series of food anxiety dreams (the way it goes is this: there are eight people coming to dinner in twenty minutes, and I am in an utter panic because I have forgotten to buy the food, plan the menu, set the table, clean the house, and the supermarket is closed). I knew that I had become a victim of the dreaded food obsession syndrome and would have to do something about it. This article is what I did.

Incidentally, I anticipated that my interviews on this would be sublime gourmet experiences, with each of my subjects forcing little goodies down my throat. But no. All I got from over twenty interviews were two raw potatoes that were guaranteed by their owner (who kept them in a special burlap bag on her terrace) to be the only *potatoes worth eating in all the world. Perhaps they were. I don't know, though; they tasted exactly like the other potatoes I've had in my life.*

September 1968

You might have thought they'd have been polite enough not to mention it at all. Or that they'd wait at least until they got through the reception line before starting to discuss it. Or that they'd hold off at least until after they had tasted the food—four tables of it, spread about the four corners of the Four Seasons—and gotten drinks in hand. But people in the Food Establishment are not noted for their manners or their patience, particularly when there is fresh gossip. And none of them had come to the party because of the food.

They had come, most of them, because they were associated with the Time-Life Cookbooks, a massive, high-budget venture that has managed to involve nearly everyone who is anyone in the food world. Julia Child was a consultant on the first book. And James Beard had signed on to another. And Paula Peck, who bakes. And Nika Hazelton, who reviews cookbooks for the *New York Times Book Review*. And M.F.K. Fisher, usually of *The New Yorker*. And Waverley Root of Paris, France. And Pierre Franey, the former chef of Le Pavillon who is now head chef at Howard Johnson's. And in charge of it all, Michael Field, the birdlike, bespectacled, frenzied gourmet cook and cookbook writer, who stood in the reception line where everyone was beginning to discuss it. Michael was a wreck. A wreck, a wreck, a wreck, as he himself might have put it. Just that morning, the very morning of the party, Craig Claiborne of the *New York Times*, who had told the Time-Life people he would not be a consultant for their cookbooks even if they paid him a hundred thousand dollars, had ripped the first Time-Life cookbook to shreds and tatters. *Merde alors*, as Craig himself might have put it, how that man did rip that book to shreds and tatters. He said that the recipes, which were supposed to represent the best of French provincial cooking, were not even provincial. He said that everyone connected with the venture ought to be ashamed of himself. He was rumored to be going about town telling everyone that the picture of the soufflé on the front of the cookbook was not even a soufflé—it was a meringue! *Merde alors!* He attacked Julia Child, the hitherto unknockable. He referred to Field, who runs a cooking school and is author of two cookbooks, merely as a "former piano player." Not that Field wasn't a former piano player. But actually identifying him as one—well! "As far as Craig and I are concerned," Field was saying as the reception line went on, "the gauntlet is down." And worst of all—or at least it seemed worst of all that day—Craig had chosen the day of the party for his review. Poor Michael. How simply frightful! How humiliating! How delightful! "Why did he have to do it today?" moaned Field to Claiborne's close friend, chef Pierre Franey. "Why? Why? Why?"

Why indeed?

The theories ranged from Gothic to Byzantine. Those given to the historical perspective said that Craig had never had much respect for Michael, and they traced the beginnings of the rift back to 1965, when Claiborne had gone to a restaurant Field was running in East Hampton and given it *one* measly star. Perhaps, said some. But why include Julia in the blast? Craig had done that, came the reply, because he had never liked Michael and wanted to tell Julia to get out of Field's den of thieves. Perhaps, said still others. But mightn't he also have done it because his friend Franey had signed on as a consultant to the *Time-Life Cookbook of Haute Cuisine* just a few weeks before, and Craig wanted to tell *him* to get out of that den of thieves? Perhaps, said others. But it might be even more complicated. Perhaps Craig had done it because he was furious at Michael Field's terrible review in the *New York Review of Books* of Gloria Bley Miller's *The Thousand Recipe Chinese Cookbook*, which Craig had praised in the *Times*.

Now, while all this was becoming more and more arcane, there were a few who secretly believed that Craig had done the deed because the Time-Life cookbook was as awful as he thought it was. But most of those people were not in the Food Establishment. Things in the Food Establishment are rarely explained that simply. They are never what they seem. People who seem to be friends are not. People who admire each other call each other Old Lemonface and Cranky Craig behind backs. People who tell you they love Julia Child will add in the next breath that of course her husband *is* a Republican and her orange Bavarian cream recipe just doesn't work. People who tell you Craig Claiborne is a genius will insist he had little or nothing to do with the *New York Times Cookbook*, which bears his name. People will tell you that Michael Field is delightful but that some people do not take success quite as well as they might. People who claim that Dione Lucas is the most brilliant food technician of all time further claim that when she puts everything together it comes out tasting bland. People who love Paula Peck will go on to tell you—but let one of *them* tell you. "I love Paula," one of them is saying, "but *no* one, absolutely *no* one understands what it is between Paula and monosodium glutamate."

Bitchy? Gossipy? Devious?

"It's a world of self-generating hysteria," says Nika Hazelton. And those who say the food world is no more ingrown than the theater world and the music world are wrong. The food world is smaller. Much more self-involved. And people in the theater and in music are part of a culture that has been popularly accepted for centuries; people in the food world are riding the crest of a trend that began less than twenty years ago.

In the beginning, just about the time the Food Establishment began to earn money and fight with each other and review each other's books and say nasty things about each other's recipes and feel rotten about each other's good fortune, just about that time, there came curry. Some think it was beef Stroganoff, but in fact, beef Stroganoff had nothing to do with it. It began with curry. Curry with fifteen little condiments and Major Grey's mango chutney. The year of the curry is an elusive one to pinpoint, but this much is clear: it was before the year of quiche Lorraine, the year of paella, the year of vitello tonnato, the year of boeuf Bourguignon, the year of blanquette de veau, and the year of beef Wellington. It was before Michael stopped playing the piano, before Julia opened L'Ecole des Trois Gourmandes, and before Craig had left his job as a bartender in Nyack, New York. It was the beginning, and in the beginning there was James Beard and there was curry and that was about all.

Historical explanations of the rise of the Food Establishment do not usually begin with curry. They begin with the standard background on the gourmet explosion—background that includes the traveling fighting men of World War Two, the postwar travel boom, and the shortage of domestic help, all of which are said to have combined to drive the housewives of America into the kitchen.

This background is well and good, but it leaves out the curry development. In the 1950s, suddenly, no one knew quite why or how, everyone began to serve curry. Dinner parties in fashionable homes featured curried lobster. Dinner parties in middle-income homes featured curried chicken. Dinner parties in frozen-food compartments featured curried rice. And with the arrival of curry, the first fashionable international food, food acquired a chic, a gloss of snobbery it had hitherto possessed only in certain upper-income groups. Hostesses were expected to know that iceberg lettuce was déclassé and tuna-fish casseroles *de trop.* Lancers sparkling rosé and Manischewitz were replaced on the table by Bordeaux. Overnight rumaki had a fling and became a cliché.

The American hostess, content serving frozen spinach for her family, learned to make a spinach soufflé for her guests. Publication of cookbooks tripled, quadrupled, quintupled; the first cookbook-of-the-month club, the Cookbook Guild, flourished. At the same time, American industry realized that certain members of the food world—like James Beard, whose name began to have a certain celebrity—could help make foods popular. The French's mustard people turned to Beard. The can-opener people turned to Poppy Cannon. Pan American Airways turned to Myra Waldo. The Potato Council turned to Helen McCully. The Northwest Pear Association and the Poultry and Egg Board and the Bourbon Institute besieged food editors for more recipes containing their products. Cookbook authors were retained, at sizable fees, to think of new ways to cook with bananas. Or scallions. Or peanut butter. "You know," one of them would say, looking up from a dinner made during the peanut-butter period, "it would never have occurred to me to put peanut butter on lamb, but actually, it's rather nice."

Before long, American men and women were cooking along with Julia Child, subscribing to the Shallot-of-the-Month Club, and learning to mince garlic instead of pushing it through a press. Cheeses, herbs, and spices that had formerly been available only in Bloomingdale's delicacy department cropped up around New York, and then around the country. Food became, for dinner-party conversations in the sixties, what abstract expressionism had been in the fifties. And liberated men and women who used to brag that sex was their greatest pleasure began to suspect that food might be pulling ahead in the ultimate taste test.

Generally speaking, the Food Establishment—which is not to be confused with the Restaurant Establishment, the Chef Establishment, the Food-Industry Establishment, the Gourmet Establishment, or the Wine Establishment—consists of those people who write about food or restaurants on a regular basis, either in books, magazines, or certain newspapers, and thus have the power to start trends and, in some cases, begin and end careers. Most of them earn additional money through lecture tours, cooking schools, and consultancies for restaurants and industry. A few appear on radio and television.

The typical member of the Food Establishment lives in Greenwich Village, buys his vegetables at Balducci's, his bread at the Zito bakery, and his cheese at Bloomingdale's. He dines at the Coach House. He is given to telling you, apropos of nothing, how many soufflés he has been known to make in a short period of time. He is driven mad by a refrain he hears several times a week: "I'd love to have you for dinner," it goes, "but I'd be afraid to cook for you." He insists that there is no such thing as an original recipe; the important thing, he says, is point of view. He lists as one of his favorite cookbooks the original *Joy of Cooking* by Irma Rombauer, and adds that he wouldn't be caught dead using the revised edition currently on the market. His cookbook library runs to several hundred volumes. He gossips a good deal about his colleagues, about what they are cooking, writing, and eating, and whom they are talking to; about everything, in fact, except the one thing everyone else in the universe gossips about—who is sleeping with whom. In any case, he claims that he really does not spend much time with other members of the Food Establishment, though he does bump into them occasionally at Sunday lunch at Jim Beard's or at one of the publishing parties he is obligated to attend. His publisher, if he is lucky, is Alfred A. Knopf.

He takes himself and food very very seriously. He has been known to debate for hours such subjects as whether nectarines are peaches or plums, and whether the vegetables that Michael Field, Julia Child, and James Beard had one night at La Caravelle and said were canned were in fact canned. He roundly condemns anyone who writes more than one cookbook a year. He squarely condemns anyone who writes a cookbook containing untested recipes. Colleagues who break the rules and succeed are hailed almost as if they had happened on a new galaxy. "Paula Peck," he will say, in hushed tones of awe, "broke the rules in puff paste." If the Food Establishmentarian makes a breakthrough in cooking methods—no matter how minor and superfluous it may seem—he will celebrate. "I have just made a completely and utterly revolutionary discovery," said Poppy Cannon triumphantly one day. "I have just developed a new way of cooking asparagus."

There are two wings to the Food Establishment, each in mortal combat with the other. On the one side are the revolutionaries—as they like to think of themselves—the home economists and writers and magazine editors who are industry-minded and primarily concerned with the needs of the average housewife. Their virtues are performance, availability of product, and less work for mother; their concern is with improving American food. "There is an awe about Frenchiness in food which is terribly precious and has kept American food from being as good as it could be," says Poppy Cannon, the leader of the revolutionaries. "People think French cooking is gooking it up. All this kowtowing to so-called French food has really been a hindrance rather than a help." The revolutionaries pride themselves on discovering short cuts and developing convenience foods; they justify the compromises they make and the loss of taste that results by insisting that their recipes, while unquestionably not as good as the originals, are probably a good deal better than what the American housewife would prepare if left to her own devices. When revolutionaries get together, they talk about the technical aspects of food: how to ripen a tomato, for example; and whether the extra volume provided by beating eggs with a wire whisk justifies not using the more convenient electric beater.

On the other side are the purists or traditionalists, who see themselves as the last holdouts for haute cuisine. Their virtue is taste; their concern primarily French food. They are almost missionary-like, championing the cause of great food against the rising tide of the TV dinner, clamoring for better palates as they watch the children of America raised on a steady diet of Spaghetti Os. Their contempt for the revolutionaries is eloquent: "These people, these home economists," said Michael Field distastefully, "—they skim the iridescent froth off the gourmet department, and it comes out tasting like hell." When purists meet, they discuss each other; very occasionally, they talk about food: whether one ought to put orange peel into boeuf Bourguignon, for example, and why lamb tastes better rare.

Although the purists do not reach the massive market available to the revolutionaries, they are virtually celebrities. Their names conjure up a sense of style and taste; their appearance at a benefit can mean thousands of dollars for hospitals, charities, and politicians. The Big Four of the Food Establishment are all purists—James Beard, Julia Child, Michael Field, and Craig Claiborne.

Claiborne, a Mississippi-born man who speaks softly, wears half-glasses, and has a cherubic reddish face that resembles a Georgia peach, is probably the most powerful man in the Food Establishment. From his position as food editor of the *New York Times*, he has been able to bring down at least one restaurant (Claude Philippe's Pavillon), crowd customers into others, and play a critical part in developing new food tastes. He has singlehandedly revived sorrel and cilantro, and, if he could have his way, he would single-handedly stamp out iceberg lettuce and garlic powder. To his dismay, he played a large part in bringing about the year of beef Wellington. "I hate the stuff," he says.

In his thirties, after too many unhappy years in public relations and the armed forces, Claiborne entered the Lausanne Hotel School to study cooking. On his return—and after a brief fling bartending—he began to write for *Gourmet* magazine and work for Ann Seranne's public-relations firm, handling such products as the Waring Blender and Fluffo the Golden Shortening. In 1957 he was hired by the *Times*, and he unabashedly admits that his job has been a dream come true. He loves it, almost as much as he loves eating, though not nearly as much as he loves cooking.

Claiborne is happiest in his Techbuilt house in Springs, East Hampton, which overlooks an herb garden, an oversized swimming pool, and Gardiner's Bay. There, he, his next-door neighbor Pierre Franey—whom he calls "my arm and my dear friend"—and a number of other chefs go fishing, swap recipes, and whip up meals for fifty guests at a time. The menus are logged into a small leatherbound notebook in which Claiborne records every meal he eats throughout the year. During the winter, Claiborne lives in Greenwich Village. His breakfasts often consist of Sara Lee frozen crois-sants. His other daily meals are taken in restaurants, and he discusses them as if he were serving penance. "That," he says firmly, "is the thing I like least about my job."

Six years ago Claiborne began visiting New York restaurants incognito and reviewing them on a star system in the Friday *Times*; since that time, he has become the most envied, admired, and cursed man in the food world. Restaurant owners decry his Francophilia and can barely control their tempers while discussing his prejudice against large-management corpora-tions and in favor of tiny, ethnic restaurants. His nit-picking constantly irri-tates. Among some of the more famous nits: his censure of a Pavillon waiter who allowed his pencil to peek out; his disapproval of the salt and pepper shakers at L'Étoile, and this remark about Lutèce: "One could wish that the owner, Monsieur Surmain, would dress in a more reserved and elegant style to better match his surroundings."

Surmain, a debonair man who wears stylish striped shirts, sputters when Claiborne's name is mentioned. "He said in a restaurant of this sort I should wear a tuxedo," said Surmain. "What a bitchy thing. He wants me to act like a headwaiter."

The slings and arrows of outrage fly at Claiborne—and not only from restaurateurs. Carping about Craig is practically a parlor game in the food world. Everything he writes is pored over for its true significance. It is suggested, for example, that the reason Craig criticized proprietor Stuart Levin's clothes in his recent review of Le Pavillon had to do with the fact that Levin fawned over him during his two visits to the restaurant. It is suggested that the reason Craig praised the clothes of Charles Masson of Grenouille in the same review had to do with the fact that Masson ignores Craig entirely too much. It is suggested that Craig is not a nice person; and a story is offered to support the thesis, all about the time he reviewed a new restaurant owned by a friend after the friend begged him to wait a few weeks. His criticisms, it is said, drove the friend to drink.

But the fact of the matter is that Craig Claiborne does what he does better than anyone else. He is a delight to read. And the very things that make him superb as a food critic—his integrity and his utter incorruptibility—are what make his colleagues loathe him.

"Everyone thinks about Craig too much," says cookbook author and consultant Mimi Sheraton. "The truth is that he is his own man and there is no way to be a friend of his. He is the only writer who is really honest. Whether or not he's reliable, whether or not you like him, he is honest. I know *Cue* isn't—I used to write for them. *Gourmet* isn't. And Michael Field is just writing for Craig Claiborne."

Whenever members of the Food Establishment tire of discussing Craig they move on to discuss Craig's feuds—though in all fairness, it must be said that Claiborne is usually the less active party to the feuds. The feud currently absorbing the Food Establishment is between Claiborne and Michael Field. Field, who burst into stardom in the Food Establishment after a career as half of the piano team of Appleton & Field, is an energetic, amusing, frenetic man whose recent rise and subsequent candor have won him few friends in the food world. Those who are not his admirers have taken to passing around the shocking tidbit—untrue—that Field had not been to Europe until 1967, when he visited Julia Child in Provence.

"Essentially," says Field, "the whole Food Establishment is a mindless one, inarticulate and not very cultivated. These idiots who attack me are furious because they think I just fell into it. Well, let me tell you, I used to make forty soufflés in one day and throw them out, just to find the right recipe."

Shortly after his first cookbook was published, Field began reviewing cookbooks for the *New York Review of Books*, a plum assignment. One of his first articles, an attack on *The Fannie Farmer Cookbook* which centered on its fondue recipe, set off a fracas that produced a furious series of argumentative letters, in themselves a hilarious inadvertent parody of letters to highbrow magazines. Recently, he reviewed *The Thousand Recipe Chinese Cookbook*— a volume that was voted winner of the R. T. French (mustard) Tastemaker Award (chosen by one hundred newspaper food editors and roughly analogous in meaning to landing on the Best Dressed List). In his attack on Gloria Bley Miller's book, he wrote: "It would be interesting to know why, for example, Mrs. Miller's recipe for hot mustard requires the cook to bring one cup of water to a boil and then allow it to cool before adding one half cup of dry mustard? Surely Mrs. Miller must be aware that drinking and cooking water in China was boiled because it was often contaminated. . . ."

Mrs. Miller wrote in reply: "I can only suggest to Mr. Field . . . that he immerse his typewriter immediately in boiling water. There are many types of virulence in the world, and 'boiling the water first' is one of the best ways to disinfect anything."

The feud between Field and Claiborne had been simmering for several years, but Claiborne's review of the Time-Life cookbook turned it up to full boil. "He has a perfect right to dislike the book," said Field. "But his attack went far beyond that, into personalities." A few months after the review was published, Field counterpunched, with an article in *McCall's* entitled "New York's Ten Most Overrated Restaurants." It is in almost total opposition to Claiborne's *Guide to New York Restaurants*; in fact, reading Field's piece without having Claiborne's book alongside is a little like reading *Finnegans Wake* without the key.

For his part, Claiborne would just as soon not discuss Field—"Don't get me started," he said. And his attitude toward the Time-Life series has mellowed somewhat: he has finally consented to write the text of the *Time-Life Cookbook of Haute Cuisine* along with Franey. But some time ago, when asked, he was only too glad to defend his review. "Helen McCully (food editor of *House Beautiful*) said to me, 'How could you be so mean to Michael?'" he recalled. "I don't give a good God damn about Michael." His face turned deep red, his fists clenched, he stood to pace the room. "The misinformation! The inaccuracies in that book! I made a stack of notes thicker than the book itself on the errors in it. It's shameful."

Claiborne was so furious about the book, in fact, that he managed to intensify what was, until then, a one-sided feud between James Beard and himself. Beard, a genial, large, round man who receives guests in his Tenth Street house while seated, Buddha-like, on a large pouf, had been carrying on a mild tiff with Claiborne for some time. Just before the first Time-Life cookbook was published, the two men appeared together on the David Susskind Show, and in the course of the program, Beard held up the book and plugged it on the air. Afterward, Claiborne wrote a letter to Susskind, with carbon copy to Beard, saying that if he had known he was going to appear on the same show with the Time-Life cookbook, he never would have consented to go on.

(That Julia Child has managed thus far to remain above the internecine struggles of the food world probably has more to do with the fact that she lives in Cambridge, Massachusetts, well away from it all, than with her charming personality.)

The success of the Time-Life cookbook series is guaranteed, Claiborne's review notwithstanding. Offered by mail order to subscribers who care not one whit whether the soufflé on the cover is actually a meringue, the series rapidly signed up five hundred thousand takers—for all eighteen books! (The *New York Times* Cookbook, itself a blockbuster, has sold only two hundred thousand copies.) "The books, whatever their limits, are of enormous quality," says Field. "Every recipe works and is honestly conceived." Yet a number of those intimately connected with the books have complained about the limits Field parenthetically refers to, and most particularly about the technique of group journalism that has produced the books: apparently, the text, recipes, and photographs of some of the cookbooks have been done independently of each other.

"It's a joke," said Nika Hazelton, who is writing the text for the *Time-Life German Cookbook*. "First there is the writer—me, in this case, but I have nothing to do with the recipes or illustrations. Then there is the photographic staff, which takes recipes from old cookbooks, changes them a little, and photographs them. Then there is the kitchen, under Michael Field's supervision. I think Michael knows about French and Italian food, but he doesn't know quite as much about other cookery. The cook is John Clancy, a former cook in a short-order house who once worked for Jim Beard. I'm the only person connected with the project who knows languages besides French. There is a consultant who hasn't been in Germany for thirty years. My researcher's background is spending three years with the Morgan Bank. It's hilarious. I'm doing it only for the money."

The money that is available to members of the Food Establishment is not quite as much as they would have you think, but it is definitely enough to keep every last one of them in truffles. James Beard—who commands the highest fees and, though a purist, has the most ties with industry—recently turned down a hundred-thousand-dollar offer to endorse Aunt Jemima mixes because he didn't believe in their products. Retainers offered lesser stars are considerably smaller, but there are many jobs, and they suffice. Nevertheless, the impression persists that there are not enough jobs to go around. And because everyone in the food world is free-lancing and concerned with putting as many eggs into his basket as possible, it happens that every time someone gets a job, the rest feel that they have lost one.

Which brings us to the case of Myra Waldo. An attractive, chic woman who lives on upper Fifth Avenue, Miss Waldo published her first cookbook in 1954, and since then she has been responsible for forty-two others. Forty-two cookbooks! In addition, she does four radio spots a day for WCBS, is roving editor of *Family Circle* magazine, is retained by Pan American Airways, and recently landed the late Clementine Paddleford's job as food editor of *This Week* magazine. Myra Waldo has never been a favorite in the Food Establishment: she is far too successful. Furthermore, although *she* once made forty-eight soufflés over a July Fourth weekend, she is not a truly serious cook. (To a visitor who wanted a recipe for a dinner party, she suggested duck in a sauce made of frozen orange juice, Melba sauce, red wine, cognac, lemon juice, and a can of Franco-American beef gravy.) For years it has been rumored that Miss Waldo produces as many cookbooks as she does because she clips recipes and pastes them right onto her manuscript pages, or because she has a gigantic staff—charges she denies. But when she landed the *This Week* job, one that nearly everyone else in the Food Establishment had applied for, the gang decided that too much was too much. Shortly afterward, she went to the Cookbook Guild party, and no one except James Beard even said hello to her.

Said Beard: "You could barely move around at that party for fear someone would bite you in the back."

How much longer life in the Food Establishment—with its back-biting, lip-smacking, and pocket-jingling—will go on is hard to tell. There are some who believe the gourmet explosion that began it all is here to stay and that fine cooking is on the increase. "Of course it will last," said Poppy Cannon, "just in the way sculpture will last. We need it. It is a basic art. We ought to have a National Academy of the Arts to represent the art of cooking."

Others are less sure. They claim that the food of the future will be quite different: precooked, reconstituted, and frozen dishes with portion control. "The old cuisine is gone for good and dying out," says Mrs. Hazelton. "Ultimately, cooking will be like an indoor sport, just like making lace and handiwork."

Whatever happens, the Food Establishment at this moment has the power to change the way America eats. And in fact, about all it is doing is showing how to make a better piecrust and fill a bigger breadbox.

"What fascinates me," says Mimi Sheraton, "is that the more interest there is in gourmet food, the more terrible food is for sale in the markets. You can't buy an unwaxed cucumber in this country, the bread thing everyone knows about, we buy overtenderized meat and frozen chicken. You can't buy a really fresh egg because they've all been washed in hot water so the shells will be clean. And the influence of color photography on food! Oil is brushed on to make it glow. When we make a stew, the meat won't sit on top, so we have to prop it up with oatmeal. Some poor clod makes it at home and it's like buying a dress a model has posed in with the back pinned closed. As a result, food is marketed and grown for the purpose of appearances. We are really the last generation who even has a vague memory of what food is supposed to taste like.

"There have been three revolutionary changes in the food world in past years," Miss Sheraton continued. "The pressure groups have succeeded in changing the labeling of foods, they've succeeded in cutting down the amounts of pesticides used on foods, and they've changed the oversized packages used by the cereal and cracker people. To me, it's interesting that not one of these stories began with a food writer. Where are they, these food writers? They're off wondering about the boeuf en daube and whether the quiche was authentic."

Yes, that's exactly where they are. "Isn't it all a little too precious?" asks Restaurant Associates president Joseph Baum. "It's so elegant and recherché, it's like overbreeding a collie." But, after all, someone has to worry about the boeuf en daube and whether the quiche was authentic—right? And there is so much more to do. So many soufflés to test and throw out. So many ways of cooking asparagus to discover. So many patés to concoct. And so many things to talk about. Myra's new book. The record Poppy is making. Why Craig finally signed on to Time-Life Cookbooks. Michael's latest article. So much more to do. So many things to talk about. . . .

Wallflower at the Orgy (1970)

Gael Greene

Lessons in Humility and Chutzpah

As restaurant critic for *New York* magazine from 1968 to 2000, Gael Greene (b. 1937) had a front-row seat for the American Food Revolution. She was also a player to watch: an enthusiastic advocate of the notion of restaurant as theater and a stylistic innovator who shrugged off the demure, recipe-heavy prose that had long been the province of female food writers and home economists. Greene's rollicking first-person accounts of her sybaritic escapades and amorous conquests—in her magazine writing, and in novels such as *Blue Skies, No Candy* (1976), and *Doctor Love* (1982)—helped to blast open the stodgy gourmet world and turned food loving into a sexy adventure. They also encouraged long-intimidated middle-class food lovers to have fun—as here, with her advice on how to neutralize an imperious maitre d' and occupy the coveted seats at a dining room's center stage. Her most recent work is a gourmandizing memoir: *Insatiable: Tales from a Life of Delicious Excess* (2006).

■ ■ ■

Telephone Power

Your secretary calls for a reservation. Your English secretary, preferably. Or your wife, cleverly passing herself off as your English secretary. "This is Mr. Ford's office. Mr. Ford would like a table for two at lunch." When the cagey maître d' asks for Mr. Ford's initial, cagey wife answers "E." Roosevelt and Vanderbilt are also good names. As Mimi Strong observes, "Not every Vanderbilt is a Vanderbilt, you know."

If you are Miss Nobody lunching with Ava Gardner or Dorothy Schiff or Happy Rockefeller, say so boldly, or slyly: "By the way, Martin, I am meeting Mrs. Rockefeller. Please watch for her in case I'm a few minutes late." And you *are* late, to insure getting a Rockefeller table instead of a nobody table. If your family name is Orlovsky, change your first name to Prince. I have a friend who has vowed to name her next son Count. "Count Kaufman's table, please." If he is stabbed by the petit-pain boy, he needn't bleed blue—just profusely, muttering darkly about hemophilia.

For really advanced knavery, it takes a rogue–"preferably Hungarian," says writer-rogue Béla von Block, John Paul Getty's ghost. "This is von Block," Béla announces, demanding a table. Then he asks for a rundown on the house's clarets, or orders champagne to be waiting in a bucket. "I ask for Pol Roger and I accept nothing older than the forties." What if the restaurant has an acceptable Pol Roger? "I doubt if five restaurants in New York have," says von Block. "If they do, you'll be stuck for about sixty dollars, but when you play Russian roulette, you've got to be ready to take an occasional shot in the wallet." Next von Block deploys a messenger with an envelope addressed to himself care of the maître d'. "I steal impressive letterheads and use a wax seal." When he arrives at the restaurant, the headwaiter takes him aside. "We have an instant intimacy."

A True-Grit Arrival

For sheer class, you may never beat the wispy plaster-casted dowager whose chauffeur carried her into La Caravelle. But sables never hurt. Jonathan Dolger, author of *The Expense Account Diet*, advocates a confident smile. "Definitely have your teeth capped."

Don't rush . . . glide. Greet the maître d' by name. As he teeters off-balance (Who are you? Should he know you?), quickly give your name. "Ford. Table for two." "Of course, Mr. Ford." (He juggles tables mentally. Perhaps you don't belong quite so deep in Siberia.)

"Good" table and "bad" table can be crucial. Ludwig Bemelmans told of a woman who was always given an undesirable table in a certain posh restaurant whenever she dined with her husband. One day she came in with another man and was immediately led to the best table in the house. Divorce inevitably followed.

Just as water seeks its own level, tables find their own status. The most desirable tables are in the heart of tumult and traffic. Not even the iron-willed Henri Soulé could de-status a table once Le Pavillon pets had charted their own perverse social topography. "They would rather dine in the telephone booth than in the dining room," he would complain. True, it's the same mousse de sole no matter where you sit, but the service can vary erratically. Of course, the snobbery of status seekers breeds reverse snobbery. At "21," says Mimi Strong, "the nouveau status-seekers will stay at the bar till they get a seat in the front room . . . they're afraid to sit down anywhere else. The most important people insist on a table upstairs with the nobodies." If you are quite clearly a nobody with not a hoot of hope for a table downstairs, do not meekly submit to the ignominious climb. Seize the reins at once. Demand a table upstairs, "in that little room where you keep the tourists, please." Your tone should suggest you are a Whitney or a Paley seeking privacy and quiet. Immediately you are less than nobody. The faked-out Kreindler brother or cousin or in-law may remember.

Money liquefies some glaciers, but not those of L'Académie Pavillon.

Money will not melt Robert Meyzen of La Caravelle: "You cannot buy a table—not for two hundred dollars," Meyzen has said. "If you belong here, you get a table."

The Mask of Belonging

Martin Decré likes simplicity. Simple black dresses and simple diamonds. Mme. Henriette of Côte Basque and the cantankerous Fayets of Lafayette have never warmed to ladies in pants. Soulé's disciples are stodgily conservative. La Grenouille is more permissive. There, in the castle of the Seventh Avenue kings, anything goes: see-through jumpsuits, unfettered bosoms, Sioux rain-dance togs. Le Pavillon under Stuart Levin has softened its formidable mien. But after five, dark suits and white shirt are still *de rigueur*. And no turtlenecks at lunch. "Not even for Sammy Davis, Jr.," Levin warned. "Of course, if he comes in dashiki I'll have to let him in . . . dashiki is national dress."

The wrong purse and a voluminous suburban bag (unless it's alligator) are dead giveaways, Mimi Strong cautions.

The lady checks her coat. Yes, even her sable. "We like to think our customers are secure," Levin observes. So, check the security blanket. Martin once demoted a very impressively dressed couple from the plains to the frozen tundra. "When he passed by I saw his rundown heels and white socks."

Even the consummate arbiters of "in" have their astigmatisms. Henri Soulé himself once seated two matrons in the farthest reaches of Outer Mongolia. They ate lunch without protest. "You have a nice restaurant—it's a pity you don't know your New York," the former Mrs. Nelson Rockefeller admonished Soulé as she exited. La Grenouille's headwaiter failed to recognize

Alice Longworth. "Howard Hughes in his dusty sneakers would probably get the same rebuff," predicts Jonathan Dolger. "I assume he'd walk around the corner, step into a phone booth and buy the block."

No reservations? The snob maître d' keeps a few empty tables for the eleventh-hour whims of his favorites. Present yourself, discreetly costumed, to the benevolent ogre. You may get the table you couldn't reserve on the phone that same morning.

How to Talk Cordon Bleu

You can never know too much about food. If you care what crosses your plate, you may fire a bored captain's imagination. I favor an academic approach. Cooking lessons . . . a year at the Cordon Bleu. A tutor in French . . . frequent research trips to France. Waverley Root is my muse and *Larousse Gastronomique* the companion of my insomnia. At the very minimum, memorize a few common terms: *florentine* (spinach); *véronique* (with white grapes); *en gelée* (jellied); *fumé* (smoked). If something is cold or singed or spoiled or rotten, send it back. If you order ris de veau expecting rice and veal, you lose points complaining that you didn't order sweetbreads. Try not to weep when you discover pamplemousse is not exotic mousse of pample but merely everyday grapefruit.

Ordering caviar is always impressive. May and June, October and November are the best months for caviar. *Malossol* means "lightly salted." Daddy O prefers the slightly less expensive caviar. Restaurants which Ari favors keep a supply on hand. Ask if the house can spare some. Champagne goes well, Polish vodka even better.

Béla von Block always demands fresh horseradish. "That throws them. Not too many places have it." If they do, he commands it cut in paper-thin curls. "Delicious with Bloody Marys. Put a strip between your teeth and drink the Bloody Mary through it."

Devastate the chocolate-mousse-swilling proles with your dessert order: "A nice crisp apple would be pleasant." Always ask to see the cheese, even if you haven't the slightest intention of actually ordering it. Frown. "That's all?" you say (a suitable comment for less than six offerings . . . for more than six a simple "Hmmmph" will do). "I don't see Bleu du Bresse," you say. (Of course not, no one serves Bleu du Bresse . . . almost no one imports it.) Say, "The Roquefort looks lean." Or when appropriate. "It looks like that Brie has had it." Or . . . spying a crumbly goat cheese, you say, "Young goat, yes . . . old goat, no." Then in a low pained voice: "I think we'd best forget about cheese and see if we can't do better on the pastry tray."

For the best possible meal, restaurateurs wish you would order ahead. "Especially if you are more than four at dinner," Stu Levin urges. "But even for a party of two." Paul Kovi at the Four Seasons outdoes himself when you say, "We put ourselves entirely into your hands." Martin at La Seine says, "We knock ourselves out for out-of-towners who confide they've come because of the *Gourmet* magazine rave, have saved for a year, and hope they won't be disappointed." Alfred Knopf, Jr., asks to meet the chef.

Points at Payoff

Overtipping the waiter is wanton. It is impossible to overtip the maître d'. Some innocents still tip 15 per cent and some tip 25 per cent. But 20 per cent (before tax) is still the going rate—15 per cent for the waiter, 5 per cent to the captain. If you sign the check, you *must* specify so much for each. Otherwise, the waiter claims it all and the captain is miffed. If there is a wine steward, he gets 15 per cent on the wine (subtracted from the waiter's total at the risk of his wrath) or a dollar (on half a bottle, more for really grand imbibing). There is infinite cachet in the invisible payoff: ask the maître d' in advance to sign your check and add the usual tips—he will be impeccably discreet. Regulars tip the maître d' $2 to $5 every three or four visits or generously at Christmas and before his vacation. A printing magnate I know hates to see his tips pocketed discreetly with minimum impact. He likes to thank the maître d' for a fine evening by sending $20 to his house with a note—"Makes the guy feel big at breakfast in front of his wife, and he remembers where it came from." He did it after an impressively flambéed evening at the Forum of the Twelve Caesars. "Now whenever I walk in, I'm the thirteenth Caesar."

If the evening was great, put it in writing—on Tiffany note paper, of course. If dinner was an outrage, definitely write. You may be invited back as guests of the house.

You can do better than gross currency. Martin's Cartier cuff links came from Mrs. Charles Engelhard. Frederick Brisson gave him tickets to *Coco*. When Martin and his wife arrived at St. Thomas on vacation, they were met at the airport by Charles Revson's chauffeured limousine and invited to lunch on the yacht that "Fire and Ice" built. When Martin visits Rome or Milan or Washington, he sees the town in a car dispatched by J. Edgar Hoover, complete with FBI men.

What have you done for your favorite maître d' lately?

Perhaps you can get his son into St. Bernard's.

In fleeting moments of sanity, the lust to be so loved in *haute* eating circles may wane. If so, take a few deep breaths. Attacks of sanity usually pass quickly.

Bite (1971)

ZUCCHINI QUICHE

1 recipe Basic Shortcut Pastry

1/4 cup grated Parmesan

1/4 cup grated Cheddar

1/2 cup dry breadcrumbs

1 1/2 to 2 lb. fresh zucchini

2 eggs, separated

1 1/2 cups sour cream

2 Tbs. chopped chives

2 Tbs. flour

1/8 tsp. cream of tartar

salt and fresh-ground black pepper

butter

This is a recipe for people who consider food a visual art. First it is constructed, then it is baked—and it's a lovely thing. When you bring it to the table, steaming hot out of the oven, it looks like a fabulous, double-crust, deep-dish pie. When you slice it into wedges, each one looks like a stone or brick wall. The first time I served this dish somebody told me I should have been a mason. (It's very good to eat, too: delicate and light, not at all like a wall.)

Prepare the pie-crust dough, combine the two grated cheeses, and add 1/2 cup of the mixture to the dough. Chill it, press into a 10-inch pie dish, and put it away to chill again. Mix the rest of the cheese with the bread-crumbs and set it aside.

Wash the zucchini and cut them into 1/4-inch slices, trying to make the slices as even in width as possible. Drop them into a kettle of boiling, salted water for 5 minutes and drain.

Beat together the egg yolks and the sour cream; add the chives, flour, salt, and pepper. Beat the egg whites with the cream of tartar until they are stiff but not dry, and fold them into the sour cream mixture.

Arrange a layer of zucchini slices on the bottom of the pie crust, placing them edge to edge, and cover with a small amount of sour cream mixture. Continue these layers, making two or three more, until it is all used up, and cover the top with the sour cream mixture. Sprinkle over it the cheese and breadcrumb mixture, dot with little slivers of butter; bake for 10 minutes in a 450-degree oven, then turn it down to 325 degrees and bake for 40 minutes more. 6 to 8 servings.

Anna Thomas, *The Vegetarian Epicure* (1972)

As the back-to-the-earth contingent began publishing recipes for heavy, tasteless bulgur casseroles and soybean loaves, Anna Thomas, a young filmmaker who was born in Germany but grew up in Michigan and California, created stylish recipes such as this one, in which a French concept and vegetarian precepts converge.

Roy Andries de Groot

The Techniques of the Kitchen—The Making of a Cook

Roy Andries de Groot (1912–1983) became a food writer partly by accident. He began his career as a general newspaper journalist and filmmaker, but during the Blitz in London, he suffered an eye injury that would eventually leave him blind. He immigrated to the United States in 1941, working at first for the U.S. State Department; but as his sight failed, his other senses grew in importance, and he turned increasingly to the subject of food. Few indeed have equaled his lovely evocations of the tastes and aromas of fine cooking. In classic books such as *Feast for All Seasons* (1966), *The Auberge of the Flowering Hearth* (1973), *Revolutionizing French Cooking* (1976), and the posthumous collection *In Search of the Perfect Meal* (1986), de Groot championed local, seasonal ingredients, and addressed himself to the secrets of culinary art with an almost mystical fervor. A whole generation of chefs, including Alice Waters, Larry Forgione, and Madeline Kammen, counted him as a major source of inspiration.

■ ■ ■

After lunch, I asked permission to visit Mademoiselle Ray in her kitchen. As I walked in, there was a noise as if someone were tap dancing on a stone floor. Her sleeves rolled up to her elbows, she was vigorously slapping a mound of dough on the marble top of her work table. On the chopping block, at the far side, the white-fleshed carcass of a baby kid goat gave off the warm smells of garlic and fresh tarragon.

A fair-sized kitchen had been made by combining two rooms of the original farmhouse. A wide window faced the mountains; another, on the west side, had been adapted as an indoor-outdoor greenhouse for potted herb plants. On sunny days the outer window could be opened. Mademoiselle Ray said: "In summer, of course, I step outside the kitchen door into our herb garden. But in winter it is my chief secret of good cooking to be able to reach out my hand and pick the fresh green leaves at the last moment before using them. Also, I always try to avoid overheating the herbs so that their oils do not evaporate. I may cut them into a sauce a few seconds before it is served. Or they may be added to the garnish of a dish just as it goes into the dining room."

Now she was kneading the dough, with firm and self-assured movements. The grey-veined slab (it must have been five feet by four and weighed a ton!) was supported by an iron frame and legs painted a bright red. When she wanted to use it for cutting, she covered the marble with a fitted sheet of thick zinc. For heavy chopping, of course, there was the large wooden block.

There was a professional cooking stove run on bottled gas. On the right of the cooker, at top-of-the-stove height, there was the *salamandre*, one of the essential tools of the French cuisine. A dish could be placed on an iron plate a few inches below a "hood" which reflected downward the heat from a powerful grill flame. The surface of the food could, within a few seconds, be made brown and bubbly, just before being served. My attention was diverted from the *salamandre* by a wild, scrabbling noise from one of the four sinks. It was half-full of water, with a few dozen crayfish crawling and swimming around. They had just been brought in from the garden tank.

On the opposite wall, there was a kitchen wine rack with more than two dozen bottles of reds and whites, dry and sweet Madeiras, Sherries and vermouths; various Armagnacs, Calvados, Cognacs, and dark Martinique rums; as well as a range of fruit brandies and liqueurs. Mademoiselle Ray said that the dry spirits could be used to add subtle touches to main dishes (even, sometimes, fish), while the liqueurs were mainly for desserts and for marinating fruits.

There were four professional refrigerators, deep and high, but there was no freezer, apart from a small box used solely for storing ice cream. Mademoiselle Ray said: "We do not believe in *les conserves industrielles*—our French name for anything canned, dehydrated, frozen, etc. All of us, of course, use some *conserves*. My own bottled fruits, jars of pickles, and marinated wild mushrooms, for example, are in fact *conserves*. Coffee beans and rice grains are in reality dehydrated. But whenever I have natural foods directly from earth or water, they are incomparably better."

Yet there was plenty of "conserving" going on in the kitchen and adjoining pantry. There was a marvelous array of pottery marmites of every size and conceivable shape. Some of them (large, lidded "berthes," or "cruches") were standing on the stone floor of the pantry, filled with mysterious pieces of this or that, soaking in marinating liquids, or preserved from the air under layers of white goose fat. Still, with all its equipment

and stores, this room had none of the coldly impersonal feeling of a professional hotel kitchen. It was *La Cuisine*—the beautifully organized and
much-loved heart of a French country home.

I asked Mademoiselle Ray: "How did you learn to be a chef? Did Mademoiselle Vivette teach you her techniques from Provence? What has been
your gastronomic experience?"

"The first thing that will shock you," said Mademoiselle Ray, "is to
know that I am half British. My mother came to the South of France from
Manchester for a short vacation. She met my father in Marseille and never
went home. My two sisters and I were born there. So you see, I am almost
as much a Provençale as Vivette."

"Was the food in your home Manchester or Marseillais?"

"Totally English. Totally garlicless. Except when my mother went away for
a few days, then my father fried Mediterranean fresh sardines in garlic-soaked
olive oil and I helped him, almost before I could reach the top of the stove. My
mother just couldn't bear the smell! Then, when my mother died, we three
girls took turns cooking for my father. We competed fiercely for his approval.
I learned one thing that my sisters missed. They tried to keep up my mother's
traditions and prepared English food for him. I sensed that he was longing to go
back to the Provençal cuisine of his childhood. I switched from butter to olive
oil. I flooded everything with garlic. I garnished everything with olives. I sauced
everything with tomatoes. I used a heavy hand with the herbs and spices. My
father demanded more and more of my cooking. I basked in the sunshine of his
approval. I was terribly shy. Cooking for me became the key to being loved."

"How did you finally get away?"

"I decided to become a nurse and went to Monaco for my training. Then
came the war and I joined the Army Nurse Service. I was sent to a military
hospital in the Alps, where I found Vivette."

Listening to the soft voice of Mademoiselle Ray and breathing in the
perfumed aromas of her kitchen—the faint odors of earthy juices, the same
essences one smelled in the breezes of the Valley—I felt I was discovering the
secret of the extraordinary cuisine of the Auberge of the Flowering Hearth.
Its heart was the combination of the strong and colorful techniques of the
country cooking of Provence with the broad character of the Mediterranean
internationalism—the subtle influences of the Arab world of North Africa,

of Greece, Italy, Spain and the Middle East—that flowed into the great port city of Marseille, all gently restrained by the careful conservatism of England. Then, when the blend of these skills and traditions was transplanted to this Alpine valley, where Nature is still so completely in command, Mesdemoiselles Vivette and Ray were influenced by a new force. Among these mountains, there remains an irresistible regional unity in the products of a particular soil in a particular place. The earth of each valley, of each mountain slope, has its own peculiar balance of minerals and salts. They seep up through the roots of the grasses, the trees, the vegetables and vines. The cows eat the grasses. The minerals and salts control the character of the meat and the milk. The milk makes the cheese, which has a slightly different character in every valley. As soon as we try to mass-produce cheese, by mixing many milks from many valleys, this character is lost.

The minerals and salts are in the grapes, which control the character of the wines. The wine from one vineyard in one place is slightly different from every other. The earth is the unity between the products. The wines of the Savoy are the perfect complement to the cheeses of the Savoy. As soon as we try to manufacture mass wines by blending among many vineyards, the character is lost.

The cuisine of this Auberge is built on the foundation of the local products from the surrounding countryside. The meats are from animals which roam on these slopes and birds which fly among these trees. The fish are from these mountain lakes. The fruits and vegetables, from these farms. . . . This is the source of the sense of unity one feels flowing through each meal—and from one meal to the next.

There is one other Golden Rule in Mademoiselle Ray's kitchen. She follows (and does not try to overthrow) Nature's natural and perfect feeding cycle. She accepts the fundamental law that the right food always comes at the right time. By submitting to this natural cycle of the seasons, she revels in a cornucopia of delicacy and variety. She joyously prepares the first wild mushrooms after the snows. The first spring lamb, the first bright-green asparagus. . . . She happily revels in the rich flood of summer fruits . . . each month has its special meaning in her kitchen. June brings the crayfish from the rivers in the high valleys. October, the game birds and venison. December, the geese. The cycle of the year is a feast for every season.

Neither Mademoiselle Ray nor any other French cook demands soggy canned asparagus or mushy frozen strawberries in December. She does not defrost a venison steak in July. The reliance on out-of-season foods, she feels, makes the gastronomic year an endlessly boring repetition. She said: "If we try to overthrow the natural cycle, we are left with nothing more than dull and tasteless foods. But if we cooperate with Nature, if we follow instead of trying to lead, the reward is one marvelous meal after another."

This seemed to be the moment to leave Mademoiselle Ray to the preparation of, one was sure, a marvelous dinner. . . .

MENU OF
A Mountain Dinner

———

APÉRITIF: PERNOD SUISSESSE

Poireaux de Meyrargues
(*Leeks with Purée of Tomatoes*)

MACONNAIS BLANC, DOMAINE BURRIER

Brochet Braisé au Champagne
(*Lake Pike in Champagne*)

Caneton Glacé aux Pêches à l'Armagnac
(*Duckling Garnished with Fresh Peaches and Flamed with Armagnac*)

Tian de Courgettes au Riz
(*Tian of Zucchini with Rice*)

MAGNUM OF RED BURGUNDY, 1964 CHAMBERTIN, CLOS DE BÈZE

Fromages:
St. Félicien de Savoie   Berrichon de Valençay
Fort aux Poireaux de Dauphiné

Croquettes de Marrons
(*Fried Chestnut Croquettes*)

Café

MARC DE POMMARD

Since the "deadliest of all drinks," absinthe, has been banned in France (and almost everywhere else in the world), Frenchmen now consume enormous quantities of its anise-flavored substitutes: Pernod and Ricard. At her miniature copper-covered bar, Mademoiselle Vivette mixed the Pernod Suissesses with one egg white per person, two jiggers of Pernod and a tiny teaspoon of sugar. It was all furiously shaken with ice until it was the lightest of foams, then served in tall chilled glasses.

The method of preparing the local white baby leeks is from the valley of Meyrargues in Provence, which an American publicist might call "The Leek Capital of France." They were lightly poached in a sauce which included green, virgin olive oil, puréed tomatoes, chopped lemon pulp, fresh bay leaves and garlic. It was served at room temperature.

This strong sauce was well matched by the strong white wine from the Burgundian region just north of Beaujolais.

The handsome large river pike, weighing about three and one-half pounds, was first larded by Mademoiselle Ray with Cognac-marinated lardoons of salt pork, as if it were a piece of meat. Then it was lightly poached with butter, shallots, and wild forest mushrooms in brut Champagne. After the fish was done and removed, the liquid was reduced, slightly thickened with heavy cream and served as the sauce. Finally, the fish was decorated with flowerets of flaky pastry and carved mushroom caps.

The main entrée was one of Mademoiselle Ray's masterpieces—the brilliant combination of the rich juiciness of a lean young duckling, fresh from a farm near Grenoble, with the accent of brandied peaches and an extraordinary sweet and sour sauce of maple syrup (a gift sent by a Canadian friend) and tarragon wine vinegar. The duck was braised on an aromatic bed of carrots, shallots and fresh tarragon, lightly moistened with dry white wine. Meanwhile, the peach halves were quickly sautéed in butter and flamed with a mixture of Armagnac and orange Curaçao. Finally, the juices of the duck were converted into the sauce with the addition of miniscule amounts of the maple syrup and vinegar before being reduced, concentrated and slightly thickened. The duck was served garnished with the peach halves, with the sauce poured over and everything beautifully glazed under the *salamandre*.

The accompanying dish of zucchini and aromatic rice was baked and served in an earthenware *tian*, the classic shallow square baking dish of

Provence. As with the word "casserole," the cooking pot gives its name to the entire dish. The chopped zucchini was folded into the rice, with cheese, onions, garlic and herbs, then baked with an enrichment of cream and beaten eggs.

Clearly, all this was worthy of one of the finest bottles from the cellar of the Auberge: a magnum from the great Clos de Bèze vineyard of Gevrey-Chambertin. Although it was still somewhat young, we all agreed that it was a very fine wine—potentially noble.

To finish such an outstanding red, Mademoiselle Vivette offered three farm-made cheeses of interesting and strong character. The Saint Félicien is an extremely rich double-cream, originally from the High Savoy village of Saint Félix but now made in several local valleys. It is shaped rather like a thin Camembert, with a bluish yellow crust and a wonderfully aromatic flavor.

The Berrichon is the most famous goat cheese of the village of Valençay, on the road from Lyon to the Loire valley. The cheese is shaped like the base of a pyramid and its crust is covered with finely powdered beechwood ash. When fresh, it is creamy and soft, but as it ages it becomes progressively harder and, finally, smells a bit like the menagerie at the circus. It was a favorite cheese of the great French statesman Talleyrand, who once owned the Château de Valençay and placed the Berrichon near the top in his "hierarchy of cheeses."

There was also the white cheese of the Dauphiné mountains, *Le Fort*, of cows' milk, perhaps given its name because it is speckled with bits of chopped leek and green peppercorns, giving it a strongly oniony, peppery flavor.

For the unusual and attractive dessert, shelled and skinned chestnuts were cooked in vanilla-flavored milk, then mashed. Next, this purée was molded into balls, each with a glacéed chestnut at its center. The balls were then rolled in fine breadcrumbs, deep-fried until crisp on the outside, sweetly luscious on the inside, and served sprinkled with powdered sugar. Each was a single luxurious mouthful.

Sensing our warm appreciation of the entire dinner, Mademoiselle Vivette was in a mood to share her greatest treasures. She brought up from the cellar a dusty unlabeled bottle which had been given her as a Christmas present by one of her Pommard suppliers in 1948, the year she took over the Auberge. She guessed that it must have been about thirty years old when she got it and was now more than fifty. Most Burgundian vignerons distill their own private brandy (called *marc*) from the mash of grape pulp and skins (also called *marc*) left in the press after the liquid wine has run off. When this *eau-de-vie de marc* is aged, it can be extraordinary. We opened this bottle with considerable anticipation. It glub-glubbed heavily into the snifters. It was deep purple. Its bouquet was superb, and it went down the throat as a pure combination of dynamite and velvet. We tottered to bed.

The Auberge of the Flowering Hearth (1973)

moong dal

SERVES 6

This is North India's most popular dal, and it is eaten with equal relish by toothless toddlers, husky farmers, and effete urban snobs. The simple recipe given below can be used for the white urad dal, the salmon-colored masoor dal, and the large arhar or toovar dal as well.

1 1/2 cups moong dal (hulled and split)

2 cloves garlic, peeled

2 slices peeled fresh ginger, 1 inch square and
*   1/8 inch thick*

1 tablespoon chopped Chinese parsley (coriander greens
*   or cilantro)*

1 tablespoon ground turmeric

1/4-1/2 teaspoon cayenne pepper (optional)

1 1/2 tablespoons salt

1 1/2 tablespoons lemon juice

3 tablespoons vegetable oil or usli ghee

A pinch ground asafetida or tiny lump asafetida

1 teaspoon whole cumin seeds

Lemon or lime wedges

Clean and wash dal thoroughly. Put dal in heavy-bottomed 3-4-quart pot, add 5 cups water, and bring to a boil. Remove the froth and scum that collects at the top. Now add the garlic, ginger, parsley, turmeric, and cayenne pepper. Cover, leaving the lid very slightly ajar, lower heat, and simmer gently for about 1 1/2 hours. Stir occasionally. When dal is cooked, add the salt and lemon juice (it should be thicker than pea soup, but thinner than cooked cereal).

In a 4-6-inch skillet or small pot, heat the vegetable oil or ghee over a medium-high flame. When hot, add the asafetida and cumin seeds. As soon as the asafetida sizzles and expands and the cumin seeds turn dark (this will take only a few seconds), pour the oil and spices over the dal and serve. (Some people put the dal in a serving dish and then pour the oil and spices over it.)

To serve: Serve with plain rice, Kheema, and a vegetable for a simple meal. Most meat and chicken dishes go well with this dal. Since some people like to squeeze extra lemon or lime juice on their dal, serve some wedges separately. Note: Finely sliced onion rings, fried until brown and crisp, are often spread over the dal as a garnish before it is served.

Madhur Jaffrey, *An Invitation to Indian Cooking* (1973)

Born in Delhi in 1933, Madhur Jaffrey did not enter a kitchen until after she went to London at 19 to study at the Royal Academy of Dramatic Arts. Since then, in addition to appearing in over 15 films, she has published a series of influential cookbooks and has almost single-handedly demystified Indian cooking for America.

Richard Olney

from Simple French Food

When Richard Olney (1927–1999) moved to the south of France in 1951, he intended to devote himself to painting and literature. But in his small house near the village of Solliès-Toucas in Provence, his interest in food–always keen–turned professional. In 1962 he began writing a column called *Un Américain (gourmand) à Paris* for the journal *Cuisine et Vins de France*, and eight years later published *The French Menu Cookbook*. Like de Groot, Olney advocated local, seasonal cooking, and while his own work was grounded in the traditional French kitchen, he was an early champion of nouvelle cuisine. His clear style and detailed deconstruction of complicated dishes made him one of the most important food writers of his era and–along with treks to M.F.K. Fisher's home in Sonoma and Julia Child's kitchen in Cambridge, Massachusetts–a visit to Richard Olney was *de rigueur* for aspiring chefs and food writers. He made taste by influencing the next generation of tastemakers, particularly some of the early practitioners of the new American and California cuisines.

■ ■ ■

The only rational translation of *pâté* into English is "pie": A *pâté de foie gras* is not liver paste. It is a whole, fat goose liver enclosed in pastry. A *terrine de foie gras* is whole liver prepared in a terrine without pastry. In serious restaurants, *pâté* on a menu still means "enclosed in pastry." Outside of that rarefied atmosphere, the confusion is so total–*pâté* can mean meatloaf, liver paste, or dog-food, and *pâté en croûte* means *pâté*–that it is not worthwhile even to attempt to respect the terminology.

To me, a true *pâté* represents an excessive amount of work to produce something that is no better than–and rarely as good as–a terrine. French puff paste (*pâte feuilletée*, not *pâte à choux*), in fact, does not rank among the foods I most worship–but, in fairness to the thing, it should be noted that it is rarely made with pure butter, often with none, and almost never with an unpasteurized, absolutely fresh, delicately perfumed, sweet butter of irreproachable quality. It is not only cheaper, but also much easier to work with margarine or other laboratory fat products and the visual result is handsomer. The taste is horrid. Furthermore, in the instance of *pâtés*, the essential spread of firmly bound forcemeat—*mousseline* or other—that rapidly forms a seal, preventing the meat juices from penetrating to the pastry and transforming it into a soggy mess, is often forgotten. A *pâté*, correctly prepared, belongs strictly to the realm of professional *grande cuisine* (interested visitors to Paris should visit the young chef Claude Peyrot in his restaurant, Le Vivarois. He is a great *saucier* and a great pastry chef—a practically unheard-of combination—and, unlike a number of world travelers, never leaves his kitchens).

The complexly organized *pâtés* and terrines of *la grande cuisine* (and largely of the past) are composed of a variety of different meats, each of which is often marinated or precooked in a different way to underline differences in character and then layered in a variety of interrelationships, alternating with two or more forcemeats, also of markedly separate characters. These *pâtés* depend, for their particular refinement, on the fine balance of intermingling and separation of flavors and textures. Typical and, perhaps, the most celebrated of its type—Dumaine revived it—is Lucien Tendret's *L'Oreiller de la Belle Aurore*, or Lovely Aurora's Pillow (Claudine-Aurore Récamier was Brillat-Savarin's mother). This dish takes its name from the pillow-like form of the *pâté*, but, in passing, may be thought to harbor a mute reference to the lady's disinclination to leave her bed where, but for the hours of sleep, she spent most of her time eating. Upon a rectangular base of puff paste, the basic dough of which has been flavored with Cognac and strengthened by the addition of egg white, two forcemeats (one identical to that of the following rabbit terrine recipe; the second, but for the addition of finely chopped mushrooms sautéed in butter, finely chopped truffles, and the stronger-flavored partridge livers, similar to the following chicken-liver terrine recipe), beginning and finishing with the first, are alternated with layers in varying combinations of strips of partridge, hare, duck, chicken, veal, and pork fillets and parboiled sweetbreads (truffle pieces, pistachios, and slivers of raw, cured ham being packed into each of these layers). The pillow covering is formed by another sheet of the same pastry (in which small, circular air vents have been cut) sealed to the borders of the basic rectangle. The "pie" is baked for two hours, and a firm meat aspic, enriched with the partridge, hare, and poultry carcasses, is poured in through the air vents while the *pâté* is still hot. It is served chilled.

A simple terrine, based on a single forcemeat and a single meat garnish, is never so good as when prepared in the easiest possible way, all of the ingredients of the composition mixed, pell-mell but intimately, together.

Chopping

Meats that are ground or chopped mechanically are always crushed. The fibrous structure of the flesh is broken, the succulent juices originally imprisoned within this structure escape, and therefore the forcemeat is always pastier in texture and drier than when composed of meats chopped by hand. The forcemeat, moreover, gains in character when the different meats in its composition are chopped more or less finely, lending a varied texture to the whole.

To chop meat by hand, scrape it free from all fragments of tendon, nervous tissue, or skin, cut it first into thin strips, cut the strips crosswise into tiny cubes, then chop, carefully and slowly at first, keeping the point of the knife in fulcrum-contact with the chopping block. When the meat is reduced to small enough pieces to form a cohesive mass, fragments of which will not fly in all directions, begin chopping more rapidly, using, preferably, two large "chef's" knives of the same size and weight, one in each hand, held somewhat above the board, chopping firmly, but not violently, with alternate knives in a rhythmic, loose-wristed motion. As the chopped mass is flattened out, regularly fold it over on itself with the blade of a knife, turn it over on the board, and begin again, continuing to fold, turn over, and chop until the desired degree of fineness is achieved. If you do not have knives of the same size and weight, chop with one hand only—the rhythm is lost with unequal weights.

I have tried a number of alternatives to hand-chopping, but I can only say this: Mechanical chopping will produce good results (all restaurant terrines are, after all, made in this way) and, I confess, some of my guests have been unable to discern the difference; the difference is, nonetheless, very marked. It is a question of whether you, the reader, will be satisfied with a decent product or whether you prefer something sublime . . . The poorest results are those of meat-grinders—a massacre—and, in my experience, the best are those of the electrical, whirring-bladed robot-cutters, although the violence of the latter tends to reduce a part of the meat to purée before the whole is sufficiently chopped—the work is done in the space of a few seconds.

Meat and poultry terrines are all made in pretty much the same way: The tender pieces of meat are left whole or cut into relatively large pieces to lend variety to the texture and are usually marinated (very often in Cognac, which lends a false, slightly rotten, gamey taste and renders the terrine indigestible—a good *eau de vie* is a valuable flavoring agent but should be incorporated only just before cooking); tougher flesh containing tendons or nervous tissue is chopped and usually combined with a certain amount of blandly flavored meat—veal or pork or both—to form the base of the forcemeat; liver lends smoothness to the texture and support to the egg binding; chopped or cubed pork fat (often about three times as much as the proportions given in any of the following recipes) is incorporated to nourish the forcemeat and prevent its drying out; breadcrumbs are too often not added but, if measured discreetly—about one ounce of crumbs per pound of flesh— so that its presence is imperceptible, it will always lend a gratifying lightness to the body of the terrine; in addition to salt, spices, and herbs, garlic, onion, pistachios, truffles, and the currently fashionable green peppercorns may lend aromatic support. The tender, unripened peppercorns are available tinned, but they are much more interesting in their highly perfumed fresh state; in Paris, M. Paul Corcellet, whose exotic foods shop at 46 rue des Petits-Champs is probably the most fantastic of its kind in the world, flies them in fresh from Madagascar, vacuum packs them in plastic envelopes, and deep freezes them. If this has not yet occurred to an American packager, it will soon.

A terrine mixture should contain only that liquid rigorously essential to its flavor; soaking breadcrumbs in milk, for instance, only adds to the liquid content and the milk adds nothing to the quality, whereas a highly reduced, gelatinous stock not only heightens the flavor, but also, when the terrine is cooled, lends binding support to the forcemeat. And when a marinade is called for, its quantity should be limited to just that necessary to moisten the surfaces of the meat pieces, well turned around in it.

The terrine is always lined and the contents covered with thin sheets of fresh fat pork, which, serving the same function as the chopped or cubed fat in the mixture, forms a wrapping that facilitates serving. The four-sided envelope of fat, however, should be removed from each slice at the time of serving. English and American cookbooks often recommend substituting slices of bacon for the sheets of fat pork, but, in fact, the quarrelsome, smoky presence will slur the clean definition of most flavors. I think of two exceptions: (1) *Guinea fowl* unites happily with bacon to the advantage of both (a terrine of guinea fowl may be prepared exactly like that of rabbit, the skinned breast being cut up like the rabbit fillets, the remainder of the flesh as well as a couple of supplementary chicken livers being passed into the forcemeat, the terrine lined with bacon strips); and (2) *Veal*, whose bland and impersonal, submissive character assumes and flatters that of many a more aggressive ally. (A number of years ago, M. René Viaux introduced at the Relais Paris-Est a veal and American-sliced bacon terrine baptized *terrine de body*–"body" being Berry dialect for veal–that has since become something of a classic. It consists in filling a bacon-lined terrine with alternate layers of very thin veal cutlets, rindless bacon slices laid lengthwise, and a mixture of finely chopped onions, chopped parsley, freshly ground pepper, and crumbled, dried herbs, finishing with a layer of bacon, dribbling a bit of white wine over the surface, and baking in a slow oven–about $1^3/_4$ hours at 325° for $1^1/_2$ pounds each of veal and bacon. It is cooled under weight and, inasmuch as there is no forcemeat binding, it must be served well chilled to ensure the slices' remaining intact.)

With the exception of the so-called *pâtés de campagne*, which are usually baked, mounded up, like American meatloaves, often wrapped in pig's caul rather than sheets of fat (for a typical *pâté de campagne*, double the pork-fat content, limit the meats to two parts of cheap cuts of pork to one of veal plus a piece of pork liver, grind everything up together, season and bind as for the rabbit terrine–bake for two hours), these terrines are always cooked in a *bain-marie* and should be cooled under weight, the better to ensure a compact, non-crumbly body, easy to slice and to serve. No one has yet bothered to invent a terrine with a reversible lid that could serve as well to weight the contents; boards should be cut to the inside dimensions of each terrine for this purpose. For small terrines, a heavy piece of cardboard may be cut to the inside dimensions and wrapped in aluminum foil. Place unopened tin cans on top for weights.

Rabbit Terrine
(Terrine de Lapin)

Any small game, furred or feathered, may replace the rabbit in this recipe—with glorious results. The ham, although still welcomed by wild rabbit, pheasant, partridge, or wild duck, no longer plays an essential supporting role in relation to those flavors, all more distinctive than that of domesticated rabbit, and it could be replaced by a supplement of pork, veal, or the primary element. Rabbits have large livers; terrines made of game birds or duck need the addition of a couple of chicken livers.

Of domesticated breeds of ducks, the barbary duck or one of the sterile hybrids is the most interesting. Our dependence on freezers has all but wiped out, on the American market, any competition to the depressingly fat, deep-frozen Long Island ducks. They are, happily, serviceable in the fabrication of a terrine: All of the fat is contained in the skin itself or, loose, in the abdomen; the flesh is lean, but, once the skin has been peeled off and discarded, there is not much of it. Two ducks should be used to replace the rabbit in this recipe, the breasts being cut up, the legs and flesh scrapings chopped for the forcemeat, and the carcasses converted into a stock. The livers of deep-frozen Long Island ducks have an inexplicably strong and acrid taste and should be discarded, only chicken livers being used in the forcemeat.

The marination of game or duck is a question of personal taste; the bland flavor of domesticated rabbit can ill do without it, but I, personally, prefer not to marinate meats of more pronounced character. Any of these terrines will gain in depth by the addition of cut-up truffles or chopped truffle peelings. They should either be marinated with the meats or mixed with the basic forcemeat (eggs and Cognac added later) and refrigerated overnight, covered by plastic, to permit the maximum penetration of their perfume before cooking. If they are conserved, add their liquid to the stock while reducing it.

This recipe will fill 2 quart-sized terrines and will provide about 20 servings—or, perhaps, a great deal less if the guests are left to their own devices.

1 rabbit, approximately 3 $\frac{1}{2}$ pounds, skinned and cleaned

Marinade	$\frac{1}{3}$ cup dry white wine
	1 tablespoon olive oil
	1 healthy pinch finely crumbled mixed herbs (thyme, oregano, savory)
	Bay leaf
	Salt, pepper
Stock	The rabbit's bones, neck, and head (split)
	Rinds from fat pork and ham
	1 quart water
	1 onion, finely sliced or coarsely chopped
	1 carrot, sliced or chopped coarsely
	Thyme, bay leaf, salt, branch celery, parsley
Forcemeat	1 large clove garlic
	2 ounces stale bread, crusts removed, crumbled
	2 ounces shelled, unroasted pistachio nuts
	10 ounces firm fresh fatback, cut into tiny cubes
	7 ounces lean veal (all fat and nervous tissue removed), chopped
	7 ounces lean raw ham (prosciutto type), finely chopped
	The remaining rabbit flesh—about 14 ounces (the flesh from the saddle and the tender white meat from the hind legs removed), finely chopped
	The rabbit's heart, liver, and lungs, finely chopped
	2 eggs
	$\frac{1}{3}$ cup Cognac
	Seasonings: 1 teaspoon mixed herbs (same as marinade), 3 heads of cloves, allspice, and a suspicion of nutmeg, all ground to a powder, freshly ground pepper to taste, a pinch of cayenne, salt

About 8 ounces thin sheets of fresh fat pork

Imported bay leaves

Melted lard (optional)

Make an incision the length of the rabbit's back to each side of the spinal ridge and carefully remove the filets (the elongated muscles stretching from the beginning of the rib cage to the tail), loosening them with a sharp paring knife, following closely the contours of the vertebrae. Remove the filets mignons (much smaller corresponding muscles clinging to the inside of the spinal column). Detach the tender, fleshy white meat from the bones of the hind legs. Cut the filets crosswise into slices of from $\frac{1}{3}$ to $\frac{1}{2}$ inch thick and cut the meat from the legs into similar-sized pieces. Mix well with the elements of the marinade and leave, covered, in the refrigerator overnight.

Remove the remaining flesh (except for the neck and the head) from the bones, scraping with a knife, and put it aside, along with the heart, liver, and lungs, to be chopped. Break or cut up the carcass and add it, along with the head, the neck, and the rinds, to the water, bring slowly to a boil, skim off the foam, add all the other ingredients, and cook, the lid slightly ajar, at a bare simmer, for from $2\frac{1}{2}$ to 3 hours. Strain the liquid, leave it to settle, carefully skim off the fat, bring back to a boil, and, keeping the saucepan a bit to the side of the flame so that a light boil continues only at one side of the surface, remove the fatty skin that forms, drawing it to the far side with a tablespoon; repeat this action several times over a period of 20 minutes or so. Turn the flame high and reduce rapidly, stirring, and, at a halfway point, transfer to your smallest saucepan. Reduce until the stock has passed the foamy boil and begins to make slurry sounds, the body noticeably thick and sticky. A scant half cup should remain.

Pound the garlic to a purée in the mortar, mix with the breadcrumbs, pour over the boiling stock and work to a thick sticky paste with the pestle.

Parboil the pistachios for a couple of minutes, rub them vigorously in a towel to loosen the skins, peel and chop them coarsely.

Combine all of the elements of the forcemeat and mix thoroughly with your hands, squeezing the mixture through your fingers. Then add the pieces of rabbit meat and continue to mix and squeeze . . .

Line the sides and bottoms of the terrines with the sheets of fat pork, pressing them firmly, fill with the mixture and tap the bottom of each terrine, smartly, two or three times against a wooden table top (or other surface softened by a couple of layers of towel) to be certain that the contents are well settled. Place one or two bay leaves on the surface of each, gently press a sheet of fat pork over all, cover, and cook in a *bain-marie* (the terrine placed in a larger receptacle—a cake tin, for instance—which is filled with boiling water so as to immerse the terrines by about two thirds) in a 325° to 350° oven, counting 1 1/2 to 1 3/4 hours. The terrines are done when the center is firm to the touch and when, if pierced by a trussing needle, the juice that appears is completely transparent.

Remove the lids, place boards cut to the inside dimensions on each surface with approximately 1 1/2 pounds of weight on each. Juices may run over the sides, so it is best to place the terrines in a shallow container while cooling. Allow to cool completely—several hours or overnight—before removing the weights and, unless the terrines are to be consumed within two or three days, pour a layer of melted lard over the surface of each, return the lids, and refrigerate. The flavor will improve if they are left for at least three or four days and, protected by the layer of lard, one may be kept, uncut, for a couple of weeks.

*   *   *

Pork and Herb "Meatballs"
(Caillettes)

A recipe typical of the Vaucluse and Ardêche country, the area west of the Rhône valley stretching from Avignon to Lyons. The mixture may also be poured into a fat-lined terrine, baked for 1 1/2 hours in a 350° oven, and cooled under weight. It becomes *la terrine aux herbes*, a specialty of Chez-Hiély-Lucullus in Avignon, one of the finest restaurants in France for the appreciation of regional cooking (and, among restaurants of quality, probably the least expensive).

The spinach is sometimes replaced, in part, by the green parts of the leaves of Swiss chard, also parboiled (10 minutes), pressed, and chopped. Caul (*crépine*) is the thin, fatty, weblike membrane surrounding the pig's intestines. You may have to go to a specialty pork butcher for it or ask your butcher to order it especially. If you cannot find caul, substitute a couple of thin strips of fatback or bacon, wrapping each *caillette* so that they cross on the top surface, the ends being tucked beneath.

Caillettes are nearly always eaten cold as a first course, but, traditionally, they are served hot at Christmastime, accompanied by a truffle sauce.

1 medium onion, finely chopped

1 tablespoon olive oil

2 pounds spinach, well picked over and washed in several waters

2 large clove garlic, crushed, peeled, finely chopped

8 ounces fresh fatback, chopped or cut into tiny cubes

10 ounces pork variety meats (liver, lungs, heart, spleen, in approximately equal quantities of those that you are able to find—sometimes only liver is used, but the result is less interesting), finely chopped

5 ounces chopped chicken livers

8 ounces lean, fresh salt-pork (uncured bacon), chopped

1 handful chopped parsley

1 teaspoon crumbled thyme

$\frac{1}{2}$ bay leaf, crumbled and finely chopped

2 eggs

Salt, freshly ground pepper

Caul

Gently cook the chopped onion in olive oil, stirring from time to time, for from 15 to 20 minutes—until yellowed and soft, but not browned.

Parboil the spinach for a couple of minutes in a large quantity of salted rapidly boiling water, drain, refresh under running cold water, squeeze the mass repeatedly in your hands to rid it of the maximum liquid, and chop it well.

Combine all of the ingredients except the caul and mix thoroughly with your hands. Form handsful of the mixture to the approximate size of a small orange and wrap each in a 5- or 6-inch square of caul (it is not always possible to cut it so mechanically—pieces may be spliced together). Pour about $\frac{1}{2}$ cup water into the bottom of a shallow baking dish, cake tin, or anything that is just large enough to hold the *caillettes* placed side by side; arrange them in the pan and bake in a hot oven (450°) for about 25 minutes. Finish with overhead heat, if necessary, to lightly brown the surfaces. Leave to cool and refrigerate. They are better served close to room temperature, so it is wise to remove them from the refrigerator an hour or so before serving.

Larded Pork Liver in Aspic
(Foie de Porc Piqué)

In view of the number of friends who nourish a passion for this preparation—a passion I understand intellectually but nonetheless fail to share
(perhaps simply because pure pork liver I like only pinkly cooked and, in
its unadorned state, pork liver does not number among those foods I most
love), an unselfish impulse has banished my hesitation to give the recipe.

You will need a highly flavored, richly gelatinous stock. If you have veal
stock on hand, use it—or a leftover *pot-au-feu* or *poule-au-pot* broth. Otherwise, make up a solid, vulgar stock out of pork and veal bones, beef, pork,
and veal parings, chicken backs and necks, etc. A veal knuckle will lend
sufficient gelatinous content or, lacking that, add a pig's foot. Prepare it as
usual, the meats and bones covered with cold water, brought slowly to a
boil, skimmed several times. Add a pound of carrots, an onion stuck with a
couple of cloves, a head of garlic, and a big bouquet garni packed with leek
greens, celery, thyme, bay leaf, any other herbs that meet your fancy, and,
by all means, if available, a branch of lovage, and coarse salt. Cook at a bare
simmer, lid ajar, for about 4 hours, and strain.

To make it in larger quantity, the proportions need not be respected to
the letter, the precise quantity of liquid necessary depending on the size and
form of the cooking vessel in relation to the liver.

Old bed sheets (cotton or linen), torn into squares, are useful both for
wrapping the meat and for straining the jelly.

> 1 teaspoon mixed herbs (thyme, savory, oregano, sage,
>   marjoram), ground to a powder
> Salt, pepper
> 5 ounces fresh fatback, cut into approximately 8-inch
>   lengths, $\frac{1}{4}$ inch square
> The large lobe of a pork liver (something over 1 pound)

Marinade
> 2 cups dry white wine
> 1 head garlic, cut crosswise in two
> $\frac{1}{3}$ cup sliced shallots
> Parsley stems and root, if possible
> Thyme

2 bay leaves

2 cloves

Several grains allspice

$^{1}/_{3}$ cup Cognac

3 cups gelatinous stock

Mix the ground herbs, the salt, and the pepper in a bowl with the strips of fatback, tossing and turning until they are evenly coated with the seasonings. Using a larding needle (not a butcher's larder, which would tear the liver to shreds), thread the strips of fat repeatedly through the length of the liver, leaving $^{1}/_{2}$-inch protrusions at either end. Work gently and unhurriedly so as not to damage or tear the liver. Marinate, covered and refrigerated, overnight or for up to 24 hours, turning the liver around in the marinade two or three times during this period.

Wrap the liver firmly in a square of cloth and tie it tightly. Place it in an oval *cocotte*, pour over the marinade, including the solid elements, the Cognac, and the melted stock—the liver should be largely submerged. Bring to the boiling point, skim, and cook, the lid slightly ajar, at the slightest suggestion of a simmer, for about $1^{3}/_{4}$ hours (2 hours or slightly over for a larger bulk of liver). Leave to cool until tepid, then remove and unwrap the liver and place it in a terrine just large enough to contain it. Pour the liquid through a strainer lined with a tightly woven cloth; it will take its time and should not be forced, but, as the weave becomes clogged with sediment, rearrange the cloth slightly so the liquid contacts new areas. Skim off any fat that may have settled on the surface. The jelly will probably have to be reduced a bit—taste for seasoning and put a teaspoonful in a small container in the coldest part of the refrigerator to check its firmness in gelatin. If, after reduction, the stock seems still somewhat troubled, pass it a second time through a cloth—the jelly should be limpid but, for a preparation of this kind, it need not be crystalline. When you are satisfied with the stock, pour it over the liver. Chill for a day before serving. If traces of fat appear on the surface, they may be wiped off with a cloth dampened in hot water. Serve sliced, the cross-sectional view studded with the squares of fat.

Simple French Food (1974)

A sweet and spicy-sharp ginger-flavored chicken stew
that comes to the table bright yellow and fragrant.
Strictly speaking it is not a kdra,
but a modern variation of a classic dish.

chicken tagine

with chick-peas ✻ [DJEJ BIL HAMUS]

INGREDIENTS

1 pound dried chick-peas or 2 twenty-ounce cans
cooked chick-peas
2 chickens, whole or quartered
5 cloves garlic, peeled
Salt
1 teaspoon ground ginger
1 rounded teaspoon freshly ground black pepper
Pinch of pulverized saffron
1 teaspoon turmeric
1/4 cup finely chopped parsley
1 cinnamon stick
1/2 cup chopped scallions, white part only
5 tablespoons sweet butter
1 Spanish onion, sliced very thin
1/2 cup black raisins (optional)

Mixing bowls
Large glass or stainless steel bowl
4-quart saucepan
5 1/2-quart casserole with cover
Deep serving dish

✻

Working time: 30 minutes
Cooking time: 1 1/2 hours
Serves: 6 to 8

1

The day before, soak the dried chick-peas in water to cover.
Using 4 cloves of the garlic and 2 tablespoons salt, prepare the
chickens as directed below. Then blend 1 teaspoon salt,
the ginger, pepper, and the remaining clove garlic, crushed,
with 2 tablespoons water and rub into the flesh of the
chickens. Place in the large glass or stainless steel bowl,
cover and let stand overnight in the refrigerator.

2

The next day, drain the chick-peas, place in the saucepan,
cover with fresh water, and cook, covered, 1 hour. Drain and
submerge in a bowl of cold water. Rub the chick-peas to
remove their skins. The skins will rise to the surface.
Discard them. (If you are using canned chick-peas, rinse,
drain, and skin them, and set them aside.)

3

Transfer the chickens and any juices in the bowl to
the casserole. Add a pinch of saffron, the turmeric, parsley,
cinnamon stick, scallions, and butter. Pour in 5 cups water and
bring to a boil. Reduce the heat, cover, and simmer 1 hour,
turning the chickens frequently in the sauce. When the
chickens are very tender, remove and keep warm.

4

Add the finely sliced onions, freshly cooked chick-peas,
and raisins to the sauce and cook until the onions are very soft
and the sauce has reduced to a thick gravy. Return the chickens
to the sauce to reheat. (If you are using canned chick-peas,
add them now.) Taste the sauce for salt, and add a pinch
of pulverized saffron for a good yellow color.

5

To serve, place the chicken parts in the deep serving dish,
forming them into a mound. Spoon over the
onion-chick-pea-raisin sauce. Serve hot with plenty
of Moroccan Bread or pita.

✳ BASIC METHOD FOR PREPARING POULTRY ✳

1

Wash the chickens or other poultry in salted water and drain.
Pound 4 cloves garlic and 2 tablespoons salt into a paste.
Rub the paste into the cavity and flesh of the poultry, at the
same time pulling out excess fat from under the skin
and from the neck and rump ends.

Pull out the thin translucent membrane from under the skin
of the breast. Rinse the poultry well under running water
until it no longer smells of garlic. (The garlic is used to
rid the poultry of any bitterness that might spoil a sauce;
it also acts to bring out its flavor, much like MSG.)
Drain the poultry well.

2

If you suspect that your poultry is tasteless on account
of "scientific breeding," use a method invented by Janet Jaidi
to improve its taste: Rub it with spices to be used in the
recipe, a little butter or oil, and marinate it overnight.
(If you do this, remember you may have to readjust the
spicing of your sauce at the end.)

3

If you are using whole poultry, it must be trussed. Trussing
poultry is easy: clip off the wing tips and discard; slip the
ends of the legs into a horizontal incision made just above the
rump (turkeys often come this way), or slip the legs into
incisions made on the lower sides of the breast.

*Note: When stuffing turkeys or squabs or chickens,
do not wash with garlic or salt.*

Paula Wolfert, *Couscous and Other Food of Morocco* (1973)

A cook's cook, Paula Wolfert has proven herself willing to travel anywhere to find the best recipe. Her quest for flavor, wrote Peggy Knickerbocker, "has drawn her across the Mediterranean, from Berber villages in the Atlas Mountains of Morocco to the plains of Slavic Macedonia, from the far reaches of the Ionian Island and Sicily through southwestern France and Catalonia."

Calvin Trillin

The Traveling Man's Burden

Although Calvin Trillin (b. 1935) did not set out to become a food writer, as the son of a grocery store owner in Kansas City, Missouri, he was more or less born into the food business. Leaving town as soon as he was old enough to get into Yale, Trillin went on to a journalism career that took him from *Time* to *The New Yorker*, where for fifteen years he traveled curious byways all over the country for "U.S. Journal." On the road, he established the posture he has always maintained when writing about food—that of a hungry amateur in a world of overwrought connoisseurs, an anti-gourmet. His first food book, *American Fried: Adventures of a Happy Eater* (1974), gave him a cult-like following. Self-deprecating and never at a loss for irony, the reluctant foodie serves slices of real life, hold the pretence.

■ ■ ■

The best restaurants in the world are, of course, in Kansas City. Not all of them; only the top four or five. Anyone who has visited Kansas City and still doubts that statement has my sympathy: He never made it to the right places. Being in a traveling trade myself, I know the problem of asking someone in a strange city for the best restaurant in town and being led to some purple palace that serves "Continental cuisine" and has as its chief creative employee a menu-writer rather than a chef. I have sat in those places, an innocent wayfarer, reading a three-paragraph description of what the trout is wrapped in, how long it has been sautéed, what province its sauce comes from, and what it is likely to sound like sizzling on my platter—a description lacking only the information that before the poor beast went through that process it had been frozen for eight and a half months.

In American cities the size of Kansas City, a careful traveling man has to observe the rule that any restaurant the executive secretary of the Chamber of Commerce is particularly proud of is almost certainly not worth eating in. Its name will be something like La Maison de la Casa House, Continental Cuisine; its food will sound European but taste as if the continent they had in mind was Australia. Lately, a loyal chamber man in practically any city is likely to recommend one of those restaurants that have sprouted in the past several years on the tops of bank buildings, all of them encased in glass and some of them revolving—offering the diner not only Continental cuisine and a twenty-thousand-word menu but a spectacular view of other restaurants spinning around on the top of other bank buildings. "No, thank you," I finally said to the twelfth gracious host who invited me to one of those. "I never eat in a restaurant that's over a hundred feet off the ground and won't stand still."

What is saddest about a visitor's sitting in the Continental cuisine palace chewing on what an honest menu would have identified as Frozen Duck à l'Orange Soda Pop is that he is likely to have passed a spectacular restaurant on the way over. Despite the best efforts of forward-looking bankers and mad-dog franchisers, there is still great food all over the country, but the struggle to wring information from the locals about where it is served can sometimes leave a traveler too exhausted to eat. I often manage to press on with a seemingly hopeless interrogation only because of my certain knowledge that the information is available—discussed openly by the residents in their own homes, the way that French villagers might have discussed what they really thought of the occupation troops they had been polite to in the shops. As it happens, I grew up in Kansas City and spent hours of my youth talking about where a person could find the best fried chicken in the world or the best barbecued ribs in the world or the best hamburgers in the world— all, by chance, available at that time within the city limits of Kansas City, Missouri. I grew up among the kind of people whose response some years later to a preposterous claim about Little Rock's having a place that served better spareribs than the ones served by Arthur Bryant's Barbecue at Eighteenth and Brooklyn was to fly to Little Rock, sample the ribs, sneer, and fly back to Kansas City.

Knowing that the information exists does make me impatient if some civic booster in, say, one of the middle-sized cities of the Southwest is keeping me from dinner by answering my simple questions about restaurants with a lot of talk about the wine cellar of some palace that has inlaid wallpaper chosen personally by a man who is supposed to be the third-best interior decorator in San Francisco. As the booster goes on about the onion soup with croutons and the sophisticated headwaiter named Jean-Pierre, my mind sometimes wanders off into a fantasy in which my interrogation of the booster is taking place in the presence of one of those ominous blond Germans from the World War II films—the ones with the steel-blue eyes and the small scars who sat silently in the corner while the relatively civilized German line officer asked the downed Allied flyer for military information. "I do hope you will now agree to tell me if there's any Mexican food worth eating around here and quit talking about the glories to be found in La Maison de la Casa House, Continental Cuisine," I tell the booster. "If not, I'm afraid Herr Mueller here has his methods."

It is common for an American city to be vaguely embarrassed about its true delights. In the fifties, a European visitor to New Orleans who insisted on hearing some jazz was routinely taken to hear a group of very respectable-looking white businessmen play Dixieland. A few years ago, I suspect, an Eastern visitor to Nashville who asked a local banker if there was any interesting music in town might have been taken—by a circuitous route, in order to avoid overhearing any of the crude twanging coming out of the Grand Ole Opry or the country recording studios—to the home of a prominent dermatologist who had some friends around every Friday night for chamber music. In most American cities, a booster is likely to insist on defending the place to outsiders in terms of what he thinks of as the sophisticated standards of New York—a city, he makes clear at the start, he would not consider living in even if the alternative were moving with his family and belongings to Yakutsk, Siberia, U.S.S.R. A visitor, particularly a visitor from the East, is invariably subjected to a thirty-minute commercial about the improvement in the local philharmonic, a list of Broadway plays (well, musicals) that have been through in the past year, and some comment like "We happen to have an *excellent* French restaurant here now." The short answer to that one, of course, would be "No you don't." An American city's supply of even competent French restaurants is limited by the number of residents willing to patronize them steadily, and, given the difficulty of finding or importing ingredients and capturing a serious chef and attracting a clientele sufficiently critical to keep the chef from spending most of his time playing the commodities market out of boredom, "an *excellent* French restaurant" will arrive in Tulsa or Omaha at about the time those places near the waterfront in Marseilles start turning out quality pan-fried chicken. In New York, where I live now, the few restaurants that even pretend to serve French food comparable to the food available in the best restaurants in France are maintained at a cost so high that dinner at any one of them seems bound, sooner or later, to face competition from the round-trip airfare to Paris or Lyon.

"I don't suppose your friends took you to Mary-Mac's on Ponce de Leon for a bowl of pot likker, did they?" I once said to a friend of mine who had just returned from her first visit to Atlanta. Naturally not. No civic-minded residents of Atlanta—which advertises itself as the World's Next Great City—would take an out-of-town guest to Mary-Mac's. Their idea of a regional eating attraction is more likely to be someplace built to look like one of the charming antebellum houses that Atlanta once had practically none of—having been, before Sherman got there, an almost new railroad terminus that had all the antebellum charm of Parsons, Kansas. Pot likker, I told my friend, is the liquid left in the bottom of the greens pot, is eaten like a soup, after crumbling some corn bread into it, and is what a Great City would advertise instead of a lot of golf courses.

"They took me to a very nice French restaurant," she said, gamely claiming that it was almost as good as the one she can go to for lunch on days she doesn't feel like walking far enough to get to the decent places.

Since "No you don't" would be considered an impolite reply to the usual boast about a city's having a three-star French restaurant, I have, in the past, stooped to such responses as "French food makes me break out." I love French food. (In fairness, I should say that I can't think of a nation whose food I don't love, although in Ethiopia I was put off a bit by the appearance of the bread, which looks like a material that has dozens of practical uses, not including being eaten as food.) But who wants to hear a skin doctor saw away at the cello when Johnny Cash is right down the street? Lately, when the local booster informs me—as the city ordinance apparently requires him to do within ten minutes of meeting anyone who lives in New York—that he would never live in New York himself, I say something like "Well, it's not easy, of course. There's no barbecue to speak of. That's because of a shortage of hickory wood, I think, although I haven't checked out that theory with Arthur Bryant. We don't really have any Mexican restaurants—I mean the kind you find in Texas, say. Oh, we have Mexican restaurants run by maybe a guy from the East Side who picked up a few recipes while he was down in

San Miguel de Allende thinking about becoming a painter, but no Mexican family restaurants. No señora in the kitchen. No Coors beer. No Lone Star. I wouldn't claim that you can live in New York and expect to drink Lone Star. There's a shortage of Chicago-style pizza south of Fourteenth Street. They don't know much about boiling crabs in New York. It's only since the soul-food places opened that we've been able to get any fried chicken, and we still don't have those family-style fried-chicken places with the fresh vegetables and the pickled watermelon rind on the table. Sure we've got problems. Grits are a problem. I'd be the last one to say living in New York is easy."

Somehow, people have listened to my entire speech and then suggested that I forget my troubles with some fine Continental cuisine at La Maison de la Casa House. I'm then forced into playing the restaurant section of the Yellow Pages—trying one system after another, like a thoroughly addicted horseplayer who would rather take his chances with a palpably bad system than give up the game altogether. I go with small listings for a while—no place that says anything like "See Advertisement Page 253 of this section." Then places called by someone's first name. Then places not called by some-one's first name. For a while, I tried a complicated formula having to do with the number of specialties claimed in relation to the size of the entry, but I could never remember whether the formula called for me to multiply or divide. Constant traveling has provided me with some information on some cities, of course, but the discovery process remains a strain. Who would have ever guessed, for instance, that the old Mexican street near downtown Los Angeles that looks as if it was restored by the MGM set department and stocked by one of the less tasteful wholesalers in Tijuana would have one place that served delicious hand-patted soft tacos packed with *picadillo* or *chicharrón*? How can an innocent traveler be expected to guess that he is going to be subjected to the old Hollywood mystery-film trick of hiding the real jewel in a case full of paste imitations?

There are some types of food that do lend themselves to sophisticated techniques of interrogation. When an Italian restaurant is suggested, for instance, I always say, "Who controls the city council here?" I suppose a good Italian restaurant could exist in a city that doesn't have enough Italians to constitute at least a powerful minority in city politics, but a man in town for only two or three meals has to go with the percentages. It is axiomatic that good barbecue is almost never served in an obviously redecorated restaurant—the reason being, according to my favorite theory on the subject, that walls covered with that slick precut paneling let the flavor slide away.

Some time ago, I found myself in Muskogee, Oklahoma, with dinner-time approaching, and I asked some people I was having a drink with if they knew of any good barbecue places. Through a system of what amounted to ethnic elimination, I had arrived at barbecue as the food most likely to see me through the evening. There is, I am relieved to say, no Continental cuisine in Muskogee, Oklahoma. The people I was having a drink with were trying to be helpful, perhaps because the liquor laws of Oklahoma see to it that citizens who are taking a bourbon in public feel so much like criminals—having skulked in through an unmarked back door and flashed some patently phony membership cards—that we had developed the closeness of conspirators. (Even states that allow grown-ups to drink in public with comparative ease expect a traveler to observe some bizarre liquor laws, of course, including at least one I approve of—the Vermont statute that makes it illegal for a customer to carry a drink from one table to another. I have found that a man who picks up his drink and moves to your table is invariably a man who is going to talk at length about how many miles his car gets to the gallon.) One barbecue place was mentioned, but something about the way it was mentioned made me suspicious.

"They have plates there?" I asked.

"What do you mean 'plates'?" one of my fellow criminal boozers asked me.

"You know—plates you eat off of," I said.

"Of course they have plates," he said.

"You have any other barbecue restaurants around here?" I asked. I have eaten fine barbecue on plates—Arthur Bryant, in fact, uses plates—but I would hesitate to eat barbecue in a place that has plates "of course" or "natu-rally" or "certainly." The next piece of information an outsider is likely to extract about such a place is that it also serves steaks and chicken and maybe even a stray lobster tail.

"Well," my partner in crime began, "there's an old colored fellow out on the highway who—"

"Tell me how to get there," I said.

It turned out to be a small diner, and if it had been a half mile closer I might have been able to locate it unassisted by following the perfume of burning hickory logs. There were, as it happened, no plates. The proprietor's version of the formal restaurant custom of including a dinner plate on top of a larger plate at each place setting was to put down a piece of butcher paper and then a piece of waxed paper and then the barbecue—first-class barbecue. It would have been a thoroughly satisfying meal except that my success in finding the place caused me to ponder all through dinner on how much happier traveling would be if only I could think of a workable formula for finding fried-chicken restaurants.

American Fried (1974)

RISOTTO

Risotto alla
parmigiana

This is the purest and perhaps the finest of all risotti. The only major ingredient added to the rice and broth is Parmesan cheese. In Italian cooking, you should never use anything except good-quality, freshly grated Parmesan cheese, but for this particular risotto you should make a special effort to obtain authentic, aged, Italian *parmigiano-reggiano* from the best supplier you know.

During the truffle season in Italy, the risotto is crowned at the table with thinly sliced fresh white truffles. Fresh truffles are sometimes available here for a few days in late November or early December. If you should have a chance at a nice large truffle, do get it for this risotto. It is going to set you back a considerable amount, but you are not likely to regret it.

5 cups Homemade Meat Broth

OR

1 cup canned chicken broth mixed with 4 cups water

2 tablespoons finely chopped shallots or yellow onion

3 tablespoons butter

2 tablespoons vegetable oil

1 1/2 cups raw Italian Arborio rice

1/2 heaping cup freshly grated Parmesan cheese

Salt, if necessary

1. Bring the broth to a slow, steady simmer.

2. Put the shallots in a heavy-bottomed casserole with 2 tablespoons of the butter and all the oil and saute over medium-high heat until translucent but not browned.

3. Add the rice and stir until it is well coated. Saute lightly, then add 1/2 cup of the simmering broth. Proceed according to the basic directions for making risotto, adding 1/2 cup of simmering broth as the rice dries out, and stirring it very frequently to prevent it from sticking. (If you run out of broth, continue with water.)

4. When you estimate that the rice is about 5 minutes away from being done, add all the grated cheese and the remaining tablespoon of butter. Mix well. Taste and correct for salt. Remember, when the cooking nears the end, not to add too much broth at one time. The risotto should be creamy but not runny. Serve immediately, with additional grated cheese, if desired, on the side.

Marcella Hazan, *The Classic Italian Cookbook* (1973)

In a country where "Italian" meant almost exclusively "Neapolitan," Marcella Hazan's recipes from Italy's northern regions created an appetite for balsamic vinegar, well-aged Parmesan, and extra-virgin olive oil, and inspired the Northern Italian restaurant craze of the 1980s.

Craig Claiborne

Just a Quiet Dinner for Two in Paris:
31 Dishes, Nine Wines, a $4,000 Check

In terms of integrity and journalistic dispassion everything before Craig Claiborne (1920–2000) is B.C.: an era when advertisers and the food industry's test kitchens largely determined the stories and recipes that would appear in print. Restaurant criticism was far less common than restaurant boosterism, which could be bought for the price of a meal. Claiborne saw no reason why one section of the paper should be exempt from the ethics and standards that guided the other pages. By insisting on just that, he turned the food section of *The New York Times* into the most powerful food authority in America, and in the process gave newspaper food writing moral fiber.

His technical expertise, graceful prose, and constitutional inability to be anything but a soft-spoken gentleman certainly helped. Born in Sunflower, Mississippi, Claiborne was raised on Southern home cooking. He attended hotel school in Lausanne, Switzerland, and went on to write for *Gourmet*; in 1957, he was named food editor of the *Times*, a position he held for 35 years. Claiborne invented the star-system still used by the newspaper; introduced the sometimes timid postwar American palate to a host of new ethnic flavors; turned people like Diana Kennedy, Paul Prudhomme, Paula Wolfert, Marcella Hazan, and Pierre Franey into celebrities; and wrote over 20 cookbooks. He was admired, reviled and, above all else, incorruptible. He had no interest in becoming part of the story, and thus was not socially or emotionally vulnerable to those he wrote about. A case in point is the story of the meal he bid on at a charity auction: a $4,000 dinner for two in Paris. Claiborne's report neither preens nor lords over; rather, it holds the cuisine to an ideal standard and, indeed, finds several dishes just shy of perfection.

■ ■ ■

If one were offered dinner for two at any price, to be eaten in any restaurant anywhere in the world, what would the choice be? And in these days of ever-higher prices, what would the cost be?

By submitting the highest bid on Channel 13's fund-raising auction last June, we found ourselves in a position earlier this week to answer these questions. The place: Chez Denis in Paris. The cost: $4,000.

Our winning bid was $300.

One factor in the selection of the restaurant should be noted quickly: The donor of the dinner that Channel 13 auctioned was American Express, which set forth as its only condition the requirement that the establishment be one that accepts its credit card.

In turn, when American Express ultimately learned what we had done, its reaction went from mild astonishment to being cheerful about the outcome. "Four thousand—was that francs or dollars?" asked Iris Burkat, a company official, at one point.

At any rate, the selection of the restaurant dominated our fantasies for weeks as in our minds, we dined on a hundred meals or more. At times we were in Paris, then in Alsace. We considered Rome, Tokyo and Hong Kong, Copenhagen and Stockholm, Brussels and London.

The consideration of restaurants competed with thoughts of the greatest of champagnes and still wines, visions of caviar and foie gras, dreams of elaborate desserts. Perhaps we would choose nothing but vodka or champagne with caviar followed by foie gras with Chateau d'Yquem—but no, any old millionaire could do that.

In addition to excluding those that did not recognize the credit card of the donor, we dismissed from our potential list of restaurants several celebrated places, simply, perhaps, because of their celebrity.

In time we considered Chez Denis, which is a great favorite among several food writers (Henri Gault, Christian Millau and Waverley Root among them), but is nonetheless not well known. It is a tiny place on the Rue Gustave Flaubert, not far from the Arc de Triomphe.

We visited Chez Denis in a party of three to reconnoiter. It was not hard to go incognito, for we suspect that the proprietor, Denis Lahana, does not credit any Americans with even the most elementary knowledge of French wine and food.

The investigatory dinner was sumptuous. There was a chiffonade of lobster (a salad of cold lobster, cubed foie gras, a touch of cognac and, we suspect, cayenne, and a tarragon mayonnaise flavored with tomato, tossed with lettuce).

In addition, there was fresh foie gras with aspic, braised sweetbreads with a light truffle sauce, roast quail and those delectable tiny birds from the

Landes region of France, ortolans. There was also a great personal favorite, andouillettes served with an outstanding sorrel sauce. The wine was a fine Pommard.

The meal having passed the test, we were able to ignore the few plastic boughs and plastic flowers tucked in beams here and there.

We wondered how it was that the place did not merit one, two or three stars in the Guide Michelin. It is not even listed. Mr. Denis would not comment on a story we had heard about inspectors from Michelin having somehow offended the proprietor and having been asked to leave.

After dinner, we asked Mr. Denis, offhandedly, how much he would charge for the most lavish dinner for two that he and his chef could prepare. He spoke in terms of $2,000 to $3,000.

We told him that we were about to celebrate a birthday and that money was no obstacle in ordering the finest dinner in Europe. Mr. Denis, with little hesitation, pulled up a chair and sat down. He took us seriously.

We asked him to consider the matter at his convenience and write to us with his proposal. When he did, his letter stated:

"In accordance with your demand, I propose to organize for you a prestigious dinner. In the land of my birth, the region of Bordeaux, one speaks of a repas de vins, a meal during the course of which a number of wines of great prestige are served, generally nine wines.

"I am suggesting nine such wines, to be served in the course of a dinner à la Française in the classic tradition. To dine properly in this style, many dishes are offered and served to the guests, chosen with the sole thought that each dish be on the same high level as the wines and those most likely to give pleasure as the wines are tasted."

He suggested a dinner of 31 dishes that would start with an hors d'oeuvre and go on to three "services," the first consisting of soups, savory, an assortment of substantial main dishes, and ices or sherbets to clear the palate.

This would be followed by the second service: hot roasts or baked dishes, vegetables, cold, light, meaty dishes in aspic and desserts.

And then the third service: decorated confections, petits fours and fruits.

The youngest wine would be a six-year-old white burgundy, the oldest a 140-year-old madeira.

Mr. Denis set a price of $4,000. This, we must hasten to add, included service and taxes. We accepted.

The proprietor suggested that the meal be served to four persons—all for the same price—because the food had to be prepared in a certain quantity and would be enough to serve as many as 10 persons, while the wines were enough for four.

We declined, because the rules set by American Express called for dinner for two. The dinner party would be made up of me and my colleague, Pierre Franey. Anything left over, we knew, would not go to waste.

Mr. Denis noted that it was not required that all foods be sampled and that the quantity of the food served would depend on the guest's appetite.

And so, we sat down to our $4,000 dinner.

The hors d'oeuvre was presented: fresh Beluga caviar in crystal, enclosed in shaved ice, with toast. The wine was a superb 1966 Champagne Comtesse Marie de France.

Then came the first service, which started with three soups. There was consomme Denis, an inordinately good, rich, full-bodied, clear consommé of wild duck with shreds of fine crepes and herbs. It was clarified with raw duck and duck bones and then lightly thickened as many classic soups are, with fine tapioca.

The second soup (still of the first service) was a crème Andalouse, an outstanding cream of tomato soup with shreds of sweet pimento and fines herbes, including fresh chives and chervil.

The first two soups were superb but the third, cold germiny (a cream of sorrel), seemed bland and anticlimactic. One spoonful of that sufficed.

The only wine served at this point was a touch of champagne. The soups having been disposed of, we moved on to a spectacularly delicate parfait of sweetbreads, an equally compelling mousse of quail in a small tarte, and a somewhat salty, almost abrasive but highly complementary tarte of Italian ham, mushrooms and a border of truffles.

The wine was a 1918 Chateau Latour, and it was perhaps the best bordeaux we had ever known. It was very much alive, with the least trace of tannin.

The next segment of the first service included a fascinating dish that the proprietor said he had created. Belon oysters broiled quickly in the shell and served with a pure beurre blanc, the creamy, lightly thickened butter sauce.

Also in this segment were a lobster in a creamy, cardinal-red sauce that was heavily laden with chopped truffles and, after that, another startling but excellent dish, a sort of Provençale pie made with red mullet and baked with tomato, black olives and herbs, including fennel or anise seed, rosemary, sage and thyme.

The accompanying wine was a 1969 Montrachet Baron Thénard, which was extraordinary (to our taste, all first-rate Montrachet whites are extraordinary).

The final part of the first service consisted of what was termed filets et sots l'y laissent de poulard de Bresse, sauce suprême aux cèpes (the so-called "fillet" strips of chicken plus the "oysters" found in the after-backbone of chicken blended in a cream sauce containing sliced wild mushrooms).

There followed another curious but oddly appealing dish, a classic chartreuse of partridge, the pieces of roasted game nested in a bed of cooked cabbage and baked in a mosaic pattern, intricately styled, of carrot and turnip cut into fancy shapes.

And a tender rare-roasted fillet of Limousin beef with a rich truffle sauce.

The wine with the meat and game was a 1928 Chateau Mouton Rothschild. It was ageless and beautiful.

The first service finally ended with sherbets in three flavors—raspberry, orange and lemon. The purpose of this was to revive the palate for the second service, and it did. We were two hours into the meal and going at the food, it seemed, at a devilish pace.

The second service included the ortolans en brochette, an element of the dinner to be anticipated with a relish almost equal to that of the caviar or the foie gras.

The small birds, which dine on berries through their brief lives, are cooked whole, with the head on, and without cleaning except for removing the feathers. They are as fat as butter and an absolute joy to bite into because of the succulence of the flesh. Even the bones, except for the tiny leg bones, are chewed and swallowed. There is one bird to one bite.

The second service also included fillets of wild duck en salmis in a rich brown game sauce. The final dish in this segment was a rognonade de veau, or roasted boned loin of veal wrapped in puff pastry with fresh black truffles about the size of golf balls.

The vegetables served were pommes Anna—the potatoes cut into small rounds and baked in butter—and a purée rachel, a purée of artichokes.

Then came the cold meat delicacies. There was butter-rich fresh foie gras in clear aspic, breast meat of woodcocks that was cooked until rare and served with a natural chaudfroid, another aspic and cold pheasant with fresh hazelnuts.

The wines for this segment consisted of a 1947 Chateau Lafite-Rothschild, a 1961 Chateau Petrus, and the most magnificent wine of the evening, a 1929 Romanée Conti.

The dinner drew near an end with three sweets—a cold glazed charlotte with strawberries, an ile flottante and poires alma. The wine for the sweets was a beautiful unctuous 1928 Chateau d'Yquem, which was quite sweet yet "dry."

The last service consisted of the pastry confections and fruits, served with an 1835 madeira. With coffee came a choice of a 100-year-old calvados or an hors d'âge cognac.

And for the $4,000, logic asks if it was a perfect meal in all respects?

The answer is no.

The crystal was Baccarat and the silver was family sterling, but the presentation of the dishes, particularly the cold dishes such as the sweetbread parfait and quail mousse tarte, was mundane.

The foods were elegant to look at, but the over-all display was undistinguished, if not to say shabby.

The chartreuse of pheasant, which can be displayed stunningly, was presented on a most ordinary dish.

The food itself was generally exemplary, although there were regrettable lapses there, too. The lobster in the gratin was chewy and even the sauce could not compensate for that. The oysters, of necessity, had to be cooked as briefly as possible to prevent toughening, but the beurre blanc should have been very hot. The dish was almost lukewarm when it reached the table, and so was the chartreuse of pheasant.

We've spent many hours reckoning the cost of the meal and find that we cannot break it down. We have decided this: We feel we could not have made a better choice, given the circumstance of time and place.

Mr. Denis declined to apply a cost to each of the wines, explaining that they contributed greatly to the total cost of the meal because it was necessary to open three bottles of the 1918 Latour in order to find one in proper condition.

Over all, it was an unforgettable evening and we have high praise for Claude Mornay, the 37-year-old genius behind the meal.

We reminded ourselves of one thing during the course of that evening: If you were Henry VIII, Lucullus, Gargantua and Bacchus, all rolled into one, you cannot possibly sustain, start to finish, a state of ecstasy while dining on a series of 31 dishes.

Wines, illusion or not, became increasingly interesting, although we were laudably sober at the end of the meal.

The New York Times, November 14, 1975

Russell Baker

Francs and Beans

Craig Claiborne's front-page report on his $4,000 dinner for two in Paris elicited a deluge of response from *New York Times* readers outraged by the seeming depravity of such excess. Four days later, *Times* columnist Russell Baker (b. 1925) chimed in with a characteristically deft lampoon. Baker, who won Pulitzer prizes both for his column in the *Times* and for his memoir *Growing Up* (1982), manages to put the grandiose aspect of Claiborne's dinner in its place while adopting the self-deprecating tone of an average Joe.

■ ■ ■

As chance would have it, the very evening Craig Claiborne ate his historic $4,000 dinner for two with 31 dishes and nine wines in Paris, a Lucullan repast for one was prepared and consumed in New York by this correspondent, no slouch himself when it comes to titillating the palate.

Mr. Claiborne won his meal in a television fund-raising auction and had it professionally prepared. Mine was created from spur-of-the-moment inspiration, necessitated when I discovered a note on the stove saying, "Am eating out with Dora and Imogene—make dinner for yourself." It was from the person who regularly does the cooking at my house and, though disconcerted at first, I quickly rose to the challenge.

The meal opened with a 1975 Diet Pepsi served in a disposable bottle. Although its bouquet was negligible, its distinct metallic aftertaste evoked memories of tin cans one had licked experimentally in the first flush of childhood's curiosity.

To create the balance of tastes so cherished by the epicurean palate, I followed with a *paté de fruites de nuts of Georgia*, prepared according to my own recipe. A half-inch layer of creamy-style peanut butter is troweled onto a graham cracker, then half a banana is crudely diced and pressed firmly into the peanut butter and cemented in place as it were by a second graham cracker.

The accompanying drink was cold milk served in a wide-brimmed jelly glass. This is essential to proper consumption of the paté, since the entire confection must be dipped into the milk to soften it for eating. In making the presentation to the mouth, one must beware lest the milk-soaked portion of the sandwich fall onto the necktie. Thus, seasoned gourmandisers follow the old maxim of the Breton chefs and "bring the mouth to the jelly glass."

At this point in the meal, the stomach was ready for serious eating, and I prepared beans with bacon grease, a dish I perfected in 1937 while developing my *cuisine du dépression*.

The dish is started by placing a pan over a very high flame until it becomes dangerously hot. A can of Heinz's pork and beans is then emptied into the pan and allowed to char until it reaches the consistency of hardening concrete. Three strips of bacon are fried to crisps, and when the beans have formed huge dense clots firmly welded to the pan, the bacon grease is poured in and stirred vigorously with a large screw driver.

This not only adds flavor but also loosens some of the beans from the side of the pan. Leaving the flame high, I stirred in a three-day-old spaghetti sauce found in the refrigerator, added a sprinkle of chili powder, a large dollop of Major Grey's chutney and a tablespoon of bicarbonate of soda to make the whole dish rise.

Beans with bacon grease is always eaten from the pan with a tablespoon while standing over the kitchen sink. The pan must be thrown away immediately. The correct drink with this dish is a straight shot of room-temperature gin. I had a Gilbey's, 1975, which was superb.

For the meat course, I had fried bologna *à la Nutley, Nouveau Jersey*. Six slices of A&P bologna were placed in an ungreased frying pan over maximum heat and held down by a long fork until the entire house filled with smoke. The bologna was turned, fried the same length of time on the other side, then served on air-filled white bread with thick lashings of mayonnaise.

The correct drink for fried bologna *à la Nutley, Nouveau Jersey* is a 1927 Nehi Cola, but since my cellar, alas, had none, I had to make do with a second shot of Gilbey's 1975.

The cheese course was deliciously simple—a single slice of Kraft's individually wrapped yellow sandwich cheese, which was flavored by vigorous rubbing over the bottom of the frying pan to soak up the rich bologna juices. Wine being absolutely *de rigueur* with cheese, I chose a 1974 Muscatel, flavored with a maraschino cherry, and afterwards cleared my palate with three pickled martini onions.

It was time for the fruit. I chose a Del Monte tinned pear, which, regrettably, slipped from the spoon and fell on the floor, necessitating its being blotted with a paper towel to remove cat hairs. To compensate for the resulting loss of pear syrup, I dipped it lightly in hot-dog relish which created a unique flavor.

With the pear I drank two shots of Gilbey's 1975 and one shot of Wolfschmidt vodka (non-vintage), the Gilbey's having been exhausted.

At last it was time for the dish the entire meal had been building toward—dessert. With a paring knife, I ripped into a fresh package of Oreos, produced a bowl of My-T-Fine chocolate pudding which had been coagulating in the refrigerator for days and, using a potato masher, crushed a dozen Oreos into the pudding. It was immense.

Between mouthfuls, I sipped a tall, bubbling tumbler of cool Bromo-Seltzer, and finished with six ounces of Maalox. It couldn't have been better.

The New York Times, November 18, 1975

Ray Kroc

from Grinding It Out: The Making of McDonald's

Health concerns, like those raised by Eric Schlosser's *Fast Food Nation* (2001) and Morgan Spurlock's documentary *Super Size Me* (2004), had barely begun to be felt when Ray Kroc (1902–1984) wrote *Grinding It Out* (1977), his account of turning McDonald's into the most successful of all fast food franchises. At that time, in the early days of fast food, nothing tasted sweeter than healthy competition and a healthy bottom line. Even so, Kroc draws the line at hot dogs: "There's no telling what's inside a hot dog's skin, and our standard of quality just wouldn't permit that kind of item." As his book makes clear, he had opinions as strong as any chef's about what could and could not contend for a spot on his menu.

■ ■ ■

Some of my detractors, and I've acquired a few over the years, say that my penchant for experimenting with new menu items is a foolish indulgence. They contend that it stems from my never having outgrown my drummer's desire to have something new to sell. "McDonald's is in the hamburger business," they say. "How can Kroc even consider serving chicken?" Or, "Why change a winning combination?"

Of course, it's not difficult to demonstrate how much our menu has changed over the years, and nobody could argue with the success of additions such as the Filet-O-Fish, the Big Mac, Hot Apple Pie, and Egg McMuffin. The most interesting thing to me about these items is that each evolved from an idea of one of our operators. So the company has benefited from the ingenuity of its small businessmen while they were being helped by the system's image and our cooperative advertising muscle. This, to my way of thinking, is the perfect example of capitalism in action. Competition was the catalyst for each of the new items. Lou Groen came up with Filet-O-Fish to help him in his battle against the Big Boy chain in the Catholic parishes of Cincinnati. The Big Mac resulted from our need for a larger sandwich to compete against Burger King and a variety of specialty shop concoctions. The idea for Big Mac was originated by Jim Delligatti in Pittsburgh.

Harold Rosen, our operator in Enfield, Connecticut, invented our special St. Patrick's Day drink, The Shamrock Shake. "It takes a guy with a name like *Rosen* to think up an Irish drink," Harold told me. He wasn't kidding. "You may be right," I said. "It takes a guy with a name like Kroc to come up with a Hawaiian sandwich . . . Hulaburger." He didn't say anything. He didn't know whether I was kidding or not. Operators aren't the only ones who come up with creative ideas for our menu. My old friend Dave Wallerstein, who was head of the Balaban & Katz movie chain and has a great flair for merchandising—he's the man who put the original snack bars in Disneyland for Walt Disney—is an outside director of McDonald's, and he's the one who came up with the idea for our large size order of french fries. He said he loved the fries, but the small bag wasn't enough and he didn't want to buy two. So we kicked it around and he finally talked us into testing the larger size in a store near his home in Chicago. They have a window in that store that they now call "The Wallerstein Window," because every time the manager or a crew person would look up, there would be Dave peering in to see how the large size fries were selling. He needn't have worried. The large order took off like a rocket, and it's now one of our best-selling items. Dave really puts his heart into his job as a director, now that he's retired and has plenty of time. There's nothing he likes more than traveling with me to check out stores.

Our Hot Apple Pie came after a long search for a McDonald's kind of dessert. I felt we had to have a dessert to round out our menu. But finding a dessert item that would fit readily into our production system and gain wide acceptance was a problem. I thought I had the answer in a strawberry shortcake. But it sold well for only a short time and then slowed to nothing. I had high hopes for pound cake, too, but it lacked glamor. We needed something we could romance in advertising. I was ready to give up when Litton Cochran suggested we try fried pie, which he said is an old southern favorite. The rest, of course, is fast-food history. Hot Apple Pie, and later Hot Cherry Pie, has that special quality, that classiness in a finger food, that made it perfect for McDonald's. The pies added significantly to our sales and revenues. They also created a whole new industry for producing the filled, frozen shells and supplying them to our stores.

During the Christmas holidays in 1972, I happened to be visiting in Santa Barbara, and I got a call from Herb Peterson, our operator there, who said he had something to show me. He wouldn't give me a clue as to what it was. He didn't want me to reject it out of hand, which I might have done, because it was a crazy idea—a breakfast sandwich. It consisted of an egg that had been formed in a Teflon circle, with the yolk broken, and was dressed with a slice of cheese and a slice of grilled Canadian bacon. This was served open-face on a toasted and buttered English muffin. I boggled a bit at the presentation. But then I tasted it, and I was sold. Wow! I wanted to put this item into all of our stores immediately. Realistically, of course, that was impossible. It took us nearly three years to get the egg sandwich fully integrated into our system. Fred Turner's wife, Patty, came up with the name that helped make it an immediate hit—Egg McMuffin.

The advent of Egg McMuffin opened up a whole new area of potential business for McDonald's, the breakfast trade. We went after it like the Sixth Fleet going into action. It was exhilarating to see the combined forces of our research and development people, our marketing and advertising experts, and our operations and supply specialists all concentrating on creating a program for catering to the breakfast trade. There were a great many problems to overcome. Some of them were new to us, because we were dealing with new kinds of products. Pancakes, for example, have to be offered if you intend to promote a complete breakfast menu. But they have an extremely short holding time, and this forced us to devise a procedure for "cooking to order" during periods of low customer count. Our food assembly lines, so swift and efficient for turning out hamburgers and french fries, had to be geared down and realigned to produce items for the breakfast trade. Then, after all the planning and all the working out of supply and production problems, it remained for the individual operator to figure out whether to adopt breakfast in his store. It meant longer hours for him, of course, and he'd probably have to hire more crew members and give the ones he had additional training. Consequently, the breakfast program is growing at a very moderate rate. But I can see it catching on across the country, and I can visualize extensions for a lot of stores, such as brunch on Sunday.

I keep a number of experimental menu additions in the works all the time. Some of them now being tested in selected stores may find their way into general use. Others, for a variety of reasons, will never make it. We have a complete test kitchen and experimental lab on my ranch, where all of our products are tested; this is in addition to the creative facility in Oak Brook. Fred Turner has a tendency to look askance at any new menu ideas. He'll usually try to put them down with some wisecrack such as, "That may be all right, but when are we going to start serving grilled bananas? We could put a little container of maple syrup on the side, and maybe for dinner we could serve them flaming." Such sarcasm doesn't bother me. I know Fred's thinking, and I respect it. He doesn't want us going hog wild with new items. We aren't going to, but we are going to stay flexible and change as the market demands it. There are some things we can do and maintain our identity, and there are others we could never do. For example, it's entirely possible that one day we might have pizza. On the other hand, there's damned good reason we should never have hot dogs. There's no telling what's inside a hot dog's skin, and our standard of quality just wouldn't permit that kind of item.

Grinding It Out: The Making of McDonald's (1977)

Edna Lewis

Morning-After-Hog-Butchering Breakfast

Edna Lewis (1916–2006), the granddaughter of an emancipated slave who had founded Freetown, Virginia, was widely hailed in the last decades of her life as one of the nation's leading authorities on Southern cooking. Leaving home as a teenager, she moved to Washington, D.C., and eventually to New York, where in 1948 she helped to open a restaurant. Presiding over the kitchen at Café Nicholson, "Miss Lewis" (as she was known) became the toast of a generation of Southerners in the city, including on occasion Truman Capote and William Faulkner, as well as other celebrities. She went on to publish *The Edna Lewis Cookbook* (1972), *The Taste of Country Cooking* (1976), *In Pursuit of Flavor* (1988), and, with her companion in her later years Scott Peacock, *The Gift of Southern Cooking* (2003)–books that were ahead of their time in their emphasis on simplicity and freshness and that helped restore Southern food to its central place at the American table.

■ ■ ■

——

Black Raspberries and Cream
Eggs Sunny-Side Up
Oven-Cooked Fresh Bacon
Fried Sweetbreads
Country-Fried Apples
Biscuits–Corn Bread
Butter
Wild Strawberry Preserves–Wild Blackberry Jelly
Coffee

——

Hog Killing

Hog killing was one of the special events of the year and generally took place in December–the exact time depending on a solid cold spell coinciding with the right time of the moon, which was when the moon was on the increase. The cold spell was essential, as the hogs could not be carved up until they

were thoroughly chilled and the meat had firmed up enough to cut properly. This took a good three days of hanging in the open air.

Aside from the special feeding, fattening, and cleaning of the hogs that
led up to the day of butchering, there were many other preparations to be
made. Scaffolds for hanging the hogs had to be erected, and wood laid for
the fires that would heat the iron drums of water needed for scalding and
cleansing the hogs after they were killed. Many families had an outdoor or
"summer" kitchen—an extra kitchen detached from the house which was
used during the hot weather so that the continuous heat coming from a
wood stove would not make the whole house unbearably hot. These summer
kitchens were also useful at hog-killing time, as there was too much fat to be
rendered, sausage meat to grind, and other cooking to handle easily in the
main house, so they would be all scrubbed and put in order ahead of time.

The butchering day was a hectic one. Every family had a dozen or more
hogs and we all joined in helping each other. After each hog was killed, it
was carefully scalded so that the bristles would scrape off easily, leaving a
smooth, unmarked skin. After this was done, the hind legs were fastened
together by a special stock called a gambrel, which was shaped like a rolling
pin with pointed ends. The stick was placed between the legs and the pointed
ends were inserted under the hocks. To hang the hog, which would be about
six feet long, two men would hoist it up, hooking the hind legs over the top
of the scaffold. The hog was then cut down the center. A large, round tub
was placed underneath for the entrails to fall into. My father would remove
the liver and the bladder, which he would present to us. We would blow the
bladders up with straws cut from reeds and hang them in the house to dry.
By Christmas they would have turned transparent like beautiful balloons.
We always handled them with care and made them part of our Christmas
decorations.

The following morning my brothers and sisters and I would rush out
before breakfast to see the hogs hanging from the scaffolds like giant statues.
The hogs looked beautiful. They were glistening white inside with their
lining of fat, and their skin was almost translucent after the scraping.

We waited with impatient excitement through the three days of hanging;
we were all looking forward to the many delicious dishes that would be
made after the hogs were cut up—fresh sausage, liver pudding, and the sweet,

delicate tastes of fresh pork and bacon. One of my favorite foods that we always had after hog killing was crackling bread. When the lard was rendered and strained, little defatted pieces were left which we called cracklings. Cut into small pieces and mixed into cornmeal batter they made a bread which was deliciously crispy and chewy. Meanwhile, we enjoyed the fresh liver, which my mother would pan-fry for breakfast or dinner.

When the three-day period of hanging ended, the hogs were carved up. The special skill that was needed for butchering was provided by an itinerant hog-killer, who would always appear a few days before the first cold spell that we waited for so eagerly, and who would often stay on for three or four weeks past hog killing. (It was not unusual for someone to arrive for a few days' visit during the winter months and stay on for several weeks—sometimes until spring.)

As soon as the hogs were butchered, a series of necessary activities ensued that kept the whole community busy for at least a week or more. Besides all the special treats we would be enjoying at mealtime, it was the highly festive feeling of everyone working together that made this one of our favorite times in the year.

The first part of the hog to be removed was the layer of white fat that had seemed to glisten so when the hogs were hanging. This fat is known as leaf lard because it peels off in thin sheets or leaves. It is very special, as its taste and texture are so fine, and we always kept it and used it for pies, biscuits, and even cakes. A group of the women would be on hand to cut the lard into small cubes as soon as it was removed and then to render it in heavy iron pots. Sometimes the pots would be hung in a fork over an outdoor fire. The fat had to cook very slowly in order to turn liquid. Then it was strained and poured into 5-gallon tins. After it cooled, it was sealed and stored in a cool, dry place.

Each piece of meat had to be carved to a certain shape, and as it was cut, trimmings flowed from the hams, shoulders, and bacon. They would form a great pile and huge pots were needed to render this fat, which would be used for frying meats and other foods that didn't require the same fineness of flavor that pastry does. It took three or four days of constant work to render all of the lard, but when it was finished there would be a good year's supply for every family.

Among the trimmings there was always some lean as well as fat, and this had to be carefully cut away. The lean from the trimmings was put into the "sausage bin," along with what we now call loin. I think that was why the sausage was so good, because it had in it pieces from all parts of the hog. Lard and sausage meat are still being prepared in the same way in this part of Virginia.

Once the lard was rendered, the women would turn to making sausage. First our meat was seasoned with sage, black pepper, and salt, then it was ground in a sausage mill and made up into cakes and canned in jars, or stuffed into casings that came from the hogs' intestines and smoked. When all of the sausage had been cooked and sealed into jars, a piece of the jowl was cooked with the liver, then finely ground and seasoned with sage and onion. The jowl is mostly fat and makes the liver softer and lighter. We called this delicate pâté liver pudding, and it was a favorite dish. Some of the jowls were cured with the hams and bacon; they were delicious sliced and oven-fried for breakfast as a change from bacon.

While the women were busy with rendering the fat and cooking the sausage and liver, the men would prepare the hams, bacon, and shoulders. These would be seasoned with salt, black pepper, saltpeter, and brown sugar and stored in a wooden meat box for about six weeks. The meat would then be cleaned with a stiff brush and hung from hooks in the smokehouse, where it would be smoked for three or four days over green hickory logs and sassafras twigs.

After the meat had been smoked, it was put into clean, white bags and tied securely to make sure no flies or other insects got into the meat. It was then left to hang in the smokehouse until it was needed, which was usually late summer. Hams were sometimes left to age for a year or two. They become quite mellow and delicious when they are left this length of time and are usually saved for special events such as family reunions, weddings, and graduations.

Black Raspberries and Cream

Raspberries grew wild along the streams and edges of the nearby woodland and they ripened later in the season than strawberries. The black raspberries were particularly good for preserving because they remained firm, so we could have them as a treat, served with cream, throughout the winter and on into the spring. We preserved them in what seemed to me a most intriguing way. We would mix the berries with equal amounts of sugar and place them in glass bottles. Then we would cork the necks with a piece of cotton and pour melted wax over the tops. We would keep the filled bottles in an opening in the ground under a board in the kitchen floor and bring them out on special occasions like hog-butchering day because the flavor was so exotic. I have never forgotten the taste of them.

Eggs Sunny-Side Up

No breakfast was complete without eggs cooked in some form: boiled, poached, or fried. Even though we didn't have to buy them, they were greatly relished. Eggs of that day were fertile and had a real flavor. Of the various ways we cooked them—including wrapping them in wet brown paper and cooking them in the ashes of the fireplace—sunny side was the most elegant. They were more like a sunny-side soufflé. They were always fried in the same pan that the bacon or ham had just been cooked in, so they would absorb whatever flavor there was left in the pan. When fresh eggs were broken into the hot fat they held their shape, and the sizzling fat would cause them to cook quickly and to puff up. We would shake the pan around while they cooked so that the hot fat splashed over the whites and this would make the eggs puff into a ball. We would then serve them quickly while still puffy.

The same technique can be used with butter as well. Heat the butter to the foaming stage; put in the egg, and tilt the pan to one side so that the egg will be enveloped in the butter. When fully puffed, serve.

Bacon

Country breakfast bacon ranged from middling, jowl, shoulder to ham. Varying the cuts kept up a lively interest in each meal because every part tasted different—and I will never forget the taste of fresh bacon, sliced thin from the middling as soon as the meat was cold enough to carve, sprinkled with salt and fresh black pepper, whose aroma filled the air during hog-butchering time. The slices were placed in a hot skillet containing 2 tablespoons of lard, then set into the oven to cook for about 18 minutes. Fresh bacon should be cut from the section of the middling that is most fat. The lean part would be a bit tough.

The jowl, shoulder, and ham all have different flavors. They are first cured and then left hanging in the meat house. Each morning we would take a piece from the hook, place it on the workbench that was in the meat house, and with a sharp knife slice enough for breakfast, trimming away the rind from each thin slice. Returning to the kitchen, the slices were washed in a little warm water to take out excess salt, placed in a medium-hot frying pan, and set into a hot oven to cook. If bread was being baked the bacon would be placed on the floor of the oven. The slices could be turned if needed. If the bread finished baking first, the meat pan would be placed upon the rack in the oven. Total cooking time would be about 15 to 18 minutes, depending upon the thickness of the slices. This is an excellent way to cook very thin bacon, as I've said before; all kinds of bacon you buy today can be done this way. The over-all heat of the oven seems to completely relax the bacon, while giving it a crispy, chewy, baked flavor. When finished, remove from the oven and drain on brown paper.

Fried Pork Sweetbreads

There was very little meat for cooking immediately after hog butchering because all of the important pieces were put down in salt or ground into sausage and the liver went into pudding. But there was an assortment of organ meats, among them the sweetbreads, that were seasoned and put into an open baking pan and cooked in the oven. When everything was cooked, the contents of the pan was all brown and aromatic. I remember tasting the sweetbreads as a child, and they were delicious to me; I never forgot the flavor. I was disappointed later when I tried veal sweetbreads, expecting them to be brown and crisp like those we did. It would be hard to duplicate that dish now, but one can prepare delicious, crisp sweetbreads.

Serves 5 to 6

2 pounds pork sweetbreads (or if available, veal)
1 cup fresh bread crumbs, sifted fine
2 eggs, beaten
$^1/_2$ cup flour

$^{1}\!/_{2}$ teaspoon salt

$^{1}\!/_{2}$ teaspoon black pepper

$^{1}\!/_{2}$ cup (1 stick) butter

1 lemon, cut in wedges

$^{1}\!/_{4}$ cup finely cut parsley

To prepare, wash the sweetbreads well in cold water, then plunge into boiling salted water for about 10 minutes. Then plunge into cold water, drain, and wipe dry. Place in freezer compartment for about 15 minutes to become firm enough to remove outer web and slice well into $^{1}\!/_{4}$-inch slices. Coat the slices in about two-thirds of the cup of fresh bread crumbs, and then in beaten egg, then in a mixture of flour, salt and pepper, and the remaining bread crumbs. Fry in butter a few minutes on each side and drain on brown paper. Serve hot, garnished with lemon wedges and finely cut parsley.

Country-Fried Apples

Serves 5 to 6

6 apples

3 tablespoons fresh bacon fat

$^{1}\!/_{3}$ cup sugar

Prepare apples by peeling, quartering, coring, and quartering again. Heat the bacon fat in a hot skillet and when sizzling add the apples. Cover and cook briskly until the apples become soft and there is juice in the pan. Timing depends upon the kind of apple you use, but you can tell the apples are soft when they begin to break up. Remove cover and sprinkle the sugar over the apples. Stir and cook with the cover off until the liquid has dried up and apples begin to brown. Cook medium-brisk until the apples are quite brown. Stir frequently. The apples should be a mixture of light and very dark amber.

Corn Bread

Serves 5 to 6

2 cups sifted white cornmeal

$\frac{1}{2}$ teaspoon salt

$\frac{1}{2}$ teaspoon baking soda

2 teaspoons Royal Baking Powder

3 eggs, beaten

1 tablespoon lard

1 tablespoon butter

2 cups sour milk, or buttermilk

9 x 10-inch pan

Sift cornmeal, salt, soda, and baking powder into a mixing bowl. Stir in the beaten eggs. At this point set the baking pan in the oven with the lard and butter added. Pour the sour milk into the cornmeal batter and stir well. Now remove the pan from the oven and tilt it all around to oil the whole surface of the pan. Pour off into the batter what fat remains. Mix well and pour the batter into the hot pan. Cornmeal batter must be poured into a sizzling hot pan, otherwise it will stick. Bake at 400° for 25 to 30 minutes. Remove and cut into squares. Serve hot.

Note: Sometimes we would add a tablespoon of lard to the baking pan and return it to the oven to heat. Then we would pour the batter in, forcing the extra fat into the corners of the pan. (When cooked, the corner pieces of bread would have a lacy, crispy edge and there would be quite a bit of competition for those pieces when it was placed on the table.)

Hog-butchering breakfast was the kind of occasion when we would open some of the wild strawberry preserves we had made in mid-May and the wild blackberry jelly we had put up in July.

The Taste of Country Cooking (1976)

Raymond Sokolov

An Original Old-Fashioned Yankee Clambake

Raymond Sokolov (b. 1941) already had a career as a Paris-based correspondent for *Newsweek* behind him when in 1973, back in the U.S., he became restaurant critic of *The New York Times*. There his erudite reporting introduced the Hunan and Sichuan dishes that were beginning to appear on Chinese menus and gave readers an early look at the rise of nouvelle cuisine. Currently a food columnist for *The Wall Street Journal*, Sokolov is also the author of *The Saucier's Apprentice* (1976), *Why We Eat What We Eat* (1991), *The Cook's Canon* (2003), and a biography of A. J. Liebling, *Wayward Reporter* (1980). Here, in a chapter from his collection *Fading Feast: A Compendium of Disappearing American Regional Foods* (1981), he looks back enticingly at a tradition almost past: the Yankee clambake.

■ ■ ■

The most exclusive and elaborate event in the American culinary calendar takes place on a tree-lined plot of land near Dartmouth, Massachusetts, in August. Last year, Wilfred Morrison, the proprietor of Davoll's General Store in the nearby hamlet of Russells Mills, was the *chef de cuisine*. He presided over a brigade of more than one hundred *sous-chefs*, who had worked for days to get this multicourse extravaganza onto the plates of five hundred lucky guests, who had signed up in time to secure a seat at one of the long wooden picnic tables across the path from Morrison's al fresco kitchen. Two thousand eager gourmets were turned away.

Unlike most modern chefs, Morrison did not cook with gas on a massive professional range. Indeed, he had no range at all, but insisted on a traditional, one might even say aboriginal, oven constructed, *à l'improviste*, from rocks, wood, and canvas. No wire whisks, copper pans, or Cuisinarts were allowed on the premises, only the canonical utensils sanctified by ninety previous years' experience: long-handled steel shovels.

The Allen's Neck Clambake began as an outing for the Sunday school of the local Quaker meeting in 1888. Originally held on Horseneck Beach, it moved slightly inland after 1903, but it is still within smelling distance of the Massachusetts shore in the state's biggest surviving agricultural region, just to the east of the Rhode Island line. Getting lost in the maze of winding country roads running around farms is inevitable the first time you visit the area. The rational highway system of modern America is only minutes away, but just far enough to preserve the area from creeping exurbia. And because of this isolation from the socioeconomic mainstream, the life of the region has been spared the worst, most deracinating shocks that have shaken much of the rest of New England. A community of dirt farmers and gentry with a conservative outlook is holding its own on the east branch of the Westport River. And the Allen's Neck Clambake is its high-water mark, a historic ritual that transcends its official purpose of raising funds for the Friends Meeting House.

When working folk and local Brahmins sit down side by side over paper plates filled with steaming clams and ears of corn redolent of rockweed, there is a spirit of old-time, small-town democracy in the salt air, the same spirit that once animated town meetings in New England. Perhaps the mood is mainly symbolic, but at least the symbolism is pure and unadulterated by slickness, shortcuts, and Chamber of Commerce hoopla. The genius of this clambake is its unremitting, stiff-necked fidelity to a method of cooking and a menu that have not changed since the dawn of the Republic, when settlers learned to cook the corn and shellfish of their newfound land in ad hoc ovens the Indians had invented and perfected on the rocks and sand of that same coast.

The New England clambake has as much claim to the title of our national feast as Thanksgiving, except that Thanksgiving flourishes everywhere, while the clambake has mostly fallen into neglect and been distorted by modern notions. Even some of the clambake's most devoted adherents will succumb to the proddings of their sensual natures and embellish the bake with lobsters. Others, hoping to simplify the cumbersome, labor-intensive process of watching and controlling the bake, conduct this chthonic cookery in a metal prison that started out as a washtub.

At Allen's Neck, the bakemaster has always held the line against lobster fancification. And teams of willing weed-rakers and rock-pilers have been turning out early and late for more than fourscore years. This combination of abundant manpower and a menu codified right down to the tripe (see recipe) has preserved the original Yankee clambake in as rugged and pristine form as modern conditions will allow.

Today, it is true, the menfolk no longer sail a catboat into Buzzard's Bay for fresh fish. And clams are no longer dug locally. The fish (mackerel) comes already filleted from a wholesaler. Clams arrive from Maine, where they were dug commercially in Machias Bay. But the corn is picked in a local field the morning of the bake. And the process of the clambake itself is militantly unchanged.

On the eve of the bake last summer, some twenty volunteers, men and boys, waded into the east branch of the Westport, collecting rockweed under the watchful eye of Karl Erickson, a retired schoolteacher with twenty years' experience on the clambake committee. He picked up a handful of rockweed and pointed out the blisters all over it. "They're full of water," he explained. "When they're heated, that water makes our bake into a natural steam pressure cooker."

It was almost nightfall before the pickup truck on the riverbank was full of rockweed. Meanwhile, other volunteers had been gathering the rocks and the hardwood for the fire.

By 7:15 a.m. the day of the bake, all of the raw materials had been assembled at the site, except for the corn, still to be picked, and the clams, which would soon be laboriously sorted and washed in a boat filled with seawater on the sand at Horseneck Beach.

At the site, a team of teenagers started building the huge fire. They began with a concrete apron covered with a platform of long green oak stringers, on which were laid alternating levels of cut hardwood and stones. One girl, hefting a granite rock as big as her head and passing it on down the line, said, "This is great. All these years we've been coming here and we never knew this was how it was done."

Eventually, she and her friends had built an oblong rock and wood structure that stood five feet high and measured about twelve feet long and four feet across. There was kindling on top and gasoline-soaked paper underneath. At 8:45 the fire was lit and roared away brightly. "Utopia," said Karl Erickson, "is when it burns so there's not a stick of wood left, just charcoal and stones." By 9:00, all the food was cut and trimmed, bagged and racked, ready to cook. J. T. Smith, ninety-one years old and a former bakemaster, looked on approvingly.

By 10:45, the fire had burned down to a pyramid of rocks. It was time for the pullers. With their long-handled shovels, they dragged the hot rocks off the cement apron so that the charcoal and ash could be cleaned away. No wood smoke should defile the bake.

Speed was crucial so that the rocks wouldn't cool any more than absolutely necessary. As soon as the cement was clean, back went the rocks. On top of them came the rockweed. The food was set out in layers on the rockweed: the racks of clams first, the delicate corn last. Then the whole sizzling pile was covered with a soaked sheet and six layers of canvas; the edges of these cloths, where they met the ground, were caulked with rockweed. Clouds of vapor rose when the sheet went on, but the extra canvas shrouding and the rockweed sealed in the steam. The last edge was tamped down at 11:45. Twenty minutes later, steam pressure made the canvas billow up taut as a sail in a good wind.

Now Ralph Macomber could rest while the clambake baked. This burly sawyer had supervised the trickiest part of the ritual, the breaking down of the fire and the piling up of the hot stones. And at 1:00, as 500 eager guests gathered round, it was his job to reach down, pull up a corner of the canvas, and gingerly extract a finger-burning clam. Out of the shell it came, and into his mouth it went. Macomber pronounced it done.

Off came the six canvases and the sheet. Ravenous diners took their places at the tables, and efficient teams of servers moved about, distributing the mountain of food. On my paper plate was a feast without equal. The clams, especially, were remarkable—fresh and tender and permeated with the aroma of rockweed and ocean. I was happy. Wilfred Morrison was happy. Karl Erickson was happy. Ralph Macomber was happy. We stuffed ourselves with an abandon that itself is part of the clambake tradition. The late Skipper Howland, a chronicler of New England life and the grandfather of my host at Allen's Neck, wrote the classic description:

> The first bowl of clams disappears with surprising speed. Another
> relay appears, reinforced with fish, corn, and potatoes from the bake,
> and slices of brown bread and helpings of onions from the center of
> the table. But from this point on how can I attempt to set down in
> words, which after all are poor things, the disposal of all these gifts

of God, which have been for the most part cooked in the good earth, seasoned by the salts thereof, uncontaminated by the impurities of civilization, fresh as the dawn; in such abundance that no one has to bolt his first helping to ensure a second, third, or even a fourth—except to say that, when every soul here gathered has filled himself or herself to comfortable capacity, and those who smoke have ignited the butt ends of Manila cheroots that have come tied in bunches with buttercup-yellow ribbands in leaden chests from the Far Eastern Isles, the day sinks softly and peacefully down toward its end in a pale blue smoky haze of contentment; a contentment that can come only from the know-how of making the most of Nature's gifts and the satisfaction arising from such knowledge, which has been acquired, not from endowed institutions of learning, but from attendance at that greatest of all universities, the outdoor world.

Clambake to Feed 500 Paying Guests Plus 125 Workers

(*From the* Allen's Neck Friends Cook Book)

A safe, smooth, convenient site	1 truckload of rockweed
1 cord of dry hardwood in 4-foot lengths	1 ½ tons of stones about the size of a cantaloupe melon

All clambakes are not alike; they vary in menu. Allen's Neck always has the same menu:

22 bushels clams	100 pounds onions
200 pounds sausage	20 large watermelons
75 pounds fish fillets	85 homemade pies
150 pounds tripe	50 pounds butter
75 dozen sweet corn	Coffee
3 bushels sweet potatoes	Milk
30 pans of dressing	

SPECIAL REQUIREMENTS

A group of enthusiastic workers willing to work from Monday through Thursday; without these people no clambake of this size would succeed.

The clams must be culled and washed in fresh seawater, in a boat at Horseneck Beach.

The sweet corn must be fresh and sweet—harvested the day of the clam-bake. The rockweed must be fresh and kept moist.

After all the food from the bake has been consumed, it is hard to imag-ine how 20 large watermelons and 85 pies can disappear, but they do! No person should ever leave an Allen's Neck Clambake unless he or she is "full to the gills."

Now the last, and most important, ingredient of all is to ask our dear Lord for good weather.

Four recipes by Harriet Tucker, adapted from the *Allen's Neck Friends Cook Book:*

Stewed Squash à la Nantucket

1 large Hubbard squash   Molasses

(1) Cut a large Hubbard squash into 6 pieces. Peel hard part off.

(2) Place in large skillet, tender side down. Cover with $^1/_3$ part molas-ses, $^2/_3$ part water. Stew uncovered for 1 hour. Turn shell side down. Con-tinue to cook until tender. Serve hot.

YIELD: 6 servings.

Corn Pudding

12 ears raw corn, grated	1 tablespoon butter
$^3/_4$ cup milk	Salt
2 eggs	Pepper
1 tablespoon sugar	

Combine all ingredients and bake in a shallow dish for 1 hour at 350 degrees.

YIELD: 6 to 8 servings.

Cape Cod Baked Beans

1 pound pea beans	3 tablespoons molasses
3 tablespoons brown sugar	$\frac{1}{2}$ teaspoon dry mustard
1 teaspoon salt	3 tablespoons catsup
1 teaspoon onion	2 cups strong coffee
$\frac{3}{4}$ pound lean salt pork, slashed through rind	

(1) Soak beans overnight.

(2) Preheat oven to 325 degrees.

(3) Add all ingredients and boil for 1 hour.

(4) Then bake for a few hours or until done, adding water as needed and pushing salt pork down into beans.

YIELD: 6 to 8 servings.

Lobster Stew

Salt	1 bay leaf
4 1½-pound lobsters	2 cloves
1 tablespoon sugar	4 tablespoons butter
2 cups clam juice	Flour
1 sprig parsley	Pepper
1 rib celery	Cayenne
1 carrot, scraped and cut in rounds	Dry Sherry
1 small onion, peeled and finely chopped	4 cups light cream

(1) Boil lobsters for 15 minutes in lightly salted water to cover, with the sugar.

(2) Remove all meat from shells. Reserve both meat and shells.

(3) In a large pot, combine clam juice, 2 cups water, parsley, celery, carrot, onion, bay leaf, and cloves. Bring to a boil, add lobster shells, and simmer for 30 minutes.

(4) While the shells are simmering, cut the lobster meat into chunks (leave the claw meat whole).

(5) In a skillet, heat the butter until it foams. When the foam subsides, add the lobster meat and sauté at low heat. While you do this, sprinkle the meat lightly with flour, salt, pepper, and a dash of cayenne. When the pepper has browned lightly, add 2 tablespoons of sherry. When that comes to a boil, add a cup of the shell cooking liquid without straining out any coral or tomalley.

(6) Add cream. When the stew is heated throughout, add more sherry and/or broth or other seasonings to taste.

YIELD: 6 to 8 servings.

Fading Feast (1981)

Guy Davenport

The Anthropology of Table Manners
from Geophagy Onward

The title of one of Guy Davenport's collections—*The Geography of the Imagination* (1981)—could easily be applied to his whole extensive body of fiction, essays, and poetry. Born in the foothills of the Appalachian Mountains in South Carolina, Davenport (1927– 2005) taught at the University of Kentucky while following his wide-ranging curiosity through the byways of history and literature. "The imagination," he wrote, "is like the drunk man who lost his watch, and must get drunk to find it. It is as intimate as speech and custom, and to trace its ways we need to re-educate our eyes." This little discourse on table manners is a splendid instance of his capacity to rove freely through an apparently limitless store of erudition.

■ ■ ■

A businessman now risen to a vice-presidency tells me that in his apprentice days he used to cross deepest Arkansas as a mere traveling salesman, and that there were certain farms at which men from his company put up overnight, meals being included in the deal. Once, on a new route, he appeared at breakfast after a refreshing sleep in a feather bed to face a hardy array of buttery eggs, biscuits, apple pie, coffee, and fatback.

This latter item was unfamiliar to him and from the looks of it he was damned if he would eat it. He knew his manners, however, and in passing over the fatback chatted with the lady of the house about how eating habits tend to be local, individual, and a matter of how one has been raised. He hoped she wouldn't take it wrong that he, unused to consuming fatback, left it untouched on his plate.

The genial Arkansas matron nodded to this politely, agreeing that food is different all over the world.

She then excused herself, flapped her copious apron, and retired from the kitchen. She returned with a double-barreled shotgun which she trained on the traveling salesman, with the grim remark, "Eat hit."

And eat hit he did.

Our traveler's offense was to reject what he had been served, an insult in practically every code of table manners. Snug in an igloo, the Eskimo scrapes gunk from between his toes and politely offers it as garnish for your blubber. Among the Penan of the upper Baram in Sarawak you eat your friend's snot as a sign of your esteem. There are dinner parties in Africa where the butter for your stewed calabash will be milked from your hostess's hair. And you dare not refuse.

Eating is always at least two activities: consuming food and obeying a code of manners. And in the manners is concealed a program of taboos as rigid as Deuteronomy. We rational, advanced, and liberated Americans may not, as in the Amazon, serve the bride's mother as the wedding feast; we may not, as in Japan, burp our appreciation, or as in Arabia, eat with our fingers. Every child has suffered initiation into the mysteries of table manners: keep your elbows off the table, ask for things to be passed rather than reach, don't cut your bread with a knife, keep your mouth closed while chewing, don't talk with food in your mouth, and on and on, and all of it witchcraft and another notch upward in the rise of the middle class.

Our escapes from civilization are symptomatic: the first rule we break is that of table manners. Liberty wears her reddest cap; all is permitted. I remember a weekend away from paratrooper barracks when we dined on eggs scrambled in Jack Daniel's, potato chips and peanut brittle, while the Sergeant Major, a family man of bankerish decorum in ordinary times, sang falsetto "There Will be Peace in the Valley" stark naked except for cowboy boots and hat.

But to children, hardest pressed by gentility at the table, a little bending of the rules is Cockayne itself. One of my great culinary moments was being taken as a tot to my black nurse's house to eat clay. "What this child needs," she had muttered one day while we were out, "is a bait of clay." Everybody in South Carolina knew that blacks, for reasons unknown, fancied clay. Not until I came to read Toynbee's *A Study of History* years later did I learn that eating clay, or geophagy, is a prehistoric habit (it fills the stomach until you can bring down another aurochs) surviving only in West Africa and South Carolina. I even had the opportunity, when I met Toynbee at a scholarly do, to say that I had been in my day geophagous. He gave me a strange, British look.

The eating took place in a bedroom, for the galvanized bucket of clay was kept under the bed, for the cool. It was blue clay from a creek, the consistency of slightly gritty ice cream. It lay smooth and delicious-looking in its pail of clear water. You scooped it out and ate it from your hand. The taste was wholesome, mineral, and emphatic. I have since eaten many things in respectable restaurants with far more trepidation.

The technical names have yet to be invented for some of the submissions to courtly behavior laid upon me by table manners. At dinners cooked by brides in the early days of their apprenticeship I have forced down boiled potatoes as crunchy as water chestnuts, bleeding pork, gravy in which you could have pickled a kettle of herring, and a *purée* of raw chicken livers.

I have had reports of women with skimpy attention to labels who have made biscuits with plaster of Paris and chicken feed that had to be downed by timid husbands and polite guests; and my venturesome Aunt Mae once prepared a salad with witch hazel, and once, in a moment of abandoned creativity, served a banana pudding that had hard-boiled eggs hidden in it here and there.

Raphael Pumpelly tells in his memoirs of the West in the good old days about a two-gunned, bearded type who rolled into a Colorado hotel with a vi- and wrapped in a bandana. This he requested the cook to prepare, and seated at a table, napkined, wielding knife and fork with manners passably Eastern, consulting the salt and pepper shakers with a nicety, gave a fair imitation of a gentleman eating. And then, with a gleam in his eye and a great burp, he sang out at the end, "Thar, by God, I swore I'd eat that man's liver and I've done it!"

The meaning of this account for those of us who are great scientists is that this hero of the West chose to eat his enemy's liver in the dining room of a hotel, with manners. Eating as mere consumption went out thousands of years ago; we have forgotten what it is. Chaplin boning the nails from his stewed shoe in *The Gold Rush* is thus an incomparable moment of satire, epitomizing all that we have heard of British gentlemen dressing for dinner in the Congo (like Livingstone, who made Stanley wait before the famous encounter until he could dig his formal wear out of his kit).

Ruskin and Turner never dined together, though an invitation was once sent. Turner knew that his manners weren't up to those of the refined Ruskins, and said so, explaining graphically that, being toothless, he sucked his meat. Propriety being propriety, there was nothing to be done, and the great painter and his great explicator and defender were damned to dine apart.

Nor could Wittgenstein eat with his fellow dons at a Cambridge high table. One wishes that the reason were more straightforward than it is. Wittgenstein, for one thing, wore a leather jacket, with zipper, and dons at high table must wear academic gowns and a tie. For another, Wittgenstein thought it undemocratic to eat on a level fourteen inches higher than the students (at, does one say, low table?).

The code of Cambridge manners could not insist that the philosopher change his leather jacket for more formal gear, nor could it interfere with his conscience. At the same time it could in no wise permit him to dine at high table improperly dressed. The compromise was that the dons sat at high table, the students at their humbler tables, and Wittgenstein ate between, at a card table, separate but equal, and with English decorum unfractured.

Maxim's declined to serve a meal to Lyndon Baines Johnson, at the time President of the United States, on the grounds that its staff did not have a recipe for Texas barbecue, though what they meant was that they did not know how to serve it or how to criticize Monsieur le Président's manners in eating it.

The best display of manners on the part of a restaurant I have witnessed was at the Imperial Ramada Inn in Lexington, Kentucky, into the Middle Lawrence Welk Baroque dining room of which I once went with the photographer Ralph Eugene Meatyard (disguised as a businessman), the Trappist Thomas Merton (in mufti, dressed as a tobacco farmer with a tonsure), and an editor of Fortune who had wrecked his Hertz car coming from the airport and was covered in spattered blood from head to toe. Hollywood is used to such things (Linda Darnell having a milk shake with Frankenstein's monster between takes), and Rome and New York, but not Lexington, Kentucky. Our meal was served with no comment whatever from the waitresses, despite Merton's downing six martinis and the Fortune editor stanching his wounds with all the napkins.

Posterity is always grateful for notes on the table manners of the famous, if only because this information is wholly gratuitous and unenlightening. What does it tell us that Montaigne glupped his food? I have eaten with Allen Tate, whose sole gesture toward the meal was to stub out his cigarette in an otherwise untouched chef's salad, with Isak Dinesen when she toyed with but did not eat an oyster, with Louis Zukofsky who was dining on a half piece of toast, crumb by crumb.

Manners survive the test of adversity. Gertrude Ely, the Philadelphia hostess and patron of the arts, was once inspired on the spur of the moment to invite home Leopold Stokowski and his orchestra, together with a few friends. Hailing her butler, she said breezily that here were some people for pot luck.

"Madam," said the butler with considerable frost, "I was given to understand that you were dining alone this evening; please accept my resignation. Good night to you all."

"Quite," said Miss Ely, who then, with a graciousness unflummoxed and absolute, set every table in the house and distributed splinters of the one baked hen at her disposal, pinches of lettuce, and drops of mayonnaise, not quite with the success of the loaves and fishes of scripture, but at least a speck of something for everybody.

I, who live almost exclusively off fried baloney, Campbell's soup, and Snickers bars, would not find table manners of any particular interest if they had not, even in a life as reclusive and uneventful as mine, involved so many brushes with death. That great woman Katherine Gilbert, the philosopher and aesthetician, once insisted that I eat some Florentine butter that Benedetto Croce had given her. I had downed several portions of muffins smeared with this important butter before I gathered from her ongoing conversation that the butter had been given her months before, somewhere in the Tuscan hills in the month of August, and that it had crossed the Atlantic, by boat, packed with her books, Italian wild flowers, prosciutto, and other mementos of Italian culture.

Fever and double vision set in some hours later, together with a delirium in which I remembered Pico della Mirandola's last meal, served him by Lucrezia and Cesare Borgia. I have been *in extremis* in Crete (octopus and what tasted like shellacked rice, with P. Adams Sitney), in Yugoslavia (a most innocent-looking melon), Genoa (calf's brains), England (a blackish stew that seemed to have been cooked in kerosene), France (an *andouillette*, Maigret's favorite feed, the point being, as I now understand, that you have to be born in Auvergne to stomach it).

Are there no counter-manners to save one's life in these unfair martyrdoms to politeness? I have heard that Edward Dahlberg had the manliness to refuse dishes at table, but he lost his friends thereby and became a misanthrope. Lord Byron once refused every course of a meal served him by Breakfast Rogers. Manet, who found Spanish food revolting but was determined to study the paintings in the Prado, spent two weeks in Madrid without eating anything at all. Some *Privatdozent* with time on his hands should compile a eulogy to those culinary stoics who, like Marc Antony, drank from yellow pools men did die to look upon. Not the starving and destitute who in wars and sieges have eaten the glue in bookbindings and corn that had passed through horses, wallpaper, bark, and animals in the zoo; but prisoners of civilization who have swallowed gristle on the twentieth attempt while keeping up a brave chitchat with the author of a novel about three generations of a passionately alive family.

Who has manners anymore, anyhow? Nobody, to be sure; everybody, if you have the scientific eye. Even the most oafish teen-ager who mainly eats from the refrigerator at home and at the Burger King in society will eventually find himself at a table where he is under the eye of his father-in-law to be, or his coach, and will make the effort to wolf his roll in two bites rather than one, and even to leave some for the next person when he is passed a bowl of potatoes. He will, naturally, still charge his whole plate with six glops of catsup, knock over his water, and eat his cake from the palm of his hand; but a wife, the country club, and the Rotarians will get him, and before he's twenty-five he'll be eating fruit salad with extended pinky, tapping his lips with the napkin before sipping his sauterne Almaden, and talking woks and fondues with the boys at the office.

Archaeologists have recently decided that we can designate the beginning of civilization in the concept of sharing the same kill, in which simple idea we can see the inception of the family, the community, the state. Of disintegrating marriages we note that Jack and Jill are no longer sleeping together when the real break is when they are no longer eating together. The table is the last unassailed rite. No culture has worn the *bonnet rouge* there, always excepting the Germans, who have never had any manners at all, of any sort.

The tyranny of manners may therefore be the pressure placed on us of surviving in hostile territories. Eating is the most intimate and at the same time the most public of biological functions. Going from dinner table to dinner table is the equivalent of going from one culture to another, even within the same family. One of my grandmothers served butter and molasses with her biscuits, the other would have fainted to see molasses on any table. One gave you coffee with the meal, the other after. One cooked greens with fatback, the other with hamhock. One put ice cubes in your tea, the other ice from the ice house. My father used to complain that he hadn't had any cold iced tea since the invention of the refrigerator. He was right.

Could either of my grandmothers, the one with English country manners, the other with French, have eaten on an airplane? What would the Roi Soleil have done with that square foot of space? My family, always shy, did not venture into restaurants until well after the Second World War. Aunt Mae drank back the tiny juglet of milk which they used to give you for coffee, and commented to Uncle Buzzie that the portions of things in these cafés are certainly stingy.

I was raised to believe that eating other people's cooking was a major accomplishment, like learning a language or how to pilot a plane. I thought for the longest time that Greeks lived exclusively off garlic and dandelions, and that Jews were so picky about their food that they seldom ate at all. Uncles who had been to France with the AEF reported that the French existed on roast rat and snails. The Chinese, I learned from a book, begin their meals with dessert. Happy people!

Manners, like any set of signals, constitute a language. It is possible to learn to speak Italian; to eat Italian, never. In times of good breeding, the rebel against custom always has table manners to violate. Diogenes assumed the polish of Daniel Boone, while Plato ate with a correctness Emily Post could have studied with profit. Thoreau, Tolstoy, and Gandhi all ate with pointed reservation, sparely, and in elemental simplicity. Calvin dined but once a day, on plain fare, and doubtless imagined the pope gorging himself on pheasant, nightingale, and minced boar in macaroni.

Honest John Adams, eating in France for the first time, found the food delicious if unidentifiable, but blushed at the conversation (a lady asked him if his family had invented sex); and Emerson once had to rap the water glass at his table when two guests, Thoreau and Agassiz, introduced the mating of turtles into the talk. Much Greek philosophy, Dr. Johnson's best one-liners, and the inauguration of the Christian religion happened at supper tables. Hitler's table-talk was so boring that Eva Braun and a field marshal once fell asleep in his face. He was in a snit for a month. Generalissimo Franco fell asleep while Nixon was talking to him at dinner. It may be that conversation over a shared haunch of emu is indeed the beginning of civilization.

To eat in silence, like the Egyptians, seems peculiarly dreadful, and stiff. Sir Walter Scott ate with a bagpipe droning in his ear and all his animals around him, and yards of babbling guests. Only the truly mad eat alone, like Howard Hughes and Stalin.

Eccentricity in table manners—one has heard of rich uncles who wear oilcloth aviator caps at table—lingers in the memory longer than other foibles. My spine tingles anew whenever I remember going into a Toddle House to find all the tables and the counter set; not only set, but served. One seat only was occupied, and that by a very eccentric man, easily a millionaire. He was, the waitress explained some days later, giving a dinner party there, but no one came. He waited and waited. He had done it several times before; no one had ever come. It was the waitress's opinion that he always forgot to send the invitations; it was mine that his guests could not bring themselves to believe them.

And there was the professor at Oxford who liked to sit under his tea table, hidden by the tablecloth, and hand up cups of tea and slices of cake from beneath. He carried on a lively conversation all the while, and most of his friends were used to this. There was always the occasional student who came to tea unaware, sat goggling the whole time, and tended to break into cold sweats and fits of stammering.

I was telling about this professor one summer evening in South Carolina, to amuse my audience with English manners. A remote cousin, a girl in her teens, who hailed from the country and had rarely considered the ways of foreigners, listened to my anecdote in grave horror, went home and had a fit.

"It took us half the night to quiet down Effie Mae," we were told sometime later. "She screamed for hours that all she could see was that buggerman under that table, with just his arm risin' up with a cup and saucer. She says she never expects to get over it."

The Geography of the Imagination (1981)

James Villas

Blessed Are We Who Serve

When James Villas (b. 1938) began writing about food and entertaining for *Town & Country* in 1972, he brought to the magazine both his Southern charm—he was born in Mecklenburg, North Carolina, and graduated from the state's university—and a streak of acerbic wit. Part snob and part country boy, Villas can be intensely fastidious about the traditions of country cooking. Here, he's a genial guide to the culture of a modern dining room, seen, for once, from the waiter's perspective.

■ ■ ■

You're seated in a fancy restaurant, and the last thing on your mind is what the captains and waiters are saying to each other—especially the things about you. Right? Well, after my week as an undercover captain in a very fancy French restaurant I now know exactly what is said. For instance:

"Forget the coffee refill on nineteen, ole buddy," directs Paul, another captain who's saucing a rack of veal at the serving table. "And how about cutting me a wagon for the dame on fourteen. For God's sake, don't do anything to raw 'em off. Dig the rock on that fat paw. Her ole man's a mark if I ever saw one—good for maybe twenty-five percent."

I'm worried that the customers might hear the crude language we tend to use among ourselves, possibly as a reaction to all the elegance and display we have to affect for the job. I'm also worried about the coffee for the couple at table nineteen.

"Forget 'em for now," Paul says. "All he cares about is snowing the chick, and besides, you can tell by the wine they're drinking he's no more than a fifteen percenter. Come on, for God's sake, step on it please with that tenderloin. . . . Quick, Jim, behind you on twenty."

I snap around just in time to pull out the table for the lady who is getting up, heading most likely for the john.

"Captain!" This is from table nineteen. "How about a little more coffee over here and a few more of those chocolate things."

I nod, back off, and go across the room to get a busboy to take care of the coffee and chocolate truffles. Then I make tracks for the silver trolley and begin carving three slices of beef. No sooner have I ladled on a bit of Bordelaise sauce and started to wipe dribbles from the edge of the hot plate than Jean-Pierre, the suave maître d'hôtel, passes by taking a new party to their table. He glances down at my handiwork, and, never for an instant losing pace with the two couples, he murmurs, "*Les bouts, n'oublie pas les bouts.*" I still haven't gotten it through my thick skull to cover the ends of the meat with sauce.

"Quick, Paul, I need vegetables," I say.

"Yeah, I know, but the bastards didn't send out enough. See if you can grab a kitchenman and . . . no, forget it . . . why don't you just run back to the kitchen yourself while I finish up the veal and I'll try to find a cover for the tenderloin. And Jim, while you're back there, for God's sake do something about that sauce on your jacket."

As I break my way through the busy waiters and busboys and pantrymen, slide across the glop in the dishwashing area, grab a wet towel to wipe the Bordelaise off my dinner jacket, and stand puffing frantically on a cigarette while waiting for a chef to spoon out the neglected vegetables, I once again have the feeling I can't make it through the evening. The blood blisters on my left foot, the excruciating pain in my lower back, the dizziness from lack of anything to eat since the cheeseburger in mid-afternoon. So far I've managed to survive this self-inflicted ordeal, and no doubt I'm convinced more than ever before that the project is both noble and constructive. To my knowledge none of us highfalutin, omnipotent, forever-complaining restaurant critics has ever made any effort to experience firsthand the actual running of a great restaurant.

Okay, I know. The customer is shelling out plenty of hard cash, and he shouldn't be expected to understand why a place happens to flop miserably on any given occasion. Correct? For years that was my way of thinking too, until, that is, I began to wonder if there weren't a few hidden facts behind the scenes that could reveal ways whereby I and everybody else just might get better food and service. So I did it, and I learned a lot. Things like this:

You should expect a maître d', captain, or waiter in any first-class restaurant to be able to do anything to enhance your pleasure, but, like it or not, no matter who you are or how fat your wallet, if you don't make some small effort yourself, you'll have a very ordinary experience. You should dress properly, meaning a suit and tie for men, a nice dress for women. Deluxe restaurants have little use for clods. You should ask the captain or waiter his name when he arrives at the table. You should smile from time to time at the people serving you. For heaven's sake, you should say thank you when they do something special. And you're even better off if you can show an intelligent interest in the menu and wine list.

It seriously upsets captains and wine stewards to see guests pouring their own wine. If your glass needs refilling and everyone on the staff is busy, try to be patient a few minutes till someone has time to pour. You shouldn't go thirsty, however, and if you must pour after a short wait, go ahead. But understand that the staff will take this as a complaint. If it's deserved, make it.

Nobody on a restaurant staff is overly fond of couples (deuces), for the simple reason that they require virtually the same amount of time that it takes to serve four, and for half the tips or less. Singles are never loved, contrary to what anybody says. Quite often a maître d' will turn down dozens of same-day requests for deuces in order to hold space for parties of four, six, or eight.

Since those working the floor receive hardly any salary to speak of (union or no union), tips matter more to them than anything else in life. Almost everywhere (except New York City) tips are pooled and distributed after lunch and dinner among either the entire floor staff (as at my restaurant) or those working their separate stations: generally a full cut for captains, waiters, and wine stewards; $3/4$-cut for kitchenmen; and $1/2$-cut for busboys. Although this means you're really tipping many for a job performed by one or two, don't try to take out your wrath on the system (unless, of course, you found the service rotten). If you automatically stiff the bill thinking the tip is basically impersonal and meaningless, remember you're only decreasing the cut (i.e., livelihood) collected by those who served you well. (Even if you palm a captain, he's expected to contribute that tip to the pool—except in New York City.) Also don't forget that knowledge of your stinginess filters down quickly among the staff, and this could have a disastrous effect on your next visit, no matter who waits on you.

Often the bottle of wine a guest orders is indicative of what the tip will be, but we prayed for 25 percent, were thankful for 20, and said ugly things about those who left only 15 (previously I had rarely tipped over 15 percent in even the finest restaurants).

The best way to tip? Most people simply add a percentage to the credit card slip (either in one lump sum or, say, 15 percent for the waiters and 5 percent for the captain), but nobody impressed us more than those who made the rare gesture of personally handing us the tips while expressing thanks. Does palming a maître d' or captain a five before you sit down guarantee special attention and possibly better food? You can bet your bottom dollar it does!

Nothing irritates a staff so much or causes a greater disruption of service than when customers jump up and leave the table for one reason or another, especially while the main courses are being served.

It hurts when an obviously satisfied customer who's leaving doesn't even have the graciousness to thank those who've provided good service—palmed tip or no palmed tip. This discourtesy is never forgotten.

Before taking on this mission I had no idea what I was getting myself into, but one thing was for sure: the plan was ingenious. Since I was determined to work totally under cover for one week in a deluxe, expensive restaurant and couldn't risk my name or face being recognized in New York, contact was made in Chicago with Jovan Trboyevic, owner of the well-known and

highly praised Le Perroquet. Now it so happened that one of Jovan's old
friends and colleagues had recently opened a new luxury restaurant in New
York, so our story was that the friend was sending this promising waiter by
the name of Jim Anderson (my alias) out to Chicago to recieve initial training
as a captain by Jovan and his veteran staff. Jovan agreed to all the terms:
nobody except Jovan himself was to have an inkling as to what I was about
(with the polite understanding that if I suspected betrayal, I'd discontinue
the project on the spot); I would stay at the Drake Hotel but there would be
a fake address and phone drop elsewhere in case someone wanted to contact
me; I would work both lunch and dinner, keeping the same hours as the
others; I would be treated by Jovan just like any other employee, even nas-
tily if necessary; and I would turn any and all tips over to the other captains
to be included in the normal distribution since, after all, I was there only for
the experience. Suffice it to say that the boys bought the story hook, line,
and sinker and were convinced from the beginning that this Anderson guy
was no more than a New York hashhouse waiter with a sloppy Southern accent who was aspiring to the restaurant big time. How did I happen to know
French? By slaving with a bunch of frogs for a year in some French dive on
New York's West Side, that's how.

From the moment I showed up for my first lunch it was pretty obvious I was working in a first-class restaurant, one of the best in the country.
On the surface Le Perroquet manifests just about what you would expect
(and more) of a luxury restaurant in this country: muted mustard and light
green murals, red velvet banquettes with appliquéd cushions, starched linen
tablecloths, fine etched crystal, silver flatware, small individual table lamps,
Lalique flower vases, silver ice buckets, bottles of mineral water on every
table, fancy complimentary hors d'oeuvres and chocolate truffles, and so
forth. It's all very high class, to say the least, but what was to amaze me continuously during my week there was the assemblage of experts who make
the place function so beautifully: three young Americans, no less, holding
down the important jobs of head chef, pastry chef, and wine steward; a per-
fectionist Mexican bartender who has no patience with staffers who don't
follow his directions on how to place drink orders; a French maître d'hôtel
who can detect (and reject) a slob after ten seconds on the phone; a brigade of
American, French, Syrian, Mexican, and Spanish waiters and busboys who

don't seem to need to speak much English in order to communicate; and, of course, the dynamic force of Jovan himself, an elegant, proud, often melancholy Yugoslav who is brutally frank in all matters, who proclaims himself a philosophical anarchist in his never-ending struggle against mediocrity and boredom, and who doesn't think twice about throwing out customers who cause unnecessary problems and embarrassment.

So there I was that first miserable day, determined to make a go of this thing yet frightened stiff that somebody on the staff (not to mention the customers) would decide there was just something too weird about this fellow. Even the most illiterate, inexperienced greasy-spoon waiter knows how to carry a full tray of drinks, write down an order, and serve food without dumping it in the guy's lap. I didn't, and in case you suffer under the illusion (as I always have) that a captain in a restaurant does no more than smile, take orders, flame an occasional duck, and grab for tips, let me clue you in. In addition to having to execute the most menial tasks, I (like everyone else in Jovan's employ) was expected to be able to cup ashtrays deftly when emptying them, hold lamp wires up with my foot while pulling out tables, pour wine across three bodies when a wall made it impossible to pass behind a customer, gracefully pick up a plate of food and place a clean napkin over a spill without drawing too much attention to the customer's sloppiness, and, of course, prepare and sauce in a matter of seconds an array of exquisite dishes on a flaming hot serving table not much bigger than a TV set.

No task, I was to learn quickly, is too demeaning for any captain who wants things to run smoothly, no matter how proud or experienced he may be. By the same token, it's understood in a great restaurant that regardless of whether you wear a tuxedo or a waiter's white jacket or a kitchenman's lowly black uniform, success (i.e., satisfying customers, keeping your job, and, above all, raking in as much money as possible from the split on tips) is determined by unrelenting teamwork. If a captain sees a dirty dish on a table, he doesn't wait for a busboy to pick it up; if a patron takes a cigarette out, a waiter doesn't hesitate to rush over and light it; and it's nothing extraordinary for a wine steward to fetch a quick pot of coffee, slice a side of smoked salmon, or help a hurried captain dish out at the serving table. As a result of this interchange, a remarkable sense of togetherness develops behind the scenes, an understanding on the part of everyone that if you expect to make a decent livelihood, you'd sure as hell better respect and help the next guy.

By the third day I had the basics pretty well under control, thanks mainly to the sympathetic help of everybody on the staff. I had grasped the technique of referring to tables and customers by number and writing down orders accordingly—vegetable terrine for #2 on table 14, for instance; I reeled off all the specialities with their exotic descriptions, encouraging customers to sample these extraordinary dishes instead of the more standard preparations listed on the menu; I learned how to decant fine red wines at the table and handle dishes and silver and crystal without so much as a tingle; I mastered the delicate art of "pushing" soufflés at dinner by telling customers how delicious they were and reminding them that, of course, these must be ordered in advance. I'd even begun to develop that inimitable look of self-confidence and authority I've always admired in a good captain.

Of course there were disasters, like when I poured '61 Haut Brion into a glass containing humble Beaujolais (the customers were given a new bottle, and I received a blast from Jovan), or when, not having any idea what to do when a slimy *crème caramel* slid off the plate onto a lady's dress, I frantically picked it up from her lap with my fingers, dropped it in a napkin, and inspired something close to hysteria on the part of Madame and staff members alike. I also had to be told constantly by a particularly concerned Mexican waiter always to stand erect when taking orders (Jovan disagreed) and never, but never, to touch the table while talking with a customer. The maître d' had to remind me time and again to be sure to clear away extra place settings, to stand by a table so as not to turn my back to customers, and never, heaven forbid, to serve my dish if the customer happened to be away from the table. These things seemed to work themselves out, however, and I felt that generally I was making fairly good progress.

I gradually became accustomed to much of the same way of life the other guys knew forty-nine weeks out of the year, every day except Saturday lunch and Sunday (when the restaurant was closed). The routine, which is no doubt generally like that in any good restaurant, is deadly and never varies. Around ten-thirty in the morning you show up to analyze the reservations with Jovan and Jean-Pierre, study the special dishes to be offered at lunch, deal with the fresh linen and setting of tables, see that the cold dishes are properly displayed and the sherbet containers spotless, answer the blasting phone and take reservations, on and on, one thing after another. If the laundry isn't delivered, you're sunk and can only pray there's still enough new stock in supply for those tables you can't fake with last night's linen. If a waiter calls in sick, you have to rechart stations and figure out who can best cover for him. If the crayfish pâté looks or tastes wrong, an equally exotic dish must be decided on and prepared in split-second time back in the kitchen. Shortly before noon you change from ratty garb to tux or uniform, exposing holes in T-shirts, pale white skin that's rarely exposed to the sun, a gut bloated from too much wee-hours beer, feet forever swollen from pacing the job some twelve to thirteen hours a day. Soon you hear on the intercom the rugged voice of the off-duty cop downstairs giving the name of the first customer coming up in the elevator. The bowing and scraping and sweeping of arms begins as the mechanics of still another lunchtime are put into motion.

You continue till three, three-fifteen, three-thirty, or till the last guests move toward the elevator. You're anxious to collect your cut of the tips (distributed after every meal around the bar or back in the pantry), and you've had nothing to eat and you're a bit pooped. Instead of sticking around to take chances on what some of the guys who never leave the place are served at four-thirty, you head out for a cheeseburger and fries, dash home, and maybe watch a little TV or soak in a hot tub before heading back to the restaurant around five-fifteen.

Friday night is booked solid, and since there is no reasonable way to turn down anybody who reserved two weeks in advance, you're stuck with far too many deuces to make the evening truly profitable in the way of tips. "Fifty-five dollars, maybe sixty apiece for the captains," guesses Paul, "but then you never know. See those two guys on four? They're weekend regulars and actually pretty nice and generous. Give 'em plenty of attention and they'll leave a good twenty-five percent. The couple on six is also around about once a week, but remember, the one thing that infuriates that guy is having the menus pushed on him till he asks for them. And the two on twelve—well, I heard those Southern accents when they arrived, and if they're like most Southerners they can't count past fifteen. No offense to you, ole buddy, but Southerners are rotten tippers, the worst."

Enter Tennessee Williams and party of three. The great man himself, and Jovan suggests privately I take on the table in hopes of reaping an interesting scenario ("But no special attention, Jim. He gets no better treatment than any other customer in this restaurant"). Williams smiles, says there'll be no cocktails, and asks what nice dry white wine I'd recommend.

"Sir, would you care to see the wine list?" I answer.

"Naw, I don't feel up to having to wrestle with a long wine list tonight," he drawls, "but you look like the type of captain who'll choose something that's very appropriate for the occasion—hee, hee."

Of course I have no idea what occasion he's talking about or why the giggle, but I nevertheless discuss it with Alain, a wine steward, and together we decide on a fairly rare but reasonably priced Pavillon Blanc du Château Margaux.

"This is superrrb," cries Williams after checking the nose like the old pro he is and taking a huge gulp. "We'll just have to have two bottles, young man, and I'll have an explanation of where you happen to be from with that marrrvelous accent. Now don't tell me. It's Georgia, or maybe South Carolina, but it's *not* Mississippi."

Suddenly I notice the man at the next table reaching for his bottle of wine in the ice bucket, so, leaving Williams's question dangling, I excuse myself momentarily and pour the wine in a flash. I have every intention of returning to Williams's table to absorb every word I can, but no sooner have I placed the bottle back on ice than a waiter who's looking deathly pale asks if I could cover his station and handle serving the soufflés on twelve while he goes to the bathroom. Action is at its peak throughout the restaurant, with not one captain, waiter, or busboy to spare. Held prisoner by two raspberry soufflés that must be spooned out immediately, I'm unable to help poor Roberto, who is struggling with both the pastry wagon and sherbet trolley for the dessert orders on sixteen. Dirty dishes should be cleaned off twenty, but it seems all the busboys are back in the pantry preparing espresso—and besides, though I know my attitude is wrong, I've really lost all desire to try to make things nice for two dolts who've nursed Martinis throughout an entire glorious meal and kept business papers spread out in every direction on the table.

"Hey, captain," I hear behind me, as I feel a hand being placed around my shoulders. "See that cute little thing sitting in front of me over there? Well, I got a big favor to ask of you. See, it's her birthday tonight, and I was just wondering if maybe the restaurant had a little special cake or something. And I was also wondering if later on you could come by and, you know, just give her a little kiss on the cheek and wish her a happy birthday. Really would give her a big thrill, and, don't worry, I'll make it all worth your time—ya know what I mean?"

"Not in this restaurant you don't!" Jovan booms at me. "You inform the guy this place is no playground." Suffice it to say I did a little hand-kissing, then watched the oaf walk out without so much as a fare-thee-well.

As I pass by twenty to check on the wine glasses, I notice the attractive party of three is still seriously involved in their comparative tasting of two first-growth Bordeaux and two fine California Cabernets. One lady, two gentlemen. Like many of the customers, they ordered their food intelligently, asked me the details of each preparation, and, in general, have conducted themselves in such a delightful manner that I find waiting on them an absolute joy. Although Le Perroquet has an exquisite selection of cheeses included in the price of dinner, I've learned not to waste my breath suggesting this course to those who obviously couldn't care less. But for the party at this table, I don't even ask but make the special effort to present the wicker tray, discuss which cheeses I feel would go nicely with the wines, and, although not doubting the ability of the waiter to cut the cheeses properly, choose to serve them myself. And, as I suspected, these sensible souls order no more than a little fresh sherbet for dessert, espresso, and a bit of Cognac. More than likely they'll tip me a ten-in-hand (which it so happens they eventually do), but even if they didn't, I would still consider it a privilege to have served them.

"Jim, do you think you can handle that scene on twenty-one?" whispers Alain.

Rushing up to Williams's table, I see that the drooping head of the guest sitting in front of the playwright is practically touching his salmon steak.

"Excuse me, captain," says Williams calmly, "but it appears that one of my companions has been stricken by an attack of acute exhaustion necessitating an immediate cup of strong black coffee." (I jotted down that line the second I got back to the pantry.) Strangely enough, the other two guests never stop their conversation or so much as glance over to see if this guy is alive, and even Mr. Williams seems too accustomed to his friend's condition to become in any way alarmed.

It's 12:30 A.M. With only one couple still lingering over coffee, Jean-Pierre and I stand in the small area behind Gino's bar where throughout the evening we've left cigarettes smoldering in a filthy ashtray. Although I know some of the boys are back in the pantry snitching food from the cooler and finishing up whatever was left on the trolleys and even on plates, I'm too exhausted to be hungry. All I want now is to go out and get drunk, relax, forget. Returning to check the dining room, I see Dan, Roberto, Alain, Paul, Zigi, all standing and waiting and praying it won't be too much longer before they can finish up, collect their tips, and leave.

Finally the time came for Jovan to reveal my cover-up to the staff–I didn't have the guts to do it myself. All the guests had left, Paul had just announced that a certain party had tipped exactly $7 on a $410 bill, and a group of us were standing at the bar bemoaning the outcome of the evening's sacred tip sheets.

"And just what do you think of that, Monsieur Villas?" bolted Jovan, putting his hand on my shoulder.

No reaction from anybody–anybody!

"Gentlemen, look here," he continued. "What would you say if I told you we've got a phony creep in the group whose name is not Anderson?"

Jean-Pierre raised his eyes, glanced at Jovan, then at me, then back to Jovan. As the explanation continued, a formidable silence came over the rather frightened men as they all glared at me in disbelief. Feeling more and more rotten, I could find nothing to say but "I'm sorry," and I was sorry, for the noble project now seemed a little distasteful. These guys had become my friends. Then Gino smiled politely for the first time and Paul offered to light my cigarette and nobody reminded me it would be my turn to buy the beer. I knew a unique experience was over.

So the week came to an end. Physically, I ached and had lost five pounds; spiritually, I'd gained invaluable insight into the special world I write about. Perhaps the most important lesson I learned at Le Perroquet is that the public is dealing with pros who, if treated right, can and will move mountains to make people feel special.

But my experience in Chicago has made me ever less tolerant of those in the business who're quite obviously out to con the public. Shortly after my arrival back in New York, for instance, I had occasion to dine for the first time in one of the city's more fashionable restaurants. At the very beginning, I attempted to establish a rapport with the captain by asking his name, soliciting his opinions on the menu, taking his wine recommendation, and generally making him feel we needed and trusted him. Nothing worked. The food was garbage, the service shoddy, and the captain totally indifferent. He never supervised anything we were served, he allowed us to pour our own wine throughout the meal, he stood chatting casually with the haughty maître d'hôtel while I motioned for him. When I finally managed to wave him over to complain that my companion's calf's liver was tough as leather, he merely shrugged and suggested that perhaps she just didn't like liver. He was hopeless and should have been jobless. When time came to pay the bill, naturally he was there, hovering, pampering, eyeing. To the amount of the bill I begrudgingly added 10 percent for the incompetent waiter only because he might have been inexperienced or sick or in love.

"Did Monsieur not enjoy his meal?" questioned the captain as we brushed by, still hoping I'd palm him a bill.

"No, Monsieur did not enjoy his meal," I snapped, "and I'd like to add that the service was inexcusable."

"But Monsieur, you don't understand. Tonight was exceptionally busy, and if you could put yourself in my place, having to take care of this many people, maybe you'd understand."

Staring him straight in the eye, I was almost tempted. Then I turned, took the lady's arm, and walked out.

American Taste (1982)

chicken
marbella

This was the first main-course dish to be offered at The Silver Palate, and the distinctive colors and flavors of the prunes, olives and capers have kept it a favorite for years. It's good hot or at room temperature. When prepared with small drumsticks and wings, it makes a delicious hors d'oeuvre.

The overnight marination is essential to the moistness of the finished product: the chicken keeps and improves over several days of refrigeration; it travels well and makes excellent picnic fare.

Since Chicken Marbella is such a spectacular party dish, we give quantities to serve 10 to 12, but the recipe can successfully be divided to make a smaller amount if you wish.

4 chickens, 2 1/2 pounds each, quartered

1 head of garlic, peeled and finely puréed

1/4 cup dried oregano

coarse salt and freshly ground black pepper to taste

1/2 cup red wine vinegar

1/2 cup olive oil

1 cup pitted prunes

1/2 cup pitted Spanish green olives

1/2 cup capers with a bit of juice

6 bay leaves

1 cup brown sugar

1 cup white wine

1/4 cup Italian parsley or fresh coriander (cilantro), finely chopped

1. In a large bowl combine chicken quarters, garlic, oregano, pepper and coarse salt to taste, vinegar, olive oil, prunes, olives, capers and juice, and bay leaves. Cover and let marinate, refrigerated, overnight.

2. Preheat oven to 350°F.

3. Arrange chicken in a single layer in one or two large, shallow baking pans and spoon marinade over it evenly. Sprinkle chicken pieces with brown sugar and pour white wine around them.

4. Bake for 50 minutes to 1 hour, basting frequently with pan juices. Chicken is done when thigh pieces, pricked with a fork at their thickest, yield clear yellow (rather than pink) juice.

5. With a slotted spoon transfer chicken, prunes, olives and capers to a serving platter. Moisten with a few spoonfuls of pan juices and sprinkle generously with parsley or cilantro. Pass remaining pan juices in a sauceboat.

6. To serve Chicken Marbella cold, cool to room temperature in cooking juices before transferring to a serving platter. If chicken has been covered and refrigerated, allow it to return to room temperature before serving. Spoon some of the reserved juice over chicken.

16 pieces, 10 or more portions

Julee Rosso & Sheila Lukins, *The Silver Palate Cookbook* (1982)

If Julia Child was a teacher, Julee Rosso and Sheila Lukins in their *Silver Palate Cookbook* were more like coaches, writing in a chatty, celebratory style but conveying a great deal of information along the way. Their Chicken Marbella is a recipe that cut a huge swath through company dinners in the 1980s and never really disappeared.

Lillian Hellman &
Peter Feibleman

from Eating Together: Recipes & Recollections

To the public, New Orleans–born Lillian Hellman (1905–1984) was known for her path-breaking plays *The Children's Hour* (1934), *The Little Foxes* (1939), *Watch on the Rhine* (1942), and *Toys in the Attic* (1960); for her long relationship with Dashiell Hammett; for her refusal to name names before the House Un-American Activities Committee in 1952; and later for her feud with Mary McCarthy. Among her friends she was also known as a good cook. In *Eating Together* (1984), she collaborated with her companion in later years, Peter Feibleman (b. 1930), a playwright and novelist who had written the Time-Life books *The Cooking of Spain and Portugal* (1969) and *American Cooking: Creole and Acadian* (1971). Recalling the meals they prepared together, they also looked back on the fights they had over them. The fights continued through the recipe testing (a task that, as a young food writer, fell to me). This passage evokes summers among the literati on Martha's Vineyard and it provides a snapshot of the blend of obsessiveness, ego, and generosity that make a meal.

■ ■ ■

Food in America is often dismissed as the least important part of what Americans call "entertaining," a term that seems to mean feeding people. "Do you entertain a lot?" is genteel jargon for "Do you ask people to eat with you?," but too much attention is paid to who's asked and not enough to what's eaten. Perhaps in response to this mistake, Lilly tends to the opposite extreme.

One Monday morning on the Vineyard I came down to find her making a guest list for a dinner she was planning the following Saturday. This did not bode well. It left six days during which she was apt to change the menu maybe fifty times, settling on it only at the very last minute, so that around five P.M. on the Saturday in question she could begin to resent the people she had invited, because they had accepted her invitation and had to be fed.

Martha's Vineyard was a curious place for a dinner party: a guest list sounded like an exercise in name-dropping. As a general rule, nobody is as impressed by celebrities as other celebrities, and the covey of famous people on the island drifted from house to house, week to week, depending largely on who had the best weekend guest to be honored. Lillian was expecting Mike and Annabel Nichols, which was considered top of the line even in that rarified atmosphere. She was an expert at seating people, but most of her friends had heard each other's stories years before. By the end of July, Vineyard gossip was hard to come by, and by mid August a certain frantic quality began to set in.

"I think," Lillian said as I reached for the coffee, "I'll ask the Herseys, Anne and Art Buchwald, Kay Graham, Bob Brustein, Jules Feiffer, Bill and Rose Styron, Tony Lewis, Walter Cronkite, Lally Weymouth, Norman Mailer—he's staying with somebody for the weekend—and Teddy Kennedy, if he's with the Styrons. What do you think?"

I said I thought that would be fine.

"Okay," she said, "about the menu. Maybe I'll cook a simple pasta dish, and just have some salad and lemon sherbet. How does that sound?"

A few seconds went by.

"Please don't stare at me that way, Peter," she said. "There's lots of fresh basil in the garden. We could begin with spaghetti and diced tomatoes and basil. Okay?"

I said okay.

Lillian wrote it down, and then lifted the pencil and looked at it. "The trouble," she said thoughtfully, "is that I ordered fresh mussels last week from a fisherman I met. He said he'd deliver them Saturday morning, he's charging me almost nothing. We *can't* have mussels *and* spaghetti with basil. That's two first courses."

"So have the mussels," I said.

"Don't answer before you think," Lillian said. "If we have mussels, what am I going to do with all the basil in the garden?—What about *that?*"

I swallowed another half cup of coffee and said she could have them both if she put them together.

"You see?" Lilly said, brightening, "if you'd just try thinking once in a while your whole life would be different. Basil and mussel sauce." She wrote it down. "Do you think we should have it as a first course . . . or as a main course?" she added, setting herself up for an impossible choice.

"A main course," I said.

"That means we don't have any first course," Lillian said.

"Skip the first course," I said.

"What's the matter with you?" Lillian said, "you're too young to cave in like that. Why am I having such a problem with it?"

"You want the problem," I said, "you don't want the solution."

"Let's not have any Woolworth Freud," Lillian said, "let's stick to the menu."

I said nothing.

"So what's the first course?" Lillian said.

An hour and three menus later, she was struggling over a choice between mussels and bluefish.

When Saturday came she sat down in the same chair at five o'clock, dressed for the party, and said: "I don't see why all those people are coming to my house expecting me to feed them. It's your fault," she said to Mike, who was coming downstairs with Annabel. "I'm only doing this for you."

"I didn't want a party," Mike said gently; "I came to rest."

"That's no excuse and you know it," Lillian said, "getting this meal ready in time has taken ten years off my life. Nobody else on the island cares about food—they'll probably hate it."

I made some inane remark about nobody hating a good meal, and Mike said he was sure Lillian's guests would like whatever she served them.

"They should all be honored you invited them," Annabel said loyally.

"Fuck all of them," Lillian said, "except the Herseys. Let's have a drink."

The social mores of the artist-intellectual set on the Vineyard are the flip side of Easthampton, which is to say that a man who wears a tie is gauche, elegance is outré, discomfort a virtue, modesty a must, casual living reigns and nobody who has air-conditioning in a bedroom admits to it. Wealth is seldom displayed except in real estate, and frayed cuffs are chic. In all countries the rules of rebellion are more strict than what is being rebelled against (nobody is as judgmental as a bohemian) and the casual life on this part of the Vineyard is more rigidly mannered than its black-tie opposite. A hostess giving a formal Easthampton buffet might go the whole hog and have an ice-sculpture swan; but Lillian had to keep things looking like just folks. In an effort to keep it plain, she had stayed in the kitchen all day and

I had made an ordinary chopped vegetable salad with one lone leftover radish stuck on top.

Just as the doorbell rang, Lillian took the radish off and buried it in the salad.

"You don't want people to think you're decorating food around here," she said. "Some of them would never speak to you again."

FOOD FOR A MODEST, UNMOVEABLE FEAST

Chopped Vegetable Salad

Serves 6

1 zucchini, cut into bite-size pieces
2 carrots, cut into bite-size pieces and lightly blanched
2 cups green beans, cleaned, cut into bite-size pieces and blanched
1 red pepper, chopped
1 green pepper, chopped
2 stalks celery, chopped
1 bunch scallions, chopped
1 bunch radishes, sliced thin
2 packages frozen mixed vegetables
2 cups Romescu sauce (recipe follows)

Combine all vegetables in a large bowl. Toss with 2 cups Romescu sauce. Refrigerate and serve well chilled.

Romescu Sauce

1 1/2 cups

1/4 cup almonds, toasted
1 clove garlic
1/2 teaspoon cayenne pepper
1 teaspoon salt
1 tomato, peeled, seeded and chopped
1/4 cup red wine vinegar
1 cup olive oil

Pulverize almonds, garlic, cayenne pepper, salt, tomato and vinegar in blender. Slowly drizzle in oil, making sure that each addition is completely absorbed. Adjust seasoning to taste with additional salt and pepper.

Pasta with Basil and Tomatoes

Serves 6

1 cup olive oil

2 cloves garlic, minced

12 tomatoes, peeled, seeded and chopped

1 bunch fresh basil leaves, minced

   salt and pepper

2 pounds pasta (angel hair or vermicelli)

   grated Parmesan cheese

Heat olive oil in a large skillet. Add garlic and cook until it begins to turn golden. Add tomatoes and basil and continue cooking over medium heat until warmed. Season with salt and pepper to taste. Cook 2 pounds thin pasta. Drain, toss with sauce, adding up to 1 additional cup of olive oil to coat. Sprinkle with grated Parmesan cheese and serve.

Eating Together: Recipes & Recollections (1984)

Waverley Root

Gillotte's

Waverley Root (1903–1982) was one of my earliest guides. He was not infallible; indeed, his massive *Food: An Authoritative and Visual History and Dictionary of the Foods of the World* (1980) represents a good deal of apocrypha and folklore as historic fact. But long before most historians, sociologists, and anthropologists gave a fig for food, there was Root, a Paris correspondent for the *Chicago Tribune* and later for *The Washington Post*, motoring around France and trying to understand its people through their cooking. His classic *The Food of France* (1958) drew on the insights of natural history, political history, social science, and geography to create a full-scale portrait of culinary culture; in later books he took a similar approach to Italy and the United States. In Paris, as a dinner companion of serious epicures like A. J. Liebling as well as scores of journalists with sights set on becoming expense-account gourmets, Root gave many Americans the beginnings of a culinary education. Here, in an excerpt from his posthumously published memoirs, he remembers Gillotte's, a favorite local haunt that offered Root himself a solid grounding in *la cuisine bourgeoise*.

■ ■ ■

As an encourager of esprit de corps, the Hôtel de Lisbonne has to be ranked only second among the Paris Edition's rendezvous, with Gillotte's, our common eating place, first. The two were twins in at least one respect: Neither was afraid of an overlay of good healthy dirt. Gillotte's had the advantage that we frequented it mostly at night, and since the lighting was dim, the dirt didn't show much.

Gillotte's was a small place directly across the street from the offices of the *Chicago Tribune*; its clientele, apart from us, was composed chiefly of the *Petit Journal* printers and, at lunchtime, taxi drivers. This was a good sign. Taxi drivers, comparatively free to roam in search of fodder, tend to nose out the best values in different parts of the city and head for the nearest one available when hunger strikes. The taxi drivers ate in the front room, relaxing before returning to labor by playing *belotte*, a French card game. We also used to play French checkers at Gillotte's among ourselves, with forty pieces on a board of one hundred squares.

It did not look like a temple of gastronomy and was not, but we ate quite well there even though the place's appearance suggested that this was an accident. It was an epoch when one ate well at all levels, even the humblest. If you had your mouth made up for truffles and foie gras the workmen's restaurants could do nothing for you, but if you were willing to put up with foods in their price range, you would get good substantial nourishment, prepared and seasoned with skill. It might be suggested that we were overimpressed, as refugees from American restaurant cooking, but there was the evidence of the choice of Gillotte's by the taxi drivers, who were French—except for some White Russians, who in those days drove a considerable proportion of Paris taxis. They all admitted to being members of the Russian nobility, a class that had some experience in eating well. What Gillotte's gave us, the French taxi drivers, and the former cronies of the czar was hearty French home cooking, *la cuisine bourgeoise.*

Gillotte's space was limited. The building was just wide enough to permit placing one small round table and two chairs at either side of the door on the sidewalk, a token terrace that obliged passersby to step down into the street to pass. Inside Gillotte's began with a front room occupied on the left side by the *zinc,* or bar, with a standing, or leaning, capacity of about a dozen average-sized drinkers. After a brief interval to allow for squeezing out from behind the bar, the rest of the left wall was occupied by a series of shelves. A display of hors d'oeuvres and pastry sat on the shelves and the cat sat on the pastry. The right half of the room contained four or five stone-topped tables set at right angles to the wall, available to the lower classes—printers, taxi drivers, and strays.

The partition that guarded the privacy of the back room was more of a symbol than a barrier, with a wide opening that had no door. It sufficed, however, to separate the riffraff from the aristocracy—in the evening, us. Three tables parallel to the wall stood on either side, and next to the wall not chairs but benches upholstered in the unidentifiable material referred to by the French as "moleskin."

The third part of this domain was the cubbyhole kitchen in the rear whose door was always open, permitting samples of the evening's menu to be wafted into the back room in the form of vapor. Nothing ever smelled unappetizing while cooking.

We often filled the whole back room, but when we did not we had a tendency to seek the kitchen end of the room, leaving unoccupied a table or two nearest the entrance that might be occupied by unknowns. The Gillottes exercised a certain censorship over those who might thus be privileged to dine in our presence. Unworthy characters were informed that the room was private, for the house did not intend to allow its day-in day-out customers to be displeased by the invasion of their quarters by citizens of dubious status. They had noted that we were not dismayed by the presence of comely young women, so table seekers who fell into this category usually got by the barrier. These customers also had the advantage for the house that their dinner checks were almost invariably paid, if not by the girls themselves, at least by somebody, though perhaps not until the end of the month.

Our financial arrangements with Gillotte's, as well as its nearness and its good cooking, accounted largely for the fact that the night staff in toto usually dined there before crossing the street and climbing the stairs to start work at 8:00 P.M. Like the Hôtel de Lisbonne it was cheap, and it gave credit. When I described the Polish restaurant near the Luxembourg Gardens as the cheapest I knew, I forgot Gillotte's, whose prices could not have been much different. But I really don't know, for I cannot recall ever having paid a bill for a single meal there. I ate on the cuff like everybody else. We were paid on the fifteenth and on the last day of the month, and on those days, each of us, as he arrived, stopped at the *zinc* and settled for his half-month's accumulation of bills, preserved by the house, to which we preferred to leave the dull chore of mathematics since we were convinced of the Gillottes' scrupulous honesty.

Only one editor, Egbert Swenson, checked the bills, one by one, against his own memoranda of his consumption, set down meticulously in microscopic script in a small black notebook. This, I think, was not because he was suspicious but because he was orderly. Or perhaps he found it hard to believe the amount of his bills, for he ate twice as much as anybody else. I had seen him plow all the way through a complete meal—hors d'oeuvre, fish, meat, salad, cheese, and dessert—pause a few seconds for reflection, and then eat the same menu from beginning to end all over again. Maybe he knew how much a single meal cost at Gillotte's, but nobody else did.

The paying of the fortnightly bill was completed by an invariable ritual. Papa Gillotte reached under the counter and produced, with a certain formality, an unlabeled bottle containing a pale yellowish-brown liquid, from which he poured, for the customer and for himself, a thimbleful each of *prunelle*, on the house. *Prunelle* was an eau de vie distilled from plums by one of his country relatives. Thus fortified, we were ready for one other half-monthly rite, paying the rent, after which we could spend what remained of our $30 on riotous living. On the sixteenth or the first we were back on the cuff again.

Papa Gillotte was one-fourth of the staff of Gillotte's, if you refrain from counting Toto the dog and Minette the cat. Toto belonged to a nameless category of dog of which a replica existed at that period in every cheap bistro—about Airedale-sized, though there was nothing else about them to suggest so distinguished an animal as an Airedale, rusty black in color and smooth-haired. They had long thrashing tails, excellent for knocking glasses off tables. I have seen none of them for years.

Toto's color seemed good camouflage against all backgrounds, and since he never barked, whined, or growled, you where usually unaware of his presence until a restive muzzle was suddenly thrust into your groin in guise of welcome. This was the only contribution Toto knew how to make to the quality of life, a disconcerting one if you were not braced for it.

Most bistro dogs in France at that period were called Toto and the cats were known as Minette, the generic name in France for cats of all kinds, best translated as "pussy." Minette had a basket behind the bar but preferred to lie on the pastry, except when she was giving birth, as she seemed to do every few weeks. The kittens gradually disappeared, a phenomenon sometimes connected by us, in purposely loud voices, with the appearance of rabbit stew on the menu. The object of this slander was to provoke the wrath of the ordinarily good-natured Mama Gillotte and provoke the display of a vocabulary unmatchable even by the taxi-driving customers. Newcomers to the staff would sometimes try to get a rise out of her by suggesting that Gillotte's beef was really horse, and were surprised at her calm indifference to this theory, until one of the veterans explained that horse meat at the time was more expensive than beef. (Nowadays it costs about the same.)

Papa and Mama Gillotte were from the Auvergne, as were almost all Paris bistro keepers. The classic story of the Paris bistro keeper was that of a peasant who arrived from the mountains of his native Auvergne and set himself up as a *bougnat* (all Parisian *bougnats* were Auvergnats too). A *bougnat* is, or was, for mighty few of them are left today, a small-scale dealer in coal and wood—small-scale enough that he would personally deliver your order, at the frequent intervals and in the small amounts dictated by the limited storage space of most apartments. This was a profitable business when a large proportion of the Paris population heated itself with fireplaces and hardly were aware of the existence of gas ranges, much less electric ones. It also made for frequent contacts with customers who might ultimately be induced to support another type of business. Once the *bougnat* had saved enough money (Auvergnats are a thrifty lot), he would sweep out the wood shavings and scrub away the coal dust from part or all of his premises, install a bar and bottles, and notify his wood and coal customers that he was now prepared to supply internal, as well as external, heat. He thus became a *limonadier*.

The Gillottes were excellent hosts, and I think they felt a certain affection for us. Indeed, they sometimes went so far as to lend us money, which was not a Parisian habit. They allowed us to convert their back room into our private club, and a very pleasant club it was. We not only dined there, we descended in full force at 10:00 P.M. for a half-hour break, and sometimes we returned after the paper had gone to press about 2:30 A.M., though at this hour we were more apt to disperse to foreign parts, sometimes even going home. I do not know if I ever enjoyed any other restaurant more thoroughly than Gillotte's. I suppose it was chiefly the company; we were a close-knit family on the Paris Edition.

Gillotte's was open twenty-three hours out of twenty-four, closing from four to five in the morning, and probably would never have closed at all if the license fee for round-the-clock cafés had not been something like double that for places that took at least an hour off. This timetable regulated the Gillotte life-style, or lack of one. They had no home except the bistro cellar, which was entered through a trapdoor behind the bar. It is probable that they had in reserve a retirement property somewhere in the Auvergne (perhaps where the *prunelle* came from) for this was the rule among the Auvergnat bistro owners of Paris, but in the capital they slept on their business premises. Papa and Mama Gillotte were both above ground at meal times and other busy moments, but in between they took turns descending to the cellar for a little sleep. They had no children.

Under this regime, Mama Gillotte looked as if she never fully wakened, except at moments of anger or laughter. A large, blowsy, friendly, tolerant woman, when she laughed she laughed all over. Papa Gillotte, who weighed in at about half the heft of his spouse, looked relatively awake, if not alert, except that his eyes were set deep into narrow slits that served to protect them from light. He was always a little outnumbered by his large blue apron, and I never saw him without a dirty oversized cloth cap on his head. Mama Gillotte's sartorial aspect I am unable to describe because there was nothing about it on which attention could be focused. All I can say is that she wore a dress, and if it was not always the same dress, it at least was always equally colorless and shapeless. If she were true to her class, she must have accumulated before marriage a plentiful trousseau that had been carefully folded and stored away in a series of bureau drawers, where it would remain until her death, lest it should deteriorate from being worn.

One of the assets of Auvergnats, for expanding their businesses as *bougnats* or *limonadiers*, is an unlimited supply of labor in the form of cousins. The rest of Gillotte's staff fell into this category. Food was transported from kitchen to tables by Raymond, who must have been about fourteen when I first became a guest of Gillotte's, a pasty-faced boy whose complexion suggested that he slept in the cellar too and had never come into contact with open air. (Papa and Mama Gillotte had in their youth in their native province acquired complexions sufficiently ruddy to last them the rest of their lives.) Raymond was full of goodwill, but easily bewildered. On the not infrequent occasions when someone tried to point out to him that the sole meunière he had brought to the table was not the roast lamb that had been ordered, his timid grin was so disarming and so uncomprehending that the diner usually ate what he had been given. Perhaps Raymond was smarter than we thought.

The keystone of the culinary department of Gillotte's was Madame Charlotte, also a member of the family, direction and distance from Mama and Papa Gillotte unknown. She presided over the kitchen, visible through its open door, her sparse gray hair escaping in unmanageable wisps from what might have been referred to charitably as her coiffure, busying herself around the heavy iron range of the type known in Parisian restaurants as "the piano," under its permanent canopy of drying female underwear.

"Madame" was a courtesy title awarded in honor of her age, which was in-determinable, anywhere from sixty to eighty, for legally Madame Charlotte was still a mademoiselle.

Madame Charlotte could be peppery and sometimes enlivened the bis-tro's atmosphere with minor eruptions. These were usually intrafamily, but among us it was Hérol Egan who seemed fated to provoke Madame Charlotte most often, as a result of a communications gap. Egan's French was more fluent than accurate.

The most widely repeated example of Egan's struggles with the French language occurred at a dinner given by sports reporters in honor of the re-tiring head of I-have-forgotten-which sports association, who happened to bear the title of count. Nobody had asked Egan to make a speech, but he was never one to stand on ceremony, so he got up and made one anyway. He knew vaguely that final consonants are often left unpronounced in French, and though the *t* in *comte* is not quite final, Egan elected to omit it anyway, just for safety's sake. The other diners managed to keep straight faces through a series of references to "*Monsieur le Con*," but when Egan described the guest of honor as "*ce vieux con usagé par le travail*," the phrase "this old cunt worn out by work" brought down the house.

One communications failure between Egan and Madame Charlotte was pure comedy. One day Egan ordered dinner only to have Madame Charlotte emerge from her lair as soon as Raymond relayed the order. "*Monsieur voulait dire* deux *oeufs, n'est-ce pas?*" she asked. Egan responded that he wanted *douze*, and Madame Charlotte executed the shrug of the shoulders that meant, "All Americans are crazy," returned to her piano, and in a trice Raymond plunked down before Egan a tremendous platter laden with twelve fried eggs.

"What the hell is this?" Egan exploded. "I ordered two eggs, and look what they've given me."

"You horse's ass," said Frantz, from across the room, "you didn't ask for two eggs, you asked for twelve eggs, and that's what you've got. You should have said *deux*; you said *douze*."

"I did not say *douze*," Egan protested. "I said *douze*."

I forget what happened to the surplus eggs. Perhaps Swenson ate them.

This was a minor incident, but on another occasion Egan nearly lost us our excellent cook with a single remark. She had been having trouble with her stove one evening, so the next day Egan, friendly though unintelligible, poked his head through the kitchen door to ask how her *poêle* was behaving. *Poêle* is a justifiable word for stove, though a Frenchman would be more likely to use it to mean a heating stove than a cooking stove, and most likely to use it to mean a frying pan. But it is a good word for a foreigner to avoid entirely, for its combination of vowels can be played only on a French larynx.

What Madame Charlotte heard was *pöils*, and she exploded from her quarters, half screaming and half crying, tore off her apron, and announced that she was quitting on the spot rather than cook for barbarians who insulted respectable women in public by discussing their pubic hair. It took all of us and both the Gillottes to unravel the misunderstanding, after which Madame Charlotte resumed her apron and returned to the kitchen, grumbling. She put off quitting for several years, when she eloped with Raymond, who was about half a century younger than she was.

The Paris Edition (1987)

Laurie Colwin

Kitchen Horrors

Laurie Colwin (1944–1992) focused in her novels and short stories on the dark little in-
terstices between what appears to be true, what we want to be true, and what in fact is
true. In her essays about cooking she likewise wrote about the absurdities of modern
living and the fate of fragile hearts. "I had no recipe to guide me, but does love need
a recipe?" she writes in "Kitchen Horrors," from her collection *Home Cooking* (1988).
"Does inspiration require instructions?" Philosophically, Colwin was torn between a
cool, rational view of life and a rosy, romantic one; personally, she alternated between
haimish mama and competitive careerist. After our long, gossipy lunches, she would
press things upon me: scraps of paper containing the contact information for "the best"
masseuse, shrink, psychic, or writing coach; boxes of chocolate truffles or fine pastries
after we'd shared hours of diet woes. It kept our lunches, as well as her salon-like dinner
parties, interesting.

■ ■ ■

Awful things happen in the kitchen all the time, even to the most experienced cooks, but when it happens to you it is not comforting to know that
you are supposed to learn from your mistakes, especially when you contemplate the lurid-looking mess in front of you.

I myself have never made a spinach pie, and therefore I have never had
the thrilling opportunity to see one catch on fire. Therefore I have never
watched my husband place his large, wet hiking boot on top of my flaming
puff pastry to keep it from burning down the house, but this did happen to
a friend. More mundane things happen to me: half the cake sticks in the
bundt pan. The pudding won't unmold from the pudding mold, and when it
does, half of it is melted.

A really first-rate disaster passes into legend. My sister and I have never
forgotten the salmon loaf our mother, an excellent cook, made when we were
little. By mistake, she reached for the cayenne pepper instead of the paprika.
I was six, my sister was ten and we remember it as if it were yesterday.

My husband recalls a dinner party he attempted to give as a young man around town. The beef stew turned into an ocean of gray juice in which tiny, hard cubes of overcooked meat floated. The dessert was to be crêpes but when he removed the batter from the refrigerator, something had gone terribly amiss. The batter had turned into cinder block, and the wooden spoon he had left in it was stuck. Later it turned out that he had used potato starch instead of flour. These things happen.

My own greatest disasters have been the result of inexperience, over-reaching, intimidation and self-absorption.

As a blithe young thing I became quite hipped on a dish called rösti— a Swiss way of frying shredded potatoes in an enormous quantity of butter. I had been introduced to this dish by an English boyfriend, who loved to entertain. One night he invited six people for dinner and I thought it would be a swell idea to make rösti.

Alone in my beloved's kitchen, I began to shred the potatoes into a big bowl. By the time my arm began to get sore, I noticed that the potatoes had taken on a pinkish tinge, but I pressed on. A few minutes later, I looked to see how many more potatoes I needed and observed that a sickly green was now the predominant shade. A few minutes later, my heartthrob appeared.

"Good gracious," he said. "What's this funny black stuff?"

There was no doubt about it. That funny black stuff was my potatoes. Into the garbage they went, and to this day I am still a little phobic about potatoes: rösti for two, potato pancakes for four is my motto.

In the middle period of my kitchen disasters, by which time I had done a lot of cooking and knew my way around the kitchen, I decided to entrap the man I would later marry by baking a red snapper, the only fish he liked. Misguided by passion, I decided I would stuff this fish with sliced grapes, small shrimp and fermented black beans. I had never stuffed a fish before, let alone baked one. I had no idea what I was doing. In fact, I must have been out of my mind. I had no recipe to guide me, but does love need a recipe? Does inspiration require instructions?

It is hard to describe the result, which was put back into the oven many times before it dried out and became inedible. Many were my maidenly blushes as I said: "Well, the inside still looks a little underdone, but I'll just pop it back in the oven for a minute." I might have said this fifteen times.

When it finally emerged from the oven, this fish looked like Hieronymus Bosch's vision of hell, with little nasty-looking things spilling out into a pallid-looking puddle of undercooked fish juices.

Years later, I entertained a newly married friend. This friend had married a goddess and lived in the country. I of course was a slob and lived in the city. The goddess had built their post-and-beam house with her own two hands, raised chickens, milked cows and was a veterinarian as well. On the side she was a glassblower. She had built her own studio. All the glassware, jugs, pitchers and vases in their house were made by her. Of course she baked her own bread, raised her own vegetables and made her own clothes, although she didn't yet know how to spin. At that news I heaved a sigh of relief.

As the burden of this woman's accomplishments was being piled ever higher on my lowly shoulders, I cooked dinner. Baked chicken, hominy in cream, steamed string beans. By the time I heard about the glassblowing, I was whipping up some butterscotch brownies for dessert.

It was the first meal I have ever cooked of which there was not enough. I don't mean that my husband and our friend polished everything off because it was so delicious. They polished everything off because there was so little to polish, and there were no seconds. My butterscotch brownies would compensate, I thought. They were cooling in their pan on a rack, and when I went to cut them, I knew that something awful had happened.

I did not think that substituting Demerara sugar for white sugar would make much of a difference, but the knife wouldn't seem to penetrate. When I finally sawed through to the bottom, I realized that the sugar had settled to the bottom and solidified. Oh, well, I thought. It will be like Scotch tablet, that delicious confection of butter and sugar.

But those butterscotch brownies were not like Scotch tablet. They were like cooked sugar that had turned into firebrick. From this experience I learned that you should never be in the kitchen with anyone married to a perfect person.

My greatest horror, however, was a culinary triumph, in my opinion. *In my opinion* are the crucial words.

I had been invited to the country for Easter. At the same time an English friend had sent me a packet of suet. With this I intended to make something called Suffolk Pond Pudding from Jane Grigson's wonderful book *English Food*.

Suffolk Pond Pudding, although something of a curiosity, sounded perfectly splendid. First, you line a pudding basin with suet crust. Then you cut butter mixed with sugar into small pieces. Next you take an entire lemon and prick it all over with a fork. Then you stick the lemon on top of the butter and sugar, surround it with more butter and sugar, stick a pastry lid on the top, tie it up in a pudding cloth and steam in a kettle for four hours. It never occurred to me that nobody might want to eat it.

I followed every step carefully. My suet crust was masterful. When unwrapped from its cloth, the crust was a beautiful, deep honey color. I turned it out onto an ornamental plate.

My hostess looked confused. "It looks like a baked hat," she said.

"It looks like the Alien," said my future husband.

"Never mind," I said. "It will be the most delicious thing you ever tasted."

The pudding was brought to the table. My host and hostess, my future husband and a woman guest looked at it suspiciously. I cut the pudding. As Jane Grigson had promised, out ran a lemon-scented buttery toffee. I sliced up the lemon, which was soft and buttery too. Each person was to get some crust, a slice of lemon and some sauce.

What a hit!, I thought. Exactly the sort of thing I adored. I looked around me happily, and my happiness turned to ash.

My host said: "This tastes like lemon-flavored bacon fat."

"I'm sure it's wonderful," said my hostess. "I mean, in England."

The woman guest said: "This is awful."

My future husband remained silent, not a good sign. I had promised him a swell dessert and here was this weird, inedible sludge from outer space. The others ate ice cream. I ate almost the entire pudding myself.

I have had a number of small horrors since then, mostly involving pie crust, something I haven't quite gotten the hang of. One of my pies fell apart. One was so odd-looking my husband took a picture of it, and one had the texture and resilience of old parchment.

Now that I am more accomplished I feel that I am in a position to gauge my kitchen disasters and choose them carefully. For my next I am either going to make Circassian chicken (poached chicken blanketed with a walnut purée) or a chocolate jelly roll which my sister assures me is a snap to make. I have never cooked either of these things before, but instinct tells me that the possibilities for something going terribly wrong in either case are endless.

Home Cooking (1988)

Sara Suleri

from Meatless Days

A distinguished academic–she is professor of English at Yale and author of *The Rhetoric of English India* (1992)–Sara Suleri (b. 1953, now Sara Suleri Goodyear) won considerable acclaim for her memoir *Meatless Days* (1989). Recalling her early years in Pakistan, Suleri weaves together personal and political history from a distance of decades and continents. She also offers a complex, lyrical evocation of a child's first tastes: the "illicit joy" she finds nibbling cauliflower buds in the garden, the "oceanic" intensities of a glass of buffalo milk. The particulars are personal, but the responses awakened by taste can be intense and visceral, cutting across the bounds of time and cultural difference.

■ ■ ■

"Sara," said Tillat, her voice deep with the promise of surprise, "do you know what *kapura* are?" I was cooking and a little cross. "Of course I do," I answered with some affront. "They're sweetbreads, and they're cooked with kidneys, and they're very good." Natives should always be natives, exactly what they are, and I felt irked to be so probed around the issue of my own nativity. But Tillat's face was kindly with superior knowledge. "Not sweetbread," she gently said. "They're testicles, that's what *kapura* really are." Of course I refused to believe her, went on cooking, and that was the end of that.

The babies left, and I with a sudden spasm of free time watched that organic issue resurface in my head—something that had once sat quite simply inside its own definition was declaring independence from its name and nature, claiming a perplexity that I did not like. And, too, I needed different ways to be still thinking about Tillat, who had gone as completely as she had arrived, and deserved to be reproached for being such an unreliable informant. So, the next time I was in the taut companionship of Pakistanis in New York, I made a point of inquiring into the exact status of *kapura* and the physiological location of its secret, first in the animal and then in the meal. Expatriates are adamant, entirely passionate about such matters as the eating habits of the motherland. Accordingly, even though I was made to feel that it was wrong to strip a food of its sauce and put it back into its bodily belonging, I certainly received an unequivocal response: *kapura*, as naked meat, equals a testicle. Better, it is tantamount to a testicle neatly sliced into halves, just as we make no bones about asking the butcher to split chicken breasts in two. "But," and here I rummaged for the sweet realm of nomenclature, "couldn't *kapura* on a lazy occasion also accommodate something like sweetbreads, which is just a nice way of saying that pancreas is not a pleasant word to eat?" No one, however, was interested in this finesse. "Balls, darling, balls," someone drawled, and I knew I had to let go of the subject.

Yet I was shocked. It was my mother, after all, who had told me that sweetbreads are sweetbreads, and if she were wrong on that score, then how many other simple equations had I now to doubt? The second possibility that occurred to me was even more unsettling: maybe my mother knew that sweetbreads are testicles but had cunningly devised a ruse to make me consume as many parts of the world as she could before she set me loose in it. The thought appalled me. It was almost as bad as attempting to imagine what the slippage was that took me from nipple to bottle and away from the great letdown that signifies lactation. What a falling off! How much I must have suffered when so handed over to the shoddy metaphors of Ostermilk and Babyflo. Gosh, I thought, to think that my mother could do that to me. For of course she must have known, in her Welsh way, that sweetbreads could never be simply sweetbreads in Pakistan. It made me stop and hold my head over that curious possibility: what else have I eaten on her behalf?

I mulled over that question for days, since it wantonly refused to disappear after it had been posed: instead, it settled in my head and insisted on being reformulated, with all the tenacity of a query that actually expects to be met with a reply. My only recourse was to make lists, cramped and strictly alphabetical catalogs of all the gastronomic wrongs I could blame on my mother; but somehow by the time I reached *T* and "tripe," I was always interrupted and had to begin again. Finally it began to strike me as a rather unseemly activity for one who had always enjoyed a measure of daughterly propriety, and I decided that the game was not to be played again but discarded like table scraps. For a brief span of time I felt free, until some trivial occasion—a dinner, where chicken had been cleverly cooked to resemble veal—caused me to remind my friends of that obsolete little phrase, "mutton dressed up as lamb," which had been such a favorite of my mother's. Another was "neither flesh nor fowl," and as I chatted about the curiousness of those phrases, I suddenly realized that my friends had fallen away and my only audience was the question itself, heaving up its head again and examining me with reproach and some scorn. I sensed that it would be unwise to offer another list to this triumphant interlocutor, so I bowed my head and knew what I had to do. In order to submit even the most imperfect answer, I had to go back to where I belonged and—past a thousand different mealtimes—try to reconstruct the parable of the *kapura*.

Tillat was not around to hear me sigh and wonder where I should possibly begin. The breast would be too flagrant and would make me too tongue-tied, so I decided instead to approach the *kapura* in a mildly devious way, by getting at it through its mate. To the best of my knowledge I had never seen *kapura* cooked outside the company of kidney, and so for Tillat's edification alone I tried to begin with the story of the kidney, which I should have remembered long ago, not twenty-five years after its occurrence. We were living in Lahore, in the 9-T Gulberg house, and in those days our cook was Qayuum. He had a son and two daughters with whom we were occasionally allowed to play: his little girl Munni I specially remember because I liked the way her hair curled and because of all the times that she was such a perfect recipient of fake *pan*. *Pan*, an adult delicacy of betel leaf and nut, can be quite convincingly replicated by a mango leaf stuffed with stones: Ifat, my older sister, would fold such beautifully simulated *pan* triangles that Munni would thrust them into her mouth each time—and then burst into tears. I find it odd today to imagine how that game of guile and trust could have survived even a single repetition, but I recollect it distinctly as a weekly ritual, with us waiting in fascination for Munni to get streetwise, which she never did. Instead, she cried with her mouth wide open and would run off to her mother with little pebbles falling out of her mouth, like someone in a fairy tale.

Those stones get linked to kidneys in my head, as part of the chain through which Munni got the better of me and anticipated the story I really intend to tell. It was an evil day that led her father Qayuum to buy two water buffalo, tethering them at the far end of the garden and making my mother beam at the prospect of such fresh milk. My older brother Shahid liked pets and convinced me that we should beam too, until he and I were handed our first overpowering glasses of buffalo milk. Of milks it is certainly the most oceanic, with archipelagoes and gulf streams of cream emitting a pungent, grassy odor. Trebly strong is that smell at milking-time, which my mother beamingly suggested we attend. She kept away herself, of course, so she never saw the big black cows, with their ominous glassy eyes, as they shifted from foot to foot. Qayuum pulled and pulled at their white udders and, in a festive mood, called up the children one by one to squirt a steaming jet of milk into their mouths. When my turn came, my mother, not being there, did not see me run as fast as I could away from the cows and the cook, past the vegetable garden and the goldfish pond, down to the farthermost wall, where I lay down in the grass and tried to faint, but couldn't.

I knew the spot from prior humiliations, I admit. It was where I had hidden twice in the week when I was caught eating cauliflower and was made to eat kidney. The cauliflower came first—it emerged as a fragrant little head in the vegetable garden, a bumpy vegetable brain that looked innocent and edible enough to make me a perfect victim when it called. In that era my greatest illicit joy was hastily chawing off the top of each new cauliflower when no one else was looking. The early morning was my favorite time, because then those flowers felt firm and crisp with dew. I would go to the vegetable patch and squat over the cauliflowers as they came out one by one, hold them between my knees, and chew as many craters as I could into their jaunty tightness. Qayuum was crushed. "There is an animal, Begum Sahib," he mourned to my mother, "like a savage in my garden. *Maro! Maro!*" To hear him made me nervous, so the following morning I tried to deflect attention from the cauliflowers by quickly pulling out all the little radishes while they were still pencil-thin: they lay on the soil like a pathetic accumulation of red herrings. That was when Munni caught me. "*Abba Ji!*" she screamed for her father like a train engine. Everybody came running, and for a while my squat felt frozen to the ground as I looked up at an overabundance of astonished adult faces. "What are you doing, Sara *Bibi?*" the driver finally and gently asked. "Smelling the radishes," I said in a baby and desperate defiance, "so that the animal can't find the cauliflower." "Which one?" "The new cauliflower." "Which animal, *bibi ji*, you naughty girl?" "The one that likes to eat the cauliflower that I like to smell." And when they laughed at me, I did not know where to put my face for shame.

They caught me out that week, two times over, because after I had been exposed as the cauliflower despoiler and had to enter a new phase of penitence, Qayuum the cook insisted on making me eat kidney. "*Kirrnee*," he would call it with a glint in his eye, "*kirrnee*." My mother quite agreed that I should learn such discipline, and the complicated ritual of endurance they imposed did make me teach myself to take a kidney taste without dwelling too long on the peculiarities of kidney texture. I tried to be unsurprised by the mushroom pleats that constitute a kidney's underbelly and by the knot of membrane that holds those kidney folds in place. One day Qayuum insisted that only kidneys could sit on my plate, mimicking legumes and ignoring their thin and bloody juices. Wicked Ifat came into the room and waited till I had started eating; then she intervened. "Sara," said Ifat, her eyes brimming over with wonderful malice, "do you know what kidneys do?" I aged, and my meal regressed, back to its vital belonging in the world of function. "Kidneys make pee, Sara," Ifat told me, "That's what they do, they make pee." And she looked so pleased to be able to tell me that; it made her feel so full of information. Betrayed by food, I let her go, and wept some watery tears into the kidney juice, which was designed anyway to evade cohesion, being thin and in its nature inexact. Then I ran out to the farthermost corner of the garden, where I would later go to hide my shame of milking-time in a retch that refused to materialize.

Born the following year, Tillat would not know that cautionary tale. Nor would she know what Ifat did when my father called from Lady Willingdon Hospital in Lahore to repeat that old phrase, "It is a girl." "It's a girl!" Ifat shouted, as though simply clinching for the world the overwhelming triumph of her will. Shahid, a year my senior, was found half an hour later sobbing next to the goldfish pond near the vegetable garden, for he had been banking on the diluting arrival of a brother. He must have been upset, because when we were taken to visit my mother, he left his penguin—a favorite toy—among the old trees of the hospital garden, where we had been sent to play. I was still uncertain about my relation to the status of this new baby: my sister was glad that it was a girl, and my brother was sad that it wasn't a boy, but we all stood together when penguiny was lost.

It is to my discredit that I forgot this story, both of what the kidney said and what it could have told to my still germinating sister. Had I borne something of those lessons in mind, it would have been less of a shock to have to reconceive the *kapura* parable; perhaps I'd have been prepared for more skepticism about the connection between kidneys and sweetbreads–after all, they fall into no logical category of togetherness. The culinary humor of kidneys and testicles stewing in one another's juices is, on the other hand, very fine: I wish I had had the imagination to intuit all the unwonted jokes people tell when they start cooking food. I should have remembered all those nervously comic edges, and the pangs, that constitute most poignancies of nourishment. And so, as an older mind, I fault myself for not having the wits to recognize what I already knew. I must have always known exactly what *kapura* are, because the conversation they provoked came accompanied with shocks of familiarity that typically attend a trade of solid information. What I had really wanted to reply, first to Tillat and then to my Pakistani friends, was: yes, of course, who do you think I am, what else could they *possibly be?* Anyone with discrimination could immediately discern the connection between *kapura* and their namesake: the shape is right, given that we are now talking about goats; the texture involves a bit of a bounce, which works; and the taste is altogether too exactly what it is. So I should have kept in mind that, alas, we know the flavor of each part of the anatomy: that much imagination belongs to everyone's palate. Once, when my sisters and I were sitting in a sunny winter garden, Tillat began examining some ants that were tumbling about the blades of grass next to her chair. She looked acute and then suddenly said, "How very sour those little ants must be." Ifat declared that she had always thought the same herself, and though I never found out how they arrived at this discovery, I was impressed by it, their ability to take the world on their tongues.

So poor Irfani, how much his infant taste buds must have colored his perception of the grimness of each day. Irfan was born in London, finally another boy, but long after Shahid had ceased looking for playmates in the home. It now strikes me as peculiar that my parents should choose to move back to Pakistan when Farni was barely a year old, and to decide on June, that most pitiless month, in which to return to Lahore. The heat shriveled the baby, giving his face an expression of slow and bewildered shock, which was compounded by the fact that for the next year there was very little that the child could eat. Water boiled ten times over would still retain virulence enough to send his body into derangements, and goat's milk, cow's milk, everything liquid seemed to convey malevolence to his minuscule gut. We used to scour the city for aging jars of imported baby-food; these, at least, he would eat, though with a look of profound mistrust—but even so, he spent most of the next year with his body in violent rebellion against the idea of food. It gave his eyes a gravity they have never lost.

Youngster he was, learning lessons from an infant's intuition to fear food, and to some degree all of us were equally watchful for hidden trickeries in the scheme of nourishment, for the way in which things would always be missing or out of place in Pakistan's erratic emotional market. Items of security—such as flour or butter or cigarettes or tea—were always vanishing, or returning in such dubiously shiny attire that we could barely stand to look at them. We lived in the expectation of threatening surprise: a crow had drowned in the water tank on the roof, so for a week we had been drinking dead-crow water and couldn't understand why we felt so ill; the milkman had accidentally diluted our supply of milk with paraffin instead of water; and those were not pistachios, at all, in a tub of Hico's green ice cream. Our days and our newspapers were equally full of disquieting tales about adulterated foods and the preternaturally keen eye that the nation kept on such promiscuous blendings. I can understand it, the fear that food will not stay discrete but will instead defy our categories of expectation in what can only be described as a manner of extreme belligerence. I like order to a plate, and know the great sense of failure that attends a moment when what is potato to the fork is turnip to the mouth. It's hard, when such things happen.

So, long before the *kapura* made its comeback in my life, we in Pakistan were bedmates with betrayal and learned how to take grim satisfaction from assessing the water table of our outrage. There were both lean times and meaty times, however; occasionally, body and food would sit happily at the same side of the conference table. Take, for example, Ramzan, the Muslim month of fasting, often recollected as the season of perfect meals. Ramzan, a lunar thing, never arrives at the same point of time each year, coming instead with an aura of slight and pleasing dislocation. Somehow it always took us by surprise: new moons are startling to see, even by accident, and

Ramzan's moon betokened a month of exquisite precision about the way we were to parcel out our time. On the appointed evenings we would rake the twilight for that possible sliver, and it made the city and body both shudder with expectation to spot that little slip of a moon that signified Ramzan and made the sky historical. How busy Lahore would get! Its minarets hummed, its municipalities pulled out their old air-raid sirens to make the city noisily cognizant: the moon had been sighted, and the fast begun.

I liked it, the waking up an hour before dawn to eat the prefast meal and chat in whispers. For three wintry seasons I would wake up with Dadi, my grandmother, and Ifat and Shahid: we sat around for hours making jokes in the dark, generating a discourse of unholy comradeship. The food itself, designed to keep the penitent sustained from dawn till dusk, was insistent in its richness and intensity, with bread dripping clarified butter, and curried brains, and cumin eggs, and a peculiarly potent vermicelli, soaked overnight in sugar and fatted milk. And if I liked the getting up at dawn, then Dadi completely adored the eating of it all. I think she fasted only because she so enjoyed the *sehri* meal and that mammoth infusion of food at such an extraordinary hour. At three in the morning the rest of us felt squeamish about linking the deep sleep dreams we had just conducted and so much grease—we asked instead for porridge—but Dadi's eating was a sight to behold and admire. She hooted when the city's sirens sounded to tell us that we should stop eating and that the fast had now begun: she enjoyed a more direct relation with God than did petty municipal authorities and was fond of declaiming what Muhammad himself had said in her defense. He apparently told one of his contemporaries that *sehri* did not end until a white thread of light described the horizon and separated the landscape from the sky. In Dadi's book that thread could open into quite an active loom of dawning: the world made waking sounds, the birds and milkmen all resumed their proper functions, but Dadi's regal mastication—on the last brain now—declared it still was night.

I stopped that early rising years before Tillat and Irfan were old enough to join us, before Ifat ran away to get married, and before my father returned to ritual and overtook his son Shabid's absent place. So my memories of it are scant, the fast of the faithful. But I never lost my affection for the twilight meal, the dusky *iftar* that ended the fast after the mosques had lustily rung with the call for the *maghrib* prayer. We'd start eating dates, of course, in order to mimic Muhammad, but then with what glad eyes we'd welcome the grilled liver and the tang of pepper in the orange juice. We were happy to see the spinach leaves and their fantastical shapes, deftly fried in the lightest chick-pea batter, along with the tenderness of fresh fruit, most touching to the palate. There was a curious invitation about the occasion, converting what began as an act of penance into a godly and obligatory cocktail hour that provided a fine excuse for company and affability. When we lived in Pakistan, that little swerve from severity into celebration happened often. It certainly was true of meatless days.

The country was made in 1947, and shortly thereafter the government decided that two days out of each week would be designated as meatless days, in order to conserve the national supply of goats and cattle. Every Tuesday and Wednesday the butchers' shops would stay firmly closed, without a single carcass dangling from the huge metal hooks that lined the canopies under which the butchers squatted, selling meat, and without the open drains at the side of their narrow street ever running with a trace of blood. On days of normal trade, blood would briskly flow, carrying with it flotillas of chicken feathers, and little bits of sinew and entrail, or a bladder full and yellow that a butcher had just bounced deftly into the drain. On meatless days that world emptied into a skeletal remain: the hot sun came to scorch away all the odors and liquids of slaughter and shriveled on the chopping blocks the last curlicues of anything organic, making them look both vacant and precise.

As a principle of hygiene I suppose it was a good idea although it really had very little to do with conservation: the people who could afford to buy meat, after all, were those who could afford refrigeration, so the only thing the government accomplished was to make some people's Mondays very busy indeed. The Begums had to remember to give the cooks thrice as much money; the butchers had to produce thrice as much meat; the cooks had to buy enough flesh and fowl and other sundry organs to keep an averagely carnivorous household eating for three days. A favorite meatless day breakfast, for example, consisted of goat's head and feet cooked with spices into a rich and ungual sauce—remarkable, the things that people eat. And so, instead of creating an atmosphere of abstention in the city, the institution of meatless days rapidly came to signify the imperative behind the acquisition of all things fleshly. We thought about beef, which is called "big meat," and we thought about mutton, "little meat," and then we collectively thought about chicken, the most coveted of them all.

But here I must forget my American sojourn, which has taught me to look on chicken as a notably undignified bird, with pimply skin and pockets of fat tucked into peculiar places and unnecessarily meaty breasts. Those meatless day fowls, on the other hand, were a thing apart. Small, not much bigger than the average quail, they had a skin that cooked to the texture of rice paper, breaking even over the most fragrant limbs and wings. Naturally we cherished them and lavished much care on trying to obtain the freshest of the crop. Once I was in Karachi with my sister Nuz when the thought that she had to engage in the social ferocity of buying chickens was making her quite depressed. We went anyway, with Nuz assuming an alacrity that had nothing to do with efficiency and everything to do with desperation. Nuz stood small and dark in the chicken-monger's shop, ordered her birds, paid for them, and then suddenly remembered her housewifely duty. "Are they fresh?" she squawked, clutching at them, "Can you promise me they're fresh?" The chicken-monger looked at her with some perplexity. "But Begum Sahib," he said gently, "they're alive."

"Oh," said Nuz, "so they are," and calmed down immediately. I have always admired her capacity to be reassured by the world and take without a jot of embarrassment any comfort it is prepared to offer. So I thought she had forgotten about the issue of freshness as we drove home (with the dejected chickens tied up in a rope basket on the back seat) and the Karachi traffic grew lunchtime crazed. But "Oh," she said again, half an hour later, "So a fresh chicken is a dead chicken." "Not too dead," I replied. It made us think of meatless days as some vast funeral game, where Monday's frenetic creation of fresh things beckoned in the burial meals of Tuesday and Wednesday. "Food," Nuz said with disgust—"It's what you bury in your body."

Meatless Days (1989)

Chris Maynard
& Bill Scheller

from Manifold Destiny

Nouvelle cuisine had degenerated into a lot of silly, overwrought dishes when photographer Chris Maynard (b. 1948) and writer Bill Scheller (b. 1949) teamed up to cook their way across the country, literally, in the late 1980s. Their hilarious fusion of car-engine maintenance and cookery was a perfect counterpoint to frou-frou food; a vague aroma of diesel fuel wafts from their recipes (which give cooking times in miles and suggested routes). The pair also collaborated on *The Bad-For-You Cookbook* (1992), a satiric riposte to the dietary police who emerged on cue as the nation turned gourmet: in America there is always a backlash, and though the puritan impulse may hibernate, it never completely dies.

■ ■ ■

Neither of us can leave Montreal without stopping first at Schwartz's, on Boulevard St.-Laurent.

Schwartz's is a little storefront deli that cures and smokes its own beef briskets, which it heaps high in the front window partly for display and partly so the countermen can quickly spear and slice them. "Smoked meat" is what Montreal prosaically calls this apotheosis of pastrami, and Schwartz's makes the best. You can eat it in the store. You can take it out and eat it at home. Or you may have to eat it on the sidewalk half a block away when the aroma coming through the butcher paper drives you nuts. What we had in mind, one summer's day in 1985, was to pack some in the car for a rest-stop picnic on our way back to Boston.

We were barely out of the city when we started to talk about what a shame it was that our pound of Schwartz's wouldn't be so alluringly hot when we pulled over for lunch. When you order this stuff the way Montreal insiders do—"easy on the lean"—room temperature just doesn't do it justice.

It was then that the idea hit. One of us remembered those stories we used to hear thirty years ago, about lonely truckers cooking hot dogs and beans on their engines. Why not Schwartz's smoked meat? It wouldn't even be cooking it—Schwartz had already done that—but just borrowing a little heat from the engine to warm it up. So we decided what the hell; if it worked for Teamsters, why not us?

We pulled off the interstate in Burlington, Vermont, bought a roll of aluminum foil, and triple-wrapped the sliced brisket. Opening the hood, we spied a nice little spot under the air filter of the '84 VW Rabbit, which seemed the perfect place to tuck in the package, and off we went. An hour later we arrived at a standard-issue Vermont highway rest stop, the kind that looks like they wash the trees, and *voilà!*—in minutes, we were putting away hot smoked-meat sandwiches that actually had steam rising off them. Best of all, we nearly made two women at the next picnic table choke on their sprouts when they saw that instead of a busted fan belt, we had actually just dragged our lunch from the Rabbit's greasy maw.

Necessity, to rewrite the old chestnut, is the mother of necessary inventions—like ways to heat smoked meat when you don't have a steam table handy. But since inspired foolishness is the *real* hallmark of civilization, it wasn't long before we were inventing necessities. For instance, a dire need to roast a pork tenderloin on I-95 between Philadelphia and Providence. Car engines, we discovered, are good for a lot more than simply heating things up.

Soon we were calling each other (not on car phones, thank God) with news of our latest accomplishments:

"I poached a fillet of sole."

"I roasted a stuffed eggplant."

"I figured out how to do game hens."

"I made baked apples."

Before long, those rest-stop stares of disbelief had been replaced by reactions infinitely more delightful to savor—like that of the toll collector who swore he smelled chicken and tarragon, but couldn't figure out where the hell it was coming from.

What we didn't realize, during those early years of random experimentation, was that our burgeoning skills as car-engine cooks were going to serve us splendidly as we competed in one of the most grueling sporting events on the planet: the Cannonball One Lap of America Rally. The One Lap is an eight-thousand-mile-plus highway marathon, seven days of nonstop driving in which participants must adhere to strict rules while reeking of spilled coffee and unchanged underwear. It might be the most exhausting and disorienting event anyone would pay money to enter, but of course it makes you feel like a kid with nothing to do except ride his bike in the park for a week—with no grown-ups around.

Trouble is, it's damned difficult to stick to the rally routes and get anything decent to eat. Most people who run the One Lap follow a regimen of truck-stop breakfasts (not necessarily eaten at breakfast time) and assorted pack-along calories drawn from the canned and bottled food groups. Our wonderful epiphany, shared by none of the fifty-seven other teams in the 1988 event, was that if we cooked on the big V-8 under the hood of our sponsor's stretch Lincoln Town Car, we could eat like epicures without screwing up our time and distance factors.

Here's what we did. Two days before the rally started in Detroit, we worked out a menu and did our shopping. Then we commandeered the kitchen of our friend Marty Kohn, a feature writer for the *Detroit Free Press*, and put together enough uncooked entrées to last us at least all the way to our midway layover in Los Angeles. Boneless chicken breasts with prosciutto and provolone, fillet of flounder, a whole pork tenderloin, a ham steak (a reversion to our simple heat-through days)—everything was seasoned, stuffed, and splashed according to our own recipes, sealed up tightly in three layers of aluminum foil, and promptly frozen. We felt like we were turning Marty's kitchen into a tiny suburban version of those factories where they make airplane food, with one big difference—our stuff was good.

The next day we transferred our frosty little aluminum packages to the kitchen freezer at the Westin Hotel in the Renaissance Center (try pulling a request like *that* on the next concierge you meet) and had them brought up with our coffee and croissants on the morning of the rally. The food went into a cooler, the cooler went into our Lincoln, and off we went. Every afternoon between Detroit and the West Coast we'd haul out another dinner, throw it on the engine, and cook it as we lopped a few hundred more miles off the route. Let our competitors use the drive-thrus at McDonald's. We ate well, very well indeed.

We would have done the same thing in L.A. for the return trip, but we didn't have the time. Anyway, it occurred to us somewhere around

Albuquerque that we *couldn't* have done it, since none of the people we know in L.A have freezers. Everyone there eats out all the time, subsisting entirely on a diet of langoustine ravioli on a coulis of roasted red peppers.

By the time the rally ended, we'd gained more fame for our means of sustenance than for our position in the final standings: Everybody, it seemed, had something to say about car-engine cooking. Half the comments were expressions of pure disbelief (and this book is an attempt to convert the disbelievers), while the rest amounted to variations on "Truck drivers have been doing that for years." *Please.* All the truck drivers we've ever heard of who cook on their diesels are still punching vent holes in cans of Dinty Moore stew.

This is not to say we refuse to acknowledge the pioneers. We are by no means the first people to cook food on car engines. The idea dates back so far, in fact, that it predates cars altogether.

The Huns of the fourth and fifth centuries lived on horseback, and subsisted to a great extent on meat. When a Hun wanted to enjoy a hunk of unsmoked brisket–say, when he was tearing around in the One Lap of the Western Roman Empire (with points for pillage)–he would take the meat and put it under his saddle cloth, and the friction between Hun and horse would have a tenderizing and warming effect. (We think they used saddle cloths. If not, well, just don't think about it.) Since this was a situation in which a "cooking" effect was achieved by the application of excess heat generated by the means of propulsion, it is clearly part of the line of descent that leads to hot lunch buckets in the cab of a steam locomotive, and to stuffed chicken breasts à la Lincoln Town Car. We can't say for sure, but it may also have been the origin of steak tartare.

But let's get back to that important qualification–*excess heat generated by the means of propulsion.* This disqualifies a lot of other attempts at mobile cookery, or at least relegates them to a different branch of evolution. We read recently, for instance, that the big, handsomely outfitted carriage Napoleon Bonaparte used during his military campaigns was equipped with an oil lantern mounted above and behind the rear seat that could be used for cooking as well as lighting. But whether or not the little corporal used his lantern to heat up leftover veal Marengo, the fact is that lanterns don't make carriages go. What Napoleon was really on to here was the ancestor of the latest yuppie doodad, the dashboard microwave. Don't laugh—these are hard upon us, touted as just the thing for people too important to waste time revving up the molecules of frozen Danish in their kitchens. The traffic accident of the future will involve some boob who, peeling a memo off his on-board fax machine, doesn't see the lady in the next lane taking a Pop-Tart out of her micro.

No such risk with car-engine cooking. Since you can't check to see if your dinner is done without getting out of the vehicle and looking under the hood, it's no more dangerous than pulling over to change a tire—a lot less dangerous, in fact, since you don't get to pick the location for a flat tire. As engine cooking spreads in popularity—which it will—interstate rest areas will take on a new, homey character. People will ask each other what smells so good, and lend each other oven mitts; those two rich farts in the Grey Poupon ad who are always borrowing each other's mustard will be joined by plenty of ordinary folks. Like most slow, low-tech enterprises, car-engine cooking will bring people together. Don't take this lightly; the only other way to promote sociability on the road is to smile at strangers in the Howard Johnson's, and God knows where that could get you.

But ultimately, gastronomy overrides sociability. The best reason to cook on your car engine is the same desire to avoid indigestion that motivated us during the rally. Unless you're carrying with you the collected works of Calvin Trillin or Jane and Michael Stern and have the time to detour to all the wonderful diners and rib joints they have chronicled, a long car trip is likely to bring you up short in the eats department. And it's not like the good old days were any better. We recently came across Henry Miller's *The Air-Conditioned Nightmare*, based on a six-month cross-country trip he took in a '32 Buick back in 1941. Miller finished the trip in Los Angeles, not only dyspeptic over the philistines and materialists he claimed to have encountered all over the republic, but with his innards devastated from eating in one greasy spoon after another. Poor devil—that '32 Buick probably had a lovely flathead six, as choice a cooking device as any six-burner restaurant range. If only he'd known. And being Henry Miller, he'd probably have felt better about America if only he'd known that in little more than a decade the philistines and materialists at Rambler were going to produce a car with a backseat that folded into a bed.

But we digress. The point is that you can make better meals for yourself, on your engine, than the vast majority of the roadside stands can make for you. Not to mention that engine cooking is a great way to sample regional foods. Think about crayfish in Louisiana. Lake perch in Wisconsin. Abalone in Northern California (look ahead, if you must, to our abalone recipe). And think of the fun you could have on vacation, with endless, monotonous rides made bearable by salivating over that dinner cooking right under your own hood. Instead of "When are we going to get there?" the kids will ask, "When will the chicken be done?" Finally, the car-engine chef is using one of the tastiest and most healthful cooking methods, simmering foods in their own juices in a sealed package—en papillote, as they say when they cook on their Renaults in France.

We could go on, maybe even mentioning the conservation benefits of cooking with heat that otherwise would be wasted—at the risk, of course, of sounding like refugees from the 1970s gas shortage Moral Equivalent of War. But who knows? If there's another energy crisis, we might be hailed as the heralds of a kinder, gentler way to cook dinner.

Manifold Destiny (1989)

Wendell Berry

The Pleasures of Eating

Many food writers describe a culinary epiphany, an encounter with a single flavor or dish that changed the way they saw the world. In my case it was not an actual taste, but rather the tastes that I imagined as I listened to Wendell Berry (b. 1934). I was an aspiring poet at a small college in Ohio. Berry was a poet, a farmer, and a professor at the University of Kentucky. Two teachers—Allen Ginsberg and Gary Snyder—encouraged me to drive south across the Ohio River and down to Kentucky to hear Berry read. Nothing has ever tasted the same since. It was several years after the shootings of the war protesters at Kent State, a time when individuals seemed small and powerless and dispensable, and corporations seemed huge and insistent and eternal. Berry—who was raised on a farm not far from the one he tends today, and has published more than 40 books of fiction, poetry, and essays—read songs for an interconnected world of human scale, a world shaped by one's own hands. "We must recover the sense of the majesty of the creation and the ability to be worshipful in its presence," he affirmed as he discussed growing and picking and cooking his food. "It is only on the condition of humility and reverence before the world that our species will be able to remain in it." I felt as if Thoreau had come back from the dead and was offering to fix dinner.

"Eating," said Berry "is an agricultural act, a political act," and as he described the food from his farm—carrots cold and gritty and sweet from the ground, skin-bursting tomatoes, corn too fresh to have lapsed into starch—I understood flavor as the result of a chain of events. It's the chatter at the farm stand, the smell of the dirt, the power to choose this-not-that, the sense of urgency, the rush home with the corn, the not-so-square meals my mother allowed on those days, those cucumber-tomatoes-corn-and-shortcake dinner days when everything tasted better than any other time. I saw that a good meal was an expression of a good life, and I decided that dinner can change everything. The country was rife with similar conversion experiences. A generation of transcendentalist gourmets was being born. It would become chic, competitive, commercial, everything that the poet of Port William, Kentucky, is not. When I get depressed about the state of food—when the bad outweighs the good, and even the good seems like just another commodity—I read Berry to remember what matters.

■ ■ ■

Many times, after I have finished a lecture on the decline of American farming and rural life, someone in the audience has asked, "What can city people do?"

"Eat responsibly," I have usually answered. Of course, I have tried to explain what I meant, but afterwards I have invariably felt that there was more to be said than I had been able to say. Now I would like to attempt a better explanation.

I begin with the proposition that eating is an agricultural act. Eating ends the annual drama of the food economy that begins with planting and birth. Most eaters, however, are no longer aware that this is true. They think of food as an agricultural product, perhaps, but they do not think of themselves as participants in agriculture. They think of themselves as "consumers." If they think beyond that, they recognize that they are passive consumers. They buy what they want—or what they have been persuaded to want—within the limits of what they can get. They pay, mostly without protest, what they are charged. And they mostly ignore certain critical questions about the quality and the cost of what they are sold: How fresh is it? How pure or clean is it, how free of dangerous chemicals? How far was it transported, and what did transportation add to the cost? How much did manufacturing or packaging or advertising add to the cost? When the food product has been "manufactured" or "processed" or "precooked," how has that affected its quality or nutritional value?

Most urban shoppers would tell you that food is produced on farms. But most of them do not know on what farms, or what kinds of farms, or where the farms are, or what knowledge or skills are involved in farming. They apparently have little doubt that farms will continue to produce, but they do not know how or over what obstacles. For them, then, food is pretty much an abstract idea—something they do not know or imagine—until it appears on the grocery shelf or on the table.

The specialization of production induces specialization of consumption. Patrons of the entertainment industry, for example, entertain themselves less and less and have become more and more passively dependent on commercial suppliers. This is certainly also true of patrons of the food industry, who have tended more and more to be *mere* consumers—passive, uncritical, and dependent. Indeed, this sort of consumption may be said to be one of the chief goals of industrial production. The food industrialists have by now persuaded millions of consumers to prefer food that is already prepared. They will grow, deliver, and cook your food for you and (just like your mother) beg you to eat it. That they do not yet offer to insert it, prechewed, into your mouth is only because they have found no profitable way to do so. We may rest assured that they would be glad to find such a way. The ideal industrial food consumer would be strapped to a table with a tube running from the food factory directly into his or her stomach. (Think of the savings, the efficiency, and the effortlessness of such an arrangement!)

Perhaps I exaggerate, but not by much. The industrial eater is, in fact, one who does not know that eating is an agricultural act, who no longer knows or imagines the connections between eating and the land, and who is therefore necessarily passive and uncritical—in short, a victim. When food, in the minds of eaters, is no longer associated with farming and with the land, then the eaters are suffering a kind of cultural amnesia that is misleading and dangerous. The current version of the "dream home" of the future involves "effortless" shopping from a list of available goods on a television monitor and heating precooked food by remote control. Of course, this implies, and indeed depends on, a perfect ignorance of the history of the food that is consumed. It requires that the citizenry should give up their hereditary and sensible aversion to buying a pig in a poke. It wishes to make the selling of pigs in pokes an honorable and glamorous activity. The dreamer in this dream home will perforce know nothing about the kind or quality of this food, or where it came from, or how it was produced and prepared, or what ingredients, additives, and residues it contains. Unless, that is, the dreamer undertakes a close and constant study of the food industry, in which case he or she might as well wake up and play an active and responsible part in the economy of food.

There is, then, a politics of food that, like any politics, involves our freedom. We still (sometimes) remember that we cannot be free if our minds and voices are controlled by someone else. But we have neglected to understand that neither can we be free if our food and its sources are controlled by someone else. The condition of the passive consumer of food is not a democratic condition. One reason to eat responsibly is to live free.

But, if there is a food politics, there are also a food aesthetics and a food ethics, neither of which is dissociated from politics. Like industrial sex, industrial eating has become a degraded, poor, and paltry thing. Our kitchens and other eating places more and more resemble filling stations, as our homes more and more resemble motels. "Life is not very interesting," we seem to have decided. "Let its satisfactions be minimal, perfunctory, and fast." We hurry through our meals to go to work and hurry through our work in order to "recreate" ourselves in the evenings and on weekends and vacations. And then we hurry, with the greatest possible speed and noise and violence, through our recreation—for what? To eat the billionth hamburger at some fast-food joint hell-bent on increasing the "quality" of our life. And all this is carried out in a remarkable obliviousness of the causes and effects, the possibilities and the purposes of the life of the body in this world.

One will find this obliviousness represented in virgin purity in the advertisements of the food industry, in which the food wears as much makeup as the actors. If one gained one's whole knowledge of food—as some presumably do—from these advertisements, one would not know that the various edibles were ever living creatures, or that they all come from the soil, or that they were produced by work. The passive American consumer, sitting down to a meal of pre-prepared or fast food, confronts a platter covered with inert, anonymous substances that have been processed, dyed, breaded, sauced, gravied, ground, pulped, strained, blended, prettified, and sanitized beyond resemblance to any part of any creature that ever lived. The products of nature and agriculture have been made, to all appearances, the products of industry. Both eater and eaten are thus in exile from biological reality. And the result is a kind of solitude, unprecedented in human experience, in which the eater may think of eating as, first, a purely commercial transaction between him and a supplier, and then as a purely appetitive transaction between him and his food.

And this peculiar specialization of the act of eating is, again, of obvious benefit to the food industry, which has good reason to obscure the connection between food and farming. It would not do for the consumer to know that the hamburger she is eating came from a steer that spent much of its life standing deep in its own excrement in a feedlot, helping to pollute the local streams, or that the calf that yielded the veal cutlet on her plate spent its life in a box in which it did not have room to turn around. And, though her sympathy for the coleslaw might be less tender, she should not be encouraged to meditate on the hygienic and biological implications of mile-square fields of cabbage, for vegetables grown in huge monocultures are dependent on toxic chemicals just as animals in close confinement are dependent on antibiotics and other drugs.

The consumer, that is to say, must be kept from discovering that, in the food industry—as in any other industry—the overriding concerns are not quality and health but volume and price. For decades now the entire industrial food economy, from the large farms and feedlots to the chains of fast-food restaurants and supermarkets, has been obsessed with volume. It has relentlessly increased scale in order to increase volume in order (presumably) to reduce costs. But, as scale increases, diversity declines; as diversity declines, so does health; as health declines, the dependence on drugs and chemicals necessarily increases. As capital replaces labor, it does so by substituting machines, drugs, and chemicals for human workers and for the natural health and fertility of the soil. The food is produced by any means or any shortcuts that will increase profits. And the business of the cosmeticians of advertising is to persuade the consumer that food so produced is good, tasty, healthful, and a guarantee of marital fidelity and long life.

It is, then, indeed possible to be liberated from the husbandry and wifery of the old household food economy. But one can be thus liberated only by entering a trap—unless one sees ignorance and helplessness, as many people apparently do, as the signs of privilege. The trap is the ideal of industrialism: a walled city surrounded by valves that let merchandise in but no consciousness out. How does one escape this trap? Only voluntarily, the same way that one went in—by restoring one's consciousness of what is involved in eating, by reclaiming responsibility for one's own part in the food economy. One might begin with Sir Albert Howard's illuminating principle that we should understand "the whole problem of health in soil, plant, animal, and man as one great subject." Eaters, that is, must understand that eating takes place inescapably in the world, that it is inescapably an agricultural act, and that how we eat determines, to a considerable extent, the way the world is used. This is a simple way of describing a relationship that is inexpressibly complex. To eat responsibly is to understand and enact, so far as one can, this complex relationship.

What can one do? Here is a list, probably not definitive:

Participate in food production to the extent that you can. If you have a yard or even just a porch box or a pot in a sunny window, grow something to eat in it. Make a little compost of your kitchen scraps, and use it for fertilizer. Only by growing some food for yourself can you become acquainted with the beautiful energy cycle that revolves from soil to seed to flower to fruit to food to offal to decay, and around again. You will be fully responsible for any food that you grow for yourself, and you will know all about it. You will appreciate it fully, having known it all its life.

Prepare your own food. This means reviving in your own mind and life the arts of kitchen and household. This should enable you to eat more cheaply and give you a measure of "quality control." You will have some reliable knowledge of what has been added to the food you eat.

Learn the origins of the food you buy, and buy the food that is produced closest to your home. The idea that every locality should be, as much as possible, the source of its own food makes several kinds of sense. The locally produced food supply is the most secure, the freshest, and the easiest for local consumers to know about and to influence.

Whenever you can, deal directly with a local farmer, gardener, or orchardist. All the reasons listed for the previous suggestion apply here. In addition, by such dealing, you eliminate the whole pack of merchants, transporters, processors, packagers, and advertisers who thrive at the expense of both producers and consumers.

Learn, in self-defense, as much as you can of the economy and technology of industrial food production. What is added to food that is not food, and what do you pay for these additions?

Learn what is involved in the *best* farming and gardening.

Learn as much as you can, by direct observation and experience if possible, of the life histories of the food species.

The last suggestion seems particularly important to me. Many people are now as much estranged from the lives of domestic plants and animals (except for flowers and dogs and cats) as they are from the lives of the wild ones. This is regrettable, for these domestic creatures are in diverse ways attractive; there is much pleasure in knowing them. And, at their best, farming, animal husbandry, horticulture, and gardening are complex and comely arts; there is much pleasure in knowing them, too.

And it follows that there is great displeasure in knowing about a food economy that degrades and abuses those arts and those plants and animals and the soil from which they come. For anyone who does know something of the modern history of food, eating away from home can be a chore. My own inclination is to eat seafood instead of red meat or poultry when I am traveling. Though I am by no means a vegetarian, I dislike the thought that some animal has been made miserable in order to feed me. If I am going to eat meat, I want it to be from an animal that has lived a pleasant, uncrowded life outdoors, on bountiful pasture, with good water nearby and trees for shade. And I am getting almost as fussy about food plants. I like to eat vegetables and fruits that I know have lived happily and healthily in good soil—not the products of the huge, bechemicaled factory-fields that I have seen, for example, in the Central Valley of California. The industrial farm is said to have been patterned on the factory production line. In practice, it invariably looks more like a concentration camp.

The pleasure of eating should be an *extensive* pleasure, not that of the mere gourmet. People who know the garden in which their vegetables have grown and know that the garden is healthy will remember the beauty of the growing plants, perhaps in the dewy first light of morning when gardens are at their best. Such a memory involves itself with the food and is one of the pleasures of eating. The knowledge of the good health of the garden relieves and frees and comforts the eater. The same goes for eating meat. The thought of the good pasture, and of the calf contentedly grazing, flavors the steak. Some, I know, will think it bloodthirsty or worse to eat a fellow creature you have known all its life. On the contrary, I think, it means that you eat with understanding and with gratitude. A significant part of the pleasure of eating is in one's accurate consciousness of the lives and the world from which food comes. The pleasure of eating, then, may be the best available standard of our health. And this pleasure, I think, is pretty fully available to the urban consumer who will make the necessary effort.

I mentioned earlier the politics, aesthetics, and ethics of food. But to speak of the pleasure of eating is to go beyond those categories. Eating with the fullest pleasure—pleasure, that is, that does not depend on ignorance—is perhaps the profoundest enactment of our connection with the world. In this pleasure we experience and celebrate our dependence and our gratitude, for we are living from mystery, from creatures we did not make and powers we cannot comprehend. When I think of the meaning of food, I always remember these lines by the poet William Carlos Williams, which seem to me merely honest:

> There is nothing to eat,
>   seek it where you will,
>   but the body of the Lord.
> The blessed plants
>   and the sea, yield it
>   to the imagination
> intact.

What Are People For? (1990)

Alice Waters

The Farm-Restaurant Connection

Without Alice Waters (b. 1944), it sometimes seems, there would be no darling baby vegetables, no proliferation of green markets, no organic chic, no pressure against agribusiness. Not only does she believe that fresh, local, seasonal food can change the world: she has proven it. Waters came of age at Berkeley (where she specialized in French cultural studies) in the 1960s, when distrust of the conventional, the corporate, and the mass-produced was endemic. Traditional class distinctions were eroding in American culture, and a generation that had known little privation was less inclined to seek career security than it was to insist on self-expression. For many, faced with the meat-and-potatoes habits of their parents, restaurant work and creative cooking suddenly made radical sense.

Traveling in France after college, Waters understood—in the lightning bolt of one simple, delicious meal—that good food is not an accident, but the result of a host of careful, conscious decisions, both personal and political. Returning to Berkeley in 1971, she opened Chez Panisse, a restaurant that featured impeccable ingredients, a menu that changed daily (and sometimes hourly), and dishes that drew heavily on French technique but were otherwise too idiosyncratic to categorize. This kind of cooking came to be known as California cuisine. To budding epicures across the country, the restaurant was an inspiration, the realization of a shared dream. Hundreds of cooks, chefs, and food writers passed through the kitchen, absorbing the notion that the only sane response to the modern global economy, with its frantic pace and its ever-increasing diminishments of the sense of place, is to eat locally and eat well.

■ ■ ■

I have always believed that a restaurant can be no better than the ingredients it has to work with. As much as by any other factor, Chez Panisse has been defined by the search for ingredients. That search and what we have found along the way have shaped what we cook and ultimately who we are. The search has made us become part of a community—a community that has grown from markets, gardens, and suppliers and has gradually come to include farmers, ranchers, and fishermen. It has also made us realize that, as a restaurant, we are utterly dependent on the health of the land, the sea, and the planet as a whole, and that this search for good ingredients is pointless without a healthy agriculture and a healthy environment.

We served our first meal at Chez Panisse on August 28, 1971. The menu was pâté en croûte, duck with olives, salad, and fresh fruit, and the meal was cooked by Victoria Wise, who, together with Leslie Land and Paul Aratow, was one of the three original cooks at the restaurant. The ducks came from Chinatown in San Francisco and the other ingredients mostly from two local supermarkets: the Japanese produce concession at U-Save on Grove Street and the Co-op across the street. We sifted through every leaf of romaine, using perhaps 20 percent of each head and discarding the rest. We argued about which olives we ought to use with the duck and settled without much enthusiasm on green ones whose source I don't recall, agreeing after the fact that we could have done better. To this day we have yet to find a source of locally produced olives that really satisfies us.

We don't shop at supermarkets anymore, but in most respects the same processes and problems apply. Leslie Land recalls, "We were home cooks—we didn't know there were specialized restaurant suppliers. We thought everybody bought their food the way we did." I think that ignorance was an important, if unwitting, factor in allowing Chez Panisse to become what it is. Often, we simply couldn't cook what we wanted to cook because we couldn't find the level of quality we needed in the required ingredients, or we couldn't find the ingredients at all. Our set menus, which we've always published in advance so customers can choose when they want to come, featured the phrase "if available" with regularity during the first seven or eight years. Since we've always felt that freshness and purity were synonymous with quality, there were few guarantees that what we needed would appear in the form and condition we wanted when we wanted it.

If, as I believe, restaurants are communities—each with its own culture—then Chez Panisse began as a hunter-gatherer culture and, to a lesser extent, still is. Not only did we prowl the supermarkets, the stores and stalls of Chinatown, and such specialty shops as Berkeley then possessed (some of which, like the Cheese Board and Monterey Market, predated us and continue to develop from strength to strength) but we also literally foraged.

We gathered watercress from streams, picked nasturtiums and fennel from roadsides, and gathered blackberries from the Santa Fe tracks in Berkeley. We also took herbs like oregano and thyme from the gardens of friends. One of these friends, Wendy Ruebman, asked if we'd like sorrel from her garden, setting in motion an informal but regular system of obtaining produce from her and other local gardeners. We also relied on friends with rural connections: Mary Isaak, the mother of one of our cooks, planted fraises des bois for us in Petaluma, and Lindsey Shere, one of my partners and our head pastry cook to this day, got her father to grow fruit for us near his place in Healdsburg.

Although most of our sources in the restaurant's early days were of necessity unpredictable, produce was the main problem area, and we focused our efforts again and again on resolving it. Perhaps more than any other kind of foodstuff, produce in general and its flavor in particular have suffered under postwar American agriculture. Although we've been able to have as much cosmetically perfect, out-of-season fruit and vegetables as anyone could possibly want, the flavor, freshness, variety, and wholesomeness of produce have been terribly diminished. With the notable exception of Chinese and Japanese markets that even in the early seventies emphasized flavor and quality, we really had nowhere to turn but to sympathetic gardeners who either already grew what we needed or would undertake to grow it for us.

Our emphasis—and, today, our insistence—on organically grown produce developed less out of any ideological commitment than out of the fact that this was the way almost everyone we knew gardened. We have never been interested in being a health or natural foods restaurant; rather, organic and naturally raised ingredients happen to be consistent with both what we want for our kitchen and what we want for our community and our larger environment. Such ingredients have never been an end in themselves, but they are a part of the way of life that inspired the restaurant and that we want the restaurant to inspire. Most of us have become so inured to the dogmas and self-justifications of agribusiness that we forget that, until 1940, most produce was, for all intents and purposes, organic, and, until the advent of the refrigerated boxcar, it was also of necessity fresh, seasonal, and local. There's nothing radical about organic produce: It's a return to traditional values of the most fundamental kind.

It had always seemed to us that the best way to solve our supply problems was either to deal directly with producers or, better still, to raise our own. By 1975, we'd made some progress with the first approach, regularly receiving, for example, fresh and smoked trout from Garrapata in Big Sur. One of my partners, Jerry Budrick, had also set up a connection with the Dal Porto Ranch in Amador County in the foothills of the Sierra Nevada, which provided us with lambs and with zinfandel grapes for the house wine Walter Schug made for us at the Joseph Phelps Winery. Jerry also acquired some land of his own in Amador, and it seemed an obvious solution to our produce needs for us to farm it. In 1977 we tried this, but we knew even less about farming than we thought we did, and the experiment proved a failure.

Fortunately, during the late 1970s some of our urban gardens were producing quite successfully, notably one cultivated by the French gardener and cook at Chez Panisse, Jean-Pierre Moullé, on land in the Berkeley hills owned by Duke McGillis, our house doctor, and his wife, Joyce. In addition, Lindsey Shere returned from a trip to Italy laden with seeds, which her father planted in Healdsburg, thereby introducing us to rocket and other greens still exotic at that time. Meanwhile, we were also learning how to use conventional sources as best we could. Mark Miller, then a cook with us, made the rounds of the Oakland Produce Market each dawn, and we discovered useful sources at other wholesale and commercial markets in San Francisco. Closer to home, we bought regularly—as we still do—from Bill Fujimoto, who had taken over Monterey Market from his parents and had begun to build its reputation for quality and variety.

It's difficult now to remember the kind of attitude to flavor and quality that still prevailed in the mid and late 1970s. When Jeremiah Tower, who was our main cook at Chez Panisse from 1973 to 1977, once sent back some meat he felt wasn't up to scratch, the supplier was apoplectic: No one had ever done that before. And Jerry Rosenfield, a friend and physician who has worked on many of our supply problems over the years, caused an uproar one morning when he was substituting for Mark Miller at the Oakland Produce Market: Jerry insisted on *tasting* some strawberries before buying them. Jerry was also a key figure in securing our sources for fish, probably the first of our supply problems that we were able to solve successfully. During the restaurant's first few years, we served very little fish at all, such was the quality available—despite our being across the bay from a city renowned for its seafood. But, in 1975, Jerry brought us some California sea mussels he'd gathered near his home, and they were a revelation. We asked him to bring us more, and in late 1976 he became our fish dealer, buying from wholesalers and fishermen ranging up the coast from Monterey to Fort Bragg. Along the way he began to be assisted by Paul Johnson, a cook from another Berkeley restaurant called In Season, who took over from Jerry in 1979 and who today sells what is arguably the best fish on the West Coast.

Our produce problem, however, remained unsolved, and we decided to have another try at farming. John Hudspeth, a disciple of James Beard who later started Bridge Creek restaurant just up the street from us, owned some land near Sacramento that he was willing to make available to us in 1980 and 1981. In some respects, this farm was a success—producing good onions and potatoes and wonderful little white peaches from a tree John had planted— but we weren't equipped to deal with the valley heat or the land's penchant for flooding. While the farm did produce, it produced unreliably, and we had to continue to obtain supplies from elsewhere. It also finally disabused us of any illusion that we were farmers. We realized that there seemed to be only two solutions available: extending and formalizing the system of ur- ban gardeners we already had in place, and establishing direct connections with sympathetic farmers who could grow what we needed—that is, farmers who, since we didn't know enough farming to do it ourselves, would farm on our behalf.

In the early 1980s, two members of the restaurant staff, Andrea Crawford and Sibella Kraus, and Lindsey Shere's daughter Thérèse established several salad gardens in Berkeley, one of which was in my backyard. These eventu- ally met most of our needs for salad greens, but for other kinds of produce we remained dependent on a hodgepodge of often-unreliable sources. Two things happened in 1982, however, that turned out to be tremendously im- portant. First, Jean-Pierre Gorin, a friend and filmmaker teaching in La Jolla, introduced us to the produce grown near there by the Chino family. And, second, Sibella Kraus became the forager for the restaurant and eventually started the Farm-Restaurant Project. Jean-Pierre happened by the Chinos' roadside stand, tasted a green bean, and arranged to have two boxes sent to us immediately. The beans were exquisite, and I flew down to find out who had grown them. We became good friends, and to this day we receive nine boxes of produce from the Chinos each week.

Meanwhile, as Sibella had become more and more involved with our salad gardens, she decided that she would like to work with produce full-time and proposed that she become the restaurant's first full-time forager, an idea we agreed to with enthusiasm. Sibella spent her time on the road locating farmers, tasting their produce, and, if we liked it, arranging for a schedule of deliveries to Chez Panisse. In 1983, we funded the Farm-Restaurant Project under Sibella's direction, which set up a produce network among a number of Bay Area restaurants and local farmers and culminated in the first Tasting of Summer Produce, now an annual event at which dozens of small, quality-conscious farmers show their produce to the food community and the general public. Sibella left us to work for Greenleaf Produce (from whom we still regularly buy) and has become an important figure in the sustainable-agriculture movement. She was succeeded as forager by Catherine Brandel, who has since become one of the head cooks in our upstairs café. During this period, Green Gulch, run by the San Francisco Zen Center, became an important supplier, as did Warren Weber, whom we continue to work with today. We were also fortunate to have Thérèse Shere and Eric Monrad producing tomatoes, peppers, beans, lettuce, and lamb for us at Coulee Ranch near Healdsburg.

During her tenure as forager, Catherine continued to develop the network Sibella had created, finding, for example, a regular source of eggs for us at New Life Farms. But she was frustrated, as we all were, by the seeming impossibility of finding meat that was both flavorful and raised in a humane and wholesome way. Since the beginning of Chez Panisse, we had been forced to rely on conventional suppliers, a continuing disappointment given how much progress we had made with other kinds of materials. But, in late 1986, Jerry Rosenfield took over as forager from Catherine, and over the next two years he made enormous strides in finding meat sources for us. Jerry had been living in the Pacific Northwest and had discovered a number of ranchers and farmers there who were attempting to raise beef, veal, and lamb without hormones and under humane conditions. In particular, the Willamette Valley between Portland and Eugene, Oregon, became a source for rabbits, lambs, goats, and beef, although Jerry also located producers closer to home, including ones for game and for that most elusive bird–a decently flavored, naturally raised chicken. We still have a way to go, but today, for the first time in our history, we are able to serve meat that really pleases us.

We have made progress on other fronts, too. In 1983, for example, we helped Steve Sullivan launch Acme Bakery, which bakes for us and for many other local restaurants. And, recently, we've realized a close approximation of our dream of having a farm. In 1985, my father, Pat Waters, began looking for a farmer who would be willing to make a long-term agreement to grow most of our produce for us according to our specifications. With help from the University of California at Davis and local organic food organizations, Dad came up with a list of eighteen potential farmers, which he narrowed down to a list of four on the basis of interviews, tastings, and visits. We settled on Bob Cannard, who farms on twenty-five acres in the Sonoma Valley.

Bob is very special, not only because he grows wonderful fruits and vegetables for us–potatoes, onions, salad greens, tomatoes, beans, berries, peaches, apricots, and avocados, to name a few–but also because he is as interested in us as we are in him. He likes to visit the restaurant kitchen and pitch in, and we send our cooks up to him to help pick. He takes all the restaurant's compostable garbage each day, which he then uses to grow more food. He is also a teacher at his local college and a major force in his local farmer's market. He sees that his farm and our restaurant are part of something larger and that, whether we acknowledge it or not, they have a responsibility to the health of the communities in which they exist and of the land on which they depend.

The search for materials continues, and I imagine it always will. We are still looking for good sources for butter, olives, oil, and prosciutto, to name a few. But, even when we find them, the foraging will continue. Ingredients will appear that we'll want to try, and we in turn will have new requirements that we'll want someone to fulfill for us. Whatever happens, we realize that, as restaurateurs, we are now involved in agriculture and its vagaries–the weather, the soil, and the economics of farming and rural communities. Bob Cannard reminds us frequently that farming isn't manufacturing: It is a continuing relationship with nature that has to be complete on both sides to work. People claim to know that plants are living things, but the system of food production, distribution, and consumption we have known in this country for the last forty years has attempted to deny that they are. If our food has lacked flavor—if, in aesthetic terms, it has been dead—that may be because it was treated as dead even while it was being grown. And perhaps we have tolerated such food—and the way its production has affected our society and environment—because our senses, our hearts, and our minds have been in some sense deadened, too.

I've always felt it was part of my job as a cook and restaurateur to try to wake people up to these things, to challenge them really to taste the food and to experience the kind of community that can happen in the kitchen and at the table. Those of us who work with food suffer from an image of being involved in an elite, frivolous pastime that has little relation to anything important or meaningful. But in fact we are in a position to cause people to make important connections between what they are eating and a host of crucial environmental, social, and health issues. Food is at the center of these issues.

This isn't a matter of idealism or altruism but rather one of self-interest and survival. Restaurateurs have a very real stake in the health of the planet, in the source of the foodstuffs we depend on, and in the future of farmers, fishermen, and other producers. Hydroponic vegetables or fish raised in pens will never be a real substitute for the flavor and quality of the ingredients that are in increasing jeopardy today. Professionally and personally, both our livelihoods and our lives depend on the preservation of what we have and the restoration of what we have lost. The fate of farmers—and with them the fate of the earth itself—is not somebody else's problem: It is our fate, too.

There is clearly so much more to do. But ultimately it comes down to realizing the necessity of the land to what we do and our connection to it. Few restaurants are going to be able to create the kind of relationship we have with Bob Cannard, but there are other routes to the same goal. I'm convinced that farmer's markets are an important step in this direction; they also contribute to the local economy, promote more variety and quality in the marketplace, and create community. As restaurateurs and ordinary consumers meet the people who grow their food, they acquire an interest in the future of farms, of rural communities, and of the environment. This interest, when it helps to ensure the continuing provision of open space near cities and the diversity of food produced on it, is to everyone's benefit. Country and city can once again become a mutual support system, a web of inter-dependent communities. That's why fresh, locally grown, seasonal food-stuffs are more than an attractive fashion or a quaint, romantic notion: They are a fundamental part of a sustainable economy and agriculture—and they taste better, too. Of course, people respond, "That's easy for you to say: In California you can have whatever you want all year round." I tell them that's true, but I also tell them that most of it tastes terrible. And, while there's no reason to forgo all non-locally-produced ingredients—I wouldn't want to give up our weekly shipment from the Chinos—local materials must become the basis of our cooking and our food; this is true for every region of the planet that has produced a flavorful, healthy cuisine.

What sometimes seem to be limitations are often opportunities. Ear-lier this year, in the lee between the early spring vegetables and those of mid-summer, we had an abundance of fava beans, which we explored in the kitchen for six weeks, served in soups, in purees, as a garnish, and, of course, by themselves—and we discovered that we had only *begun* to tap the possi-bilities. There was a stew of beans with savory and cream, a fava-bean-and-potato gratin, fava bean pizza with lots of garlic, a pasta fagioli using favas, a rough puree of favas with garlic and sage, and a vinaigrette salad, to name a few. The point is that what constitutes an exciting, exotic ingredient is very much in the eye of the beholder and that few things can be as compelling as fresh, locally grown materials that you know have been raised in a respon-sible way.

When I was first thinking about opening what would become Chez Panisse, my friend Tom Luddy took me to see a Marcel Pagnol retrospective at the old Surf Theater in San Francisco. We went every night and saw about half the movies Pagnol made during his long career, including *The Baker's Wife* and his Marseilles trilogy—*Marius, Fanny,* and *César.* Every one of these movies about life in the south of France fifty years ago radiated wit, love for people, and respect for the earth. Every movie made me cry.

My partners and I decided to name our new restaurant after the widower Panisse, a compassionate, placid, and slightly ridiculous marine outfitter in the Marseilles trilogy, so as to evoke the sunny good feelings of another world that contained so much that was incomplete or missing in our own—the simple wholesome good food of Provence, the atmosphere of tolerant camaraderie and great lifelong friendships, and a respect both for the old folks and their pleasures and for the young and their passions. Four years later, when our partnership incorporated itself, we immodestly took the name Pagnol et Cie., Inc., to reaffirm our desire to recreate a reality where life and work were inseparable and the daily pace left time for the afternoon anisette or the restorative game of *pétanque*, and where eating together nourished the spirit as well as the body—since the food was raised, harvested, hunted, fished, and gathered by people sustaining and sustained by each other and by the earth itself. In this respect, as in so many others, the producers and farmers we have come to know not only have provided us with good food but have also been essential in helping us to realize our dreams.

The Journal of Gastronomy, Summer-Autumn 1989

Daniel Pinkwater

Where Is the Grease of Yesteryear?

Daniel Pinkwater (b. 1941) has become widely known for his wry and affecting commentary on National Public Radio's "All Things Considered." This Proustian disquisition on grease, with its exquisite cataloging of "patties of semiliquid fat and gristle" and "scary bright-green pickle relish," restores a lost corner of American food history in all its cholesterol-rich grandeur.

■ ■ ■

When I was fourteen, my family left Los Angeles, where we'd lived for five or six years, and moved back to Chicago. Naturally, I was glad to leave L.A., but I was miserable and lonely in Chicago.

I didn't know anybody. The high school I transferred to was a hotbed of early Elvis-worshippers and thugs. My parents rented an ugly apartment in a brand-new, shoddily built high-rise—a place I hated from the first day. And I was entering the state of adolescent crisis that lasted until I was thirty-two years old.

I spent my time wandering the streets. I liked walking through city streets, especially at night—and do so to this day. It was about this time that I began an earnest pursuit of the other activity which has characterized and shaped my life—gluttony.

My funds were limited, but I was able to sample many truly frightening varieties of 1950s junk food. When I hear experts inveigh against the fast food of today, which, if a little light in nutritional content, is at least fairly sanitary and made mostly of thing you can eat, I remember such haunts of mine as Fred's Red Hots.

Fred's Red Hots was not far from the apartment building. It was in one of those triangular buildings you see where two streets converge diagonally. There were never a lot of customers at Fred's. Just Fred. Angry face. Big nose. Grease-soaked apron. White paper cap. Mumbling.

Grease was the motif at Fred's. Instantly I would enter the place, a fine mist of grease suspended in the air would adhere to my eyeglasses—diffracting the light—so I always remember Fred's as a pointillist painting.

A monster fan over the door blasted grease-laden air out into the street, and made a roaring sound.

The red-hots I regarded more as objects of art than something to eat. Bright red, they tended to snap and squirt hot fat when you bit into them, and left a strange chemical taste in the mouth for days. Even I knew they were deadly, and left them alone.

I was a cheeseburger customer. Fred dispensed the cheapest cheeseburgers in Chicago. They came as singles, doubles, triples and quadruples. This referred to the number of patties of semiliquid fat and gristle. I believe a quadruple was under a dollar with a heap of dripping French fries, nearly raw in the middle, a limp quarter-pickle, and a bun with one last redundant gleam of schmaltz on top.

To make a balanced meal of a Fredburger, one could spoon on ketchup and scary bright-green pickle relish from bowls on the counter, thus adding vital trace minerals.

A quadruple contained more cholesterol than the average Copper Eskimo gets in a month. And indeed, most of my memories of Fred's are also of wild blizzards and eyeball-freezing February Chicago nights.

Not only did I thaw out at Fred's, and fortify myself for further wandering through the whiteout—Fred himself was, for the first few months I lived in Chicago, the only person I knew to speak to. I would tell Fred of my life, my suffering, my hopes and dreams.

"Yeh? So what?" Fred would ask, and give me a free limp, warm pickle spear.

It was good to know someone who listened.

Even after I began to make friends with various other misfits and delinquents, and have places to go and things to do, I would stop in at Fred's for a double or triple to fill the gap between the end of school and suppertime—or late at night, on my way home from committing an act of vandalism, I might drop by for one last infusion of lipids to help me sleep.

Probably the last time I visited Fred's was about the time I defied the predictions of guidance counselors and juvenile officers and left for college.

Seventeen or eighteen years later I was in Chicago with my wife. I drove Jill around the old neighborhood, and told her stories of my youth, which was at the very least misguided.

There was Fred's. Unchanged. I was charmed and filled with nostalgia.

"Let's go in," Jill said.

"Let's," I said. "But don't eat anything."

"Don't?"

"If you value your life."

We entered. I felt the grease-cloud envelop me. It was all exactly the same. Fred was exactly the same. It smelled exactly the same. The little greasy dust icicles hung from the transom exactly the same. Four or five Chicago cavemen sat at the counter, gnawing cheeseburgers.

"It's like stepping back in time," I whispered.

Jill, overcome with nostalgia on my behalf, ordered a red-hot.

"No!"

"It's fine," she said. "Just like the Bronx."

There is no arguing with Jill. She does as she pleases. Fred handed her the red-hot. Later she would pay the price of her arrogance.

"Do you recognize this man?" Jill asked Fred.

Fred eyed me.

"My husband used to come in here all the time, twenty years ago. He always talks about you. He says you were his only friend."

"Yeh? So what?" Fred replied.

It's not that you can't go home again. It's that most people know better.

Fish Whistle (1989)

philadelphia pepperpot soup

If you enjoy the taste of tripe, and perhaps even if you think you don't but are open-minded, then you must surely try Philadelphia Pepperpot Soup. It was first issued to General Washington's troops when they were on the brink of starvation and freezing to death during the great winter battle at Valley Forge, Pennsylvania, during the War of Independence. This is how the story goes. One day, after making an inspection of his troops, Washington furiously demanded to see the cook and ordered him to feed the men. The cook replied that all he had was some tripe and some peppercorns. So out of necessity came this original creation. To my mind this makes the cook a real war hero, since without his ingenuity Washington's men wouldn't have been able to outlast the British, win a decisive victory, and go on to win the war.

Everyone I know in Philadelphia makes Pepperpot Soup differently. Some use up to a dozen large potatoes while others add up to 4 lb (2 kg) of tripe. My Aunt Ella says that the soul way to cook tripe is to boil it till it's nice and tender, then roll it in seasoned flour and fry it.

But I'd like to give you the recipe that I created to pass a cooking exam back in school. The main change I made was to add a variety of peppers. This enhances the flavor of the soup and also seems to alter the texture. The recipe also contains more herbs and spices than General Washington's cook was probably able to obtain. But then, we're no longer at war with the British either.

Now to the soup!

serves 4

4 slices of fatty bacon
1 large green bell pepper, finely chopped
1/2 cup onion, finely chopped (1 medium onion)
1/2 cup (2 1/2 oz, 75g) celery, finely chopped
1 teaspoon paprika
1/2 teaspoon thyme
2 tablespoons parsley, finely chopped
1/2 teaspoon marjoram
1 lb (500 g) honeycomb tripe, cooked and
    finely shredded
8 cups (3 1/2 pints, 2 l) beef bouillon or
    chicken stock
1 bay leaf
1/2 teaspoon black peppercorns,
    finely pounded (this time!)
1/2 teaspoon red pepper flakes, crushed
2 teaspoons salt
1 cup raw white potatoes, peeled and cubed
2 tablespoons butter or margarine
2 tablespoons all-purpose flour
1/2 cup (4 fl oz, 120 ml) heavy (double) cream

"... out of necessity came this original creation ..."

Cut up your bacon into tiny bits and saute them in a skillet until they are transparent but not totally crisp. Throw in your green peppers, onion, and celery, and continue to sauté for another 5 minutes or so, until all your vegetables are tender. Now stir in your paprika, thyme, parsley, and marjoram; then set your frying pan aside for the time being.

Place your shredded cooked tripe in a large pot along with the bouillon or stock, bay leaf, black and red pepper, and salt. Bring the mixture to a boil, then put in your cubed potatoes. When it boils again reduce the heat and gently simmer, uncovered, until your potatoes are nice and tender, about 15 minutes.

Melt your butter or margarine in a small pan over low heat and stir in the flour to make a roux. Tip it into the pot of tripe. Bring this back to the boil, pour in your bacon and vegetable mixture, reduce the heat again, and mix well. Adjust your seasoning at this point.

Just before you are ready to serve, warm the cream. Take the pot of soup off the heat and stir in the cream. Don't allow the soup to boil again.

variation

This soup is truly a main course and really needs no accompaniments. But Grandma Battle used to add these dumplings to hers, and they do make a delicious addition. Simply sift 1 cup (4 1/2 oz, 130 g) all-purpose flour with 1/2 teaspoon salt and 1/2 teaspoon baking powder. Cut in 2 tablespoons butter, margarine, or bacon grease, and add enough water to make a soft dough. Shape into small balls no more than 1 in (2.5 cm) across and add to the pot 15 minutes before you add the cream. Raise the heat for a few seconds to return the soup to a simmer, then lower it again.

Sheila Ferguson, *Soul Food: Classic Cuisine from the Deep South* (1989)

Before chefs became rock stars, there was Sheila Ferguson of Philadelphia, lead singer of the all-girl soul group The Three Degrees. Many celebrities, major and minor, have written cookbooks, but few hold up as well as Ferguson's.

Jeffrey Steingarten

Primal Bread

The lack of decent bread was one of the great laments in the early days of America's gourmet revolution. Words like *crusty*, *wood-fired*, and most of all *Poilâne* (the fabled bread baker of Le Cherche-Midi in Paris) were intoned like the names of lesser gods, while words like *sliced*, *white*, and *Wonder* were spat out as if they were the devil's own handiwork. Beginning in the late 1970s, people—particularly men—began baking bread. Some, seeking to appease feminist wives, brought to this activity a sense of meditation, the hope of acquired gentleness and, if nothing else, some credit for contributing to the housework. Others kneaded with a sanctimonious vigor—take that, you multinational bread-baking conglomerate! Still others brought a connoisseur's diligence, sometimes misdiagnosed as obsessive-compulsive disorder, to the enterprise. Writing about the phenomena in the early 1980s, I visited one wacko who slept with his starter and another, a surgeon in Chicago, who'd flown a team of masons in from France to build a Poilâne-style oven in his backyard. But Jeffrey Steingarten (b. 1942) is the only man I've met who almost turned down tickets to a Madonna concert because it might upset his natural sourdough starter. Once on a case (he graduated from Harvard Law School in 1968 and approaches food a bit like William Kunstler approaches the bench), Steingarten is indefatigable. Being served the best, and eating it with impunity is, he believes, an inalienable right. And Steingarten, an old-school curmudgeon and long-time food columnist for *Vogue*—his writings have been collected in *The Man Who Ate Everything* (1997) and *It Must've Been Something I Ate* (2003)—will go to any lengths to defend that right.

■ ■ ■

> Wherefore do ye spend money for that which is not bread? . . . Eat that which is good, and let your soul delight itself in fatness.
>
> Isaiah 55:2.

The world is divided into two camps: those who can live happily on bread alone and those who also need vegetables, meat, and dairy products. Isaiah and I fall into the first category. Bread is the only food I know that satisfies completely, all by itself. It comforts the body, charms the senses, gratifies the soul, and excites the mind. A little butter also helps.

Isaiah was a first-class prophet but untrained as a dietitian. A good loaf of bread will not delight your soul in fatness. It contains almost no fats or sugars—mainly proteins and complex carbohydrates—because it is made from three elemental ingredients: flour, water, and salt. If you wonder why I left out the yeast, you have discovered the point of my story.

Every year I have an intense bout of baking, but these episodes now seem just a prelude, a beating around the bush, a period of training and practice for this year's assault on the summit: *le pain au levain naturel*, naturally leavened bread. I have slipped into a foreign language here because this is a bread most commonly associated with the Paris baker Lionel Poilâne and his ancient wood-fired oven at 8 rue du Cherche-Midi, the most famous bakery in the world. When the baking is going well, Poilâne's bread defines the good loaf: a thick, crackling crust; a chewy, moist interior; the ancient, earthy flavors of toasted wheat and tangy fermentation; and a range of more elusive tastes—roasted nuts, butterscotch, dried pears, grassy fields—that emanate from neither flour, water, nor salt, but from some more mysterious source. This is the true bread of the countryside, Poilâne writes, the eternal bread. This is the bread I can eat forever, and often do.

Pain au levain was the first leavened bread, probably discovered in Egypt six thousand years ago. Professor Raymond Calvel, in his definitive *La boulangerie moderne*, places this breakthrough "*chez les Hébreux au temps de Moïse*," which is when *les Hébreux* were enslaved by *les Egyptiens*. I would love to believe this account but find it improbable. My own *pain au levain* adventure began much more recently.

Saturday, October 7, 1989   I amass thirty recipes for creating a starter, or as the French call it, *le chef*. This is a piece of dough in which wild yeast and lactic acid bacteria live happily in symbiosis, generating the gases, alcohols, and acids that give this bread its complex taste and chewy texture. Commercial yeast is bred to produce clouds of carbon dioxide for a speedy rise, at the expense of other aromatic compounds. But your first loaf of *pain au levain* can take six days to make from start to finish.

Then each new batch of bread is leavened with a piece of risen dough saved from the previous baking. Compared with using commercial yeast, *pain au levain* is unpredictable, slow, and prey to variations in weather, flour, temperature, and the seasons. 'Playing with wild yeast is like playing with dynamite,' I was warned by the technical manager of a giant US milling company.

Chez Panisse Cooking has a lucid and detailed recipe contributed by Steve Sullivan, owner of the Acme Bread Company in Berkeley and a stupendous baker; he uses organic wine grapes to activate the starter. I am in luck: the New York State grape harvest is under way. I order a variety of excellent flours from Giusto's Specialty Foods in San Francisco, which supplies flour to Acme, and when they arrive I walk around the corner to the Union Square Greenmarket, buy several bunches of unsprayed Concord grapes, tie them in cheesecloth, lower the cheesecloth into a batter of flour and water, squeeze the grapes to break their skins, put the bowl near a pilot light on the stove, and go away for the weekend.

Two days later   What a mess! My mixture of flour and grapes has overflowed, sizzling and seething over the stove and running into those little holes in the gas burners from which the flames are supposed to emerge. I start again. There is something terrifying about the violent life hiding in an innocent-looking bowl of flour and grapes, and I lie awake at night wondering where it comes from.

My computer has collected 236 scientific abstracts on naturally leavened bread, but none has a definitive answer—as many as 59 distinct species of wild yeast and 238 strains of bacteria have been spotted in sourdough cultures. The truth is vital to me. Wild yeast living on the wheat berry would make Montana-Idaho country bread, because that's where Al Giusto says his wheat is grown. If they live on the grapes, it would be upstate New York country bread. But my goal is to bake *Manhattan* country bread with a colony of wild bacteria and yeast that can grow and flourish only here. I apply to *Vogue* for the funds to run DNA traces and gas chromatographs on all my breads and starters. I have received no reply as of the present writing. Maybe tomorrow.

Saturday, October 14   I have made a few loaves of bread with my grape starter—the early ones were pale purple—but must abandon the project in a few days when I leave New York to eat in Paris for three weeks. Besides, I am extremely suspicious of yeast that live on grapes. They are too fond of wine rather than wheat. I am looking for yeast that love bread as much as I do.

Monday, April 2, 1990   In the August 1989 issue of his indispensable newsletter, *Simple Cooking*, John Thorne gives instructions for *pain au levain* based on the methods that Poilâne himself employs. But I will wait until I can get hold of Poilâne's paperback handbook, *Faire son pain*. My friend Miriam promises to find one for me in Paris.

Meanwhile, I turn to *The Laurel's Kitchen Bread Book* . . . and its recipe for *desem* (the Flemish word for *levain*), which is fastidiously designed to develop the yeast that live on stoneground whole-wheat. Everything must be kept below 60 degrees until the final rise to discourage the growth of acid-generating bacteria that thrive at higher temperatures, and everything must be sealed to avoid colonization by airborne yeast.

I telephone Giusto's and ask them to send me a sack of whole-wheat flour by overnight mail the moment it is milled. Then I walk around the house testing the temperature. Bread writers who live in the country typically tell you that the perfect place for this rising or that is on the creaky wooden stairs going down to your root cellar. Don't they know that most people live in apartments? At last I create a zone of 55 degrees by piling a twenty-four-quart stockpot on a cardboard box at the edge of my desk with the air conditioner set to turbofreeze.

Late April   It is a balmy spring, but I am wearing a winter coat at my desk so that *Laurel's Kitchen desem* will feel comfortable. My wife has the sniffles.

Early May   Both of us have come down with serious colds, complete with fever. The *desem* starter smells terrific, a fresh fruity scent unlike anything I've made before, and the bread is rough and wheaty, full of complex aromas. But like all whole-grain breads, the strong taste of unrefined flour obscures the more delicate flavors I am after. Long ago I concluded that the only bread worth its name is made with good white flour; small amounts of barley, whole-wheat, or rye can be added for their flavor and color. John Thorne calls whole-grain bread "a kind of aerated gruel." If Isaiah were alive today, I'm sure he would agree.

Friday, June 1, late morning   Miriam and *Faire son pain* have arrived from Paris. Step One: create a bowlful of life. Poilâne's instructions have you make a small piece of dough with one-ninth of the total flour and water and leave it covered for two to three days while the wild yeast and bacteria awaken and multiply to form an active culture.

Bakers weigh everything because flour can be packed densely or lightly in a measuring cup and doughs can be tight or aerated; it is their weight that matters. I dust off my electronic kitchen scale and set it to grams. Poilâne says that all ingredients at all stages should be between 22 and 24 degrees centigrade, which equals 72 to 75 degrees on Dr Fahrenheit's thermometer—a nice, moderate room temperature. Now I can turn off the air conditioner.

I weigh 42 grams of water and 67 grams of unbleached white flour, about a half cup, put them in a large bowl, and squish them together with the fingers of my right hand until the dough comes together into a rough ball.

I knead the *chef* with extra flour on my wooden counter for two minutes, put it into a rustic brown ceramic bowl, cover the bowl with a wet kitchen towel, secure the towel with a rubber band, and go about my business. This nonchalance lasts for five minutes, and then I am back in the kitchen, peeking under the towel to see if anything is happening. Twenty peeks and several broken rubber bands later, I scrape the *chef* into a clear glass bowl. It looks less like something from a French farmhouse but does facilitate obsessive observation.

I wash my rustic bowl in hot water and learn a lasting lesson: utensils coated with flour or dough are easily washed in *cold* water; hot water makes the starch and gluten stick to everything, including itself. If the dough has hardened, *soak* the utensils in cold water. If you leave them long enough, your wife may get disgusted and clean them up herself. Do it too often and there will be a price to pay.

For the rest of the day, at three-minute intervals, I search for the appearance of tiny bubbles against the glass.

Saturday, June 2, immediately after waking   In just twenty-four hours, the kitchen towel has grown dry and stiff, the dough has darkened and crusted over, and two spots of pale blue mold have appeared on it. This is not the life-form I had in mind.

I make the morning coffee and start all over. This time I use bottled spring water. New York City tap water is rated among the most delicious in the nation, but chlorinated water of any kind can inhibit the growth of yeast. And weeks later, when I grow attuned to small differences in the taste of my breads I find that you can recognize things like chlorine in the crust, where flavors are concentrated.

Instead of white flour I weigh out some organic whole-wheat flour: organic because pesticides and fungicides deal death to microbes, and whole-wheat because if yeast do actually live on the wheat berry, it is on the outer bran layer that they will, I figure, be found. Instead of a colorful, charming kitchen towel, I use plastic wrap this time. It may prevent a friendly air-borne microbe or two from settling on the *chef*, but it keeps the dough from crusting over.

Sunday, June 3   Is that a bubble in the *chef* or a flaw in the glass of the bowl? The *chef* still smells like wet whole-wheat flour, nothing more.

Monday, June 4   The *chef* has swelled and smells tangy, somewhere between beer and yogurt.

Tuesday, June 5   No further change. Maybe I have failed. Maybe my *chef* is dead. But it is time for Poilâne's Step Two, doubling the earlier quantities and building the *chef* into what Poilâne calls the *levain*, which you leave from twenty-four to forty-eight hours to ferment.

Wednesday, June 6, bright and early   The thing is alive! I think it is trying to talk to me. In only twenty-four hours the *levain* has risen to the top of the bowl and is pressing up against the plastic wrap. Large bubbles proudly show themselves through the glass. There can be no doubt about it: I have created life in a bowl in my kitchen!

In Step Three you build the *levain* into two pounds of bread dough, tripling its weight by dissolving it in 252 grams of water and working in 400 grams of flour and 15 grams of salt. Now that a happy fermentation has begun, I shift to Giusto's white organic unbleached bread flour. The kneading begins, twenty long minutes of it, stretching the dough away from my body with the heel of my hand, folding it back toward me, giving the dough a quarter turn, and doing it again and again. Besides aerating the dough, this motion unkinks the protein molecules and lines them up next to each other, where they link into a network of gluten. The dough becomes satiny and elastic so that as the yeast produces more carbon dioxide it can stretch and expand around bubbles of gas.

I find twenty minutes of kneading unendurable. Mine is not the attitude of a true artisan. Hand kneading puts the baker in touch with his living dough, you read, endows him with responsibility for his bread. Soon I will switch to my KitchenAid K5A heavy-duty home mixer equipped with a dough hook. It pummels and whirls instead of kneading, but it does produce acceptable results, especially when I take over for a few minutes at the end.

Seven o'clock that evening   Poilâne is fuzzy on forming a round loaf, so I follow the standard procedure—flattening the dough with the smooth domed surface facedown and rolling and stretching it into a tight spherical package. I have bought a *banneton,* a professional linen-lined rising basket, from French Baking Machines to replace my makeshift two-quart bowl lined with a kitchen towel. I flour it heavily and lower the loaf into it, smooth side down. Then, to create a moist, draftless environment, I inflate a large Baggie around the whole thing and tie it tightly. My loaf will rise until midnight.

I spend part of the evening in a state of wonder. The first miracle is that a handful of wheat flour contains everything needed to create the most satisfying and fundamental of all foods. Then I marvel a while about yeast. Why does the yeast that feeds on wheat produce a harmless leavening gas and appealing flavors rather than poisons? And why does wild yeast seem to do best at room temperature? Yeasts were created long before rooms were. Is this a coincidence or part of Somebody's master plan? Last, I wonder at the role of salt. Nearly all recipes call for about 1 percent salt by weight—much more and you kill the yeast and bacteria, much less and the yeast grow without restraint and exhaust themselves too soon. Is it mere chance that the chemically ideal level of salt is precisely the amount that makes bread taste best?

Midnight   The loaf has barely budged and I am getting worried. Better give it another two hours. My wife has already gone to bed. She sees this as a dangerous precedent. But several weeks will pass before my compulsive baking threatens to destroy the marriage.

2 a.m.   Through the inflated Baggie I can see that the loaf has swelled by half. I have preheated the oven to 500 degrees with a thick 16-inch terra cotta tile on the oven shelf and a Superstone backing cloche on top of it. This device, manufactured by Sassafras Enterprises, is an unglazed ceramic dish with a domed cover that creates something like the even, penetrating, steamy heat of a brick oven. The tile underneath increases the stored heat in the oven and protects the bottom of the bread from burning. Elizabeth David's *English Bread and Yeast Cookery* has a photograph of a nearly identical baking cloche from 500 B.C., excavated from the Agora in Athens.

I invert the *banneton* on the fiery base of the cloche, slash the top of the loaf in a checkerboard pattern with a razor blade to encourage a good rise in the oven, pour a quarter-cup of warm water over the loaf to create extra steam (a frightening but successful gesture I learned from *The Laurel's Kitchen Bread Book*), sprinkle flour over the top for decoration, and cover with the preheated dome.

2:30 a.m.   I lower the heat to 400 and uncover the bread to let it brown. It has not risen as much as I would have liked and my slashes have become deep valleys.

3:00 a.m.   My first *pain au levain* is done! When I tap the bottom of the loaf with my forefinger, it sounds hollow, a sign that the starch has absorbed all the excess water, turning from hard crystals into a soft gel.

As I know unequivocally from both book learning and experience, bread is not at its best straight from the oven. Complex flavors develop as it cools, and if you love your bread warm, you should reheat or toast it later.

3:05 a.m.   Just this once, I cut a slice of hot bread. The crust is crisp and tender, the aroma and taste are complex and nutty if a little bland. But it is overly sour and its crumb is dense and gray. Yet I am not disappointed. Butter improves matters, as it does everything in life but one's health, and I know that the flavor will improve by the morning. Which it does.

3:20 a.m.   I am falling toward slumber when my heart starts racing and a wave of dread washes over me. I forgot to hold back part of the dough as the *chef* for my next loaf!

3:21 a.m.   I can't fall asleep. I drag myself into the kitchen and whip up a new *chef*. This time it takes two minutes, and I am confident it will work perfectly. I eat another piece of bread and sleep contentedly. In the morning, my wife objects to crumbs on the pillow.

Thursday, June 21   I am baking as fast as I can, six generations so far with my new *chef.* With each baking the *chef* grows more vigorous and its flavor more assertive but a bit less acidic.

My wife feels that my baking schedule has prevented us from going away on sunny summer weekends. She says it is like having a newborn puppy without the puppy. She has always wanted a puppy. And she is unhappy that every surface in the apartment has a delicate dusting of Giusto's bread flour. But it is only when I nearly turn down tickets to the Madonna concert for fear that Madonna will interfere with my first rising that she puts her foot down. I refrigerate the dough overnight, as I've done with other breads, and find that the final flavor has, if anything, improved. But my bread is still too dense, and I do not know what to do about it.

Tuesday, July 31   I throw myself upon the mercy of experts. Noel Comess left the post of chef de cuisine at the Quilted Giraffe four years ago, at the age of twenty-eight, to start the Tom Cat Bakery in an abandoned ice cream factory in Queens, and his sourdough *boule* is the best in the city. He agrees to let me snoop around one evening. His room temperature is 85 degrees, much warmer than Poilâne's, and the proportion of old risen dough to new at each stage is less than I have learned to use. I watch him form several loaves and realize that beating down the dough is the last thing that naturally leavened bread needs. We pore over his books. Noel loves baking bread and the continuous, self-renewing process of *pain au levain.*

Back at home I round my loaves more gently and find that they bake higher and with a more varied texture. But they still look like my bread, not like Noel's. A warmer rising temperature sometimes helps and sometimes doesn't. And my *chef* is simply not active enough to use the proportions that Noel does.

I turn to Michael London. From 1977 to 1986 Michael and his wife, Wendy, ran a patisserie in Saratoga Springs, New York, called Mrs London's Bake Shop–Craig Claiborne once compared their creations favorably to Wittamer's in Brussels and Peltier's in Paris–and now from the makeshift kitchen of their Federal-period brick farmhouse in nearby Greenwich they run the Rock Hill Bakehouse, where they bake three times a week. I cannot count the mornings I have rushed down to Balducci's or over to the Green-market to buy a giant loaf of Michael's Farm Bread before they disappear.

An unstable and sweltering little plane carries me to upstate New York. I am bearing a Baggie filled with 4 ounces of *chef* and my latest loaf of bread. Michael and Wendy critique the loaf I have brought, and then we eat it with butter from their cow. Their percipient and blonde seven-year-old daughter, Sophie, loves my bread. I watch Michael make his *levain*, and he shows me how to invigorate my starter. As you build the dough from one stage to the next, the *chef*, the *levain*, and the dough should always be used just at the peak of their activity. We sleep for a few hours, wake at one in the morning, make a ton of dough, sleep until five, when his four helpers arrive, and begin shaping loaves for the final bake.

Michael builds my 4 ounces of strengthened starter into *levain* and then into 20 pounds of dough. He bakes several loaves with it, and they look just like Michael's other breads, not like mine at all. The secrets, it seems, lie in the baker's art and intuition, not just in the bacterial composition of the air, the flour, or the grapes. A professional French hearth oven does not hurt either.

Thursday, September 6 My baking schedule is less frenzied, twice a week now, and my wife eagerly awaits the finished product. My *chef* is happy and strong and aromatic, the man from UPS has got used to lugging up a 50-pound bag from Giusto's every week or two, and I have vacuumed most of the organic bread flour out of my word processor. Most days the bread is more than good enough to eat, and some days it is so good that we eat nothing else.

Ray Gonzalez

Mama Menudo

Hangovers are part of the job, an occupational hazard as inevitable for the traveling epicure as jet lag, weight gain, and the occasional case of food poisoning. I wish I'd read Ray Gonzalez (b. 1952) before touring the mescal distilleries in Juchipila, Mexico. There we were, eating corn tortillas and praying to the Virgin of Guadeloupe, when all we really needed was menudo, or, as the poet says, "Mama menudo." Gonzalez is the author of many books of poetry as well as the memoir *Memory Fever: A Journey Beyond El Paso del Norte* (1993), from which this chapter is taken.

■ ■ ■

The mescal night inspires you to get up on an early Sunday morning, hot Texas sun shining, making you crazier than the hangover your brain kisses. You hear yourself gasp, "*¡Menudo! ¡Mama Menudo!*" You must go to La Paloma Café and wave your pained face over a big steaming bowl of hot, quivering chunks of menudo. It is an emergency. Your soul calls for it, prays to it, waits for the red spirit of the Menudo God to bless you and save you from the big mescal death.

You know menudo is the greatest thing anyone has ever sunk his teeth into. Nothing else comes close. Nothing else forces you to get into your car to drive a couple of miles down Paisano Street on a day when everyone else is in church praying. They listen to the Padre whose church sells menudo in the dining hall after *la misa. Los señores y señoras, sus hijos, los vatos*—they all pray first before thinking of eating menudo.

Not you. Your stomach moves like a dying river, a settling of flowing juices needing fresh slices of cow tripe to rise again and be reborn, putting life back into your existence, the magical source of survival in the desert.

Paisano Street is a wide, empty road of newspapers, trash, old tires, and dust. It is nearly empty of traffic, a Sunday morning in south El Paso looking like an abandoned movie lot, cardboard buildings warping in the heat, the parking lot behind La Paloma stinking of dog shit, half a dozen empty bottles of Carta Blanca reminding you of last night, the mescal and the limes.

You enter La Paloma because Mama Menudo is waiting, the sweet smell of a Mexican restaurant dampening your head. You are glad to see the place is nearly empty. The only other customer is an old Mexican sitting heavily at the counter, his huge body pressing into the stool, a bright cloud of steam rising from the bowl of menudo he hugs with thick hands.

You don't care that your favorite booth has a new tear in the old vinyl seat. None of the springs have popped through yet. It is the right place to sit.

Sylvia, the young waitress, knows what you want. She spots the menudo gleam in your red eyes and smiles beautifully at you. "¿Café y un plato de menudo?"

"Sí, por favor." You smile back, the smell of sizzling chorizo and fresh tortillas sprinkling through your nose, preparing you for the taking of the holy food, a transcendence you have tried to describe to your friends—a state of menudo mind you share with your family, and with only a few converted friends.

Sylvia takes your order and you wait, this period very important, a silent oath of patience calming your heart to ease the hangover. The old man is hunched over his bowl. John F. Kennedy smiles at you from his portrait above the door. The painting of a pigeon, la paloma, reflects over the long mirror that stretches the length of the café.

Sylvia brings the silverware and the revolving cup holder, each container holding the magic ingredients that are part of the ceremony. You look into the cup of freshly cut onion, glad to see it is as full as the cups of oregano, chili piquin, and lemon slices. You set it on the right side of the table, the place it must always be. As you spread your arms over the table, Sylvia comes out on cue with the smoking bowl of menudo.

You hear the bells of the church ring down the street as she sets the offering before you. "Gracias." She leaves the bowl to steam into your eyes, knows you must eat alone, and quickly pours the coffee. You wait for her to leave.

The ritual begins. Two spoons of oregano flake into the bowl. The menudo is finely cut this morning, thin square strips floating among the posole. The soup is a dark red. You know it is a message from Mama that this mixture comes from a hot chili. Two spoons of chili piquin follow spoons of onion bits. The thing looks like a collage of chili, meat fat, jello, and black and green grains that emerge from the oregano. An innocent, ignorant person would say it looks like dog vomit and leftover cooking grease! But you love it and that person will never know the meaning of life, never understand why eating Mama Menudo is wild ecstasy and greedy pleasure—and most of all—it saves your life!

You slurp it like an anteater slurps ants, like a vacuum cleaner slurps dirt, like a monkey eats a banana, like a man slurps himself into sleep to wake up in search of his mama. Your right hand boasts of great skill. It digs spoonfuls of menudo straight into your mouth. The stuff is hot. You sigh as the chunks burn your tongue on their way down your throat. It does not take long. It never can. No one takes his time eating menudo. It is a creation of consumption, a snortling and grinding of the senses. The chili makes your eyes water, your ears pop, and it magically takes away the hangover. Your pupils blossom awake. Your heart beats proudly into the world. Your stomach flips awake like a dog that spots a cat and sprints for it!

It vanishes in a final gulp. A thin film of red grease that looks like blood glitters over the inside of the empty bowl. You touched the coffee only twice. You came up for air once. Your nose runs. You are safe and happy. Something moves inside you. You sit still for a few moments, arms resting quietly on the table. A huge burp tries to leap out of you. You hiss it through your teeth. Sylvia appears a final time to see that everything has fallen into place. At the cash register, you pay the dollar fifty. As she counts the change, you pull your pants higher at the waist and see the old man waddle toward you, his ancient body having accepted grace from Mama Menudo as boldly as you have.

Sylvia gives you the change. As you tip her, the old man stands behind you to pay. You turn to say "*Buenos dias,*" and your eyes are filled with the color he wears on his gray shirt, the red badge of courage. A couple of menudo stains shine on his chest and chin.

"Yes," you cry in your heart, "this man knows." He is one of Mama Menudo's lost sons who has returned. You wait in the morning sun for the old man to step out of La Paloma. Standing by your car, you watch him move slowly down the sidewalk. He pauses at the corner, turns around to face you. He raises his right arm slowly and points a friendly finger at you. He smiles and crosses the street as you climb into your car. Before starting the engine, you look down at your T-shirt. It is a clean white, not a single drop on it. You look at the doorway of La Paloma and something moves in your stomach, tells you to come back to reclaim the red badge of menudo stain and wear it on your chest.

Memory Fever (1993)

Maxine Kumin

Enough Jam for a Lifetime

Weekend after weekend, I am invited to this home and that: "We'll cook!" the host promises in the same tone in which, only a decade earlier, he might have declared, "We'll play tennis!" What, I wondered, is so restorative and special about cooking together? The luxury of a day whose only deadline is dinner? The chance to show off? The calming effect of repetitive tasks? Perhaps all of these. Give me a hundred heads of garlic, a paring knife, and a deadline, and I will give you a woman in no need of sleeping aids, anti-depressants, or even a spa. More than anything, though, the power of cooking lies in connection. It connects people to places, one generation to another, and, in the case of something seasonal like the jam-making that the poet Maxine Kumin describes here, revives lost memories. Here, she makes enough jam for a lifetime, and making it takes long enough to recall a lifetime. Born and raised in Philadelphia, Kumin (b. 1925), who won a Pulitzer Prize in 1973 and has published many novels and volumes of poetry, has long been known for her crystalline focus on daily life and her bond with the landscapes of New England, tendencies that have deepened since 1976 when she and her husband moved to a farm in Warner, New Hampshire.

■ ■ ■

January 25. Three days of this hard freeze; 10 below at dawn and a sullen 2 above by midday. After the morning barn chores, I start hauling quart containers of wild blackberries up from the basement freezer. I am a little reluctant to begin.

Last August, when the berries were at their most succulent, I did manage to cook up a sizable batch into jam. But everything peaks at once in a New England garden, and I turned to the importunate broccolis and cauliflowers and the second crop of bush beans, all of which wanted blanching and freezing straightaway. Also, late summer rains had roused the cucumber vines to new efforts. There was a sudden spurt of yellow squash as well.

Victor went on picking blackberries. Most mornings he scouted the slash pile along upturned boulders, residue from when we cleared the last four acres of forage pasture. We've never had to fence this final field, for the brush forms an impenetrable thicket on two sides and deep woods encircle the rest.

We've always had blackberries growing wild here and there on the property, good-sized ones, too. But never such largess, such abundance. I wondered what this bumper crop signified, after a drought-filled summer. Were the Tribulation and the Rapture at hand?

Long ago I wrote in a poem, "God does not want / His perfect fruit to rot," but that was before I had an addicted picker on my hands—whose enthusiasm became my labor. It is the habit of the deeply married to exchange vantage points.

Even the horses took up blackberries as a snack. Like toddlers loose in a popcorn shop, they sidled down the brambly row, cautiously curling their lips back so as to pluck a drooping cluster free without being stabbed in the muzzle by truly savage thorns. It was a wonderful sight.

Making jam—even though I complain how long it takes, how messy it is with its inevitable spatters and spills, how the lids and the jars somehow never match up at the end of the procedure—is rich with gratifications. I get a lot of thinking done. I puff up with feelings of providence. Pretty soon I am flooded with memories.

My mother used to visit every summer during our pickling, canning, freezing, and jamming frenzy. She had a deep reservoir of patience, developed in another era, for repetitive tasks; she would mash the blender-buzzed, cooked berries through a strainer until her arms were as weary as a weightlifter's at the end of a grueling workout. She prided herself on extracting every bit of pulp from the purple mass.

I find myself talking to her as I work. I am not nearly as diligent, I tell her, thumping the upended strainer into the kitchen scraps pile, destined for compost. I miss her serious attention to detail.

Scullery work used to make my mother loquacious. I liked hearing about her childhood in the southwestern hilly corner of Virginia at the turn of the century, how the cooking from May to October was done in the summer kitchen, a structure loosely attached to the back of the house, much as many New England sheds and barns connect to the farmhouses they supplement. I liked hearing about my grandfather's matched pair of driving horses— Saddlebreds, I gather, from the one surviving snapshot that shows my mother's three youngest brothers lined up on one compliant horse's back. My mother talked about the family pony that had a white harness for Sundays. I wonder aloud what a white harness was made of in the 1890s. Perhaps she had imagined this item, but fabricated it lovingly so long ago that it had become real.

One spectacular late summer day we took my mother down North Road along Stevens Brook in search of elderberries. We hiked up and down the sandy edge of the water in several locations before coming upon an enormous stand of the berries, ripe to bursting, branches bent double with the weight of them. After filling the five-gallon pail we had brought with us, greedily we started stuffing whole racemes of berries into a spare grain bag.

I had not thought much about dealing with the booty until we had lugged it triumphantly home. Mother sat at the kitchen table well past midnight, stripping the berries from their slender finger filaments into my biggest cooking pot. Even so, the great elderberry caper took two more days to complete. We prevailed, eventually boiling the berries with some green apples from our own trees so that the released pectin would permit the mass to jell. I don't believe in additives and scorn commercial pectin, but I will lean on home-grown apples or rhubarb in order to thicken the berry soup.

It was amazing what those elderberries had reawakened in my mother; she was transported. There was the cold cellar, there stood the jars of pickled beets, the Damson plum conserve larded with hazelnuts; there, too, the waist-high barrel of dill pickles weighted down with three flatirons atop a washtub lid. Potatoes and sweet potatoes, carrots, onions, and apples were stored in areas appropriate to their needs—apples in the dark far corner which was the driest (and spookiest), and so on. There was the springhouse, where milk from the family cow cooled unpasteurized in a metal can set down in a cavity of rocks, and a butter churn which took hours of push-pulling the paddle to turn the cream into a finished product.

It was never an idyll Mother described. She remembered sharply and wryly the labor, the peonage of childhood, when the most menial and least absorbing tasks were invariably assigned to the smallest children, especially the girls. She could not escape the chores of housekeeping for the imagined dramas of field and barn. But interestingly, chickens seemed always to have been relegated to the care of females.

Mother loathed the chickens that pecked her feet when she went into the coop to scatter their scratch. She detested egg gathering, having to shoo brood hens off their nests and then be quick about plucking the eggs into the basket; eggs from which fluff, feathers, and bits of crusty manure had to be removed. I never saw my mother eat an egg, boiled soft or hard, poached, or sunny-side up. They were a bit too close to nature for her taste.

Another kitchen thing I hear my mother say as I work, this cold January noon: "Warm the plates!" she croons to me from the Great Beyond. She abhorred the common practice of serving hot food on cold china. *Common* is the epithet she would have applied to it, a word that carried powerful connotations of contempt.

This wintry day, then, I reduce five gallons of blackberries to serviceable pulp, measure out three cups of sugar to every four of berry mash, and set it boiling. We will have successive batches on the stove the rest of this day. I have already rummaged for suitable jars from the cellar shelves and these I will boil for fifteen minutes on a back burner. Toward the end I will grow more inventive about jars, for there are never enough of the good, straight-sided variety.

But for now, the jam puts up lacy bubbles, rolling around the top third of my giant cooking pot at a full boil. Despite candy thermometers, the only way I trust to gauge when the jam is ready is dip and drip. From a decent height, off a slotted spoon, I perform this test until the royal stuff begins to form a tiny waterfall. This is known as sheeting; all the cookbooks describe it, but it's a delicate decision to arrive at. Stop too soon and you have a lovely blackberry sauce to serve over ice cream, sponge cake, or applesauce. Continue too long and you have a fatally overcooked mess of berry leather.

There is no quality control in my method. Every batch is a kind of revisionism. It makes its own laws. But the result is pure, deeply colored, uncomplicated, and unadulterated blackberry jam, veritably seedless, suitable for every occasion. After it has cooled, I pour melted paraffin on top of it, tilting the glass to get an airproof seal. Modern science frowns on so casual an approach to shutting out microbes, but I don't apologize. If the wax shows a spot of mold growing on top after a few months on the shelf, I can always remove it, wipe the sides clean, and pour a new layer of wax over all.

My mother would go home from her summer visits with a package of pickles and jams for her later delectation. When she died, there were several unopened jars in her cupboard. I took them back with me after the funeral. We ate them in her stead, as she would have wanted us to. Enough jam for a lifetime, she would say with evident satisfaction after a day of scullery duty. It was; it is.

Women, Animals, & Vegetables (1994)

YELLOWFIN

TUNA

BURGERS

with

Ginger-Mustard

Glaze

If necessity is the mother of invention, then Union Square Cafe's tuna burger is one of our menu's most successful children. Thanks to the overwhelming popularity of our Fillet Mignon of Tuna—which we butcher only from the front, fat end of the tuna—we've always had an enormous supply of expensive, delicious, but oddly shaped tuna tail meat left over. We needed to figure out a way to sell the back end of the tuna to avoid doubling our menu price for the fillet mignon. For years, we floundered with experimental tuna recipes that tasted better than they looked. We came up with such unmemorable ideas as sashimi niçoise, tuna sloppy joes, and tuna chili. None of them worked. Then one day, our friend Pierre Franey asked if we had ever considered doing tuna burgers. We worked up the following recipe, which has been a signature lunch dish ever since. The tuna burger is so popular that we actually now need to cut into our fillet mignon supply just to have enough tuna to meet the demand.

Ginger-Mustard Glaze

1/3 CUP TERIYAKI SAUCE

2 TEASPOONS MINCED GINGER

1/2 TEASPOON MINCED GARLIC

1 TABLESPOON HONEY

1 TABLESPOON DIJON MUSTARD

1/2 TEASPOON WHITE WINE VINEGAR

* * *

Tuna Burgers

1 1/2 POUNDS YELLOWFIN TUNA,
FREE OF ANY SKIN OR GRISTLE

2 TEASPOONS MINCED GARLIC

3 TABLESPOONS DIJON MUSTARD

1/2 TEASPOON CAYENNE

1 TEASPOON KOSHER SALT

1/4 TEASPOON FRESHLY GROUND BLACK PEPPER

1/4 CUP OLIVE OIL

4 FRESH HAMBURGER BUNS WITH SEEDS

1/4 CUP JAPANESE PICKLED GINGER,
AVAILABLE IN JAPANESE SPECIALTY FOOD SHOPS (OPTIONAL)

Combine all the ginger-mustard glaze ingredients in a 1-quart sauce-pan and bring to a boil. Lower the heat and simmer until the glaze coats the back of a spoon, about 5 minutes. Strain through a sieve and reserve in a warm place until tuna burgers are cooked. Can be prepared up to 2 days ahead and stored, covered, in the refrigerator.

②

Grind the tuna in a meat grinder or chop with a large sharp knife to the texture of hamburger meat. Do not use a food processor, which will shred the tuna rather than chop it.

③

Transfer the ground tuna to a bowl and combine with the garlic, mustard, cayenne, salt, and pepper. Mix thoroughly. Divide the tuna into four equal portions. Using your hands, roll each part into a smooth ball and then flatten into a compact patty.

④

Heat the olive oil in a large skillet over medium-high heat and sear the tuna burgers until browned and medium rare, 3 to 4 minutes a side. Serve each burger on a buttered toasted bun and spread with a tablespoon of warm glaze. Garnish the burgers with equal amounts of pickled ginger slices.

Danny Meyer & Michael Romano, *The Union Square Cafe Cookbook* (1994)

Invented when health concerns had Americans searching for leaner cuisine, the Yellowfin Tuna Burger is merged cuisine: a nod both to the American icon and to the rage for sushi and sashimi. The dish has become a staple of restaurants nationwide as well as in grocery store frozen-food cases; I've yet to taste one as good as the original, though.

Laura Shapiro

Do Women Like to Cook?

Laura Shapiro's work focuses on the trajectory of cooking from the late 1800s to the present. In *Perfection Salad* (1986) she explored the role of science and industry in defining nutrition, home economics, and women's role in the kitchen, and in the more recent *Something from the Oven* (2004), she takes a long hard look at the major food companies' collaboration with advertising to convince housewives to embrace ready-made products. This essay, in which Shapiro (b. 1946) exercises her penetrating sense of humor, raises the question so often asked now, "Does anyone cook?" And more importantly now what *is* home cooking? No one uses the word "glamorized" anymore to describe combinations of frozen, packaged, and canned food to make a main dish or dessert, and the definition of "from scratch" has surely shifted in the past 50 years.

■ ■ ■

Until recently, the question "Do women like to cook?" wouldn't have been asked and couldn't have been answered. When it was time to feed the family, women cooked and that was that. But during the years immediately following the Second World War, cooking—an activity long seen as so immutably female it was practically a secondary sex characteristic—became, for the first time, a choice. With the advent of packaged and semi-prepared foods, it became possible to put meals on the table while doing very little actual cooking. These new products were promoted on the premise that cooking was an odious chore, one that women couldn't wait to drop, and indeed many women greeted the arrival of gingerbread mix and dehydrated mashed potatoes with glad relief. But it took considerable persuasion to convince most women that packaged-food cuisine was real cooking. Whether or not they liked to cook, most women liked *feeling* as though they were cooking. And they worried about leaving out the most powerful ingredient in any dish served at home—the ingredient one newspaper food writer called "a wife and mother's love for her family."

By the mid-1940s, the American food industry had a single overriding ambition: to create a mass market for the processed food that had been developed originally to feed the armed forces. The technology for freezing and drying food, ensuring a long shelf life and general indestructibility, was available; whether or not it extended any real benefits to consumers who didn't have to dine in foxholes was immaterial. All that remained for manufacturers to figure out was how to convince the post-war American woman that she needed canned hamburgers and frozen Welsh rarebit (to name two of the earliest technical triumphs). What the advertising industry, women's magazines and the home economics profession came up with was a theme that has enjoyed one of the longest runs in the history of marketing: "too busy to cook."

Homemakers had always been busy, especially years earlier when their kitchens had no running water or refrigeration, and the wood for the stove was stacked outdoors. Now, at the twentieth century's halfway mark, with all-electric kitchens increasingly commonplace, women became so extraordinarily busy that they could barely get around to making dinner. "Where it was possible, once upon a time, to spend hours planning meals, marketing, then cooking, today we simply cannot repeat the pattern and live," wrote Beverly Pepper in *The Glamour Magazine After Five Cookbook*, published in 1952. "Either we are working at jobs outside the home or we have other interests." By the end of the 1950s, forty per cent of all adult women were employed, including nearly a third of all married women. But Beverly Pepper was one of the few food writers to acknowledge paid employment as a factor in women's suddenly full schedules. For the most part, the women of the 1950s were depicted as frantic creatures racing from bridge parties to parent–teacher meetings to shopping sprees—an image that kept clear the distinction between earning money, seen as man's responsibility, and spending it, woman's greatest glory. Indeed, many authorities went quite far out of their way to avoid mentioning paid work when they conjured the typical daily challenges faced by wives. "Emergency meals are inevitable," counselled *Redbook* in 1956. "Whether they're caused by unexpected company, an over-busy day or something as drastic as a hurricane, be prepared with stored meals on your pantry shelf or in your food freezer."

As the time available for cooking mysteriously dried up, so the awful potential for drudgery also vanished. The more quickly women prepared dinner using packaged foods, the more delightful the work and the greater the rewards. Labour for hours making a strawberry shortcake and what do you have at the end? Dessert. But with Bisquick and frozen berries, it was a "dessert masterpiece," according to a 1954 advertisement. "And Reddi-wip tops your masterpiece with exciting glamour at the touch of a finger."

Exciting glamour was very much in order, according to numerous prescriptions in the women's magazines. A harried-looking wife who was perpetually fussing over the children would be boring—dangerously boring— to even the most devoted and selfless husband. Just look at "Susan and Howard Brown," advised an article in *Woman's Day* in 1954. Susan insisted on going to bed early every night because the three children were up at seven. So Howard was forced to go out alone. "Susan began to worry about their relationship. She tried to bring it back to life, but she didn't quite know how." Sure enough, one night Howard met someone else, and the Browns divorced. "Now Susan is a tragic figure, and her children are being raised without a father because she allowed her marriage to get away from her."

The message to women was clear: drudgery and despair—*their* drudgery and despair—could be fatal to their marriages. It was a message that set the stage nicely for a new ideal in domesticity: home life as bright and charming as the post-war housewife herself, at least as she was regularly drawn and photographed in the women's magazines. *Better Food* showed an example in 1946: there she stood before a new "electric cabinet sink" in high heels, apron and puffed sleeves, attentively washing a dish. Below the sink, the cabinet door had been opened to reveal a General Electric Disposall, which would neatly and invisibly do away with her garbage.

Quick and easy cooking was crucial to this iconography, but in truth, most women had been practising quick and easy cooking all their lives. Americans had been sitting down to pretty much the same uncomplicated meals for decades, and the standard cookbooks were full of the recipes: meatloaf, liver and onions, steaks and pork chops, leftovers made into hash. Fantasy-laden salads and desserts were sometimes on the menu, and these could be laborious projects, but day-to-day cookery tended to get right to the point. And as some of the first processed foods became widely available, they suited such menus very well. Canned peas, frozen french fries and instant chocolate pudding were

genuinely convenient products for the women who used them, whether or not
the results contributed much flavour or finesse to the prevailing cuisine.

If women were now so pressed for time that they needed to cook even more
quickly, one possibility might have been to learn to cook better—in general,
she cooks fastest who knows most about ingredients and techniques. But
amassing substantive culinary expertise held little appeal in an era of convenience. "Your Blendor takes the place of years of experience and skill,"
promised a Waring blender cookbook in 1957. And the food industry stood
ready to do a lot more than seal peas in a can or dehydrate milk for a pudding. In the course of the 1950s and early 1960s, a new cuisine began to
show up in households across the country, a curiously abstract cuisine derived almost entirely from recipes developed in test kitchens. Its purpose
was to make use of specific products, not to put a meal on the table, so many
of the new dishes were unrecognizable as breakfast, lunch or dinner. Some
were unrecognizable as food. "Start making your reputation as a cook right
now!" urged a *Woman's Day* column aimed at teenagers, called "How to be
a Girl." An appropriate dish for a beginner—at both cooking and being a
girl—was Chick-Ham à la Princesse, which involved mixing cubes of Spam
with canned cream of chicken soup and evaporated milk. Only a few decades earlier, young girls would have been taught how to make white sauce
and baking-powder biscuits, but by the 1950s there was no need to learn
how to cook such pedestrian items. Basic foods of every sort were available
ready-made, and it was a foolish, old-fashioned housewife, according to the
women's magazines, who felt reluctant to take advantage of them. "The
thousands of people working in canneries, creameries, packing plants and
frozen-food plants are just as much your servants as if they were under
your roof," explained *House Beautiful* in 1951. "For the hard, dirty, exacting
work of food preparation is done there by them. Only the easy part is left
for you to do."

Many of the new recipes were indeed easy, calling for the simplest manipulation of packages and cans. Still, in the spirit of what the magazines
called "creativity," the food itself rapidly sank into confusion. "Add a touch of
your own," urged *Woman's Day* in a 1954 article on imaginative use of everyday processed foods. Perhaps some women did cut frankfurter rolls crosswise

into half-inch slices, toast them in a waffle-iron and add melted butter, cinnamon and sugar, but it's unclear what the cook was actually supposed to do with what she had made. Nothing in the combination signalled whether it was a meal, a snack, an accompaniment or a dessert. An advertisement for Nabisco crackers anticipated this problem by designating one suggestion "an *easy* dessert," although the concept itself—a saltine topped with cottage cheese and a strawberry—could not have been very convincing in this category. But packaged-food cuisine existed outside most gastronomic categories and followed its own logic. Hence a 1956 article in *Redbook* on foods that could be prepared and frozen ahead of time didn't stop with casseroles but plunged right on into salads. The inspiration came from the freezer, not the food. So women were advised to empty a can of cranberry sauce into the blender, pour the blended sauce into a cake pan, top it with whipped cream and nuts, and freeze the whole thing. At mealtime, they would serve a chunk on a lettuce leaf, a presentation long employed to make otherwise inscrutable mixtures, or even lone foods, instantly recognizable as the salad course.

One reason many women were tempted to try packaged-food cookery was that it promised what was often termed "sophisticated" food. This was a wandering standard—arranging the strawberry on the saltine was described as a way to "sophisticate" the fruit—but the term usually implied expensive ingredients, long cooking time, difficult procedures and an imprecise air of foreignness. From very early on, the food-processing industry was able to freeze or can just about anything from beef stew to bouillabaisse but, as *House Beautiful* cautioned in 1951, most packed products were created for the mass market, not for lovers of fine food. "The only safe course for the food manufacturer is to 'play the middle of the road'—to season for the common-denominator, taste-bland, unstartling, careful," the magazine explained. But smart women knew what to do with these products—"glamorize them." For instance, heat up a can of cream of mushroom soup, a can of cream of tomato soup, a pound of crabmeat, season the mixture with curry powder and add sherry. "It's as gourmet as anything, yet it can be put together in about ten minutes," *House Beautiful* promised. By the end of the decade, everyone was glamorizing, including the women in the congregation of Trinity Church in Topsfield, Massachusetts, whose fund-raising cookbook, *Landmarks in Cooking*, featured a casserole called Gourmet Crab. This called for packaged spinach to be layered with canned crab, then moistened with canned cream of mushroom soup into which had been blended the contents of a small jar of Cheez Whiz. It was the crab that made this dish relatively expensive, hence desirable; but it was utilitarian canned soup, festively mixed with Cheez Whiz, that made the dish gourmet.

Opening boxes and cans, no matter how ingeniously the contents might be transubstantiated, was nevertheless a long way from home cooking, and most women knew it. Putting a frozen pie on the table might look like serving dessert, but did it count? What did it really mean for a woman to feed a family, beyond apportioning nutrients to a husband and each child? The industry was aware from the start that women were unlikely to accept its products without a struggle. Documenting the advances in frozen food as early as 1946, *Better Food* noted that two kinds of frozen pies were available, one that was fully baked and only had to be heated up, and another in which raw pastry was filled and frozen uncooked. "This type of pie is actually baked by the purchaser and permits a greater degree of self-expression than the pre-baked variety," observed the magazine approvingly. Over time, packaged-food cuisine absorbed women's worries and built into both the products and the advertising a great many signs and symbols of domestic "self-expression." The directions on cake mixes, for instance, called for the addition of a real, from-the-refrigerator egg long after the technology was in place to make adding fresh eggs unnecessary. Sure enough, cake mixes were among the first products successfully to change their identities, slipping imperceptibly across the border from packaged-food cookery into the culinary realm known as cooking from scratch.

One of the important mechanisms for helping packaged food exude an aura of traditional domesticity was the use of a fictional corporate spokeswoman, whose pen-and-ink portrait often accompanied the advertising. The most famous was, and is, Betty Crocker, but she had many colleagues as self-assured and inventive as she was, including Mary Blake (for Carnation) and Carol Drake (for Safeway stores). Sometimes, it was implied, these women got together and cosily traded recipes. "Certainly one of the great recipes of the year is Dutch Pantry Pie, a new one-dish dinner developed by my good friend Betty Crocker of General Mills," Mary Blake told readers in a 1954 advertisement. (The pie carried a hefty dose of Carnation evaporated milk.) More often, advertisements simply trumpeted how very home-made the products looked and tasted, though this claim had to be made with some tact: if home-made was so superior, why should anyone buy a boxed version? Swans Down cake mixes got around this problem handily by evoking the impressive world of science and technology. "The secret of extra-home-made-ness? Ingredients made especially for our new mixes. Ingredients so special you can't buy 'em in the store!"

But the food company that engineered one of the most successful promotions of the century made no effort to fool women into thinking that boxed was best. Instead, Pillsbury celebrated outright women's traditional ties to the kitchen by inviting Americans who loved to cook and enjoyed showing off their skill to enter a national baking contest that came to be known as the Pillsbury Bake-Off. Launched in 1949, the Bake-Off required contestants to submit original recipes using Pillsbury flour; two hundred thousand people entered the first year, and the Bake-Off is still going strong today.

At the fourth Bake-Off, in 1953, a contestant named Mrs. Robert R. Wellman of Kenosha, Wisconsin, triumphed with a dish that did much of what packaged-food cuisine was trying to do, but did it from the heart. The authentic emotion generating this dish was plain from the name: Liver and Onion Dinner. Nobody ever cooked liver and onions for effect: this was dinner at home. But there was plenty of glamour in the presentation, certainly by 1953 standards: the cooked liver was ground with spices and catsup and spread over a rolled-out biscuit dough. Then the dough was rolled up into a log, shaped in a single, giant crescent and baked. Mrs Wellman suggested topping it with a quickly made sauce of hot canned tomato soup, left undiluted, and she served bacon alongside. Here was a dish Betty Crocker or Mary Blake would have been proud to invent, yet it demanded enough hands-on work to make a woman feel as though she mattered. In later years, the Bake-Off was to inspire countless recipes obedient to the principles of packaged-food cookery, but dishes like Mrs Wellman's kept turning up, too—emblems of emotional resistance to a wholly artificial cuisine. Alas, the very year Mrs Wellman won her prize, Swanson introduced the first TV dinner: roast turkey with mashed potatoes and peas, each in a separate compartment of a metal tray that lent its peculiarly acrid flavour to the food. By 1960, the company had selected a distinctly chilling slogan: "Only Swanson comes so close to your own home cooking." It was starting to verge on truth.

Granta, Winter 1995

Victor M. Valle & Mary Lau Valle

from Recipe of Memory

Recipe of Memory (1995) is at once cookbook, family chronicle, and social history. We are told not only what ingredients and processes go into the making of Mexican food, but what pressures and circumstances have shaped its history. The passage excerpted here concerns Victor Valle's grandmother Delfina, who left Mexico for Los Angeles in the early 20th century for economic reasons, splitting up her family and experiencing a decline in her social standing: "Delfina found herself shoulder to shoulder with women she would have hired as maids in Guadalajara. And they knew it. They took pleasure in denying her the deference to which she was accustomed." In remarkable detail Victor (b. 1950) and Mary Lau (b. 1950) Valle tell a complex story almost entirely through food.

■ ■ ■

Delfina's decision to stay in Los Angeles proved humbling. She could not find steady work after walking away from her rag-sorting job, so she had no choice but to move in with her aunt, Juanita, and her husband, José. Delfina's waning independence added a sense of desperation to her heartache.

Now "she fretted about becoming a burden to their family," Estela recalls. "She didn't know where to turn, where to find work. She was a stranger here." But she was too proud to go back.

Juanita understood Delfina's predicament, so she asked her sons to see what they could do. They secured one of the two-bedroom wood-frame shacks provided to dairy workers with families. Now Delfina and the kids could have a place of their own, even if it was drafty and built on a flea-infested riverbed. Since the dairy gave Juanita's sons free room and board, they could afford to pay Delfina to cook their meals on a stove that flavored everything with a hint of kerosene. So the shack became a dining hall for Juanita's sons, who'd by now grown tired of fried chicken with mashed potatoes and gravy, and the other Americano foods the dairy cooked for its Mexican workers.

Other milkers quickly got wind of Delfina's cooking. During the work week, Delfina cooked for Juanita's sons and four other milkers. To meet the demands, Delfina kneaded and rolled out more than one hundred pounds of flour tortillas each week, and then found several more egg crates to seat her new guests. On these crates sat six men eager to pay a bit extra for thinly sliced steaks grilled with onions, refried beans spiked with chards of toasted *chilacate* chile and crumbled, homemade cheese; *sopa de fideos* in garlicky chicken broth, steaming columns of hand-rolled flour tortillas, and burnt-orange, pan-roasted *chile de árbol*. Not surprisingly, milk was plentiful, as was stringy beef from freshly slaughtered dairy cows.

On Sundays, friends and relatives came, bearing groceries so that they'd be sure to have a place at Delfina's table. Later, the *verdurero*, the produce peddler, might drive his truck to the ranch to bet on the rooster fights behind the corrals. Before betting, the vendor sold Delfina string beans, tomatoes, or serranos for that day's *guisado*—what we now call steak *picado*, a pan-fried and stewed combination of chopped steak, tomato, onion, garlic, and available vegetables. Fresh produce marked a special occasion. Big meaty Anaheims grown in San Fernando—roasted and stuffed with homemade cheese, coated and fried in beaten egg white—were served in a tomato sauce of sliced onions, dried oregano, and a few pickled chiles.

And if supplies ran low, there was always enough milk—at least ten gallons per family per week, more sometimes—for Delfina to run a small cheese-making operation. With the help of her children, she made *panela*, a simple hoop cheese best eaten fresh, *queso casero*, a salty cheese made for drying and aging and selling to other Mexican families, or the ultimate treat, *chongos en almibar*, fresh curd simmered in a cinnamon- or citrus-flavored sugar syrup. From the whey left over from cheesemaking, they made *requesón*, a ricotta-like cheese.

In addition to feasting, Sundays were for attending mass and shopping. My father and Estela remember rattling into downtown Los Angeles in Rafael's hard-wheeled Model T. Their destination: Nuestra Señora de Los Angeles, the eighteenth-century Franciscan mission that presides over the plaza by the same name. After being closeted in flickering candles, florid perfumes, and perspired shirt collars, they stepped out across Main Street, once La Principal, to La Luz del Día, a dry goods store, and La Esperanza, a bakery catering to a growing Mexican population. In the plaza itself, local vendors sold fresh fruits and vegetables, hawked ears of roast corn, tacos, tamales, and barbecued beef heads from pushcarts, a reminder of their own village marketplaces. A few blocks away on Spring Street, La Nacional sold a variety of dried legumes, including black beans, lard in bulk, 100-pound sacks of whole white corn, several brands of wheat flour, and *ristras* of strung dried California chiles; everything, in other words, for those who made their tortillas and tamales at home.

The Grand Central Market on Broadway was the closest thing to a bustling communal marketplace. Besides its labyrinth of stalls piled high with fragrant fruits and vivid vegetables and aisles filled with haggling shoppers, the Grand Central was known for its fresh fish and so-called variety cuts. Immigrant shoppers came for the thick cow's tongues, languid and speckled; glistening, convoluted cow's brains, marbled oxtails and pinkish pig's feet, white honeycombed tripe, jewel-like kidneys, stiff-clawed chicken feet, and other suspicious organ meats. Here immigrants could boast to each other of secret victories. Here *arrechera*, the belts of skirt steak girding a cow's voluminous intestines, was considered a cheap variety cut like kidneys or liver. (The early Californios prized the belts of fatty, tender muscle as the ideal range delicacy, since it was easy to remove after skinning, and easier to skewer over a fire.) Crates of dried *bacalao* (salt cod), popeyed cow cods, thick sea bass, halibut steaks ribboned in thick succulent skin, and inky tubs of squid, could always be had.

The goods came from Mexico, Latin America, and even Spain. On rail lines from Central Mexico boxcars hauled in *chile mulato, chile pasilla, chile ancho, chile guajillo*, mesquite-smoked *chile chipotle*, dried tamarind pods, *pinole* (ground and toasted corn to which milk can be added as a breakfast food), dried corn husks, and *piloncillo*, or cones of raw sugar. From the mountains of Sinaloa and Sonora came the incendiary round berrylike *chile piquín de bolita*, dried cooking and medicinal herbs, and whole unroasted coffee beans from southern Mexico. Baja supplied Los Angeles with various styles of dried beef, canned seafood, including pickled squid and eels, and Latin American trade goods unloaded on its docks at Ensenada; *chicharrones de vieja* (big, crunchy pork rinds), hand-churned butter wrapped in maize leaves, *panela, queso añejo* (a salty aged cheese), chile-spiced *queso enchilado* for enchiladas, and "Jijona" brand *turrón*, or Spanish-style nougat.

A handful of companies also packed Mexican foods locally. The Cotera Brothers ran a mail-order business out of El Paso that advertised Mexican chocolate, coffee, moles, and other dry foodstuffs in *La Opinión*, while La Victoria Packing Company advertised *Mole Poblano, Pipian Ranchero, Salsa del Diablo Rojo, Chilitos en Escabeche, Tomatillo* (presumably canned), *Salsa Serrana,* and *Cajeta de Membrillo* (candied quince). In 1906, Emilio C. Ortega moved his chile roasting operation from his father's home in Ventura to Los Angeles, where he founded the Ortega Chile Company, the first to develop a system for canning fire-roasted green chile. Del Monte, one of the first national canners, begins to advertise its Chile Verde Pelado, or canned and peeled green chile, by 1919 in *El Heraldo de México.* But Del Monte represented a rare exception of a national canning company producing a Mexican food product for a regional market. For the most part, the job of industrializing the production of Mexican foods and condiments was being carried out by a handful of pioneering Mexican business owners, like Rose Ramírez, who teamed up with Ernie Feraud in 1923 to establish the Ramírez & Feraud Chili Company, which specialized in red chile and enchilada sauces. But there was one essential part of her Central Mexican diet which Delfina could not buy while living at the dairy's labor camp—corn tortillas. For these she would have to wait until Sunday to go buy them in Los Angeles, where the demand was great enough to sustain a fledgling industry.

Even with the abundance and variety of imported dry goods, low milker's wages (about $45 a month in 1927) drastically limited Delfina's cooking options. She spent most of their money on such staples as flour, beans, rice, and so on. After all, her customers could only afford to pay her so much for meals. Beyond the staples, Delfina improvised. *Cilantro* was hard to get. Dried California (Anaheims) substituted for Jalisco's hotter *chilaca* pods; spinach replaced *romeritos*, a tiny wild herbal green. Fresh fruits such as plantain or mango were simply unobtainable.

Still, Delfina and her family could always count on a few seasonal delicacies. For a few weeks in late spring and early summer, tender, bright green *nopalitos*, or beavertail cactus leaves, burst forth from the arms of weathered opuntia, thorny markers planted decades earlier by preceding Mexicans. After removing their immature spines, diced and cooked *nopalitos* were traditionally simmered with *tortas de camarón*, small, pan-fried soufflés of dried pulverized shrimp held together by beaten egg whites. In late fall, after a season of good rains, the same beavertail cactus produced purple, crimson, and yellow-green *tunas* or prickly pears. Two persons holding a pair of dried mustard stalks partially disarmed the fruit of its fiberglass-like spines by rolling it on the grass. After rinsing and peeling, the *tunas* could be eaten whole, or seeded and blended into a refreshing drink, or cooked down into a candy.

Few Mexicans at that time owned land, which more or less precluded home gardening. Many lived in labor camps, often hidden from view by orange or lemon groves. The community's social invisibility allowed a lot of respectable folks to view Mexicans as foreigners. That they clung to this notion even as they dreamed of California as a "Spanish" Eden shouldn't seem odd. They had long swallowed the myth of "Spanish" romance, *sans* Mexicans.

Yet Delfina's son, Manuel, hardly recalls being shunned or deprived. Roger Jessup's dairy near Glendale gave him the supportive company of his uncles, and a chance to be a kid again. He loved squeezing warm milk from a cow he had tamed, then scrambling up a high mound of bakery surplus—broken cookies, almonds, dried figs, apples, apricots—piled high inside the dairy's feed barns. Reclining at the top of the mound, he would take his fill of milk and cookies and dried fruit destined for the feed troughs.

It was different for Delfina. "My mother suffered a lot," Estela recalls. "Can you imagine. From having known almost nothing about housework to washing men's work clothes by hand, to making them breakfast, lunch, and dinner. In Guadalajara she had maids to help her with everything." She staved off loneliness and despair by escaping into fiction. Each night, after having cleared the table, she waited for her audience to arrive—the milker's wives and her aunts and cousins—before she gave her dramatic readings of *Les Misérables* and other novels in installments.

Recipe of Memory: Five Generations of Mexican Cuisine (1995)

John Thorne

The Toll House Cookie

Iconic American foods—hamburgers, hot dogs, the ice-cream cone, apple pie—tend to have a myth of origin. These myths often involve a "eureka!" moment and turn sometimes, as in the case of the chocolate-chip cookie, on the unexpected upside that redeems a mistake. In the year 1930, Ruth Wakefield of the Toll House Inn in Wakefield, Massachusetts, added chunks of semi-sweet chopped chocolate to a buttery drop-cookie batter, expecting them to melt. Mrs. Wakefield was making chocolate cookies but though she baked them well, the chocolate remained intact, creating little islands of molten goo. Ruth was surprised and embarrassed, but her customers couldn't get enough of her mistake. Americans love luck and happy endings as surely as we love chocolate-chip cookies. John Thorne (b. 1943), the assiduous food writer from Maine, deftly combines memory and cookbook research in his retelling of the myth, revealing not only Mrs. Wakefield's discovery but its prehistory—the chocolate-chip cookie "yearning, struggling to be born."

■ ■ ■

When I was a kid, my absolute favorite cookie was the chocolate-chip cookie. In some ways, I suppose—at least in terms of durable attraction—it still is, but at age ten there was simply no competition. My mother liked them, too, but her taste was more catholic. The cookie jar might just as well be filled with brownies, peanut-butter cookies (my second favorite), sugar cookies, or *oatmeal* cookies.

I can remember coming home from school, catching the telltale scents of baking day, and rushing into the kitchen. There they were, spread out on the cooling racks, dozens of hot, brown-edged cookies, covered with dark, melty dots. Only, when I went to snatch one, I discovered that the dots weren't what I expected. My mother had made her own favorite, oatmeal cookies, the traitor cookie that looked like my favorite but tasted like . . . well, like porridge patties with raisin plops.

Hard to believe, but for my mother, while all these other cookies were old familiars from her childhood, the chocolate chipper was a novelty item, first encountered when she was a teenager in the late 1930s. In fact, although this won't appear on many calendars, the year 2000 will mark the seventieth anniversary of the fabled moment when Ruth Wakefield pulled the first batch of chocolate-chip cookies out of the oven at the Toll House Inn in Wakefield, Massachusetts.

If you know this legend, you know that no one was more surprised at this turn of events than Ruth herself. She had expected the chocolate to melt into the cookie. Instead, out came a crisp, buttery cookie shot through with molten nuggets. Lacking the advantage of hindsight, she christened it the "Chocolate Crunch Cookie."

In 1930, of course, there were no morsels or chips or nuggets; Ruth Wakefield had to break up a chocolate bar to get her bits—specifically, a bar of Nestlé's semisweet Yellow Label Chocolate. According to the official (i.e., Nestlé) account, the cookie became so popular with customers and neighbors that a sales rep finally came by to find out who exactly was buying all those chocolate bars. He discovered Ruth baking up a storm at the Toll House Inn . . . and struck a deal. Let's hope she drove a good Yankee bargain for herself, because Nestlé made out all right; by the cookie's fiftieth anniversary in 1980, the company was producing 350 million morsels a *day.**

Nestlé's first move was to produce that bar scored into tiny squares, packaging it with a special tool to help break it up. By 1939, they finally landed the hammer directly on the nail and began cranking out the familiar already-formed morsels, in packages that still bear the color of the now-forgotten Yellow Label, and printed the recipe for "The Famous Toll House Cookie" on the back. An American classic was born.

My question, though, is: *why*? Why is the chocolate chip cookie *my* favorite cookie, *your* favorite cookie, nearly *everybody's* favorite cookie? Why have at least three separate entrepreneurs (not counting Ruth herself) made it the foundation of their cookie-chain empires? Why isn't it Famous Amos's Pecan Sandies, Mrs. Fields' Benne Wafers, David's Gingersnaps?

Looking for the answer, I spent some time searching through a batch of early-twentieth-century New England cookbooks, the sort that might have roosted on top of Ruth Wakefield's Frigidaire. The amazing thing is how

---

*Ruth Wakefield continued to hope that the same bolt of lightning might strike her twice. Among her subsequent attempts was the "Toll House Ting-a-Ling," made with prunes, walnuts, ginger, chocolate chips, and cornflakes.

clearly we can now see the chocolate-chip cookie yearning, struggling, to be born. Here are Boston cookies with the familiar combination of brown and white sugar . . . here are chocolate walnut wafers, also very similar, but still not quite right . . . here are drop brownies, so close, so close . . . and so on.

The idea wasn't so much to get *chocolate* into the cookie as to get *intensity* into it. After a meal of roast beef and gravy, potatoes mashed with milk and butter, creamed onions, and hot rolls and butter, a slice of, say, pound cake comes as a bit of a letdown, something easy to refuse. So affronted home bakers brought out of the kitchen the triple layer cake covered with fudge frosting. No one was going to turn that down! And no one did . . . and mostly still can't.

To grasp what was going on, imagine a homemaker with a bowl of fudge frosting in one hand and a cookie in the other, trying to push the two together. Cookies don't take to being frosted; there's not enough *cookie* in a cookie to stand up to so much sweetness. If only you could bake a cookie with little lumps of fudge frosting all through it. You can't do that with frosting, of course, but you can with plain chocolate. *Voilà*, the cookie every home baker was waiting for, the cookie that was more than just another sweetened cracker, another teatime snack.

Like our national anthem, our national cookie demands more skill than many of us can muster. Cooks have always had trouble with the Toll House Cookie, and for good reason—it is really too rich for its own good. Although it evolved from a drop cookie and is still made like one, it is in truth closer to a refrigerator cookie—but without that cookie's ease of making. As Ruth Wakefield revised her Toll House cookbook, she kept pushing it in this direction, instructing that the dough be refrigerated overnight and the "drops" of dough be flattened by hand once they were put on the cookie sheet. Even so, as any cookie maker will know, there is no really foolproof method.

Interestingly, the many subsequent variations of the Toll House Cookie all seem bent on recapturing that initial experience of richness. The original recipe called for each cookie to be made with only half a teaspoon of dough; commercial versions such as David's and Mrs. Fields are much larger, demanding a proportional increase in the size of the chocolate chunks.* This

---

*For instance, in her *Mrs. Fields Cookie Book*, directed to the home cook, Debbi Fields makes each cookie with a tablespoon of dough, or six times the original amount.

meant, at first, a return to the old method of breaking bars up into genuine chunks, but recently Nestlé and other chocolate companies have bowed to the trend and begun producing mega-morsels.

This craving for richness piled upon richness is strictly an American one, and the chocolate-chip cookie, on the whole, has remained an unabashedly American taste. Unlike the hamburger, which has been an eager cross-cultural proselytizer, the Toll House Cookie has mostly stayed at home. European chocolate does not necessarily improve it; European *pâtissiers* are incapable of grasping its generous innocence.

This is because in Europe a cookie is generally considered a delicate thing: a tiny, subtle, bite-sized pastry meant to nestle at the edge of the teacup or even the brandy snifter. The blurb on the canisters of those Italian confections *amarettini di Saronno* recommends them as choice company for "fine wine and after-dinner liqueurs" . . . hardly something we'd want to pair up with a couple of chocolate chippers. *Their* best accompanying beverage is an icy glass of milk; their most appropriate milieu, the kitchen table.

Europeans, reminiscing about childhood treats, call up visions of nursery food or, perhaps, a slice of bread wrapped around a square of chocolate. Over there, dessert seems mostly an adult prerogative, and their cookies reflect this attitude. As much as they may call attention to themselves, such cookies have a certain *délicatesse*, as befits something baked to play the accompaniment to a tiny scoop of sorbet, a ripe pear, or a bowl of strawberries and Devonshire cream.

Mention the word "dessert" to an American, however, and what comes to mind? Memories of hot-fudge sundaes, coconut-frosted layer cakes, apple pie and ice cream, and Mother saying, "Clean your plate, dear—or no dessert." At the end of supper our appetite suddenly assumes a child's face. And what could be more of a kid pleaser than a handful of buttery crunchy cookies filled with chocolate chips?

The original chocolate-chip cookie recipe, of course, isn't the one printed on the back of the Nestlé package, since the Toll House Cookie predates the Toll House morsel. Here, for the record, is the recipe Ruth Graves Wakefield, Dietitian and Lecturer, first set down in *Toll House Tried and True Recipes* back in 1938.

Chocolate Crunch Cookies

Cream 1 cup of butter. Add ³⁄₄ cup each of brown and granulated sugar and 2 eggs beaten whole. Dissolve 1 teaspoon of baking soda in 1 teaspoon hot water and mix alternately with 2 ¹⁄₄ cups flour sifted with 1 teaspoon salt.* Lastly, add 1 cup chopped nuts and 1 pound of Nestlé's Yellow Label Chocolate, semisweet, cut into pieces the size of a pea. Flavor with 1 teaspoon vanilla and drop by the half-teaspoonful onto a greased cookie sheet. Bake 10 to 12 minutes in a pre-heated 375°F oven. Makes 100 cookies.

*If this sentence seems a little confused, no wonder: Ruth Wakefield is directing us to alternately mix the flour-salt mixture and that little spoonful of baking-soda paste into the creamed butter and sugar. When she first created the recipe, this awkward approach was mandated by the coarse texture of baking soda. Since then, producers have learned to mill it fine enough so that it can be simply sifted into the flour with the salt. Amusingly, this posed later food writers with an unexpected problem: what to do with the now redundant teaspoon of water. Most dared not simply omit it, and so, decade after decade, you find chocolate-chip cookie recipes with a mysterious teaspoon of water separately stirred into the batter.

Serious Pig (1996)

Shirley Geok-lin Lim

Boiled Chicken Feet and Hundred-Year-Old Eggs: Poor Chinese Feasting

In this homage to the down-home cooking of her youth in the ethnic Chinese community of Malaysia, the poet and memoirist Shirley Geok-lin Lim (b. 1944) goes beyond the egg rolls and fortune cookies of Americanized "Chinese food" to less readily assimilable fare. From "scraps, offal, detritus, and leftovers saved from the imperial maw," she argues, her family eked out a "fragrant and mouth-watering survival." American cooking also has a history in which the humble vies with the luxurious (sometimes the humble *becomes* a luxury, or vice versa). But the lesson is clear: even out of the cheapest cuts, "triumphant feasting" is always a possibility.

■ ■ ■

You mustn't eat chicken feet until you are a married woman!" my aunts warned me. "Otherwise you will grow up to run away from your husband."

They sat around the dining table, an unstable jointure of old planks stained by years of soya-sauce drips and scorched by the ashy embers that always fell out of the small coal oven under the metal hot-pot which was fetched out once a year for Chinese New Year family feasts. They chewed on gold-brown chicken feet that had been boiled with ginger, garlic, sugar, and black soy. The feet looked like skinny elegant batons with starred horny toes at one end, their speckled skins glossy with caramelized color, but chicken feet all the same. My aunts and stepmother gnawed at the small bones, grinding the jellied cartilage of the ligaments audibly, and the bone splinters piled up beside their plates.

I would not stay to watch them. I had seen hens and roosters pick their feet through fungal monsoon mud, stepping on duck and dog and their own shit.

My stepmother raised poultry on our leftovers and on chopped swamp vegetation which sprouted lavishly in the greenish slimy wasteland behind our house, and on festival days she slaughtered at least two fat chickens for us—her five stepchildren, two sons, and cherished husband. Chicken was a luxury we tasted only on these days, on Chinese New Year, Ch'ing Ming, the Mid-Autumn Festival, and the Feast of the Hungry Ghost. And then, as my aunts told us was the practice even when they were children, the chickens were divided according to gender, the father receiving the white breast meat, the sons the dark drumsticks, and the daughters the skinny backs, while the women ate the feet and wings.

As the only daughter in a family (then) of seven boys, I was excused from such discrimination and took my turn equally with the drumsticks, the favorite meat for all of us. Chicken was always sold whole and freshly slaughtered, and no one imagined then that one could make a dish solely of drumsticks or of chicken breasts. Such mass marketing was possible only with the advent of refrigeration, and although coffee shops in town held large industrial-sized refrigerators for serving shaved iced concoctions and cold sodas, popular refreshments among Malaysians to fend off the humid equatorial temperatures, Chinese Malaysians, like most Asians in the 1950s, would eat only fresh food. We thought of frozen meat as rotten, all firm warm scented goodness of the freshly killed and gathered gone, and in its place the monochromatic bland mush of thawed stuff fit only for the garbage pail.

Still, while no one sold chicken parts separately, fresh chicken feet were always available in the wet market; you could buy them by the kilos, a delicacy to be enjoyed, according to my elders, only by married women. Well, let my aunts and stepmother suck on those splintery bones. I was never comfortable at the table when those feet appeared, when the women waved me away from them. My mother had run away from her husband. A bad woman, a runaway wife, a lost mother. A young girl, I was not to be trusted with those chicken feet, not when I had my mother's history in my blood, my mother's face on my face, still recognizable to my aunts, my father's brothers' wives, good wives and mothers, even though it had been five, six, seven years since she ran away.

I could not face the leathery skin, tightly bound to the long femurs after hours of simmering. And the soft padded soles that my aunts delighted in chewing—it was here that the chicken came closest to the human anatomy: pads like the fat feet of my stepmother's babies. Even now, now that I have grown to become a wife and mother like my aunts and stepmother, like my runaway mother, I will not eat chicken feet, no matter how much wine, cardamom, cumin, honey, or ginger has steeped them. I remember the tiny bones, the crunch of skin and cartilage. I remember my mother.

Almost forty years later, living in the United States, I am constantly reminded of how "Chinese" has become a fetish for Americans looking for a transcending experience of difference and otherness. Ranging from white models with stark black eye-liner and chopsticks in their chignons to "happy" dressing gowns that copy karate-type uniforms, things associated with Chinese culture pervade mainstream American imagination, suggesting, through the fixed acquirement of a traditional middle-class taste—for blue willow-pattern china, for instance, or take-out shrimp in lobster sauce—that Americans are omnivorous consumers rather than Eurocentric ideologues.

Purveyors of such U.S. "multiculturalism," however, usually disguise the material sources of their goods. Difference has to be softened, transformed, before it can be assimilated into Middle America. So also with Chinese food, which, before Nixon's visit to China in 1972, was sold in thousands of small restaurants outside of Chinatowns as egg rolls, egg foo yung, chow mein, and fortune cookies, none of which was recognizable to me who had grown up eating home-cooked Chinese food in Malaysia. Influenced by the increase in Asian immigration to the United States after the 1965 Hart-Celler Act, and thirty years after Mao Tse-tung intoxicated the Nixon presidential party with *maotai* and exotic ten-course banquets, many Americans have learned to dine on "authentic" Chinese food across a number of regional cuisines, from the mild, flavorful fresh steamed dishes of Canton, to the salty fiery peppers of Szechwan and Hunan and the rich elaborate food of the Shanghainese. But mid-Manhattan restaurants and Chinese cookbooks never note the particular dishes peculiar to Old One-Hundred-Name, what the Chinese call the man in the street. These dishes have been the ordinary fare for billions of poor Chinese through the centuries, and for myself as a hungry child in a family of too many children and never enough money.

While the chicken feet my aunts feasted on was forbidden to me, I was repeatedly coaxed to taste *pei ta-an*, the only other dish in my famished childhood that I could not eat. These duck eggs, imported from China, had been selected for their large size, covered with a mix of mud and straw, then stored in a darkened space for at least a month, covered with cloth that had been impregnated with sodium carbonate. You had to knock the dried grey mantle of mud gently off, wash the eggs in cold water, then crack and peel the bluish-white shells. What emerged was a clear glistening gelatinous black oval enclosing a purple-green-black yolk, and a sharp reek of sulfuric vapor, a dense collection of chemicals from decaying things, like the airborne chemical traces that trigger the salivary glands of scavenging wolves or turkey buzzards.

Father was especially fond of *pei ta-an*, what the expensive restaurants called hundred-year-old eggs, which my stepmother always served sliced thin in sections of eighths accompanied by shredded pinky young ginger pickled in sugared vinegar. He believed it was *poh*, full of medicinal properties that stimulated blood circulation, cleansed the liver and kidneys, sharpened the eyesight and hearing, and elevated the male libido, and my stepmother, a generation younger than he, diligently served it as a cold relish to accompany steaming rice porridge, or alone, as a late-night snack.

Occasionally Father shared this delicacy with us. My brothers hung greedily over him, waiting for their one-eighth sliver of slippery shining jet-black egg, which was served draped with a vinegary-moist ginger shred. Approaching *pei ta-an* for the first time, I thought its glistening black carapace and iridescent green-black yolk beautiful, a magical gem cut open for inspection. But then its acrid stench shot up my olfactory glands opening passageways more powerfully than a tongueful of green mustard, and I gagged, as close to vomiting over food as I would ever get. Unlike boiled chicken feet which I could ignore by resolutely leaving the table, *pei ta-an* pursued me out of the kitchen, out of the living area, and out of the house, a smell of pollution I feared each time Father called out for us to come and eat some hundred-year-old egg.

At some point in my childhood, however, drawn by my brothers' lust for *pei ta-an*, I pinched my nostrils closed and opened my mouth for the sliver. Its flavor and texture was like nothing I had ever tasted, the combination of the jellied white-turned-to-black and the tightly packed purple-black heart igniting on my taste buds as in intricate instantaneous sensation of bitter and sweet, rawly and densely meaty, yet as delicate as air-spun cotton-candy, primitively chemical and ineffably original. I was hooked. But *pei ta-an*, although not expensive, was what my stepmother bought for Father alone: for his health, his pleasure, his libido. A morsel would always be our share of this pleasure.

Late on the evening that I first tasted *pei ta-an* I walked out to the Chinese grocery store at the corner of the main road and spent some of my cache of coins hoarded from the dollars that my mother far away in another country mailed me once or twice a year. I bought two eggs jacketed in mud and straw. While my brothers were playing Monopoly in the front room, I sneaked into the kitchen, broke open the armor, carefully crazy-cracked the shells, peeled the pair, all the time marveling at the scent that had set my saliva flowing, and ate them slowly, reveling in the gentle chewy texture of the albumin and the heavy metallic yolky overload. My stepmother was right. Eating *pei ta-an* was a libidinous experience.

I have grown accustomed to the absence of strong flavor and scent in food, living in the United States. Many Americans appear to prefer their meals as antiseptic as their bathrooms. The movement toward "health foods" seems to me to be yet another progression toward banning the reek, bloodiness, and decay of our scavenging past and installing a technologically controlled and scientifically scrutinized diet. In some future time, humans may live to a hundred and fifty years, dining on a mass-produced nutritious cuisine of "natural foods" based on grains, vegetables, and roots. Boiled chicken feet and chemically preserved eggs will become gross memories from a horrible history of animal abuse and carcinogenic poisoning. But in the meantime, millions of Asians are still eating these dishes in search of, if not, as my poor father who died young of throat cancer believed, health and longevity, at least a diverse diet that can keep them body and soul.

Thus my eldest brother, by now middle-aged and middle-class prospering, promised me a memorable breakfast when I visited him in Malacca in 1989. It was Sunday, as in the West a day for leisurely gatherings and perhaps some family feasting. We drove to the center of town, up through a narrow side-lane, and parked by an open ditch. Under a galvanized tin roof, crowding with other families, we sat on low stools around a small round wooden table, as scarred and stained as the table around which we ate in our childhood. The hawker, a Chinese Malaysian, was busy stirring an enormous blackened iron pot from which clouds of steam puffed up. Smaller pots containing various dark and green mashes sat on smaller grills, all fueled by a propane tank. Pouring the boiling liquid from the teapot, Eldest Brother rinsed the bowls, cups, spoons, and chopsticks set before us. Then a woman—the hawker's wife? daughter?—filled our bowls with plain white rice porridge, watery, the grains soft but still separate rather than broken down into a glutinous mass. From the many pots she brought different bowls—salted cabbage cooked to a dark-green slush with slabs of pork fat edged with a little lean; salted pickled cucumber crunchy and sweet; hard-cooked and browned bean curd less chewy than the meat it was processed to imitate; salted dried anchovies smaller than my little finger, fried crisp with their heads on. Nothing was fresh, everything was freshly cooked.

A light in my head flashed and lit something I had always known but never understood. How poor the masses of ordinary Chinese have been for millennia and how inventive hunger has made them. How from the scraps, offal, detritus, and leftovers saved from the imperial maw, from dynastic overlords who taxed away almost everything, peasant Chinese have created a fragrant and mouth-watering survival: dried lily buds and lotus roots, tree cloud fungus and fermented bean mash, dried lichen and salted black beans, pickled leeks and seaweed dessert; fish maw and chicken feet; intestines and preserved eggs. No wonder as a child I was taught to greet my elders politely, "Have you eaten yet, Eldest Auntie? Have you eaten rice, Third Uncle?" Speaking in our dialect, my stepmother still greets me, newly arrived from rich America, thus, "Have you eaten?"

The cook himself approached our table bearing two dishes especially ordered by my brother for me: soy-boiled chicken feet chopped into bite-sized pieces, and *pei ta-an* cut in eighths with a mound of pickled ginger on the side. My eldest brother had figured me out; that, even after decades of American fast foods and the rich diet of the middle class, my deprived childhood had indelibly fixed as gastronomic fantasies those dishes impoverished Chinese had produced out of the paltry ingredients they could afford. This is perhaps the instruction to an increasingly consuming and consumed planet that the cuisine from China offers: to eat is to live. And we multiplicious billions will all have to learn to eat well in poverty, turning scarcity and parsimony to triumphant feasting. Facing my morning's breakfast of preserved vegetables and hundred-year-old eggs, boiled chicken feet, and rice gruel, I knew my brother was offering me the best of our childhood together.

Soy-Boiled Chicken Feet*

10 pairs of chicken feet

1 teaspoon salt

1 ½ teaspoon pepper

one knob ginger as big as a large walnut

4 cloves garlic

¼ cup sherry

1 tablespoon sesame oil

2 teaspoons sugar

1 cup soy sauce

5 star-anise or 1 teaspoon five-spice powder (optional)

1. Wash chicken feet well, making sure that claws are clipped off and any small feathers plucked with tweezers. Strip the yellow outer epidermis off legs.

2. Fill a large pot with water and set it on high heat. When water boils, place chicken feet in the pot and cook for about 15 minutes, then drain.

3. Peel brown skin off ginger and slice thin in rounds. Peel garlic and crush lightly.

4. Put soy sauce, sherry, ginger, garlic, salt, pepper, sugar, star-anise or five-spice powder, sesame oil, and chicken feet in a large flat saucepan. Bring to a light simmer and leave simmering for about 30 minutes, by which time meat should be falling off the bones.

5. Cool, then chop into bite-sized pieces.

Serves 4 to 6.

*The same recipe can be used for chicken drumsticks, substituting eight drumsticks for the feet, and skipping the initial boiling.

Through the Kitchen Window, Arlene Voski Avakian, ed. (1997)

CREOLE GUMBO

5 lb fresh heads-on shrimp (or 4 lb frozen shrimp tails)

12 live crabs (or 1 lb frozen crabmeat)

4 dozen oysters and their liquor

1 chicken, about 2 lb

1 lb stewing beef, diced small

1 meaty hambone

1/2 lb country ham, diced

4 strips bacon   **[SERVES 12 OR MORE]**

3 large onions, chopped

2 green peppers, chopped

6 scallions with their green leaves, chopped

4 cloves garlic, minced

1 cup chopped celery

1/4 cup chopped parsley

3 lb fresh (or 4 pkg frozen) okra, sliced

4 large Creole tomatoes, peeled and diced (or a 32-oz can)

2 bay leaves

1 tsp thyme

2 tbsp Worcestershire sauce

1/2 tsp cayenne

1 tsp freshly ground black pepper

4 tbsp salt (or more)

6 quarts stock or water (or more)

4 tbsp butter and 4 tbsp flour (for the roux)

steamed rice

The operation requires several utensils, a big skillet, a big stew pot, and several smaller pots for steaming.

First the roux: Melt the butter in the skillet, add the flour, and stir until dark brown, keeping the fire very low. To the roux in the skillet add the chopped onions, green peppers, scallions, garlic, and celery and stir them in well. Adding more butter if necessary, cook the vegetables until they're limp and transparent, but don't brown them. Add the okra and keep cooking until the okra loses its gummy consistency. Put this mixture into the large stew pot. Clean the skillet, and fry the strips of bacon and the diced country ham slowly until browned. Add the ham to the pot, and drain the bacon on a paper towel. Crumble it and add to the pot. Shake the diced stewing beef in a paper bag with seasoned flour, coating it well, and add it to the bacon grease in the skillet. Sear the beef until it's browned on all sides, and add it to the pot.

While you were doing all the above, your assistant cooks should have been performing the following operations: Cut the chicken into pieces, place them in a pot, and cover with water, adding a teaspoon of salt. Boil for 30 to 40 minutes, or until tender. Remove the chicken and add its cooking stock to the big pot. Remove the skin from the chicken, cut the skin into very small pieces, and add it to the pot. Remove the chicken meat from the bones, dice it, and add it to the pot.

Wash the shrimp and cover them with water in a pot, adding a little salt. Bring to the boil and cook for five minutes, or until they're pink and easy to peel. Take them out and cool them in the sink. Save the shrimp stock in the pot. Peel the shrimp and set them aside. Take the heads and the shells off the shrimp, place them in some sort of flat-bottomed container, and crush them thoroughly with a pestle or an empty bottle. Pour this mixture into the shrimp water in the pot, and boil it vigorously for 15 minutes. Strain the liquid through triple cheesecloth into the big stew pot.

The stuff inside the shrimp's head is like the tomalley of a lobster— a nectar of the gods—and this stock will really give kick to the gumbo. So will the crab stock.

Wash the live crabs thoroughly, put them in a pot, cover with boiling water, and boil for 20 minutes. Remove the crabs and pour the stock into the large stew pot. Clean the crabs. Remove the top shells and scrape the spongy gills off. Break off the mouth parts, and remove the "apron" on the bottom of the crab. Twist off the fins, legs, and claws. Crack the claws and put them in the main pot. Break the body into two halves and drop them in. Be sure you've scraped out all the crabfat from the corners of the top shells and from the body cavity and added it to the pot, because a gumbo wouldn't be fit to eat without this delicious stuff. Crush the crab shells, legs, and fins in the bottom of a pot as you did the shrimp shells. Cover them with water and boil vigorously for 15 minutes. Strain the liquid and add it to the main cooking pot.

Add the oyster liquor to the pot. Get as much of this stuff from your oyster dealer as you can, a quart or two if possible, but if you can't get that much, the chicken, shrimp, and crab stock (plus water if needed) will do.

You are now ready to light the fire under the big stew pot. Add the tomatoes, parsley, hambone, and all the flavoring elements except the salt. The liquid should cover everything in the pot by about two inches, so add more liquid if necessary. You can use fish stock, oyster liquor, chicken bouillon, a combination of all these, or just plain water. Bring the pot to a boil, then lower the heat, place an asbestos pad under the pot to prevent scorching, and boil gently for 1 1/2 to 2 hours. You can't overcook it; the longer it cooks, the better. Stir it occasionally and scrape the bottom with a metal kitchen spoon. If there's a black residue on the tip of your spoon, it means you're scorching it, and you'd better slow down. If it really begins to burn and has an acrid, scorched smell, you must cut off the heat, remove the gumbo from the pot, clean all the burned material off the bottom of the pot, rinse it out, replace the gumbo, and start cooking again. Thus chastened, you'll use moderation and sense.

A stew containing roux will always scorch if you don't keep a close watch on it and cook slowly.

About 30 minutes before the gumbo is done, start cooking your rice. Bring 12 cups of water to a boil, and add a tablespoon of vegetable oil (keeps the grains separated), 4 teaspoons of salt, and 6 cups of rice. Stir the mixture vigorously, and when it return to the boil, turn the heat very low, cover the pot tightly, and cook for 15 minutes or until all the water is absorbed. Let it set for a few minutes, and then taste for doneness. Never stir steaming rice until it's done.

Ten minutes before serving the gumbo, add the shrimp and the oysters to the pot, and stir them in.

Now comes the last and critically important act: adjusting the salt. A good gumbo must have plenty of salt in it if it's to be as savoury as it should be. Keep adding salt to the pot and stirring it in until it achieves this deep, rich savour. Don't be timid! A bland gumbo is a disaster.

Serve the gumbo in large preheated soup bowls. Place a half cup of rice in the bottom of each bowl and ladle the gumbo over it, making sure that each bowl gets a generous share of all the elements—shrimp, crab, and oysters. (Option: Many hosts prefer to pass around a bowl of hot rice and let the guests add exactly the amount they want.)

I like a good full-bodied imported red Burgundy with my gumbo, but many prefer the lighter white wines.

Howard Mitcham, *Creole Gumbo and All That Jazz: A New Orleans Seafood Cookbook* (1997)

Howard Mitcham, chef, writer, and artist, was born in Winona, Mississippi, and grew up in New Orleans. He lost his hearing to spinal meningitis as a child, and the loss seemed to amplify his other senses: nothing but flavor impressed him, and he believed that the traditions he knew well–the New Orleans cooking of his childhood and the New England cuisine he learned over many summers in Provincetown–had long since figured out the best way of coaxing flavor from food.

Judith Moore

Adultery

A bittersweet account of yearning, indulgence, and remorse at a moment when the gourmet revolution and sexual liberation seemed to be happening all at once, this chapter from *Never Eat Your Heart Out* (1997), by Judith Moore (1940–2006), is one of my favorite pieces of recent food writing. I have returned to it many times, always finding something new to admire: its unflinching, intimate, generous tone; its deft, multilayered revelations and awakenings, the emotions and the senses feeding off each other. Reading Moore is like having a wise, older friend in the kitchen; more than almost anyone, she understands that food is one of the more important matters of the heart.

■ ■ ■

I don't think I ever better got the feel for that complicated business of insinuating cold butter into flour and thence into a high-pitched oven (500 degrees for the first five–ten minutes!) that produces *mille-feuilles* pastry, don't think I ever stirred, sniffed, and tasted my way to a more provocative lime-ginger-garlic-soy-molasses marinade for duck than during the year I went out on my husband. Our daily menus, already intriguing, grew more complex. I dared myself beyond the great American mamas, Fannie Farmer and Irma Rombauer and Irma's daughter Marion Rombauer Becker, beyond rib roasts and sweating pork butts and pineapple-and-clove-stuck hams, beyond mashed potatoes pouring out lavas of fat-gilded gravy. I acquired soufflé dishes. I bought a mandoline. I bought whisks. I learned to scrape ginger root. I turned the aforementioned *mille-feuilles* into elephant ears; into a delicate casing for baked apple cored out and filled with rum-soaked raisins; into tidy squares with custard between them, the flaky squares drizzled with a translucent strawberry sauce.

Nights, I studied Elizabeth David's *Summer Cooking*, with its advice on scattering chopped basil across *ratatouille en salade* and suggestions for hors d'oeuvres of mushrooms marinated in olive oil. I read the *Larousse Gastronomique* and marveled at all the things you could do with eggplant, and went ahead and did them, even eggplant soufflé. The latter puffed up past the white collar I'd wound around the soufflé dish, and once on the tongue, the eggy fluff released the purple eggplant's sharp, dolorous smoke.

During the adultery year my husband, Jack, gained eighteen pounds. The younger of our two daughters, who ate heedlessly, without cost to her figure, said, "I'm having to watch it, Mom, at the old trough." Nights when we gave dinner parties, our belly-heavy company crawled from the dining-room table. Their lips glistened with lamb fat and Elizabeth David's mint butter ("Pound," she writes, the fresh mint leaves and butter "to a smooth *ointment*"). Raspberry purée dribbled down shirtfronts, *crème caramel* freckled bosoms. Our friends threw themselves down into the living-room couches and sighed among the poppy-printed pillows.

"Such is the way of an adulterous woman; she eateth, and wipeth her mouth, and saith, I have done no wickedness." (Proverbs 30:20) Let me assure you, I do think I did "wickedness." Let me assure you, I didn't go unpunished. The adultery ended up in a godawful mess, that I'll tell you right now.

The affair, circumstantially, began in cooking. Summers, I put up pickles, preserves, salsas, chutneys, jellies, jams, fruit. The September noon that I ran into the gentleman who became my partner, my adultery angel, adultery demon, love of my life, also destroyer, the temperature was in the mid-seventies. The sky offered that visibility-unlimited cloudless blue that makes you tilt your head backward. You look up and think how illimitable, how without measure and sempiternal the world is, and how happily mortal you are; a medium-range contentment puts a wriggle in your walk that flips the hem on your faded blue denim wrap skirt and raises your chest beneath your favorite Liberty of London print blouse. Breezes floated down off surrounding hills and carried cidery scents off pear and apple orchards that soldiered down the green hills. When I looked out those windows bosomy hills made you feel sleepy; I could have rested on their softness. The mountains that rose behind the hills *didn't* look soft. They seemed ill-tempered and dangerous, and were; almost every year somebody slipped down into a crevasse and died before the whirring Life Flight helicopter could rope him up to safety. I used to wonder what it was like, to lie curled up, crushed between black basalt, breathing raspily with a broken rib poked into your lung, thinking about your wife, your baby, your mother, how you'd done no good in your life; then maybe, when your head rolls backward, you see a vulture ride the air above you.

When you flew above Coraville in a light plane, as I had, and looked down, you saw church steeples and college bell tower, parks' viridescing squares, trim ribbons of streets, the two supermarkets' asphalt parking lots, the water tower graffitied by that year's Coraville High graduating class, the two-story stucco Elks Lodge atop Cora Hill, the aforementioned orchards, and beyond them, farms and ranches and plotted fields, fences, and along the fences the yellow wild mustard and shelterbelts of wind-twisted trees. Easily, you could pick out your own house, your evergreens and quivering aspen and weeping willow, and your friends' houses, your children's schools. I recall that the afternoon I went up in the plane, I could see my back-yard garden and count eight rows of Country Gentleman corn. I couldn't see the pole beans that I planted between corn rows to let the cornstalks serve as supports, but I wanted to.

The supermarket lot where I parked wasn't crowded in the way city people imagine crowds. Maybe twenty cars and pickup trucks, keys dangling from ignitions, nosed between the white lines on the asphalt lot.

Glancing neither left, right, nor forward, Peter floated out through the store's whiny automatic doors, his hands fidgeting open a sack of pipe tobacco. I rushed toward the same doors. What I had in mind was twenty pounds of sugar, rings for my old mason jars, and, if any were left, two maple-frosted doughnuts for whose pleasure I'd forgone a hunk of Oregon Gold Cheddar and the bowl of leftover black-bean soup that awaited Jack when he bicycled the six blocks from his office for lunch and nap. I intended to eat the doughnuts after I stowed the sugar and jar rings in the passenger seat and while I drove up in the hills to Potts's orchard to collect three flats of Bartlett pears for preserves and chutney (green and red bell peppers chopped fine, grate fresh ginger root, raisins, mustard seed, pear chunks) and the fourteen quarts of mint pears I put up every year. I was dreaming of those frosted-with-maple doughnuts and how the cool scratchless icing would melt across my tongue and down the walls of my cheeks, and Peter was fiddling with the tobacco packet.

We were each as happy then as people need to be and didn't know it.

We bumped. I was gazing into his tie, an ugly non-silk item striped brown and gold. I remember thinking what a viciously ugly tie it was and that you rarely saw a pretty tie in Coraville like the pretty ties in *The New Yorker*. At the time I *didn't* think the following, although I had before and since: that in Coraville men who *did* wear suits, ties, white shirts regarded the tie as a sign of the step up from manual labor to authority over other, lesser men and women. As in any area dependent upon agriculture, Coraville's outskirts convulsed with fattening hogs, breeding rabbits, sheep, mad bulls, dairy cows, alfalfa, potato, corn, and dryland wheat. The men and women who guided this brute vigor to market came to town in rusty mud-splattered pickups. Cow manure and straw stuck to their boots. The Coraville men tied into their ties from J. C. Penney's and the Sears catalogue sat at desks in city and county offices, stood behind counters in banks and stores, and lorded it over those country folk. These city men, too, over lunches at The Alcazar and Papa's Steakhouse, told jokes that featured bulls and rams and roosters. This fecund blood-dangerous world was always threatening to invade the tiny town, break into churches and hardware emporiums; the seed of farm children, likewise, threatened the virginal beds of city daughters. Nobody wanted his daughter to marry a farmer. A rancher, maybe, but not a farmer. Ranchers, often, were rich.

We literally bumped into each other. He stepped right down on my navy-blue Ked. We were both standing on the sensored flooring, so Safeway's door stayed open while we apologized, Peter doing most of the apology, since I was the principally injured. Peter, his six-foot five-inch Ichabod Crane frame bowed at the waist, addressed me with old-fashioned formality. He bit down on his pipe stem, studied me.

Aware we were keeping the door open and straining Safeway's air-conditioned chill, I touched Peter's jacketed arm with my fingertips, said, "Well, nice to have seen you," and turned to go into the store.

Peter grabbed my elbow, turned me around, and propelled me a few feet into the parking lot. "Have you seen my new car?" He pointed toward a navy-blue Alfa-Romeo. "It's used, but it's new to me."

Before I knew it, I had agreed to forgo my pears and climb into his Alfa-Romeo and lean back into the leather seat and drive to the river, to play, as he put it, smiling down on me as if he were sunshine itself, "a little hooky on a lovely afternoon."

When I said, "Okay, why not?" he grinned and pitched his keys in the air and caught them with a jingle, and then smiled at me again and put one of his long skinny arms around my shoulders and squeezed.

We'd talked at Friday-afternoon town-gown parties whose stated goal was getting faculty from the teachers college and town burghers together (and whose unstated purpose was booze and mild dalliance). I had chatted with him and his handsome wife at Democratic precinct meetings. I'd never given him a second thought. My only memory of him before the ride in the Alfa-Romeo was thinking he looked like Abraham Lincoln with blond hair and that he had a charming way of leaning over from his great height to talk with me.

Certainly, I never thought he was interested in me sexually. First, he was a serious and voluble churchman and nature preservation do-gooder (that's what Coravilleans called preservationists, "do-gooders"). Second, he was fifteen years my senior. Third, I never imagined men as interested in me sexually. I was always shocked when men did flirt; they would have to come right out and say it straightforwardly so that I could not but believe it.

He pushed the top down on the car. The drive from town to river took us past cornfields. Black crows flew up from the corn's stiff, stubborn rows and then settled, on their wide, tarry wings, onto air currents. Ten minutes brought us to the river. The water twisted below us. The water shone. Peter talked jubilantly of the new car, how much he liked his job, the good grades his three children still at home made, and his daughter's marriage. He even exulted over a line of poplars he'd planted in his back yard two years earlier, which had grown, he said, four feet.

I asked, teasingly, "Isn't there *anything* wrong with your life?"

Had I not asked that, I swear nothing would have happened.

He slowed the car. He took his glance from the winding uphill road to look at me. His eyes were the blue color you see in old marbles. "I have a terrible need for affection." I still remember how that sounded, said by him in a low tone with a quick vibrato, as if said by a talking cello. I know this is cornball and in bad taste, but there's that moment during Handel's *Messiah* where the chorus sings, "And the heavens were rent." That's what that moment felt like when Peter said, "I have a terrible need for affection." The heavens were rent, as if God had reached in under His big flowing white God robes and took out from one of His secret pockets a buck knife and just reached down and ripped a mile-long slash across that cloudless blue sky.

You can't believe what a homey person I was then. I always seemed to smell of the starch I sprayed on my husband's shirts when I ironed them and the bread I baked every day, big high loaves that rose and rose. I baked every kind of bread, and cinnamon rolls, and soft, eggy brioche, and French bread in long narrow tins; for the French bread, I'd put a bowl of water in the oven to make steam and whip egg whites and take my pastry brush and paint the loaves with the egg whites to make the loaves shiny.

He slowed, steered into a graveled turnoff, and stopped. He said, "Let's get out and walk." I nodded a yes and he took out his key, which jangled on a ring filled with keys, grabbed a tan poplin jacket folded behind his seat. I pulled myself up out of the car, which felt tinny when I shut its door. I brushed down the back of my wrap skirt, which had wrinkled sweatily under me. He offered me his hand, which was dry and cool, and we walked uphill, away from the turnoff, our feet crunching on the gravel. The ascent put him out of breath.

I can't remember what we said. I remember only the rattling in his chest, his rapid indrawn breaths. I knew enough about men his age not to ask if he wanted to rest. At some point he stopped. He asked, "Is it all right if I hold your hand?" I nodded a yes. I couldn't see why not. We reached a rise that looked down over the olive-green river that ran from mountains, down into the valley along Coraville's edge. We meandered down a few feet onto a patch of grass under droopy cottonwoods. We'd not had much rain that year. The grass was brown. We looked onto the catarrhal rush of quick water through basalt canyons.

Did I know we were going to kiss? No.

His mouth tasted of metal. My heart sank. I'd gone this far, I figured I had to keep on. My tongue found rough fillings, bridgework, the ridged plastic of a partial plate. When I pulled away from his embrace as if to catch my breath, he asked, "What's wrong?"

"Nothing," I said.

He bowed his head against the shoulder of my blouse. I looked down. I could see pink scalp between his graying hairs as he kissed the skin that lay bare in the V of my shirt. Over his shoulder I watched rust-colored ants crawl out of a rotted log.

After it was all over, cottonwood leaf clung to his prim beard and his hair had the tousle of someone risen from a night of fever. He said, "Thank you," and nodded, his thank you as formal as if I'd passed him a crystal bowl heaped with pastel after-dinner butter mints. He patted my bare arm the way you'd pat a child who'd behaved well while the doctor gave her a polio shot. And, believe me, I felt rather that way, like a child dragged to the doctor who'd squinched her eyes and swallowed her medicine.

He asked, "Do you mind if I have a pipe?" and when I said I didn't, he said, "My wife and my boys don't like the pipe."

The river gurgled, breezes lifted the branches on scrub trees, he pulled on his pipe. I fussed with the space where he'd spread out his jacket, straightening the poplin sleeves as I would tidy rumpled doilies on an easy chair's arms. I pulled a leaf and a blade of dead grass from his hair. I didn't know what else to do with my hands. I was thirsty but didn't say so.

He began running his hand up and down my legs. He said, "You don't have varicose veins."

"Why would I?"

"My wife," he said, "has varicose veins."

Driving home, the navy-blue car spiraling down through the hills, I asked, "Do you do this often?"

He didn't, he said, frowning. He had, he added, never done it. And asked me, rather prissily, "You?"

"No."

He asked when he could see me again, and I didn't know what to answer. So he said, "Well, how about tomorrow?"

"Okay," I said, waved a silly little wave, got back into my car, and drove winding roads up into the hills to get my pears. I was worried Mr. Potts might have sold them to someone else, but he hadn't.

That night I lay awake while Jack slept. That I'd committed adultery, and with a man I knew only to speak with in the most banal social manner, did not then seem so outlandish as in fact it was. Peter felt familiar, not as if I'd known him since childhood, but rather as if all these years I'd been expecting him, that he had been promised to me, and so I was not so much surprised, perhaps, as relieved that the promise had been fulfilled. He for whom I waited had arrived.

After that first afternoon we contrived to meet or talk on the telephone almost every day.

We didn't, mind you, start saying "I love you" right away. We didn't say that at all, not for months. We flirted. We played hard to get. We turned moody on each other. But never, for more than a day, did we turn away or try to turn back. It was as if after that first coupling, which was not in any way "lovemaking" but rather what an animal might have done and no more pleasurable for me than the rooster's entry for the hen, we had caught a disease, a fever, that made it impossible for us not to see each other.

I wasn't unhappy with my husband. Jack was dainty and beautiful, built small, low to the ground. We could have lived in houses with six-foot ceilings and jumped up and down and still never bumped our heads. He had perfect little hands, size-eight feet with well-formed toes whose nails more than once when I was feeling silly he permitted me to polish bright red. He rescued me from my miserable childhood and I rescued him, he said, from coming home and marrying someone he sat next to in first grade.

For a novice to adultery, I proved remarkably apt at fitting into my life Peter's and my meetings. I was well organized and thrifty. My ability to knit complicated Aran Isle patterns while reading, my petit bourgeois shrewdness at stretching a roast loin of pork (baked with prunes that I'd soaked in burgundy) to a second meal of ersatz-Chinese sweet-and-sour pork served me well in arranging Peter into an otherwise ordinary domestic life.

Fall rains began. The air turned cold. Soon we could no longer go to the river. Peter was too tall for lovemaking in my old Volvo or his Alfa-Romeo. No way we could use the town's two motels. The hotel had burned down years earlier. The entire downtown had burned down twice.

I found a place to meet, an A-frame far out in the country that belonged to a gay male friend. He used the house—"the chalet," he called it—in summer and on weekends. The chalet' original owner had built the two-story structure as a hideaway, and hide it did, off the county road, down an unmarked driveway that twisted a half mile through scrub timber and blackberry bushes grown wild. "No more than a sheep path," Peter would sometimes say, and add, wincing, that the ruts were hard on his car's under-carriage. The chalet rested in a deep hollow. Trees, distance, and the hollow hid its high-peaked blue roof from the road.

Sometimes I met Peter at the chalet. But more often he drove into our alley, parked, walked through the roofed patio to our back door, and knocked, as if he were any friend of the family. I'd always be ready and somewhat anxious at having him hang about at the back of the house, in the laundry room, pantry, and kitchen. When our affair began, I offered to meet him. He said no, that would be "cheap." He said that unless something came up that made it impossible for him to pick me up at my house and deliver me back, that is what we would do. He said, "Gentlemen call for ladies." He said, "You start acting guilty, people start wondering what you're guilty of."

Peter didn't think we were guilty of anything. "We're enhancing each other's life," he said. And later, he said, "We bring each other joy."

I came from that generation of women who believe men know best. Peter said, "Don't worry." I always ended up believing Peter. That, and I didn't want to stop. I wanted to go on forever, seeing him.

In no time, we had our routine. Peter's job was such that he could disappear for several hours without question. Given that my children were in high school and that my husband came home for lunch, ate, and then napped and returned to his office, we began to meet two–three times per week at a few minutes after one.

A fifteen-minute drive brought us to the chalet. We drove quickly past city limits onto a two-lane county blacktop and past the abandoned one-room schoolhouse my father-in-law had attended, the first spot where we could safely lean across the gear-shift and kiss. Then we passed barns and silos, passed a high, blinking radio antenna in a deserted field, a stinking slaughter-house, more barns, then sheep and cattle and horses munching pasture, then cornfields dotted in fall with crows. Once in one of these corn-fields we saw a hawk soar down and plunk a mouse out from between the rows and ascend with the mouse wriggling in its beak.

At the chalet, Peter took the key from me and unlocked the door. If my friend's fat Siamese glowered at us from his filthy cushion in the living room, Peter grabbed the cat by the loose skin on the back of his neck, carried him through the kitchen, opened the back door, and tossed him out. If I'd brought Peter's lunch, I'd set it on a table that looked out onto pasture. Peter washed his hands. "To get the cat off," he'd say, and then take his Swiss Army knife from his pocket and uncork the wine he'd brought, wrapped in brown paper. I walked to the cupboard and took down glasses.

We made love, sometimes on the double bed upstairs, with a beach towel stretched across the plaid coverlet, or downstairs on the couch or floor. What I liked with him was that what I thought of as "love" seemed to be the impetus for, the precursor of, the "sex." He didn't seem simply horny and hankering.

But what do I know? Maybe it was that he was older. I'd come out of a generation of women who worked at sexual proficiency, took pride in orgasm. To know how to do what I thought of as "sex tricks" pasted a big shining star in one's crown. The more daring, the more athletically challenging; the dirtier, the better. But for Peter sex was won, earned even, by romance. He didn't try fancy positions or ask me to wear garter belts.

As September, then October and November passed, things between us grew increasingly serious. With each step up or step down, depending on how you want to look at this, one of us, for a day or two, turned bitter toward the other. We didn't want to be in love.

Back then, though, I believed I couldn't help myself. I believed love was weather, what insurance adjusters call an "act of God," a tornado or cyclone, and that the best you could do was curl up in a culvert or run down into a storm cellar until the big wind passed over. Now I don't think that. But now isn't then.

One problem adulterers face is explaining where they've been during the hours they're busy with adultery. In my case, nobody asked. My husband was at work until five or five-thirty. The girls got home at four.

Another problem adulterers face is that they become liars, if nothing else, by omission. I lied daily, constantly, by omission. Worse yet in its comment on me is that I *wanted* to tell my husband, but for the wrong reason. I wanted to tell him because he was, or had been, my best friend. I wanted to tell him how happy I was.

All that fall and winter, when I should have looked more and more harried, because I was a liar, a cheat, and because the housekeeping, cooking, and gardening I normally did in the afternoon had to get done in the morning, all I did was bloom. I have a photograph of myself taken shortly before Christmas. I am standing on our front porch. Snow covers the flower beds and hummocks of straw I'd spread, that fall, over the lily beds. I had cinched my black velveteen trench coat tightly at the waist. My face is pale but lovely and my eyes are open wide. I don't guess I ever looked prettier than I did then. Everyone said so, even my daughters, even Jack.

I think there are women, and I was one of them, who lose their virginity, bear babies, suffer deaths of those close to them, *and* are not yet women but still girls. They are, and I was, still innocent. Their experience, for whatever reason, has not yet cut deeply into them. They might well be sixth-graders in pigtails; all the pubic moss and sweat and menstrual fluids are mummery that masks a child.

It's easy to say that I was restless, nearing forty, that I was foolish, that I was flattered by the attention Peter paid me. That my children were getting ready to leave home, that I was frightened about who I would be, what I would do, when they left. All that's true. But I don't think any of the psychological explanations entirely serve. Even now, when I look back on that year, with horror at what I did and the pain I caused, all I can tell you is that I loved him. The hours with Peter, bit by bit, became my real life. As that happened, the light changed on the other hours. Every staple item of life appeared transformed, transubstantiated even, newly lit, radiant.

Somebody might suggest I cooked that year the most superb dinners of my housewifely life because I was trying to atone for my adultery. I wish I could say that was true. The fact is, I cooked so lavishly because I was so happy. The eggplant soufflés, the baked apples filled with rum-soaked raisins, the translucent strawberry sauce were overruns of my happiness.

I became something of a Luddite. Previous to adultery, I had given over the chopping, shredding, blending chores to the Cuisinart. Jack had given me the powerful professional model for Christmas several years before. He wrapped the huge box in shiny bells-and-holly paper, and then on Christmas Eve day, before the stores closed, he collected green and red cabbages, carrots, onions, apples, hunks of Cheddar and chocolate, and a quart of cream from the dairy for me to chop and dice and shred and thicken. That Christmas morning, once we'd eaten our cranberry muffins, pork sausages, eggs-over-easy and been to church, where, even singing my favorite, "Break forth, O beauteous heav'nly light, and usher in the morning; / Ye shepherds, shrink not with affright, / But hear the angel's warning," I couldn't keep my mind off what I'd chop with the Cuisinart.

After that hour under the drooping cottonwoods, I used the Cuisinart less and less. When, for instance, I made coleslaw, I couldn't bring myself to abandon the veined cabbage head to the Cuisinart blade. I took out my knife and shredded. Before adultery, I hurried through garden and kitchen tasks. After, I took pains. I felt engaged in something beyond myself, something sacramental. Martin Buber makes the distinction between "I and It" and "I and Thou." Beets and baking hens and butter lettuces, Dungeness crabs, plums—all turned to Thous, to numinous, hallowed visible forms bestowing invisible grace. Recipes began to hint at ritual formula, as in John Peale Bishop's "The ceremony must be found / that will wed Desdemona to the huge Moor."

Holidays aren't easy for adulterers. That Christmas my friend was ensconced in his chalet, Peter and I had family and social obligations. We saw each other briefly, at parties, from several days before Christmas until almost a week after New Year's Day. Peter called from pay phones. He said, "I miss you." He said "I'm counting the days."

The first afternoon that we were able to meet again, we almost forgot to make love because we held on to each other and said, again and again, "I missed you so much." Before this, we'd never said, "I love you." Now we did. I cried. Peter cried, big tears dribbled down his cheeks. "What's wrong," Peter said, "is we've fallen in love." His hands shook when he lit his pipe.

Hardly a thought was given to how things looked. We did whatever it took, no matter how foolish or dangerous, to see one another. The phrases "crazy in love" and "fool of his senses" come to mind. As do the judgments "immoral," "selfish to the core." In present-day courts, you perhaps could even make a case for our suffering "diminished capacity."

No sooner did my husband leave for work and the children for school than Peter would pull into the alley and rush through the back gate, back yard, across the uneven brick patio to the back door, and grab me and kiss me. We'd make love on the couch, the stairs, anywhere but my husband's and my bed. We'd sit afterward at the small round kitchen table where I read cookbooks and made grocery lists and fed my husband his lunch and the children did their homework. We'd drink coffee and chat, for all the world as if we were a blissful married couple in our own home. Sometimes we talked about what life would have been like if we'd met in our twenties and married. "Do you think we'd have been happy?" I asked.

"We would have," he said.

Afternoons when we drove out to the chalet, we sometimes stayed so late that Peter would call someone with whom he had an appointment and say he was stuck somewhere. We got out my friend's Barbra Streisand records and danced, slowly, over the carpets. Peter, one afternoon, took my face between his cool palms. "I adore you," he said. "I live on the idea of you."

So we went from winter's end, through spring and summer. Off and on, we seemed to come to our senses and use some caution. But we could never stay away from each other for long. I think we tried. I really do.

At Jack's and my house, we had company for days at a time, all summer, picnics out on the lawn and floats down the river. My friend was spending a month of vacation in his chalet. I had trouble getting away to see Peter. We talked on the telephone, we wrote each other notes and sent them through the mail. I made Elizabeth David's rice salads. I concocted sandwiches from pork loin and slices of apple sautéed in butter. Early mornings, I baked chickens I'd marinated all night in lemon juice and garlic. I contrived huge composed salads from the garden, with red-jacketed new potatoes, with green beans, yellow crookneck squash, white pattypan squash, cherry tomatoes, and Japanese eggplant. I made apricot ice cream and herb sherbets and blackberry cobbler and raspberry shortcake and strawberry cream pies. Everyone ooh'ed and ah'ed and asked, "May I have just one more, please?"

I grew more ambitious with my canning. The Big Boys put out so many and such heavy red fruit that August that I even tried catsup. I sat at the little kitchen table with my bare feet on the chair where Peter had sat. You name it—say, for instance, a pear—and I pulled one after another cookbook from the kitchen shelf and read recipes that called for pears. I read these recipes as if my waiting Bartletts, Anjous, Boscs, Comices, or Seckels were heroes or heroines, eager to star in the complex narrative twists of a great novel. I wanted the plot of chutney, grainy rough butter, or a pale honeyed preserve buoying up pear chunks. I wanted a cast of characters that would engage these Boscs or Bartletts in action thick with subtextual and mythic underpinnings. For pears, I wanted happy endings, I wanted weddings

where bridesmaids wore wreaths wound from white daisy and blue hare-
bell, I wanted dancing.

I considered the nameless ebon-skinned plums from my father-in-law's
trees. For years, these plums had called for a chutney deeper, more tragic,
than any I'd been able to concoct. The plums' flesh, dark as aged beef, demanded some catastrophe from which they would emerge, solemn and serious, ready to be wedded to duck breasts or a dry Virginia ham. I steeped
them in a few spoons of Burgundy and added onion, mustard seed, brown
sugar, malt vinegar, cloves, cinnamon, allspice, golden raisins, green and
red bell peppers, raisins, grated ginger, walnuts. I put the plum chutney up
in wide-mouth half-pint jars. First, I thought I'd give some for Christmas.
Then I thought, No, I can't bear to.

Of course this all had to end, and end badly, and it did. It was that time
of year when company quit coming and we put away the picnic gear and
the rafts and oars and put the storm windows back up. It was that time of
year, too, when we ordered cords of orchard woods for the fireplace, and in
late afternoon the girls and I stacked apple and cherry and pear tree trimmings. Nights began to turn cold. The garden got puny, the squash leaves
yellow. Pole beans were long gone, the second planting of bush beans, too.
I dug up the glad corms and dahlia tubers. I piled hay on the lily beds. Any
morning you could expect to walk out into the garden and find tomato vines
blackened. The girls were back in school. I was thinking about airing winter
clothes on the back-yard line, to get out the mothball smell. And Peter and I,
we'd whisper to each other, were still in love.

You can bet that many nights, many long days, I've looked back and asked
myself if I sensed what was coming. I didn't. The day came and I didn't even
guess at it. The day was watery, windy, not raining yet, but it would. Early
morning after Jack left for work and Rebecca and Sarah for school, I'd picked
out of the dewy garden a fat warted Hubbard squash, leaving its frayed
umbilical vine attached. I'd been watching it for months. I carried it into the
kitchen. The vine scratched my arm. The squash must have weighed six
pounds.

I've had a lot of time to go back over that day.

All morning I was in and out of back yard and kitchen. Clouds gradually deepened. Hornets whirred up under the eaves of the patio roof, and

I told myself to remember to get Jack to use a hornet bomb on them that weekend.

I made up a batch of whole-wheat bread—three cups white flour, three cups whole wheat. I'd rubbed down four game hens with olive oil and garlic. I stood one of the fat little hens on its end, where its head had been chopped off. Sunlight from the kitchen windows slanted down and illuminated the hen's interior. The ribs curved to meet like cathedral arches in a matchstick miniature Rouens. James Taylor's brother Livingston was singing "Please Come to Boston" on the record player while I melted butter in the big iron skillet. I chopped the hens' gizzards and livers, and when the butter pooled in the skillet, I tossed in the innards and sautéed them with diced onion and garlic. Into my big stoneware mixing bowl I tore up the last of the sourdough French bread I'd baked earlier in the week. I chopped dried apricots and added them, along with a handful of white raisins, to the bread.

I got dressed. I would guess I sucked in my stomach and looked at myself in the mirror. I was wearing a new dress, a red stamp-size plaid buttoned down the front with tiny jet buttons. I liked the dress a lot. I closed all the upstairs windows against the coming rain. I had a new raincoat and, at the last minute, grabbed it.

One-thirty, on the dot, the little car scattered alley gravel as Peter nosed its hood in under the garage canopy.

"That's just a very pretty dress," he said.

At the chalet, we heard thunder roll across the valley. The chalet living room darkened. Peter's fingers were cool.

Our drive back into town was uneventful except that Peter drove faster than he normally would. He saw me glance at the speedometer. "I've got an appointment at four," he said. It was already ten to four. We made plans for the next day, to meet. In my alley I jumped out, raincoat over my shoulders. I pushed open the back gate, walked across the patio bricks, stopping to lean over and pluck dead heads from the French marigolds. The rain spit against the patio roof.

I went into the kitchen and lifted the towel off the bread dough I'd left rising. I drew in a long breath of the yeast aroma. I poked a finger into the puffed-up dough, which was soft as a new baby. My fingertip dimpled the dough. I remember, distinctly, how happy I was, all the places we'd kissed each other, what a good time we'd had.

Nobody was home. I ran upstairs and changed into my jeans. Back down in the kitchen, I sifted flour out onto the marble slab. I gathered the sticky web from the bowl and plopped it onto the field of flour, dipped my hands into the flour, and began kneading. I made bread a little wet, with not quite as much flour as recipes called for. My husband and daughters didn't like what they derided as "health bread." They liked their bread soft. So I cheated some on the flour.

I buttered the tins, put in the dough. I broke an egg, its yolk with the red spot in it indicating the egg had been fertilized by some antic rooster. I whipped the egg white with my whisk and with the pastry brush painted the beaten white over the top of the loaf. As the loaves baked the egg whites would make them shine. I put the bread on the middle rack in the warm oven, set at 375 degrees. The heat radiated onto my face.

The wind lifted the curtains off the sills. Fruit flies circled above ripening tomatoes stacked in the windowsill above the sink. I was singing, along with Livingston Taylor, about Boston in the springtime.

The phone rang. I answered. It was Peter. I thought he'd called because he wanted to say how wonderful the afternoon had been. I could hear people talking. I asked, "Where are you?"

"Phone booth. Out by the freeway." He spoke roughly. He said, "We're busted."

Peter, a few days later, was permitted to resign and left town. After I confessed to Jack, he forgave me. But I had broken the bond between us, and it never mended. My daughters were embarrassed, wounded, disappointed, repelled. Even my father was disgusted with me. He said, "No man is going to want you after what you've done." Eventually I packed up and left home. Years passed before I cooked much of anything again.

About adultery, I don't recommend it. I also have to confess that for that year I was happier than I'd ever been before or have been since.

Never Eat Your Heart Out (1997)

Betty Fussell

from My Kitchen Wars

"The trick was to be a lady in the dining room, yet an amateur-pro in the kitchen," writes Betty Fussell (b. 1927) in *My Kitchen Wars* (1999), her memoir of her sometimes harrowing married life. Fussell's substitution of "kitchen" for "bedroom" in the familiar maxim reflects the fact that gourmet cooking in the era of Julia—when women vied for dinner-party preeminence to advance their husbands' careers—was not only a sign of status, but a way to bat one's eyelashes. Within a decade writers (food writers, at least) began proclaiming that food had replaced sex. But first came the moment of the amateur gourmet, and here Fussell provides a finely wrought sketch of a time when cooking was becoming an art as well as a form of social one-upmanship.

■ ■ ■

Dinner parties were important ammunition in the fierce competition among our husbands—and ourselves. While wives in sexy low-cut dresses were still a plus, now the aim was to look like a hot tomato while remaining cucumber-cool within. You had to keep cool to cook for, lay out, and clean up after parties that required weeks of preparation, parties that consumed infinite time and energy and passion in the one-upmanship of friends.

A key rule of this demanding sport was that she who plays the hostess must also cook and serve. You were allowed some help for serving, but it was a cheat to hire cooking help, especially if you could afford to. If you didn't cook it yourself, the food didn't count. Anybody could hire a caterer. But not everybody could act, and you had first to be an actor in a ritually shared pretense. Pretend there'd been no labor, no expense, no fatigue, no sweat. All dishes, especially showpieces like soufflés, must appear as if by miracle, with a wave of Ariel's wand. And although it was understood among the women guests that each would assist from time to time in shuttling dishes to and fro, no one knew better than we did who'd done the work, and just how much work it was.

But it was work in the guise of leisure. What we were doing in our home kitchens had nothing to do with the calibrated hierarchies, from apprentice to chef, of the professional French kitchen. We weren't about to go off and apprentice ourselves, as a later generation of Americans would, to the great chefs of Europe. Nor were we about to go off and enroll in professional cooking classes, although an occasional foray into Chinese or Indian or some other ethnic venue was permissible. A one point, a group of us used my kitchen for Chinese cooking classes taught by a pro we'd hired to come down once a week from New York. She couldn't understand how we got through so much wine in the space of four short hours, because she didn't realize we were having a party in the guise of a cooking class.

The trick was to be a lady in the dining room, yet an amateur-pro in the kitchen. The distinctions between amateur, amateur-professional, and all-out professional were obscure but vital. An amateur was not skilled. And we were. But a professional was paid for his services. We were not. Like doing other good works inside and outside the house, cooking at any level had to be voluntary to count. To count, that is, in the class warfare that distinguished between blue and white collars for guys and pink and white aprons for gals. Pink signified Volunteer Hospital Aide, white signified cleaning lady. I never wore an apron while I cooked, partly to ease the oscillation between hostess and cook, but also to refuse the badge of household drudge.

The solution to the drudge problem was to make cooking an art, or at the very least a craft, like watercolor painting, embroidery, pottery making, basket weaving, leather tooling, all those genteel accomplishments that distinguished the ladies who chatted in the parlors of Jane Austen from their servants. A lady could become extremely accomplished in any of these arts, even in writing novels, as long as no one took her work seriously or paid money for it, which was much the same thing. Our dinner parties were baroquely elaborated gifts, like the human-hair embroidery of weeping willows and cenotaphs that validated the gentility of Victorian hands.

We didn't want to be professional chefs. We wanted to be artists, and Julia was there to show us how cooking could be elevated to art. We'd called Julia Child by her Christian name the moment *Mastering the Art of French Cooking* appeared in 1961, because she seemed to be talking directly to us. In a very American way, she translated the tools of a traditionally male guild, as regimented and hierarchical as the military, into the milieu of "the servantless

American cook," the woman who does her own work. Overnight, she turned our amateur bouts into professional matches within the ropes of our own kitchens. She insisted that if we wanted to do the job right we must have professional tools, the *batterie de cuisine* of a French kitchen. We must equip ourselves the way a soldier must procure his rifle, a carpenter his hammer and saw, a violinist his fiddle and bow, a professor his Ph.D. She sent us scurrying to hotel and restaurant supply houses. She gave us courage to face down even the billy-goat gruff who inhabited the Bridge Company in Manhattan and to demand from him, in our most imperious suburban station-wagon voices, tin-lined copper pots with no less than one-eighth-inch-thick bottoms.

This was no undertaking for the poor. Such equipment cost money, and we weren't looking for bargains. All we wanted, like Jacqueline Kennedy, was the best. Julia warned us away from cheap pots. She taught us that a pot with a copper bottom less than one-eighth inch thick was worse than useless, which meant that a copper wash on stainless steel was there only for show. Out went the Revere Ware at the first Hospital Charity Sale. In came the costly thick copper pots, which were hell to polish if you actually used them to cook in, and which had tin linings that were hell to renew as the tin wore off and the copper came through and potentially poisoned any food that remained too long in the pot.

In came the costly sets of Le Creuset, its heavy cast-iron glazed with red enamel outside and creamy white enamel within, each pot with its special purpose: oval casseroles (*cocottes*) with lids shaped to condense vapor on the roast inside, gratin dishes (*plats à gratin*) that would take broiler heat, saucepans (*casseroles*) with lips for pouring, chef's skillets (*poêles*) with sloping sides for browning, sauté pans (*sautoirs*) with straight sides for frying. Never mind that you had to become instantly bilingual, at least in the kitchen. And never mind that some of the larger casseroles were so heavy they broke your back lifting them from the oven. No sacrifice was too great for the advancement of your husband's career and of your own newfound Art.

A complete *batterie* required specialty firearms like soup kettles (*marmites*), multidisked food mills (*moulins*), vegetable slicers (*mandolines*), double-handled chopping knives (*hachoirs*), wooden-rimmed drum sieves (*tamis*) for creating purees, straight boxwood rolling pins (*rouleaux*), olive pitters (*chasse-noyaux*), fine-meshed conical sieves (*chinois*), poultry shears for deboning chickens for galantines, larding needles (*lardoires*) for barding spaghetti-thin strips of pork fat through a roast, and a complete dud of a metal garlic press sold to the American market before we discovered we could do a better job with the side of a cleaver and the edge of a knife.

We didn't wait for Julia's second volume of instruction to reinforce our initial emplacements. In the affluent sixties, gourmet stores sprouted like mushrooms in the wild. A campaign abroad to purchase arms in Elizabeth David's shop off Sloane Square and in Dehillerin's near Les Halles was obligatory. On our own shores we had already procured a heavy-duty professional mixer, with its wire whip for egg whites, flat beater for pastry doughs, and dough hook for breads and brioches. Only with a mixer could you beat egg yolks with sugar until they formed "a slowly dissolving ribbon." My KitchenAid mixer still stands like a veteran on my kitchen counter, wheezing when called upon to knead a stiff dough, but, like me, proud of long service.

The one sure sign of a Serious Competitive Cook, however, was the copper bowl and wire whisk. You had to have at least one large unlined copper bowl (*bassine*) in which to beat egg whites with a wooden-handled balloon whisk (*fouet*), to foam what looked like snot into a shiny white satin mountain. The chemical reaction between copper and albumin was said to produce creamier and airier whites than could be produced in any other way. So we practiced the specified wrist action, necessary to keep shoulders and arms from aching, with the assiduity of a piano player practicing Bach. We hid our old handheld electric beaters in a drawer, where they pushed our manual Dover beaters to the rear.

The showiest dish you could make with bowl and whisk was a soufflé, the pièce de résistance of our show-off menus and the emblem of our paradox. Literally, the French phrase meant the climax of a series, or a piece of artillery with staying power. A dessert soufflé was a good climax, all right, but its staying power was nil. It held only two or three minutes before collapse. And what was it, after all? An airy nothing, inflated for a momentary display as ephemeral as fireworks, leaving nothing behind but an image in the mind and a memory on the tongue. A soufflé was time's victim, not its resister. And yet, and yet . . . even now I can taste the first *soufflé au Grand Marnier* we ever ate, at a small Michelin two-star restaurant in Paris, Chez

Allard, and even now I can remember the pride with which I created the first one in my own kitchen, presenting it in all its quivering brown-crusted puffery before it collapsed within the buttered and sugared eight-cup porcelain mold.

As we moved up the ladder of class and competence, we graduated from plain pâtés to *pâtés en croûte*. It wasn't enough to simply enclose one of our usual brandy-laden mixtures in a crust, or to shape the crust into a hinged oval pâté mold (*moule à pâté*). No, serious climbers had to first bone a duck, leaving the entire skin intact, then stuff it with truffles and pork and veal, stitch it with thread and a trussing needle, wrap it in pastry dough, and decorate it with little pastry fans cut with a cooky cutter to conceal the seam where we pinched the top and bottom pastry ovals together. A meat thermometer, inserted in a paper funnel through the dough and into the meat, told us when the meat was done. And since this was a dish for a cold buffet, we had then to chill the pâté, remove the top crust, take out the duck, take out its stitches, carve it into slices, and tuck it back into the crust. No sweat. See Julia's Volume 1, pages 471 and following.

Veau Prince Orloff was another display piece consumptive of enough money and time to garner status. This one, Julia assured us, could be made in the morning and reheated the same evening–provided you did nothing else all day. It required you to bone and tie a five-pound roast of veal, prepare a *soubise* of rice and onions, a *duxelles* of mushrooms, and a *velouté* from a *roux* enriched with heavy cream and a pinch of nutmeg. You pureed the *soubise* and the *duxelles* together to spread on each slice of the roasted meat, then covered the entire roast with thick sauce and grated Swiss cheese so that it would brown when you reheated it. The dish was so rich that after the first two mouthfuls you were ready to gag or go home, but these were headier times, less obsessed with cardiovascular health and liposuctioned bodies than with strutting your stuff with the best ingredients money could buy.

In food terms, we middle Americans were all nouveaux riches, giddy with a cornucopia of goods and techniques that poured in from Europe, along with its refugees, after the Second World War. To put it another way, we didn't know how poor we'd been until we hit it rich. Rich at the markets in terms of what we could buy, rich in the kitchen in terms of what we were now equipped to prepare. It was a time when more was better and a lot more was best. And so we overdressed our meals wildly and decked them out with too much flash. While the very notion of haute cuisine was new to us, to Europeans it was as old as haute culture, so we went bonkers over all things French. To cook French, eat French, drink French (California wines didn't yet count, and couldn't be mentioned in polite conversation unaccompanied by the word "varietal") was to become versant in the civilized tongues of Europe as opposed to America's barbaric yawp.

The cocktail party with its baroque hors d'oeuvres evolved speedily into the rococo buffet. Julia choreographed the production, plotting the time of preparation for each stage of each dish, detailing what could be prepared ahead, what frozen, what chilled. We each felt we had Julia in our corner, and if your keenest rival led with a buffet of baked ham and roast turkey, you knew how to counter with a *jambon persillé*, presliced and molded into a beautiful green-flecked mountain, or a boned turkey stuffed with veal forcemeat larded with truffles. The more baronial the buffet, the better, and it didn't matter a hoot if guests didn't know or like what they were eating because they could always try something else. My tables were as overblown as a Manuelesque cathedral. No matter how reasonable my initial plan, I always made more dishes, and more, and more, to make sure there was always too much.

Spendthrift of time, I took pride in multistepped preparation that extended over many days and required much special equipment. I delighted in galantines and ballottines because they demanded an artist's patience and a surgeon's skill to bone out the flesh of a chicken or turkey without breaking its skin, to stuff it and sew it and wrap it and poach it and weigh it and chill it and glaze it with stock. I jumped at the chance to sculpt a whole salmon or sea bass into a mammoth pastry crust decorated with scales and fins and mouth and eye, or to paint the snowy canvas of a *chaud-froid* chicken with a spring bouquet of vegetables cut paper-thin to resemble flowers. I reveled in piping the heart-shaped layers of a nutted meringue stacked with mocha and praline-flavored butter creams and enclosed in a bittersweet chocolate frosting, decorated with rosettes and leaves and swags pushed through the various metal tubes of a pastry bag.

We didn't count the weeks we spent on cassoulets, preparing what Julia called "the order of battle." Yes, we made our own sausage cakes of spiced ground pork and Armagnac, and put up our own duck or goose confit months in advance to have it ready in its crock of fat, and teased our butcher into getting us a chunk of fresh bacon and fresh pork rind, and searched for imported French white beans and then for an earthenware casserole large enough to hold a pork loin, a shoulder of mutton, the confit, the chunk of bacon and rind, half a dozen sausage cakes, plus two quarts of beans and vegetables and wine and stock, covered with bread crumbs and pork fat to make a crust, which we dutifully pushed under every ten minutes during the baking because the crust, the crust, dear reader, was the measure of a true cassoulet.

So many parties. So much art down the gullet. Cocktails with light hors d'oeuvres or with heavy hors d'oeuvres or with buffets, Sunday brunches and Sunday suppers, tailgate picnics and beer barbecues and football parties, Christmas Eve and all-night New Year's Eve and New Year's Day parties. Hangover parties, birthday parties, political fund-raising and charity parties. Halloween and Thanksgiving and Easter and Boxing Day and Valentine's Day and Fourth of July and Labor Day parties. Costume and theme parties, transatlantic shipboard farewell parties, and welcome-home-from-abroad parties. Formal and informal sit-down dinner parties for four, six, eight, twelve, twenty-four, forty-eight—but that was really pushing it. Each kind of party demanded its own props, choreography, costumes, mise-en-scène, and menus, at a time when women dressed for dinner in long dresses as a matter of course. Often the planning, as in Eliot's *The Cocktail Party*, was more fun than the event, and you worked up such a head of steam getting ready for curtain time that the moment the first guest rang the bell you wanted to go upstairs and take off your clothes and go to bed.

No event was too small to be sanctified by a party. We gave parties back to back: Farewell to the Cottage one month and At Home in the New House the next. The Farewell was to be an informal come-as-you-are party for our regular gang of eight to ten couples, because the rugs were already rolled, half the furniture was gone, and packing cases lined the walls. Perfect for a dancing party. So instead of finishing the packing, I cooked up a *pissaladière niçoise*, with pounds of onions sautéed with garlic and herbs, piled in a pastry shell and topped with anchovy filets and black olives. Then a *gigot de pré-salé farci*, since a boned lamb leg was easy to slice and its rice and kidney stuffing was splendidly exotic. And it was a pleasure to test your skill in cutting into the red flesh to locate the bones—pelvic, rump, knuckle, leg, shank, and tail— because you were learning about your own bones and how the ball joint fit into the hip and how the hipbone was connected to the tailbone and how flesh was covered with fat and fell. *Charlotte aux pommes* was a good finisher, with strips of white bread soaked in butter to line the charlotte mold filled with a thick puree of apples and apricot preserves and dark rum and more butter.

Our Farewell Party was no big deal, but it turned into an all-nighter, what with the dancing and the euphoria, or maybe it was hysteria, of clearing out and starting over. We talked our last guest out the door around 5 a.m., his wife having given up and gone home hours before. So we were a bit groggy when Tucky woke us up at nine to say, "There's a strange man in my bed." Our guest, it turns out, had dropped his keys when he went to start his car and couldn't find them, so he climbed through an open window above the kitchen sink, fell into the piles of dirty dishes, and made his way upstairs and into the first bed he saw. When we went into Tucky's room, there he was, fully dressed and snoring away. That was when I remembered that we had six people coming for lunch.

Our first At Home party on Lilac Lane was a big deal, home-cooked food and drink for two hundred. It was a test to see if the flow flowed. While Paul tended bar in the kitchen and guests helped themselves at a secondary bar in the living room, I spread the dining table with a blockbuster array of Julia. At one end of the table, a *suprêmes de volaille en chaud-froid, blanche neige*, the breasts sliced and covered with jellied cream for a checkerboard of black truffles. At the other end, a *mousseline de poisson*, its texture as light as a quenelle, from a puree of scallops and wine and cream and white button mushrooms, shaped into a curved fish and beached on a bed of fresh tarragon. To fill the gaps between: a bowl of *céleri-rave rémoulade*, a plate of endives and artichokes *à la grecque*, a platter of asparagus, the stalks neatly skinned, the heads aligned and scarfed with a *mayonnaise verte*. There was room for a colorful ratatouille and a rice pilaf, baked with butter and minced onion in a Creuset casserole in good chicken stock that I'd made, of course, from scratch.

My Kitchen Wars (1999)

Rick Bragg

Dinner Rites

Born and raised in Alabama, Rick Bragg (b. 1959)–a big-city dweller until just recently, winner of a 1996 Pulitzer Prize for his *New York Times* features, and author of the memoirs *All Over But the Shoutin'* (1997) and *Ava's Man* (2001)–goes back home for a Thanksgiving meal with an aunt and uncle in this powerfully nostalgic piece. What he finds is not "magazine-cover food" but honest home cooking in abundance. And he eats "until it hurts," as one should on such an occasion, but also like a man hungry for something he has lost.

■ ■ ■

The meal we all live for, the one we gather for in my momma's house after the first frost and gentle fall have faded the splendid green from the foothills of the Appalachians, is really born months before in the damp, thick hot of an Alabama summer. People here still call that time of late summer the dog days, a time when the sun glares white, like an old man's blind eye, on the pine barrens and frame houses, until the afternoon thunderstorms come down like a fist and then blow themselves out, quick, leaving the ground to steam. Thanksgiving is just a cool dream, then, for most of us, except for the man in the garden, a hoe in his hand, planning ahead.

It all begins, that wonderful November meal, with that tall, thin man, his silver hair hidden by a straw hat, moving slowly between rows of sweet corn and tomatoes and beans, being careful with his feet because any fool knows that the copperheads like to rest there, among the stalks, waiting on a field mouse. The man, my uncle John, is not afraid of snakes, but they can flat spoil an otherwise uneventful day. Besides, as I have heard men say here, in summer it's just too damn hot to get bit.

Corn is a science, maybe even an art. Pick it too soon and you waste it because there will not be enough on the cob to shave off even with the sharpest, oldest butcher knife, and people who grew up poor cannot live with themselves if they waste food. Pick it too late and all it's fit for is hogs. But pick it just right, Lord God Almighty, and it is a reason to live. My aunt

Jo will boil it until it turns creamy, from the starch in it, and put it in the freezer to keep.

Uncle John Couch and my aunt Jo, who helped raise me, along with my uncle Ed Fair and my aunt Juanita and my aunt Edna, know the garden the way their mommas and daddies knew it, by feel, by smell, by something almost like magic. To say this is a simple life is a city person's ignorance. There is nothing simple about working a shift at Goodyear and then toiling bent over until the heat and the sweat bees run you into the house. But it is a rich life, rich because the food that will line the countertops in my momma's kitchen on Thanksgiving Day comes from the red dirt just outside the door, which beats the bald hell out of anything else. The tomatoes, the beans, the peppers will all be canned in kitchens where the air is spiced with salt and vinegar and set in a cool, dry place until November. Everyone knows it will be the turkey, swimming in pale yellow butter, that will steal the show, but without those steaming pots of vegetables crowding around it, the main attraction would be, well, nekkid.

Like I said, my uncle John knows gardens. He also knows turkeys. Uncle John, on the fourth Thursday in November, is a valuable man.

The women usually rule the kitchens in the houses that perch on the hills and inside the valleys that make up the counties of Calhoun, Cleburne, Clay, Cherokee, St. Clair and Talladega here in the northeastern part of Alabama, not far from the Georgia line. But one day a year, many of them grudgingly allow their men to enter that sacred, mysterious domain to help with the turkey, just the turkey. I do not really know why this is, why these pipe fitters, steelworkers, rubber workers, farmers, cotton-mill workers and shade-tree mechanics are brought into the kitchen on this one particular day. I have asked and been told simply, "Well, they just are. Go sit down."

Men do cook here, but outside. They are allowed to flip the hamburgers, turn the ribs and spin the pig but are usually not trusted with anything, as we say, "lectric." "Your aunt Jo says I can mess up a kitchen boiling water," says Uncle John, in explanation. Aunt Jo is a small woman, but it is best not to mess with her.

I asked Aunt Jo, before I asked Uncle John for the recipe, if there was any secret to the turkey, anything he might not share with me, out of cussedness. There was one thing, she said. "Your pan has to be at least 30 years old. We won ours at Coleman's Service Station. Every time you bought gas, you put your name in. And we won." The pan, once a shiny stainless steel, has been burned gold by four decades of Thanksgivings and Christmases. "Twice a year. That's all we use it. That's why it's lasted."

Funny to think that that pan will outlive me, will be passed down and down. It's nice, thinking that.

It is a covered pan with a small opening in the lid to let steam in and out, and that is one tiny secret to the turkey's tenderness. The important thing, Aunt Jo said, is not to care what it looks like when it comes out of the oven. "The legs always fall off," she said, because it is so tender.

In our house, presentation doesn't count for a real whole lot.

It is the cooking that matters, and Uncle John has done exactly the same thing for 40 years. Listen to him: "The first thing I do is slide a whole pound of butter inside the turkey, which is laying back-down. Then I coat the whole thing all over with poultry seasoning. That's black pepper, garlic powder, onion salt, some paprika and a little bit of sage."

I am beginning to taste it now.

The bird is a beautiful gold, specked with sage and black pepper, and when he raises the lid, the steam billows out and permeates the kitchen, the dining room, everything. And you hope, hard, that the pre-meal prayer will be a short one.

The dressing is my aunt Jo's job, and she does not cook it so much as she creates it. Listen to her: "Start the night before with a big pan of corn bread cooked in an iron skillet. The day of Thanksgiving, mix in some chicken juice—broth, but I call it chicken juice. Dice up an onion, a big onion, and mix in the sage and some salt, because we're salt eaters. Edna said last year I used too much sage, but I didn't hear nobody else complaining."

She bakes it in the oven in a shallow pan until the top is crispy, gold-brown, and the inside is pale yellow, creamy. "Some people go to the store and buy dried bread cubes and call that stuffing," she says, and I get the feeling she would rather eat a bug.

My momma handles it from there. She makes biscuits, called catheads, that are too good to be described by mere words, and though she is never satisfied with them—"Lord," she will say, "I sure did let y'all down on them biscuits"—I cannot remember a single time in my life when there was one left.

She makes the best mashed potatoes I have ever tasted, just butter, milk, salt, black pepper and—for reasons I have never understood but know better than to argue with—a teaspoon of mayonnaise. Every Thanksgiving, I scrape the pan.

The legacy of the garden, and that hot summer, sits steaming on a side table. There are the green beans, cooked to death, with pork, and the corn, simmered with butter. The tomatoes my uncle John threaded his way through months ago are now pickled in quart jars, bright green and heavy with dill. They look down from a high counter, waiting for someone with strong hands to pry them open.

And we will have macaroni and cheese, which is a vegetable in the South, and, one of the best things on earth, a big pot of pinto beans, a massive ham bone swimming in the middle for seasoning. The only fresh vegetable, the only cold thing except for the cranberry sauce, which is chilled, can and all, in the refrigerator, is cabbage slaw.

"Thank you, Lord, for this food for the nourishment of our bodies," my uncle John will say, and every head is bowed.

Plates overflow. We drink sweet tea—this is a Protestant house, and the only alcohol is in the medicine cabinet. Dessert is pumpkin pies, pecan pies, coconut cake and a chilled strawberry shortcake. I almost never eat dessert, because I am never able. I live in big cities, in New York, Los Angeles, Boston, Atlanta, Miami, so I do not see this food the rest of the year. I eat until it hurts, and my brother Sam will grin at me, because he lives here, works at the cotton mill, and can eat it all the time.

Kinfolks stop by, seldom the same ones every year. Everybody eats. Everyone says it was better than last year, and, because of the gray I see in their hair, in mine, I suppose it is. This is not magazine-cover food. It is the food of my youth, my life. I guess I would live longer if I didn't eat it, but the life would be so bland. I would rather eat the pages of the magazines.

We sit and tell stories then, because it is all we are able to do. Some of the people we talk about have passed on, like Grandma Bundrum, who I still miss terrible, and my uncle John's daddy, Homer Couch, who was a live wire of a man, a storyteller who could make you feel good just standing in his shadow.

"Daddy used to tell this story," my uncle John says, "about this man who wanted a turkey for Thanksgiving, and every day the man would say, 'Lord, please send me a turkey.' And as the weeks went by, no turkey came. So finally, it was a week before Thanksgiving, and the man had to change his prayer. 'Lord,' he said, 'please let me go and get my own self a turkey.' And the Lord did. That might not be funny, unless you knew Daddy."

I would like to be the man trusted with the turkey some day, and maybe some day I will be. For now, I'll just have to be the man praying for one.

STEAMED PORK LOAF
WITH SALTED DUCK EGGS

THIS DISH IS WELL KNOWN to many of my fellow Chinese-Americans. It should become a favorite of all Americans, hyphenated or not. I am sure the recipe was first put together a long time ago in the kitchen of a South China peasant family and was the centerpiece of a celebratory feast. Meat loaf may be common on American tables, but in China both pork and duck eggs are rather expensive special treats, hardly the ordinary fare of even wealthy peasants.

UNLIKE OUR FAMILIAR MEAT LOAF, this pork loaf is not baked but steamed with an array of exciting seasonings. In this recipe I follow my mother's customary use of salted duck eggs, which can be found at Chinese groceries. Preserved in brine, the egg yolks harden, and tempting flavors suffuse the whole egg. The eggs thus add much to the already zestful blend of robust pork and spices. The result is a pleasantly rich and aromatic dish that is a true centerpiece for any special meal. One needs only plain rice and a vegetable to make a complete, balanced, nutritious dinner.

1 pound fatty ground pork

1 pound fresh water chestnuts, peeled and coarsely chopped

3 tablespoons finely chopped scallions

1 tablespoon light soy sauce

2 teaspoons Shaoxing rice wine or dry sherry

2 teaspoons salt

1 teaspoon sugar

2 teaspoons cornstarch

2 teaspoons Asian sesame oil

1/2 teaspoon freshly ground black pepper

2 salted duck eggs (see recipe introduction)

IN A FOOD PROCESSOR, mix the pork with the water chestnuts until they are finely chopped. Scrape this mixture into a large stainless-steel bowl and toss in the scallions, then pour in the soy sauce and rice wine. Toss in the salt, sugar, cornstarch, sesame oil, and pepper. With your hands, mix well, then turn the meat onto a deep heatproof plate and shape it into a flat loaf. Crack open the duck eggs, discard the whites, and cut the yolks in half. Distribute the yolks over the top of the meat, pressing them into the loaf.

SET UP A STEAMER by putting a rack inside a wok or deep pan. Fill it with about 2 inches of water. Bring the water to a boil, then reduce the heat to a low simmer. Gently set the platter with the loaf in the steamer, cover, and steam vigorously for 20 minutes, or until the pork is done.

SERVE IMMEDIATELY

Ken Hom, *Easy Family Recipes from a Chinese-American Childhood* (1997)

Hom made a celebrity career for himself hosting food programs for the BBC, opening restaurants, and writing more than a dozen cookbooks. Although there were plenty of Chinese recipe books, Hom's introduced basic methods with the clarity of an experienced instructor.

Grace Young

The Breath of a Wok

In this elegant meditation on stir-frying from her cookbook *The Wisdom of the Chinese Kitchen* (1999), Grace Young goes beyond the mere how-to of ordinary recipes. Instead, she evokes the essence of the techniques she learned growing up in a Chinese-American family in San Francisco, and in extensive interviews with family members since. Here that essence involves a flash-heat that almost singes the exterior of the ingredient but leaves its energy intact. Young offers a fascinating glimpse into the complexities of Cantonese culinary aesthetics, and opens the door between Eastern and Western cultures a little wider.

■ ■ ■

All my life I have heard Baba speak about *wok hay*, the *breath* of a wok. No matter whether he is in a restaurant or his own home, when a stir-fried dish comes to the table, the sight of the heat rising from the food always causes him to smile and say, "Ahhh, *wok hay*." I know that many people dislike piping-hot food and prefer their food to cool before eating it, but most Chinese are just the opposite—the hotter, the better.

Wok hay is not simply hot food; it's that elusive seared taste that only lasts for a minute or two. It reminds me of the difference between food just off the grill and grilled food that has been left to sit. *Wok hay* occurs in that special moment when a great chef achieves food that nearly, but not quite, burns in the mouth. For the Chinese, if the dish doesn't have the prized taste of the wok's aroma, it isn't an authentic stir-fry.

As a child, I clearly understood that when dinner was announced there was no excuse for tardiness. It was totally unacceptable to explain that you wanted to see the last five minutes of a television show, finish a phone conversation, or even do a few more minutes of homework. Hot food was serious business, and the idea of missing the *wok hay* was unthinkable. The dishes were choreographed for completion at the moment we sat at the table and the piping-hot rice arrived. I always imagined *wok hay* as a special life force that, when consumed, provided us with extra energy, *hay*. Some readers may be familiar with the Mandarin word for *hay*, which is *qi*, as in *qigong*. *Qi* (pronounced "chee") is the Chinese concept of vital energy that flows through the body.

When my parents entertained, they cooked in tandem, bringing out each dish as it was stir-fried. Douglas and I were left to "entertain" the guests, and I recall thinking how uncomfortable we and our American friends felt. Our guests seemed more intent on socializing and, although they enjoyed the food, they couldn't comprehend my parents' refusal to eat one morsel until all the food was on the table. It puzzled them to see my parents cook one dish at a time, disappearing into the kitchen and not sitting until everything was done. When Chinese friends came over, however, they would agree, after politely refusing to eat, that sacrificing the *wok hay* was inappropriate and they would gladly eat dish by dish with gusto. Forgoing their own enjoyment of *wok hay* was my parents' gift to their guests.

Even today, whenever my family attends a Chinese banquet, I can guarantee that shortly after the dinner my parents will comment first on the crispness of the Peking duck, then on the amount of shark's fin in the shark's fin soup (versus the filler ingredients), and, finally, on the *wok hay* of the stir-fried dishes. Later the same evening, the critique will continue by telephone with a few of my uncles and aunts. The discussion will be brief, but no one in the family can resist commenting on the quality of the food. If the dishes were outstanding, then the evening was memorable. I have heard my family fondly recall meals from years ago where the shark's fin was extra thick or abalone was prepared particularly well. Baba likes to sit closest to the kitchen when we go to a restaurant, especially for dim sum. This way, he can get the freshest food the moment it leaves the kitchen. If there is no table available near the kitchen, Mama will occasionally ask one of us to go to the dim sum cart as it emerges to retrieve the piping-hot food ourselves. Why wait for the lifeless food that arrives by the time the waitress makes her way to us? My Uncle Sam reminds me that the family still laments the change in what was once a favorite restaurant. The establishment was so successful that it expanded to three floors, moving the kitchen to the basement. Same chefs, same cooking technique, but now the *wok hay* had disappeared, because the distance between the kitchen and the dining area was too far for the "breath" to last.

To achieve *wok hay*, it is necessary to learn a few secrets of successful stir-frying. Stir-frying, like sautéing, is cooking bite-sized pieces of meat or vegetables in a small amount of oil over high heat for a brief period of time. Stir-frying, especially, requires keeping the food in constant motion, tossing it with a metal spatula, to ensure that everything cooks evenly and quickly, preserving the vitamins and vibrancy of the ingredients. The wok must be sufficiently hot for the food to sizzle vigorously the moment it hits the oil. The ingredients must be dry, especially the vegetables. If there is any water left clinging to them after washing, the oil will splatter when the vegetables are added, and then they will steam, rather than stir-fry. For this reason, Mama washes vegetables early in the day to allow time for them to dry. It's best to have all the ingredients at room temperature and everything cut into uniform pieces to ensure the same cooking time. Some dishes, like Baba's Stir-Fried Butterfly Fish and Bean Sprouts or Stir-Fried Squid, must cook in very small quantities because the home stove cannot produce the same amount of heat as a restaurant wok. Crowding food in the wok requires more heat and longer cooking time and results in braised food rather than stir-fried food.

My parents do not use a wok for stir-frying. They use an old fourteen-inch Farberware skillet or an eight-inch-wide, four-inch-deep metal pot that protects them from oil splatters. The traditional wok used in China was cast-iron, preferred because it adds iron to food and conducts heat well. Chinese cast-iron woks can be purchased in some cookware shops in Chinatown; they are thinner and lighter in weight than Western cast-iron pans. Today carbon-steel woks are more common; each time food is stir-fried the wok becomes seasoned, as the ingredients and oil leave a delicate varnish on the wok's surface. Unlike a cast-iron skillet that simply becomes black with use, a carbon-steel wok develops a rich mahogany patina after about six months of regular use. A well-seasoned cast-iron or carbon-steel wok is a Chinese chef's most treasured utensil, for the more you use it, the more it becomes like a nonstick pan, requiring less and less oil for stir-frying. Be sure never to use a well-seasoned wok for steaming, as the water will strip the wok of its seasoning. The important advice here is that fancy equipment is not necessary to stir-fry. Choose a twelve- to fourteen-inch skillet that conducts heat evenly on high heat, or a fourteen-inch flat-bottomed cast-iron, carbon-steel, or stainless-steel wok. Never use a nonstick or an electric wok. It's dangerous to heat most nonstick pans on high heat, and electric woks do not generate enough heat; without adequate heat the food cannot properly stir-fry. Also avoid the traditional round-bottomed wok popular in restaurants, because it is impossible to heat sufficiently on a household stove. A gas stove is always preferable to an electric one because the heat level can be regulated instantaneously; however, for years, my parents successfully cooked on an electric stove.

The time-honored way of seasoning a new cast-iron wok is to wash it with mild soap, rinse, and let dry. Warm the wok and lightly grease it with vegetable oil. Place in a 300-degree oven and season 40 minutes. To season a carbon-steel wok, wash it in mild, soapy, hot water to remove the protective coating of oil from the factory. Dry the wok thoroughly before heating it over high heat until hot but not smoking. Add two tablespoons of vegetable oil and stir-fry a bunch of Chinese chives, *gul choy*, and discard the vegetables after cooking. This onion-like vegetable miraculously removes the metallic taste from the wok. Wash the wok in hot water and never use soap again. Be sure to dry it thoroughly. To wash a cast-iron or carbon-steel wok after cooking, soak the wok in hot water or rice water, then wash with a soft bristle brush. Scrub it well, as any excess food or oil left in the wok will become rancid with time.

In my own family, the level of cooking tension escalates as the stir-frying begins. I always think of the Cantonese as the Italians of the Far East, and cooking certainly brings out their "Mediterranean" emotions. Voices rise as the drama of the cooking performance commences. My parents cook with a high degree of difficulty, ranked for Olympic competition. Sometimes I will cringe at the possible dangers. Their Chinese slippers offer no protection from hot spills, and Baba, who always wears a sports jacket, is equally formally attired when he cooks. One parent will precariously carry the steamer of boiling water from the stove to the sink, while the other stir-fries, often leaning over the front gas burner to tame a pot on the back burner. Their voices rise with urgency as they react to the demands of each moment, against the backdrop of the exhaust fan and the sound of a reporter discussing some world crisis on the CBS *Evening News*. Suddenly, Mama climbs the kitchen ladder to reach into the cabinet for a platter and Baba matches her exploit by pouring boiling water over the platter to heat it. (Hot food can never be served on a cold platter.) Miraculously, my parents arrive at the table unscathed, along with the stir-fried dish, rice, the steamed dish, and a piping-hot saucepan of soup. Within seconds, it seems, everything is on the table, masterfully executed. If more than one dish is to be stir-fried, the second is cooked after we have sampled these first dishes.

Timing is the most essential technique to master for stir-frying. Prepare carefully, and never try to chop or measure anything at the last minute, especially while you are stir-frying. The moment the wok is hot, turn on the exhaust fan, swirl in the oil, and immediately add the food. One of the secrets for preventing food from sticking in the wok is to have the wok hot, but the oil cool. Do not heat the oil but heat the wok. Stay calm as the first crackle is heard as the food touches the oil. Sometimes the oil smokes or sputters. If you feel anxious, simply pull the wok off the heat and regroup.

Stir-frying is full of life and energy, and requires quick reactions. Garlic, ginger, and vegetables require immediate stir-frying; but poultry, meat, and seafood should cook undisturbed for a minute or two, so that the ingredient sears slightly before stir-frying. If you immediately start stirring, the meat will surely stick and tear, yet too much hesitation will result in food that is overcooked. Always swirl sauce ingredients down the sides of the wok to prevent the temperature of the pan from dropping. Stay focused, pay attention, follow these tips, and you will master the art of stir-frying. Eventually, too, you will achieve *wok hay* and understand why the Chinese have for centuries revered the experience of food that still breathes its life force.

The Wisdom of the Chinese Kitchen (1999)

Anthony Bourdain

from Kitchen Confidential

Anthony Bourdain (b. 1956) embodies the late-20th-century shift in American restaurant culture. The self-proclaimed bad boy of gourmet-dom was a drug-pushing, vodka-guzzling, two-pack-a-day smoker when, after dropping out of Vassar, he landed in a restaurant kitchen in 1974. He fit right in. With few exceptions, restaurant kitchens were at that time blue-collar sweatshops with their fair share of ex-convicts and alcoholics—men, I wrote in my memoir *Mostly True* (2006), "who wore boots with steel-reinforced toes, men too ungovernable to work corporate jobs, men full of pathos, unrealized ambition, and rage." Things had begun to change somewhat by the mid-1970s; by the time Bourdain and I arrived on the scene (we worked in the same kitchen in Provincetown), we were not the only liberal arts students whose tastes had been inflamed on trips to Europe and who had afterward been attracted to the Wild West of restaurant work. Bourdain straightened himself out (sort of), enrolled at the Culinary Institute of America, and worked his way up the food chain of New York's finer eateries—a trajectory he recounts in his provocative and amusing memoir *Kitchen Confidential* (2000). What I love about his writing is not its shock value but its innocence. Bourdain sucks up life with an open heart and responds without ambivalence: if he likes it he inhales it, if he doesn't he spits it out. As familiar as he is with the seedy underside of the restaurant world, Bourdain is constitutionally incapable of turning cynic. He seeks redemption, tirelessly and fearlessly, and finds it in food and the people who have the pride and love and courage to make it well. Here Bourdain captures the Culinary Institute's transition from trade school to the would-be Harvard of cuisine.

■ ■ ■

My knives set me apart right away. I had my by now well-worn high-carbon Sabatiers rolled in with the cheap school-supply junk: hard-to-sharpen Forschner stainless steel, peeler, parisienne scoop, paring knife and slicer. I was older than most of my fellow students, many of whom were away from home for the first time. Unlike them, I lived off campus, in Poughkeepsie with the remnants of my Vassar pals. I'd actually worked in the industry— and I'd had sex with a woman. These were not the cream of the crop, my fellow culinarians. It was 1975 and CIA was still getting more than their share of farm boys, bed-wetters, hicks, flunk-outs from community colleges and a few misfits for whom CIA was preferable to jail or juvenile detention. Hopeless in the kitchen, happy in their off-hours to do little more than build pyramids of beer cans, they were easy marks for a hard case like myself. I nearly supported myself during my two years in Hyde Park playing seven-card stud, Texas hold-em, no-peek and acey-deucey. I felt no shame or guilt taking their money, selling them beat drugs or cheating at cards. They were about to enter the restaurant industry; I figured they might as well learn sooner rather than later. If the Mario crew ever got hold of some of these rubes, they'd have the fillings out of their teeth.

It was very easy going for me. The first few months at CIA were spent on stuff like: "This is the chef's knife. This is the handle. This is the blade," as well as rote business on sanitation. My food sanitation instructor, an embittered ex-health inspector (judging from the scars on his face, the last honest man in that trade), regaled us with stories of pesticide-munching super rats, the sex lives of bacteria and the ever present dangers of unseen filth.

I took classes in food handling, egg cookery, salads, stocks, soups, basic knifework. But after spending way too many hours deep in the bowels of Marioland, peeling spuds, making gallons of dressings, chopping vegetables and so on, I knew this stuff in my bones.

Of course, my stocks in class always tasted far better than my classmates'. No one could figure out how I coaxed such hearty flavor out of a few chicken bones, or made such wonderful fish fumet with fish racks and shrimp shells, all in the limited time available. Had my instructors given me a pat-down before class they might have learned my secret: two glassine envelopes of Minor's chicken and lobster base inside my chef's coat, for that little extra kick. They never figured it out.

The CIA of 1975 was very different from the four-year professional institution it is today. Back then, the desired end product seemed to be future employees at a Hilton or Restaurant Associates corporate dining facility. A lot of time was spent on food destined for the steam table. Sauces were thickened with roux. Escoffier's heavy, breaded, soubised, glacéed and over-sauced dinosaur dishes were the ideal. Everything, it was implied, *must* come with appropriate starch, protein, vegetable. Nouvelle cuisine was practically unheard of. Reductions? No way. Infusions? Uh-uh. We're talking two years of cauliflower in Mornay sauce, saddle of veal Orloff, lobster thermidor, institutional favorites like chicken Hawaiian, grilled ham steak with pineapple ring and old-style lumbering classics like beef Wellington. The chef/instructors were largely, it seemed, burnouts from the industry: bleary-eyed Swiss, Austrian and French ex-cronies, all ginblossoms and spite—along with some motivated veterans of major hotel chains, for whom food was all about cost per unit.

But it was fun. Pulled sugar, pastillage work, chaud-froids, ice-carving. You don't see a lot of that in the real world, and there were some really talented, very experienced old-school Euro geezers at CIA who passed on to their adoring students the last of a dying style. Charcuterie class was informative and this old style was well suited to learning about galantines and ballottines and socles and pâtés, rillettes, sausage-making and aspic work. Meat class was fun; learning the fundamentals of butchering, I found for the first time that constant proximity to meat seems to inspire black humor in humans. My meat instructor would make hand puppets out of veal breast and his lamb demo/sexual puppet show was legendary. I have since found that almost everybody in the meat business is funny—just as almost everyone in the fish business is not.

They'd let us practice our knifework on whole legs of beef, my novice butcher classmates and me absolutely destroying thousands of pounds of meat; we were the culinary version of the Manson family. Fortunately, the mutilated remains of our efforts were—as was all food at CIA—simply passed along to another class, where it was braised, stewed or made into soup or grinding meat . . . before ending up on our tables for dinner. They had figured out this equation really well. All students were either cooking for other students, serving other students or being fed by other students—a perfect food cycle, as we devoured our mistakes and our successes alike.

There were also two restaurants open to the general public, but a few fundamentals were in order before the school trusted us with inflicting our limited skills on the populace.

Vegetable Cookery was a much-feared class. The terrifying Chef Bagna was in charge, and he made the simple preparing of vegetables a rigorous program on a par with Parris Island. He was an Italian Swiss, but liked to use a German accent for effect, slipping quietly up behind students mid-task and screaming questions at the top of his lungs.

"Recite for me . . . *schnell!* How to make pommes dauphinoisee!!"

Chef Bagna would then helpfully provide misleading and incorrect clues, "Zen you add ze *onions*, ya?" He would wait for his flustered victim to fall into his trap, and then shriek, "*Nein! Nein!* Zere is *no* onions in ze potatoes dauphinoisee!" He was a bully, a bit of a sadist and a showman. But the man knew his vegetables, and he knew what pressure was. Anyone who couldn't take Chef Bagna's ranting was *not* going to make it in the outside world, much less make it through the penultimate CIA class: Chef Bernard's "E Room."

Another class, Oriental Cookery, as I believe it was then called, was pretty funny. The instructor, a capable Chinese guy, was responsible for teaching us the fundamentals of both Chinese *and* Japanese cooking. The Chinese portion of the class was terrific. When it came time to fill us in on the tastes of Japan, however, our teacher was more interested in giving us an extended lecture on the Rape of Nanking. His loathing of the Japanese was consuming. In between describing the bayoneting of women, children and babies in World War II, he'd point at a poster of a sushi/sashimi presentation on the wall, and say in his broken, heavily accented English, "That a raw a fish. You wanna eat that? Hah! Japanese *shit!*" Then he'd go back into his dissertation on forced labor, mass executions and enslavement, hinting darkly that Japan would pay, sooner or later, for what it had done to his country.

The joke went that everyone gained five pounds in baking class. I could see what they meant. It was held in the morning, when everyone was starving, and after a few hours of hard labor, hefting heavy sacks of flour, balling and kneading dough, loading giant deck and windmill ovens with cinnamon buns, croissants, breads and rolls for the various school-operated dining rooms, the room would fill with the smell. When the finished product started coming out of the ovens, the students would fall on it, slathering the still-hot bread and buns with gobs of butter, tearing it apart and shoveling it in their faces. Brownies, pecan diamonds, cookies, profiteroles—around 10 percent of the stuff disappeared into our faces and our knife rolls before it was loaded into proof racks and packed off to its final destinations. It was not a pretty sight, all these pale, gangly, pimpled youths, in a frenzy of hunger and sexual frustration, shredding bread. It was like *Night of the Living Dead*, everyone seemed always to be chewing.

If there was an Ultimate Terror, a man who fit all of our ideas of a Real Chef, a monstrous, despotic, iron-fisted Frenchman who ruled his kitchen like President for Life Idi Amin, it was Chef Bernard. The final class before graduation was the dreaded yet yearned-for "E Room," the Escoffier Room, an open-to-the-public, three-star restaurant operated for profit by the school. Diners, it was said, made reservations *years* in advance. Here, classic French food was served à la carte, finished and served off *guéridons* by amusingly inept students. Our skipper, the mighty septuagenarian Chef Bernard, had, it was rumored, *actually worked with Escoffier himself.* His name was mentioned only in whispers; students were aware of his unseen presence for months before entering his kitchen.

"Wait till 'E Room'," went the ominous refrain, "Bernard's gonna have your ass for breakfast."

Needless to say, the pressure, the fear and the anticipation in the weeks before Escoffier Room were palpable.

It was an open kitchen. A large window allowed customers to watch the fearsome chef as he lined up his charges for inspection, assigned the day's work stations, reviewed the crimes and horrors and disappointments of the previous night's efforts. This was a terrifying moment, as we all dreaded the soufflé station, the one station where one was assured of drawing the full weight of Chef Bernard's wrath and displeasure. The likelihood of a screwup was highest here, too. It was certain that at least *one* of your *à la minute* soufflés would, under real working conditions, fail to rise, rise unevenly, collapse in on itself—in some way fail to meet our leader's exacting standards. Students would actually tremble with fear before lineup and work assignments, praying, "Not me, Lord. Not today . . . please, not the soufflé station."

If you screwed up, you'd get what was called the "ten minutes." In full view of the gawking public and quavering comrades, the offending soufflé cook would be called forward to stand at attention while the intimidating old French master would look down his Gallic shnozz and unload the most withering barrage of scorn any of us had ever experienced.

"You are a shit chef!" he would bellow. "I make two cook like you in the *toilette* each morning! You are deezgusting! A *shoemaker*! You have destroyed

my life! . . . You will *never* be a chef! You are a *disgrace!* Look! Look at this
merde . . . *merde* . . . *merde!*" At this point, Bernard would stick his fingers into the offending object and fling bits of it on the floor. "You *dare* call
this cuisine! This . . . this is grotesque! An abomination! You . . . you
should kill yourself from shame!"

I had to hand it to the old bastard, though, he was fair. *Everyone* got ten
minutes. Even the girls, who would, sad to say, invariably burst into tears
thirty seconds into the chef's tirade. He did not let their tears or sobs deter
him. They stood there, shaking and heaving for the full time while he
ranted and raved and cursed heaven and earth and their ancestors and their
future progeny, breaking them down like everybody else, until all that remained was a trembling little bundle of nerves with an unnaturally red face
in a white polyester uniform.

One notable victim of Chef Bernard's reign of terror was a buddy of
mine—also much older than the other students—who had just returned from
Vietnam. He'd served in combat with an artillery unit and returned state-
side to attend the CIA under the GI Bill and had made it through the whole
program, had only *four days* to go before graduation, but when he saw that
in a day or two *his* number would be up and *he*, without question, would be
working the dreaded soufflé station, he folded under the pressure. He went
AWOL, disappearing from Hyde Park forever. Boot camp and the Viet Cong
had not been as bad as Chef Bernard's ten minutes, I guess.

When my time came to stand there in front of my fellow students, and
all the world, and get *my* ten minutes, I was ready. I could see Chef Bernard
looking deep into my eyes as he began his standard tirade, could see him
recognize a glimmer of *something* familiar somewhere in there. I did the
convict thing. The louder and more confrontational the authority figure
got, the more dreamy and relaxed I became. Bernard saw it happening. I may
have been standing at rigid attention, and saying all the right things, "*Oui*,
Chef! *Non*, Chef!" at all the right moments, and showing the right respect,
but he could see, perhaps in my dead fish-eye gaze, that he wasn't getting
anywhere with me. I think the old bastard might have even smiled a little
bit, halfway through. There seemed to be a twinkle of amusement in his
eyes as he finally dismissed me with feigned disgust. He knew, I think, that
I had *already* been humiliated. He looked in my eyes and saw, perhaps, that

Tyrone and the Mario crew had done his work for him. I liked Chef Bernard and respected him. I enjoyed working under him. But the fat bastard didn't scare me. And he knew it. He could have smacked me upside the head with a skillet and I would have smiled at him through broken teeth. He saw that, I think—and it ruined all the fun.

Kitchen Confidential (2000)

David Sedaris

Today's Special

In his collections *Naked* (1997), *Me Talk Pretty One Day* (2000), and *Dress Your Family in Corduroy and Denim* (2004), David Sedaris (b. 1956) has proven himself to be one of the nation's sharpest observers of popular culture. Here, he turns his wit loose on dinner in Soho, at a moment when restaurants were specializing in what Sedaris describes as "fifteen-word entrees" and food ran the risk of becoming all but unrecognizable. Not long after writing the essay, Sedaris and his partner moved to France, and restaurant cooking in downtown New York took a rustic turn.

■ ■ ■

It is his birthday, and Hugh and I are seated in a New York restaurant, awaiting the arrival of our fifteen-word entrées. He looks very nice, dressed in the suit and sweater that have always belonged to him. As for me, I own only my shoes, pants, shirt, and tie. My jacket belongs to the restaurant and was offered as a loan by the maître d', who apparently thought I would feel more comfortable dressed to lead a high-school marching band.

I'm worrying the thick gold braids decorating my sleeves when the waiter presents us with what he calls "a little something to amuse the palate." Roughly the size and color of a Band-Aid, the amusement floats on a shallow, muddy puddle of sauce and is topped with a sprig of greenery.

"And this would be . . . what, exactly?" Hugh asks.

"This," the waiter announces, "is our raw Atlantic swordfish served in a dark chocolate gravy and garnished with fresh mint."

"Not again," I say. "Can't you guys come up with something a little less conventional?"

"Love your jacket," the waiter whispers.

As a rule, I'm no great fan of eating out in New York restaurants. It's hard to love a place that's outlawed smoking but finds it perfectly acceptable to serve raw fish in a bath of chocolate. There are no normal restaurants left, at least in our neighborhood. The diners have all been taken over by precious little bistros boasting a menu of indigenous American cuisine. They call these meals "traditional," yet they're rarely the American dishes I remember. The patty melt has been pushed aside in favor of the herb-encrusted medallions of baby artichoke hearts, which never leave me thinking, Oh, right, those! I wonder if they're as good as the ones my mom used to make.

Part of the problem is that we live in the wrong part of town. SoHo is not a macaroni salad kind of place. This is where the world's brightest young talents come to braise carmelized racks of corn-fed songbirds or offer up their famous knuckle of flash-seared crappie served with a collar of chided ginger and cornered by a tribe of kiln-roasted Chilean toadstools, teased with a warm spray of clarified musk oil. Even when they promise something simple, they've got to tart it up—the meatloaf has been poached in seawater, or there are figs in the tuna salad. If cooking is an art, I think we're in our Dada phase.

I've never thought of myself as a particularly finicky eater, but it's hard to be a good sport when each dish seems to include no fewer than a dozen ingredients, one of which I'm bound to dislike. I'd order the skirt steak with a medley of suffocated peaches, but I'm put off by the aspirin sauce. The sea scallops look good until I'm told they're served in a broth of malt liquor and mummified litchi nuts. What I really want is a cigarette, and I'm always searching the menu in the hope that some courageous young chef has finally recognized tobacco as a vegetable. Bake it, steam it, grill it, or stuff it into littleneck clams, I just need something familiar that I can hold on to.

When the waiter brings our entrées, I have no idea which plate might be mine. In yesterday's restaurants it was possible both to visualize and to recognize your meal. There were always subtle differences, but for the most part, a lamb chop tended to maintain its basic shape. That is to say that it looked choplike. It had a handle made of bone and a teardrop of meat hugged by a thin rind of fat. Apparently, though, that was too predictable. Order the modern lamb chop, and it's likely to look no different than your companion's order of shackled pompano. The current food is always arranged into a senseless, vertical tower. No longer content to recline, it now reaches for the sky, much like the high-rise buildings lining our city streets. It's as if the plates were valuable parcels of land and the chef had purchased one small lot and unlimited air rights. Hugh's saffron linguini resembles a miniature turban, topped with architectural spires of shrimp. It stands there in the center while the rest of the vast, empty plate looks though it's been leased out as a possible parking lot. I had ordered the steak, which, bowing to the same minimalist fashion, is served without the bone, the thin slices of beef stacked to resemble a funeral pyre. The potatoes I'd been expecting have apparently either been clarified to an essence or were used to stoke the grill.

"Maybe," Hugh says, "they're inside your tower of meat."

This is what we have been reduced to. Hugh blows the yucca pollen off his blackened shrimp while I push back the sleeves of my borrowed sport coat and search the meat tower for my promised potatoes.

"There they are, right there." Hugh uses his fork to point out what could easily be mistaken for five cavity-riddled molars. The dark spots must be my vegetable.

Because I am both a glutton and a masochist, my standard complaint, "That was so bad," is always followed by "And there was so little of it!"

Our plates are cleared, and we are presented with dessert menus. I learn that spiced ham is no longer considered just a luncheon meat and that even back issues of *Smithsonian* can be turned into sorbets.

"I just couldn't," I say to the waiter when he recommends the white chocolate and wild loganberry couscous.

"If we're counting calories, I could have the chef serve it without the crème fraîche."

"No," I say. "Really, I just couldn't."

We ask for the check, explaining that we have a movie to catch. It's only a ten-minute walk to the theater, but I'm antsy because I'd like to get something to eat before the show. They'll have loads of food at the concession stand, but I don't believe in mixing meat with my movies. Luckily there's a hot dog cart not too far out of our way.

Friends always say, "How can you eat those? I read in the paper that they're made from hog's lips."

"And . . . ?"

"And hearts and eyelids."

That, to my mind, is only three ingredients and constitutes a refreshing change of pace. I order mine with nothing but mustard, and am thrilled to watch the vendor present my hot dog in a horizontal position. So simple and timeless that I can recognize it, immediately, as food.

Me Talk Pretty One Day (2000)

Jhumpa Lahiri

Indian Takeout

A child of Bengali immigrants to Rhode Island, Jhumpa Lahiri (b. 1967)—later to write the Pulitzer Prize–winning story collection *The Interpreter of Maladies* (1999)—grew up at a time when Indian groceries were largely unavailable in the United States. Thus the Food Suitcase: a humble piece of luggage that served as a lifeline between worlds, crammed on flights back from India with everything her parents missed in their adopted home. Today, as ethnic specialty markets have stepped in to satisfy demand and many other supermarkets have expanded their Indian offerings, the exotic "treasures" of Lahiri's youth have begun to seem less precious, more ordinary. Walking the crowded streets of Jackson Heights, though, in New York—the produce bins full of fresh turmeric root, mangoes, curry leaves, mustard greens—it seems like a very fortunate fall.

■ ■ ■

I am the daughter of former pirates, of a kind. Our loot included gold, silver, even a few precious gems. Mainly though, it was food, so much that throughout my childhood I was convinced my parents were running the modern equivalent of the ancient spice trade. They didn't exactly plunder this food; they bought it in the bazaars of Calcutta, where my mother was born and to which we returned as a family every couple of years. The destination was Rhode Island, where we lived, and where, back in the Seventies, Indian groceries were next to impossible to come by.

Our treasure chest, something we called the Food Suitcase, was an elegant relic from the Fifties with white stitching and brass latches that fastened shut with satisfying clicks. The inside was lined in peach-colored satin, had shirred lingerie pockets on three sides and was large enough to house a wardrobe for a long journey. Leave it to my parents to convert a vintage portmanteau into a portable pantry. They bought it one Saturday morning at a yard sale in the neighborhood, and I think it's safe to say that it had never been to India before.

Trips to Calcutta let my parents eat again, eat the food of their childhood, the food they had been deprived of as adults. As soon as he hit Indian soil, my father began devouring two or three yellow-skinned mangoes a day, sucking the pits lovingly smooth. My mother breakfasted shamelessly on sticky orange sweets called *jelebis*. It was easy to succumb. I insisted on accompanying each of my meals with the yogurt sold at confectioners in red clay cups, their lids made of paper, and my sister formed an addiction to *Moghlai parathas*, flatbread folded, omelet-style, over mincemeat and egg.

As the end of each visit neared, our focus shifted from eating to shopping. My parents created lists on endless sheets of paper, and my father spent days in the bazaars, haggling and buying by the kilo. He always insisted on packing the goods himself, with the aura of a man possessed: bare chested, seated cross-legged on the floor, determined, above all, to make everything fit. He bound the Food Suitcase with enough rope to baffle Houdini and locked it up with a little padlock, a scheme that succeeded in intimidating the most assiduous customs inspectors. Into the suitcase went an arsenal of lentils and every conceivable spice, wrapped in layers of cloth ripped from an old sari and stitched into individual packets. In went white poppy seeds, and resin made from date syrup, and as many tins of Ganesh mustard oil as possible. In went Lapchu tea, to be brewed only on special occasions, and sacks of black-skinned Gobindovog rice, so named, it is said, because it's fit for offering to the god Govinda. In went six kinds of *dalmoot*, a salty, crunchy snack mix bought from big glass jars in a tiny store at the corner of Vivekananda Road and Cornwallis Street. In, on occasion, went something fresh, and therefore flagrantly illegal: a bumpy, bright green bitter melon, or bay leaves from my uncle's garden. My parents weren't the only ones willing to flout the law. One year my grandmother secretly tucked *parvals*, a vaguely squashlike vegetable, into the Food Suitcase. My mother wept when she found them.

My parents also bought utensils: bowl-shaped iron *karhais*, which my mother still prefers to ordinary pots and pans, and the areca-nut cracker that's now somewhere in the back of the silverware drawer, and even a *boti*, a large curved blade that sits on the floor in Bengali kitchens and is used instead of handheld knives. The most sensational gadget we ever transported was a *sil-nora*, an ancient food processor of sorts, which consists of a massive clublike pestle and a slab the size, shape and weight of a headstone. Bewildered relatives shook their heads, and airport workers in both hemispheres must have cursed us. For a while my mother actually used it, pounding garlic cloves by hand instead of pressing a button on the Osterizer. Then it turned into a decorative device, propped up on the kitchen counter. It's in the basement now.

The suitcase was full during the trip from Rhode Island to Calcutta too, with gifts for family. People there seldom asked for any food from America; instead they requested the stuff of duty-free, Dunhills or Johnnie Walker. We brought them Corning Ware plates and bowls, which, in their eyes, were exotic alternatives to the broad, gleaming stainless steel dishes they normally used. The only food we packed for ourselves was a big jar of Tang, which my father carried with him at all times and stirred obsessively into the bitter purified water.

In spite of everything we managed to haul back, the first meal we ate after returning from India was always a modest affair. My mother prepared the simplest of things: rice, some quartered potatoes, eggs if she was motivated, all boiled together in a single pot. That first meal was never an occasion to celebrate but rather to mourn, for the people and the city we had, once again, left behind. And so my mother made food to mirror our mood, food for the weary and melancholy. I remember thinking how strangely foreign our own kitchen felt that first night back, with its giant, matching appliances, water we could safely drink straight from the tap and rice which bore no stray stones. Just before we ate, my mother would ask my father to untie the ropes and unlock the suitcase. A few pappadams quickly fried and a drop of mustard oil drizzled over the potatoes would convert our survivalist meal into a delicacy. It was enough, that first lonely evening, not only to satisfy our hunger but to make Calcutta seem not so very far away.

My parents returned last August from their 13th visit to India in their 30-odd years abroad. When I asked my mother what foods they'd brought back she replied, with some sadness, "Nothing, really." My father observed matter-of-factly that most everything was sold here these days. It's true. Saffron and cardamom grace supermarket shelves, even in the small towns of Rhode Island. The world, the culinary world in particular, has shrunk considerably. Still, when my cousin's mother recently visited New York City, she packed several pieces of fried *ruhi*, the everyday fish of Bengal, into her bags. Of course, the Indian markets of Jackson Heights, Queens, were only a subway ride away, but the fish had been sliced, salted and fried in Calcutta. This was what mattered.

Today the Food Suitcase sits in our basement, neglected, smelling of cumin. When I opened it on my last trip home, a few stray lentils rolled around in one corner. Yet the signs were still visible, in the cupboards and the refrigerator, that my parents have not abandoned their pirating ways. You would know as much, were you to visit them yourself, by the six kinds of *dalmoot* my mother would set out with tea and the mustard oil she would offer to drizzle on your potatoes at dinner.

Patricia Volk

Hersheyettes

The child of restaurateurs, novelist and short-story writer Patricia Volk (b. 1943) brings a light touch, in this excerpt from her memoir *Stuffed* (2001), to what is, in America more than anywhere else, an increasingly common problem: obesity. Caught, as if in a vise, in a culture in which billboards for oozing burgers and glistening donuts compete with the "airbrushed perfectionism" of a "supermodel norm," weight was "never not an issue" for Volk when she was growing up. She recounts her history in terms of diets and pounds as well as years.

■ ■ ■

My mother calls to tell me my sister weighs 150 pounds: "I don't think her husband could like it very much," my mother says. "Do you?"

My sister calls to tell me she's starting Jenny Craig: "I met with my diet counselor and told her she could have every piece of jewelry I had on if she could get me thin enough to wear her jeans."

The next morning my sister calls to tell me the diet's not working: "You have to buy all the food from Jenny Craig, and it's horrible."

"My friend Brenda is on the English Red and Green Diet," I tell her. "You eat five fruits and five veggies every day. But on green days you add things that grow. And on red days you add things that walk."

"I don't need a diet," my sister says. "I know every diet. Here's the trick, okay? Here's all you have to know: Eat less."

Since my sister and I like to invent things–Cuzzles, the Cookie Puzzle for Kids; the *10 Meals in 10 Minutes for 10 Dollars Cookbook* revised to the *20 Meals in 20 Minutes for 20 Dollars Cookbook*; the book about sisters somebody else did; the movie about sisters we didn't know enough about movies to make; reading glasses that beep when you press a locator button so you can find them; the Hoseable Apartment, where floors gently slope toward a drain and everything is waterproof, even the books; Airplane Dating so when you book your seat, you get to say what kind of person you'd like to sit next to–since we like to hatch schemes, I say, "Why don't we do a book of all the diets we've been on? Fifty-two diets, a new one every week."

We start naming diets: The Nine-Egg-a-Day, the Grapefruit, the Beverly Hills, the Atkins, the Modified Atkins, the Ornish, the Pineapple, the Scarsdale, the Sauerkraut, the Red Soup, the Mayo Clinic, the Duke Rice Diet, the Vanderbilt Rotation Diet, the Hilton Head Metabolism Diet, the Substitution Diet, Weight Watchers, Weight Watchers Quick Start, the Watermelon, the Loma Linda, Fit for Life, Sugar Busters!, Dr. Hevert's Famous Diet (modified Atkins), the Chew Everything 30 Times Diet, the Blood-type Diet, the Bloomingdale's Eat Healthy Diet, Dr. Berger's Immune Power Diet, Dr. McDougall's 12-Day Diet Meal Plan, the Carbohydrate Addicts Diet, the Hollywood 48-Hour Miracle Diet (ten pounds in a weekend), the Cyberdiet, the Stillman, Optifast, Dexfenfluramine HCI, the Nutri/System Diet Plan, the Zone Diet, Medifast, Metrecal, Slim-Fast, Ultra Slim-Fast, Richard Simmons Deal-A-Meal, the 8-Glasses-of-Water-a-Day, the Pritikin Diet, HMV, Horse Hoof Protein, the Liquid Protein. I especially like the one where you eat nothing but fruit till noon and then all the protein you want. Or all the protein you want till noon, and nothing but fruit the rest of the day. One diet my sister was on allowed her to eat unlimited bacon. Microwaves had just come out. She kept those rashers going in on paper towels. DING! Four rashers came out, four rashers went in. For dinner she ate steak with a sooty black crust. The weight fell off. Her breath smelled like nail polish remover. "That was the Acetone Breath Diet," my sister says. "Do you think I have A.D.D.?"

"Attention Deficit Disorder?"

"Attention *Diet* Disorder," she says.

When you watch your weight, you literally watch it. We are masters of the scale. Bend one knee, you weigh less. Lean sideways, that's worth a pound. If you weigh yourself before breakfast after going to the bathroom and walking twice around the reservoir, that's the least you'll weigh all day. You weigh less after a shower than you do before, provided your hair is dry. If you hold your breath and suck in your gut, the needle on the scale heads west. You can weigh less from blowing your nose, brushing your teeth, cutting your cuticles, and thinking light thoughts. You can lose (or gain) weight stepping off the scale, then getting right back on.

People like my sister and me know our weight at any given time. The sixth grade, before the musical at camp, during the SATs, first day of college, first date with husband-to-be, wedding weight, post-honeymoon weight, pre- and post-baby weights, weight at grandmother's funeral. Give us a year, we'll give it back to you in pounds. Give us a *day*.

"We've had thirty years of fat and thin," my sister says.

"I've got a distorted body image," I tell her. "I think I look good."

Weight was never not an issue. It was there, every morning, like the *New York Times*. At Weight Watchers they tell you, "Nothing tastes as good as thin feels." But my sister has decided she prefers eating to looking skinny, that eating gives her more pleasure, even if she wears only bespoke black. Once, when we rented a movie, she bought a bag of Hershey's Hugs. I told her not to buy anything Hershey, because when I'd done the advertising for the company, I'd invented the name Hershey's Hugs for a candy to be sold alongside Hershey's Kisses—Hugs and Kisses—and I never got credit for it. I did get credit for inventing the name "Whatchamacallit" for a new candy bar. "Hershey's Whatchamacallit. You can ask for it by name," the logo line went. It was my major contribution in eighteen years of advertising. But Hershey stole the Hugs name, so I've been boycotting them for twelve years. "If you buy Hugs," I told my sister, "it's the same as crossing a picket line. If you buy Hugs, you're a scab."

She bought the Hugs. In the car she unwrapped eight and palmed them into her mouth.

"Why are you doing that?" I asked her.

"I love the sensation of the chocolate filling my mouth, the area around my teeth, of it melting on my tongue, and sliding hot and liquidy down my throat. I love the taste. I love the feel."

What could I say? By the time she pulled into her driveway, the bag was empty.

In 1996, while cleaning out a dresser drawer, I came across a small locked metal box. The box had moved to four apartments with me. I couldn't remember the last time I'd seen it. I shook it in my hand. Something was inside. It sounded like paper. A hundred-dollar bill? A secret? A last will and testament? On top of my dresser there's a small tray filled with mystery keys. I tried the little ones. None of them worked. I got a screwdriver. That didn't work either. Finally I pried the box open with the claw of a hammer. Inside, there was a yellowed three-by-five card. Written on it were the words "All-time High: 143."

By the fourth grade my sister was taller than all her teachers. She's still tall. Recently she had her skeleton weighed. A doctor glued electrodes over key bones and ran a charge through them. "It felt prickly," she says. "Like when your foot falls asleep, then starts to wake up." A strip of paper chattered out of the machine. My sister's skeleton weighed 117 pounds. The doctor was stunned. "For a person your height," he said, "your skeleton should weigh eighty-eight. This is the largest female skeleton I've ever seen." So now at least we have proof: My sister is big-boned.

In high school we dieted in earnest. We wore full skirts with crinolines made rigid by soaking them in a bathtub full of sugar water. Then we'd tuck in a sweater or blouse and buckle on a four-inch cinch belt. Because the skirts ballooned out, our waists looked tiny. My sister could get hers down to twenty-two inches. I could get mine under twenty. Still we thought we were fat.

There was an obstetrician/gynecologist in town who stopped doing ob/gyn to become a diet specialist full-time. Dad went to him and started losing weight. We convinced Mom to take us. The doctor prescribed a small pink pill. A lot of girls in our high school were taking the small pink pill. It made you not interested in food. You just didn't think about it. When you went for fries after school, they lacked appeal. When you went for pizza after the movies, you couldn't finish a slice. The weight fell off. Desserts lost their glow. Our waists got smaller. People stopped us to tell us how thin we were. The first week, I lost 8½ pounds, my sister, 7. The doctor praised us. He prescribed more pink pills. Mother seemed pleased. Even so, she kept our chocolate shelves loaded.

The pink pills had no impact on our need for chocolate. There was a small cabinet in the kitchen. The upper shelf was for my sister's Tootsie Rolls, the bottom shelf was for my Hersheyettes. Hersheyettes were the Hershey Company's answer to M&M's. They were drops of chocolate covered with a pastel sugar shell stamped H. Three things set Hersheyettes

apart: one, the Hershey association. Two, the sugar shells were Easter colors—
pink, lavender, baby blue. And three, the shape was unusual—two small
cones stuck together at their wide part. Looking head-on at a Hersheyette,
it was shaped like a diamond. I preferred the chocolate in M&M's. But there
was more to Hersheyettes. You could spin them on your tongue like a top.

Hersheyettes seemed to take off. During my senior year in high school,
they replaced M&M's in the vending machines at Jones Beach. I thought I'd
always have them. On Mom's weekly visits to the supermarket, she'd pick
me up a one-pound bag. She wanted us to lose weight, she was happy we
were successes at the diet doctor's, but she understood the need for chocolate too. Besides, even with the candy, as long as you took a little pink pill
every day, you'd keep losing weight. My candy shelf was well stocked. Then
I left for college, and when I came home for Thanksgiving, Hersheyettes
had vanished.

In college I made an accidental discovery. I forgot to take a pink pill one
morning. When I remembered, it was late afternoon. That night, I couldn't
sleep. If you took a pink pill late in the day, it kept you up. You could pull
an all-nighter. Something in the diet doctor's pink pills made it possible to
study all night before a final. You didn't feel sleepy at all. If anything, you felt
energized and smarter.

The disappearance of Hersheyettes is a mystery. It may have been a
shelf-space problem. Shelf space in the supermarket is an ongoing, filth-
ily fought, kill-or-get-killed battle. Often a new product can launch itself
by out-couponing preexisting products. Consumers will keep buying the
new product despite brand loyalty to the old product because the new one is
so much cheaper with a coupon. The company giving the discount coupon
is willing to take a loss because it's hard to change established buying patterns, especially for "parity" products like glass cleaners or club soda or a
tiny sugarcoated milk chocolate candy. The Mars Company, which puts out
M&M's, may have fought back with its own coupon war. No Hersheyettes ad
campaign comes to mind like the M&M spot with the little naked M&M and
its friend the peanut M&M diving into a swimming pool of chocolate. "First
we're drenched in creamy milk chocolate," the plain M&M, the brainy one,
says. They grab the pool ladder and swing their little chocolate bodies back

and forth until all the extra chocolate flies off and they zip up their sugar shells. "Melts in your mouth, not in your hand."

In the end, what may have killed Hersheyettes was unmemorable advertising. Or poor distribution. Or maybe not enough people liked them. You'd think anyone who liked a Hershey bar would have liked Hersheyettes. The Hershey name has chocolate equity. Hershey *means* chocolate. M&M's don't have any chocolate connection or brand-name recognition beyond M&M's. So Hersheyettes should have been a natural, a "line extension," like Wrigley's spearmint gum coming out with a breath mint. Or Nike bridging the Dr. Scholl's or Spenco market. The Hershey name alone was permission to believe a Hersheyette would be a morsel of America's favorite candy bar. And that may have been the problem. When I did the advertising for Hershey, I was told that not all Hershey milk chocolate is the same. Premium milk chocolate goes into the gold-wrapped candy, a lesser grade is used for the familiar brown- and silver-wrapped bars. When other flavors are added, say wafers with KitKat or puffed rice and penuche with Whatchamacallit, the quality of the chocolate plummets. Hershey uses cheaper chocolate with a lower cocoa fat content in these bars because consumers can't tell the chocolate isn't first-rate when it's mixed with so much other stuff. The worst chocolate goes into Mr. Goodbar, Chicago's number-one candy bar. The peanuts taste so strong, people don't notice the chocolate's not up to speed. A Hersheyette tasted different from a Hershey bar.

Hersheyettes vanished. The little pink pills disappeared too. Preludins turned out to be amphetamines that caused birth defects. The diet doctor lost his New York State license in a sting. He sold one thousand Preludins to a federal agent. He moved to California, got a license there, and went back to the practice of obstetrics and gynecology. I stopped taking Preludins eight years before I had children. My kids seem pretty normal despite the airbrushed perfectionism of their supermodel norm, despite growing up without ever seeing an unwanted hair, the heartbreak of psoriasis, a cellulite dimple, or a backside you could serve tea off of.

Stuffed: Adventures of a Restaurant Family (2001)

Eric Schlosser

from Fast Food Nation

"Do we really need to know how much bad it takes for something to taste so good?" In her later years, Julia Child often asked me that question. She was obsessed with the diet police, the forces she called "joy killers" who were, she said, out to destroy the simple pleasures of the table. I share her uneasiness, and if, like Julia, most Americans relished a big plate of McDonald's french fries twice a year, there would be little need for a book like Eric Schlosser's *Fast Food Nation* (2001). But as Schlosser (b. 1959) shows in his passionate and well-reported exposé, it is not occasional indulgence that fuels the fast food industry; a wholesale transformation of the American diet is at stake. Just as Upton Sinclair's *The Jungle* (1906) changed the meat-packing industry, Schlosser's book (which was recently made into a movie) aims to change fast food. In addition to his energetic and relentless investigative skill, Schlosser has the ability to make the reader taste his subject: the mouth first waters and then, as the portrait grows sharper and more frightening, the tongue begins to itch and the throat to close—not without some sadness for those of us who once viewed the occasional McDonald's fry as one of life's guilty pleasures.

■ ■ ■

The taste of McDonald's french fries has long been praised by customers, competitors, and even food critics. James Beard loved McDonald's fries. Their distinctive taste does not stem from the type of potatoes that McDonald's buys, the technology that processes them, or the restaurant equipment that fries them. Other chains buy their french fries from the same large processing companies, use Russet Burbanks, and have similar fryers in their restaurant kitchens. The taste of a fast food fry is largely determined by the cooking oil. For decades, McDonald's cooked its french fries in a mixture of about 7 percent cottonseed oil and 93 percent beef tallow. The mix gave the fries their unique flavor—and more saturated beef fat per ounce than a McDonald's hamburger.

Amid a barrage of criticism over the amount of cholesterol in their fries, McDonald's switched to pure vegetable oil in 1990. The switch presented the company with an enormous challenge: how to make fries that subtly taste like beef without cooking them in tallow. A look at the ingredients now used in the preparation of McDonald's french fries suggests how the problem was solved. At the end of the list is a seemingly innocuous, yet oddly mysterious phrase: "natural flavor." That ingredient helps to explain not only why the fries taste so good, but also why most fast food—indeed, most of the food Americans eat today—tastes the way it does.

Open your refrigerator, your freezer, your kitchen cupboards, and look at the labels on your food. You'll find "natural flavor" or "artificial flavor" in just about every list of ingredients. The similarities between these two broad categories of flavor are far more significant than their differences. Both are man-made additives that give most processed food its taste. The initial purchase of a food item may be driven by its packaging or appearance, but subsequent purchases are determined mainly by its taste. About 90 percent of the money that Americans spend on food is used to buy processed food. But the canning, freezing, and dehydrating techniques used to process food destroy most of its flavor. Since the end of World War II, a vast industry has arisen in the United States to make processed food palatable. Without this flavor industry, today's fast food industry could not exist. The names of the leading American fast food chains and their best-selling menu items have become famous worldwide, embedded in our popular culture. Few people, however, can name the companies that manufacture fast food's taste.

The flavor industry is highly secretive. Its leading companies will not divulge the precise formulas of flavor compounds or the identities of clients. The secrecy is deemed essential for protecting the reputation of beloved brands. The fast food chains, understandably, would like the public to believe that the flavors of their food somehow originate in their restaurant kitchens, not in distant factories run by other firms.

The New Jersey Turnpike runs through the heart of the flavor industry, an industrial corridor dotted with refineries and chemical plants. International Flavors & Fragrances (IFF), the world's largest flavor company, has a manufacturing facility off Exit 8A in Dayton, New Jersey; Givaudan, the world's second-largest flavor company, has a plant in East Hanover. Haarmann & Reimer, the largest German flavor company, has a plant in Teterboro, as does Takasago, the largest Japanese flavor company. Flavor Dynamics has a plant in South Plainfield; Frutarom is in North Bergen; Elan Chemical is in Newark. Dozens of companies manufacture flavors in New Jersey industrial parks between Teaneck and South Brunswick. Indeed, the area produces about two-thirds of the flavor additives sold in the United States.

The IFF plant in Dayton is a huge pale blue building with a modern office complex attached to the front. It sits in an industrial park, not far from a BASF plastics factory, a Jolly French Toast factory, and a plant that manufactures Liz Claiborne cosmetics. Dozens of tractor-trailers were parked at the IFF loading dock the afternoon I visited, and a thin cloud of steam floated from the chimney. Before entering the plant, I signed a nondisclosure form, promising not to reveal the brand names of products that contain IFF flavors. The place reminded me of Willy Wonka's chocolate factory. Wonderful smells drifted through the hallways, men and women in neat white lab coats cheerfully went about their work, and hundreds of little glass bottles sat on laboratory tables and shelves. The bottles contained powerful but fragile flavor chemicals, shielded from light by the brown glass and the round plastic caps shut tight. The long chemical names on the little white labels were as mystifying to me as medieval Latin. They were the odd-sounding names of things that would be mixed and poured and turned into new substances, like magic potions.

I was not invited to see the manufacturing areas of the IFF plant, where it was thought I might discover trade secrets. Instead, I toured various laboratories and pilot kitchens, where the flavors of well-established brands are tested or adjusted, and where whole new flavors are created. IFF's snack and savory lab is responsible for the flavor of potato chips, corn chips, breads, crackers, breakfast cereals, and pet food. The confectionery lab devises the flavor for ice cream, cookies, candies, toothpastes, mouthwashes, and antacids. Everywhere I looked, I saw famous, widely advertised products sitting on laboratory desks and tables. The beverage lab is full of brightly colored liquids in clear bottles. It comes up with the flavor for popular soft drinks, sport drinks, bottled teas, and wine coolers, for all-natural juice drinks, organic soy drinks, beers, and malt liquors. In one pilot kitchen I saw a dapper chemist, a middle-aged man with an elegant tie beneath his lab coat, carefully preparing a batch of cookies with white frosting and pink-and-white sprinkles. In another pilot kitchen I saw a pizza oven, a grill, a milk-shake machine, and a french fryer identical to those I'd seen behind the counter at countless fast food restaurants.

In addition to being the world's largest flavor company, IFF manufactures the smell of six of the ten best-selling fine perfumes in the United States. It makes the smell of Estée Lauder's Beautiful, Clinique's Happy, Ralph Lauren's Polo, and Calvin Klein's Eternity. It also makes the smell of household products such as deodorant, dishwashing detergent, bath soap, shampoo, furniture polish, and floor wax. All of these aromas are made through the same basic process: the manipulation of volatile chemicals to create a particular smell. The basic science behind the scent of your shaving cream is the same as that governing the flavor of your TV dinner.

The aroma of a food can be responsible for as much as 90 percent of its flavor. Scientists now believe that human beings acquired the sense of taste as a way to avoid being poisoned. Edible plants generally taste sweet; deadly ones, bitter. Taste is supposed to help us differentiate food that's good for us from food that's not. The taste buds on our tongues can detect the presence of half a dozen or so basic tastes, including: sweet, sour, bitter, salty, astringent, and umami (a taste discovered by Japanese researchers, a rich and full sense of deliciousness triggered by amino acids in foods such as shellfish, mushrooms, potatoes, and seaweed). Taste buds offer a relatively limited means of detection, however, compared to the human olfactory system, which can perceive thousands of different chemical aromas. Indeed "flavor" is primarily the smell of gases being released by the chemicals you've just put in your mouth.

The act of drinking, sucking, or chewing a substance releases its volatile gases. They flow out of the mouth and up the nostrils, or up the passageway in the back of the mouth, to a thin layer of nerve cells called the olfactory epithelium, located at the base of the nose, right between the eyes. The brain combines the complex smell signals from the epithelium with the simple taste signals from the tongue, assigns a flavor to what's in your mouth, and decides if it's something you want to eat.

Babies like sweet tastes and reject bitter ones; we know this because scientists have rubbed various flavors inside the mouths of infants and then recorded their facial reactions. A person's food preferences, like his or her personality, are formed during the first few years of life, through a process of socialization. Toddlers can learn to enjoy hot and spicy food, bland health food, or fast food, depending upon what the people around them eat. The human sense of smell is still not fully understood and can be greatly affected by psychological factors and expectations. The color of a food can determine the perception of its taste. The mind filters out the overwhelming majority of chemical aromas that surround us, focusing intently on some, ignoring others. People can grow accustomed to bad smells or good smells; they stop noticing what once seemed overpowering. Aroma and memory are somehow inextricably linked. A smell can suddenly evoke a long-forgotten moment. The flavors of childhood foods seem to leave an indelible mark, and adults often return to them, without always knowing why. These "comfort foods" become a source of pleasure and reassurance, a fact that fast food chains work hard to promote. Childhood memories of Happy Meals can translate into frequent adult visits to McDonald's, like those of the chain's "heavy users," the customers who eat there four or five times a week.

The human craving for flavor has been a largely unacknowledged and unexamined force in history. Royal empires have been built, unexplored lands have been traversed, great religions and philosophies have been forever changed by the spice trade. In 1492 Christopher Columbus set sail to find seasoning. Today the influence of flavor in the world marketplace is no less decisive. The rise and fall of corporate empires—of soft drink companies, snack food companies, and fast food chains—is frequently determined by how their products taste.

The flavor industry emerged in the mid-nineteenth century, as processed foods began to be manufactured on a large scale. Recognizing the need for flavor additives, the early food processors turned to perfume companies that had years of experience working with essential oils and volatile aromas. The great perfume houses of England, France, and the Netherlands produced many of the first flavor compounds. In the early part of the twentieth century, Germany's powerful chemical industry assumed the technological lead in flavor production. Legend has it that a German scientist discovered methyl anthranilate, one of the first artificial flavors, by accident while mixing chemicals in his laboratory. Suddenly the lab was filled with the sweet smell of grapes. Methyl anthranilate later became the chief flavoring compound of grape Kool-Aid. After World War II, much of the perfume industry shifted from Europe to the United States, settling in New York City near the garment district and the fashion houses. The flavor industry came with it, subsequently moving to New Jersey to gain more plant capacity. Man-made flavor additives were used mainly in baked goods, candies, and sodas until the 1950s, when sales of processed food began to soar. The invention of gas chromatographs and mass spectrometers—machines capable of detecting volatile gases at low levels—vastly increased the number of flavors that could be synthesized. By the mid-1960s the American flavor industry was churning out compounds to supply the taste of Pop Tarts, Bac-Os, Tab, Tang, Filet-O-Fish sandwiches, and literally thousands of other new foods.

The American flavor industry now has annual revenues of about $1.4 billion. Approximately ten thousand new processed food products are introduced every year in the United States. Almost all of them require flavor additives. And about nine out of every ten of these new food products fail. The latest flavor innovations and corporate realignments are heralded in publications such as *Food Chemical News, Food Engineering, Chemical Market Reporter,* and *Food Product Design.* The growth of IFF has mirrored that of the flavor industry as a whole. IFF was formed in 1958, through the merger of two small companies. Its annual revenues have grown almost fifteenfold since the early 1970s, and it now has manufacturing facilities in twenty countries.

The quality that people seek most of all in a food, its flavor, is usually present in a quantity too infinitesimal to be measured by any traditional culinary terms such as ounces or teaspoons. Today's sophisticated spectrometers, gas chromatographs, and headspace vapor analyzers provide a detailed map of a food's flavor components, detecting chemical aromas in amounts as low as one part per billion. The human nose, however, is still more sensitive than any machine yet invented. A nose can detect aromas present in quantities of a few parts per trillion—an amount equivalent to 0.000000000003 percent. Complex aromas, like those of coffee or roasted meat, may be composed of volatile gases from nearly a thousand different chemicals. The smell of a strawberry arises from the interaction of at least 350 different chemicals that are present in minute amounts. The chemical that provides the dominant flavor of bell pepper can be tasted in amounts as low as .02 parts per billion; one drop is sufficient to add flavor to five average size swimming pools. The flavor additive usually comes last, or second to last, in a processed food's list of ingredients (chemicals that add color are frequently used in even smaller amounts). As a result, the flavor of a processed food often costs less than its packaging. Soft drinks contain a larger proportion of flavor additives than most products. The flavor in a twelve-ounce can of Coke costs about half a cent.

The Food and Drug Administration does not require flavor companies to disclose the ingredients of their additives, so long as all the chemicals are considered by the agency to be GRAS (Generally Regarded As Safe). This lack of public disclosure enables the companies to maintain the secrecy of their formulas. It also hides the fact that flavor compounds sometimes contain more ingredients than the foods being given their taste. The ubiquitous phrase "artificial strawberry flavor" gives little hint of the chemical wizardry and manufacturing skill that can make a highly processed food taste like a strawberry.

A typical artificial strawberry flavor, like the kind found in a Burger King strawberry milk shake, contains the following ingredients: amyl acetate, amyl butyrate, amyl valerate, anethol, anisyl formate, benzyl acetate, benzyl isobutyrate, butyric acid, cinnamyl isobutyrate, cinnamyl valerate, cognac essential oil, diacetyl, dipropyl ketone, ethyl acetate, ethyl amylketone, ethyl butyrate, ethyl cinnamate, ethyl heptanoate, ethyl heptylate, ethyl lactate, ethyl methylphenylglycidate, ethyl nitrate, ethyl propionate, ethyl valerate, heliotropin, hydroxyphrenyl-2-butanone (10 percent solution in alcohol), α-ionone, isobutyl anthranilate, isobutyl butyrate, lemon essential oil, maltol, 4-methylacetophenone, methyl anthranilate, methyl benzoate, methyl cinnamate, methyl heptine carbonate, methyl naphthyl ketone, methyl salicylate, mint essential oil, neroli essential oil, nerolin, neryl isobutyrate, orris butter, phenethyl alcohol, rose, rum ether, γ-undecalactone, vanillin, and solvent.

Although flavors usually arise from a mixture of many different volatile chemicals, a single compound often supplies the dominant aroma. Smelled alone, that chemical provides an unmistakable sense of the food. Ethyl-2-methyl butyrate, for example, smells just like an apple. Today's highly processed foods offer a blank palette: whatever chemicals you add to them will give them specific tastes. Adding methyl-2-peridylketone makes something taste like popcorn. Adding ethyl-3-hydroxybutanoate makes it taste like marshmallow. The possibilities are now almost limitless. Without affecting the appearance or nutritional value, processed foods could even be made with aroma chemicals such as hexanal (the smell of freshly cut grass) or 3-methyl butanoic acid (the smell of body odor).

The 1960s were the heyday of artificial flavors. The synthetic versions of flavor compounds were not subtle, but they did not need to be, given the nature of most processed food. For the past twenty years food processors have tried hard to use only "natural flavors" in their products. According to the FDA, these must be derived entirely from natural sources—from herbs, spices, fruits, vegetables, beef, chicken, yeast, bark, roots, etc. Consumers prefer to see natural flavors on a label, out of a belief that they are healthier. The distinction between artificial and natural flavors can be somewhat arbitrary and absurd, based more on how the flavor has been made than on what it actually contains. "A natural flavor," says Terry Acree, a professor of food science technology at Cornell University, is a flavor that's been derived with an out-of-date technology." Natural flavors and artificial flavors sometimes contain exactly the same chemicals, produced through different methods. Amyl acetate, for example, provides the dominant note of banana flavor. When you distill it from bananas with a solvent, amyl acetate is a natural flavor. When you produce it by mixing vinegar with amyl alcohol, adding sulfuric acid as a catalyst, amyl acetate is an artificial flavor. Either way it smells and tastes the same. The phrase "natural flavor" is now listed among the ingredients of everything from Stonyfield Farm Organic Strawberry Yogurt to Taco Bell Hot Taco Sauce.

A natural flavor is not necessarily healthier or purer than an artificial one. When almond flavor (benzaldehyde) is derived from natural sources, such as peach and apricot pits, it contains traces of hydrogen cyanide, a deadly poison. Benzaldehyde derived through a different process—by mixing oil of clove and the banana flavor, amyl acetate—does not contain any cyanide. Nevertheless, it is legally considered an artificial flavor and sells at a much lower price. Natural and artificial flavors are now manufactured at the same chemical plants, places that few people would associate with Mother Nature.

Calling any of these flavors "natural" requires a flexible attitude toward the English language and a fair amount of irony.

The small and elite group of scientists who create most of the flavor in most of the food now consumed in the United States are called "flavorists." They draw upon a number of disciplines in their work: biology, psychology, physiology, and organic chemistry. A flavorist is a chemist with a trained nose and a poetic sensibility. Flavors are created by blending scores of different chemicals in tiny amounts, a process governed by scientific principles but demanding a fair amount of art. In an age when delicate aromas, subtle flavors, and microwave ovens do not easily coexist, the job of the flavorist is to conjure illusions about processed food and, in the words of one flavor company's literature, to ensure "consumer likeability." The flavorists with whom I spoke were charming, cosmopolitan, and ironic. They were also discreet, in keeping with the dictates of their trade. They were the sort of scientist who not only enjoyed fine wine, but could also tell you the chemicals that gave each vintage its unique aroma. One flavorist compared his work to composing music. A well-made flavor compound will have a "top note," followed by a "dry-down," and a "leveling-off," with different chemicals responsible for each stage. The taste of a food can be radically altered by minute changes in the flavoring mix. "A little odor goes a long way," one flavorist said.

In order to give a processed food the proper taste, a flavorist must always consider the food's "mouthfeel"—the unique combination of textures and chemical interactions that affects how the flavor is perceived. The mouthfeel can be adjusted through the use of various fats, gums, starches, emulsifiers, and stabilizers. The aroma chemicals of a food can be precisely analyzed, but mouthfeel is much harder to measure. How does one quantify a french fry's crispness? Food technologists are now conducting basic research in rheology, a branch of physics that examines the flow and deformation of materials. A number of companies sell sophisticated devices that attempt to measure mouthfeel. The Universal TA-XT2 Texture Analyzer, produced by the Texture Technologies Corporation, performs calculations based on data derived from twenty-five separate probes. It is essentially a mechanical mouth. It gauges the most important rheological properties of a food—the bounce, creep, breaking point, density, crunchiness, chewiness, gumminess, lumpiness, rubberiness, springiness, slipperiness, smoothness, softness, wetness, juiciness, spreadability, spring-back, and tackiness.

Some of the most important advances in flavor manufacturing are now occurring in the field of biotechnology. Complex flavors are being made through fermentation, enzyme reactions, fungal cultures, and tissue cultures. All of the flavors being created through these methods—including the ones being synthesized by funguses—are considered natural flavors by the FDA. The new enzyme-based processes are responsible for extremely life-like dairy flavors. One company now offers not just butter flavor, but also fresh creamy butter, cheesy butter, milky butter, savory melted butter, and super-concentrated butter flavor, in liquid or powder form. The development of new fermentation techniques, as well as new techniques for heating mixtures of sugar and amino acids, have led to the creation of much more realistic meat flavors. The McDonald's Corporation will not reveal the exact origin of the natural flavor added to its french fries. In response to inquiries from *Vegetarian Journal*, however, McDonald's did acknowledge that its fries derive some of their characteristic flavor from "animal products."

Other popular fast foods derive their flavor from unexpected sources. Wendy's Grilled Chicken Sandwich, for example, contains beef extracts. Burger King's BK Broiler Chicken Breast Patty contains "natural smoke flavor." A firm called Red Arrow Products Company specializes in smoke flavor, which is added to barbecue sauces and processed meats. Red Arrow manufactures natural smoke flavor by charring sawdust and capturing the aroma chemicals released into the air. The smoke is captured in water and then bottled, so that other companies can sell food which seems to have been cooked over a fire.

In a meeting room at IFF, Brian Grainger let me sample some of the company's flavors. It was an unusual taste test; there wasn't any food to taste. Grainger is a senior flavorist at IFF, a soft-spoken chemist with graying hair, an English accent, and a fondness for understatement. He could easily be mistaken for a British diplomat or the owner of a West End brasserie with two Michelin stars. Like many in the flavor industry, he has an Old World, old-fashioned sensibility which seems out of step with our brand-conscious, egocentric age. When I suggested that IFF should put its own logo on the products that contain its flavors—instead of allowing other brands to enjoy the consumer loyalty and affection inspired by those flavors—Grainger politely disagreed, assuring me such a thing would never be done. In the absence of public credit or acclaim, the small and secretive fraternity of flavor chemists praises one another's work. Grainger can often tell, by analyzing the flavor formula of a product, which of his counterparts at a rival firm devised it. And he enjoys walking down supermarket aisles, looking at the many products that contain his flavors, even if no one else knows it.

Grainger had brought a dozen small glass bottles from the lab. After he opened each bottle, I dipped a fragrance testing filter into it. The filters were long white strips of paper designed to absorb aroma chemicals without producing off-notes. Before placing the strips of paper before my nose, I closed my eyes. Then I inhaled deeply, and one food after another was conjured from the glass bottles. I smelled fresh cherries, black olives, sautéed onions, and shrimp. Grainger's most remarkable creation took me by surprise. After closing my eyes, I suddenly smelled a grilled hamburger. The aroma was uncanny, almost miraculous. It smelled like someone in the room was flipping burgers on a hot grill. But when I opened my eyes, there was just a narrow strip of white paper and a smiling flavorist.

Fast Food Nation (2001)

Corby Kummer

Cheese: Cindy and David Major, Vermont

Corby Kummer (b. 1957) brings to his column in the *Atlantic* and pieces in newspapers and magazines a passionate interest in the authentic, traditional, and delicious. Whether he is writing about coffee, olive oil, or artisanal cheese, he is always drawn to quality, and is careful to describe the pains taken to produce the best possible product. Along with other American food people like Alice Waters and Eric Schlosser, Kummer was an early advocate of the Slow Food movement, which began in Italy as a reaction to the fast food of the United States. His earlier writing and *The Pleasures of Slow Food* (2002) have brought to American consciousness the benefits of cheese made from unpasteurized milk, the mystery of ice wine, and the real probability that political and social action may be needed to protect these foods.

■ ■ ■

The milking parlor at Major Farm, a weathered wood cabin on a long and verdant rise, looks like an illustration for a lullaby about counting sheep. Fourteen sheep at a time scamper from an adjoining barn onto a knee-high platform and calmly put their heads into metal headlocks so that they can be milked. Then David Major pulls a lever like the one on a voting booth to release the sheep, who scamper out as the next fourteen come in.

Great cheese has always been made with great milk, and Major and his wife, Cindy, want both. They know what Roberto Rubino knows—that milk is better if the cow or sheep or goat grazed on green grass under an open sky. The cheese the Majors will make with the milk from those scampering sheep, who grazed in the storybook (and now very valuable) hills near Putney, Vermont, is a big proud wheel called simply Vermont Shepherd. It's America's finest sheep's milk cheese, with a firm but creamy texture, beautiful pale straw color, and the sweet, nutty overtones that come only from wild grass.

For that full spectrum of flavors to shine through, the milk not only must be from grazing animals but also must be raw—milk whose flavor-giving bacteria haven't been killed by pasteurization. This is another thing Rubino and the Majors know.

The matter is urgent in America, where the huge dairy industry is leading a worldwide fight to ban raw milk in cheese. Before World War II, almost all American cheese was made with raw milk, as it was in Europe for hundreds of years, with no ill effects to people's health. Lactic acid in milk and the salt used to flavor and preserve any aged cheese kill most harmful bacteria. Pasteurization for fluid milk that will be drunk fresh has been the rule all over the world for a century. Raw milk, with its superior flavor, has been the rule for cheese aged more than two months.

With industrialization, and especially after World War II, America left raw milk in the backward, rural past. In 1998, an industrial trade group proposed that all U.S. cheese, fresh and aged, be defined by law as beginning with pasteurized milk. This makes perfect sense for a cheese factory, which produces tens of thousands of pounds of cheese a day and combines tanks of milk from dozens of dairies. It makes no sense for an individual cheese maker who works with milk from his or her own small herd of cows, sheep, or goats and whose goal is to produce the best cheese possible. Pasteurization equipment is very expensive, and is unnecessary if the dairy follows sensible sanitation guidelines.

Cindy and David Major are important members of a small but growing band of American artisans opposing any ban on raw milk. They've joined the battle in the most effective way they know: making a sheep's milk cheese to rival any Sardinian pecorino or Lacaune *brebis*, and teaching other farmers how to do it, too. Their efforts are on a smaller scale than Roberto Rubino's but they closely mirror his, down to ripening the cheeses of many farmers in one carefully built room. And the Majors have pioneered, on their own, the idea of a Slow Food Presidium, giving instruction and marketing help to artisans who would otherwise be unable to practice their craft.

The Majors may be unusually attractive and Major Farm unusually beautiful, but the difficulties they faced in trying to keep a farm alive and make a traditional food with integrity are typical of artisans everywhere—and especially in a country that has not valued Slow ways.

After studying international development at Harvard, Major, whose fine, almost delicate features are only accentuated by the ruddy effects of Vermont wind and winter rain, returned to his parents' farm in 1983. He had grown up helping tend and shear sheep, and now he wanted to find a way to make the farm pay for itself, something it had never done; his father sold real estate to support it. He also wanted to help imperiled neighboring farms. He took a job at a woolen mill in Putney. But his salary there, and shearing and slaughtering on the farm, were not enough.

Cindy Schwartz, who has the poignant face and long brown curls of a Van Eyck angel, learned about processing and selling milk, yogurt, and cheese at her father's dairy business in Queens, New York. Soon after she began attending a Vermont college, she met David at a contra dance. They married and settled at David's farm. Cindy's father was the one who made the outlandish suggestion that the Majors milk their sheep. In Vermont, sheep were for wool and meat. The breeds that thrived in its climate produced relatively small amounts of milk. But, as with Podolico cows in Italy, that milk was full of flavor, and could make great cheese.

Thinking something can be great is a long way from making it great, especially if you're working in an absence of traditions that could point the way and have to invent your own—the situation in which most American food artisans find themselves. For a number of years, Cindy tried making one style of cheese after another, with dismal results. "The Gouda wasn't good," she says, "and the bleu wouldn't turn blue. I buried a lot of cheese in the manure pile."

These were the wrong kinds of cheese. Cindy hadn't talked with Rubino, of course, to have the benefit of his motto: Read the Landscape.

She did pour out her heart in a letter to another wise man of cheese, Patrick Rance, the late godfather of the revival of farmhouse cheeses in England and the author of definitive guides. Rance wrote back and advised her to visit the Pyrenees, where geographic, climatic, and possibly economic conditions were similar to the ones she had described.

Using a French-speaking student who had lived with them for a summer as a translator, and Rance's *The French Cheese Book* (Macmillan) as an address book, the couple went to France in 1992. They packed a rented car with their two small children, samples of maple syrup from the sugar house on Major Farm, photographs of the farm and their sheep, and bits of experimental cheese. "The French people were so warm and receptive," Cindy says. "They really wanted to teach us how to do it right." This might have been because they tasted her samples. "How threatening can two people be," she asks, "with little kids and bad cheese?"

Generosity is typical of the story of artisans everywhere, who face similar challenges and believe that the least they can do is help others. Following the detailed advice she received in France, Cindy started making a cut-curd, natural-rind cheese aged for four months. The process of cutting curds with wires into neat little cubes and stacking them into circular forms is the one used to make Cheddar and other English farmhouse cheeses. A natural rind means that rather than being inoculated with a specific mold, the cheese is aged under controlled conditions, so protective, flavor-giving white molds form; it is brushed daily, so undesirable molds do not.

The next year, Cindy decided she was ready to enter the premier competition of U.S. artisanal cheeses, at the annual conference of the American Cheese Society—something she had never before dared to do. She chose the darkest and ugliest of her first group of just-ripened rounds from which to take a sample, so as not to jinx things. "Oh my gosh," she says, recalling her first mouthful. "It tasted so rich, creamy, and sweet. I just knew we'd finally figured it out." Vermont Shepherd received the society's blue ribbon, and Major Farm couldn't fill all its orders.

A string of awards has helped the couple spread their gospel. In 2000, the American Cheese Society gave Vermont Shepherd its best-of-show award; it had already given them its award for best farmhouse cheese in five out of seven years.

The Majors viewed their inability to meet the demand as a chance to help fellow farmers. With grants from the state agricultural department and the Vermont Land Trust, they set up a teaching center to show neighboring sheep farmers how to make cheese. Again similar to Rubino in southern Italy, they built a ripening "cave"—actually a closed cheese-storage room with controlled temperature and humidity—where the cheese would all be aged. This would be the domain of Cindy and their assistant Charlie Parent.

Five farms within a thirty-five-mile radius of Major Farm now make cheese three times a week using the Majors' recipe. The Majors regularly send technical advisers to the five other farms during production season. The farms deliver seven-day-old rounds to the cave, where Cindy, Charlie, and helpers (apprentice cheese makers—Cindy's way of passing on the generosity her French hosts showed her) brush them daily. After four months, a panel of three rates each of the cheeses; only the highest-scoring ones are sold as Vermont Shepherd. Slightly lower-scoring cheeses are sold under the name Shepherd's Tomme, and the remainder go to the manure pile. The system is based on one used by L'Etivaz, a Swiss mountain cooperative that makes Gruyère. It's another example of American artisans borrowing traditions.

Each round of cheese from each farm tastes different—proof of Rubino's point that the grass makes the cheese, and proof of Carlo Petrini's point that helpful microbes floating through the air create different flavors everywhere. Some of the Vermont Shepherd wheels are mushroomy and earthy. Some are much more aggressively flavored and salty than the mild, creamy cheese that made Vermont Shepherd's name. All are worth eating.

The Majors have added two kinds of cow's milk cheese to their repertory, so that neighboring farms can make cheese during the six months that sheep stay indoors and can't graze: a French-style *tomme*, creamy-textured and a bit tangy, and Timson, something like a Camembert, with a golden, buttery paste and a brown-orange "washed" rind. These cheeses are works in progress, continuing collaborations with other farmers and ways for them all to thrive and learn—and they all use raw milk.

The Majors exemplify the Slow Food battle plan: Think global, fight local. Help your neighbor. Make something that tastes so good that anyone who takes a bite will join the struggle.

The Pleasures of Slow Food (2002)

Gary Paul Nabhan

from Coming Home to Eat

Among serious and environmentally concerned food people, the typical American supermarket—aisle upon aisle of out-of-season produce, flown in unsustainably from halfway around the world and bred for shelf-life and appearance rather than what ought to matter, *taste*—is definitely not the place to shop. But once you've determined to live off the grid, what next? Gary Paul Nabhan (b. 1952), an ethnobotanist who co-founded Native Seeds/SEARCH and now directs the Center for Sustainable Environments at Northern Arizona University, has become a leading voice of indigenous eaters through such books as *Gathering the Desert* (1985), *Enduring Seeds* (1989), and *Cultures of Habitat* (1997). Here, he recounts some of his adventures in pursuit of native foods.

■ ■ ■

When I first met him, Javier was parked on the roadside eight miles below our home. He had a table set up in front of the local clinic, and he sat under a parasol attached to the back of his lawn chair. I had stopped because of the hand-lettered FRESH TORTILLAS FOR SALE sign he had set up right next to the pavement.

"*Me gustaría comprar dos docenas.*" I said to him, putting down three dollar bills. He passed one back to me, then handed me two bags full of tortillas the size of dinner plates. The bags felt warm to my touch. I opened one bag, pulled out a soft, floury wheat tortilla, folded it in half, and sampled it right then and there. It nearly melted in my mouth.

"*Que milagro!*" I blurted out.

"*Gracias, mi amigo.*" And then he added in perfect English, "Thank you, my friend."

"Thank *you*, they're very fresh."

"No, I will thank for you my wife and my daughter, Esperanza. They don't let me sell their tortillas unless they are fresh and warm like this. As soon as they get them done, they send me out of the house with them."

"Do you live nearby?"

"Well, we have a place off Sandario on Calle Lucido, but we are from a little ranch down by Agua Prieta, Sonora."

"I thought so. They seem like the kind of tortillas I've eaten in the *zona serrana* of eastern Sonora."

"Yes, that's right. We don't make those *gorditas* they do elsewhere."

"Well, I hope I can buy some more from you."

"Well, if you don't find me here, look for me down on Sandario about five in the evening. You know, by the mailboxes there where you turn off Ajo Way."

"That's on my way home from work. We'll look for each other. *Nos vemos pronto.*"

I did look for that man and his pickup truck for days on end, without any luck. And then, the following Saturday, I saw a lovely dark-haired woman parked in a car at the same place Javier had parked. She was also selling tortillas, under his parasol.

"Are you Esperanza?" I asked.

"How do you know my name?"

"Is that man who sells tortillas here your father?"

"His name is Javier. Yes he is. Would you like to buy some more?"

"Yes, I would . . . I think they're the best tortillas I ever had. Do you only make wheat tortillas?"

"We don't make corn. Is that what you mean?"

"No, I'm not interested in corn tortillas. Let me show you what I mean." I went over to my car and brought out a twelve-pound bag of mesquite flour and a two-pound box of grain amaranth flour. I did not mention that the early Catholic priests in Mexico banned the traditional use of amaranth grain as a ceremonial tithing by the Aztecs. Until the ban families under Aztec rule would provide bushels of grain that the emperor's workers would mix with wild honey and the blood of humans ritually sacrificed on feast days. They would shape this sticky mix into statues of the gods, and called them candies of happiness, or *alegrias*.

"I know your mother probably doesn't make tortillas with these, but if anyone could make good tortillas with them, I bet she could. This is flour from the *péchita*, you know, the *mesquite*, and this is from the *alegria* seeds that they pop and make into candies. It's called *amaranto*, like the greens of one of the *quelites*."

"Sure, I know *péchita* and those *quelites*. They are all over our ranch. I know my mother used to eat both when she was a child, so she might be willing to try making tortillas with them. Why do you want them?"

I said nothing for a moment, not knowing how to explain myself. "I'm kinda on a special diet."

"Like for diabetes or something?"

"Like that. I am trying to eat the native foods that lower blood sugars and cholesterol, but also because I'm trying to eat only what grows around here."

"Well, I can't guarantee you that we can do it, but if you want me to take this home, we'll try."

"Thank you. If it works, I'd love to buy three or four dozen a week. Here's my phone number."

"We'll see. I just don't know. We'll see."

I received a call from Esperanza a week later. Her voice burst across the wire with excitement.

"We have some mesquite tortillas for you! We kept trying to make them different ways, but we finally got something I think you will like. The first ones were too brittle. Finally my father, who likes to join in experiments, he had us change to olive oil and to mix the masa differently. Where can I meet you to give them to you?"

"How about at the mailboxes on Sandario."

"Fine. We'll meet you there in fifteen minutes."

Javier and Esperanza were both there waiting for me when I arrived.

"We used up a lot of your flour in the trials, but I think we can make them on a regular basis without too much trouble," Javier explained in hesitant English. "They taste just like the foods my grandmother used to make with the *péchita*, the mesquite beans. Tell me, where do you get that flour?"

"For now I get it from a friend, Carlos Nagel, who has been working to market mesquite for years. But I have a special grinding mill that can break the seeds free from the flour in the *vainas*, the pods. I'll show it to you when it comes."

"That would be good, because I want to try to make my own. I am somewhat of a machinist. I mean, I design small machines to help me with my work."

"How much do I owe you?"

"You decide! We used up most of your flour," Esperanza said, gesturing her inability to even guess anything appropriate.

I gave them fifteen dollars and promised to bring them more flour. We decided when and where to rendezvous next, as if we had become partners in some crime against the commercial food lords. The clandestine transfer of hot tortillas outside the reach of the global economy. No checks, no receipts, no taxes, no food handler's permits.

I got back into the old Blazer, and opened up one of the bags. The unmistakable aroma of mesquite wafted into the air, filling the entire cab with its bouquet. I took out one tortilla and ate it. It was sweet and smoky, not as soft as a flour tortilla, but not as brittle as a wafer. It was like a Grandma Moses painting, a homemade masterpiece. I tenderly cradled these first warm bags of mesquite tortillas in my lap, the first evidence that an ancient desert food had been revived in my neighborhood.

If a native food tasted this good, why did it ever fall out of favor? When the Spaniards and Moors first encountered foods made from mesquite in their early explorations of American deserts, they thought its pods tasted like those of another legume tree found on the arid edges of the Mediterranean: the carob tree, also known as Saint John's bread. And so, they first referred to the mesquite tree in print by the name *algarroba*, derived from the more ancient Arabic term, *al-jarruba*. They initially recognized its food value and prized its richly hued heartwood for making church beams, furniture, and crosses. Today, however, most Americans think of mesquite only as something that imparts a smoky flavor to grilled steak and fish. What had happened in the interim?

It was hard to say why mesquite went into decline as a foodstuff in the nineteenth century, after ten thousand years of dominating desert diets in the New World. Over the last twenty years I have asked dozens of food historians, anthropologists, and ecologists why mesquite's popularity slipped away, but none of them have offered an airtight answer explaining away the winds of change. However, they all agree that somehow our ancient connection with mesquite as a food was off course by the nineteenth century, blown off the superhighway along which modern American society had chosen to drive.

Perhaps the simplest reason for mesquite's demise had nothing to do with the intrinsic taste, yield, or nutritional value of mesquite as a food. It simply became less and less in vogue for the *gente de razón*, the "civilized residents" of the desert Southwest, to eat wild foods. Both mesquite and amaranths became hardly more than fodder for their farm animals. As some farmers and ranchers grew wealthy, they used as a sign of their sophistication the fact that their own diets were based on something other than what sustained their livestock.

We were weird creatures, ones who habitually assert our otherness by distancing our tastes from those of other creatures. If hogs like mud baths, we must proclaim that taking mud baths is a piggish pursuit, even if the feel of mud on our bare skin was delicious. When Spanish missionaries observed Indians celebrating the emergence of amaranth greens by getting down on all fours and grazing on them while they were still attached to the earth, they themselves would not stoop to this same ecstatic pursuit. Instead, the priests condemned their brethren as "little more than wild animals." It did not matter that their own predecessors—the earliest monastics in the Middle East—also foraged on their hands and knees, delighted by the delicious wild greens their Lord blessed them with. Those monks believed that they were literally following Christ's instruction to imitate the birds of the air and herds of the field, and they took refuge in caves and trees to experience fully the sacredness all around them.

Amaranths and mesquite were once the most abundant, widely eaten wild foods during the summer months, but modern Christian sensibilities had suppressed their inclusion in the diets of desert dwellers over the last few centuries. I recalled the root meaning of *amaranth*, "the flower that does not fade," and only wished it had meant "the flour that did not fade away from use."

Nevertheless, the thrill of my encounter with Javier and Esperanza redoubled my drive to find other local food producers hidden in the fabric of my neighborhood. I soon became a devoted customer of "the Egg Lady," an attractive blond woman in her late thirties who always seemed to have a bunch of muscular men and boys resting on her couches when I knocked at her door. There were always a couple of her sons or her husband's coworkers around, and they all seemed exceedingly comfortable in the nest she had made. And yet most of these guys seemed bewildered whenever I came to ask for eggs, as if they didn't know what I was talking about. Sometimes I wondered if I was the only man in the valley who responded to the EGGS FOR SALE signs at either end of Ms. Soto's circular driveway; the rest of the males around here seemed so smitten by her warmth and beauty that they had not even noticed her deep devotion to raising turkeys, ducks, chickens, and geese.

Each time I knocked Ms. Soto would soon appear from a back room and take me to a fridge filled with distinctive duck eggs, sizable turkey eggs, over-size goose eggs, colored Aracauna eggs, and little bantam eggs. The prices always seemed to change from one visit to the next, perhaps because each breed of poultry had its particular season. As I placed in her smooth, delicate hands a pile of quarters or a few crumpled dollar bills, Ms. Soto always told me to come more often, expressing disappointment that so many eggs were piling up in her fridge. She didn't know anyone else in the valley raising birds for eggs, and was glad to hear that I had picked up turkey keeping as an avocation. She offered me tips about how to deal with the peculiarities of my poults, still months away from being able to produce any eggs of their own.

There were other weekly contacts besides Javier, Esperanza, and the Egg Lady. They were a scattered, motley crew: the folks at the National Fruit Market at Twelfth and Ajo Way, whose vegetables and fruit came from a dozen farm towns within two hours' drive of South Tucson. The old Chinese grocery that sold venison from Globe, Arizona, one hundred miles northeast, and shrimp from—of all places, Gila Bend, Arizona—down the dry river from me another one hundred miles. The Rodriguez fish market, which featured Gulf of California catches brought in daily from Rocky Point, Sonora, which is Arizona's adopted seaport, since it lies within an hour of the international border. All this reminded me of simple fact: While I was busy obtaining four out of five of my meals within a half day's drive or a ten-day walk of my home, most of my fellow citizens in Arizona were sourcing four out of every five of their meals from distant lands. By 1980 Arizonans were already gaining less than a third of their food supplies from Arizona crops, livestock, poultry, and eggs. Since then the balance has shifted even further. The restaurant offerings planned for New Year's Eve 1999 in Phoenix, Arizona, were more like what my brothers shared with me at the Club Du Lubnan in the ancient Phoenician port of Juniye than they were like what Arizonans ate a century ago.

Nevertheless, I no longer doubted that there were others in my neigh-borhood, county, state, or country who preferred informal food exchange networks to purchasing groceries at supermarket chains. As Laurie and I spoke on the telephone with family neighbors and friends living in other re-gions of the continent, they would tell us of their delight in finding similar networks where they lived: a small harbor on the Atlantic seaboard where you could purchase fish directly from the boat on which it was caught; flea markets, swap meets, and garage sales where berries, jerked meat, and sour mash whiskey could be purchased out of the trunks of cars, amid used ex-ercise equipment, paintings on velvet, and eight-track tapes of Elvis live in Las Vegas. Church bazaars where old farmers would auction off their home-cured hams, or a couple of spinsters would offer the sassafras root beer they had brewed. Without involving any advertising agencies, shipping firms, fancy packaging, or middleman markups, millions of pounds of American foods have been bought with cash in hand, bartered for, or given away as gifts every summer of our lives. It is the true commerce of the continent, the kind that Walt Whitman would have loved: these cactus pickers, turkey smokers, and egg gatherers, and all the fishmongers, ham curers, bootleggers, and mushroomers, all the root beer brewers, persimmon pluckers, ginseng diggers, clammers, nocturnal crawfish prowlers, and crab potters still out and about in the shallows, woods, and little fields, happily working the "land of ten million virgin farms–to the eye at present wild and unproductive . . . [but able to] last longer, fill the esthetic sense fuller, precede all the rest, and make North America's characteristic landscape."

Coming Home to Eat (2002)

Ana Menéndez

Celebrations of Thanksgiving: Cuban Seasonings

Sooner or later, and for better or worse, immigrants to the United States tend to forget their native food habits and pick up American ones. But cultural assimilation is always complicated, and what counts as "American" is often altered in the process—even in the case of the most traditional American meal, Thanksgiving. Here, Ana Menéndez (b. 1970), who writes for the *Miami Herald* and is the author of a novel, *Loving Che* (2003), turns a brief history of her family's Thanksgiving celebration into a moving example of what is lost and what is gained as foodways change. Torn between Cuban and American traditions—between the ancestral roast pig and the Yankee turkey—her family comes up with a recipe that negotiates the gap between the two. The result offers a new Thanksgiving possibility for those enervated by generations of oyster, sage, or cornbread stuffing.

■ ■ ■

We called it "Tansgibin" and to celebrate, we filled our plates with food that was strenuously—almost comically—Cuban: black beans and rice, fried plantains, yucca. Back then we didn't know enough to know we were being ethnic, much less trendy. This was simply the kind of food we ate, secure in our culinary superiority, and heirs to a long kitchen tradition that expressed everything from annoyance ("You're making my life a yogurt") to ubiquity ("Like parsley, he's in all the sauces") in terms of food. Thanksgiving, in our own small context, seemed the perfect holiday. And if we were a bit embarrassed at not having invented it ourselves, we went about transforming it with the religious zeal of people finding themselves suddenly, woefully, far from home.

At the center of the party was, of course, the pig. In the early years, when my parents still dreamt of returning to their island, Tansgibin was celebrated, as were all major holidays in Cuba, with roasted pork. This was a time when the family was closest and largest, still bound by common memories and hopes, and a 50-pound pig roasting in the backyard seemed perfectly natural.

The day before, the men would drive out to Homestead to pick out a live pig for slaughter. The pig was then cleaned, split down its rib cage (a process I never witnessed), and laid out over newspapers and a large tray in the kitchen to marinate. The marinade, the mojo, was the most important part of the equation and families lived and died by their mojo recipes. Today you can buy a strange chemical syrup in bottles labeled "mojo"—of which the best one can say about it is that it's another sad example of the banality of exile.

Mojo is not complicated to make, at any rate. And it makes up in exuberance for whatever it lacks in subtlety. First, several heads of garlic are peeled and then mashed with a little salt (to keep them from jumping) in a large mortar. If one is marinating pork, and therefore large quantities are called for, the garlic goes into a blender along with fresh sour orange juice. Cumin might be added, perhaps dried oregano. This is blended well and the whole thing poured over the pig. In the years before concern over food poisoning, the pig was covered and left on the table all night. As a girl, I was so addicted to the salty mojo that I often would sneak down to the kitchen and scoop up dripping fingerfuls of the stuff from the wells of the pig's open ribs.

The following day, the men would dig a hole in the backyard, light a fire, and set the pig to roasting over a grill, covered with banana leaves, and later foil. It had every aspect of ritual, as well as dress rehearsal—for come Christmas Eve the whole thing would be repeated with far more ceremony and purpose. These were long, warm days in Miami. The men—shirtless and drinking beer as they told jokes and reminisced—tended to the roasting from morning until evening. The rest of the meal was up to the women and the day was a whirlwind of pots and rice makers and sizzling sazón (seasonings) and smells and the "hish hish" of the pressure cooker hurrying along its charge of black beans, and then of yucca. It was a happy, bantering gathering, as I remember all women's efforts in the kitchen; and perhaps I'm one of the few women of my generation who does not consider the kitchen a chore or an affront to my independence, but rather a place of warmth and sustenance.

Those were happy days, colored as they were by the brief honeyed hour of childhood, and when I look back on them now I have a strange sense of them having taken place not in America, but in the Cuba of my parents' memories. But change, always inevitable and irrevocable, came gradually. As usual, it was prefigured by food. One year someone brought a pumpkin pie from Publix. It was pronounced inedible. But a wall had been breached. Cranberry sauce followed. I myself introduced a stuffing recipe (albeit composed of figs and prosciutto) that to my current dismay became a classic. Soon began the rumblings about pork being unhealthy. And besides, the family was shrinking: first through sicknesses and then death, and finally through misunderstandings and the pressures of a life that became more hurried and graceless by the day. A whole pig seemed suddenly an embarrassing extravagance, a desperate and futile grasping after the old days.

And so came the turkey. I don't remember when exactly. I do recall that at the time, I had been mildly relieved. I had already begun to develop an annoyance with my family's narrow culinary tastes—which to me signaled a more generalized lack of curiosity about the wider world. I had not yet discovered M.F.K. Fisher, and at any rate, I wasn't old enough to understand that a hungry man has no reason to play games with his palate. I remember that soon after that first turkey appeared, there was much confusion over how to cook this new beast. The problem was eventually resolved by treating the bird exactly as if it were a pig. In went the garlic and the sour orange, the night-long mojo bath. When this didn't seem quite enough to rid the poor turkey of its inherent blandness, someone came up with the idea of poking small incisions right into the meat and stuffing them with slivered garlic. Disaster, in this way, was mostly averted. And to compliment the cook one said, "This tastes just like roast pork."

I moved away from Miami almost 10 years ago. I've only been back for one or two Christmas Eve celebrations. But somehow I've always found myself in the city on Thanksgiving. My sister still claims it as her favorite holiday, even if the past few years she's used the occasion to leave town. The celebrations wax and wane. Occasionally we can still muster large crowds, though we haven't had pork for years now. Sometimes it is another occasion to see the larger family, and also to witness the ravages. It was on one such Thanksgiving that I overheard my father's mother ask him, "Tell me, have we been in this country a long time?" I was in the library of my parents' home, writing what would become my first book, and I immediately put the line into a story. None of us knew it then, but she had already begun the long decline into the forgetting illness that would eventually finish tearing apart the family as she babbled quietly in a corner, "Is this Tia Cuca's house? I have to return home, my mother is expecting me in Cardenas . . ."

This last Thanksgiving was the smallest on record. We gathered, for the first time in memory, not at a massive folding table in the porch, but around the regular dining room table at my parent's home. It was just me, my parents, my mother's mother, and her sister. My husband was in Iraq, covering the war. My sister was in Aruba with her boyfriend. My grandmother's husband was dead, as was her sister's. And my other grandmother had been temporarily shut in a nursing home, a final act of forgetting which my father could not stomach on Tansgibin.

When it came time to say grace, my father refused. "You have nothing to be thankful for?" my mother asked, angrily. "Plenty," my father said through clenched teeth. The old women eyed each other nervously. In the silence, the one agnostic among us began to pray. Probably I expressed an ironic thanks for family and asked that there be peace in the world. I've forgotten the smirking details. I do remember that the rest of the meal passed in awkward silence. There was war within and war without and there is a lot about that Thanksgiving that I wish could have been different. But the turkey was delicious. I realized, with a pang of nostalgia that surprises me still, that it tasted just like roast pork.

Recipe for Mojo

(Measure: 1 cup = 237 milliliters)

Two whole heads of garlic, separated into cloves and peeled

1 tablespoon salt

4 cups sour orange juice (or a 50-50 mix of lime juice and orange juice)

½ cup olive oil (my own family skips the oil, but it's good for warming the spices)

1 teaspoon whole cumin seeds

2 teaspoons dried oregano (2 bay leaves or a few rosemary sprigs, while not traditional, can be substituted)

Toast the cumin seeds in a dry skillet. Pound the seeds in a mortar and pestle and stir into the olive oil along with the bay leaves or rosemary, if using. In the same mortar and pestle pound the garlic and salt into a smooth paste; depending on the size of your mortar, you may have to work in batches. In a saucepan, heat the oil with the spices until fragrant. Do not let it boil. Let cool, pull out the bay leaves or rosemary sprigs, if using, and then pour the oil into a blender along with the sour orange juice and the garlic paste. Blend well. Makes 4 $\frac{1}{2}$ cups, enough to marinate a whole turkey. Or a small pig.

Lady Bird Johnson's

▪▪▪▪ Pedernales Chili ▪▪▪▪▪▪▪▪▪▪▪▪▪▪▪

During the ranch era, the Dutch oven and cast-iron skillet became common cooking utensils. The new cookware made it possible to brown the meat before cooking the chili, which improved the color and flavor. Here's a classic cowboy chili recipe that Lady Bird Johnson used to give out.

> 4 pounds chili meat (beef chuck ground through the
>   chili plate of a meat grinder or cut into 1/4-inch dice)
> 1 large onion, chopped
> 2 garlic cloves
> 1 teaspoon dried Mexican oregano
> 1 teaspoon ground cumin
> 2 tablespoons chili powder
> 1 1/2 cups canned whole tomatoes and their liquid
> 2 to 6 generous dashes of liquid hot sauce
> Salt
>
> **Makes 12 cups**

Saute the meat, onion, and garlic in a large skillet over medium-high heat and cook until lightly colored. Add the oregano, cumin, chili powder, tomatoes, hot sauce, and 2 cups hot water. Bring to a boil, lower the heat, and simmer for about 1 hour. Skim off the fat while cooking. Salt to taste.

Robb Walsh, *The Tex-Mex Cookbook* (2004)

As a food writer in Texas, Walsh has chronicled everything from chili pepper societies to hot-sauce competitions, and has spent decades studying the place of chili in Texas culture and the American psyche. This recipe from a former first lady epitomizes the mix of cultures (Mexican and American), the elegance of the affordable, and the importance of meat.

Ruth Reichl

from Looking for Umami

There is a lighthearted hint of the cloak-and-dagger to this account–by *Gourmet* editor and former *Los Angeles Times* and *New York Times* restaurant critic Ruth Reichl (b. 1948), from her book *Garlic and Sapphires* (2005)–of a superlative sushi lunch. Led to her destination not by word of mouth or other buzz, Reichl instead spots an elegantly dressed Japanese lady, follows her to a restaurant, and orders another of the same. Such undercover stealth was one of Reichl's trademark contributions to the *Times*: most famously, in 1993, she noted the widely disparate experiences she had at Le Cirque, first in disguise, looking like an average member of the reading public, and then as herself, the powerful reviewer. In addition to her influential journalism, Reichl is the author of a now hard-to-find cookbook, *Mmmmm: A Feastiary* (1972), and two moving memoirs, *Tender at the Bone* (1998) and *Comfort Me with Apples* (2001).

■ ■ ■

I spent the better part of a year looking for the perfect sushi bar, the one that would persuade Claudia to try raw fish. Then, in the spring of 1995, it found me.

It was one of those days when the sky looks as if it has been washed clean and the air is so pure it pulls you along, forcing you to stay outside. I walked across Central Park, past all the delirious children on the carousel, exited at Fifth Avenue, and continued downtown. Just as I passed Bergdorf Goodman, the door opened to disgorge a stylish Japanese fashion plate. From her Manolo Blahnik shoes to her Hermès scarf, she was dressed entirely in designer clothing. As she tripped elegantly along I found myself following her, and when she turned west on Fifty-fifth Street, some impulse made me turn with her. Her destination, it turned out, was a modest restaurant I had never noticed halfway down the block.

I blinked when I walked in; it was quite dark, and quite empty. When my vision cleared I saw two Japanese men at one end of the sushi bar, and a bearded American wearing Birkenstocks in the middle. Vacant seats stretched between them.

The sushi chef was an older man, and when he looked up and saw the fashion plate, his lined round face was illuminated with fierce joy. He bowed very deeply and intoned, "*Hajimemashite.*"

The woman bowed back, but much less deeply. "*Genki-Deju,*" she said, tucking herself into a seat directly in front of the chef and carefully arranging her legs.

An older woman in a kimono appeared from behind a curtain and bowed to the new customer. Then she noticed me standing in the doorway, and said discouragingly, "Only sushi."

"That will be fine," I replied.

"No tempura. No noodles. Only sushi," she reiterated in a voice that held no invitation.

"Only sushi," I agreed. "Fine." She led me to the far end of the bar, the one that was not occupied. "Only sushi," she said again, warningly.

"May I have tea?" I asked, giving a sidelong glance to the chic woman, who was now engaged in what seemed like polite Japanese chitchat with the old man.

He had laid a long bamboo leaf in front of her and was grating a pale green wasabi root against a traditional sharkskin grater. Seeing this, I suddenly understood that this was going to be an expensive meal; ordinary sushi bars do not use fresh wasabi.

It took me a while to convince the waitress that I wanted whatever the chic woman was having. It took me even longer to persuade her that I could afford it. "Very expensive," she said, shaking her head. I said that would be fine. She shook her head and went down the counter to convey my wishes to the chef, who turned to give me a long appraising stare.

He ambled down the bar toward me, smiled, and stared frankly into my face. Then he asked, "You have eaten sushi before?"

I told him that I had, and struggled to say something that would reassure him. I knew that he was worried that when the bill came I would not be able to pay it, that he was embarrassed to tell me that when he said "expensive" he meant that my lunch was likely to cost more than a hundred dollars. What could I say to him? I tried this: "I have spent time in Japan."

This did not seem to reassure him. I tried again. I bowed and said, "*Omakase,* I am in your hands."

A broad smile moved across his face. I had found the code. He spread the bamboo leaf in front of me and, leaning forward, said softly, "Sashimi first?"

"Of course," I said, and he began grating the wasabi. Patting it into a pale green pyramid, he placed it precisely on the leaf, added pickled ginger, and retreated to the center of the counter to survey his fish.

From a drawer beneath the counter he extracted a wrapped rectangle and began peeling off the plastic to reveal a pale pink slab of tuna belly. As his knife moved unerringly through the flesh, the waitress glided up to me. "Notice," she said, "that Mr. Uezu does not cut toro as other chefs do. He cuts only *with* the grain of the fish, never across it." I scrutinized the squares of fish the chef placed on the leaf. They were the pale pink of pencil erasers, with no telltale traces of white sinew snaking through them. When I put the first slice on my tongue it was light, with the texture of whipped cream. It was in my mouth—and then it had simply vanished, faded away leaving nothing but the sweet richness of the fish behind. "Oooh," I found myself moaning, and the waitress allowed herself a tight little smile.

The chic woman said something to the sushi chef, and he grinned and said "*Hai*," as he bent to take something from the glass case before him. It was a small silvery fish, only a few inches long, that I had never seen before. He filleted it quickly, pulled the shining skin back in one quick zipping motion, and chopped the fish into little slivers that he scooped into two hollowed-out lemons. He placed one lemon before her, along with a little dish of chopped ginger and scallions, and then he came to my end of the bar and did the same.

"*Sayori*," he said.

"No wasabi," said a voice in my ear. The waitress had glided up so silently that I had not heard her. She pointed to the soy sauce. "Sayori is very delicate and Mr. Uezu does not want you to eat wasabi with this fish."

I picked up a cool sliver, dipped it into the ginger mixture, and placed it in my mouth. It was smooth and slick against my tongue, with a clear, transparent flavor and the taut crispness of a tart green apple.

"Oh," I murmured in surprise, and again the waitress gave a tight little smile.

"You have not had this before," she said. "Mr. Uezu has secret ways of obtaining fish that no one else can get." I had a fleeting vision of the small, sweet-faced man rampaging through the Fulton Fish Market with a snub-nosed pistol.

"No," I agreed, "I have not had this before." As I said it a look of horror, quickly replaced by a less potent look of mere disapproval, flashed across her face. Following her glance I saw the man in Birkenstocks plunk his sushi rice-side-down into the soy sauce, and as he put it in his mouth we could both see that the rice had turned a deep brown. The waitress made a quick, sharp intake of breath and turned away.

Mr. Uezu was in front of the fashion plate now, prying a tiny abalone out of its thick shell and slicing it so thinly you could practically see light through the slices. He was creating a little still life, his knife slashing through the long neck of a geoduck clam until he had created little stars snuggling next to the abalone. Now he laid a bright red Japanese Aogi clam beside it, and next to that two tiny octopuses the size of marbles. Finally an assistant handed him a pair of minuscule crabs, no larger than my thumbnail, on a little square of white paper; he placed them on the plate. The woman became more animated, smiling and bowing in a way that let me know that something he had given her was really out of the ordinary. I wondered if he would deign to repeat the still life for me

He did. The abalone was like no creature I've ever eaten, hard and smooth, more like some exotic mushroom than something from the ocean, with a slightly musky flavor that made me think of ferns. Beside it the geoduck was pure ocean—crisp and briny and incredibly clean—so that what I thought of was the deep turquoise waters of the Caribbean. Next to the pure austerity of these two, the Japanese clam seemed lush and almost baroque in its sensuality.

Mr. Uezu pointed to the miniature crabs. "*Sawagani*," he said "One bite, one bite. Whole thing."

I picked up one of the crabs with the tips of my chopsticks. They had been deep-fried, and they crunched and crackled in my mouth like some extraordinary popcorn of the sea. When the noise stopped, my mouth was filled with the faint sweet richness of crabmeat, lingering like some fabulously sensual echo.

"More?" asked Mr. Uezu. And I suddenly realized that no matter what the beautiful woman might be eating, I did not want more, that I wanted to keep these tastes in my mouth, to savor them as the day wore on. And so I shook my head no, I was finished. "One handroll?" he asked. How could I resist?

He filled a crisp sheet of nori with warm rice and spread it with umeboshi, the plum paste that is actually made from wild apricots. Then he covered that with little sticks of yama imo, the odd, sticky vegetable the Japanese call "mountain yam." It tastes as if a potato had been crossed with Cream of Wheat—changing, in an instant, from crisp to gooey in your mouth. The chef added a julienne of shiso leaf, wrapped it all up, and handed it across the counter.

It was an extraordinary sensation, the brittle snap of the seaweed wrapper giving way to the easy warmth of the rice and then the crunch of the yama imo, which almost instantly turned into something smooth and sexy. Meanwhile the flavors were doing somersaults in my mouth: the salt of the plum, the sharp of the vinegar, and the feral flavor of the herb.

"*Umami*," the waitress whispered in my ear. Again she had glided silently up.

"Excuse me?" I asked.

"*Umami*," she said again. "It is the Japanese taste that cannot be described. It is when something is exactly right for the moment. Mr. Uezu," she continued proudly, "knows *umami*."

Paying the bill, I held the tastes in my mouth, along with the knowledge that this was, absolutely, the place to bring Claudia.

Garlic and Sapphires (2005)

Michael Pollan

My Organic Industrial Meal

From the moment the counterculture took a rural turn in the late 1960s, counter-cuisine—which celebrated the farm-raised and the hand-made and shunned the industrial and the processed—was inevitable. Perhaps just as inevitably, the food industry has responded to changing tastes: since the 1960s, these pastoral impulses have become big business. Here Michael Pollan (b. 1955), in an excerpt from *The Omnivore's Dilemma* (2006), goes behind the scenes and asks tough questions about the organic movement. Aware that "organic" is not simply a way of growing but is also, like any fashion in food, a cultural marker, part of a mind-set or even a morality play, he delves into the many issues at stake as he serves his family a simple winter supper.

■ ■ ■

My shopping foray to Whole Foods yielded all the ingredients for a comforting winter Sunday night dinner: roast chicken (Rosie) with roasted vegetables (yellow potatoes, purple kale, and red winter squash from Cal-Organics), steamed asparagus, and a spring mix salad from Earthbound Farm. Dessert would be even simpler: organic ice cream from Stonyfield Farm topped with organic blackberries from Mexico.

On a hunch it probably wasn't quite ready for prime time (or at least for my wife), I served the Cascadian Farm organic TV dinner I'd bought to myself for lunch, right in its microwaveable plastic bowl. Five minutes on high and it was good to go. Peeling back the polyethylene film covering the dish, I felt a little like a flight attendant serving meals, and indeed the entrée looked and tasted very much like airline food. The chunks of white meat chicken had been striped nicely with grill marks and impregnated with a salty marinade that gave the meat that slightly abstract chicken taste processed chicken often has, no doubt owing to the "natural chicken flavor" mentioned on the box's list of ingredients. The chicken chunks and allied vegetables (soft carrots, peas, green beans, and corn) were "blanketed in a creamy rosemary dill sauce"—a creaminess that had evidently been achieved synthetically, since no dairy products appeared among the ingredients. I'm

717

betting it's the xanthan gum (or maybe the carrageenan?) that bears responsibility for the sauce's unfortunate viscosity. To be fair, one shouldn't compare an organic TV dinner to real food but to a conventional TV dinner, and by that standard (or at least my recollection of it) Cascadian Farm has nothing to be ashamed of, especially considering that an organic food scientist must work with only a tiny fraction of the synthetic preservatives, emulsifiers, and flavor agents available to his colleagues at Swanson or Kraft.

Rosie and her consort of fresh vegetables fared much better at dinner, if I don't mind saying so myself. I roasted the bird in a pan surrounded by the potatoes and chunks of winter squash. After removing the chicken from the oven, I spread the crinkled leaves of kale on a cookie sheet, sprinkled them with olive oil and salt, and slid them into the hot oven to roast. After ten minutes or so, the kale was nicely crisped and the chicken was ready to carve.

All but one of the vegetables I served that night bore the label of Cal-Organic Farms, which, along with Earthbound, dominates the organic produce section in the supermarket. Cal-Organic is a big grower of organic vegetables in the San Joaquin Valley. As part of the consolidation of the organic industry, the company was acquired by Grimmway Farms, which already enjoyed a virtual monopoly in organic carrots. Unlike Earthbound, neither Grimmway or Cal-Organic has ever been part of the organic movement. Both companies were started by conventional growers looking for a more profitable niche and worried that the state might ban certain key pesticides. "I'm not necessarily a fan of organic," a spokesman for Grimmway recently told an interviewer. "Right now I don't see that conventional farming does harm. Whether we stay with organic for the long haul depends on profitability." Philosophy, in other words, has nothing to do with it.

The combined company now controls seventeen thousand acres across California, enough land that it can, like Earthbound, rotate production up and down the West Coast (and south into Mexico) in order to ensure a twelve-month national supply of fresh organic produce, just as California's conventional growers have done for decades. It wasn't many years ago that organic produce had only a spotty presence in the supermarket, especially during the winter months. Today, thanks in large part to Grimmway and Earthbound, you can find pretty much everything, all year round.

Including asparagus in January, I discovered. This was the one vegetable I prepared that wasn't grown by Cal-Organic or Earthbound; it had been grown in Argentina and imported by a small San Francisco distributor. My plan had been a cozy winter dinner, but I couldn't resist the bundles of fresh asparagus on sale at Whole Foods, even though it set me back six dollars a pound. I had never tasted organic South American asparagus in January, and felt my foray into the organic empire demanded that I do. What better way to test the outer limits of the word "organic" than by dining on a spring-time delicacy that had been grown according to organic rules on a farm six thousand miles (and two seasons) away, picked, packed, and chilled on Monday, flown by jet to Los Angeles Tuesday, trucked north to a Whole Foods regional distribution center, then put on sale in Berkeley by Thursday, to be steamed, by me, Sunday night?

The ethical implications of buying such a product are almost too numerous and knotty to sort out: There's the expense, there's the prodigious amounts of energy involved, the defiance of seasonality, and the whole question of whether the best soils in South America should be devoted to growing food for affluent and overfed North Americans. And yet you can also make a good argument that my purchase of organic asparagus from Argentina generates foreign exchange for a country desperately in need of it, and supports a level of care for that country's land—farming without pesticides or chemical fertilizer—it might not otherwise receive. Clearly my bunch of asparagus had delivered me deep into the thicket of trade-offs that a global organic marketplace entails.

Okay, but how did it taste?

My jet-setting Argentine asparagus tasted like damp cardboard. After the first spear or two no one touched it. Perhaps if it had been sweeter and tenderer we would have finished it, but I suspect the fact that asparagus was out of place in a winter supper made it even less appetizing. Asparagus is one of a dwindling number of foods still firmly linked in our minds to the seasonal calendar.

All the other vegetables and greens were much tastier—really good, in fact. Whether they would have been quite so sweet and bright after a cross-country truck ride is doubtful, though the Earthbound greens, in their polyethylene bag, stayed crisp right up to the expiration date, a full eighteen days after leaving the field—no small technological feat. The inert gases, scrupulous cold chain and space-age plastic bag (which allows the leaves to respire just enough) account for much of this longevity, but some of it, as the Goodmans had explained to me, owes to the fact that the greens were grown organically. Since they're not pumped up on synthetic nitrogen, the cells of these slower-growing leaves develop thicker walls and take up less water, making them more durable.

And, I'm convinced, tastier, too. When I visited Greenways Organic, which grows both conventional and organic tomatoes, I learned that the organic ones consistently earn higher Brix scores (a measure of sugars) than the same varieties grown conventionally. More sugars means less water and more flavor. It stands to reason the same would hold true for other organic vegetables: slower growth, thicker cell walls, and less water should produce more concentrated flavors. That at least has always been my impression, though in the end freshness probably affects flavor even more than growing method.

To serve such a scrupulously organic meal begs an unavoidable question: Is organic food better? Is it worth the extra cost? My Whole Foods dinner certainly wasn't cheap, considering I made it from scratch: Rosie cost $15 ($2.99 a pound), the vegetables another $12 (thanks to that six-buck bunch of asparagus), and the dessert $7 (including $3 for a six-ounce box of black-berries). Thirty-four dollars to feed a family of three at home. (Though we did make a second meal from the leftovers.) Whether organic is better and worth it are certainly fair, straightforward questions, but the answers, I've discovered, are anything but simple.

Better for what? is the all-important corollary to that question. If the answer is "taste," then the answer is, as I've suggested, very likely, at least in the case of produce—but not necessarily. Freshly picked conventional produce is bound to taste better than organic produce that's been riding the interstates in a truck for three days. Meat is a harder call. Rosie was a tasty bird, yet, truth be told, not quite as tasty as Rocky, her bigger nonorganic brother. That's probably because Rocky is an older chicken, and older chickens generally have more flavor. The fact that the corn and soybeans in Rosie's diet were grown without chemicals probably doesn't change the taste of her meat. Though it should be said that Rocky and Rosie both taste more like chicken than mass-market birds fed on a diet of antibiotics and animal by-products, which makes for mushier and blander meat. What's in an animal's feed naturally affects how it will taste, though whether that feed is organic or not probably makes no difference.

Better for what? If the answer is "for my health" the answer, again, is probably—but not automatically. I happen to be lieve the organic dinner I served my family *is* healthier than a meal of the same foods convention-ally produced, but I'd be hard-pressed to prove it scientifically. What I could prove, with the help of a mass spectrometer, is that it contained little or no pesticide residue—the traces of the carcinogens, neurotoxins, and endocrine disruptors now routinely found in conventional produce and meat. What I probably can't prove is that the low levels of these toxins present in these foods will make us sick—give us cancer, say, or interfere with my son's neu-rological or sexual development. But that does not mean those poisons are *not* making us sick: Remarkably little research has been done to assess the effects of regular exposure to the levels of organophosphate pesticide or growth hormone that the government deems "tolerable" in our foods. (One problem with these official tolerances is that they don't adequately account for children's exposure to pesticides, which, because of children's size and eating habits, is much greater than adults'.) Given what we do know about exposure to endocrine disruptors, the biological impact of which depends less on dose than timing, minimizing a child's exposure to these chemicals seems like a prudent idea. I very much like the fact that the milk in the ice cream I served came from cows that did not receive injections of growth hormone to boost their productivity, or that the corn those cows are fed, like the corn that feeds Rosie, contains no residues of atrazine, the herbicide commonly sprayed on American cornfields. Exposure to vanishingly small amounts (0.1 part per billion) of this herbicide has been shown to turn normal male frogs into her-maphrodites. Frogs are not boys, of course. So I can wait for that science to be done, or for our government to ban atrazine (as European governments have done), or I can act now on the presumption that food from which this chemi-cal is absent is better for my son's health than food that contains it.

Of course, the healthfulness of a food is not simply a question of its tox-icity; we have also to consider its nutritional quality. Is there any reason to

think my Whole Foods meal is any more nutritious than the same meal prepared with conventionally grown ingredients?

Over the years there have been sporadic efforts to demonstrate the nutritional superiority of organic produce, but most have foundered on the difficulty of isolating the great many variables that can affect the nutritional
quality of a carrot or a potato—climate, soils, geography, freshness, farming
practices, genetics, and so on. Back in the fifties, when the USDA routinely
compared the nutritional quality of produce from region to region, it found
striking differences: carrots grown in the deep soils of Michigan, for example, commonly had more vitamins than carrots grown in the thin, sandy
soils of Florida. Naturally this information discomfited the carrot growers
of Florida, which probably explains why the USDA no longer conducts this
sort of research. Nowadays U.S. agricultural policy, like the Declaration of
Independence, is founded on the principle that all carrots are created equal,
even though there's good reason to believe this isn't really true. But in an
agricultural system dedicated to quantity rather than quality, the fiction
that all foods are created equal is essential. This is why, in inaugurating the
federal organic program in 2000, the secretary of agriculture went out of
his way to say that organic food is no better than conventional food. "The
organic label is a marketing tool," Secretary Glickman said. "It is not a statement about food safety. Nor is 'organic' a value judgment about nutrition or
quality."

Some intriguing recent research suggests otherwise. A study by University of California–Davis researchers published in the *Journal of Agriculture and Food Chemistry* in 2003 described an experiment in which identical
varieties of corn, strawberries, and blackberries grown in neighboring plots
using different methods (including organically and conventionally) were
compared for levels of vitamins and polyphenols. Polyphenols are a group of
secondary metabolites manufactured by plants that we've recently learned
play an important role in human health and nutrition. Many are potent
antioxidants; some play a role in preventing or fighting cancer; others exhibit antimicrobial properties. The Davis researchers found that organic
and otherwise sustainably grown fruits and vegetables contained significantly higher levels of both ascorbic acid (vitamin C) and a wide range of
polyphenols.

The recent discovery of these secondary metabolites in plants has brought our understanding of the biological and chemical complexity of foods to a deeper level of refinement; history suggests we haven't gotten anywhere near the bottom of this question, either. The first level was reached early in the nineteenth century with the identification of the macronutrients—protein, carbohydrate, and fat. Having isolated these compounds, chemists thought they'd unlocked the key to human nutrition. Yet some people (such as sailors) living on diets rich in macronutrients nevertheless got sick. The mystery was solved when scientists discovered the major vitamins—a second key to human nutrition. Now it's the polyphenols in plants that we're learning play a critical role in keeping us healthy. (And which might explain why diets heavy in processed food fortified with vitamins still aren't as nutritious as fresh foods.) You wonder what else is going on in these plants, what other undiscovered qualities in them we've evolved to depend on.

In many ways the mysteries of nutrition at the eating end of the food chain closely mirror the mysteries of fertility at the growing end: The two realms are like wildernesses that we keep convincing ourselves our chemistry has mapped, at least until the next level of complexity comes into view. Curiously, Justus von Liebig, the nineteenth-century German chemist with the spectacularly ironic surname, bears responsibility for science's overly reductive understanding of both ends of the food chain. It was Liebig, you'll recall, who thought he had found the chemical key to soil fertility with the discovery of NPK, and it was the same Liebig who thought he had found the key to human nutrition when he identified the macronutrients in food. Liebig wasn't wrong on either count, yet in both instances he made the fatal mistake of thinking that what we knew about nourishing plants and people was all we needed to know to keep them healthy. It's a mistake we'll probably keep repeating until we develop a deeper respect for the complexity of food and soil and, perhaps, the links between the two.

But back to the polyphenols, which may hint at the nature of that link. Why in the world should organically grown blackberries or corn contain significantly more of these compounds? The authors of the Davis study haven't settled the question, but they offer two suggestive theories. The reason plants produce these compounds in the first place is to defend themselves against pests and diseases; the more pressure from pathogens, the more polyphenols a plant will produce. These compounds, then, are the products of natural selection and, more specifically, the coevolutionary relationship between plants and the species that prey on them. Who would have guessed that humans evolved to profit from a diet of these plant pesticides? Or that we would invent an agriculture that then deprived us of them? The Davis authors hypothesize that plants being defended by man-made pesticides don't need to work as hard to make their own polyphenol pesticides. Coddled by us and our chemicals, the plants see no reason to invest their resources in mounting a strong defense. (Sort of like European nations during the cold war.)

A second explanation (one that subsequent research seems to support) may be that the radically simplified soils in which chemically fertilized plants grow don't supply all the raw ingredients needed to synthesize these compounds, leaving the plants more vulnerable to attack, as we know conventionally grown plants tend to be. NPK might be sufficient for plant growth yet still might not give a plant everything it needs to manufacture ascorbic acid or lycopene or resveratrol in quantity. As it happens, many of the polyphenols (and especially a subset called the flavonols) contribute to the characteristic taste of a fruit or vegetable. Qualities we can't yet identify in soil may contribute qualities we've only just begun to identify in our foods and our bodies.

Reading the Davis study I couldn't help thinking about the early proponents of organic agriculture, people like Sir Albert Howard and J. I. Rodale, who would have been cheered, if unsurprised, by the findings. Both men were ridiculed for their unscientific conviction that a reductive approach to soil fertility—the NPK mentality—would diminish the nutritional quality of the food grown in it and, in turn, the health of the people who lived on that food. All carrots are *not* created equal, they believed; how we grow it, the soil we grow it in, what we feed that soil all contribute qualities to a carrot, qualities that may yet escape the explanatory net of our chemistry. Sooner or later the soil scientists and nutritionists will catch up to Sir Howard, heed his admonition that we begin "treating the whole problem of health in soil, plant, animal and man as one great subject."

So it happens that these organic blackberries perched on this mound of vanilla ice cream, having been grown in a complexly fertile soil and forced to fight their own fights against pests and disease, are in some quantifiable way more nutritious than conventional blackberries. This would probably not come as earthshaking news to Albert Howard or J. I. Rodale or any number of organic farmers, but at least now it is a claim for which we can supply a scientific citation: *J. Agric. Food. Chem.* vol. 51, no. 5, 2003. (Several other such studies have appeared since.)

Obviously there is much more to be learned about the relationship of soil to plant, animals, and health, and it would be a mistake to lean too heavily on any one study. It would also be a mistake to assume that the word organic on a label automatically signifies healthfulness, especially when that label appears on heavily processed and long-distance foods that have probably had much of their nutritional value, not to mention flavor, beaten out of them long before they arrive on our tables.

The *better for what?* question about my organic meal can of course be answered in a much less selfish way: Is it better for the environment? Better for the farmers who grew it? Better for the public health? For the taxpayer? The answer to all three questions is an (almost) unqualified yes. To grow the plants and animals that made up my meal, no pesticides found their way into any farmworker's bloodstream, no nitrogen runoff or growth hormones seeped into the watershed, no soils were poisoned, no antibiotics were squandered, no subsidy checks were written. If the high price of my all-organic meal is weighed against the comparatively low price it exacted from the larger world, as it should be, it begins to look, at least in karmic terms, like a real bargain.

And yet, and yet . . . an industrial organic meal such as mine does leave deep footprints on our world. The lot of the workers who harvested the vegetables and gathered up Rosie for slaughter is not appreciably different from that of those on nonorganic factory farms. The chickens lived only marginally better lives than their conventional counterparts; in the end a CAFO is a CAFO, whether the food served in it is organic or not. As for the cows that produced the milk in our ice cream, they may well have spent time outdoors in an actual pasture (Stonyfield Farm buys most—though not all—of its milk from small dairy farmers), but the organic label guarantees no such thing. And while the organic farms I visited don't receive direct government payments, they do receive other subsidies from taxpayers, notably subsidized water and electricity in California. The two-hundred-thousand-square-foot refrigerated processing plant where my salad was washed pays half as much for its electricity as it would were Earthbound not classified as a "farm enterprise."

But perhaps most discouraging of all, my industrial organic meal is nearly as drenched in fossil fuel as its conventional counterpart. Asparagus traveling in a 747 from Argentina; blackberries trucked up from Mexico; a salad chilled to thirty-six degrees from the moment it was picked in Arizona (where Earthbound moves its entire operation every winter) to the moment I walk it out the doors of my Whole Foods. The food industry burns nearly a fifth of all the petroleum consumed in the United States (about as much as automobiles do). Today it takes between seven and ten calories of fossil fuel energy to deliver one calorie of food energy to an American plate. And while it is true that organic farmers don't spread fertilizers made from natural gas or spray pesticides made from petroleum, industrial organic farmers often wind up burning more diesel fuel than their conventional counterparts: in trucking bulky loads of compost across the countryside and weeding their fields, a particularly energy-intensive process involving extra irrigation (to germinate the weeds before planting) and extra cultivation. All told, growing food organically uses about a third less fossil fuel than growing it conventionally, according to David Pimental, though that savings disappears if the compost is not produced on site or nearby.

Yet growing the food is the least of it: only a fifth of the total energy used to feed us is consumed on the farm; the rest is spent processing the food and moving it around. At least in terms of the fuel burned to get it from the farm to my table, there's little reason to think my Cascadian Farm TV dinner or Earthbound Farm spring mix salad is any more sustainable than a conventional TV dinner or salad would have been.

Well, at least we didn't eat it in the car.

So is an industrial organic food chain finally a contradiction in terms? It's hard to escape the conclusion that it is. Of course it is possible to live with contradictions, at least for a time, and sometimes it is necessary or worthwhile. But we ought at least face up to the cost of our compromises. The inspiration for organic was to find a way to feed ourselves more in keeping with the logic of nature, to build a food system that looked more like an ecosystem that would draw its fertility and energy from the sun. To feed ourselves otherwise was "unsustainable," a word that's been so abused we're apt to forget what it very specifically means: *Sooner or later it must collapse.* To a remarkable extent, farmers succeeded in creating the new food chain on their farms; the trouble began when they encountered the expectations of the supermarket. As in so many other realms, nature's logic has proven no match for the logic of capitalism, one in which cheap energy has always been a given. And so, today, the organic food industry finds itself in a most unexpected, uncomfortable, and, yes, unsustainable position: floating on a sinking sea of petroleum.

The Omnivore's Dilemma (2006)

SOURCES AND ACKNOWLEDGMENTS

The editor wishes to thank Gary Allen and other members of the Association for the Study of Food and Society for their generous suggestions; Laura Shapiro, for sharing her research into the role of women and technological change in the American kitchen; and Anne Mendelson, for her invaluable help in identifying recipes that document the story of food in America.

Great care has been taken to locate and acknowledge all owners of copyrighted material included in this book. If any such owner has inadvertently been omitted, acknowledgment will gladly be made in future printings.

Henry Adams, from *History of the United States: History of the United States of America during the Administrations of Thomas Jefferson*, Earl N. Harbert, ed. (New York: The Library of America, 1986), pp. 31–34. First published in 1884.

Nelson Algren, from *America Eats: America Eats* (Iowa City: University of Iowa Press, 1992), pp. 30–37. Copyright © 1992. Reprinted by permission of the University of Iowa Press.

Mary Antin, from *The Promised Land: The Promised Land* (New York: Houghton Mifflin, 1912), pp. 90–93.

Russell Baker, "Francs and Beans": *The New York Times*, November 18, 1975. Copyright © 1975 by The New York Times Co. Reprinted with permission.

Joel Barlow, from "The Hasty-Pudding": *The New-York Magazine, or Literary Repository* 1.1 (January 1796): 41–45.

James Beard, "Beef Stroganoff": *The James Beard Cookbook* (New York: Dell, 1959), pp. 246–47. Copyright © 1959. Appears by permission of the publisher, Marlowe & Company, a division of Avalon Publishing Group. From *Delights and Prejudices: Delights and Prejudices* (New York: Atheneum, 1964), pp. 176–89. Copyright © 1964 by James Beard. Reprinted by permission.

Henry Ward Beecher, "Apple-Pie": *Eyes and Ears* (Boston: Ticknor & Fields, 1862), pp. 251–55.

John Berry, "Toward Fried Chicken": *The Artists' & Writers' Cookbook*, Beryl Barr & Barbara Turner Sachs, eds. (Sausalito: Contact Editions, 1961), pp. 84–87. Reprinted by permission of Ynez Johnston.

Wendell Berry, "The Pleasures of Eating": *What Are People For?* (San Francisco: North Point Press, 1990), pp. 145–52. Copyright © 1990 by Wendell Berry. Reprinted by permission of North Point Press, a division of Farrar, Straus and Giroux, LLC.

Beverly Hills Woman's Club, "Chop Suey": *Fashions in Foods in Beverly Hills* (Beverly Hills: Beverly Hills Woman's Club, 1930), p. 73.

Anthony Bourdain, from *Kitchen Confidential*: *Kitchen Confidential: Adventures in the Culinary Underbelly* (New York: Bloomsbury USA, 2000), pp. 37–43. Copyright © 2000 by Anthony Bourdain. Reprinted by permission of Bloomsbury USA.

Peg Bracken, from "Good Cooksmanship, or How To Talk a Good Fight": *The I Hate to Cook Book* (New York: Harcourt, Brace, & World, 1960), pp. 150–56. Copyright © 1960 by Peg Bracken. Reprinted by permission of Lescher & Lescher, Ltd. All rights reserved.

Rick Bragg, "Dinner Rites": "Bragging Rites," *Food & Wine*, November 1999, pp. 32–39. Later retitled. Copyright © 1999 by Rick Bragg. Reprinted by permission of International Creative Management, Inc.

Jean Anthelme Brillat-Savarin, "Exploit of the Professor": *The Physiology of Taste; or, Meditations on Transcendental Gastromony*, M. F. K. Fisher, tr. (New York: Heritage Press, 1949), pp. 81–85. First published in 1825. Copyright © 1949 by The George Macy Companies, Inc. Used by permission of Alfred A. Knopf, a division of Random House, Inc.

Helen Evans Brown, "Gazpacho": The West Coast Cook Book (Boston: Little, Brown, 1952), p. 344. Copyright © 1952 by Helen Evans Brown, copyright © 1991 by Philip Brown, Executor of the Estate of Helen Evans Brown. Used by permission of Alfred A. Knopf, a division of Random House, Inc.

John Burroughs, "My Sugar-Making Days": *Signs and Seasons* (Boston: Houghton Mifflin, 1886), pp. 256–58.

Tunis G. Campbell, "To Make Corn Bread": *Hotel Keepers, Head Waiters, and House-keepers' Guide* (Boston: Coolidge & Wiley, 1848), p. 104.

George Washington Carver, "Puree of Peanuts Number Two (Extra Fine)": *How To Grow the Peanut and 105 Ways of Preparing It for Human Consumption* (Tuskegee Institute Experimental Station, Bulletin 31, 1916).

Willa Cather, from *My Ántonia*: *Early Novels and Stories*, Sharon O'Brien, ed. (New York: The Library of America, 1987), pp. 758–63. First published in 1918.

Samuel Chamberlain, from *Clémentine in the Kitchen*: *Clémentine in the Kitchen* (New York: Hastings House, 1943), pp. 81–90. Copyright © 1943. Reproduced with permission of Hastings House / Daytrips Publishers.

Buwei Yang Chao, "Fried Scallion Cake": *How To Cook and Eat in Chinese* (New York: John Day, 1945), pp. 215–16. Reprinted by permission of Professor Rulan Chao Pian.

Julia Child, Louisette Bertholle, Simone Beck, "Coq au Vin": *Mastering the Art of French Cooking* (New York: Alfred A. Knopf, 1961), pp. 263–65. Copyright © 1961 by Alfred A. Knopf, a division of Random House, Inc. Used by permission of Alfred A. Knopf, a division of Random House, Inc. "About the Television Series": *The French Chef Cookbook* (New York: Alfred A. Knopf, 1968), pp. viii–xiii. Copyright © 1968 by Julia Child. Used by permission of Alfred A. Knopf, a division of Random House, Inc.

Lydia Maria Child, "To make a chowder": *The Frugal Housewife* (Boston: Carter & Hendee, 1830), p. 61. First published in 1829.

Craig Claiborne, "Just a Quiet Dinner for Two in Paris: 31 Dishes, Nine Wines, a $4,000 Check": *The New York Times*, November 14, 1975. Copyright © 1975 by The New York Times Co. Reprinted with permission.

Laurie Colwin, "Kitchen Horrors": *Home Cooking* (New York: Alfred A. Knopf, 1988), pp. 140–45. Copyright © 1988 by Laurie Colwin. Used by permission of Alfred A. Knopf, a division of Random House, Inc.

Mrs. John E. Cooke, "Perfection Salad": Janet McKenzie Hill, comp., *Dainty Desserts for Dainty People [Salads, Savories, and Dainty Dishes made with Knox Gelatine]* (Johnstown, New York: Charles B. Knox Co., n.d.), p. 31. First published ca. 1905.

Frank Hamilton Cushing, from *Zuñi Breadstuff*: *Zuñi Breadstuff* (New York: Museum of the American Indian, Heye Foundation, 1920), pp. 556–63. First published in *The Millstone*, 1884–85.

Guy Davenport, "The Anthropology of Table Manners from Geophagy Onward": *The Geography of the Imagination* (San Francisco: North Point Press, 1981), pp. 345–52. Reprinted by permission of the Estate of Guy Davenport.

Emily Dickinson, "Black Cake": *The Letters of Emily Dickinson*, Thomas H. Johnson, ed. (Cambridge: Harvard University Press, 1986), pp. 783–84. Copyright © 1958, 1986, The President and Fellows of Harvard College; © 1914, 1924, 1932, 1942 by Martha Dickinson Bianchi; © 1952 by Alfred Leete Hampson; ©1960 by Mary L. Hampson. Reprinted by permission of the publishers.

Frederick Douglass, from *My Bondage and My Freedom*: *Autobiographies (Narrative of the Life of Frederick Douglass, an American Slave; My Bondage and My Freedom; Life and Times of Frederick Douglass)*, Henry Louis Gates Jr., ed. (New York: The Library of America, 1994), 188–89, 190–93. First published in 1855.

Paul Laurence Dunbar, "Possum": *Howdy Honey Howdy* (New York: Dodd, Mead, 1905).

John M. Duncan, "A Virginia Barbecue": *Travels through Part of the United States and Canada in 1818 and 1819* (London: Hurst, Robinson, 1823), vol. 1, pp. 296–300.

Clarence E. Edwords, "Around Little Italy": *Bohemian San Francisco: Its Restaurants and Their Most Famous Recipes, The Elegant Art of Dining* (San Francisco: Paul Elder, 1914), pp. 66–75.

Ralph Ellison, from *Invisible Man: Invisible Man* (New York: Random House, 1952), pp. 198–202. Copyright © 1947, 1948, 1952 by Ralph Ellison. Copyright renewed © 1975, 1976, 1980 by Ralph Ellison. Used by permission of Random House, Inc.

Nora Ephron, "The Food Establishment: Life in the Land of the Rising Soufflé (Or Is It the Rising Meringue?)": *Wallflower at the Orgy* (New York: Viking Press, 1970), pp. 1–19. Copyright © 1970 by Nora Ephron. Reprinted by permission of International Creative Management, Inc.

Rufus Estes, "Baked Bananas, Porto Rican Fashion": *Good Things To Eat* (Chicago: Rufus Estes, 1911), p. 120.

Fannie Merritt Farmer, "Eggs à la Goldenrod": *The Boston Cooking-School Cook Book* (Boston: Little Brown, 1896), p. 96.

Edna Ferber, from "Maymeys from Cuba": *Buttered Side Down* (New York: Frederick A. Stokes, 1912), pp. 122–38.

Sheila Ferguson, "Philadelphia Pepperpot Soup": *Soul Food: Classic Cuisine from the Deep South* (London: Weidenfeld & Nicolson, 1989), pp. 78–80. Copyright © 1989 by Sheila Ferguson. Reprinted by permission of Grove/Atlantic, Inc.

Michael Field, "Vichyssoise": *Michael Field's Cooking School* (New York: M. Barrows, 1965). Copyright © 1965 by Michael Field. Reprinted by permission of Henry Holt and Company, LLC.

Abby Fisher, "Chicken Croquettes": *What Mrs. Fisher Knows about Old Southern Cooking* (San Francisco: Women's Co-operative Publishing Office, 1881), pp. 17.

M. F. K. Fisher, "A Lusty Bit of Nourishment": *Consider the Oyster* (New York: Duell, Sloan, and Pearce, 1941); "Define This Word": *Gastronomical Me* (New York: Duell, Sloan, and Pearce, 1943). Copyright © 1941, 1943 by M. F. K. Fisher. Reprinted by permission of John Wiley & Sons, Inc.

George G. Foster, "The Eating-Houses": *New York in Slices; by an Experienced Carver* (New York: W. F. Burgess, 1849), pp. 66–69.

Betty Fussell, from *My Kitchen Wars: My Kitchen Wars* (New York: North Point Press, 1999), pp. 152–63. Copyright © 1999 by Betty Fussell. Reprinted by permission of North Point Press, a division of Farrar, Straus and Giroux, LLC.

Euell Gibbons, "How to Cook a Carp": *Stalking the Wild Asparagus* (New York: D. McKay, 1962), pp. 256–59. Copyright © 1962. Used by permission of Alan C. Hood & Co., Inc., Chambersburg, Pennsylvania 17201.

Mrs. F. L. Gillette & Hugo Ziemann, "Roman Punch No. 1," "Roman Punch No. 2": *The White House Cook Book* (Chicago: Werner, 1887), p. 415.

Ray Gonzalez, "Mama Menudo": *Memory Fever: A Journey Beyond El Paso Del Norte* (Seattle: Broken Moon Press, 1993), pp. 115–18. Copyright © 1993 by Ray Gonzalez. Reprinted with permission of the author.

John Gould, "Baked Beans": *Monstrous Depravity: A Jeremiad and a Lamentation* (New York: William Morrow, 1963), pp. 209–10. Copyright © 1963 by John Gould. Reprinted by permission.

Gael Greene, "Lessons in Humility and Chutzpah": *Bite: A New York Restaurant Strategy for Hedonists, Masochists, Selective Penny Pinchers and the Upwardly Mobile* (New York: W.W. Norton, 1971), pp. 46–50. Copyright © 1971. Reprinted by permission of the author.

Roy Andries de Groot, "The Techniques of the Kitchen–The Making of a Cook": *The Auberge of the Flowering Hearth* (Indianapolis: Bobbs-Merrill, 1973), pp. 36–44. Copyright 1973 © Roy Andries de Groot. Used by permission of the Estate of Roy Andries de Groot.

Randolph Harrison, from "The Philosophy of Frying": "The Philosophy of Frying," *Southern Planter and Farmer*, April 1876, pp. 264.

Marion Harland (Mary Virginia Terhune), "Tomato Catsup": *Common Sense in the Household: A Manual of Practical Housewifery* (New York: Scribner, Armstrong, 1873), p. 196. First published in 1871.

Nathaniel Hawthorne, "This Day's Food": *The American Notebooks*, Claude M. Simpson, ed. (Columbus: Ohio State University Press, 1972), pp. 344–46. Reprinted by permission of the Ohio State University Press.

Marcella Hazan, "Risotto alla parmigiana": *The Classic Italian Cookbook* (New York: Harper's Magazine Press, 1973), pp. 181–82. Copyright © 1976 by Marcella Hazan. Used by permission of Alfred A. Knopf, a division of Random House, Inc.

Ella Rita Helfrich, "Tunnel of Fudge Cake" (1966 Pillsbury Bake-Off winner) *Pillsbury: Best of the Bake-Off Cookbook* (New York: Clarkson Potter, 1996) p. 262. Copyright © 1996, 2001, 2004 by General Mills, Inc., Minneapolis, Minnesota. Used by permission of Clarkson Potter Publishers, a division of Random House, Inc.

Lillian Hellman & Peter Feibleman, from *Eating Together: Recipes & Recollections* *Eating Together: Recipes & Recollections* (Boston: Little, Brown, 1984), pp. 94–98.

Copyright © 1984 by Left Leg, Inc., and Frog Jump, Inc. Reprinted by permission of Little, Brown and Co., Inc.

Sheila Hibben, "Eating American": *New Republic*, April 6, 1932, pp. 204–5; "Cape Cod Turkey" (Stuffed Codfish): *The National Cookbook: A Kitchen Americana* (New York: Harper & Brothers, 1932), p. 87.

Annabella P. Hill, "Peach Leather": *Mrs. Hill's New Cook Book* (New York: Carleton, 1872), pp. 327–28. First published in 1867.

Ken Hom, "Steamed Pork Loaf with Salted Duck Eggs": *Easy Family Recipes from a Chinese-American Childhood* (New York: Alfred A. Knopf, 1997). pp. 195–96. Copyright © 1997 by TAUROM Incorporated. Used by permission of Alfred A. Knopf, a division of Random House, Inc.

Langston Hughes, from "Soul Food": *Simple's Uncle Sam* (New York: Hill & Wang, 1965), pp. 113–17. Copyright © 1965 by Langston Hughes. Copyright renewed along with compilation © 1993 by Arnold Rampersad and Ramona Bass. Reprinted by permission of Hill and Wang, a division of Farrar, Straus and Giroux, LLC.

Evan Hunter, "Pancakes": *The Artists' & Writers' Cookbook*, Beryl Barr & Barbara Turner Sachs, eds. (Sausalito: Contact Editions, 1961), pp. 262–64. Copyright © 1961 by Evan Hunter. Reprinted by permission of the Estate of Evan Hunter. All rights reserved.

Madhur Jaffrey, "Moong Dal": *An Invitation to Indian Cooking* (New York: Alfred A. Knopf, 1973), pp. 249–50. Copyright © 1973 by Madhur Jaffrey. Used by permission of Alfred A. Knopf, a division of Random House, Inc.

Thomas Jefferson, "Ice cream": Holograph manuscript, ca. 1780s, Library of Congress (Thomas Jefferson Papers, Series 1, General Correspondence).

Owen Johnson, from "The Great Pancake Record": *The Prodigious Hickey* (New York: Dodd, Mead, 1908).

LeRoi Jones, "Soul Food": *Home: Social Essays* (New York: William Morrow, 1966), pp. 101–4. Copyright © 1963, 1966 by LeRoi Jones. Reprinted by permission of HarperCollins Publishers.

Pehr Kalm, from *Travels into North America*: *Travels into North America*, John Reinhold Forster, tr. (Warrington: William Eyres, 1770).

Lizzie Kander, "Matzos Pudding": Mrs. Simon Kander & Mrs. Henry Schoenfeld, comps. *The Way to a Man's Heart [The "Settlement" Cook Book]* (Milwaukee, Wisconsin: "The Settlement," 1903), p. 105.

Alfred Kazin, from *A Walker in the City*: *A Walker in the City* (New York: Harcourt, Brace, 1951), pp. 30–34. Copyright © 1951, renewed © 1979 by Alfred Kazin. Reprinted by permission of Harcourt, Inc.

Mrs. E. E. Kellogg, "Bran Jelly": *Science in the Kitchen: A Scientific Treatise on Food Substances and Their Dietetic Properties* (Chicago: Modern Medicine Publishing, 1893), p. 91.

Elizabeth Stansbury Kirkland, "Mother's Rice Pudding": *Six Little Cooks; or, Aunt Jane's Cooking Class* (Chicago: Jansen, McClurg, 1877), pp. 212–13.

Ray Kroc, from *Grinding It Out: The Making of McDonald's: Grinding It Out: The Making of McDonald's* (Chicago: Henry Regnery, 1977), pp. 163–66. Copyright © 1977 by Ray Kroc. Reprinted by arrangement with Contemporary Books, Inc.

Maxine Kumin, "Enough Jam for a Lifetime": *Women, Animals, & Vegetables: Essays and Stories* (New York: W. W. Norton, 1994). Copyright © 1994 by Maxine Kumin. Used by permission of W. W. Norton & Company, Inc.

Corby Kummer, "Cheese: Cindy and David Major, Vermont": *The Pleasures of Slow Food: Celebrating Authentic Traditions, Flavors, and Recipes* (San Francisco: Chronicle Books, 2002), 36–39. Copyright © 2002 by Corby Kummer. Reprinted by permission of Chronicle Books, LLC, San Francisco. Visit ChronicleBooks.com.

Jhumpa Lahiri, "Indian Takeout": *Food & Wine*, April 2000, pp. 44–51. Copyright © 2000 by Jhumpa Lahiri. Reprinted by permission of the author.

George Martin Lane, "The Lay of the One Fish-Ball": *Harper's* 11.62 (July 1855): 281.

Esther Levy, "Irish Potato Pudding": *Jewish Cookery Book* (Philadelphia: W. S. Turner, 1871), p. 86.

Edna Lewis, "Morning-After-Hog-Butchering Breakfast": *The Taste of Country Cooking* (New York: Alfred A. Knopf, 1976), pp. 181–89. Copyright © 1976 by Edna Lewis. Used by permission of Alfred A. Knopf, a division of Random House, Inc.

Meriwether Lewis, from *The Journals of Lewis & Clark: The Journals of the Lewis & Clark Expedition*, Gary E. Moulton, ed. (Lincoln: University of Nebraska Press, 1987), vol. 4, pp. 130–31. Copyright © 1987 by the University of Nebraska Press. Reprinted by permission.

A. J. Liebling, from "The Modest Threshold": *Between Meals: An Appetite for Paris* (New York: Simon & Schuster, 1962), pp. 133–41. Copyright © 1962 by A. J. Liebling. Reprinted by permission of the author c/o Russell & Volkening, Inc.

Shirley Geok-lin Lim, "Boiled Chicken Feet and Hundred-Year-Old Eggs: Poor Chinese Feasting": *Through the Kitchen Window: Women Writers Explore the Intimate Meanings of Food and Cooking*, Arlene Voski Avakian, ed. (Boston: Beacon Press, 1997), 217–25. Copyright © 2005. Reprinted by permission of Berg Publishers, Oxford.

Mary Lincoln, "Chicken Chartreuse": *Mrs. Lincoln's Boston Cookbook* (Boston: Roberts Brothers, 1884), pp. 269–70.

Isabel Ely Lord, "Nut Loaf": *Everybody's Cook Book: A Comprehensive Manual of Home Cookery* (New York: Henry Holt, 1924), p. 581. Copyright © 1924, renewed 1952 by Isabel Ely Lord.

Ward McAllister, "Success in Entertaining": *Society As I Have Found It* (New York: Cassell, 1890), pp. 255–64.

Betty MacDonald, "That Infernal Machine, the Pressure Cooker": *The Egg and I* (Philadelphia: J.B. Lippincott, 1945), pp. 182–85. Copyright © 1945 by Betty McDonald. Copyright renewed 1973 by Donald C. McDonald, Anne Elizabeth Evans, and Joan Keil. Reprinted by permission of HarperCollins Publishers.

John McPhee, from *Oranges*: *Oranges* (New York: Farrar, Straus & Giroux, 1967), pp. 6–16. Copyright © 1967, renewed 1995 by John McPhee. Reprinted by permission of Farrar, Straus and Giroux, LLC.

Jerre Mangione, from *Mount Allegro: A Memoir of Italian American Life*: *Mount Allegro: A Memoir of Italian American Life* (Boston: Houghton Mifflin, 1943), 127–34. Copyright © 1942, 1952, 1963, 1972 by Jerre Mangione. Reprinted by permission.

Frederick Marryat, from *A Diary in America*: *A Diary in America, with Remarks on Its Institutions* (London: Longman, Orme, Brown, Green & Longmans, 1839), vol. 1, pp. 105–10.

Chris Maynard & Bill Scheller, from *Manifold Destiny*: *Manifold Destiny* (New York: Villard, 1989), pp. 3–11. Copyright © 1989 by Chris Maynard and Bill Scheller. Reprinted by permission of the authors.

Herman Melville, "Chowder": *Redburn, White-Jacket, Moby-Dick*, G. Thomas Tanselle, ed. (New York: The Library of America, 1983), pp. 862–65. First published in 1851.

H. L. Mencken, "The Home of the Crab": *Baltimore Evening Sun*, June 13, 1927. From *A Second Mencken Chrestomathy*. Copyright © 1944 by the estate of H. L. Mencken. Used by permission of Alfred A. Knopf, a division of Random House, Inc. "Hot Dogs": *Baltimore Evening Sun*, Nov. 4, 1929. From *A Second Mencken Chrestomathy*. Copyright © 1944 by the estate of H. L. Mencken. Used by permission of Alfred A. Knopf, a division of Random House, Inc.

Ana Menéndez, "Celebrations of Thanksgiving: Cuban Seasonings": *U.S. Society & Values*, 9.4 (July 2004): 13–15. Copyright © 2004 by Ana Menéndez. Reprinted by permission of the author.

Danny Meyer & Michael Romano, "Yellowfin Tuna Burgers with Ginger-Mustard Glaze": *The Union Square Cafe Cookbook* (New York: HarperCollins, 1994), pp. 124–25. Copyright © 1994 by Danny Meyer and Michael Romano. Reprinted by permission of HarperCollins Publishers.

Carey D. Miller, Katherine Bazore, Mary Bartow, "Pineapple Pie": *Fruits of Hawaii: Description, Nutritive Value, and Use* (Honolulu: University of Hawaii Press, 1955), p. 136. Copyright © 1955 by the University of Hawaii Press. Reprinted with permission.

Howard Mitcham, "Creole Gumbo": *Creole Gumbo and All That Jazz: A New Orleans Seafood Cookbook* (Gretna: Pelican Publishing, 1997), pp. 40–41, 44. Copyright © 1997 by Howard Mitcham. Reprinted by permission of Sabina Donnamario.

Joseph Mitchell, "Mr. Barbee's Terrapin": *New Yorker*, October 28, 1939, pp. 38–48. Copyright © 1939 by Joseph Mitchell. Reprinted by permission of the Estate of Joseph Mitchell.

Gary Paul Nabhan, from *Coming Home To Eat*: *Coming Home to Eat: The Pleasures and Politics of Local Foods*: (New York: W.W. Norton, 2002), pp. 119–25. Copyright © 2002 by Gary Paul Nabhan. Used by permission of W. W. Norton & Company, Inc.

Ogden Nash, "The Strange Case of Mr. Palliser's Palate": *The New Yorker*, March 13, 1948, p. 38. Copyright © 1948 by Ogden Nash. Reprinted by permission of Curtis Brown, Ltd.

National Cookery Book, "A Michigan Receipt for Making Shortcake in Camp": *National Cookery Book* (Philadelphia: Women's Centennial Executive Committee, 1876), pp. 136–37.

Richard Olney, from *Simple French Food*: *Simple French Food* (New York: Atheneum, 1974), pp. 60–74. Copyright © 1974 by Richard Olney. Reprinted by permission of the Estate of Richard Olney.

Clementine Paddleford, from *A Flower for My Mother*: *A Flower for My Mother* (New York: Henry Holt, 1958), 36–42. Copyright © 1958 by Clementine Paddleford. Copyright © 1958 by Clementine Paddleford. Reprinted by permission of Henry Holt and Company, LLC.

Elizabeth Robins Pennell, "Spring Chicken": *The Feasts of Autolycus: The Diary of a Greedy Woman* (London: John Lane, 1896), pp. 135–42.

S. J. Perelman, "Avocado, or the Future of Eating": *Crazy Like a Fox* (New York: Random House, 1944), pp. 238–41. Copyright © 1937 by S. J. Perelman. Copyright renewed 1964 by S. J. Perelman. Reprinted by permission of Harold Ober Associates Incorporated. First published in *The New Yorker*.

The Picayune's Creole Cook Book, "Cranberry Sauce"; "Calas": *The Picayune's Creole Cook Book* (New Orleans: The Picayune, 1901), pp. 162–63; 184.

Daniel Pinkwater, "Where Is the Grease of Yesteryear?": *Fish Whistle: Commentaries, Uncommentaries, and Vulgar Excesses* (New York: Addison–Wesley, 1989), pp. 6–9. Reprinted by permission of the author.

John Pintard, Letters to His Daughter, 1819–32: *Letters from John Pintard to His Daughter, Eliza Noel Pintard Davidson, 1816–1833*, Dorothy C. Barck, ed. (New York: New-York Historical Society, 1940), vol. 1, pp. 247–48, 317, 337–38, 341–43, vol. 2, pp. 14–15, 46, 124, 301, vol. 3, p. 207, vol. 4, pp. 6–7, 16–17. Published with permission of the New-York Historical Society.

Michael Pollan, "My Organic Industrial Meal": *The Omnivore's Dilemma: A Natural History of Four Meals* (New York: Penguin Press, 2006), pp. 173–84. Copyright © 2006 by Michael Pollan. Used by permission of The Penguin Press, a division of Penguin Group (USA).

Hester Price, "Old-Fashioned Hickory Nut Cake": "A Bachelor's Thanksgiving Dinner," *The Good Housekeeping Hostess* (Springfield, Massachusetts: Phelps Publishing, 1904), p. 268.

Charles Ranhofer, from *The Epicurean*; "Lobster à la Newberg or Delmonico": *The Epicurean: A Complete Treatise of Analytical & Practical Studies on the Culinary Art* (New York: Charles Ranhofer, 1894), pp. 7–8; 411.

Marjorie Kinnan Rawlings, from *Cross Creek Cookery*: *Cross Creek Cookery* (New York: Charles Scribner's Sons, 1942), pp. 100–11. Copyright © 1942 by Marjorie Kinnan Rawlings. Copyright renewed © 1970 by Norton Baskin and Charles Scribner's Sons. Reprinted with permission of Scribner, an imprint of Simon & Schuster Adult Publishing. All rights reserved.

Ruth Reichl, from "Looking for Umami": *Garlic and Sapphires: The Secret Life of a Critic in Disguise* (New York: Penguin Press, 2005), pp. 72–76. Copyright © 2005 by Ruth Reichl. Used by permission of The Penguin Press, a division of Penguin Group (USA).

Kenneth Roberts, from "Down-East Ambrosia": "Down-East Ambrosia," *The Saturday Evening Post*, March 19, 1938. Copyright © 1938 The Saturday Evening Post Society. Reprinted from *The Saturday Evening Post* with permission.

Irma Rombauer and Marion Rombauer Becker, "Almond Torte": *The Joy of Cooking* (Indianapolis: Bobbs Merrill, 1952), p. 650. Copyright © 1931, 1936, 1941, 1943, 1946, 1951, 1952, 1953, 1962, 1963, 1975 by Simon & Schuster Inc. Copyright © 1997 by Simon & Schuster Inc., The Joy of Cooking Trust and The MTB Revocable Trust. Reprinted with the permission of Scribner, an imprint of Simon & Schuster Adult Publishing Group. All rights reserved.

Waverley Root, "Gillotte's": *The Paris Edition: The Autobiography of Waverley Root, 1927–1934*, Samuel Abt, ed. (San Francisco: North Point Press, 1987), pp. 107–13. Reprinted by permission.

Sarah Tyson Rorer, "Hamburg Steak": *Mrs. Rorer's New Cook Book: A Manual of Housekeeping* (Philadelphia: Arnold, 1902), pp. 156–57.

Julee Rosso & Sheila Lukins, "Chicken Marbella": *The Silver Palate Cookbook* (New York: Workman, 1982), p. 86. Copyright © 1979, 1980, 1981, 1982 by Julee Rosso and Sheila Lukins. Used by permission of Workman Publishing Co., Inc., New York. All rights reserved.

Sarah Rutledge, "To Dress Macaroni à la Sauce Blanche": *The Carolina Housewife; or, House and Home* (Charleston: W. R. Babcock, 1847), pp. 110–11.

James M. Sanderson, "Above All Other Birds": *Mirror for Dyspeptics; from the Diary of a Landlord* (Philadelphia: G.B. Zieber, 1844), pp. 26–27.

George Augustus Sala, "The Tyranny of Pie": *America Revisited: From the Bay of New York to the Gulf of Mexico, and from Lake Michigan to the Pacific* (London: Vizetelly, 1886), pp. 92–94. First published in 1882.

May Sarton, "Sukiyaki on the Kona Coast": *The Reporter* 16.13 (June 27, 1957): 37–39. Copyright © 1957 by May Sarton, renewed © 1985 by May Sarton. Reprinted by permission of Russell & Volkening as agents for the author.

Eric Schlosser, from *Fast Food Nation: Fast Food Nation: The Dark Side of the All-American Meal* (New York: Houghton Mifflin, 2001), pp. 120–29. Copyright © 2001 by Eric Schlosser. Excerpted and reprinted by permission of Houghton Mifflin Company. All rights reserved. First published in the *Atlantic Monthly,* January 2001.

David Sedaris, "Today's Special": *Me Talk Pretty One Day* (New York: Little, Brown, 2000), pp. 120–24. Copyright © 2000 by David Sedaris. Reprinted by permission of Little, Brown and Co., Inc.

Maria Sermolino, from *Papa's Table d'Hôte: Papa's Table d'Hôte* (Philadelphia: J.B. Lippincott, 1952), pp. 123–32. Copyright © 1952 Maria Sermolino.

Laura Shapiro, "Do Women Like To Cook?": *Granta,* Winter 1995, pp. 155–62. Copyright © 1995 by Laura Shapiro. Reprinted by permission of International Creative Management, Inc.

Amelia Simmons, "Johny Cake, or Hoe Cake": *American Cookery* (Hartford: Simeon Butler, 1798), pp. 34. First published in 1796.

Gary Snyder, "How To Make Stew in the Pinacate Desert, Recipe for Locke & Drum": *The Back Country* (New York: New Directions, 1968): pp. 28–29. Copyright © 1968 by Gary Snyder. Reprinted by permission of New Directions Publishing Corp.

Raymond Sokolov, "An Original Old-Fashioned Yankee Clambake": *Fading Feast: A Compendium of Disappearing American Regional Foods* (New York: Farrar Straus Giroux, 1981), pp. 137–46. Introduction and compilation Copyright © 1981 by Raymond Sokolov. Reprinted by permission of Farrar, Straus and Giroux, LLC.

Henrietta Sowle, from *I Go A-Marketing: I Go A-Marketing* (Boston: Little, Brown, 1900), pp. 128–31.

Gertrude Stein, from "American Food and American Houses": *New York Herald-Tribune*, April 13, 1935. Copyright © 1935 New York Herald Tribune, Inc. All rights reserved. Reproduced by permission.

John Steinbeck, "Breakfast": from *The Long Valley* (New York: Viking, 1938). Reprinted in *The Grapes of Wrath and Other Writings, 1936–1941* (New York: The Library of America, 1996), pp. 58–60. Copyright © 1938, renewed 1966 by John Steinbeck. Used by permission of Viking Penguin, a division of Penguin Group (USA).

Jeffrey Steingarten, "Primal Bread": *The Man Who Ate Everything* (New York: Alfred A. Knopf, 1997), pp. 19–32. First published in *Vogue*, November 1990. Copyright © 1997 by Jeffrey Steingarten. Used by permission of Alfred A. Knopf, a division of Random House, Inc.

Rex Stout, "Planked Porterhouse Steak": *Too Many Cooks* (New York: Farrar & Rinehart, 1938). Copyright © 1938 by Rex Stout. Used by permission of Bantam Books, a division of Random House, Inc.

Harriet Beecher Stowe, from "Cookery": Christopher Crowfield (pseud.), *House and Home Papers* (Boston: Ticknor & Fields, 1865), pp. 244–256.

William Styron, "Southern Fried Chicken": *The Artists' & Writers' Cookbook*, Beryl Barr & Barbara Turner Sachs, eds. (Sausalito: Contact Editions, 1961), pp. 87–92. Copyright © 1961 by William Styron. Reprinted by permission of Don Congdon and Associates.

Sara Suleri, from *Meatless Days*: *Meatless Days* (Chicago: University of Chicago Press, 1989), pp. 22–33. Copyright © 1989. Reprinted by permission.

Annie D. Tallent, "Bill of Fare on the Plains": *The Black Hills; or Last Hunting Ground of the Dakotahs* (St. Louis: Nixon-Jones Printing, 1899).

Anna Thomas, "Zucchini Quiche": *The Vegetarian Epicure* (New York: Alfred A. Knopf, 1972), p. 154. Copyright © 1972 by Anna Thomas. Used by permission of Alfred A. Knopf, a division of Random House, Inc.

Edith M. Thomas, "Bucks County Apple Butter": *Mary at the Farm and Book of Recipes Compiled During Her Visit among the "Pennsylvania Germans"* (Norristown, Pennsylvania: John Hartenstine, 1915), p. 404.

Henry David Thoreau, "Bread": *A Week on the Concord and Merrimack Rivers; Walden; The Maine Woods; Cape Cod*, Robert F. Sayre, ed. (New York: The Library of America, 1985), pp. 371–74; "Watermelons": *Wild Fruits: Thoreau's Rediscovered Last Manuscript*, Bradley P. Dean, ed. (New York: W. W. Norton, 2000), pp. 107–10. Copyright © 2000 by Bradley P. Dean. Used by permission of W. W. Norton & Company, Inc. *Walden* first published in 1854; "Watermelons" manuscript written 1859–62.

John Thorne, "The Toll House Cookie": John Thorne with Matt Lewis Thorne, *Serious Pig: An American Cook in Search of His Roots* (New York: North Point Press, 1996), pp. 389–92. Copyright © 1996 by John Thorne. Reprinted by permission of North Point Press, a division of Farrar, Straus and Giroux, LLC.

Alice B. Toklas, "Food in the United States in 1934 and 1935": *The Alice B. Toklas Cookbook* (New York: Harper, 1954), pp. 123–135. Copyright © 1954 by Alice B. Toklas, renewed © 1982 by Edward M. Burns. Foreword copyright © 1984 by M.F.K. Fisher. Publisher's note copyright © 1984 by Simon Michael Bessie. Reprinted by permission of HarperCollins Publishers.

Calvin Trillin, "The Traveling Man's Burden": *American Fried* (Garden City: Doubleday, 1974). Copyright © 1994 by Calvin Trillin. Reprinted by permission of Lescher & Lescher, Ltd. All rights reserved.

Marion Cabell Tyree, "Meat-flavoring": *Housekeeping in Old Virginia* (Richmond: J. W. Randolph & English, 1878), p. 116.

Victor M. Valle & Mary Lau Valle, from *Recipe of Memory: Five Generations of Mexican Cuisine*: *Recipe of Memory: Five Generations of Mexican Cuisine* (New York: New Press, 1995), pp. 114–17, 120. Copyright © 1995 by Victor Valle and Mary Lau Valle. Reprinted with permission of The New Press. www.thenewpress.com.

James Villas, "Blessed Are We Who Serve": *American Taste: A Celebration of Gastronomy Coast to Coast* (New York: Arbor House, 1982), pp. 309–19. Copyright © 1982 by James Villas. Used by permission of Robin Straus Agency, Inc., as agents for James Villas.

Patricia Volk, "Hersheyettes": *Stuffed: Adventures of a Restaurant Family* (New York: Alfred A. Knopf, 2001), pp. 109–13. Copyright © 2001 by Patricia Volk. Used by permission of Alfred A. Knopf, a division of Random House, Inc.

Robb Walsh, "Lady Bird Johnson's Pedernales Chili": *The Tex-Mex Cookbook* (New York: Random House, 2004), p. 54. Copyright © 2004 by Robb Walsh. Used by permission of Broadway Books, a division of Random House, Inc.

Eugene Walter, "The Gumbo Cult": *Gourmet*, April 1962. Copyright © 1962 by Eugene Walter. Reprinted by permission of Don. W. Goodman. Originally published in *Gourmet*.

Alice Waters, "The Farm-Restaurant Connection": *The Journal of Gastronomy* 5.2 (Summer / Autumn 1989): pp. 113–22. Copyright © 1989. Reprinted by permission of the author.

Joseph Wechsberg, "Dinner at the Pavillon": *Dining at the Pavillon* (Boston: Little, Brown, 1962), pp. 219–27. Copyright © 1952 by Joseph Wechsberg. Reprinted by permission.

Walt Whitman, "A Great Treat of Ice Cream": *The Wound Dresser: A Series of Letters Written from the Hospitals in Washington during the War of Rebellion*, Richard Maurice Bucke, ed. (Boston: G. P. Putnam, 1898), pp. 190–92.

Estelle Woods Wilcox, comp. "Hayes Cake," "Tilden Cake": *Buckeye Cookery and Practical Housekeeping* (Minneapolis: Buckeye Publishing, 1877), pp. 54, 61.

Thomas Wolfe, from *Of Time and the River*: (New York: Charles Scribner's, 1935). Copyright © 1935 by Charles Scribner's Sons. Copyright renewed © 1963 by Fred Gitlin, Administrator, C.T.A. Reprinted with permission of Scribner, an imprint of Simon & Schuster Adult Publishing Group. All rights reserved.

Paula Wolfert, "Chicken Tagine with Chick-Peas": *Couscous and Other Good Food from Morocco* (New York: Harper & Row, 1973), pp. 203–4. Copyright © 1973 by Paula Wolfert. Reprinted by permission of HarperCollins Publishers.

Jade Snow Wong, from *Fifth Chinese Daughter*: *Fifth Chinese Daughter* (New York: Harper, 1950), pp. 54–60. Copyright © 1950 by Jade Snow Wong. Reprinted by permission of Curtis Brown Literary Agency.

Grace Young, "The Breath of a Wok": *The Wisdom of the Chinese Kitchen: Classic Family Recipes for Celebration and Healing* (New York: Simon & Schuster, 1999), 20–23. Copyright © 1999 by Grace Young. Reprinted with the permission of Simon & Schuster Adult Publishing Group. All rights reserved.

INDEX

The names of authors of selections and their respective page numbers appear in boldface type.

An asterisk (*) preceding an entry indicates a recipe.